COMPENSATION FOR CRIMINAL INJURY

COMPENSATION
FOR
CRIMINAL INJURY

by

D. S. GREER, LL.B., B.C.L.

Professor of Common Law in the Queen's University of Belfast

BELFAST
SLS Legal Publications (N.I.)
1990

Published by SLS Legal Publications (NI), Faculty of Law, The Queen's University of Belfast, Belfast BT7 1NN, Northern Ireland, and printed by W. & G. Baird Ltd., Greystone Press, Antrim, Northern Ireland.

ISBN 0 85389 336 5

To Sheena and Kevin

Contents

Preface

When the first edition of this work was published by off-set lithograph in the Autumn of 1976, the publishers frankly acknowledged that they were experimenting with that method of production as a possible solution to the traditional difficulty of legal publishing in a small jurisdiction. That problem has now been solved in this jurisdiction by the SLS Programme, which was inaugurated in 1980 and thus celebrates this year its first decade of fruitful collaboration. The author is grateful to this Programme for enabling this second edition of his work to be published in a more traditional – and presentable – form.

As before – but on this occasion deprived by her departure to Bristol of the invaluable assistance of Mrs Valerie Mitchell – I have tried to provide a comprehensive and detailed commentary on the current Northern Ireland legislation and to include, where relevant, references to the non-statutory Scheme in operation south of the border. In recent years, however, the Northern Ireland scheme has moved even closer to that in operation in Great Britain and for that reason I have on this occasion made more extensive reference to decisions of the Criminal Injuries Compensation Board, which seem likely to be considered in the interpretation and application of the Northern Ireland law. Unfortunately, it was only after the manuscript had gone to press that it was decided to postpone the implementation of the statutory provisions set out in the Criminal Justice Act 1988 and instead to proceed with an amended non-statutory Scheme for the time being. I have nonetheless been able to take account of most of these developments, save the publication earlier this year of a "Guide" to the new Scheme to replace the Board's explanatory "Statement" of its interpretation of the previous Scheme. Fortunately, on most points of substance little has changed. Those who wish to know more about the 1990 Scheme in Great Britain are invited to consult my commentary on it, shortly to be published by Messrs Sweet & Maxwell.

In the preparation of this edition I have become indebted to many people for their advice and assistance. I would especially like to acknowledge the co-operation of the officials of the Compensation Division of the Northern Ireland Office, and in particular Mr Kevin Ham, Mr Oswyn Paulin and Mr John Hodgson; they have provided me with a great deal of practical information and the details of many unreported cases and they patiently answered many queries. I am grateful also to the Secretary of the Criminal Injuries Compensation Tribunal in Dublin, and to Mr Richard Ryan of the Department of Justice, for their assistance in relation to aspects of the Irish law and practice. The Secretary of the Criminal Injuries Compensation Board in London kindly provided me with information on the operation of the British Scheme. In all cases, however, the analysis of the law and any opinions expressed are mine alone, as is the responsibility for any errors or omissions.

On the production side my thanks go to my secretary Ms Karen Agnew for doing wonders with her word-processor; to Mrs Sara Gamble for her editing and production assistance; to Mr Barry Valentine for compiling the index (and offering many helpful comments on the text) and to Messrs W. & G. Baird Ltd for their efficiency in having the manuscript converted into print.

I have attempted to state the law as on 31 March 1990, but in some instances I have been able to incorporate later developments.

D. S. Greer

Bertha House
June 1990

Table of Cases

Table of Statutes

1. STATUTES OF THE PARLIAMENT OF IRELAND

2. Statutes of the Parliaments of England, Great Britain and The United Kingdom

EXTRA-STATUTORY SCHEME FOR COMPENSATING VICTIMS OF CRIMES OF VIOLENCE (1990)

3. STATUTES OF THE PARLIAMENT OF NORTHERN IRELAND

[including Orders in Council made under the Northern Ireland
(Temporary Provisions) Act 1972 and under the Northern Ireland Act 1974]

4. Statutes of the Oireachtas of the Irish Free State and of Ireland

Scheme of Compensation for Personal Injuries Criminally Inflicted
(as amended with effect from 1 April 1986)

5. Other Statutes

Table of Statutory Regulations and Rules of Court

1. United Kingdom and Northern Ireland

2. Republic of Ireland

List of Abbreviations

1

Historical Background

EARLY LEGISLATION

Statutory provision for the compensation of persons suffering personal injury as the result of the criminal activity of others dates in Ireland from the seventeenth century. There had, of course, been earlier legislation providing for the payment of public compensation to victims of crime – in Ireland, as in England, the starting point is the Statute of Winchester 1285[1] – but that legislation dealt primarily, if not exclusively, with loss of or damage to property. This preference for the protection of property was in fact to remain, with some exceptions, until well into the twentieth century.[2] In the unsettled conditions of the seventeenth century, therefore, it was "robbery petitions" which first attracted the attention of Parliament. When it was found that the Statute of Winchester was "being of late days more commonly put in execution than heretofore", steps were taken to improve the procedure whereby victims could obtain compensation from the inhabitants of the area where the robbery had taken place.[3] Parliament turned again to this principle of local liability after the Treaty of Limerick, when the government was anxious to restore law and order, and to encourage settlers to come to or stay in Ireland. An Act of 1695[4] recited that "frequent robberies, murders

---

1. 13 Edw 1, stat 2, c 2 (extended to Ireland by writ in 1308). For some time this common law approach had to vie with the Brehon law principle of "kin liability" (*cin comfocuis*) – see e.g. 10 Hen 7, c 11 (Ir) 1495; Binchy, "Secular Institutions" in Dillon (ed), *Early Irish Society* (1959), pp 62–3; Hand and Treadwell, "His Majesty's Directions for Ordering and Settling the Courts within His Kingdom of Ireland 1622" (1970) 26 *Anal Hib* 179, 184 and 206. Kennedy, *The Presidency of Munster under Elizabeth and James I* (MA Thesis 1973), p 68 suggests that the Brehon principle was applied in the Presidency Court as late as 1620.

2. See generally, Greer and Mitchell, *Compensation for Criminal Damage to Property* (1982), chapter 1.

3. An Act for the Following of Hue and Cry

(10 and 11 Chas 1, c 13 (Ir)). For an earlier attempt to reform the procedure, see *CSPI* 1625–1632, p 335. The Act of 1635 substantially enacted for Ireland the English Hue and Cry Act of 1584 – see e.g. Holdworth, *A History of English Law* (1924), vol 4, p 521; MacNally, *A Justice of the Peace for Ireland* (2nd ed 1812), vol 2, pp 420–35. A precedent for making a "robbery petition" was included in the *Instructions to be duly observed by the Judges of every . . . Court of Justice . . . in Ireland* published by the Commonwealth Commissioners in 1653 (p 15).

4. An Act for the better suppressing Tories, Robbers and Rapparees, and for preventing Robberies, Burglaries and other heinous crimes (7 Will 3, c 21 (Ir)). The language of the preamble closely resembles that of the Statute of Winchester.

1

and other notorious felonies . . . hath greatly discouraged the re-planting of this Kingdom" and alleged that local inhabitants chose "rather to suffer strangers to be robbed and despoiled of their goods than to apprehend and convict the offenders . . . ". The scope of local liability was as a result extended to cover not only robberies, but also burglaries, the burning of houses or haggards of corn, and the killing and maiming of cattle. An Irish dimension was also added to the local liability principle to enable compensation for the depredations of "Popish" and "Protestant" offenders to be collected from the "Popish" or "Protestant" inhabitants respectively.[5]

In spite of the wording of the preamble, the 1695 Act made no provision for murder victims as such. However, in 1697,[6] it was acknowledged that "there is not in the [earlier legislation] sufficient provision made for the prevention of murders and maims", and it was therefore enacted that:

> "Where any person . . . shall . . . be murdered, maimed or dismembered by any robber, tory or rapparee, and the offender or offenders . . . shall not be killed or apprehended [within six months] . . . the respective grand juries . . . shall [at the assizes] . . . present and charge upon the popish or protestant inhabitants of such county [where the crime was committed] respectively and proportionably . . . the sums following:
>
> . . . in case of murder, such sum or sums of money not exceeding £20, and in case of maim or dismembering any person, such sum or sums of money, not exceeding £10, as such grand juries on consideration had of the quality of the person murdered, maimed and dismembered, and circumstances of his family, shall think fit; such sum, in case of murder, to be paid to and for the use of the widow and children of the party murdered . . . and in case of maim or dismembering . . . to be paid to the use of the person . . . so maimed or dismembered . . . "

This legislation changed not only the scope of compensation but also the procedure for obtaining it. The Statute of Winchester and subsequent legislation (including the 1695 Act) entitled the injured party to sue any inhabitant of the hundred or barony.[7] This procedure was found in Ireland to be "tedious, difficult and chargeable".[8] The 1697 Act therefore provided for the injured party, having first given due notice of the crime,[9] to present a petition giving details of the offence and the amount of his loss, damage or injury, to the judge of assize to be examined by him in open court in the presence of the grand jury. Evidence would be given on oath by any interested party[10] and the grand jury then retired to consider the matter

---

5. *Ibid*, s 1. See Newark, "An Old Precedent Book" (1967) 18 *NILQ* 330.

6. An Act to Supply the Defects, and for better Execution of an Act . . . for the better suppressing Tories and Rapparees, and for preventing Robberies, Burglaries and other heinous crimes (9 Will 3, c 9 (Ir)).

7. The action was tried by judge and jury – see e.g. 1695 Act, s 2. If found liable, the selected defendant could recover an appropriate contribution from the other inhabitants: 1635 Act, s 3; 1695 Act, s 3.

8. 1697 Act, ss 2, 9.

9. To some nearby inhabitants "within 24 hours or within a reasonable time after he shall be at liberty", and to a Justice of the Peace within 4 days of the first report: 1695 Act, s 4.

10. Section 4 of the 1697 Act required written notice of the claim to be given at least 8 days before the sitting of the Assizes to enable local inhabitants to adduce evidence against the claim.

"amongst themselves". Following such deliberation, the grand jury "presented" such sum of money as the person "ought to have or receive", indicating further by what persons, "whether papists or protestants", such sum ought to be paid.[11] The procedure for the collection of this sum was to be that previously been laid down by an Act of 1635:

> "Two justices of the peace . . . [are] to assess and tax rateably and proportionably according to their discretions, all and every the towns, parishes, villages and hamlets as well as the . . . hundred or barony, where any such robbery shall be committed . . . to and towards an equal contribution to be had and made for the relief of the said inhabitant or inhabitants . . . and that after such taxation made, the constable or constables, head-borough or head-boroughs of every such town [etc] . . . shall . . . have full power and authority within their several limits rateably and proportionably to tax and assess, according to their abilities, every inhabitant and dweller in every such town [etc] . . . "[12]

This method of taxation was not peculiar to Ireland;[13] what was new was the role allocated to the grand jury. By the end of the seventeenth century it was becoming clear that local administration in Ireland could not be left to the justices of the peace as in England. Administrative duties were imposed on grand juries from 1634[14] and it was they who formed the basis of county government in Ireland until 1898. But there was another, more immediate, reason for involving the grand jury in the procedure for awarding criminal injuries compensation – the close relationship between compensation provisions and the enforcement of law and order. The grand jury, of course, were required to pass on bills of indictment before these were tried at assizes or quarter sessions and it was a short step from this to involve them in law enforcement and crime prevention. One of the original purposes for involving the grand jury in the criminal injuries scheme was to ensure publicity – the grand jury on receiving the details of the offence were then "to give the best description they can . . . of such malefactors, to the end they may be brought the speedier to justice . . . ".[15] The grand jury were left with a certain amount of discretion as to the persons who should pay the compensation – especially on sectarian grounds – and could therefore punish those who were in a broad sense responsible for the crime.[16] On the other hand,

---

11. Any person aggrieved by a presentment which exceeded £5 could "appeal" against it by "traverse" to be tried "at the same or the next ensuing assize, as the judge . . . who shall allow the same, shall think fit . . . ": 1697 Act, s 3.

12. 10 and 11 Chas 1, c 13 (Ir), s 3.

13. The Irish Act of 1635 followed an English Act of 1584 (27 Eliz I, c 13) – see above, n 3.

14. 10 Chas 1, sess 2, c 26 (Roads and Bridges). "From this commencement a whole code of local legislation peculiar to Ireland has arisen": *Report of the Select Committee on the Local Taxation of Ireland* (1867–8) BPP, lviii, 763. Nolan, *The County Cork Grand*

Jury 1836–1899 (MA Thesis, 1974), p 3 has suggested that the grand jury was brought into local government by Wentworth, to soften reaction to the refusal to grant the Graces by giving extra power to local magnates.

15. 1695 Act, s 5. Persons proclaimed by the grand jury who did not surrender themselves within a specified time were deemed guilty of high treason (s 6). If the victim knew the offender's identity, he had to undertake to bring a prosecution (s 4).

16. Section 1 of the 1695 Act indicated that most offenders were clearly expected to be "popish", and provided that compensation could in such cases be levied from the "popish" inhabitants of the locality.

they were equally given power to give rewards in order to encourage inhabitants to apprehend and prosecute or even kill suspected offenders.[17] The central role of the grand jury in this secondary system of criminal justice – their power to impose "fines" or give rewards – has tended to be underestimated. The more usual explanation is to emphasise the principle of "collective responsibility" underlying the Statute of Winchester and its successors and to explain that it was necessary as a means of securing law and order in the absence of an organised police force.[18] But this is perhaps to overlook the importance of involving at every turn in the administration of criminal justice the most substantial men in the county. By continually involving them in decisions relating to the award of compensation, the making of rewards and the imposition of levies to pay for these, was the legislature not constituting them as the local "police" as opposed to the local inhabitants who merely paid the sums as required by the grand jury?

Be that as it may, the legislation of the 1690s formed the basis of compensation for criminal injuries to persons for the greater part of the eighteenth century,[19] reflecting the fact that "for the first sixty years of the century the greater part of the country was free from disturbance".[20] As anyone familiar with Irish history would suspect, the system was subject to a certain amount of abuse. Fraudulent claims were sufficiently common to require remedial legislation which attempted to reduce the "trade of obtaining robbery-money from the country".[21] There was also some abuse in the distribution of the levy to pay for the compensation awarded by the grand jury.[22] The remedies adopted to tackle these abuses do not seem to have

---

17. 1695 Act, s 6, "provided such sums do not exceed £20 for any one tory . . . ".

18. See e.g. Sir John Ross C in *McKnight* v *Armagh CC* [1922] 2 IR 137, 147. The principle of collective responsibility was extensively relied on in England until the 19th century, when "this method of stimulating local inhabitants to make better provision for the preservation of the peace ceased to be of any practical importance": Radzinowicz, *A History of English Criminal Law and its Administration from 1750* (1956), vol 2, p 167. See also Boyle, "Police in Ireland before the Union" (1972) 7 *IJ* 115.

19. The Acts of 1695 and 1697 were originally enacted for a limited period only; but they were regularly continued – for irregular periods – and were in force for most of the period until 1776. See 2 Anne, c 13 (Ir) (1703 – continued Acts for 7 years); 6 Anne, c 11 (Ir) (1707 – 7 years); 6 Geo 1, c 12 (Ir) (1719 – another 7 years); 12 Geo 1, c 6 (Ir) (1725 – 11 years); 9 Geo 2, c 6 (Ir) (1735 – 21 years); 29 Geo 2, c 8 (Ir), s 2 (1755 – 21 years).

20. Beckett, *The Making of Modern Ireland*

1603–1923 (2nd ed, 1981), p 176. But *cf* 9 Anne, c 11 (Ir) (modification of 1695 Act, to deal with outbreak of cattle maiming in parts of Co Galway).

21. 6 Anne, c 11 (Ir), s 2 (1707). The remedy was to tighten up the notice requirements. As well as notifying some local inhabitants "with as much speed as may be" and a local Justice of the Peace within 20 days of the alleged offence (as required by 1635 Act, s 9), the claimant was further required to notify the high constable of the barony within 5 days of the offence.

22. The 1707 Act further recited (s 3) that "the principal and chief inhabitants of each parish" when applotting the money to be levied "do usually lay the whole burden on the poorer sort, that are least able to bear it, or able to resist or pursue the tories . . . "; the remedy was an appeal to the next going judge of assize. *Cf* in England, it was apparently the custom to levy the damages from the most solvent inhabitants – see Holdsworth, *A History of English Law* (1924), vol 4, pp 521–2.

been altogether successful,[23] and indeed the whole grand jury system became – and remained until its substantial abolition in 1898 – the subject of constant criticism and debate.

An Act of 1709[24] provides one of the first examples of another occasion for the payment of compensation associated with criminal injuries schemes. This Act "for the Encouraging the Discovery and the Apprehending of Housebreakers" attempted to reduce the number of burglaries and house-breakings by offering a reward of £5 to any person discovering, apprehending and prosecuting to conviction any person guilty of such an offence. There was nothing remarkable in this provision;[25] however, section 2 further provided:

> "That in case any watch-man or any other person or persons shall happen to be killed by any such burglar or house-breaker, such watch-man or other person or persons endeavouring to apprehend, or in making pursuit after him, her or them, that then the executors or administrators of such person or persons so killed . . . shall receive the sum of £20 . . . "

The power to make such awards rested with the judge of assize or two justices of the peace. In 1721[26] further provision was made for the payment of £20 to the executors or administrators of any person killed in the pursuit or apprehending of any murderer or robber. In such cases the money was to be raised by presentment of the grand jury. Although similar in nature, it was not until the end of the century that compensation for such injuries was amalgamated with the earlier scheme for payment of compensation for criminal injuries.

The next chapter in the history of criminal injuries compensation reflects the fact that widespread agrarian crime began to trouble Ireland from the 1760s onwards.[27] As in the 1690s, the legislature dealt first with the problem of compensation for damage to property.[28] However an Act of 1765 passed in an attempt "to prevent for the future tumultuous Risings of Persons within this Kingdom"[29] recited that:

---

23. Further legislation was soon required – see 6 Geo 1, c 12 (Ir), s 6 (1719); 8 Geo 1, c 9 (Ir), s 4 (1721). For a brief description of the grand jury system in the 18th century see McCracken, "The social structure and social life, 1714–60" in Moody and Vaughan (eds), *A New History of Ireland* (1986), vol iv, ch 2.

24. 8 Anne, c 8 (Ir).

25. A similar provision is to be found in the 1695 Act, s 6. This power to pay rewards was said in 1719 to "have been the occasion of many offenders . . . being brought to condign punishment", and the law was clarified and extended: 6 Geo 1, c 12 (Ir), s 7. See also 8 Geo 1, c 9 (Ir), s 3 and generally, Radzinowicz, *op cit* n 18, pp 67–8.

26. 8 Geo 1, c 9 (Ir), s 5.

27. For a more detailed discussion of criminal law enforcement during this period, see

Boyle, "Police in Ireland before the Union – II" (1973) 8 *IJ* 90.

28. See e.g., Unlawful Combinations Act 1755 (27 Geo 2, c 12 (Ir)). But Acts mainly designed to protect property also included some provision for personal injury. Thus, the Weavers Protection Act 1779–80 made it an offence (*inter alia*) "wilfully and maliciously [to] maim or wound any person concerned in carrying on any manufacture on account of his working at or being concerned in the same, or any person concerned in using, carrying or protecting any of the said manufactures . . . " etc (s 5). By s 6 any person who sustained any injury from one of these offences "may sue for and recover satisfaction and amends for the injury . . . at the next assizes . . .".

29. 5 Geo 3, c 8 (Ir).

" . . . it has frequently happened of late in different parts of this kingdom, that several persons as well by night as in the day time have in a riotous, disorderly and tumultuous manner assembled themselves, and being so assembled and met together have abused and injured many persons by assaulting, wounding, or otherwise maltreating their persons, or by destroying or injuring their property . . . and have forceably imposed sundry oaths contrary to law . . . "

The Act made it a capital offence for "any persons to the number of five or more [to] meet, and go by night, and assault, injure or otherwise maltreat any person or persons by wounding, beating, tying or by any other act of cruelty, whereby the life or limb of the person assaulted may be in danger".[30] It then provided, by section 3, that:

"Whereas it may tend to discourage such insurgents from perpetrating their wicked and unlawful intentions, and in some measure prevent their being guilty of the above mentioned offences, if the damage done by them on such occasions was recovered off the county or barony wherein the same was committed . . . "

therefore, if the local inhabitants did not apprehend or cause to be apprehended one at least of the offenders, the person so injured, "upon such notice given to the high constable . . . as in the case of robbery petitions", shall be entitled to have and recover satisfaction for his loss, to be presented by the grand jury and levied upon the county at large, or upon a barony. This Act expired in 1775 when it was replaced by the well-known Whiteboy Act of that year.[31] That Act also created a number of statutory offences in connection with unlawful assemblies, including in particular making it a capital offence for anyone "either by day or by night wilfully or maliciously [to] shoot at, maim or disfigure any person or persons in any dwelling house or other place . . . ".[32] Section 8 further provided:

"And in order to prevent for the future the several outrages and offences herein before mentioned be it further enacted . . . that satisfaction and amends may be made . . . to . . . every person . . . for all and every injury and damage . . . against his . . . person or . . . property . . . by any offender or offenders against this Act."

The procedure for deciding which persons were entitled to "satisfaction and amends" and for the raising of the sums so awarded was similar to that under the 1697 Act as amended, though it is perhaps worth noting that the grand jury were to present the amount which in their opinion the claimant ought to have and receive for his injury or loss "to be raised either on the county, barony, town or towns, parish or parishes in or near which such offence shall have been committed, and in such proportions as they shall think fit . . . "[33]

---

30. Section 1. The Act also made wilful or malicious damage to property, animals and crops a capital offence.
31. 15 and 16 Geo 3, c 21 (Ir). The earlier Act had been found "insufficient for the purposes thereby intended, and for preventing and punishing such wicked and unlawful practices . . . ". Supplementary legislation to deal with more localised incidents had been introduced on a temporary basis for counties Antrim, Down, Armagh, Londonderry and Tyrone in 1771 (11 and 12 Geo 3, c 5 (Ir), ss 1 and 10) – repealed in 1774 (13 and 14 Geo 3, c 4 (Ir)).

32. Section 3.

33. Section 8.

– a further refinement on the concept of "collective responsibility". The Whiteboy Act also continued existing policy by providing for compensation to be paid for persons wounded, maimed or killed when apprehending or prosecuting offenders under the Act;[34] the maximum payable was, however, raised to £100 on death or £50 for injury.[35]

It was intended that this "emergency provisions" Act should continue in force no longer than "public necessity shall require", but its operation was regularly extended[36] and eventually made perpetual in 1800 by one of the last Acts of the Irish Parliament.[37]

The third "strand" in the legislative development of compensation for criminal injuries to persons appeared in 1796 as part of the Insurrection Act of that year.[38] This Act, passed at a time of increasing tension which culminated in the rising of the United Irishmen in 1798, recited (*inter alia*) that:

> "Whereas in several instances persons who have given information against persons accused of crimes have been murdered before trial of the persons accused, in order to prevent their giving evidence and to effect the acquittal of the accused, and some magistrates have been assassinated for their exertions in bringing offenders to justice . . . "[39]

and enacted that:

> "If it shall appear to the satisfaction of any grand jury at any assizes . . . that any person giving information or evidence against persons charged with offences against the public peace, shall have been murdered or maimed previous to giving their evidence on any trial or on account of any such evidence given, or that any magistrate or other peace officer shall be murdered or maimed on account of his exertions to bring disturbers of the public peace . . . to justice . . . the grand jury [may] . . . present such sum or sums of money as they shall think just and reasonable to be paid to the personal representative of such witness [etc] who shall be murdered, or to such witness [etc] who shall be maimed, having regard to the rank, degree, situation and circumstances of such witness, magistrate or peace officer . . . to be raised on the county at large, barony, half-barony or parish in which such murder or maiming shall respectively have been perpetrated, at the discretion of such grand jury."[40]

---

34. Section 18. See also 25 Geo 3, c 54 (Ir), s 7 (Dublin Grand Jury empowered to present £20 as reward for apprehending persons guilty of robbery or murder, or injured while attempting to do so).

35. In 1784 special provision was made for the compensation of soldiers who had been "houghed . . . by cutting the tendons and sinews of their legs across . . . ". If the offenders were not apprehended within six months, the grand jury had to raise from the local inhabitants an *annual* sum of £20 during the life of the soldier: 23 and 24 Geo 3, c 56 (Ir), s 1.

36. To 1780 by 17 and 18 Geo 3, c 36 (Ir), s 8; to 1783 by 19 and 20 Geo 3, c 14 (Ir), s 5; to 1787 by 21 and 22 Geo 3, c 40 (Ir), s 1; to 1793 by 26 Geo 3, c 24 (Ir), s 72; to 1800 by 34 Geo 3, c 23 (Ir).

37. 40 Geo 3, c 96 (Ir). This legislation was not finally repealed until 1967 – see Criminal Law Act (NI) 1967, s 15(2), Sch II, Part I.

38. 36 Geo 3, c 20 (Ir).

39. Section 12, which amended the rules of evidence to allow informations or examinations taken on oath from such persons to be admitted at a subsequent trial.

40. Section 14.

This Act, also a temporary one, was likewise extended[41] and then made perpetual in 1800.[42]

One cannot leave the turbulent period of the late 1790s without one further reference. At the end of 1798, Commissioners were appointed to enquire into property losses suffered during the rebellion, and to award reasonable compensation to legitimate claimants.[43] The powers of these Commissioners were subsequently extended – in 1800[44] – to include the payment of compensation to subjects who had "materially suffered in their persons in the rebellion" and to widows and orphans of others who lost their lives thereby. This development, too, created a precedent for later "emergencies".

The position in 1800 can therefore be summarised as follows: compensation in respect of criminal injuries to persons could be awarded in each of the following circumstances:

(i)   For the murder, maiming or dismembering of any person by any robber, tory or rapparee, where the offender had not been killed or apprehended, and subject to a maximum of £20 for death, and £10 for injury (1697 Act);

(ii) "Rewards" were by various statutes payable in many circumstances to persons injured (or to the representatives of persons killed) while endeavouring to apprehend, or when pursuing or prosecuting offenders;

(iii) For the wilful or malicious shooting, maiming or disfiguring of any person under the Whiteboy Act 1775;

(iv) For the murder or maiming of witnesses, magistrates and other peace officers in certain circumstances under the Insurrection Act 1796.

In all cases (except in some reward situations) the procedure was similar: the injured person presented his petition to the judge of assize; after investigation and the hearing of any evidence, the grand jury retired to decide in private what amount (if any) to award; the sum so awarded was levied off the county at large, or the barony, half-barony or parish in which the offence had been committed. There was an appeal against such presentment by way of traverse to the judge of assize.

THE GRAND JURY (IRELAND) ACT 1836

During the early years of the nineteenth century the system of local government in Ireland was subjected to almost continuous criticism.[45] It was

---

41. 38 Geo 3, c 21 (Ir).

42. 40 Geo 3, c 96 (Ir).

43. 38 Geo 3, c 68 (Ir), as amended by 39 Geo 3, c 65 (Ir).

44. 40 Geo 3, c 49 (Ir).

45. See e.g. *Reports from the Select Com-*

mittee on Grand Jury Presentments in Ireland (1815) BPP, *vi*, 1661 and (1822) BPP *vii*, 1; *Report of the Select Committee to enquire into the State of Ireland* (1826) BPP, *v*, 659 and *Report from the Select Committee on Grand Jury Presentments in Ireland* (1826–7) BPP, *iii*, 4.

pointed out that the members of the grand jury were not representative of the general body of ratepayers, that it had no continuous existence (coming together only at the twice-yearly assizes), that the amount of work (both administrative and legal) to be got through at each assizes meant that there was little or no time to look closely at each presentment, and that such consideration as was given was carried out behind closed doors. Another major weakness was the basis on which presentments were levied on the local inhabitants.[46] These were apportioned by an equal acreage tax levied on the land; but this method of assessment had become the cause of great inequality not only by the development of complex rules (so that, for example, "unproductive" lands were calculated in reduced acres) but also because the surveys on which the acreages were based had been made in the seventeenth and eighteenth centuries and not revised. A new general survey was set in train in the 1820s, but it was not until 1852[47] that a modern and uniform valuation of land and tenements, to be used for all public and local assessments, was established. Reform of the presentment procedure was effected more speedily. Measures were taken in 1819[48] and again in 1833[49] to deal with the obvious weaknesses in the system and these reforms were consolidated by the Grand Jury (Ireland) Act 1836. By this legislation, some representation of ratepayers was established, a start made on providing a permanent secretariat and administrative offices, much of the work was diverted from the grand jury to presentment sessions, and such deliberations of the grand jury as took place now did so in open court.

In all of these discussions the provision of criminal injuries compensation by presentment of the grand jury was not a major concern. This was no doubt due primarily to the comparatively small sums involved.[50] In addition, while the scope of compensation for damage to property was somewhat increased in the early nineteenth century, that same period saw a consider-able *reduction* in the scope of compensation for personal injuries. Although

---

46. See especially *Second Report from the Select Committee on Grand Jury Presentments in Ireland* (1816) BPP, *ix*, 5–6; 1822 Report, *supra* and for the 19th century generally *Minutes of Evidence taken before the Royal Commission on Local Taxation – Part I (Memorandum by the Local Government Board for Ireland)* (1898) BPP, *xlii*, 139.

47. Valuation (Ir) Act 1852.

48. Roads and Public Works (Ir) Act.

49. Grand Jury (Ir) Act.

50. Although annual returns of the expenditure of grand jury presentment moneys were required by statute (4 Geo 4, c 33, s 18), malicious injury claims came under the heading of "Miscellaneous". Some indication may, however, be gained from the following figures for Co Cork, which detail the average annual levy for *all* malicious injuries (i.e. including damage to property):

	Malicious Injuries £	Total Levy £	Malicious Injuries as % of Total Levy
1824–8	1,331	79,611	1.7
1829–33	340	70,783	0.5
1834–8	313	71,534	0.4
1839–43	463	80,154	0.6
1844–8	1,202	90,907	1.3

See Murphy, *Remarks on the Irish Grand Jury System* (1849). Since the total sum levied by grand juries in 1826 was £814,631 (see *Report from the Select Committee on Grand Jury Presentments in Ireland* (1826–27) BPP, *iii*, 4), these figures suggest that the criminal injuries bill for the whole country was less than £14,000 pa. By 1849, the total sum raised by grand juries had increased only to £1,319,050 (see (1850) BPP, *li*, 466–7); in 1859, it had fallen to £1,059,647 (see (1860) BPP, *lxi*, 574–5).

the 1697 Act was still technically in force,[51] it does not seem to have had much effect in relation to personal injuries.[52] The Whiteboy Act of 1775 was first given a restricted interpretation,[53] and then in 1831, insofar as it made wilful or malicious shooting, maiming or disfiguring a capital offence, the Act was repealed,[54] thus putting an end to the power to award compensation for such injuries. There remained only the provisions of the Insurrection Act of 1796. These were substantially re-enacted in 1807.[55] In 1810[56] the Chief Secretary for Ireland announced that the "Government of Ireland" no longer felt it necessary to continue with these emergency powers. He added, however, that the Acts did contain some provisions which it would be proper to re-enact, and one of these was the section providing for compensation to witnesses and magistrates. This was re-enacted with minor amendments in the Unlawful Oaths etc (Ireland) Act 1810,[57] and it is this provision which became the basis of criminal injuries compensation for the remainder of the nineteenth century and for the early twentieth century through its re-enactment in the Act of 1836.[58] By section 106 of that Act, the grand jury were empowered to pay by way of compensation such sum as they "shall think just and reasonable, having regard to the rank, degree, situation and circumstances" of the claimant where:

(i)   "any person, having given information or evidence against any person or persons charged with any offence against the public peace shall have been murdered or maimed previous to the trial of the person or persons accused . . . or on account of any such evidence given"; or

(ii) "any magistrate or other peace officer shall be murdered or maimed on account of his exertions, as such magistrate or peace officer, to bring disturbers of the public peace to justice".

Section 137 of the Act added a strict notice requirement,[59] but otherwise the Act marks no departure from the pre-existing law. The scope of section 106 is discussed in detail below. At this stage we may note just one peculiarity;

---

51. It was not formally repealed until 1878.

52. When, for instance, the Acts of 1695 and 1697 were extended to Dublin, their scope was restricted to certain kinds of damage to property – see Burning of Houses (Dublin) Act 1841.

53. *In re Roe* (1824) Sm & Bat 97.

54. Tumultuous Risings (Ir) Act 1831. The effect of this Act on the provisions relating to compensation for injuries to the person was uncertain. In *In re Cowens* (1836) 4 Law Rec (ns) 151 Bushe CJ appears to have overlooked the Act of 1831 when he observed that the compensation provisions of the Whiteboy Act had not been repealed by the Grand Jury (Ir) Act 1833. But *cf In re Neil* (1836) Jebb CC 180.

55. Insurrection and Disturbances (Ir) Act, s. 8.

56. 17 Cobbett's Parl Deb, col 202 (30 May 1810).

57. 50 Geo 3, c 102, s 6.

58. "Its provisions, though repealed, give a clue to the nature and scope of the [1836] legislation": *Murphy v Cork CC* [1903] 2 IR 445, 448, *per* Lord Ashbourne C. See below, p 16.

59. Details of the injury and the victim's knowledge (if any) of the offenders had to be given to a Justice of the Peace "within three days after the commission of the . . . injury, unless prevented by illness or other sufficient cause . . . ". This requirement was strictly interpreted – see e.g. *In re Tobin* (1860–4) Res Cas 2; *In re Walpole* (1890) 24 *ILTSJ* 329.

the compensation provisions of the 1836 Act did not apply to the City and County of Dublin, nor to the City of Belfast.[60] Steps were taken to deal with compensation for damage to property in these areas[61] – but until 1898 no provision was made for compensation for personal injury in Dublin or Belfast – an illogical and anomalous omission.[62]

In general the scheme of local taxation introduced by the 1836 Act was for all requests for money from ratepayers to go first to Baronial or County Presentment Sessions, to be heard by a body of magistrates and representative ratepayers.[63] After scrutiny, they were then sent to the grand jury for approval, amendment or rejection. The grand jury's decision was subject to the "fiat" of the judge of assize. This general procedure, designed to provide a more thorough and representative control over local taxation, was modified in relation to compensation for personal injuries. Whereas claims for damage to property were, as other presentments, subject to control both before reaching the grand jury[64] and afterwards,[65] personal injury claims went straight to the grand jury, and could not be traversed.[66] The grand jury had no power to refuse an award if the applicant satisfied the requirements of the Act; but they did have considerable discretion as to the amount of compensation to be awarded[67] and as to the ratepayers from whom the requisite sums were to be levied.[68] Their decisions had to be approved by the judge of assize who could, in turn, refer any difficult legal issue to the Court for Crown Cases Reserved.[69]

The narrow scope of section 106 suggests that public compensation for personal injuries during the nineteenth century was viewed primarily as an adjunct to the criminal process. Such compensation was payable not to the victims of violent crime as such, but rather to those whose active co-operation was vital to the apprehension, prosecution and conviction of suspected offenders. Intimidation of Crown witnesses was seen as a major problem in obtaining convictions and the availability of compensation for those who stood up to it and paid the penalty was the least that could be done

---

60. See Grand Jury (Ir) Act 1837, s 2; *In re Miller* (1840) 2 Ir LR 306.

61. See County Dublin Grand Jury Act 1844, s 37; Burning of Houses (Dublin) Act 1841, and County Antrim and Belfast Borough Act 1865, ss 34–5.

62. *In re Morton's Presentment* (1873) IR 7 CL 195. The position in Belfast was particularly anomalous since it was policed by the RIC; Dublin at least had its own police force.

63. See generally Hackett, *The Irish Grand Jury System* (1898).

64. By the Presentment Sessions. The *Report from the Select Committee on Grand Jury Presentments in Ireland* (1867–8) BPP, *x*, 47, 49 observed in relation to grand juries that "practically those bodies now form courts of

appeal from the decisions arrived at at presentment sessions".

65. Aggrieved parties could traverse the presentment and have the claim retried by the Judge of Assize and a petty jury (either common or special). See e.g. *In re McGrath* (1841) 2 Cr & D 201.

66. *In re Leahy* (1888) 22 ILTR 89 (previous application to presentment sessions not necessary); *In re Anthony* (1886) 20 ILTR 14 (no power to traverse presentment).

67. *In re Nolan* (1890) 24 *ILTSJ* 623.

68. *In re Presentment of the Barony of Portnahinch* (1889) 23 ILTR 45.

69. As e.g. in *In re McKenna's Presentment* (1871) IR 5 CL 401; *In re Nolan* (1890) 24 *ILTSJ* 623.

to encourage such witnesses to come forward.[70] Similarly, the payment of compensation to magistrates and police officers injured or killed in the execution of their duty was an obvious response to the recognised difficulties faced by them in enforcing the law, particularly during times of agrarian unrest.[71] In addition, the power to fine the community "responsible" for allowing such crimes to occur was officially believed to encourage the local population to keep the peace.

This reasoning may have been undermined by the growth, from 1836 onwards, of a professional police force and by the movement towards a professional magistracy.[72] Whether for this or some other reason the limited provisions in the 1836 Act for public compensation – particularly in relation to damage to property – began for the first time to give rise to critical comment. In particular, it was alleged that malicious injury presentments were "a fertile source of jobbing and perjury" and the virtual abolition of compensation for malicious damage to property by fire was recommended.[73] The efficacy of the local liability principle also came under question:

> "Conflicting evidence has been taken before your Committee on the subject of these presentments for malicious injuries; on the one side it has been contended that by this system of compensation, the innocent may be made to pay for the guilty, and that as the injured person looks forward to be indemnified for the loss he has sustained, the detection of the offender becomes a matter of small importance to him. On the other hand it is urged by witnesses of great experience that the present state of the law does away with inducements to commit malicious injuries, which generally result from the ill-will of neighbours. It is manifest that a man will be likely to abstain from acts of destruction towards the property of his neighbour, when he is aware that not only will the person injured be, in all probability, indemnified for his loss, but that he, the offender, may have to contribute to that indemnity. All the neighbours have thus an interest in preventing malicious injury to property . . . "[74]

This Committee concluded, however, that to do away with the present system would, in 1868 as in 1842, be injurious to the security of property in Ireland. No criticism was apparently made of the provision of compensation

---

70. See e.g. Gash, *Mr Secretary Peel* (1961), pp 171–4; Beames, *Peasants and Power: The Whiteboy Movements and their Control in pre-Famine Ireland* (1983), ch 2. Those who did give evidence frequently had to emigrate at public expense – see e.g. (1829) BPP, *iv*, 147, 202 (Evidence of a Crown Solicitor to the Select Committee on Irish Miscellaneous Estimates).

71. See e.g. Williams, *Secret Societies in Ireland* (1973), p 33: "Nearly one hundred policemen were killed and five hundred wounded in suppressing secret societies in the twenty years before the Famine . . . ". See also Rudé, *Protest and Punishment 1788–1868* (1978), ch 2.

72. The Constabulary (Ir) Act 1836 had estab-lished the basis for a modern police force in Ireland.

73. *Report of the Commissioners appointed to revise the several laws under or by virtue of which moneys are now raised by Grand Jury Presentments in Ireland* (1842) BPP, *xxiv*, 59, 181.

74. *Report of the Select Committee appointed to enquire into the several laws under which Monies are now raised by Grand Jury Present-ments in Ireland etc* (1867–8) BPP, *x*, 59. Similar divergences of views were expressed in Parliament – see e.g. 161 HC Debs, cols 1676 *et seq* (8 March 1861). The Irish judges, however, never apparently doubted the effi-cacy of the principle – see e.g. *R v Recorder of Cork* (1863) 16 ICLR 1, 13, *per* Lefroy CJ.

for personal injuries – but its abolition would no doubt have been opposed as injurious to the maintenance of law and order.

More general recommendations were made for changes in the overall system of local government.[75] Although the 1836 Act had effected considerable improvements, it left unresolved many fundamental problems, particularly in relation to its representative – or rather, its non-representative – character. Political developments in Ireland were beginning to ensure that major reforms were inevitable.

THE LAND PROBLEM 1870–1885

Controversy over the wisdom and efficacy of local liability had, in the mid-nineteenth century, focused almost entirely on the provisions for public compensation for damage to property. But the onset of "agrarian outrages" in the course of the land "wars" of the 1870s and 1880s brought compensation for personal injuries to centre stage, as never before. The catalyst was the Peace Preservation (Ireland) Act 1870, section 39 of which provided:

> "Where it shall appear that any person has been murdered, maimed or otherwise injured in his person, and that such murder, maiming or injury is a crime of the character commonly known as agrarian, or arising out of any illegal combination or conspiracy, the grand jury . . . shall, upon application,[76] . . . present such sum or sums of money as they shall think just and reasonable to be paid to the personal representative of the person so murdered, or to the person so maimed or injured, having regard to the rank, degree, situation and circumstances of such person . . . "

This considerable extension of the local liability principle was criticised in Parliament, where some Irish members condemned it as giving grand juries an unbridled power to fine the innocent inhabitants of troubled districts.[77] In fact, this "temporary" provision, which remained in force for ten years,[78] gave rise to relatively few claims, except perhaps in 1871 and 1873.[79] In any

---

75. See e.g. Malley, "On the Expediency of the Total Abolition of Grand Juries in Ireland" (1871) 5 *JSSISI* 11.

76. Which could be made by or on behalf of the victim or (as never before, in order to avoid the effects of intimidation) by the Crown Solicitor of the county or by any person in that behalf authorised by the Lord Lieutenant (*ibid*).

77. See e.g. 200 HC Debs, cols 691–2 (21 March 1870). Others thought that the power should not be given to grand juries, but to the assistant barristers (*ibid*, col 483) or to the Lord Lieutenant in Council (*ibid*, col 690). Cf "The grand juries, who added to their local knowledge a deep interest in the maintenance of tranquillity in their counties . . . were the only bodies to whom it could prudently or safely be entrusted." (*ibid*, col 689).

78. The 1870 Act was continued, by the Peace Preservation (Ir) Acts 1873 and 1875, to 1880, when it was allowed to lapse.

79. The amounts claimed and granted in the years 1870–1875 were as follows:

	Amount Claimed	Amount Granted
	£	£
1870	800	700
1871	16,050	6,945
1872	5,300	1,740
1873	26,600	5,115
1874	5,000	1,685
1875	5,250	1,705

See (1875) BPP, *lxii*, 160 *et seq*. The largest award was for £1,200 to a claimant who had been "feloniously fired at, maimed and injured."

case, the section was almost immediately amended[80] to allow the necessary sums (for the first time) to be levied by yearly or half-yearly instalments, instead of in a single lump sum as hitherto. In addition, section 39 was further amended in 1875 so that no award could be made –

> "unless the grand jury . . . shall be of opinion that material evidence concerning the murder, maiming or injury . . . is withheld by a person resident within the district proposed to be charged."[81]

The 1875 Act went on to bring the local liability principle to a new level of refinement by providing that any presentment had to set forth the valuation of the district proposed to be charged, the number of instalments required to raise the sum presented, the poundage rate necessary for levying those instalments and "the grounds upon which the same has been charged upon such district".[82] All these factors had to be "carefully considered" by the Judge of Assize before he affirmed, varied or perhaps disallowed the presentment.

These refinements did little to assuage the critics of the system, and the inclusion of similar provisions in the Prevention of Crime (Ireland) Act 1882[83] added to an already bitterly controversial debate.[84] On this occasion, however, the power to award compensation was *not* given to the grand juries; instead, the Lord Lieutenant was to nominate "such person or persons being or one of whom shall be a practising barrister of at least six years' standing . . . to investigate the application . . . ".[85] After hearing all parties "whom he or they deem to be interested", a report was presented to the Lord Lieutenant, who "may award such sum for compensation as he thinks just". The 1882 Act makes no reference to the particular factors enumerated in the 1870 and 1875 Acts; but it was made clear that, in deciding whether to award compensation, the Lord Lieutenant had a wide discretion and could take into account, for example, "the amount of direct and indirect complicity which lies upon the neighbourhood", and the ability of the district to bear any given "fine".[86]

The objects of this provision were clear; to provide compensation and to punish "guilty" districts "because the liability to payment of the kind not only converted every man into a detective to discover crime after it had

---

80. Protection of Life and Property (Ir) Act 1871, ss 12 and 13.

81. Peace Preservation (Ir) Act 1875, s 3. In spite of this restriction, compensation awarded in the three years to 1880 averaged £3,240 per annum: (1884) BPP, *lxiiii*, 529.

82. Section 3.

83. Section 19. By s 19(6) these provisions applied to murders etc committed after 1880 and also to those committed before 1880 where a notice of intention to apply for compensation under the Peace Preservation Acts had been issued.

84. See especially 271 HC Debs, cols 780–894 (29 June 1882).

85. It was argued that since the grand jury met only twice a year, there would be delays in dealing with claims, "during which the purposes contemplated by this clause would be extremely prejudiced" (*ibid*, col 816). But delays in the *payment* of compensation were inevitable since the necessary funds had still to be levied by the grand jury – see e.g. *Herbert* v *Hungerford* (1886) 20 LR Ir 100 (application made in October 1882; compensation not finally paid until October 1885).

86. 271 HC Debs, cols 830, 834 (29 June 1882).

occurred, but made him also a constable for its prevention."[87] It was consistent with these objectives that compensation should not be limited to actual loss:

> "Something more than mere pecuniary compensation ought to be given to the injured person. The compensation ought to take the shape, in some respect, of a *solatium* for the misery, the life-long misery, inflicted on the friends and relatives of the murdered man – the compensation involved that consideration, and it also involved the consideration of the penalty of the deed itself."[88]

The introduction of an overt executive discretion, the removal of judicial control and comments such as the above suggest that, under the 1882 Act, which remained in force for only three years, criminal injuries compensation moved from the legal to the political sphere. Whether this be so or not, this provision – as indeed the Act as a whole – was bitterly opposed by Irish nationalist MPs, and thereafter they were to press consistently for repeal of criminal injuries compensation, even of the limited variety under the Grand Jury (Ireland) Act 1836, to which the law reverted as more peaceful conditions returned to Ireland.

The Local Government (Ireland) Act 1898

The frequent attempts to reform local government in Ireland finally came to fruition in 1898. By the Local Government (Ireland) Act of that year, the administrative functions of the grand juries were transferred to elected county councils, jurisdiction over criminal injuries was given to the county courts, and the grand jury was remaindered to its criminal function of scrutinising bills of indictment prior to trials at Assizes or Quarter Sessions.[89] Although the 1898 Act considerably extended the occasions on which compensation could be awarded for damage to property, the personal injury provisions of section 106 were not added to in any *substantive* way. However section 5(9) of the Act removed the geographical anomaly by providing that the criminal injuries code, including section 106, "shall extend to the whole of Ireland".[90] By section 80, the procedure for raising

---

87. *Ibid*, cols 862–3.

88. *Ibid*, col 843. The analogy with the assessment of damages under the Fatal Accidents Act 1846 was expressly rejected (*ibid*, col 848). In fact, in the period to 20 June 1883, there were 33 awards for death (totalling £22,450 and ranging from £200 to £3,000) and 77 awards for injuries (totalling £20,185 and ranging from £10 to £3,000) – (1884) BPP, *lxiii*, 531. The average awards (£680 for death and £260 for injuries) were only marginally higher than those awarded under the Peace Preservation Acts in 1878–1880 (£660 and £190 respectively).

89. This function was removed when grand juries in Northern Ireland were finally abolished by the Grand Jury (Abolition) Act (NI) 1969.

90. See above, p 11. It was predicted that this provision, which ended a "ridiculous" and "absurd" anomaly, would lead to "a large increase of litigation and a large increase of taxation": Brett, *Law and Procedure relating to Compensation for Criminal Injuries* (1899), *viii–ix*. For the legal effect of the provision see *Mairs v Belfast Corp* [1901] 2 IR 1; *Representative Church Body v Dublin CC* [1901] 2 IR 255.

the necessary funds was modernised.[91] In addition, the rule-making power conferred by section 5)7) of the Act had a significant effect on the administration of the scheme:

> "The power to make these [county court] rules, and the express provision that non-compliance with them shall not render any proceeding void unless the Court . . . shall so direct, and the powers given to the judges to amend irregularities, and to extend the various periods of time for the service of notices and so forth, have had the effect of practically destroying the rigidity which characterised the procedure prior to the passing of the . . . Act."[92]

The transfer of jurisdiction from the grand jury to the county courts[93] (with an appeal to the judge of assize and a further appeal to the Court of Appeal) also brought the substantive provisions of the criminal injuries code before the courts to a much greater extent than hitherto. In this legal, as opposed to administrative, setting attention came to be more closely focused on the interpretation of the legislation and the philosophy on which it was based.

The restriction of section 106 to "maiming" was apt to exclude a number of less serious injuries, but the courts modified the originally strict interpretation of this term.[94] Conversely, a more generous approach[95] was brought to an end when the Court of Appeal in *Murphy* v *Cork CC*[96] restrictively interpreted the requirement that a magistrate or other peace officer be murdered or maimed "on account of his exertions . . . to bring disturbers of the public peace to justice". In holding that a police officer maimed by a suspect attempting to escape from arrest was not entitled to compensation, Lord Ashbourne C observed:

---

91. Cf R *(Vance)* v *Dublin Corp* (1906) 40 ILTR 57 (applicant not entitled to be paid out of general funds raised for a different purpose); *R (Bennett)* v *Kings CC* [1908] 2 IR 176 (decree did not create an immediate debt or liability to pay, but only a duty to raise, levy and then pay). See also *Sullivan* v *Giltrap* (1902) 36 ILTR 26.

92. Moloney and Lee, *The Law Relating to Compensation for Criminal Injuries* (1912), p 10. " . . . The words in s 5(7) are purposely inserted in order to put a stop to the scandalous cases of failure of justice by reason of non-compliance with technical points": *per* FitzGibbon LJ in *Manders* v *Kildare CC* (1909) 43 ILTR 9.

93. By the County Court Rules 1899, r 14, criminal injury applications were governed by existing county court practice in equity cases. This meant that they were heard and determined by the county court judge sitting without a jury. Cf Local Government (Ir) Act 1898, s 5(5) provided that the Judge of Assize on appeal could impanel a jury to try any issue of fact arising on the appeal. In *Midland Rly Co (Ir) Ltd* v *Roscommon CC* (1904) 38 ILTR

52, 53 Palles LCB observed: "Since the passing of the [1898] Act . . . the functions formerly discharged by judge and jury are consolidated and discharged by . . . the judge [alone] . . . ".

94. See e.g. *Stafford* v *Belfast Corp* (1903) 37 ILTR 129 (injury need not be permanent); *English* v *Kerry CC* (1900) 34 ILTR 76 (scalp wound amounted to "maiming"); *McCabe* v *Dublin Corp* (1901) 1 NIJ 88 (stab wound on arm constituted maiming).

95. In the period 1881–1901 there were 182 claims for criminal injuries compensation by injured policemen; compensation was refused in only 12 cases (a further 2 claims were withdrawn). The total compensation paid was £38,275, ranging from £3,000 (to an injured District Inspector) to £5: (1901) BPP, *lxi*, 392–408. For some individual cases see e.g. 43 HC Debs, cols 123–5 (20 July 1896), 286 HC Debs 1015 (28 March 1884), 4 HC Debs 513 (20 March 1893) and 303 HC Debs 1181 (18 March 1886).

96. [1903] 2 IR 445, followed in *Power* v *Tipperary CC* (1904) 4 NIJ 159 and *Maguire and Walsh* v *Limerick CC* (1908) 42 ILTR 197.

" . . . the motive of this resistance, which caused the injury, is not to be traced to any special feeling of ill-will towards the constables for bringing the man to justice, but to the ordinary desire to escape from arrest."[97]

The courts also confirmed a pre-1898 decision that under section 106, which makes no express reference to "compensation" as such, a successful applicant was entitled only to such sums as are "just and reasonable", this being something less than "full compensation".[98]

Underlying these particular decisions were some general views on the philosophy and purpose of the criminal injuries code. In *Murphy* the judges had stressed the exceptional nature of the provision for compensation – had it been intended to compensate all police officers injured in the execution of their duties "this section [106] would be found in the ordinary law of the country, and not in special legislation . . . ".[99] To put it another way:

"It should be understood that the law is not that a constable is entitled to compensation by way of insurance from the public for injuries received in the discharge of his duties generally."[1]

Where compensation was payable, the courts had to take into account the special juridical nature of the claim. Thus, under section 106:

" . . . the people of the county or locality in which the injury was committed were not treated as wrongdoers. They were not considered responsible, in point of law, for the wrongful act which caused the injury. It was a misfortune that the legislature had put it upon them that they had to bear the burden, or part of the burden, incident to that misfortune."[2]

This view of local liability seems at odds with the original concept,[3] and suggests that in the early twentieth century the Irish judges were seeking to restrict that principle both in its application and extent,[4] at a time of relative peace and prosperity. This did not mean, however, that injured policemen

---

97. [1903] 2 IR 445, 449. *Cf* this reasoning might not apply where a police officer was injured by a third party – compensation was awarded in such circumstances in *Stafford* v *Belfast Corp* (1903) 37 ILTR 129; *Kennedy* v *Limerick CC* (1903) 3 NIJ 87 and *Cremin* v *Cork CC* [1908] 2 IR 61.

98. *In re Nolan* (1890) 24 *ILTSJ* 623 (one-fifth of "full" compensation awarded); *English* v *Kerry CC* (1900) 34 ILTR 76, 78 (two-thirds of "full" compensation awarded); *Wallace* v *Limerick CC* (1920) 54 ILTR 75 (widow of murdered constable earning £280 pa awarded sum calculated to yield £120 pa).

99. [1903] 2 IR 445, 450, *per* Lord Ashbourne C. Both the Lord Chancellor and Holmes LJ (at p 453) specifically referred to the origins of s 106 in the Unlawful Oaths (Ir) Act 1810.

1. *Maguire and Walsh* v *Limerick Corp* (1908) 42 ILTR 197, 199, *per* FitzGibbon LJ. See also Walker LJ in *Murphy* (at p 452): "This section is a branch of the law of compensation for malicious injury and not an insurance clause for policemen."

2. *English* v *Kerry CC* (1900) 34 ILTR 76, 78, *per* Palles CB.

3. See e.g. *Mason* v *Sainsbury* (1782) 3 Dougl 61, 64, *per* Lord Mansfield.

4. Details of claims and awards are given in the annual reports on Civil Judicial Statistics for Ireland 1900–1920. On average, 4 or 5 decrees were made each year for personal injuries and the total annual compensation awarded was about £300–£400. (*Cp* for damage to property the corresponding figures were 500 and £14,000 respectively.)

should go uncompensated; rather, this objective should be attained by other methods. In particular, the risk or fact of injury could be taken into account in the assessment of police pensions.[5] On this basis the principle of local liability (of ratepayers) would be replaced by the principle of central (or, at that time, "Imperial") governmental responsibility (of taxpayers).

From a political point of view the principle of local liability was vigorously opposed, during this period, by Irish nationalists. A half-hearted attempt had been made in 1898 to have section 106 repealed;[6] more serious attempts were made in 1908[7] and again in 1909[8] to repeal the criminal injuries code on the basis that this would assimilate Irish and English law (from which the local liability principle had been virtually eliminated in 1886[9]). All these attempts at repeal failed;[10] but as the political complexion of the new county councils – the "defendants" in all criminal injuries cases – began to reflect the increasing strength of Irish nationalism, the need for *some* reform developed accordingly.

THE STRUGGLE FOR IRISH INDEPENDENCE 1916–1924

1. 1916–1920

Practical (and political) difficulties in operating the 1836 and 1898 Acts were manageable while the number of claims, and the sums of money involved, remained low and the new system of local government worked satisfactorily, as they did for the first 15 years of the new century. But the events of Easter Week 1916 made alternative arrangements desirable and the Government, no doubt taking cognizance of the precedent set as far back as 1798, determined that claims both for property damage and personal injury suffered during the rising should be dealt with by a special tribunal. By section 1(6) of the Law and Procedure (Emergency Provisions) (Ireland) Act 1916:

---

5. *English* v *Kerry CC* (1900) 34 ILTR 76, 78, *per* Palles CB. It was also asked in Parliament – "Why should there not be an insurance fund for the purpose [of compensation] amongst the policemen themselves?" 130 HC Debs, col 1439 (1 March 1904). See generally Miers, "Compensating Policemen for Criminal Injuries" (1972) 7 *IJ* 241.

6. See 57 HC Debs, col 54 (2 May 1898). A Nationalist motion to repeal the criminal injuries code as "involving an unjust and iniquitous burden on innocent persons" was debated – and defeated – in 1904 – see 130 HC Debs, cols 1433–1462 (1 March 1904).

7. Malicious Injuries (Ir) Bill 1908 – see 183 HC Debs, col 542 (2 Feb 1908) and 188 HC Debs, col 1670 (18 May 1908). The Bill lapsed after its first reading.

8. Police (Malicious Injuries) (Ir) Bill 1909 –

see 5 HC Debs, col 729 (21 May 1909) – defeated at second reading.

9. The liability of the hundred to pay compensation had been virtually abolished by the Remedy against the Hundred Act 1827 and the Riot (Damages) Act 1886; that which remained extended to certain kinds of damage to property only. An attempt in 1914 to extend the Irish scheme to Great Britain to deal with the damage caused by militant suffragettes was rejected as "not desirable": 59 HC Debs, col 1049 (10 March 1914).

10. The Government seemed to consider this a matter for agreement between the Irish parties; at least in 1916 the Chief Secretary indicated that if they could agree, he would be happy to consider legislation to put criminal injuries compensation in Ireland on the same footing as in England: 87 HC Debs, col 823 (15 Nov 1916).

"No claim for compensation under any of the enactments relative to compensation for criminal or malicious injuries shall lie against a local authority in respect of any injury to person or property sustained in the course of the recent disturbances in Ireland."

Instead, the Government in October 1916 appointed a committee, chaired by the President of the Incorporated Law Society, to inquire into and report with regard to applications for payment out of public funds on an *ex gratia* basis to –

(a) persons who have suffered loss by reason of personal injuries sustained by them without misconduct or default on their part in the recent rebellion, and

(b) dependants of deceased persons who without misconduct or default on their part were killed or injured in the recent rebellion.[11]

Four points may be noted. First, compensation was not restricted to "criminal" injuries, but was also to be paid to innocent civilians killed or injured by the army; these terms of reference thus went considerably beyond the existing scope of public compensation for personal injury.[12] Secondly, this appears to have been the first time an express requirement was imposed that the death or injury be "without misconduct or default" of the victim.[13] Thirdly, the cost of compensation was to be borne by the central exchequer: "it has been thought equitable and just that this burden should be taken off the shoulders of the rate-payers".[14] Finally, compensation was based on that payable under the Workmen's Compensation Acts, *viz* a maximum of £300 in case of death[15] and weekly payments not exceeding one-half of pre-injury earnings and "measured on the degree of impairment of earning capacity"[16]

---

11. See 86 HC Debs, cols 393–4 (17 Oct 1916). For details of the casualties, see e.g. Lyons, *Ireland since the Famine* (1971), p 375. A separate committee was set up to deal with claims for damage to property.

12. The Attorney General for Ireland had stressed that, so far as personal injury was concerned, s 1(6) of the 1916 Act had deprived no one of any benefit, since "There is no machinery and no law in Ireland to-day existing . . . that enables any person merely because he has been injured in a civil commotion or any action of the military to recover damages for that from any local authority . . . ": 85 HC Debs, col 2214 (17 Aug 1916).

13. The Dublin Metropolitan Police provided the Committee with a report on the applicant's background and, in particular, indicated whether he was known to be a member of any "disloyal" organisation or had played any part in the rebellion.

14. 85 HC Debs, col 760 (7 Aug 1916).

15. The basic sum was three years' loss of earnings, but this was subject to a maximum of £300 – and a minimum of £150. Thus, the widow and children of a man killed at age 35 who had been earning £2 per week were awarded £300: National Archives SPO: CSORP 1922/R103.2.

16. 98 HC Debs, col 1317 (30 Oct 1917). Compensation could also be awarded for medical expenses, but *not* for pain and suffering or loss of amenities. The injury was assessed by a medical referee who classified the applicant's earning capacity as (i) totally destroyed; (ii) materially impaired; (iii) impaired or (iv) slightly impaired, and compensation was assessed accordingly. The weekly payments could be commuted to a lump sum if the incapacity lasted more than six months. Thus, a married woman earning 15/- per week who had her left leg amputated above the knee was awarded 7/6 per week for some 11 months and then a lump sum by way of commutation of £210-10-3: National Archives SPO: CSORP 1922/R103.2.

in case of injury.[17] The relevant sums were paid to trustees, to be administered by them for the benefit of the victims.[18]

The Committee had substantially completed its work by 1917[19] and for a short time normality appeared to have been restored. But in December 1918 the overwhelming victory of Sinn Fein in the general election "transformed the face of Irish politics".[20] On 21 January 1919 was held the first session of Dail Eireann, at which a Declaration of Independence was approved. On the same day two members of the RIC were killed in an ambush.[21] Further attacks on the security forces[22] – and on the magistracy – followed and this escalating violence led (*inter alia*) in April 1919 to a substantial extension of the scope of criminal injuries compensation. Section 1(1) of the Criminal Injuries (Ireland) Act 1919, in terms not too dissimilar from those of the Prevention of Crime (Ireland) Act 1882,[23] provided that compensation was payable in respect of incidents occurring after 1 January 1917[24]–

"(*a*) where a judge, magistrate, police constable, member of the . . . [armed] forces or the civil service[25] of the Crown has been murdered, maimed or maliciously injured in his person in the execution of his duty or on account of his being, acting or having acted as a judge, magistrate, police constable or member of such forces or service; [and]

(*b*) where any other[26] person has been murdered, maimed or maliciously injured in his person, and the murder, maiming or injury is a crime arising out of any combination of a seditious character or any unlawful association [or assembly[27]]."

---

17. See generally Hanna, *The Law of Workmen's Compensation* (2nd ed, 1907), ch 6.

18. See Irish Times, *Sinn Fein Rebellion Handbook* (1917), p 249. This requirement applied both to minor and adult victims. The proceedings of the Committee, which dealt in all with 450 claims, were conducted in private: *ibid*.

19. See 95 HC Debs, col 401 (27 June 1917). But some claims took much longer to settle – see e.g. that of a Mrs Wigoder for medical expenses, which was finally determined only in 1920: National Archives SPO: CSORP 1920/24762.

20. Lyons, *op cit*, n 11, p 399.

21. The resulting claims for compensation ended up in the Court of Appeal – see *O'Connell* v *Tipperary CC* [1921] 2 IR 103, discussed below.

22. The RIC appear to have been particularly vulnerable – see Hawkins, "Dublin Castle and the RIC 1916–1922" in Williams (ed), *The Irish Struggle 1916–1926* (1966), ch 14.

23. See above, p 14. This connection was explicitly acknowledged by the Attorney

General for Ireland – see 114 HC Debs, col 2187 (9 April 1919).

24. So provided by s 1(6).

25. Later held to include a postman: *McCann* v *Antrim CC* (1930) 64 ILTR 31.

26. The shooting dead of a magistrate on his way to church showed that the literal application of this word operated to the disadvantage of those listed in subsection (*a*) (see 134 HC Debs, col 743 (5 Nov 1920)), and s 7(*a*) of the Criminal Injuries (Ir) Act 1920 subsequently provided, on a retrospective basis, that the classes of persons listed in (*a*) were also entitled to compensation if injured in the circumstances described in (*b*). *Cf* in June 1920 the Government had refused to pay an extra charge (of £2% pa) for life insurance imposed on a magistrate on account of the risks of his occupation – see PRO Ms T192/7.

27. The words "or assembly" were added, retrospectively, by the Criminal Injuries (Ir) Act 1920, s 7(*a*) to avoid difficulties revealed by two cases in 1919 – see *Deehan* v *Londonderry CC* (1921) 55 ILTR 29 and *Mangan* v *Kerry CC* (1921) 55 ILTR 31.

The wording of paragraph (a) was designed to remove the limiting effect of the decision in *Murphy v Cork CC*.[28] A further provision in section 1(3) was designed to reverse the decisions in *Nolan* and *English*[29] by stipulating expressly that the power to make a decree for such sum as the county court judge thinks just and reasonable "shall include power to make a decree for full compensation".[30] This wording was clearly designed to authorise the courts to raise the level of compensation, but the judges could not agree on the new scale. The obvious approach was to award compensation on the same basis as in common law and Fatal Accidents Act cases; but the Court of Appeal appeared to consider that section 1(3) went further than this, at least in cases of compensation for murder. In *O'Connell v Tipperary CC*[31] the Court awarded compensation to the relatives of a murdered policeman on a more generous basis than would have applied under the Fatal Accidents Act.[32] Molony CJ specifically rejected this analogy:

" . . . An examination of that Act and of the cases under it will show that, while analogous in several respects, there are very material differences . . . "

Instead:

"Each case must depend upon its own facts, and the Court must determine, considering all the circumstances in a just and reasonable spirit, what is the full compensation to be paid to the applicant in each particular case."[33]

O'Connor LJ was less than enthusiastic about this open-ended approach and clearly would have preferred to follow the Fatal Accidents Act cases.[34] Later courts tended to prefer this obviously sensible solution.[35]

---

28. [1903] 2 IR 445, discussed above p 16. "The ten peaceful years which came to an end in 1906 [*sic*] presented no great number of cases in which the narrowness of this construction caused hardship or attracted attention; but it is at the present time . . . desirable that a construction so harsh to the officers concerned, and . . . so intolerable in the present circumstances . . . should be removed." Lord Birkenhead LC, 34 HL Debs, cols 307–8 (14 April 1919). Note, however, that the "third party" exception to *Murphy* (see n 97 above) had been recently followed to allow the payment of compensation in *Mills v Dublin Corp* (1919) 53 ILTR 113. The effect of the new provision is clearly demonstrated in *Dempsey v Londonderry CC* [1942] NI 90.

29. See above p 17. These cases had recently been applied in *Leahy v Roscommon CC* (unreported, but referred to by Molony CJ in *O'Connell v Tipperary CC* [1921] 2 IR 103) and in *Mills, supra*.

30. Section 2(1) further provided for the recovery of certain medical expenses.

31. [1921] 2 IR 103, discussed Veitch, "Interests in Personality" (1972) 23 *NILQ* 423.

32. Compensation was awarded to non-dependent relatives. Lord Ashbourne C further suggested that compensation could be awarded to dependent non-relatives ("persons connected by the ties of . . . friendship" – see p 117) and (*ibid*) that a widow could be compensated for "the loss of consortium, or nervous or physical breakdown through grief or shock", contrary to *Blake v Midland Rly* (1852) 18 QB 93. But neither issue actually arose for decision in *O'Connell*.

33. [1921] 2 IR 103, 126. Molony CJ seems to have been influenced in particular by Brett J's injunction in *Rowley v LNW Rly Co* (1873) LR 8 Ex 221 that damages under the Fatal Accidents Acts should not attempt "perfect", but rather "fair", compensation. See also Ronan LJ at p 129.

34. See especially at p 133.

35. See e.g. *Hunt v Tipperary CC* (1920) 54 ILTR 63, 65, *per* Moore J (decided before *O'Connell*) and *McCann v Antrim CC* (1930) 64 ILTR 31.

To these extensions of the substantive law the 1919 Act added a number of procedural reforms designed to facilitate the obtaining of criminal injuries compensation.[36] But the effectiveness of all these changes depended on the co-operation of the county councils as defendants and rate collectors. In most cases this was no longer forthcoming after Sinn Fein swept the board in the local elections held in the first half of 1920.[37] Local government bodies controlled by Sinn Fein quickly repudiated "British" authority and declared their allegiance to Dail Eireann. By November 1920, as the armed struggle reached its bloodiest stage, most councils were neither contesting applications for compensation nor paying the sums decreed by the county courts.[38] To circumvent these tactics, "provisions of the most drastic character"[39] were enacted in the Criminal Injuries (Ireland) Act 1920. Section 1 reiterated that the amount of compensation decreed "shall be a debt due by the council and payable . . . on demand" and went on to provide that it could be paid out of any moneys under the council's control.[40] The Act further provided that outstanding sums could be recouped either directly by deduction from various public funds *before* these were paid to the council, or by attachment of rates or any other debts due to the council.[41] Other amendments were also introduced to facilitate the making of applications[42]

---

36. See e.g. s 1(2) which, like the 1870 and 1882 Acts, provided that an application could be made "by the Attorney General for Ireland or any person authorised in that behalf by him". To speed up the payment of compensation, s 1(4) provided that a decree of the County Court was payable on demand, instead of after the requisite sum had been levied off the ratepayers. This provision did not work satisfactorily, and had to be replaced by s 1(2) of the Criminal Injuries (Ir) Act 1920 – see *R (Barham)* v *Leitrim CC* [1920] 2 IR 41, and Note (1920) 54 *ILTSJ* 193. But delays still occurred – see 134 HC Debs, col 209 (2 Nov 1920) (pending assessment of compensation the Government guaranteed minimum payments to the widow and children of murdered policemen).
37. See e.g. Lyons, *op cit* n 11, p 409.
38. Following orders issued by the Dail Minister for Local Government – see Hanna, *The Statute Law of the Irish Free State 1922–1928* (1929), p 62. See also Note (1921) 54 *ILTSJ* 31 and *Hosie* v *Kildare CC* [1928] IR 47, 58, *per* Murnaghan J. For specific examples, see *Lyons* v *Mayo CC* (1921) 55 ILTR 40; *Mangan* v *Kerry CC* (1921) 55 ILTR 31. The Dail courts, however, had no machinery for dealing with criminal injury claims; applicants were advised to lodge a claim with the secretary of the appropriate county council and informed that this would not be regarded as "recognition" of the British courts – see National Archives, DEC11/243 (Letter from Assistant Minister for Home Affairs, 23 Jan 1922).

39. So described in Editorial (1921) 55 *ILTSJ* 13. See further 134 HC Debs, cols 737 *et seq*.
40. Section 1(1), thus repealing the previous restriction whereby councils could pay compensation only out of funds specially applicable thereto (above, n 91).
41. Section 2(1) (applicable to payments from the Local Taxation (Ir) Account, any fund administered by any government department and any parliamentary grant) and s 3(1) (provided the decree was first removed on *certiorari* to the High Court). The Dail Government responded with a "Solemn warning" against "holders of decrees of Enemy Courts for Criminal and Malicious Injuries" and their agents who sought to enforce those decrees and thereby deprive the poor, the sick and the aged of the essential community services for which the rates had been collected – see National Archives, DEC26/10 Proclamation (nd) signed by L T MacCosgair, Minister for Local Government.
42. Section 6 repealed the three-day notice requirement laid down in the Grand Jury (Ir) Act 1836, s 137; the courts had no power to dispense with that requirement (*Shaw & Co* v *Wicklow CC* [1919] 2 IR 414) which often caused hardship to applicants – see e.g. *Rearcross Co-operative Creamery Co Ltd* v *Tipperary CC* (1920) 54 ILTR 193. Section 6 also conferred power to re-hear an application which had already been heard and refused under the pre-1920 law or due to the claim having been abandoned because of threats to or intimidation of the applicant.

and to encourage the payment of compensation.[43] These amendments had limited effect;[44] with the exception of north-east Ireland, the system of local government created by the 1898 Act had simply ceased to function.

The British Government's political response to the situation in Ireland came in two stages. During 1920 Parliament debated proposals for "home rule" and those were ultimately enacted in the Government of Ireland Act. This divided Ireland into two parts, each with its own Parliament with limited legislative powers. Intended as a temporary solution, the Government of Ireland Act was reluctantly accepted in Northern Ireland and came into effect in June 1921.[45] But in Southern Ireland the passing of the Act served only to intensify the armed struggle for independence. Attempts to end this war ultimately succeeded and a truce came into effect on 11 July 1921. Negotiations between the two sides occupied the next five months until, on 6 December 1921, Articles of Agreement for a Treaty between Great Britain and Ireland were signed, establishing the Irish Free State.

The effects of these developments on the provision of compensation for criminal injuries must be considered separately in relation to each of the new jurisdictions.

2. The Irish Free State

Given the previous opposition of Irish nationalists to many aspects of the criminal injuries code, and the unprecedented scale of damage to property and of personal injury, it was clear that radical steps would have to be taken by the new government. Three distinct phases must be considered.

(a) *Injuries sustained between 21 January 1919 and 11 July 1921*

For injuries sustained between the date of the first meeting of Dail Eireann and the date on which the Truce came into operation (the "pre-Truce period"), the framework for compensation was set in January 1922 by the Working Arrangements between the British and Irish Governments for implementing the Treaty.[46] Section 3 provided:

> "That the principle should be admitted that fair compensation is to be paid in respect of injuries which are the subject of compensation under the enactments relating to criminal injuries . . . "

More specifically, section 4 provided that, as respects personal injuries:

> "(*a*) Each Government should deal with and should be responsible for the payment of compensation in respect of personal injuries to its own supporters.[47]

---

43. E.g. sections 1(2) (power to pay by instalments over a period of up to five years), 4 (interest to be awarded on unpaid decrees) and 5 (power to levy rates at any time or to borrow money for the payment of compensation).

44. "The powers given in that Act [of 1920] were not much availed of. Some people were afraid to avail of them, others had a degree of decency which prevented them availing of them." 1 Dail Debs, col 1355 (6 Oct 1922) (Mr E Blythe, Minister for Local Government).

45. See below, p 28.

46. See *Heads of Working Arrangements for Implementing the Treaty* (Cmd 1911, 1923).

47. In cases where the injured person was not clearly a supporter of one or other government, half the amount of the decree would be paid by each government: see 52 HC Debs, col 68 (28 Nov 1922).

(b) Awards already given should stand.

(c) The provisions as to liability under *(a)* should be retrospective to apply to awards already satisfied."

It was further agreed (section 7) that all court proceedings for compensation would be barred, and steps were immediately taken by the Provisional Government to give effect to this provision.[48]

For its part, the British Government paid in full all decrees which had been awarded by the county courts to "its own supporters" for personal injuries inflicted during the pre-Truce period.[49] Cases in which final decrees had not been obtained were referred to two nominated members of the Compensation (Ireland) Commission which had been set up to deal with claims for damage to property during this period.[50] The amounts awarded by them were also paid by the British Government.

Similar payments were envisaged for supporters of the Irish Government, since the prohibition on proceedings under the Criminal Injuries Code enacted by the Damage to Property (Compensation) Act 1923 was stated not to "apply to or prevent the presentation or prosecution of a claim to or before any Commission of Inquiry ...".[51] Such a commission – the Compensation (Personal Injuries) Committee – had in fact been appointed in February 1923 under the chairmanship of a county court judge[52] –

"I [To] receive, investigate and consider applications for compensation presented by any person who has suffered loss by reason of having been injured in his person or by the dependants of any person who has died in consequence of having been so injured . . . since the 21st January, 1919 . . .

(1) Where the injury was an injury to which the Criminal Injuries Acts would have . . . applied . . .

---

48. See Public Notice No 1 (20 Jan 1922) and No 2 (11 Feb 1922), reproduced in Bolton, *The Criminal Injuries (Ir) Acts 1919 and 1920* (1922), pp *vi–vii*. The Provisional Government (Criminal Injuries) Decree No 10 made in October 1922 prohibited any use of the powers contained in the Criminal Injuries (Ir) Act 1920 – "a war measure . . . [which] contained provisions which if put into operation are calculated to seriously hamper . . . the administration of local government in Ireland . . . ": 1 Dail Debs, cols 1350–4 (6 Oct 1922). These were interim measures pending the enactment of permanent legislation in the Damage to Property (Compensation) Act 1923, s 1. For the effect of these measures see *Leen* v *President of the Executive Council* [1928] IR 408; *Galway CC* v *Minister for Finance* [1931] IR 215.

49. See Memorandum, *Irish Free State: Compensation for Injury to Persons and Property* (Cmd 1844, 1923), p 2. The amount involved

was stated to exceed £2.6m. Despite complications resulting from the Government of Ireland Act, the Criminal Injuries Acts continued to operate in southern Ireland after 1920 – see e.g. *Farrelly* v *Monaghan and Fermanagh CC* (1922) 56 *ILTSJ* 219.

50. For the work of the Shaw (and later the Ward–Renton) Commission, see Greer and Mitchell, *Compensation for Criminal Damage to Property* (1982), pp 16–18. The personal injury claims were dealt with by Mr Howell Thomas (Deputy Chief Valuer to the Board of Inland Revenue, appointed by the British Government) and Mr James Dowdall (Member of the Incorporated Chamber of Commerce and Shipping, appointed by the Irish Government).

51. Section 1(6).

52. His Honour Judge Johnston KC; the other two members were medical practitioners (Dr T Hennessy and Dr H Kennedy).

(2) Where the injured person was or was likely to be excluded from the benefit of the Criminal Injuries Acts . . . by reason only of the injury having been inflicted by members of the British military or police forces.

(3) Where the injury was sustained without default on the part of a person being a non-combatant in the course of belligerent action between the British forces and the Irish National forces . . .

II The Committee will recommend to the Minister of Finance[53] what sums should in reason and fairness be paid . . . regard being had to (inter alia) the actual earning capacity of the injured person prior to the injury and to the impairment of earning capacity attributable to the injury and to the actual extent of dependency of dependants upon the deceased person prior to the death or injury . . . and to any effective provision made by the deceased person for his dependants by way of insurance or otherwise.[54]

III The Committee shall in general recommend awards by way of lump sum, but shall also recommend in the alternative monthly or quarterly allowances in cases of injury considered likely to be permanent . . .

IV The Committee shall not recommend an award in any of the following cases:–

(1) Cases eligible for any award under any Act making provision for army pensions.

(2) Cases in which a final decree under the Criminal Injuries Acts was obtained prior to 12th February, 1922, and

(3) Cases in which the British Government have undertaken full liability."[55]

It will be noted that this arrangement made criminal injuries compensation a national responsibility[56] and gave it as such rather lower priority than compensation for damage to property:

"The restoration of the [damaged] property is no loss and no extravagance, generally speaking, because of the employment it gives. [But] huge payments for personal injuries mean sending out huge sums of money for which there is no immediate need. . . . If a person is to get a sum of money into his pocket in respect of which he is to restore nothing to the nation there is much greater liability to be extravagant than in other cases . . . [The] steps we have taken to ensure that the property will be restored, and the wealth of the nation will not be lessened indicates the difference in our appreciation of the thing."[57]

---

53. "We are not accepting a legal liability in respect of this . . . There will be *ex gratia* payments . . . As such it may be stopped at any moment . . . ": 2 Dail Debs, cols 2101–3 (7 March 1923).

54. In short, on a much less generous basis than envisaged by the 1919 Act, as interpreted in *O'Connell* – see above, p 21.

55. See Memorandum referred to in n 49 above.

56. The Government (2 Dail Debs, col 1614

(22 Feb 1923)) indicated that it wanted to relieve the local authorities of their liabilities. It also hoped, by having the claims dealt with by a single tribunal, to achieve consistency of awards: "Where there are 26 or 27 County Court Judges it is quite possible that the same case . . . in counties far apart would get different treatment from different . . . Judges." *ibid*, col 1392 (8 Feb 1923).

57. *Ibid*, col 1618. The President denied the suggestion that he was putting human life on a lower rating than property (col 205).

(b) *Injuries sustained between 11 July 1921 and 20 March 1923*

The Working Arrangements agreed in January 1922 envisaged that claims in respect of criminal injuries, whether to person or property, sustained after the Truce came into operation, would be dealt with in the usual way by the county courts.[58] That agreement was made on the assumption of a return to "normal civil life" in Ireland. Such hopes were dashed by the onset of the civil war in June 1922, as a result of which the Irish Government resolved to continue dealing with compensation for personal injury on a national basis. Section 17 of the 1923 Act prohibited proceedings under the Criminal Injuries Acts[59] in respect of all injuries to the person which occurred after 11 July 1921 and on or before 20 March 1923.[60] But section 17(6) again permitted the presentation of such claims to or before any Commission of Inquiry. The Johnston Committee, established in February 1923, was empowered to deal also with personal injuries sustained before 12 May 1923[61] and, in addition to the terms of reference quoted above, applications for compensation could be considered where the injury was sustained without default by a non-combatant "in the course of operations by the National forces against persons engaged in armed rebellion against the Government of Saorstat Eireann . . . ".[62]

The British Government accepted that responsibility for dealing with post-Truce injuries rested with the Irish Government, but "they could not divest themselves of a duty to see that such claims are met equitably and as promptly as inevitable difficulties allow".[63] In particular the two governments agreed to refer to a special tribunal those cases where –

(a) personal injury or death of members of the British Forces had been maliciously caused, in breach of the Truce, in the area under the jurisdiction of the Irish Government, and

(b) personal injury or death of other persons in the same area which had been maliciously caused in breach of the Truce by members of the British Forces.[64]

The net result of these arrangements – apart from the delay involved – was that the "full compensation" provided for criminal injuries by the Act of 1919 was no longer obtainable.[65] In particular, no compensation could be

---

58. See *Letter to the Provisional Government on Compensation for Malicious Injuries in Ireland* (Cmd 1736, 1922), para 3.

59. I.e. under the 1836 Act, but not under the Acts of 1919 and 1920 – see *Hosie* v *Kildare CC* [1928] IR 47, 66, *per* Murnaghan J.

60. As a result of what appears to have been an oversight this date was *not* extended to 12 May 1923 when that date was substituted for other purposes of the 1923 Act by the Damage to Property (Amendment) Act 1923, s 1(1).

61. The date on which the 1923 Act became law.

62. See *Memorandum on Compensation for Injury to Persons and Property in the Irish Free State* (Cmd 1844, 1923), pp 5–6.

63. *Letter to the Provisional Government on Compensation for Malicious Injuries in Ireland* (Cmd 1736, 1922), para 4.

64. See 52 HL Debs, col 70 (28 Nov 1922).

65. See generally *Report of a Committee on Irish Free State Compensation* (Cmd 2748, 1926) hereafter referred to as "*Dunedin Committee Report*").

given by the Johnston Committee where serious personal injury had been sustained, but there was little or no loss of "actual earning capacity". More forceful criticisms were made of the provisions for property damage compensation and the British Government was forced to take remedial action. In May 1922 an Irish Distress Committee had been set up in London to assist refugees from Ireland, and in 1923 this was reconstituted as the Irish Grants Committee, with power (*inter alia*) "to recommend to the Secretary of State for the Colonies . . . what advances should be made to claimants for compensation under the Criminal . . . Injuries Acts or other legislation for the time being in force in Ireland . . . ".[66] Further discussion followed, and in 1925 a committee was set up to enquire and report whether further action should be taken by the British Government in respect of compensation for post-Truce injury to person and property in Ireland. The committee recommended[67] that individual cases should be considered on an *ex gratia* basis, and for this purpose a (new) Irish Grants Committee[68] was set up in 1926:

> "to consider claims from British subjects . . . who, on account of their support of H.M. Government prior to 11 July 1921 sustained hardship and loss by personal injuries [or by damage to property] . . . in the area of the Irish Free State between . . . 11 July 1921 and 12 May 1923 being . . . injuries of such a nature as would have given rise to a claim for compensation under [the Criminal Injuries Acts then] in force . . . or who have otherwise suffered special hardship and loss on account of such support . . . and to advise H.M. Government in each case, taking into account the degree of hardship suffered by the claimant, whether, in addition to any grants or compensation already awarded[69] . . . any further *ex gratia* grant should in reason and fairness[70] be made to the claimant by H.M. Government . . . "

This Committee completed its work by 1930,[71] by which time, as a result of

---

66. *Dunedin Committee Report*, pp 3–4.

67. *Ibid*, p 9.

68. Consisting of Sir Alex Wood-Renton (Chairman), Sir James Brunyate and Sir John Oakley. The Committee had the assistance of a "Contradictor" to cross-examine claimants and their witnesses and to put a formal argument expressing the Treasury view in each case. A full report of the Committee's work was made in 1930 (hereafter referred to as "IGC Report").

69. Normally claimants had to show that they had made a claim for compensation under the Criminal Injuries Acts; but failure to do so due to ignorance, threats, intimidation or other reasonable cause was excused: *IGC Report*, p 33. *Cp* Criminal Injuries (Ir) Act 1920, s 6, discussed above, n 42.

70. In measuring the compensation to be recommended, the Committee had regard to "the factors usually taken account of in the assessment of compensation in such cases,

and, in some measure, to what may be called the conventional scale of compensation established by a long history of similar outrages": *IGC Report*, p 97. But notwithstanding *Ballymagauran Co-op Agricultural Soc* v *Cavan and Leitrim CC* [1915] 2 IR 85, insurance payments *were* taken into account "in the comparatively small number of cases in which the issue has arisen": *ibid*, p 34. Following the Damage to Property (Compensation) Act 1923, s 13(3), no allowance was made for sums deducted by the Irish Free State in respect of income tax.

71. The Committee recommended the payment of grants totalling £2.2m in 2237 cases coming within its terms of reference. Separate figures are not given for personal injury claims, but an Appendix estimated the amount expended on "Irish Compensation" in respect of personal injuries as £3.27m paid by the British Government and £2.5m paid by the Irish Free State Government: *IGC Report*, p 14 and *Appendix*.

further representations,[72] the British Government had agreed to pay its recommendations in full.

(c) *Injuries sustained after 20 March 1923*

By the spring of 1923, the civil war was coming to an end.[73] The Damage to Property (Compensation) Act 1923 was passed on 12 May 1923. Thereafter claims could be made in the courts for compensation in respect of personal injuries sustained after 20 March 1923[74] – but only on the basis of the pre-1919 law. The Criminal Injuries (Ireland) Acts of 1919 and 1920 were permanently repealed,[75] so that section 106 of the Grand Jury (Ireland) Act 1836 once more applied, without the benefit of the declaration in favour of "full compensation" and in the restricted sense as laid down in *Murphy* v *Cork CC*.[76] As a result the new system of local government inaugurated by the Local Government Act of 1925 had virtually no responsibility to provide public compensation for personal injury resulting from crime. The local liability principle still, however, survived to a considerable extent in relation to compensation for damage to property.[77]

3. Northern Ireland

The problems which had given rise to the Criminal Injuries (Ireland) Act 1920 were comparatively rare in the north-east of the island, and none of the special arrangements found necessary in Southern Ireland after 1920 applied to criminal injuries compensation in Northern Ireland.[78] Instead, the new jurisdiction created by the Government of Ireland Act 1920 simply took over the existing law[79] – the 1919 and 1920 Acts remaining fully in force.[80]

---

72. The British Government had originally set aside £400,000 for such payments. In 1927 it announced that the "Sumner principle" would be applied, *viz* the first £250 would be paid in full, 50% of the next £750 and 30% of any further amount up to £49,000. (This had been the basis of compensation adopted by the Sumner Commission for World War I damage claims.) The application of this principle was criticised and the Government, by stages, eventually adopted a more generous approach: see generally, *IGC Report*, pp 14–18.

73. The date of Mr de Valera's "proclamation" (24 May 1923) is usually taken as the end of hostilities.

74. Section 17(5).

75. Section 22(1), and see *Hosie* v *Kildare CC* [1928] IR 47.

76. See above, p 16, and e.g. *Smith* v *Cavan CC* (1924) 58 ILTR 107; *Mooney* v *Dublin Corp* [1939] IR 520; *Foley* v *Dublin Corp* [1939] IR 516 and *Hyland* v *Dublin Corp* (1940) 74 ILTR 248.

77. Greer and Mitchell, *Compensation for Criminal Damage to Property* (1982), pp 21–3.

78. In June 1922, it was reported that a special commission on the lines of the Compensation (Ir) Commission had been suggested to deal with claims for compensation for property damage in Northern Ireland, but this idea was rejected by the Government of Northern Ireland, for the reason that such claims "were all being tried by the County Court Judges throughout the length and breadth of our area . . . ": 2 HC Debs (NI), col 812 (22 June 1922).

79. Law and order services were transferred to the Government of Northern Ireland on 22 November 1921; see generally McColgan, *British Policy and the Irish Administration 1920–1922* (1983), ch 4.

80. Compensation was also paid on an *ex gratia* and extra-statutory basis for kidnapping (and looting) – see 5 HC Debs (NI), col 60 (11 March 1925).

Although the province then experienced serious "troubles" of its own, in which many people were killed and injured, claims for criminal injuries compensation continued to be dealt with by the courts.[81] Since, however, a significant element in the communal strife resulted from "southern aggression"[82] by the IRA, the British Government made available £2m to provide a 60% subsidy for Northern Ireland ratepayers in respect of compensation for criminal injuries (both to person and property) which had occurred between 1 June 1920 and 14 October 1922.[83] Local authorities were recouped in this way only if they had effectively contested the claims made against them[84] – not all councils in Northern Ireland were anxious to make the system work. But this subsidy, together with additional freedom to raise loans and to spread the cost of compensation over a five-year period,[85] enabled the local councils to weather the storm. By 1924[86] Northern Ireland too had returned to relative peace.

THE DEVELOPMENT OF THE PRESENT SYSTEM OF COMPENSATION

1. Northern Ireland

The relative calm within Ireland as a whole after 1924 resulted in a considerable reduction in the amount of criminal injuries litigation, and this is reflected both in the absence of legislation and in the relative paucity of reported cases – at least as regards personal injury claims – during the next thirty years. By the mid-1950s, the total annual cost in Northern Ireland of *all* criminal injuries compensation – that is, for both personal injury and damage to property – was in the region of £20,000.[87] Then – in 1956 – the IRA commenced a fresh campaign of shooting and bombing. This campaign had two characteristics which led to a fundamental alteration of the rationale for criminal injuries compensation in Northern Ireland. First, there was the comparative severity of the campaign – the bill for compensation was multiplied 20 times over in less than a year.[88] The impact on the local

---

81. See e.g. *Leyburn* v *Armagh CC* (1922) 56 ILTR 28 (June 1921); *Cummings* v *Armagh CC* (1922) 56 ILTR 64 (summer 1921); *Kerr* v *Belfast Corp* (1922) 56 ILTR 140 (July 1922).

82. See 2 HC Debs (NI), col 912 (5 July 1922).

83. 3 HC Debs (NI), col 1493 (16 Oct 1923), expended in roughly equal amounts in 1922–23, 1923–24 and 1924–25 – see *Ulster Year Book* (1929), p 198.

84. See Ministry of Home Affairs, *Circular to Local Authorities*, 23 Feb 1922, reprinted in Bolton, *The Criminal Injuries (Ireland) Acts 1919 and 1920* (5th ed 1922), pp *x-xi*.

85. *Ibid*. Sums received by local authorities by way of loans for criminal injuries compensa-

tion during the period 1921–1925 exceeded £600,000 – see *Ulster Year Book* (1929), p 200.

86. Expenditure by local authorities on criminal injuries compensation declined from almost £1.5m in 1922–23 to £0.3m in 1924–25 (*ibid*, pp 201–2) and to £61,000 by 1926–27 (*Ulster Year Book* (1932), p 230).

87. According to the then Minister of Home Affairs – see 40 HC Debs (NI), col 2617 (1 Nov 1956).

88. Claims for compensation amounted to £350,000 by May 1957 – 41 HC Debs (NI), col 1108 (14 May 1957). The number of criminal injury compensation claims heard in the county courts in 1957 was 1,148 (as compared with 952 in 1956, and 508 in 1955): *Ulster Year Book* (1957–1959), p 262.

rate-payers threatened to be intolerable.[89] Secondly, the campaign was essentially a "border" one, many of the attacks being launched from outside Northern Ireland. The traditional theory of "collective responsibility" was obviously inapplicable.[90] It was therefore abandoned – though with obvious reluctance – and only "until such times as conditions return to normal". The Criminal Injuries Act (NI) 1956 took the first step by providing that where compensation was awarded for damage to property or injury to persons "caused by or as a result of any combination of persons mainly residing outside Northern Ireland", the county court could direct the compensation to be paid by all the county councils in Northern Ireland in proportion to their respective net annual rates, and that the Ministry of Home Affairs might, out of money provided by Parliament, pay to each county council a grant not exceeding one-half of any such sums paid by the council.[91]

The changeover was taken one step further by the Criminal Injuries Act (NI) 1957 which, though a temporary provision, was continued from year to year until 1970.[92] By virtue of sections 6 and 7 of this Act, the Ministry of Home Affairs was empowered to make a grant of the full amount paid out by a county council as compensation for certain kinds of damage to property or for certain injuries to persons. The 1957 Act also extended the scope of the scheme – compensation became payable where any person was murdered, maimed or maliciously injured "by a malicious person acting on behalf of or in connection with any unlawful association"[93] and introduced the important device of the Inspector-General's "Certificate". This enabled the Inspector-General of the Royal Ulster Constabulary to certify that the murder, maiming, etc had in his opinion been caused by a malicious person acting for any unlawful association and this certificate was evidence that the murder, etc had been so caused, until the contrary was proved.[94]

Peace returned to Northern Ireland in 1962,[95] and it was just at this time that other legislatures began to make provision for the awarding of compensation to victims of crime – though only in cases of personal injury. The Criminal Injuries Compensation Scheme introduced in Great Britain in 1964[96] followed shortly after the enactment of the Criminal Injuries Com-

---

89. The county councils had apparently for some time maintained that the burden of compensation should be borne by the central government.

90. "There is nothing unreasonable . . . in the local authority contention that these affairs are, as near as may be, acts of war which the local people are powerless to prevent . . . ": 40 HC Debs (NI), col 2617 (1 Nov 1956). The principle had been relied on officially as late as 1919: "The effect . . . [of this Bill] will be that the country and the district which have screened the perpetrators of these crimes . . . should pay compensation to the widows and orphans of the men who have been assassinated": 114 HC Debs, col 2187–8 (9 April 1919).

91. Sections 6(1) and 11(2).

92. See s 9 and the annual Expiring Laws Continuance Acts (NI) 1957–1968 and Criminal Injuries (Continuance of Temporary Provisions) Act (NI) 1969.

93. Section 3(1). "Unlawful association" was defined as "any association declared by or under any enactment to be unlawful" (s 4).

94. Section 3(2), later amended by s 2(3) of the Criminal Injuries (Amendment) Act (NI) 1958.

95. In fact, by 1959 the number of criminal injury compensation cases had dropped to 306: *Ulster Year Book* (1960–62), p 273.

96. For a general description and analysis of this scheme see Greer, *Criminal Injuries Compensation* (1990). See also Atiyah, *Accidents, Compensation and the Law* (4th ed, 1987), ch 13.

pensation Act 1963 in New Zealand.[97] In the calm of the mid-1960s the decision was taken to bring the Northern Ireland legislation into line with these modern developments, and this step was effected with the passing of the Criminal Injuries to Persons (Compensation) Act (NI) 1968. The general policy underlying this Act was thus explained by the Minister of Home Affairs:

> "Our courts have long experience of criminal injury claims and this Bill simply extends their existing jurisdiction in that respect. This increase in jurisdiction is, however, a substantial and important one . . . The Bill would extend compensation entitlement to people injured through any criminal offence except a motoring offence . . . and to any one injured in trying to prevent such an offence or in helping the police to arrest the offender . . . Generally the intention is not that the State should be given the same liability for compensation as the offender but that the State should so far as is reasonable ensure that the victim does not suffer undue hardship."[98]

It was further explained that the Act followed, in broad terms, the provisions of the British Scheme, with some reference to the New Zealand Act.[99] As a result the 1968 Act represents a point of departure from the previous criminal injuries "code". In particular it marks the final break from the "local liability" principle; as in Great Britain (and New Zealand) criminal injuries compensation was henceforth payable "out of money provided by Parliament";[1] the "temporary" shift of responsibility from ratepayer to taxpayer was made permanent and has since been accepted without question. But the Act still preserved some traditional Irish characteristics; the scheme remained a statutory one and continued to be administered by the courts and not by a special tribunal. Some particular provision continued to be made for "political" violence.[2] Nonetheless the 1968 Act was in general conceived and enacted as a modern scheme, for application in "normal" times, to compensate victims of all crimes of violence and also those injured or killed assisting the police to enforce the law. It was, therefore, rather ironic that shortly after it came into force, the present period of political violence commenced and the Act had to operate almost from its inception in circumstances substantially different from those for which it was designed.[3] The effect of "the troubles" in this context is readily apparent from the comparison between the Northern Ireland and British schemes in Table 1.1.

---

97. Chapter 134.

98. 68 HC Debs (NI), col 626 (31 Jan 1968).

99. See generally Greer and Mitchell, *Compensation for Criminal Injuries to Persons in Northern Ireland* (1976) and Miers, "Compensation for Victims of Crimes of Violence: the Northern Ireland model" [1969] *Crim LR* 576, and "Criminal Injuries to Persons (Compensation) Act (NI) 1968" (1969) 20 *NILQ* 201.

1. 1968 Act, s 9. *Cp* British Scheme, para 2; New Zealand Act, s 22.

2. 1968 Act, s 4(5)(*a*). See now 1988 Order, Art 8(2), discussed below pp 173 *et seq.*

3. As Kennedy CJ had pointed out with reference to earlier legislation: "the Criminal Injuries Acts were pressed into service as a sort of War Losses Compensation Code . . . ": *Kennedy* v *Minister for Finance* [1925] 2 IR 195, 199.

Table 1.1

Compensation for Criminal Injuries in Northern Ireland and Great Britain
1969–1978[4]

	Northern Ireland		Great Britain	
	Total Compensation paid (£)	Amount per 1000 population (£)	Total Compensation paid (£)	Amount per 1000 population (£)
1969–70	131,876	86	1,992,402	37
1970–71	443,474	288	2,098,032	39
1971–72	724,470	471	3,300,948	61
1972–73	2,173,524	1,421	3,449,544	63
1973–74	3,927,946	2,572	4,048,069	74
1974–75	6,022,556	3,952	5,059,396	92
1975–76	7,937,751	5,208	6,476,680	118
1976–77	6,307,724	4,142	9,677,389	177
1977–78	7,529,349	4,944	10,106,513	185

For a short period during the mid-1970s the total amount of criminal injuries compensation paid in Northern Ireland actually exceeded that in Great Britain; for the whole of the period the relative rate of compensation (per 1,000 population) in Northern Ireland was much higher than in Great Britain – in 1975–76 by a factor as high as 44. It appears that approximately one-third of the compensation paid in Northern Ireland went to members of the security forces or their dependants;[5] the remainder was paid to "civilians" and represents a horrendous degree of violent injury and death in a population of some 1.5 millions. Although no precise figures are available, it was estimated that some 90% of applications for compensation in Northern Ireland arose from terrorist or "sectarian" offences.[6]

From a legal and practical point of view these circumstances created certain difficulties in the interpretation and application of the 1968 Act.[7] Thus the frequency of terrorist incidents gave rise to a large number of claims for compensation for "nervous shock" and it proved difficult under

---

4. In this Table, the figures for Northern Ireland are derived from Parliamentary Written Answers (see especially 63 HC Debs, col *593* (11 July 1984)) and information supplied by the Northern Ireland Office; those for Great Britain are taken from the Annual Reports of the Criminal Injuries Compensation Board. The population is as indicated in the *Annual Abstract of Statistics* (1989), Table 2.1.

5. By 1976 total compensation of over £21 million had been paid under the 1968 Act; of

this, some £4.9 million (or 23%) had been paid to members of HM Forces or their dependants, and £1.7 million (or 8%) to police officers or their dependants: 911 HC Debs, col *261* (13 May 1976).

6. Information provided by the Northern Ireland Office.

7. See generally the debate on the 1977 proposed Draft Order – HC Debs (NI Committee), cols 1–106 (16 Feb and 2 March 1977) (hereafter referred to as "*NI Committee Debate*").

the 1968 Act to distinguish genuine claims from more doubtful ones.[8] Other problems arose not from "the Troubles" but from legal ingenuity; it was found e.g. that compensation could be obtained under the 1968 Act for injuries resulting from what were clearly not in any sense crimes of violence.[9] Public attention came to focus on two other matters – the effect of the full deduction of "collateral benefits" on the amount of compensation which could be awarded to widows of members of the security forces (and, in particular, to the widows of murdered soldiers),[10] and uncertainty as to the extent to which the 1968 Act precluded the payment of compensation to injured persons who were connected with proscribed organisations or otherwise thought to have been engaged in acts of terrorism.[11] Practical difficulties also arose from the large number of cases required to be heard and determined by the county courts and there was criticism of the time taken to dispose of claims and pay compensation.[12] All these matters were apparently considered by a Working Party set up within the Northern Ireland Office,[13] which reported to the Secretary of State in the summer of 1976. The Report was never published, but in due course a "Proposal" for new legislation was introduced.[14] This contained a number of new provisions designed to remedy the defects in the 1968 Act. In particular, the Secretary of State was to be given power (to operate retrospectively) to make "discretionary payments" to "top up" the amount payable to a widow whose compensation had been reduced below a prescribed minimum by the deduction of other benefits received on the death of her husband. The payment of compensation to those engaged in terrorism was to be expressly prohibited. Initial responsibility for determining claims for compensation

---

8. "In the past 12 months . . . 42 per cent of all claims have been for nervous shock . . . ": *NI Committee Debate*, cols 5–6. For the continuing problems in this respect see Greer, "A Statutory Remedy for Nervous Shock?" (1986) 21 *IJ* 57 and below, pp 55–61 and 68–77.

9. See e.g. *Owens* v *Sec of State* Unreported, Cty Ct (Judge Rowland), 4 Nov 1975 (applicant awarded compensation for injury when knocked down by bicycle without effective brakes contrary to Road Vehicle (Traffic) Regulations). See also *Porter* v *Sec of State* Unreported, Cty Ct (Judge Brown), 3 March 1978 (compensation awarded to passenger injured when car collided with cattle on road contrary to Summary Jurisdiction (Ir) Act 1851, s 10). Such cases arose from the wording of the 1968 Act, s 11(1), which defined a criminal injury as including "an injury . . . directly attributable to . . . *a criminal offence* . . . " (emphasis added).

10. Particularly in comparison with awards of common law damages to suspected terrorists who had been treated unlawfully by the secur-

ity forces – see e.g. 907 HC Debs, col 1528 (18 March 1976), 912 HC Debs, col 621 (27 May 1976) and 919 HC Debs, col 944 (22 Nov 1976).

11. Particularly in connection with *Cahill* v *Sec of State* [1977] NI 53, where an applicant thought to have been shot because of his connection with a proscribed organisation was eventually refused compensation on the ground that that connection was a "relevant circumstance" for the purposes of the 1968 Act, s 1(2). See further below, p 107.

12. By 1977 some 13,000 claims were outstanding, "in or around 2,000 [of which] are likely to require a full hearing in the courts": *NI Committee Debate*, col 94.

13. With terms of reference "To review the [1968 Act] . . . to recommend in what respects, if any, the Act should be amended, taking into account the parallel review of the Criminal Injuries Compensation Scheme currently being undertaken in Great Britain, and to put forward interim proposals."

14. Proposal for a Draft Criminal Injuries (Compensation) Order (NI) 1976.

was to be transferred from the county courts to the Secretary of State,[15] who was also to have substantial discretion in dealing with those claims. The existing "small claims" exclusion was to be increased by disallowing not only the first £100 of compensation for pecuniary loss but also the first £250 of compensation for non-pecuniary loss. Other proposed changes were also included in what amounted to a substantial revision of the Northern Ireland scheme. It may be noted that the main focus of these proposals was directed to particularly Northern Ireland problems and, by being published in advance of more general reviews,[16] they tended not to involve broader considerations. This "local" focus may have contributed to the fact that many of the proposals attracted considerable public interest and much critical comment within the province.[17] When the new legislation appeared in its final form it became clear that much of this criticism had been taken on board.[18] But a number of the major proposals for change remained substantially in place with the result, in particular, that from 1977 the Northern Ireland scheme was to be administered primarily by the Secretary of State – in practice, by the Criminal Injuries Branch of the Northern Ireland Office – though with an extensive right of "appeal" to the courts. To that extent, at least, the new legislation preserved the Irish tradition of a court-based scheme. The final draft of the new legislation met little opposition[19] and became law in August 1977.[20]

A general picture of the operation of the 1977 Act and the scope of its application is given in Table 1.2. This shows a distinct change in the pattern of development as between Northern Ireland and Great Britain during the past decade. While the number of awards made, and the total amount of compensation paid, in Great Britain increased steadily and apparently inexorably, the compensation paid in Northern Ireland has only recently exceeded that paid in 1978–1979. This pattern may be compared with the changes related to the rate of crime involving personal violence, as indicated by Table 1.3.

---

15. As had been done for claims for criminal damage to property by the Criminal Injuries to Property (Compensation) Act (NI) 1971 – see Greer and Mitchell, *Compensation for Criminal Damage to Property* (1982), p 295. Although that change had aroused little controversy and appeared to be working satisfactorily, the proposal to apply it to criminal injury claims provoked considerable opposition, especially from the legal profession in Northern Ireland – see e.g., "Criminal Injuries Law Row Brews" *Belfast Telegraph*, 26 Jan 1977; "Attack on changes in injury law" *Belfast Telegraph*, 4 Feb 1977.

16. In spite of the terms of reference (n 13 *supra*) the Working Party's report was completed before the Report of the Review of the British scheme was published in 1978. The Working Party appeared to pay little attention to the Law Commission's *Report on the*

Assessment of Damages in Personal Injury Litigation (Law Com No 56, 1973) and, of course, the whole review had been completed before the *Report of the Royal Commission on Civil Liability and Compensation for Personal Injury* (the Pearson Report) was published in March 1978.

17. See generally *NI Committee Debate*.

18. In particular, the "small claims" exclusion was reduced to £150 – but a new minimum of £1,000 was introduced for certain nervous shock claims; the scope of the Secretary of State's discretion was reduced to some extent, and a special provision was inserted to prevent undue delays in the determination of claims.

19. See 934 HC Debs, cols 751–777 (1 July 1977).

20. Criminal Injuries (Compensation) (NI) Order 1977.

Table 1.2

Compensation for Criminal Injuries in Northern Ireland and Great Britain 1979–1989[21]

	Northern Ireland		Great Britain	
	Total Compensation paid (£)	Amount per 1000 population (£)	Total Compensation paid (£)	Amount per 1000 population (£)
1978–79	10,612,634	6,936	13,045,641	238
1979–80	8,737,357	5,700	15,737,363	287
1980–81	10,009,218	6,508	21,462,464	392
1981–82	6,251,314	4,065	21,976,696	401
1982–83	7,138,764	4,627	29,444,675	537
1983–84	8,495,517	5,477	32,820,772	598
1984–85	9,262,917	5,947	35,293,451	641
1985–86	13,887,904	8,868	41,559,996	753
1986–87	11,466,532	7,280	48,241,764	871
1987–88	12,925,016	8,180	52,042,581	937
1988–89	14,968,319	9,470	69,381,286	1,246

Table 1.3

Crime Rate per 100,000 Population[22]

Jurisdiction	Year	Homicide	Rape	Robbery	Aggravated Assault
Northern Ireland	1980	6	4	83	116
	1982	7	5	125	165
	1984	4	6	130	182
	1986	6	8	140	195
	1988	7	6	135	212
England and Wales	1980	1	2	30	191
	1982	1	3	46	214
	1984	1	3	50	224
	1986	1	5	60	244
	1988	1	6	63	312
Republic of Ireland	1980	1	1	33	60
	1982	1	2	55	53
	1984	1	2	55	55
	1986	1	2	43	41
	1988	1	2	46	45

21. In this Table, the figures for Northern Ireland are derived from Parliamentary Written Answers (see especially 63 HC Debs, col *593* (11 July 1984)) and from information supplied by the Northern Ireland Office; those for Great Britain are taken from the Annual Reports of the Criminal Injuries Compensation Board.

22. Adapted from *A Commentary on Northern Ireland Crime Statistics 1988* (1989), Table 7.1 (p 70).

Table 1.2 however indicates that the amount of compensation paid *per head of population* is still substantially higher in Northern Ireland. Neither Table reveals the change within the Northern Ireland scheme of the ratio between "terrorist" and "non-terrorist" claims; whereas before 1977 terrorist claims represented some 90% of the total number of claims, by 1984 they represented only 25–30% of the total.[23] Terrorist incidents do remain the major cause of death by violent crime, where (as indicated in Table 1.3) the rate in Northern Ireland is very high by comparison with England and Wales; but most criminal injuries are now caused by "ordinary" crimes of violence, which have increased significantly in recent years.

It is therefore clear that the context in which the 1977 Order has operated is again rather different from that which, to some extent at least, had given rise to its enactment. However, the most immediate concerns with its operation in practice arose not from the general social or political context, but from technical considerations. As a court-based scheme the Northern Ireland legislation had adopted the traditional "once-and-for-all" principle of the common law; awards of compensation, once made, could not be re-opened. In 1979 a different approach had been taken in the British Scheme,[24] but it was decided in 1981 that there was no basis for a similar provision in Northern Ireland.[25] A more responsive note was struck (albeit tardily) in relation to the new "discretionary payments" for widows; when the new provision in the 1977 Order was found to be difficult to apply in practice,[26] it was replaced in 1982[27] by a more satisfactory formula. Shortly thereafter – and even though the Order had by then been in operation only for five years or so, another Working Party of officials from the Northern Ireland Office was requested by the Secretary of State to embark on a general review of the new scheme. Once more the investigation was an internal and *ex parte* enquiry; no evidence was sought of the views of victims or their representatives, and no attempt was made to obtain a detailed and objective assessment of the operation of the Order.[28] It may, of course, have been intended that the Working Party should consider only the extent to which the Northern Ireland scheme should be modified in the light of recent changes in the British Scheme[29] and changes in the general law of damages

---

23. Information supplied by Northern Ireland Office. Conversely, the amount of compensation paid under the 1977 Order to members of the security forces or their dependants remained at approximately one-third of the total compensation paid – see 63 HC Debs, col *593* (11 July 1984), 139 HC Debs, col *822* (4 Nov 1988) and 151 HC Debs, col *325* (21 April 1989).

24. British Scheme, para 13, following a recommendation in the 1978 *IWP Report*, para 4.6.

25. See 3 HC Debs, cols 626–632 (27 April 1981) and below, p 155.

26. The problem was acknowledged as early

as February 1978 and an extra-statutory solution adopted – see 943 HC Debs, col 1649 (9 Feb 1978).

27. Criminal Injuries (Compensation) Amendment (NI) Order 1982, discussed below, p 215.

28. See Standing Advisory Commission on Human Rights, *13th Annual Report 1986–1987* (HC 298, 1988), (hereafter referred to as *SACHR Report*), pp 80 and 91–2.

29. As introduced in 1979, following the 1978 *IWP Report*. Further changes were recommended in the 1986 *IWP Report* – see generally Greer, *Criminal Injuries Compensation* (1990).

for personal injuries and death implemented by the Administration of Justice Act 1982.[30]

In any event, the Working Party completed its report early in 1984 and (although this report too was not published) most of the changes ultimately introduced in 1988 stem from its considerations. The Working Party decided that further modifications were required to improve the administration of the Northern Ireland scheme by closing certain loopholes or by tightening up procedural requirements.[31] In this and in certain other respects the scheme was to retain – and after the 1988 Order does retain – a number of provisions peculiar to Northern Ireland.[32] But there is also evident a concern to maintain a high degree of consistency between the Northern Ireland and British schemes and, by way of corollary, with developments in the general law of damages for personal injury and death. It was possibly for this reason that the new provisions proposed for enactment in 1988, in contrast to those in 1976–7, gave rise to little public discussion.[33] Be that as it may, the nature of these provisions is such that the origin of most of them is to be found not in any general re-assessment of any special needs arising in the Northern Ireland context, but in committee recommendations or legislation affecting the private law of damages,[34] or in proposals made and implemented in the British criminal injuries compensation scheme.[35] To this extent at least the 1988 Order has further reduced the individual character of the Northern Ireland scheme and it seems likely that for its interpretation and further development we shall have to look increasingly to the jurisprudence of other schemes.

2. The Republic of Ireland

The continued effect of the terms of reference of the Compensation (Personal Injuries) Committee and of section 22(1) of the Damage to Property (Compensation) Act 1923 meant that compensation for criminal injuries sustained in the Irish Free State after 12 May 1923 could only be awarded in the limited circumstances covered by section 106 of the 1836 Act.

---

30. Following recommendations made by the Law Commission and the Pearson Commission, and extending to Northern Ireland – see Greer, *The Administration of Justice Act 1982 and the Assessment of Damages for Personal Injuries* (1983).

31. *SACHR Report*, pp 86 and 90–91.

32. In particular, further restrictions on the award of compensation for nervous shock – see below pp 55–61 and 68–77.

33. See, however, the critical comments made by the Law Society as summarised in *The Writ* (April 1987), p 1. The debate of the Draft Order was short and straightforward – see 128 HC Debs, cols 540–544 (25 Feb 1988). For an analysis of the changes made by the 1988

Order, see Greer, "The Criminal Injuries (Compensation) (NI) Order 1988" (1988) 39 *NILQ* 372.

34. See above n 30. See especially the provision for the award of compensation for bereavement, discussed below, p 199.

35. In particular the introduction of a power (included in the British Scheme since 1964) to refuse compensation on grounds of the applicant's character or way of life (discussed below, p 125). Curiously, however, the 1988 Order was enacted *before* the Criminal Justice Act 1988. The provisions of that Act and of the amended non-statutory Scheme mean that there is still a degree of difference between the two jurisdictions.

This restricted cover was partly a reaction to the "penal" effect of the 1919 and 1920 Acts, and partly a result of a policy to reduce the financial burden on local authorities. But attacks on members of the new police force – the Garda Siochana – underlined the restrictive nature of section 106, as interpreted in *Murphy* and other pre-1919 decisions, which the courts of the new state felt obliged to follow.[36] At first the effect of these restrictions could be, and was, offset by the making of *ex gratia* payments in certain cases.[37] But matters came to a head in 1940–1941 when within a short period three policemen were murdered and another three seriously injured in circumstances in which *Murphy* precluded the award of any compensation under the 1836 Act.[38] Instead of following the precedent set in 1919–1920, however, the Government introduced a unique compensation scheme to remedy "this rather illogical and unsatisfactory state of affairs".[39] The Garda Siochana (Compensation) Act 1941 excluded the gardai from the operation of section 106 of the 1836 Act[40] and instead provided for the payment of compensation for malicious injury to, or the death of, a member of the police force–

(a) in the performance of his duties as such member while actually on duty, or

(b) while exercising powers or otherwise acting in his general capacity as a policeman when off duty or on leave or otherwise not actually on duty, or

(c) while on duty or off duty or on leave or at any other time because of anything previously done by him as a member of the Garda Siochana or merely because of his being such a member.[41]

Although these provisions effectively reversed *Murphy*, they do not cover all injuries to police officers. Thus, the injury must still have been caused *maliciously*, and so, for example, in *Conway* v *Minister for Finance*[42]

---

36. See e.g. *Hyland v Dublin Corp* (1940) 74 ILTR 248. The applicant had also to be "maimed" – see *Mooney* v *Dublin Corp* [1939] IR 520.

37. See 84 Dail Debs, cols 2192 *et seq* (23 July 1941) and 25 Sen Debs, cols 2063–6 (31 July 1941), *per* Minister for Justice.

38. See e.g. 25 Sen Debs, col 2059 (31 July 1941), *per* Minister for Justice.

39. *Harrington* v *Minister for Finance* [1946] IR 320, 323, *per* Davitt J.

40. Section 11(1).

41. Section 2(1). The 1941 Act applied retrospectively to injuries or deaths sustained from 1 Jan 1940 – s 2(2). The Government refused to extend the Act to earlier cases, but promised to review all claims made before 1940 – 95 Dail Debs, col 2137 (2 Feb 1945). The Act did, however, extend to any *former*

member of the Garda Siochana killed or injured after 1940 because of something done by him as a member of the force or because of his having been a police officer – s 2(1)(*b*), (*d*). For a general commentary on the Act, see Miers, "Compensating Policemen for Criminal Injuries" (1972) 7 *IJ* 241, especially pp 252–3 and 256–61.

42. [1953] IR 153. It was recommended in 1970 that compensation should be paid if a Garda was accidentally injured while on duty, provided that the accident was not due to any default or lack of care on his part: see Commission on the Garda Siochana, *Report on Remuneration and Conditions of Service* ("*the Conroy Report*") (Prl 933, 1970), para 1169. This recommendation has not been implemented as such, but the Social Welfare Act 1989, s 18 now provides that members of the Garda Siochana *are* eligible for certain occupational injuries benefits.

compensation was refused to a guard *accidentally* injured by a cyclist. Davitt J held that an applicant had to establish either a conscious intent to injure him or such negligence as to involve in a high degree the risk of substantial personal injury to others (i.e. recklessness). A second requirement is that the injury must be inflicted on the officer in the performance of his duties as a member of the Garda Siochana. In *Harrington v Minister for Finance*[43] no compensation was payable under the Act to the widow of a police officer killed by another officer for apparently "personal and private" reasons. Section 2 of the Act was designed only –

> "to deal with the case of a Guard injured or murdered while in the course of performing some duty or function as a Guard, as well as the case of a Guard injured or murdered because he *had* so performed some function or duty as a Guard, or merely because he *was* a Guard."[44]

The mere fact that the applicant's husband had been murdered during working hours was neither sufficient by itself to prove nor raised a presumption that he had been killed in the performance of some official police duty.

Compensation under the Act is payable not by the local authority, but by the state:

> "It is a much more rational scheme that members of the police force, which is a State force and paid out of State funds, should be compensated out of State funds rather than out of local funds as provided by the Grand Juries Act 1836."[45]

A claim is made formally against the Department of Finance,[46] but the scheme is administered by the Department of Justice.[47] It is to that Department that an application for compensation is made on the prescribed form.[48] The claim is then investigated by the Garda Commissioner, who in due course submits a full report (including a medical report made by the Garda Surgeon) to the Minister for Justice. If the claim is in respect of "minor" injuries sustained in the course of performance of a duty not involving "special risk", no compensation is payable.[49] If the injuries are minor, but a special risk was involved, the Minister himself may award compensation of

---

43. [1946] IR 320.

44. *Ibid*, p 323, *per* Davitt J.

45. 25 Sen Debs, col 2061 (31 July 1941) and 1941 Act, s 14.

46. 1941 Act, s 7(2)(*e*). From 1973 to 1987 this responsibility was transferred to the Department of the Public Service; but it was transferred back to the Department of Finance on the abolition of the Department of the Public Service in 1987.

47. 1941 Act, s 4, and see *Conroy Report*, paras 1141 *et seq.*

48. Garda Siochana (Application for Compensation) Regulations 1941.

49. 1941 Act, s 6(1)(*b*)(i). It is for the Minister to decide whether an injury is "minor"or the result of a "special risk". The *Conroy Report*, para 1166 recommended the repeal of this provision, or at least its amendment so that either question would be determined by the courts. This recommendation was not implemented, but the fact that the limit of the Minister's power has never been increased from the £100 stipulated in 1941 (see next footnote) means that the provision no longer has any practical significance.

up to £100.[50] In all other injury cases, and in all cases where a police officer had been killed, the Minister has to refer the case to the High Court for the issue of entitlement and the quantum of compensation to be determined by a judge sitting without a jury.[51] There is no appeal from the judge's decision, but a case on a point of law may be stated for the opinion of the Supreme Court;[52] the judge's decision is also subject to review in an appropriate case.[53]

The level of compensation payable caused some difficulty. The 1941 Act did not specify a general rule, but listed a number of considerations to be taken into account.[54] These provisions seem to have been intended to overrule *Nolan*,[55] but in *O'Brien* v *Minister for Finance (No 1)*,[56] the Supreme Court held that compensation was to be measured only in terms of pecuniary loss. In assessing the compensation payable to the widow of a murdered police officer Maguire P in the High Court had said that he –

> "did not accept the contention that the principles enunciated by Campbell LC in *O'Connell's* case were applicable to the present Act. Neither did I accept the view that the rules proper to a claim under Lord Campbell's Act should apply . . . I was unable to take the view that I should award compensation to the utmost pecuniary amount. I felt that the figures at which I arrived were just, reasonable and generous."[57]

The Supreme Court endorsed this approach and also agreed that the value of certain financial benefits (such as an insurance policy or a house) not specified in the Act had also to be taken into account. This was not what had been intended, and amending legislation was introduced "to make provision for compensation on a wider basis, so that a judge . . . will not be compelled to consider only the purely financial loss".[58] The Garda Siochana (Compensation) (Amendment) Act 1945 provided retrospectively[59] that the compensation to be awarded "shall be such sum as the judge thinks reasonable having regard to all the circumstances of the case". In fixing this amount he

---

50. 1941 Act, s 6(1)(*b*)(ii). The original intention of this provision was benevolent: "The compensation is really more for the risk taken than as a measure of the injury which was inflicted", and for this reason the amount awarded could be more than "the [minor] injuries received would justify . . . " – see 84 Dail Debs, cols 2396–7 (24 July 1941) and 25 Sen Debs, col 2060 (31 July 1941). But the £100 limit has never been raised (in spite of a recommendation in the *Conroy Report*, para 1165), and the effect of inflation has been to render this provision virtually inoperative.

51. 1941 Act, ss 7, 8. The claims are in practice heard by the President of the High Court; most are uncontested.

52. Sections 7(2)(*f*) and 9. In *Harrington* v *Minister for Finance* [1946] IR 320, 325, Davitt J refused to state a case because "the circumstances of this case are peculiar and

unlikely to recur" and in any case the question of interpretation did not involve "any real doubt or difficulty such as to require a decision by the highest court."

53. See e.g. *Conroy* v *Commissioner of An Garda Siochana* [1989] IR 140 (declaration that earlier decision based on erroneous assumption; additional compensation awarded).

54. In section 10(1)(*a*), (2) and (3). See also Social Welfare Act 1989, s 18(2).

55. See 84 Dail Debs, col 2191 (23 July 1941) and also 95 Dail Debs, col 2119 (2 Feb 1945). *Nolan* is discussed above p 17.

56. [1944] IR 392.

57. *Ibid*, p 398.

58. 29 Sen Debs, col 1101 (14 Feb 1945), *per* Minister for Justice.

59. By s 3 cases decided under the 1941 Act could be reconsidered.

was still to have regard to any pension, allowance or gratuity out of public funds payable in respect of the death or injury,[60] but "no account shall be taken of any property (including assets of the deceased) to which the applicant has become entitled by reason of the [victim's] death".[61] In addition the court was to "have regard to any loss (other than financial loss) sustained by the applicant".[62] The net effect of these provisions was considered in *O'Brien* v *Minister for Finance (No 2)*,[63] where Maguire P rejected the argument that he should now approach the question of compensation on the same basis as that laid down in *O'Connell*. The learned judge pointed out that the Act of 1919, on which *O'Connell* was based, had referred expressly to the award of "full" compensation; the 1945 Act had not used such language:

> "It is evident that the legislature deliberately refrained from enacting that full compensation should be given. In my opinion this has the effect of ruling out of consideration such an element as the shock which the widow must have received as a result of the tragic death of her husband. It is, however, open to me to consider . . . the effect upon the health of the widow of this initial shock.
> Furthermore . . . the words of [section 2(2)(iv)] . . . enable me to award compensation for the loss to the applicants, in the case of the widow for the loss of her husband, and in the case of the children for the loss of their father, and in the case of both, for the break-up of the home and the loss of parental guidance, help and other advantages."[64]

These subtle variations again seemed to result in a level of compensation somewhat lower than the Government had intended,[65] but no further

---

60. Section 10(3)(*a*). In *O'Looney* v *Minister for the Public Service* [1986] IR 543 the Supreme Court held (by a majority of 4–1) that this provision covered a special (enhanced) pension awarded to an injured Garda and that the full value of that pension should therefore be deducted from the compensation payable. Cf *McLaughlin* v *Minister for the Public Service* [1985] IR 631, where a similar special pension awarded to the widow of a murdered Garda was *not* deducted (see further n 61 below).

61. Section 2(1) and (2). This wording was intended to exclude both real and personal property generally, and in particular to leave out of account any house (as in *O'Brien (No 2)*) or insurance policy maturing on death – see 95 Dail Debs, cols 2454–5 (9 Feb 1945). In *McLoughlin* v *Minister for the Public Service* [1985] IR 631 Henchy J (for the Supreme Court) considered that "any property" in s 10(1)(*a*) includes any special pension and allowances payable to a widow on the death of her husband. The learned judge was "unable to align" this provision with s 10(3)(*a*) (see previous footnote), but considered that any

"want of congruity" should be resolved in favour of s 10(1)(*a*) as representing "the later thinking of the Oireachtas, having been inserted . . . by the Act of 1945." There is much to be said for the argument put in *O'Looney* that the decision in *McLoughlin* is *per incuriam* on the basis that *O'Brien (No 2)* (which was not discussed in *McLoughlin*) makes it clear that the purpose of s 10(1)(*a*) was to cover property received by descent and not other matters such as pensions specifically dealt with elsewhere in the Acts.

62. Section 10(1)(*a*)(iv) of 1941 Act, substituted by 1945 Act, s 2(2).

63. [1946] IR 314.

64. *Ibid*, p 318. See further White, *Irish Law of Damages* (1989), vol 1, pp 412–4.

65. "Our advice is that that [the phrase "any loss (other than financial loss)" in the substituted s 10(1)(*a*)(iv)] would take in any loss in addition to financial loss that the court wishes to take notice of . . . It would cover loss of companionship and that sort of thing . . . ": 95 Dail Debs, col 2136 (2 Feb 1945), *per* Minister for Justice.

amendments were introduced. When the matter was reviewed in 1970, the level of compensation awarded by the courts under the 1945 Act was considered "adequate"; the sensible proposal that the compensation should be assessed on the same basis as damages under the Civil Liability Act 1961 was rejected.[66]

The 1836 and 1941/1945 Acts provided the only statutory basis for criminal injuries compensation after 1923; but compensation was payable on an *ex gratia* basis by the Minister for Justice to persons injured while coming to the aid of the Gardai, and by the Minister for Finance, at his discretion, to "persons employed in the Civil Service" (or their dependants) injured or killed in the course of their duties.[67]

All these provisions (and those providing compensation for criminal damage to property) came under scrutiny when, in 1960, the Minister for Justice set up an interdepartmental committee to consider whether the criminal injuries code should be amended or repealed. The Committee, which reported in 1963,[68] was concerned primarily with reducing the scope of compensation for property damage. But it also considered the arguments in favour of a more comprehensive scheme of compensation for personal injuries, and indeed noted as "apparently illogical" the fact that the existing law covered property damage more extensively than personal injury. In the event, however, the Committee decided to consider each scheme "separately, on the criteria appropriate to each". It noted that a general scheme of compensation for personal injuries was not provided in any European country and that its cost would be unjustifiable. In addition it drew attention to the "real and substantial difficulties" in the way of administering such a scheme and in particular expressed concern at the danger of fraudulent claims and of compensation being paid to "undeserving persons". Two members of the Committee felt, however, that the 1941/5 Acts should, by analogy with the Acts of 1919 and 1920, be extended to provide statutory compensation for *all* State officials maliciously injured in the execution of or in connection with their official duties, and for members of the public maliciously injured while coming to the aid of the Gardai. The other two members of the Committee disagreed; the relatively few cases which arose were dealt with satisfactorily under existing *ex gratia* arrangements. The Committee as a whole agreed that the cost of paying compensation under the 1836 Act should remain with the local authorities.

This report was completed before the extra-statutory scheme was adopted in Great Britain; the Committee was aware of some of the discussions which led to the introduction of that scheme, but felt that the case was not convincing. In addition there appears to have been little public pressure for such a scheme; indeed some of the local authorities were pressing for repeal of the whole criminal injuries code.[69] It is therefore not surprising that the

---

66. *Conroy Report*, para 1170.
67. Interdepartmental Committee on Malicious Injuries, *Summary of Report* (Pr 8142, 1964), para 33.
68. The full report of the Committee does not appear to have been published; a Summary was published in 1964 (see previous footnote); personal injuries are discussed in Chapter VII (pp 16–19).
69. *Ibid,* pp 8–9.

report was put on the shelf. As crime increased, however, and many jurisdictions adopted some form of compensation scheme it was perhaps inevitable that Ireland would follow suit. The immediate catalyst appears to have been the bomb explosions in Dublin at the end of 1972 and the beginning of 1973 in which a number of persons were killed or injured.[70] In these circumstances the Government gave compensation for personal injury priority over damage to property,[71] and in February 1974 introduced an extra-statutory "Scheme of Compensation for Personal Injuries Criminally Inflicted".[72] Under this Scheme, which applied retrospectively to injuries sustained on or after 1 October 1972, compensation is payable *ex gratia* in respect of personal injury or death directly attributable (i) to a crime of violence, (ii) to assisting or attempting to assist a police officer or to prevent crime, or (iii) to saving human life. With the exception of category (iii) – a unique provision[73] – the scope of the new Scheme was similar to the non-statutory scheme then in operation in Great Britain. Despite their *statutory* entitlement to compensation under the 1941/5 Acts, police officers were not precluded from claiming under the 1974 Scheme. Double compensation was, however, avoided by providing that any statutory award must be taken into consideration when compensation is being assessed under the non-statutory scheme.[74] It would appear that most claims by members of the Garda are still dealt with under the statutory scheme alone,[75] even though additional compensation is, at least in theory, recoverable under the 1974 Scheme in certain cases.[76]

As in other local jurisdictions the Irish Scheme contains a number of exclusionary provisions – e.g. compensation is not payable in respect of family violence or road accidents, and may be refused where the conduct of the victim, his character or his way of life make it inappropriate that he should be granted an award.[77]

Entitlement to, and assessment of, compensation are determined by the Criminal Injuries Compensation Tribunal, the Chairman and six members

---

70. See 270 Dail Debs, col 515 (12 Feb 1974), *per* Minister for Justice.

71. So stated at 264 Dail Debs, col 1460 (13 Dec 1972).

72. The current version of the Scheme is that laid before the Oireachtas in March 1986; with one exception (see n 80 below) this is identical to the Scheme introduced in 1974. For a commentary on the 1974 Scheme see Osborough, (1978) 13 *IJ* 320.

73. See further *State (Creedon)* v *CICT* [1988] IR 51.

74. 1974 Scheme, para 5.

75. This may reflect the fact that costs are normally payable under the Acts (1941 Act, s 7(2)(h)), but not under the Scheme (para 27). There may also be a feeling that a High Court

judge may be more generous than the Criminal Injuries Compensation Tribunal.

76. Thus, in respect of the assessment of pecuniary loss, the value of certain pensions is deducted from the compensation payable by statute (1941 Act, s 10(3)(a), though see the cases referred to in nn 60 and 61, above) but not from that payable under the Scheme (paras 15–16); and where a police officer has been killed, his widow can recover compensation for mental distress under the Scheme (by reason of the reference in para 6 to the Civil Liability Act 1961 – see below, p 199 but not under the Acts (*cp* 1941 Act, s 10(1)(a)).

77. 1974 Scheme, paras 10, 12 and 14 respectively – see e.g. *State (McNamara)* v *CICT*, Unreported, Sup Ct (Walsh, Griffin and Hederman JJ), 1 July 1988; *State (McDonagh)* v *CICT*, Unreported, High Ct (Keane J), 25 Jan 1980.

of which are appointed by the Minister for Justice and must be practising solicitors or barristers. The Tribunal's decision is final; but although there can be no appeal against or review of the decision as such, an order of the Tribunal can be judicially reviewed by the High Court on *certiorari* if the Tribunal acts in excess of or without jurisdiction or determines any matter arising under the Scheme contrary to the principles of natural justice.[78]

The Scheme expressly provides that compensation is to be awarded by way of a lump sum assessed on the same general basis as damages in tort are awarded under the Civil Liability Acts. But it stipulates a number of exceptions to this principle – in particular, compensation is not payable by way of exemplary, vindictive or aggravated damages, the value of social welfare benefits to which the victim or claimant is entitled is deducted in full, and any sick pay which the victim is entitled to receive from his employer is taken into consideration "to the extent determined by the Tribunal".[79] A further and major departure from the Civil Liability Acts took effect from 1 April 1986 – as an economy measure, compensation in respect of injuries sustained on or after that date is no longer payable in respect of pain and suffering.[80]

The operation of the Scheme – and of the 1941/5 Acts – in recent years is summarised in Table 1.4. The figures for the operation of the 1974 Scheme in 1987 reflect the difficulties encountered by a scheme of public compensation in times of serious financial constraint. The earlier 1980s had seen a substantial and continuing increase in the number of new applications, but this was not matched by any corresponding increase in resources. As a result the time taken to deal with the applications has lengthened, and a substantial backlog has now developed. In addition budgetary constraints have meant that awards cannot always be paid immediately, and some successful applicants have had to wait for more than a year after accepting an award before receiving payment thereof.[81] It was in the context of this unsatisfactory state of affairs that the Scheme was amended in 1986 to exclude any payment of compensation for pain and suffering, and it is this amendment, rather than any reduction in the number of crimes of violence, which appears to be the main cause of the significant drop in the number of new "injury" applications received in 1987. The Irish Scheme is, therefore, at something of a cross-roads at present; unless there is a noticeable infusion of government support or public pressure, it may well be the target for a future round of public expenditure reductions.

---

78. So held in *State (Hayes)* v *CICT* (1977) [1982] ILRM 210. The onus is on the claimant to show that the Tribunal failed to observe the rules of natural justice: *State (O'Leary and O'Driscoll)* v *CICT*, Unreported, High Ct (Lynch J), 28 April 1986. This onus was satisfied, and the Tribunal's decision quashed, in *State (Hill)* v *CICT* [1990] ILRM 36; *State (Creedon)* v *CICT* [1988] IR 51; *State (McDonagh)* v *CICT (supra); State (Waters)* v *CICT*, Unreported, High Ct (Gannon J), 28 Nov 1983; *State (McNamara)* v *CICT (supra)*.
79. 1974 Scheme, paras 6 and 15 respectively.
80. See Scheme as amended with effect from 1 April 1986 (PI 3920, 1986), para 6(*e*).
81. The legality of this practice was unsuccessfully challenged in *State (O'Toole)* v *CICT*, Unreported, High Ct (Carroll J), 20 Jan 1988.

Table 1.4
Criminal Injuries Compensation in Ireland 1981–1987[82]

	1981		1983		1985		1987	
	1974 Scheme	1941–5 Acts	1974 Scheme	1941–5 Acts	1974 Scheme	1941–5 Acts	1974 Scheme	1941–5 Acts
New applications	676	157	1417	107	1975	207	243	242
Injury	659	157	1383	107	1950	207	229	242
Death	17	–	34	–	25	–	14	–
Number of awards made	393	na	851	na	811	na	430	na
Claims pending at end of year	932	na	1719	na	3895	na	4187	na
Compensation paid (£m)	1.815 ⎫		3,490 ⎫		3,977 ⎫		2,606 ⎫	
Administration costs (£m)	0.044 ⎭ 0.165		0.068 ⎭ 1.172		0.071 ⎭ 0.858		0.072 ⎭ 1.249	

82. The 1974 Scheme details are taken from Criminal Injuries Compensation Tribunal, Annual Reports (published by the Stationery Office); the figures relating to the Garda Siochana (Compensation) Acts 1941 and 1945 were kindly provided by the Department of Justice. The figures suggest that the approximate rate of compensation paid per 1,000 population in Ireland in 1981 was £575 (as compared to £6,500 in NI and £400 in GB), rising to £1,300 in 1985 (when £6,000 in NI and £650 in GB) – see above pp 32 and 35.

2

Entitlement to Compensation

INTRODUCTION

The general scope of entitlement to compensation for criminal injuries in Northern Ireland was settled some 20 years ago by the Criminal Injuries to Persons (Compensation) Act (NI) 1968.[1] The provisions of this Act (and the non-statutory scheme adopted in the Republic in 1974[2]) mark a break in the history of the Irish criminal injuries compensation code and put it on the modern footing of most such schemes;[3] compensation was now to be payable to victims of crimes of violence[4] and to those injured or killed when assisting the police in the enforcement of the law. The Irish Scheme did, however, go one stage further; compensation was to be paid (and is still payable) for injuries received "because of, or in the course of, attempting to save human life".[5] These criteria paid little regard to the traditional bases for public compensation in Ireland prior to the 1960s, *viz* "the Troubles", intimidation of witnesses, etc and "agrarian outrages", though they are, of course, apt to cover most injuries or deaths arising from crimes committed for such purposes. In two respects, however, the new Northern Ireland scheme did hold true to the Irish tradition – it was a *statutory* scheme, and it provided that entitlement to compensation in any particular case was a matter for decision not by a special Tribunal but by the ordinary courts. This meant not only that an injured person had a legal right to compensation if he satisfied

---

1. 1968, c 9 (hereafter referred to as "the 1968 Act"). For further discussion of the background to the Act, see above pp 31–2.

2. *Scheme of Compensation for Personal Injuries Criminally Inflicted* (1974, as amended in 1986) (hereafter "the Irish Scheme").

3. See especially the *Scheme for Compensating Victims of Crimes of Violence* adopted in Great Britain in 1964 (as amended in 1989) (hereafter "the British Scheme") and the Criminal Justice Act 1988, Part VII ("the 1988 Act"). The Northern Ireland Act of 1968 drew particularly on the British Scheme and on the New Zealand Criminal Injuries Com-

pensation Act 1963. For other schemes, see e.g. Edelherz and Geis, *Public Compensation to Victims of Crime* (1974) and Burns, *Criminal Injuries Compensation* (1980).

4. Strictly speaking, the 1968 Act applied to injuries arising from a criminal offence, although intended only to cover crimes of violence.

5. Irish Scheme, para 4(*d*), as applied e.g. in *State (Creedon)* v *CICT* [1988] IR 51. Ireland has also had a unique *statutory* scheme for compensating police officers injured or killed in the execution of their duty – see Garda Siochana (Compensation) Acts 1941 and 1945, discussed above, pp 38–42.

the conditions laid down in the Act but also, in more general terms, that the provisions of the scheme were subject to regular judicial scrutiny and the usual canons of statutory interpretation. In this respect, the 1968 Act could still be regarded as part of an Irish criminal injuries compensation "code" which had developed over a period of more than a century.

However, shortly after it was enacted, the 1968 Act was pressed into service for a purpose for which it had not been designed – the payment of public compensation to those injured and killed in the new era of "Troubles" which began in 1970. This unforeseen development led to the operation of the Act being reviewed in the mid-1970s,[6] but little substantial change in the scope of entitlement resulted when new legislation was enacted in 1977.[7] However, the Troubles had given rise to one particular "entitlement" problem – an unprecedented number of claims for compensation for "nervous shock" arising from bombing or shooting incidents. It was felt necessary to qualify the scope of "injury" in order to exclude many such claims which were thought to be undeserving as insufficiently serious or possibly even spurious.[8]

In general terms, however, the most significant – and controversial[9] – aspect of the 1977 Order was that it substantially diminished the judicial character of the scheme by effecting a change which harked back to the days of the grand jury. Initial determination of entitlement became a matter for private decision by the Compensation Division of the Northern Ireland Office. Although that decision remained subject to judicial control by way of an extensive right of appeal to the courts on questions of fact as well as on questions of law,[10] the change inevitably introduced a bureaucratic flavour to the administration of the scheme. The principal justification for the change – which followed the precedent set for property damage compensation claims in 1971[11] – was to speed up the payment of compensation in the vast majority of cases where the claim was agreed by the parties.

This break with the tradition of the past 80 years was modified by acceptance of the principle that decisions would still for the most part be made in accordance with judicial pronouncements as to the meaning and scope of the various statutory provisions – and indeed, the scheme has come to be administered professionally by solicitors in the Compensation Division of the Northern Ireland Office. However, the change from judicial to administrative determination was also accompanied by the introduction – in at least four instances – of a substantial degree of "executive discretion"

6. The review was not published.

7. Under the Criminal Injuries (Compensation) (NI) Order 1977 ("the 1977 Order"), compensation was payable only in respect of "violent crimes", whereas the 1968 Act had applied to "any" criminal offence. But the change was largely theoretical – few claims had been made under the 1968 Act in respect of non-violent criminal offences.

8. See below, pp 55–61 and generally Greer, "A Statutory Remedy for Nervous Shock?" (1986) 21 *IJ* 57.

9. See especially HC Debs (NI Cttee), 16 Feb 1977. Local newspaper articles were published under such headlines as "Criminal Injuries Law Row Brews", "Solicitors slam damages proposals" and "Attacks on changes in injury law" (*Belfast Telegraph*, 26 and 28 Jan and 4 Feb 1977).

10. See below, p 315.

11. Criminal Injuries to Property (Compensation) Act (NI) 1971 – see generally Greer and Mitchell, *Compensation for Criminal Damage to Property* (1982).

much less amenable to judicial scrutiny.[12] Such discretionary powers cannot, of course, be exercised in any way that is arbitrary or unreasonable, but they do derogate from the "right" to compensation and therefore cause concern, for four reasons. In most instances the 1977 Order neither expressly nor impliedly prescribed any purpose for the granting of the discretion; it merely stated that the Secretary of State "may" do something. Secondly, the new scheme was to be administered not by an independent or semi-autonomous Board, but by a government department. Thirdly, the Order made no provision for the publication of an annual report, so that public knowledge of the manner in which the scheme as a whole is being administered and the particular ways in which the discretionary powers are being exercised depend on the unsystematic and limited information revealed in response to parliamentary questions. Finally, judicial review of the Secretary of State's initial decision can be invoked only when the applicant feels aggrieved by the decision; favourable or generous decisions are, in practice, immune from judicial – or public – scrutiny. As a result the criticisms and controversy surrounding the change made by the 1977 Order have not been entirely allayed, and continue to come to the surface from time to time.

These discretionary powers indirectly qualify the right to compensation by reference to the refusal or reduction of the compensation to which an applicant is otherwise entitled; as such, they are discussed more fully in Chapter 3. The primary entitlement provisions of the 1977 Order proved far less controversial and were re-enacted almost unchanged in the Criminal Injuries (Compensation) (NI) Order 1988. However, claims for nervous shock have been further restricted[13] and it has been specifically provided that many injuries accidentally incurred in the course of law enforcement do not come within the scheme.[14] These particular changes gave rise to some comment at the time when the Order was being enacted,[15] and they may yet prove to have been ill-judged.

The 1988 Order governs injuries sustained on or after 1 July 1988,[16] injuries sustained before that date are still governed by the 1977 Order. Subject to the two particular points mentioned in the previous paragraph

---

12. I.e., to pay compensation to a member of an unlawful association or to a person who had engaged in terrorism (below, pp 128–137), to make "discretionary payments" to widows and children in certain cases (below, pp 215–217), to withhold the payment of compensation in certain cases (below, pp 138–141), and to deduct certain unpaid public debts from the compensation otherwise payable (below, pp 148–149).

13. See below, pp 76–77.

14. See below, pp 79–82.

15. See especially Standing Advisory Commission on Human Rights, *13th Annual Report 1986–87* (HC 298, 1988), pp 26–27.

16. Article 3(1) states that the Order applies "where a person sustains a criminal injury . . . after the coming into operation of this Order ...". By Art 1(2) "this Order shall come into operation on such day . . . as the Secretary of State may by order appoint." By the Interpretation Act (NI) 1954, s 14(2), "Where an enactment is expressed to come into force or operation on a particular day . . . the enactment shall be construed as coming into force immediately on the expiration of the day before that particular day." The Criminal Injuries Compensation (1988 Order) (Commencement) Order (NI) 1988 provides that the day appointed for the coming into operation of the Order is 1 July 1988; it would thus appear that injuries sustained *on* 1 July 1988 were sustained after the 1988 Order came into operation.

there appears to be no difference in the scope of entitlement, but the analysis which follows is based throughout on the 1988 Order. This may be said to provide that compensation is payable whenever (i) a person (ii) sustains in Northern Ireland (iii) an injury (iv) directly attributable to (v) a violent offence or (vi) certain acts of law enforcement.

INJURY TO PERSONS IN NORTHERN IRELAND

1. "A Person"

By Article 3(1) of the 1988 Order compensation is payable to any "person" who sustains a criminal injury in Northern Ireland. The word "person" is not defined; but while the term in general is wide enough to include a company or corporation[17] such legal persons cannot sustain injury as defined in the Order. Prior to 1977 it was not clear whether an unborn child was a "person", but that issue was put beyond doubt in Article 2(2) of the 1977 Order, a provision now replicated in the definition of "victim" in Article 2(2) of the 1988 Order.[18] It is somewhat unfortunate, however, that this bare stipulation leaves unresolved many of the matters expressly settled in respect of common law claims by the Congenital Disabilities (Civil Liability) Act 1976.[19] Thus, neither the 1977 Order nor the 1988 Order states whether it is a condition precedent to a claim that the injured child be subsequently born alive. This particular issue, however, arose for consideration in *Gilmour* v *Secretary of State*[20] – a claim under the 1968 Act. The applicant's mother, when 37 weeks pregnant, was shot in the abdomen. The applicant was subsequently born with a bullet lodged in her back, but after several operations made a complete recovery. The learned county court judge held that she was entitled to compensation in her own right:

> "I am satisfied that the law in the jurisdiction is that an unborn child, *if subsequently born alive* . . . is a person within the meaning of the 1968 Act. I do not read the phrase in the 1977 Order as increasing the class of persons who could claim under the 1968 Act but rather as being inserted in the Order for purposes of clarification of the existing position."[21]

This, with respect, seems eminently sensible and correct, and would now appear to be corroborated in the special procedural provisions for claims in respect of injuries to unborn children contained in Article 5(7) of the 1988 Order. The decision in *Gilmour* also suggests that an unborn child who is

---

17. Interpretation Act (NI) 1954, s 37(1).

18. The Irish Scheme, para 6 provides likewise, by incorporating the Civil Liability Act 1961, s 58 of which declares that damages may be awarded in respect of an unborn child "provided the child is subsequently born alive".

19. See e.g. Street, *The Law of Torts* (8th ed, 1988), pp 176-7.

20. Unreported, Cty Ct (Judge Babington), 1 Nov 1979.

21. Emphasis added. Note, however, that McMahon and Binchy, *The Irish Law of Torts* (2nd ed, 1990), p 605 point out that the Civil Liability Act 1961, s 58 is stated to be declaratory only and should not necessarily be interpreted as excluding the possibility of a cause of action even where the child is not subsequently born alive. Such a cause of action is recognised in some US jurisdictions – see e.g. Prosser and Keeton, *The Law of Torts* (5th ed, 1984), pp 369–70.

injured and not subsequently born alive has not "died" for the purposes of Article 3(3) or (4). But the point is not unarguable. Similarly, the Order offers no definition of a "child" e.g. for the purposes of Article 10(1), where, however, consistency would seem to require the word to be interpreted as co-extensive with those entitled to compensation. Equally Article 9(3) refers to "a minor"; it seems likely that a bereavement award cannot be made in respect of the "death" of an unborn child.[22]

Some of these uncertainties would have been removed had the 1976 Act been incorporated by reference, as appears to have been the case in England and Wales.[23] So too would the question whether the child's claim is affected by negligent or provocative behaviour by his mother.[24] Article 6(1)(*a*) refers solely to ". . . behaviour *of the victim*"; however, such behaviour by the mother might be regarded as a "relevant circumstance" to be taken into consideration under the general provision in Article 6(1), although the extent to which the conduct of one person is "relevant" in determining whether compensation should be paid to another person (if at all) does not appear yet to have been considered by the courts.

Unlike many European criminal injuries compensation schemes,[25] the 1988 Order lays down no nationality or residence requirements; it is sufficient to found a claim that the person concerned was in Northern Ireland when he was injured.

2. "Sustains in Northern Ireland"

"Northern Ireland" is defined in section 1(2) of the Government of Ireland Act 1920 in the following terms:

> "For the purposes of this Act, Northern Ireland shall consist of the parliamentary counties of Antrim, Armagh, Down, Fermanagh, Londonderry and Tyrone, and the parliamentary boroughs of Belfast and Londonderry . . . "

It has, however, been accepted that—

> "the rights over the territorial waters off Northern Ireland passed with the six named counties in Northern Ireland subject to the limitations and exceptions expressly imposed and excepted by the 1920 Act . . . "[26]

---

22. *Bagley* v *North Herts Health Authority* (1986) 136 *NLJ* 1014. *Cf* Fortin, "Legal protection for the unborn child" (1988) 51 *MLR* 54, 76–80.

23. See 1978 *IWP Report*, para 10.9; 1988 Act, Sch 7, para 8.

24. By the 1976 Act, s 1(7) the damages payable to an injured child are reduced if "the parent affected shared the responsibility for the child being born disabled . . . ".

25. Nor do the British or Irish schemes. The restrictions in continental schemes were noted by the CICB in their *18th Annual Report* (1981–82), para 27, but a major step forward has recently been made in *Cowan* v

Le Tresor Public, The Times, 2 Feb 1989, where the European Court of Justice held that where EC law guarantees the freedom of a person to travel to another member state, the integrity of that person (and his right to compensation if it is infringed) must be protected in that state under the same conditions as that of its own nationals. Mr Cowan was subsequently awarded compensation of £7,000: *The Times*, 29 April 1989.

26. *DPP* v *McNeill* [1975] NI 177, 192, *per* Jones LJ. Although technically an obiter dictum, this was the learned judge's "firm view" and it was also accepted by Lowry LCJ and Curran LJ.

Any person injured within these territorial confines is entitled to compensation – at least, if the violent offence or relevant act of law enforcement which occasioned the injury has also occurred in Northern Ireland:

> "Grammatically the offence does not have to occur in Northern Ireland, but the whole Criminal Injury Code over the years has worked on this basis – see for example *Fermanagh CC* v *Farrendon*[27], and the general tenor of the Act of 1968 proceeds on this basis . . . "[28]

Much the same comment can be made about the "general tenor" of the 1988 Order – especially as reflected in the definition of "violent offence" in Article 2(2), and in Articles 8(3), 17(1) and 18(2). But the grammatical position remains the same and at least one provision envisages the conviction of the offender in a court outside Northern Ireland.[29] It remains to be seen, therefore, whether the 1988 Order will be interpreted "grammatically" or purposively. An important factor in this context may be the scope of the British and Irish schemes, and the question whether the applicant may – or may not – qualify for compensation thereunder. A number of different cases may be suggested:

(i) A, standing in Northern Ireland, is injured by a shot fired from outside Northern Ireland. This indeed is what happened in *Farrendon* and compensation was awarded under the Grand Jury (Ireland) Act 1836, on the ground that –

> "if a man fires at another with intent to wound, the intent is present during every fraction of space and moment of time that is traversed by the bullet from the moment it leaves the lethal weapon until it strikes or passes its victim."[30]

Although doubt was cast on the correctness of this analysis,[31] the law, if not the precise reasoning, has since been confirmed in *R* v *Baxter*[32] and *DPP* v *Stonehouse*,[33] where Lord Keith stated:

> " . . . if a person, on the Scottish bank of the Tweed . . . were to fire a rifle at someone on the English bank, with intent to kill him, and actually did so, he would be guilty of murder under English law."[34]

A would, therefore, appear to be entitled to compensation even on a non-"grammatical" interpretation of the Order.

---

27. [1923] 2 IR 180, referring to the Grand Jury (Ir) Act 1836 which, however, required an award to be made where "such murder or maiming shall have been committed".

28. *Murphy* v *Sec of State* Unreported, High Ct (MacDermott J), 23 April 1976.

29. Article 19, discussed below, p 292.

30. [1923] 2 IR 180, 184, *per* Moore LJ.

31. Miers, "Paying for Malicious Injury Claims" (1970) 5 *IJ* 50, 52, n 11.

32. [1971] 2 All ER 359.

33. [1977] 2 All ER 909.

34. *Ibid*, p 939. His Lordship stated the general rule to be that "where a state of affairs which the law of England regards as criminal has been brought into existence abroad and continues to exist in England, without ever having come to rest, by reason of its effects being intentionally felt there, then any person whose act caused that state of affairs has committed an offence under English law . . . ".

(ii) B is in Northern Ireland when he suffers nervous shock directly attributable to a bomb explosion in the Republic of Ireland. Assuming that the bomb was not designed to injure or alarm B, no offence appears to have been committed in Northern Ireland,[35] but B has sustained injury here. B will recover compensation (if at all) only if a "grammatical" interpretation of the Order is adopted.[36]

(iii) C is outside Northern Ireland when he suffers nervous shock as a result of being told that his wife has been killed in an explosion in Northern Ireland. In *Gristwood* v *Secretary of State*[37] it was contended that compensation is not payable in such a case. It did not become necessary to decide this point, but the contention appears to be correct.

(iv) D is kidnapped in Northern Ireland, taken across the border into the Republic, and there injured or killed. D appears to have sustained no injury in Northern Ireland and is, therefore, not entitled to any compensation under the Order. This argument was raised in *Scarlett* v *Fermanagh CC*,[38] but the claim was rejected on other grounds without reference to this point.

(v) E is kidnapped and injured in Northern Ireland, then taken across the border and subsequently further injured. This is what happened in *Murphy* v *Secretary of State*,[39] where the applicant was abducted in Newry and taken by car to Dundalk. In the course of the journey she was verbally abused, her life was threatened and she was physically assaulted. She was thrown out of the car at Dundalk, where she was further assaulted, and an attempt was made to rape her. It was agreed that the proper total award in respect of the applicant's injuries was £3,000; but MacDermott J held that she was entitled only to compensation in respect of those injuries proved to have been sustained in Northern Ireland. The learned judge was satisfied on the evidence that the bulk of the injuries had occurred within the jurisdiction and he awarded compensation of £2,000.[40]

---

35. In Lord Keith's example in *Stonehouse*, if the rifle misfired, there would be no offence under English law (provided the intended victim was unaware of the attempt to shoot him) because no effect would have been felt in England. But if the intended victim knew the rifle was pointed at him and was put in a state of alarm, an offence would have been committed in England.

36. Compensation would not be payable under the Irish Scheme, para 1 of which requires the injury to have been sustained "within the State".

37. Unreported, Cty Ct (Judge Hart), 29 Jan 1986. Such an injury may not, in any case, be "directly attributable" to the explosion – see further below, pp 74 *et seq*. C's entitlement to compensation under the British Scheme raises the same question as to whether it requires the offence to be committed in Great Britain.

38. [1923] 2 IR 48. See the criminal damage cases discussed in Greer and Mitchell, *Compensation for Criminal Damage to Property* (1982), pp 44–46. Compensation will, of course, be payable under the Irish Scheme.

39. Unreported, High Ct (MacDermott J), 23 April 1976.

40. The learned judge noted that the 1968 Act thus provided less generously for such cases than previous legislation (see e.g. *Plumb* v *Fermanagh CC* [1923] 2 IR 54 and *Orr* v *Fermanagh, Cavan, Monaghan and Tyrone CC* [1923] 2 IR 54) and commented: "It may well be that the Secretary of State may wish to consider whether or not the 1968 Act provides reasonable protection for those who may be abducted from Northern Ireland and killed or injured in the Republic." No change in the Northern Ireland scheme has, however, resulted from these remarks.

(vi) F is injured in a fight aboard a ferry from Belfast to a port in England. If the injury is sustained outside Northern Ireland territorial waters, compensation is not payable under the 1988 Order (though it may be payable under the British Scheme).[41] But if the injury is sustained *within* Northern Ireland territorial waters, it appears that a claim may now be made under the 1988 Order or under the British Scheme.

3. "Injury"

By Article 2(2) of the 1988 Order compensation may be awarded to a person who sustains "an injury (including an injury which results in death) . . . ", and "injury" is stated to include "any disease, any impairment of a person's physical or mental condition and pregnancy". This follows the approach taken in the 1977 Order,[42] and gives rise to little difficulty in practice. There are, however, two areas of possible uncertainty.[43]

First, what constitutes an "impairment" of a person's "physical condition"? Although this wording has been used not just in criminal injuries legislation but in a great number of other statutes over at least the past 50 years,[44] its precise meaning seems to have arisen in only one reported case. In *Brazier* v *Ministry of Defence*[45] D's negligent use of a hypothermic syringe caused P "occasional discomfort". McNair J held that this could "be fairly comprised in the definition . . . 'any impairment of a person's physical . . . condition'". This suggests a fairly generous approach which tends to be supported for criminal injury purposes by *O'Neill* v *Secretary of State*.[46] A police officer was kidnapped and left, bound and gagged, in a field at night for four and a half hours. He was then released. He sustained no physical injury, but suffered from "a fluey cold" which kept him off work for a short time. The learned county court judge held that he was entitled to compensation under the 1977 Order. In practice, of course, even if such minor "impairments" do constitute an "injury", compensation will not be payable

---

41. *Watson* v *Sec of State* Unreported, Cty Ct (Judge Doyle), 1 May 1980. The British Scheme (para 4) applies to "Great Britain" and to injuries on board a British vessel or aircraft – see Greer, *Criminal Injuries Compensation* (1990), paras 2.06 *et seq. Cf* 1988 Act, s 110(2) applies to *United Kingdom* territorial waters. A similar overlap may occur with the Irish Scheme – see para 1 and Maritime Jurisdiction (Amendment) Act 1988.

42. Article 2(2). *Cf* of the 1968 Act, s 11(1), following the New Zealand Act of 1963, s 2(1), had defined "injury" as meaning "actual bodily harm and includes pregnancy and mental or nervous shock". The Irish Scheme (para 1) provides only that "'injury' . . . includes a fatal injury", but the Civil Liability Act 1961, s 2(1) defines "personal injury" as including "any disease and any impairment of a person's physical or mental

condition . . . ". In Great Britain, the 1988 Act, s 109(1) states that "personal injury" includes "any disease, any harm to a person's physical or mental condition and pregnancy".

43. The question of when an injury may be said to "result" in death is discussed below, p 186 as being relevant to the assessment of compensation rather than to entitlement.

44. See e.g. Law Reform (Miscellaneous Provisions) Act 1934, s 3. A LEXIS search of the definition in 1987 yielded 83 items at Level 1.

45. [1965] 1 Lloyds Rep 26.

46. Unreported, Cty Ct (Judge Russell), 8 Sept 1983. *Cf Scarlett* v *Fermanagh CC* [1923] 2 IR 48 where Andrews LJ held that the words "injured in his person" in s 1(1) of the Criminal Injuries (Ir) Act 1919 did not apply "to ailments or illnesses such as colds or chills or temporary discomforts". The authority of this case today, however, is doubtful.

in many cases because the minimum threshold set by Article 5(13) of the 1988 Order will not be passed.

The more difficult problem of uncertainty arises, however, from the words "any impairment of a person's . . . mental condition . . . ".[47] In addition this phrase must now be understood in the context of the new requirement laid down in Article 5(12)(*a*) of the 1988 Order that for certain purposes compensation is only payable where the victim has sustained "a serious and disabling mental disorder". It is suggested that the best approach is to consider first the courts' interpretation of the general definition prior to the 1988 Order and then examine the precise impact thereon of the new provision.

In fact it does not appear that the Northern Ireland courts have ever attempted to provide a precise definition of mental "impairment". Rather they have followed the approach taken by the English courts in relation to claims for damages in tort for "nervous shock".[48] That approach has now been authoritatively laid down by the House of Lords in *McLoughlin* v *O'Brian*,[49] where Lord Wilberforce stated:

> "Although we continue to use the hallowed expression 'nervous shock', English law, and common understanding, have moved some distance since recognition was given to this symptom as a basis for liability . . . [I]t is now accepted by medical science that recognisable and severe physical damage to the human body and system may be caused by the impact, through the senses, of external events on the mind. There may thus be produced what is as identifiable an illness as any that may be caused by direct physical impact."[50]

---

47. *Cf* "I do not understand what that means, nor do I accept that it is the definition of nervous shock that the courts have been working on . . . I do not like the reference to 'impairment' and 'mental condition' which raise Mental Health Act implications that are not relevant ...": HC Debs (Standing Cttee F), col 778 (24 Feb 1987) (Mr Mellor). It was, apparently, as a result of this observation that the 1988 Act, s 109(1) uses the word "harm" instead of "impairment"; it is difficult to see how this change of wording facilitates interpretation.

48. As already indicated (above, n 42) the 1968 Act expressly referred to "mental or nervous shock" and it was thus natural for the Northern Ireland courts to apply tort concepts thereto. The change in wording in the 1977 Order could have brought about a different approach, but (and it is submitted, correctly) did not do so. *Cf* Street, *The Law of Torts* (8th ed, 1988), p 504 appears to agree, in relation at least to the interpretation of the identical phrase in the Limitation Act 1980, s 38(1): "It is thought that the Act contemplates illness and disease of the mind or body, and that injuries to feelings, if unaccompanied by illness, are not 'personal injuries' for the purposes of the Act."

49. [1982] 2 All ER 298, a decision which

seems likely to be followed in Ireland – see *State (Keegan and Lysaght)* v *Stardust Victims' Compensation Tribunal* [1986] IR 642 (where the Tribunal, with the Attorney General's concurrence, followed Lord Wilberforce's judgment; but note that the Supreme Court *expressly* observed that it was not necessary to decide the question). For further analysis of *McLoughlin* see Trindade, "The principles governing the recovery of damages for negligently caused nervous shock" [1986] *Camb LJ* 476 and Teff, "Liability for negligently inflicted nervous shock" (1983) 99 *LQR* 100. For a detailed survey of "nervous shock" in the criminal injuries compensation context see Greer, "A Statutory Remedy for Nervous Shock?" (1986) 21 *IJ* 57.

50. [1982] 2 All ER 298, 301. For a medical view of psychiatric illnesses arising out of the "troubles" in Northern Ireland, see e.g. Kee *et al*, "Victims of Violence: A Demographic Study" (1987) 27 *Med Sci and Law* 241; Cairns and Wilson, "Psychiatric Aspects of Violence in Northern Ireland" (1985) 1 *Stress Med* 193; Lyons, "Terrorist Bombing and the psychological sequelae" (1974) 67 *J Ir Med Ass'n* 15 and Loughrey and Curran, "The Psychopathology of Civil Disorder" (1987) 20 *Recent Advances in Medicine* 1.

Lord Bridge explained further:

> "The common law gives no damages for the emotional distress which any
> normal person experiences when someone he loves is killed or injured.
> Anxiety and depression are normal human emotions. Yet an anxiety neurosis
> or a reactive depression may be recognisable psychiatric illnesses, with or
> without psychosomatic symptoms. So, the first hurdle which a plain-
> tiff . . . must surmount is to establish that he is suffering not merely grief,
> distress or any other normal emotion, but a positive psychiatric illness."[51]

These dicta in fact only restate the existing law, and the distinction drawn by
Lord Bridge had been clearly applied in *Hinz v Berry*.[52] The plaintiff's
husband had parked the family dormobile in a lay-by while the plaintiff and
one of her children crossed the road to pick some flowers. As they were
doing so a car, out of control, crashed into the dormobile, killing her
husband and injuring the other children. The plaintiff heard the crash and
rushed to do what she could. As a result of the incident she suffered severe
depression. Pearson LJ identified five separate factors in the plaintiff's
mental state:[53]

(i)   Her own inevitable grief and sorrow at the death of her husband.
(ii) Her anxiety for the welfare of her injured children.
(iii) Financial stress resulting from the loss of the bread-winner.
(iv) The need to adjust herself to a new life.

None of these factors was compensable.[54] However the plaintiff also suffered

(v)   A severe morbid depression caused by the shock of witnessing the
      accident.

This was a "positive psychiatric illness" and was therefore compensable.
Lord Denning MR explained how this compensation should be assessed:

> "Somehow or other the court has to draw a line between sorrow and grief for
> which damages are not recoverable, and nervous shock . . . The way to do
> this is to estimate how much the plaintiff would have suffered if, for instance,
> her husband had been killed in an accident . . . 50 miles away; and compare it
> with what she is now, having suffered all the shock due to being present at the
> accident."[55]

This approach has been adopted in a number of criminal injuries cases. In
McQuoid v Secretary of State[56] the applicant was a publican who was

---

51. [1982] 2 All ER 298, 311. In *Attia v British Gas plc* [1987] 3 All ER 455 the phrase "psychiatric damage' was preferred; no change of meaning appears to have been intended. But *cf Whitmore v Euroways Express Coaches Ltd The Times*, 4 May 1984 and also *Bond v Chief Constable of Kent* [1983] 1 All ER 456, discussed below, p 244.

52. [1970] 1 All ER 1074.

53. *Ibid*, p 1076.

54. Damages (and criminal injuries compensation) could now be awarded in respect of (i)

for bereavement – see 1988 Order, Art 9(3), discussed below, p 199.

55. [1970] 1 All ER 1074, 1075. *Cf* in *Attia v British Gas plc* [1987] 3 All ER 455, 457, Dillon LJ stated: "Where exactly the line is to be drawn between possibly extravagant grief, distress or other normal emotion and a positive psychiatric illness may perhaps be difficult to discern in what may . . . be a matter of degree."

56. [1983] 5 *BNIL* 27. See also *McLernon v Sec of State* Unreported, Cty Ct (Judge Johnson), 25 May 1977; *Cochrane v Sec of State* Unreported, Cty Ct (Judge Russell), 18 Jan 1984.

attacked and struck on the head with a bottle while working in a bar. He was physically injured, and also alleged that he had suffered nervous shock as a result of the incident. The evidence showed that he had become tense and nervous and did not like to be alone with strangers in the bar. His sleep had been upset and he dwelt on what could have happened to him. Compensation was awarded only in respect of his physical injuries – the learned judge was not satisfied that the reaction suffered by the applicant was nervous shock rather than the fear which is a natural consequence of such an incident. In *Meikle* v *Secretary of State*[57] the applicant, a married woman, claimed compensation when a bomb exploded nearby without warning, and a gas cylinder came through the window of the room in which the applicant was feeding her baby, embedding itself in a wall. The applicant was "very emotionally distressed" by the incident; she experienced panic attacks, episodes of nausea, uncontrollable tremulousness of the legs, irritability, insomnia and a general reluctance to go out socially. All this was in marked contrast to her behaviour before the incident. In addition her father was dying of cancer, and generally she was having difficulties adjusting to other circumstances in her life. The learned judge considered it "vital" to analyse the applicant's condition carefully so as to distinguish between the "nervous shock" resulting from the incident and the "grief and sorrow" caused by it, from her father's condition and the other circumstances. He was satisfied on the evidence that the applicant had suffered severely as a result of the explosion, and he awarded compensation of £6,500.

Further examples of "nervous shock" are summarised in Table 2.1 (overleaf). It is obvious that the decision whether an applicant has sustained "a positive psychiatric illness" will turn on the medical evidence. If this is not in dispute (for example, because the applicant has been admitted to hospital or undergone psychiatric treatment) the matter will normally be determined by agreed medical reports.[58] But where for any reason the applicant's condition is "a live issue", the case may well proceed to the courts, where the medical witnesses will normally be required to give oral evidence, on which they can be cross-examined.[59] The burden of proof of injury lies on the applicant; in an otherwise borderline case it may well be that the court will look for an "objective guarantee of genuineness" in the circumstances which gave rise to the application.[60]

This, at least, was the interpretation given to "any impairment of a person's . . . mental condition" *before* the enactment of Article 5(12) of the 1988 Order, which provides:

---

57. Unreported, Cty Ct (Judge McKee), 4 Dec 1984.

58. As e.g. in *Hughes* v *Sec of State* Unreported, Cty Ct (Judge Russell), 3 May 1985 and *Cochrane* v *Sec of State* Unreported, Cty Ct (Judge Russell), 18 Jan 1984.

59. See e.g. *Doyle* v *Sec of State* Unreported, Cty Ct (Judge Johnson), 9 July 1976 – an approach endorsed by the House of Lords in *McLoughlin* (see e.g. Lord Bridge at p 311).

60. The phrase is American (see especially *Richardson* v *Gates* (1986) 719 P2d 193), but the phenomenon may be seen at work e.g. in *Cochrane* (below, p 75).

Table 2.1

Specimen Awards in Nervous Shock Cases

Case	Summary	Award
Tracey[61]	Gunman plantcd bombs at dcpot managcd by A. A suffered moderately severe anxiety state; nervous and anxious and took sleeping tablets for a month. Fears another attack.	£1,250
Devine[62]	A held at gunpoint and threatened. Suffered insomnia, became nervous, wary and anxious. Full recovery may take some time.	£1,300
K[63]	Lorry hijacked and driver (A) threatened; became sleepless and in acute anxiety state for some time.	£2,500
W[64]	Elderly housewife heard explosion under son's car. He escaped injury but she became anxious, afraid of noises, suffered persistent headaches and sleeplessness. Anxiety for son continues and little improvement anticipated.	£3,000
Maguire[65]	A abducted and held for 3 days before release; blindfolded throughout ordeal and life threatened. Suffered sleeplessness, fear of crowds and strangers, reluctant to socialise, tense, nervous and had tremor in his hand; memory affected.	£3,500
S[66]	Wife arrived on scene shortly after husband shot dead. Suffered intense depression which, after 3 years, showed little or no sign of improvement.	£15,000

"No compensation shall be paid to any person by virtue of Article 3(2)(*a*)(iv) [i.e. for 'pain and suffering and loss of amenities'] in respect of any injury which is caused by his mental reaction to the act arising out of which the application for compensation is made, or to the consequences of that act, unless –

(*a*) the injury amounts to a serious and disabling mental disorder;

(*b*) he sustained the injury by virtue of being present when that act was committed; and

(*c*) the amount of compensation which, but for this sub-paragraph, would be payable by virtue of Article 3(2)(*a*)(iv) in respect of that injury is at least £1,000."[67]

---

61. [1988] 10 *BNIL* 8.

62. [1988] 6 *BNIL* 29.

63. [1988] 1 *BNIL* 32.

64. [1988] 2 *BNIL* 13.

65. [1985] 9 *BNIL* 14.

66. [1986] 5 *BNIL* 15.

67. *Cf* 1988 Act, s 109(2) also restricts the right of recovery for nervous shock, but does so in a different way – see below, p 77. There is no express restriction of any kind in the Irish Scheme.

It is suggested that (*a*) and (*c*) qualify the meaning or scope of "injury", whereas (*b*) relates to causation, which is discussed in the next section of this chapter.

Article 5(12)(*c*) replicates Article 6(4) of the 1977 Order, which was introduced to reduce the number of "nervous shock" claims:

> "We are having to contend with an ever-increasing number of 'nervous shock' cases in which value quantification is most difficult and proof of genuineness virtually impossible. It is a weakness in the system which must be removed."[68]

The £1,000 limit appears to have substantially reduced the number of nervous shock claims – some examples of its operation are given in Table 2.2.

Table 2.2

Specimen Cases where Nervous Shock assessed at under £1,000

Case	Summary	Award
McDevitte[69]	Husband and wife threatened by masked men. Caused H to become anxious and agitated with regular nightmares. W had some sleep difficulties and suffered some anxiety.	H: £1,200 W: Not above £1,000
Tully[70]	Housewife aged 59 attacked by two men and injured. As result of attack, nervous and depressed, unable to sleep, go out or stay at home alone.	£1,250 for physical injury; nervous shock not worth £1,000
Mearns[71]	Shop manager aged 67 attacked by man. Suffered physical injury. Also as result of attack became insecure, sleep was disturbed, afraid to go out alone or to socialise. Residual anxiety state likely to continue for some time.	£7,450 for physical injuries; no award for nervous shock
Barr[72]	Bus hijacked and bomb placed on board. Driver suffered shock, became irritable and anxious, felt emotionally drained and unable to sleep; medical evidence suggested condition not severe.	None

---

68. HC Debs (NI Cttee), col 98 (2 March 1977). It was estimated that 42% of all claims received during 1976 were in respect of nervous shock, and that 92.6% of the settled nervous shock cases were for less than £500. See also 934 HC Debs, col 754 (1 July 1977).

69. [1988] 6 *BNIL* 29.

70. [1983] 5 *BNIL* 24.

71. [1983] 6 *BNIL* 28.

72. [1983] 4 *BNIL* 22.

But it was, apparently, considered that (c) alone did not provide a sufficient remedy for this "weakness" and the two additional requirements will further reduce the scope for such claims. This new formula has yet to be analysed by the courts, but the following interpretations are suggested in relation to the scope of "injury" for the purposes of the 1988 Order:

(a) Article 5(12)(a) qualifies the meaning of "injury", presumably as defined in Article 2(2). Thus it requires the applicant to have suffered "an impairment of his . . . mental condition" which amounts to "a serious and disabling mental disorder". It has already been suggested that the former phrase has been treated by the Northern Ireland courts as equivalent to "a positive psychiatric illness". On this basis Article 5(12)(a) applies only where such an illness may be regarded as "serious and disabling". If this is correct, Article 5(12)(a) hardly seems necessary; there cannot be many serious and disabling psychiatric illnesses for which compensation of less than £1,000 is appropriate. It is, therefore, possible that Article 5(12)(a) is intended to define "nervous shock" by a verbal formula other than that approved in *McLoughlin*. If this is the case, the way has been opened to give "impairment of a person's mental condition" a more extensive meaning than hitherto.[73] Such an approach would seem to be a recipe for chaos and it is suggested therefore that for this reason, if for no other, the first interpretation is that which ought to be adopted. Where Article 5(12) applies, therefore, three questions must be considered:

(i)   Has the applicant suffered a recognised psychiatric illness?

(ii) If so, is it "serious and disabling"?

(iii) If so, is the compensation payable in respect thereof (i.e. excluding for this purpose any aspects of the illness which are not "serious and disabling"[74]) in excess of £1,000?

(b) Article 5(12) applies only to nervous shock as such, and not to the "ordinary" pain and suffering which results from physical injury. The latter is not covered by the formula " . . . any *injury* . . . caused by his mental reaction to the act . . . or to the consequences of that *act* . . . " and this interpretation tends to be confirmed by the wording of Article 5(12)(b).

---

73. E.g. the approach apparently preferred by Comyn J in *Whitmore* v *Euroways Express Coaches Ltd, The Times*, 4 May 1984. Street, *The Law of Torts* (8th ed, 1988), p 178n suggests that *Whitmore* "must be explained as (a) an aberration, (b) creating a new class of 'ordinary' shock distinct from true 'nervous' shock or (c) an example of compensation for mental distress consequent on physical injury." See also *Bond* v *Chief Constable of Kent* [1983] 1 All ER 456, discussed below p 244.

74. This appears to be the consequence of the inclusion of the phrase "but for this *sub-paragraph*" in Art 5(12)(c). If Art 5(12) is satisfied it is not entirely clear whether the compensation is then assessed only for the severe or disabling mental disorder (as under Art 5(12)(a)) or for all aspects of the impairment of the applicant's mental condition (as implied by the main part of Art 5(12)).

(c) The restricted definition of nervous shock applies only to the assessment of compensation under the head of pain and suffering and loss of amenities; compensation continues to be payable for any appropriate expenses or pecuniary loss which results from "ordinary" nervous shock, subject to the minimum threshold laid down in Article 5(13).[75] No such compensation can be taken into account in determining whether the applicant has exceeded the £1,000 threshold laid down in Article 5(12)(c); but if Article 5(12)(c) is satisfied, the compensation payable thereunder *does* count for the purposes of Article 5(13).[76]

(d) Article 5(12) applies if the applicant has suffered nervous shock alone or in addition to physical injury. This was so held in relation to the 1977 Order in *Rodgers* v *Secretary of State*,[77] and that decision appears equally applicable to the 1988 Order. The applicant had suffered minor physical injury and nervous shock when she was threatened and assaulted in her home by a masked intruder. The applicant contended that such a case did not come within Article 6(4). MacDermott J disagreed – but held on the evidence that the compensation payable to the applicant for nervous shock did in fact exceed £1,000.

What then is meant by a "serious and disabling mental disorder"?[78] It is suggested above that this phrase should be interpreted as a recognised psychiatric illness which is serious and disabling. How much this will add to the pre-existing £1,000 restriction remains to be seen. The courts may take the view that where Article 5(12) applies compensation should now be awarded only in fairly exceptional cases; certainly the intention of the legislature appears to have been to impose an additional restriction.[79] On the other hand, they may well take the view that the retention of the £1,000 limit suggests that the legislature must have considered that some mental disorders which could be regarded as "serious and disabling" might nonetheless merit an award of compensation of less than £1,000,[80] and thus adopt a less restrictive interpretation.

---

75. *Cf* 1988 Act, s 109(2) which stipulates the scope of "harm to a person's mental condition" for all purposes.

76. Article 5(13) refers to compensation payable under any head. In *Rodgers* v *Sec of State* Unreported, High Ct (MacDermott J), 13 Feb 1979 it was suggested that the thresholds for physical injury and nervous shock should be applied independently. But it is contended that a person whose nervous shock justifies compensation of (say) £1,200 and has physical injury worth £200 is entitled to compensation of £1,400.

77. *Ibid.*

78. Article 5(11)(a) of the Proposed Draft of the 1988 Order used the formula "a serious and disabling mental disorder of a description included in the International Classification of Diseases . . . published by the World Health Organisation . . . ". This reference to what is known as ICD-9 was criticised as inappropriate and unhelpful – see especially Greer, "A Statutory Remedy for Nervous Shock?" (1986) 21 *IJ* 57, 89. In any case the additional reference failed to clarify the meaning of "serious and disabling".

79. For an example of a precise, stipulative definition of "seriously and permanently disabled" see Coal-Mining (Subsidence) Act 1957, s 12. It is noticeable that the 1988 Order does not refer to a "permanently" disabling condition.

80. It may well be that the phrase originated in the 1986 *IWP Report*, para 4.12 where it is used as synonymous with a "recognised" psychiatric illness.

"Directly Attributable"

The 1988 Order, like its predecessors, provides that the applicant's injuries must be "directly attributable" to a violent crime or to one of the specified acts of law enforcement.[81] In most cases, this causal requirement gives rise to no difficulties. But problems have arisen in certain cases, particularly where the applicant is claiming compensation for nervous shock alone (where he has sustained no physical injury) or for an injury arising out of or in connection with an act of law enforcement. In both these situations, the general requirement of "directly attributable" is now qualified in certain cases by particular provisions of the 1988 Order.[82] We deal first with the general requirement.

Two preliminary points seem clear enough. First, the test does *not* depend upon what the offender or any other person might have been reasonably expected to foresee; in tort terms, the relevant case is not *Wagon Mound*[83] but (if anything) *Polemis*.[84] As Lord Lowry LCJ has observed:

> " . . . at common law . . . the need to prove foreseeability and the possible resort to public policy considerations confront a plaintiff in a way in which they cannot obstruct a criminal injury claimant . . . "[85]

Secondly, the use of the word "directly" is intended to strengthen the causal connection:

> "One would expect those words to require a closer connection between the injury and the [qualifying] events . . . than would be the position had the word 'directly' been omitted."[86]

Whether an injury is "attributable" to a violent crime or act of law enforcement is essentially a question of fact to be determined by the evidence in a particular case, if necessary by applying the familiar "but for"

---

81. 1968 Act, s 11(1); 1977 Order, Art 2(2). The British Scheme, pending the introduction of the 1988 Act, uses the same phrase, as does the Irish Scheme, para 1 and even the European Convention on the Compensation of Victims of Violent Crimes (1983), Art 2(1)(a). But the 1988 Act, s 109(1) requires simply that the injury be "caused by" a qualifying event. This is contrary to the 1986 *1WP Report*, para 4.10 which recommended that "the statutory scheme should include a more stringent test of remoteness which clearly conveys the need for a very close and immediate link between the offence and the consequent injury". The draftsman came up with the phrase "immediately caused by or closely connected with" but this was ultimately rejected.

82. See below, pp 76 and 79 respectively.

83. *Overseas Tankship (UK) Ltd* v *Morts Dock & Eng'g Co* [1961] 1 All ER 404.

84. *In re Polemis and Furness Withy & Co* [1921] 3 KB 560.

85. *O'Dowd* v *Sec of State* [1982] NI 210, 214. A similar point was made in relation to the British Scheme by Cumming-Bruce LJ in *R* v *CICB, ex parte Parsons, The Times*, 25 Nov 1982 (and see CICB, *19th Annual Report* (1982–83), para 17, where the judgment is quoted extensively).

86. *Martin* v *Ministry of Home Affairs* (1970) [1979] NI 172, 174, *per* Jones J. Cumming-Bruce LJ also made the same point in *Parsons, supra*. See also Ogus and Barendt, *The Law of Social Security* (3rd ed, 1988), p 319 in relation to war pensions: "Before . . . 1943, the injury had to be 'directly attributable to service'; the removal of the qualifying adverb was one of the relaxations introduced . . . to ease the conditions for entitlement . . . ".

test.[87] A good example is provided by *Gristwood* v *Secretary of State*,[88] where the applicant's daughter was in December 1982 seriously injured in an explosion. As a result of seeing her daughter's condition the applicant suffered nervous shock, for which she received psychiatric treatment for some 10 months. She was then "discharged", but unfortunately subsequently suffered further psychiatric illness. The learned judge considered the medical evidence very carefully before concluding that that evidence had not established on the balance of probabilities that the later illness was caused by her reaction to her daughter's plight. Compensation was, therefore, payable only in respect of the earlier condition.

It is, however, the "qualifying adverb" which has given rise to most of the problems, and its impact has been assessed in a number of important cases.[89] The starting point is *Martin* v *Ministry of Home Affairs*,[90] where the applicant, together with three other police officers, went to premises following a report of an attempted burglary. A climbed on to the roof of the premises and there found three men who were attempting to hide. He thereupon arrested them. They came quietly, but as they were descending the roof gave way under A and he fell through to a concrete floor some 15 feet below. His claim for compensation under the 1968 Act was rejected by the Court of Appeal on the ground that his injury was directly attributable not to the arrest of the three suspects but to the condition of the roof. But the precise reasoning of the Court is not particularly clear. Both Lord MacDermott LCJ and Jones J started from an interpretation of "directly attributable" given in *McGregor* v *Board of Agriculture for Scotland*,[91] where the court was faced with the meaning of that phrase as used in the Agriculture Act 1920. Lord Alness stated:

"To paraphrase statutory words is at all times a hazardous enterprise . . . But there is no harm in saying that . . . one is remitted by these words (directly attributable) to the task of discovering the effective or immediate cause of the loss sustained . . . And if that is so, then I think [the use of the word 'directly'] points to the operation not of a *causa sine qua non* but of a *causa causans*."[92]

Both Lord MacDermott LCJ and Jones J agreed with and adopted this approach – but both then immediately acknowledged that the matter was

87. See especially *R* v *CICB, ex parte Penny*, [1982] *Crim LR* 298 (A, a prison officer, would have been injured even if prisoner not guilty of assault).

88. Unreported, Cty Ct (Judge Hart), 29 Jan 1986. See also *McCullough* v *Sec of State* Unreported, Cty Ct (Judge Higgins), 3 Feb 1981; [1981] 3 *BNIL* 21 (stroke suffered by A following explosion not shown to be attributable to explosion). See also *Beecham* v *Hughes* [1988] 6 WWR 33 P's depression not caused by shock of accident).

89. See also Greer, *Criminal Injuries Compensation* (1990), paras 2.17 *et seq*.

90. (1970) [1979] NI 172, discussed by Miers, "Three cases on the Criminal Injuries to Persons (Compensation) Act (NI) 1968" (1971) 22 *NILQ* 186.

91. 1925 SC 613.

92. *Ibid*, p 620. Lord Anderson (at p 623) also stated that "what must be sought is the immediate cause of the loss – the *causa causans*". In the case a tenant's crops were purchased by the landlord when the tenant had to quit the holding; the quantity of the crops was underestimated by an arbitrator. It was held that the tenant's loss was directly attributable to the arbitrator's error and not to the tenant's quitting of the holding.

one of degree and that much would depend on the particular facts of the case. The learned judges attached significance to the facts that the injury to A happened after the arrest had been made and that the place where the incident occurred was not one of particular danger or involve any exceptional risk or hazard. We deal with these particular points below.

The *McGregor* test was also applied by the English courts in *R v Criminal Injuries Compensation Board, ex parte Schofield*.[93] A woman about to enter a store was knocked down and injured when two men – a store detective chasing a shop-lifter – ran out of the store. Lord Parker CJ held that the knocking down of the applicant in the course of the arrest was a *causa causans* of her injuries:

> "In my view it certainly was a cause, and indeed was the only cause, because it could not be said that her presence accidentally, about to go into the shop, was in any way a cause at all."[94]

Then, in *R v Criminal Injuries Compensation Board, ex parte Ince*[95] A, a police constable, was driving a police car at speed towards premises at which men had been reported to be acting suspiciously as if about to break in. In his haste to get there, A drove through a set of red traffic lights and was killed in a collision with another police car answering the same call. The English Court of Appeal held that A's death could be held to have been directly attributable to the prevention or attempted prevention of an offence.[96] Somewhat curiously, there was no reference to *McGregor, Martin* or *Schofield*, nor to the Latin terms approved therein. Rather, Lord Denning MR reasoned:

> "In my opinion 'directly attributable' does not mean 'solely attributable'. It means directly attributable, in whole or in part to the state of affairs . . . If the death of PC Ince was directly attributable to his answering the call for help, it does not cease to be so attributable because he was negligent or foolish in crossing the lights. In such case there were two causes: (i) the call for help; (ii) his negligence, or foolishness. His widow can rely on the first, even though the second exists."[97]

Megaw LJ adopted a similar approach – an injury is directly attributable to a qualifying event if that event –

> "is, on the basis of all the relevant facts, a substantial cause of personal injury. It does not need to be the sole cause. By the word 'substantial' I mean that the relationship between the particular cause and the personal injury is such that a reasonable person, applying his common sense, would fairly and seriously regard it as being a cause."[98]

---

93. [1971] 2 All ER 1011.

94. *Ibid*, p 1013.

95. [1973] 3 All ER 808.

96. The case was remitted to the Criminal Injuries Compensation Board for a decision on the facts.

97. *Ibid*, pp 812–3.

98. *Ibid*, pp 815–6. This was, therefore, the test adopted by the British Board – see *Statement*, para 4C(1): "Personal injuries [are] . . . 'directly attributable' to [a qualifying event] . . . if [that event] would be considered, by a reasonable person who knew all the facts, to be a substantial cause of the injury, but not necessarily the only cause." See also para 4C(2), referred to below, n 6.

Although *Martin* is distinguishable on at least two grounds (there, the initial arrest had been made, and there was no particular risk involved), one cannot help feeling that the English Court of Appeal would have allowed Martin's case to succeed.[99] The difference between the two approaches, it is submitted, is that in *Martin* the court was looking for "*the cause*" of the injury; in *Ince* the court was satisfied by "*a substantial cause*".[1]

It must however be said that this opinion has not been accepted by the Northern Ireland courts which have concluded that *Martin* and *Ince* are not inconsistent. The precise scope of the earlier cases arose in *Niland* v *Secretary of State*.[2] The applicant was a soldier who formed part of the infantry escort which accompanied a bomb disposal team to a suspected booby-trap. A car had been stolen and was found parked on top of a mound of earth; the leader of the bomb disposal team suspected that an explosive device had been placed in or under the car or in the mound of earth. He decided to pull the car off the mound. For this purpose a hook on the end of a nylon rope was attached to the car, and the other end of the rope attached to an armoured car. The armoured car began to pull, the rope stretched and the hook straightened out and on being freed from the suspect car flew back and hit A, seriously injuring him. Hutton J in the High Court held that the injury was directly attributable to the giving of help to the bomb disposal team in preventing or attempting to prevent an offence. The learned judge held that that conclusion was warranted both by *Ince* and by *Martin*, and further considered that "although different phraseology was employed in the two cases, there is no basic conflict between the judgments . . . ".[3]

Following *Martin* it might have been thought that "direct" means "immediate in point of time".[4] But, as has been pointed out:

> "In *Martin's* case, neither Lord MacDermott LCJ nor Jones J specifically said that 'directly attributable to' could only relate to the immediate cause of the injury. The reference by Lord MacDermott to what 'in the law of tort' would be a *causa causans* is significant. In the law of negligence a negligent act may create liability and therefore be a *causa causans* though it is not the immediate cause of the injury if it is a cause which in the chain of events is the real cause."[5]

---

99. See the examples given in Miers (1971) 22 *NILQ* 186, 193. In *Murphy* v *Sec of State* Unreported, High Ct (MacDermott J), 23 April 1976 the learned judge accepted that the two tests differed, but nothing turned on this difference on the facts of that case. According to the 1986 *1WP Report*, para 4.10: "Following the decision . . . in . . . *Ince* it is clear that the word 'directly' has become virtually without effect."

1. The more stringent effect of *Martin* may also be seen in *McGarvey* v *Sec of State* [1978] 2 NIJB where A went to help police officers whose landrover had been bombed. He found the officers badly injured and he tended them until an ambulance arrived. McGonigal LJ held that the nervous shock which he suffered was "directly attributable" not to the explosion but to the sight of the injured men. That

decision would not be followed today – see *Halliday* v *Sec of State*, discussed below, p 73.

2. [1982] NI 181.

3. *Ibid*, p 192. However the learned judge distinguished *McGarvey* and other nervous shock cases as based on policy considerations which did not apply to physical injury.

4. See e.g. Hart and Honoré, *Causation in the Law* (2nd ed, 1985), pp 178–9.

5. Johnson, "Injuries 'directly attributable' to a criminal offence" (1981) 32 *NILQ* 264, 266. Hart and Honoré, *op cit*, p 179 quote Prosser as defining "direct" to mean "following in sequence from the effect of the defendant's act upon conditions existing and forces already in operation at the time, without the intervention of any external forces which come into active operation later."

As has frequently been observed in the law of tort, an injury may be attributable to the original event even if there is an intervening act of the injured person or of a third party, provided that that intervening act is not "something unwarrantable, a new cause which disturbs the sequence of events, something which can be described as either unreasonable or extraneous or extrinsic."[6] On this basis, Hutton J concluded in *Niland* that:

> " . . . in trying to tow the car off the mound of earth, in the way in which he did, [the leader of the bomb disposal team] acted in a manner which was reasonable in the circumstances . . . he did not do anything which was outside the exigencies of the situation."[7]

Finally, in *O'Dowd* v *Secretary of State*[8] Lord Lowry LCJ, for the Court of Appeal, endorsed the approach taken by Hutton J in *Niland* as applicable both in physical injury *and* nervous shock cases, so that:

> " . . . an act *can* be an effective cause (*causa causans*) of damage, even if it is preceded, accompanied or followed by another act (whether negligent or not) of the injured party or a third party: whether the act complained of *is a causa causans* is a question of fact and degree."[9]

This salutary reminder that the issue is in any particular case "a question of fact and degree" suggests that any further examination of the scope of "directly attributable" should have reference to the immediate context in which it arises.

1. "Directly Attributable" to a Crime of Violence: Physical Injury

Where there has been no intervening act between the violent crime and an applicant's physical injury, the courts appear to have adopted a fairly generous approach. Thus in *Cochrane* v *Secretary of State*,[10] stones and bottles had, during a riot one evening, been thrown at passing army vehicles. The following morning, while the street was still littered with glass and debris, the applicant, a young boy, left his home unaccompanied and set off across the street to go to a nearby playground. In the course of crossing the street, he fell and injured himself on the broken glass. Gibson LJ in the High Court held that the injury was directly attributable to a criminal offence – there had been nothing to break the chain of causation from the riot. This rather generous decision was upheld by the Court of Appeal.

---

6. *The Oropesa* [1943] P 32, 37–8, per Lord Wright. See e.g. Salmond and Heuston, *The Law of Torts* (19th ed, 1987), pp 614–5. *Cf* the explanatory *Statement* to the British Scheme, para 4C(2) states: "If another, and, in particular, a subsequent cause is the negligence or wrongful act of the applicant or a third party, the injury may still be attributable to the original event and give rise to a claim for compensation. It only ceases to be so when the intervening event is so powerful a cause as to reduce the original offence to a piece of history."

7. [1982] NI 181, 192.

8. [1982] NI 210.

9. *Ibid*, pp 214–5.

10. Unreported, High Ct (Gibson LJ), 8 Oct 1976; CA, 25 May 1977 (in both cases oral judgments only appear to have been delivered).

Where there has been an intervening act, we have seen from *Niland* that the injury may still be directly attributable to the original crime of violence, provided that the intervening act is not "something which can be described as either unreasonable or extraneous or extrinsic".[11] This test has arisen more in relation to acts of law enforcement (as in *Niland*), but there are some cases to illustrate its application in relation to crimes of violence. Thus, in *Fennell* v *Secretary of State*[12] a three-year-old boy found a hand-gun lying underneath a car parked in the street outside his house. The gun went off and the boy was shot in the head. Compensation was awarded – nothing which the boy had done was "unreasonable or extraneous". The chain of causation was, however, broken in *McCaughey* v *Ministry of Home Affairs*[13] where rioters threw stones at the police. The police baton-charged the rioters and the applicant (who was not involved in the stone-throwing) was injured by a police baton. It was held that this injury was not directly attributable to the rioters' offence.[14] The chain of causation was also broken by the "bizarre" events in *Caldwell* v *Secretary of State*.[15] The owner of a garage showed A two suspicious bags which he had found in the garage. Instead of clearing the building and notifying the police the two men decided to take the smaller bag to the police station. While en route they decided to call at A's house, where they opened the bag to examine its contents. The bag contained a hand grenade, bullets, detonator cord and some objects which looked like spent bullet cases, but were in fact detonators. A hit one of the detonators with a hammer; it exploded and caused such severe injuries to A that he was blinded in both eyes. The learned judge stated:

> "If [A] . . . had misguidedly tried to remove the offending material to a place of safety and if he had been injured while so moving the material then as a question of fact and degree it is likely that a court would have taken the view that the chain of causation had not been broken, and that even if he had performed the task in a negligent manner, he would be entitled to recover a degree of compensation. But in my judgment there were five decisive voluntary acts by [A] . . . which broke the chain of causation so as to render the original offence of possession [of the explosive substances] truly a *causa sine qua non* of [A's] injuries rather than the *causa causans* of such injuries."

A similar conclusion was arrived at in *Clarke* v *Secretary of State*.[16] Two police landrovers stopped on being attacked with missiles and the police dismounted. A, who had been throwing missiles, ran off and the police gave chase. One of the police officers thought he heard a shot, and they therefore considered they were pursuing a gunman. After some time they caught sight

---

11. [1982] NI 181, 191, *per* Hutton J.

12. Unreported, Cty Ct (Judge Johnson), 22 May 1979. See also *Crean* v *Sec of State* [1987] 4 *BNIL* 19 (A in car struck by petrol bomb thrown at police vehicle; A strained her neck when she ducked in response to the attack: compensation awarded for injury to neck); *McConville* v *Sec of State* [1983] 6 *BNIL* 25 (A fell onto floor of bus to avoid stone thrown through window: compensation awarded).

13. Unreported, Cty Ct (Judge Johnson), 27 Nov 1969.

14. But A's injury *was* directly attributable to the attempted prevention of an offence.

15. Unreported, Cty Ct (Judge Russell), 23 Nov 1982.

16. [1986] 13 NIJB 93.

of A and, believing he was the gunman, called on him to halt. A failed to halt and the police opened fire, hitting A in the legs. In fact A was unarmed and Hutton J considered that "the probability [was] that no gunman had fired at" the police. Thus A's injury could not be attributed to a violent offence. But the learned judge added:

> "Even if a gunman had fired at the police . . . I am satisfied that the conduct of the applicant in running off and in leading the police officers a chase through the maze of streets and alleyways severed any chain of causation between the firing by the gunman . . . and the subsequent firing by the police at the end of the chase . . . Therefore . . . the firing by the gunman was not a *causa causans* of the injury to the applicant . . ."[17]

2. "Directly Attributable" to a Crime of Violence: Nervous Shock

It has already been stated that the 1988 Order, building on a policy first introduced in 1977, restricts the scope of compensation for "nervous shock", only in relation to compensation for pain and suffering and loss of amenities.[18] We must, therefore, consider the scope of "directly attributable" in nervous shock cases (i) generally, and then (ii) with particular regard to the special provision in Article 5(12)(*b*).

(a) *The general causal requirement*

The leading case on the scope of entitlement to compensation for nervous shock remains *O'Dowd* v *Secretary of State*,[19] a decision under the 1968 Act. Two masked gunmen invaded B's home and shot and killed two of B's sons and B's brother (J), as well as seriously injuring B himself. N (another of B's sons) returned home shortly after the shooting and was met at the door of the house by his mother, who had been in the house at the time, but had not been shot. She told N to fetch his uncle "as his father and them have all been shot dead". The uncle lived about a mile away, and N went there immediately. He returned with the uncle and two more of B's sons (P and R) who had been at the uncle's house. All four entered B's house where they saw the three bodies and the injured B. N, P and R all suffered nervous shock, for which they claimed compensation. So also did a son of J who, at the time of the shooting, had been in his own home about three miles away. He was told of the shooting very soon after it had happened and he hurried to B's house, where he saw that his father and two cousins had been shot dead and his uncle seriously injured.

The problem facing the applicants was that they had not been present when the shooting took place. In many cases prior to 1982,[20] the presence of

---

17. On appeal Kelly LJ agreed with this reasoning – see [1988] 5 NIJB 24, 29 (the applicant in fact accepted this part of Hutton J's decision).

18. *Cf* 1988 Act, s 109(2) provides a stipulative definition applicable in *all* cases where harm to a person's mental condition will be treated as arising from a qualifying event.

19. [1982] NI 210.

20. *McAllister* v *Ministry of Home Affairs* Unreported, Cty Ct (Judge Patton), 27 April 1970; *Osborne* v *Sec of State* Unreported, Cty Ct (Judge Rowland), 5 Sept 1975; *Doyle* v *Sec of State* Unreported, Cty Ct (Judge Johnson), 9 July 1976 – all apparently following a distinction drawn in *Hambrook* v *Stokes Bros* [1925] 1 KB 141.

the applicant at the scene of the crime had been held essential for the nervous shock to be "directly attributable" to that crime. During the mid-1970s this requirement had for a time been modified at county court level to allow recovery where the applicant had come on the scene in the "immediate aftermath" of the crime, at least where that crime had resulted in the injury or death of a close relative of the applicant.[21] This modification was not, however, accepted in the High Court.[22] The Court of Appeal could have decided *O'Dowd* as an "immediate aftermath" case – but Lord Lowry LCJ preferred a more robust approach. The decision of the House of Lords in *McLoughlin* v *O'Brian* now meant that –

> "the need for the claimant's initial presence at the scene of the disaster in nervous shock cases has been consigned to the lumber room of rejected legal fallacies."[23]

There was, therefore, no valid reason to give to "directly attributable" an "artificially narrow meaning" in nervous shock cases. Since the ordinary meaning of that test was satisfied in this case, the applicants were, therefore, entitled to compensation.[24]

This approach has a beguiling simplicity; "presence" may no longer be required, but it seems unlikely that the courts will not turn to other "special" factors in nervous shock cases. The general issue was neatly explained by Lord Bridge in *McLoughlin* when he identified two possible approaches to the causal issue in such cases. As adapted to criminal injury compensation:

> "The first is that the judge should receive the evidence of psychiatrists as to the degree of probability that the particular cause would produce the particular effect, and apply to that the appropriate legal test [of directly attributable] . . . The second is that the judge, relying on his own opinion of the operation of cause and effect in psychiatric medicine, as fairly representative of that of the educated layman, should . . . form his own view from the primary facts whether the proven chain of cause and effect was [direct] . . ."[25]

According to Lord Bridge there was much to be said "in principle" for the first approach which would, in effect, make the question of directness one of fact. But judicial authority was all in favour of the second, for the reason that

---

21. *Hanna* v *Sec of State* Unreported, Cty Ct (Judge Higgins), 22 Sept 1976; *Jamieson* v *Sec of State* Unreported, Cty Ct (Judge Johnson), 1 Dec 1976; *McLernon* v *Sec of State* Unreported, Cty Ct (Judge Johnson), 25 May 1977 – drawing on such common law decisions as *Boardman* v *Sanderson* [1964] 1 WLR 1317 and *Marshall* v *Lionel Enterprises Inc* [1972] 2 OR 177.

22. In *McGarvey* v *Sec of State* [1978] 2 NIJB McGonigal LJ held that compensation was *not* payable where nervous shock had been caused to an applicant coming on the scene of

an explosion and seeing people injured by it. In *O'Dowd* itself, Gibson LJ had rejected the applicants' claims on the basis that they had not been present when the shooting occurred.

23. [1982] NI 210, 214.

24. Although Lord Lowry considered that the applicant had "a strong case", he preferred to follow the procedure in *Ince* and remit the case for the High Court to decide on the facts: *ibid*, p 215.

25. [1982] 2 All ER 298, 312.

"the consensus of informed judicial opinion is probably the best yardstick available to determine whether, in any given circumstances, the emotional trauma [was directly attributable] . . . ". On this basis "directness" is a matter of judgment, so that even after *O'Dowd*, the scope of "directly attributable" in nervous shock cases may be governed or affected by "objective" controlling factors. Certain factors were indeed (with differing degrees of emphasis) identified as relevant in *McLoughlin*,[26] and as we shall see these have also been taken into account to some extent in criminal injuries cases since 1982. It has to be said, however, that psychiatrists do not analyse the cause of their patients' condition in similar terms, with the result that it is often impossible to fit a particular case into a clear "legal" category.

The most straightforward case remains that in which the applicant is present at the scene when the crime is committed and suffers nervous shock as the result of fear of immediate death or injury to himself. This category includes nervous shock resulting from assassination attempts,[27] violent threats,[28] being held captive or taken hostage,[29] hijacking[30] and the planting of explosives.[31] It also includes sexual assaults.[32] It would also appear that a person present at the scene of a shooting or of an explosion qualifies for compensation if he suffers nervous shock due simply to the traumatic nature of the crime – i.e. even if not put in fear for his own safety (or that of another person).[33]

The next category of case involves applicants also present at the scene of the crime whose nervous shock results from fear for the safety of another person. The strongest cases in this category are those where the other person is a close relative of the applicant, and compensation has frequently been awarded in such circumstances.[34] But compensation has also been awarded

---

26. In particular, the proximity of the tie or relationship between the plaintiff and the injured person, the proximity of the plaintiff to the accident both in time and place, and the proximity of communication of the accident to the plaintiff through sight or hearing of the event or its immediate aftermath.

27. See e.g. *Burke* v *Sec of State* [1981] 6 *BNIL* 21.

28. See e.g. *McDevitte* v *Sec of State* [1988] 6 *BNIL* 29; *M* v *Sec of State* [1988] 1 *BNIL* 33; *O'Neill* v *Sec of State* [1986] 2 *BNIL* 13; *C* v *Sec of State* [1983] 3 *BNIL* 16; *Murray* v *Sec of State* [1983] 1 *BNIL* 23; *McCann* v *Sec of State* [1981] 3 *BNIL* 20.

29. E.g. *D* v *Sec of State* [1989] 4 *BNIL* 15; *Devine* v *Sec of State* [1988] 6 *BNIL* 29; *Maguire* v *Sec of State* [1985] 9 *BNIL* 14; *Tease* v *Sec of State* [1985] 6 *BNIL* 22; *McGill* v *Sec of State* [1982] 8 *BNIL* 14

30. E.g. *Lavelle* v *Sec of State* [1989] 7 *BNIL* 23; *K* v *Sec of State* [1987] 10 *BNIL* 22; *Osborne* v *Sec of State* [1985] 4 *BNIL* 16; *Grimason* v *Sec of State* [1986] 9 *BNIL* 13;

Barr v *Sec of State* [1983] 4 *BNIL* 22; *Blee* v *Sec of State* [1983] 1 *BNIL* 23.

31. E.g. *Tracey* v *Sec of State* [1988] 10 *BNIL* 8; *George* v *Sec of State* [1986] 8 *BNIL* 23; *McCormick* v *Sec of State* [1985] 6 *BNIL* 22; *Lawson* v *Sec of State* [1985] 1 *BNIL* 15. Nervous shock caused by discovering a hoax bomb is also compensable – see e.g. *Martin* v *Sec of State* [1987] 3 *BNIL* 27.

32. E.g. *F* v *Sec of State* [1989] 7 *BNIL* 24; *P* v *Sec of State* [1985] 10 *BNIL* 18; *M* v *Sec of State* [1981] 6 *BNIL* 20; *E* v *Sec of State* [1981] 4 *BNIL* 25.

33. E.g. *G* v *Sec of State* [1987] 3 *BNIL* 27; *Moley* v *Sec of State* [1983] 8 *BNIL* 14; *Craig* v *Sec of State* [1982] 8 *BNIL* 14; *Campbell* v *Sec of State* [1981] 9 *BNIL* 29; *Stott* v *Sec of State* [1981] 8 *BNIL* 23.

34. E.g. *B* v *Sec of State* [1989] 4 *BNIL* 16 (husband); *McS* v *Sec of State* [1988] 6 *BNIL* 29 (father); *McN* v *Sec of State* [1985] 1 *BNIL* 15 (mother); *Baldrick* v *Sec of State* [1987] 10 *BNIL* 22 (husband); *McGuinness* v *Sec of State* [1987] 4 *BNIL* 20 (daughter).

where the person injured or killed is a close friend[35] or colleague[36] of the applicant. In *McLoughlin*[37] Lord Wilberforce emphasised the importance of a close relationship, and suggested that "other cases . . . must be very carefully scrutinised . . . ". As a result it is usually suggested that an "ordinary bystander" cannot recover damages for nervous shock resulting from his presence at an incident in which a "stranger" is injured or killed.[38] However, in *McCann v Secretary of State*,[39] compensation may have been awarded in such a case. The applicant was sitting in a social club when gunmen entered; they shot dead one man, and injured several others. None of these persons was related to the applicant in any way. She was awarded compensation for resulting nervous shock – but it may just be that that shock resulted solely from her fear for her own safety.

Another case which at least comes close to this point is *Bellew v Secretary of State*.[40] The applicant was a 15-year-old schoolboy living in a rural area. As he knew, a police constable had been kidnapped by terrorists in the area. As he was cycling to school the applicant saw at the side of the road what appeared to him to be a body, and which he assumed was that of the missing police officer. He informed the police and went on to school. After school it was found that he was suffering delayed shock – and in fact he was unable to return to school for a month. The "body" was in fact a dummy, part of a booby-trap for the security forces; but the body of the murdered constable was found nearby two days later. Compensation was awarded, apparently[41] on the basis that the applicant's nervous shock was directly attributable to his seeing the dummy and his (reasonable) belief that it was the body of the kidnapped constable.

There is, indeed, some clear judicial support for the "ordinary by-stander". As long ago as 1925 Atkin LJ stated that he could –

> " . . . see no reason for excluding the bystander in the highway who receives injury in the same way from apprehension of or the actual sight of injury to a third party. There may well be cases where the sight of suffering will directly and immediately physically shock the most indurate heart."[42]

More recently, in *McGarvey v Secretary of State*, McGonigal LJ stated:

> "It does not appear to me that that question [of directly attributable] is determined by any relationship between the person injured by the explosion and the person coming on the scene. A severely mutilated body could as easily cause nervous shock to a stranger as to a relative though the emotional aspect in the latter might be greater."[43]

---

35. *McCartan v Sec of State* [1986] 9 *BNIL* 13 or *Boggs v Sec of State* [1981] 9 *BNIL* 29 may come into this category.

36. *Poston v Sec of State* [1981] 4 *BNIL* 25 may be such a case. Damages have been awarded at common law in such cases – see e.g. *Dooley v Cammell Laird & Co Ltd* [1951] 1 Lloyds Rep 271; *Carlin v Helical Bar* (1970) 9 KIR 154.

37. [1982] 2 All ER 298, 304.

38. See e.g. Trindade, *op cit* n 49, pp 488–9.

39. [1982] 9 *BNIL* 12.

40. [1985] 6 NIJB 86.

41. The booby-trap bomb exploded, and the applicant heard the explosion; it is not made clear if this had any effect on his condition.

42. *Hambrook v Stokes Bros* [1925] 1 KB 141, 157–8.

43. [1978] 2 NIJB.

However, both these statements were made in a context in which other constraints were being imposed on recovery for nervous shock, and it remains to be seen whether *McLoughlin* or *O'Dowd* will be extended in this way.[44]

The final situation in this category of cases involving an applicant present at the scene of the crime arises when the nervous shock results not from fear for himself or another person, but from fear of damage to his property. In an older case – *McAllister* v *Ministry of Home Affairs*[45] – the applicant's house had been maliciously set on fire and destroyed. The incident occurred while A was away from home and she did not herself see it on fire, but she suffered nervous shock when told what had happened. Compensation was refused on two grounds: first, the applicant had not seen the crime committed nor did she observe with any of her (unaided) senses any of the results of the crime. We deal with this matter below. But the application was also refused on the ground that the applicant had never felt any fear of any physical danger to herself or to her husband, nor was she in fact in any danger. It is not clear if this second ground would still be accepted. In *McGlinchey* v *Secretary of State*[46] the applicants were a husband and wife whose home was endangered by fire. Some wooden boxes stored against the wall of the applicants' yard were set alight by a petrol bomb during a riot, and the fire spread to the applicants' car. Because of the riot the fire brigade took three hours to reach the scene. Both applicants were in the house during this time, and both suffered nervous shock. Compensation was awarded, without any analysis of the cause of the applicants' condition. It may be that they were afraid for their own safety; but it is also possible that they feared that their home would be burned down. A decision on the latter basis would go further than the existing common law as represented by *Attia* v *British Gas plc*.[47] In that case it was held that a plaintiff may, in an appropriate case, recover damages for nervous shock caused by witnessing her home and possessions being damaged or destroyed by a fire caused by the defendant's negligence.

A common element in all the cases so far considered is the applicant's presence at the scene of the crime. Since *O'Dowd* such presence is no longer necessary (unless required by Article 5(12)(*b*)), but *McLoughlin* suggests that the courts may still have regard to the applicant's proximity in time and space to the commission of the crime, and to the method by which the applicant learned of the crime or of its consequences. We may take *O'Dowd* itself as the starting point for this discussion; it may be categorised as a case where the applicants came upon the scene in the immediate aftermath of the crime and observed with their own unaided senses the consequences of the crime as it affected close relatives.[48] A number of subsequent

---

44. In *McLoughlin* (p 422), Lord Wilberforce considered that "such persons must be assumed to be possessed of fortitude sufficient to enable them to endure the calamities of modern life." See further Teff, (1983) 99 *LQR* 100, 104–5; Trindade, [1986] *CambLJ* 476, 487–9.

45. Unreported, Cty Ct (Judge Patton), 27 April 1970.

46. [1986] 2 *BNIL* 13.

47. [1987] 3 All ER 455. *Cf* under the British Scheme "shock directly attributable to the loss of possessions is not within the scheme": *Statement*, para 4B(2) (retained after the decision in *Attia*). Such shock is also precluded by the terms of the 1988 Act, s 109(2).

48. As indeed may *McLoughlin*, and *Jaensch* v *Coffey* (1984) 54 ALR 417.

cases may be similarly classified. Thus *Smith* v *Secretary of State*[49] is a clear "immediate aftermath" case. The applicants were the widow and daughter of a part-time member of the security forces who was shot dead outside their home. Both applicants arrived on the scene immediately after the murder and saw the mutilation caused by gunshots to the head; both were awarded compensation. Other cases have applied similar reasoning where other close relatives were involved.[50] But in *Halliday* v *Secretary of State*[51] there was no such relationship. The applicant was walking along a road when a bomb exploded nearby. He immediately went to help the injured and as a result came upon parts of human bodies blown up by the bomb. Compensation was awarded for the resulting shock, presumably by analogy with the common law "rescue" cases.[52] By way of contrast compensation was refused in *Maguire* v *Secretary of State*.[53] The applicant, "a very decent but somewhat frail old lady", was in her home when she heard a commotion. She went outside and heard that a man had been shot; then she saw a person being carried away in a blanket. The learned judge considered three features of the case to point against recovery, *viz* (i) the applicant had not seen the shooting; (ii) the person shot was not a member of her family, and (iii) all that the applicant had seen was the body of an unknown man wrapped in a blanket being carried out of a neighbouring house. In the words of the learned judge, "the death by criminal act of a total stranger reported to the claimant but not witnessed must . . . be too remote".

Where close relatives are concerned and the applicant is fairly closely involved with the incident, compensation may be awarded. In *W* v *Secretary of State*[54] the applicant was in her house when she heard the explosion and saw the smoke from a bomb which exploded under her son's car, which was parked just outside the house. Her husband had been unloading the car and she feared that either he or their son had been killed or injured. (In fact her husband was injured, but not too seriously.) Being crippled with osteoarthritis the applicant could not go to the scene, but she was held nevertheless to be entitled to compensation. In *Hughes* v *Secretary of State*[55] there was rather less proximity in time and space. A bar belonging to the applicant's husband was destroyed by an explosion. At the time the applicant was at home, some 10 miles away. She learned of the explosion from her mother, who could not tell her if her husband had been injured or killed. She immediately went to the bar, but it was only after some time that she found that her husband was safe and well. Compensation for her nervous shock

---

49. Unreported, Cty Ct (Judge Russell), 13 March 1986; [1986] 5 *BNIL* 15.

50. E.g. *C* v *Sec of State* [1983] 5 *BNIL* 13 (schoolboy came downstairs on hearing shots and found dying father); *Short* v *Sec of State* [1985] 2 *BNIL* 18 (husband working at car outside house when shooting started; wife heard shooting and ran out of house to find husband shot in leg).

51. [1986] 8 *BNIL* 23 – in effect "reversing" *McGarvey* v *Sec of State* [1978] 2 NIJB.

52. E.g. *Chadwick* v *British Rlys Board* [1967] 2 All ER 945; *Mt Isa Mines* v *Pusey* (1970) 125 CLR 383. It should, however, be noted that there is nothing in *Halliday* to suggest that the applicant actually engaged in "rescue" work.

53. Unreported, Cty Ct (Judge Curran), 6 July 1984.

54. [1988] 2 *BNIL* 13.

55. Unreported, Cty Ct (Judge Russell), 31 May 1985.

was awarded. The learned judge considered that the applicant's depressive illness was not exclusively referable to what she had been told at home (had it been he would probably have refused compensation), but was "far more" caused by what she had seen and experienced at the bar. Thus, "she had direct perception of some of the events which comprised the incident as an entire event . . . ".

The "immediate aftermath" cases were taken one stage further in *Gristwood* v *Secretary of State*.[56] Shortly before midnight A's daughter was seriously injured in an explosion. A, who lived in England, was informed of her daughter's plight at about 6.00 am the following morning. A and her husband immediately rushed to their daughter's bedside. The daughter was in a coma for five weeks, but eventually made a good recovery. A and her husband stayed in Northern Ireland and visited their daughter daily for some three weeks. As a result of these circumstances A suffered serious psychiatric illness. The learned judge was satisfied that A's condition was caused in part by her being told of what had happened to her daughter, and in part by seeing her condition and watching her slow (and for a time uncertain) recovery. He appears to have accepted that A was not entitled to compensation for nervous shock arising from what she had been told;[57] but he held that it was sufficient that what A saw was also *an* effective cause of her illness[58] – provided that it was sufficiently proximate. To answer this latter question the learned judge compared the facts of the case with those in *McLoughlin*, and concluded:

> "In my opinion, the only significant difference . . . is that whereas Mrs McLoughlin arrived at the hospital about an hour after the injuries were inflicted, Mrs Gristwood did not see the effect of the injuries for some hours after she learnt of their infliction, probably by mid-afternoon of the following day. No doubt it could be said that the passage of some hours is sufficiently significant to distinguish *McLoughlin* . . . from this case, but I do not consider that this is so . . . I consider that where the passage of time was as short as it was in this case between the infliction of the injuries, the communication of the news and the perception by the appellant of the effects, that taking all of these circumstances together it could be reasonably said that the appellant in this case did witness the aftermath of the criminal offence when one applies the test outlined by Lord Wilberforce [in *McLoughlin*]."

On this basis, Mrs Gristwood was entitled to compensation. But it may be argued that the learned judge has gone beyond the facts in *McLoughlin*, where Lord Wilberforce had been careful to point out that the plaintiff had seen the members of her family "in the same condition [caused by the

---

56. Unreported, Cty Ct (Judge Hart), 29 Jan 1986.

57. The learned judge quoted (with apparent approval) from the judgment of Lord Wilberforce in *McLoughlin*: "There is no case in which the law has compensated shock brought about by communication by a third party. In *Hambrook* v *Stokes Bros* [1925] 1 KB 141 indeed, it was said that liability would not arise in such a case, and this is surely right."

58. Referring in particular to the statement by Megaw LJ in *Ince* (above, p 64) that the violent offence need not be "the sole cause" of the applicant's injury. Query whether the situation in *Gristwood* is what Megaw LJ had in mind.

accident], covered with oil and mud, and distraught with pain . . . ".[59] Be that as it may, *Gristwood* may still be characterised as a case where an applicant, "very soon" after a violent offence has caused serious injury to a close relative, perceives for herself the after-effects of that offence. A couple of cases seem to go even further.

In *Cochrane* v *Secretary of State*,[60] the applicant's husband was a part-time member of the UDR whose place of work was some three miles from home. One morning the applicant was told that her husband had not arrived at work. Her fears that he had been abducted were confirmed when his motor-cycle helmet and gloves were found on the roadside. The IRA then issued a statement that the applicant's husband was in their hands. One week later a body was found on the roadside and a photograph of this body was published in a newspaper which the applicant saw; she identified the body as that of her husband. Compensation was awarded for her resulting shock; the learned judge accepted that the applicant was not present at the scene of any crime nor did she have "personal perception" of any crime. But she was aware of the finding of her husband's motor-cycle, she knew of the IRA statement and had seen the photograph of her husband's body. The learned judge concluded that these facts established that the applicant's condition was "directly" attributable to the crimes against her husband.[61]

Cochrane may be seen as a further extension of the "aftermath" principle, but in *Mackin* v *Secretary of State*[62] the court had to deal directly with nervous shock caused solely by what an applicant had been told. The applicant's husband had gone one evening to speak to a neighbour about a job. He did not return home that night. The next morning the applicant was told that her husband's car had been seen stopped on a lonely back road, and with a body in it. Soon afterwards, she was told that her husband had been murdered. The learned judge held that she was entitled to compensation; he appears to have attached particular importance to the fact that the applicant was the wife of the deceased and thus "within the limited class entitled to bring a claim in this type of case". It further appears that this reasoning was also applied by MacDermott J in *McNeill* v *Secretary of State*[63] when he awarded compensation to a mother who suffered nervous shock on learning

---

59. [1982] 2 All ER 298, 302. In *Jaensch* v *Coffey* (1984) 54 ALR 417, 462–3, Deane J stated that "the aftermath", both in that case and in *McLoughlin*, "extended to the hospital to which the injured person was taken and persisted for so long as he remained in the state produced by the accident up to and including immediate post-accident treatment." For criticism, see Trindade, *op cit* n 44, p 491.

60. Unreported, Cty Ct (Judge Russell), 18 Jan 1984.

61. In *McLoughlin*, Lord Bridge (at p 320) gave a similar example in which damages would be awarded, *viz* a wife, knowing that her husband was staying in a certain hotel,

reads in a newspaper that that hotel has been destroyed by a disastrous fire, and she sees photographs of victims who had been trapped on the top floor, waving for help; she is told shortly after that her husband had perished in the fire. See also *Saunders* v *Air Florida Inc* (1983) 558 F Supp 1233 (accident seen on TV).

62. Unreported, Cty Ct (Judge Rowland), 3 April 1985.

63. Unreported, High Ct (MacDermott J), 15 May 1986 (semble, only oral judgment given) *Cf State (Waters)* v *Criminal Injuries Compensation Tribunal*, Unreported, High Ct (Gannon J), 28 Nov 1983 (mother told of son's murder refused compensation).

of the murder of her son. On this basis, the Northern Ireland courts appear to be giving *McLoughlin* v *O'Brian* a more flexible interpretation than that suggested by Lord Wilberforce.[64]

There is perhaps one final point to be made on this topic. In tort cases difficulties have sometimes arisen as to the foreseeability of nervous shock in relation to a plaintiff who had a prior history of mental illness.[65] In criminal injuries compensation cases, however, such problems do not arise; the Secretary of State must simply take the victim as he finds him. As was said in *Malcolm* v *Broadhurst*,[66] "there is no difference in principle between an egg-shell skull and an egg-shell personality". The applicant will, however, still have to prove that his present condition was caused by a violent crime or other qualifying event and is not simply the recurrence or continuation of a pre-existing illness. A case in point is *Wilson* v *Secretary of State*[67] where the applicant had previously been diagnosed as having an immature personality. He had (apparently successfully) undergone a course of electro-convulsive therapy. Following the criminal incident the applicant suffered severe neurosis. After examining the medical evidence the court was satisfied that this condition was directly and solely attributable to the crime, and compensation was, therefore, awarded. In that case there was no connection between the pre- and post-incident condition of the applicant; but it would appear that compensation is also payable if the criminal incident exacerbates a pre-existing condition.[68]

(b) *The special causal requirement under Article 5(12)(b)*

Article 5(12)(*b*) of the 1988 Order in effect stipulates a new and special definition of "directly attributable" for cases coming within that paragraph, *viz* the applicant must have sustained the injury (as there defined) "by virtue of being present when that act [*sc* the act arising out of which the application

---

64. In *McLoughlin*, Lord Wilberforce suggested that damages are not, as a matter of principle, payable in such circumstances; the other Law Lords seemed prepared to treat the matter as one of fact and degree. *Cf* in *Jaensch* v *Coffey* (1984) 54 ALR 417, 457, Deane J observed that "Expert evidence is available to support [the proposition] . . . that the most important explanation of nervous shock resulting from the injury to another is the existence of a close, constructive and loving relationship with that person (a 'close relative') and that it is largely immaterial . . . how he or she learns of [the accident] . . .". The learned judge considered (p 463) that the question whether recovery is allowed where reasonably foreseeable psychiatric injury is sustained as a consequence of being told about the death or injury "remains . . . an open one". Legislation in some Australian jurisdictions specifically gives a spouse or parent the right to recover damages in such circumstances – see e.g. Law Reform (Miscellaneous Provisions) Act (NSW) 1944, s 4(1). In *McLoughlin* Lord Scarman observed that there was "much to be said" for this approach.

65. See e.g. *Brice* v *Brown* [1984] 1 All ER 997.

66. [1970] 3 All ER 508, 511, *per* Geoffrey Lane J. For a psychiatrist's view of an "egg-shell personality" see e.g. Kee *et al*, "Victims of Violence: A Demographic and Clinical Study" (1987) 27 *Med Sci Law* 241, 246.

67. Unreported, Cty Ct (Judge Babington), 19 Dec 1975. See also *McAloon* v *Sec of State* [1990] 2 *BNIL* 24; *Hughes* v *Sec of State* Unreported, Cty Ct (Judge Russell), 31 May 1985; *McNeill* v *Sec of State* Unreported, High Ct (MacDermott J), 15 May 1986.

68. As in *Malcolm* v *Broadhurst*, *supra*.

for compensation is made] was committed . . . ".[69] The intention of this provision seems clear – to reverse *O'Dowd* and other "immediate aftermath" decisions[70] to the extent that compensation under Article 3(2)(*a*)(iv) may no longer be awarded for pain and suffering and loss of amenities in such cases. Whether or not this intention has been achieved will depend on the courts' interpretation of "being present" at an explosion, shooting or other criminal incident. The most obvious case is where the applicant was physically at the scene of the explosion, shooting, etc. But it seems likely to be accepted that an applicant who was sufficiently close to see or hear the incident with his own unaided senses is also included.[71] It also seems likely that the victim of an assassination attempt will be held to have been "present" at the shooting, even if the shot was fired from some distance away.[72] But it would appear that the only basis on which applicants such as those in *O'Dowd* will recover under Article 5(12)(*b*) is if the courts are willing to stretch the concept of "being present" to include some such relationship as that the applicant was so close to the incident in time, space and circumstances as to render his experience an integral part of that incident.[73] Such an interpretation might be adopted (as it was in the mid-1970s) to avoid what might be considered the arbitrary injustice of continuing to award compensation in cases such as *McGlinchey*[74] while refusing it to the O'Dowds (or Mrs McLoughlin).

A second feature of Article 5(12)(*b*) is that the shock must be sustained "by virtue of" being present.[75] Logically, this precludes the award of compensation where a person present at the scene suffers shock not as a result of being present but because e.g. of the death of a loved one. It seems unlikely, however, that the courts will expect such a logical and precise diagnosis of the cause of the applicant's condition.

3. "Directly Attributable" to an Act of Law Enforcement

We may begin with some salutary remarks by Lord MacDermott LCJ:

> "This . . . is the more difficult limb of the definition [of criminal injury]. The relevant factor under it need not be an offence at all and this in itself makes paragraph (*b*) more vague in its scope and less definite than paragraph (*a*). I

---

69. *Cf* 1988 Act, s 109(2): "Harm to a person's mental condition is only a criminal injury if it is attributable – (*a*) to his having been put in fear of immediate physical injury to himself or another; or (*b*) to his being present when another sustained a criminal injury other than harm to his mental condition."

70. Discussed above, pp 68–76.

71. As was the case before *McLoughlin* and *O'Dowd* – see above, p 68. See also Restatement, *Torts* (2d) (1965), s 436(3), relying on *Hambrook* v *Stokes Bros* [1925] 1 KB 141, *Cf* the "presence" requirement for

robbery, as applied e.g. in *Smith* v *Desmond* [1965] 1 All ER 976.

72. On the analogy of *Farrendon*, above p 52.

73. A test suggested by *Hughes* (above p 74). But *cf Archibald* v *Sec of State* [1990] 2 *BNIL* 26 (A heard explosion and feared for husband's safety; compensation refused because A not "present").

74. Above, p 72.

75. See also 1988 Act, s 109(2)(*b*) above.

think it is this circumstance that makes the requirement that the injury shall be 'directly attributable' to the arrest etc . . . capable of creating difficulty on occasion . . . "[76]

As we have seen, the question is one of degree and much will depend on the particular facts of each case. Although in theory involvement in an act of law enforcement could cause nervous shock, claims made under this head are invariably for physical injury. In such cases the courts appear to have regard to two particular factors:

(i) Causative potency – i.e. the extent to which the injury to the applicant may be said to have been brought about by the arrest, attempted arrest, etc. It appears that this is what Jones J had in mind in *Martin* when he observed:

> "I do not think that one can draw any clear line between an injury received before an arrest is effected and one which, in point of time, follows the arrest, though, in practice, the condition of direct attributability may be easier of fulfilment before, rather than after, an arrest has been made."[77]

It is indeed noticeable that in most of the cases where compensation has been awarded the applicant had been injured as a result of conduct required by the exigencies of effecting or trying to effect an arrest, etc. A good case in point is *Stitt* v *Secretary of State*,[78] where police officers, including the applicant, were investigating a reported burglary. As they approached the premises, the intruder ran out. A gave chase in order to arrest him. They crossed a bowling green and then came to a sudden rise in the ground. In the darkness, A thought that the rise was a fence and as a result he slipped and fell, injuring himself. The intruder at that stage was about 15 feet in front of A. The court held that A's injury was directly attributable to his attempted arrest of the intruder:

> "I have no doubt that a spectator of the incident would . . . [say], 'he injured himself whilst trying to capture the intruder'."

Similarly, in *Hutchinson* v *Secretary of State*,[79] the applicant was one of two police constables who saw some suspicious figures and decided to follow them. In order to do so the constables had at one stage to climb over a wall. When A was on top of the wall he slipped and fell some 10 feet to the street below. Carswell J held that his resulting injuries were directly attributable to his attempted prevention of an offence:

> "I consider that if one applies the test of selection of the *causa causans*, it may be said that the reason why the applicant was on the wall at all was his pursuit of suspected terrorists."[80]

---

76. *Martin* v *Ministry of Home Affairs* (1970) [1979] NI 172, 176.

77. *Ibid*, p 175.

78. Unreported, Cty Ct (Judge Higgins), 4 Nov 1987.

79. [1988] 11 NIJB 64.

80. The learned judge added (p 70) that: "In *Martin's* case itself a different result might have been produced by greater emphasis upon the danger inherent in walking upon a fragile roof and the necessity for the applicant to venture upon it in order to effect the arrest."

(ii) Particular danger – i.e. to what extent did the situation involve special risk to the applicant? In *Martin*, Jones J noted that "the judge did not make any finding that the place where the affair occurred was one of particular danger or that the appellant's presence there with his captive created any particular risk or hazard".[81] This factor was also mentioned by Lord MacDermott LCJ, and this later led Carswell J to observe:

> "The Court of Appeal [in *Martin*] was concerned to propound a test that would exclude injuries sustained in the course of a police officer's duties which are the common lot of mankind, such as slipping on ice, and at the same time include those which result from unusually hazardous activities in which the officer has to engage in order to perform those duties."[82]

Compensation will, therefore, normally be refused where the applicant has suffered accidental injury while attempting to effect an arrest "in normal conditions of no particular danger or difficulty . . . ". In *Martin*, it was suggested that this would be the case where e.g. the applicant had slipped on an icy patch on the road, or fallen through a defective manhole in the footpath.[83] In *Darragh* v *Secretary of State*[84] compensation was refused to a police officer who slipped and injured his hand when walking down a gravel slope on his way to apprehend some children who had been setting fire to bushes. Similarly, in *Breen* v *Secretary of State*[85] a police officer fell while trying to get out of a police landrover. The landrover was responding to a call that a shot had been fired. At the time of the accident it stopped at a road junction, there was no particular peril from a gunman and the applicant had not been ordered to leave the landrover. Compensation was refused.

A police officer in hot pursuit of a suspect will normally be refused compensation for any accidental injury if the *locus* presents no particular danger. Thus, in *Millar* v *Secretary of State*[86] a police car came to a house in response to a call that there was an intruder at the back of the house. The car stopped at the front of the house and the applicant got out and began running towards the back. As he did so his foot went down a pot-hole and he fell heavily. It was held that his injury was not directly attributable to the attempted arrest of the intruder.

The need for a particular danger or unusual hazard has now been written into the 1988 Order, Article 5(15) of which provides:

> "No compensation shall be paid where the victim accidentally sustains an injury which is a criminal injury only by virtue of sub-paragraph (*b*) of the definition of 'criminal injury' . . . unless the Secretary of State is satisfied that the risk which the victim was taking when the injury was sustained was an exceptional risk for him to take."

---

81. (1970) [1979] NI 172, 175–6. *Cp* CICB, *11th Annual Report* (1974–75), para 7 (police officer climbed on to back of lorry to search for suspected thief; found nothing, but on way down caught hand on hook; compensation awarded).

82. In *Hutchinson, supra* n 79.

83. [1979] NI 172, 175, *per* Jones J, who added however that "Of course each case depends on its own facts . . . ".

84. [1986] 1 *BNIL* 11.

85. [1986] 3 *BNIL* 18.

86. Unreported, Cty Ct (Judge Pringle), 21 Oct 1985.

This provision has its origins in a review of the British Scheme published in 1978:

> "In some of the cases that have been brought within the scope of the Scheme in recent years, the link between the injury sustained and the criminal event has been only a slender one; such cases have had more in common with other cases of accident . . . which, though they may excite justified sympathy, should not attract compensation from a scheme with the objects of the present one."[87]

The proposed remedy was to require the victim to show that his injuries arose because at the time he was taking some exceptional risk, *and* that the risk which he was taking was justified in relation to the circumstances. This requirement was duly incorporated into the British Scheme in 1979 (and 1990)[88] and has been enacted as section 110(6) of the 1988 Act.

The 1988 Order thus brings Northern Ireland broadly[89] into line with the British Scheme on this point. The new provision will particularly affect claims by police officers, and their representatives, both in Great Britain and in Northern Ireland, have castigated this restriction as unfairly prohibiting the payment of compensation to police officers injured in the course of duty through no fault of their own.[90] These criticisms were rejected when the British Scheme was reviewed in 1986:

> " . . . the change made in 1979 was in the right direction . . . Accidental injuries incurred in the course of employment ought not to fall within the scope of the Scheme at all . . . [particularly since] police pay [is] intended to reflect the stresses and dangers of police work."[91]

It was however suggested that compensation *should* be paid to members of the public accidentally injured when going to the assistance of a police officer or otherwise attempting to prevent crime or to arrest an offender.[92] Both the 1988 Order and the British Scheme fail to draw this distinction, but it may be that in the case of accidental injuries sustained by "civilians" the Secretary of State will be more easily satisfied that the applicant was taking an "exceptional risk":

---

87. 1978 *IWP Report*, paras 5.22–5.23 (one of the cases is summarised in n 81 above). See also 1986 *IWP Report*, paras 6.8 *et seq.*

88. Paragraph 6(*d*), discussed Greer, *Criminal Injuries Compensation* (1990), paras 2.27–2.32.

89. *Cf* in Great Britain, the risk must not only be exceptional, but also be one "which was justified in all the circumstances" – see 489 HL Debs, cols 795-8 (2 Nov 1987).

90. See e.g. the comments in 1986 *IWP Report*, para 6.11.

91. 1986 *IWP Report*, para 6.12. When the

1988 Order was being discussed in Parliament, it was stated that "Although it is true that the restriction will mostly affect police officers, the number of such cases will undoubtedly be comparatively few, and those officers will be no worse off financially than any other policeman injured in the normal course of duty. In addition . . . there are other benefits to which a police officer may be entitled . . .": 128 HC Debs, col 543 (25 Feb 1988) (Mr Stanley). Atiyah, *Accidents, Compensation and the Law* (4th ed, 1987), pp 300–1 argues that the scheme should exclude *all* accidental injuries.

92. 1986 *IWP Report*, para 6.13.

> "Helping the police to arrest a criminal or to prevent a crime would not be a normal activity for a member of the public. In those circumstances, the risk taken would be regarded as exceptional in probably all cases . . . "[93]

However, compensation has been refused in Britain in at least one such case.[94] The applicant, a woman aged 33, was asleep in her home when a brick was thrown through the bedroom window. She leapt from her bed and ran to the stairs to go down to the front door in an attempt to catch the culprit. At the top of the stairs she slipped on a toy car belonging to her child, and fell down the stairs. The Board considered that even if the lights were off at the time, it could not be said that the applicant was taking an exceptional risk in trying to apprehend the offender.

As regards police officers it seems that the issue is still one of degree and that much will depend on the particular facts of the case. Until a body of Northern Ireland case law has been established, however, the following guidelines adopted by the British Board may be helpful:

> "1. Persons who fall over when walking or running towards an incident or going to apprehend an offender, will usually not be taking an exceptional risk[95] nor will a person who is injured when escorting a prisoner who is not violent.
>
> 2. Persons who are injured when climbing or jumping over things such as walls or fences will usually not be taking an exceptional risk. But a person who jumps over something when he does not know and cannot see what is on the other side will often be taking an exceptional risk, especially at night.[96]
>
> 3. A person who falls through a roof or from a height will usually have been taking an exceptional risk.[97]

---

93. 128 HC Debs, col 546 (25 Feb 1988).

94. CICB, *23rd Annual Report* (1986-87), para 22.

95. See e.g. CICB, *24th Annual Report* (1987–88), para 28 (police officer chasing a suspect suddenly slipped and fell; refused compensation); *18th Annual Report* (1981–82), para 37 (police officer chasing escaped prisoner put on an extra spurt, and fell over; compensation refused); *ibid*, para 36 (police officer chasing suspected thief tripped over a small kerb; compensation refused). *Cf 24th Annual Report* (1987–88), para 29 (police officer fell while chasing suspected thief along beach path; ground uneven and wet, path poorly maintained and no lighting; compensation awarded).

96. See e.g. CICB, *21st Annual Report* (1984–85), para 30 (police officer rushing to scene of police alarm opened a door and was injured when the plate glass in it smashed; compensa-

tion refused); CICB, *18th Annual Report* (1981–82), para 38 (woman police officer taking part in line search for suspected offender slipped while negotiating a barbed wire fence and was injured; compensation refused). *Cf* CICB, *21st Annual Report* (1984–85), para 29 (police officer chasing suspect had to climb garden fences about 5 feet high; his weight on one fence dislodged garden rake and on jumping down from fence he was impaled on handle of rake; compensation awarded); *19th Annual Report* (1982–83), para 30 (police officer chasing suspected thief followed him over high wall; very dark on other side of wall and as officer descending from wall became entangled in wires and fell heavily; compensation awarded).

97. As e.g. in CICB, *18th Annual Report* (1981–82), para 40 (police officer climbed on to roof of warehouse in poor light to search for intruders; fell through skylight to floor 15 feet below; compensation awarded).

4. In the case of car crashes, the nature of the incident will often prove decisive. Answering a 999 call relating to intruders in an unoccupied building will usually not constitute an exceptional risk, unless the premises call for such risk being taken e.g. an armoury. Chasing or attempting to intercept a car which has refused to stop will usually be within the Scheme.[98]

5. Acts which would not be regarded as constituting an exceptional risk in daylight, may well be so at night.[99]

6. Factors such as the gravity of the incident and suspected danger to the public at the hands of the offender will be relevant."

A VIOLENT OFFENCE

1. General Definition[1]

By Article 2(2) of the 1988 Order "violent offence" means –

"(*a*) any offence which was intended to cause death, personal injury or damage to property;

(*b*) any offence committed by causing the death or injury of any person, or damage to property, where the state of mind of the person committing the offence consisted of recklessness as to whether he caused death, personal injury or damage to property;

(*c*) any offence under the Explosive Substances Act 1883;

(*d*) any offence under the Firearms (NI) Order 1981;

(*e*) riot, rout or unlawful assembly;

(*f*) kidnapping or false imprisonment;

(*g*) rape; or

(*h*) aiding, abetting, counselling, procuring or inciting the commission of, or attempting to commit, any offence mentioned in sub-paragraphs (*a*) to (*g*),

but does not include a traffic offence."

With the exception of the specific inclusion of rape, this replicates the definition introduced by the 1977 Order[2] – a definition which has given rise

---

98. See especially *R v CICB, ex parte Emmett*, Unreported, Div'l Ct, 16 Dec 1988 (A driving police car in pursuit of stolen car, which stopped suddenly without warning; A forced to stop police car in middle of road and injured when another car collided with police car; decision by Board that A not taking exceptional risk held not unreasonable). See also CICB, *22nd Annual Report* (1985–86), para 24 (suspect Mini chased by police stopped and police car drew up alongside; police officer got out and opened driver's door of Mini; Mini moved forward, causing officer to hit head on driver's door; driver's action not deliberate; compensation refused).

99. See e.g. CICB, *18th Annual Report* (1981–82), para 39 (police officer searching for suspected intruders in lorry depot in total darkness fell into inspection pit; compensation awarded).

1. I am grateful to my colleague Dr John Stannard for his comments and assistance on this section.

2. Article 2(2).

to little difficulty in practice and which, indeed, has been adapted for the British Scheme by the 1988 Act.[3] It will, however, be noted that the Northern Ireland scheme expressly embraces offences of violence to property as well as to persons; this is a broader approach than has hitherto pertained in Great Britain,[4] but it has the advantage of avoiding some of the difficulties which have arisen in that jurisdiction.[5]

Difficulties may, however, arise if headings (a) and (b) are subjected to closer scrutiny. As to (a), there appears to be a double requirement:

(i)   Did D commit an offence?

(ii) If so, did he intend thereby to cause death, personal injury or damage to property?

In other words, heading (a) is drafted so that, if taken literally, it is the *offence*, not D's *act*, which must have been intended to cause death, etc.[6] Such an interpretation brings *all* crimes potentially within the ambit of "violent offence", but most will in practice be excluded because the necessary intent is lacking. Thus, an employee who "wilfully and without reasonable cause" does an act "likely to endanger himself and others" as a result of which A is injured may have committed an offence under the Factories Acts,[7] but A cannot claim compensation under heading (a) unless he can show that in committing the offence the employee *intended* to injure him.[8] Similarly if D threw a piece of iron at X intending merely to frighten him, and accidentally killed A as he unexpectedly came through the doorway, D

---

3. 1988 Act, s 109(1)(a)(ii) and (3). The 1986 *IWP Report*, para 4.7 considered the Northern Ireland approach to provide "the most satisfactory basis for a statutory definition of a crime of violence". *Cf* the 1990 Scheme (para 4) still refers only to "a crime of violence".

4. The 1988 Act, s 109(1)(a)(ii) does not refer to damage to property.

5. See e.g. *R* v *CICB, ex parte Clowes* [1977] 3 All ER 854, where a police officer was injured by an explosion while investigating the death of a person who had committed suicide by breaking a gas stand-pipe in his house. Compensation was refused on the ground that the deceased had not intentionally or recklessly endangered the life of another; but he had intentionally or recklessly damaged property. The reasoning in *Clowes* was not followed in *R* v *CICB, ex parte Warner* [1986] 2 All ER 478 but the emphasis in that case also focused on the need for an intention to injure or recklessness as to whether an injury was caused. See generally Greer, *Criminal Injuries Compensation* (1990), paras 2.33–2.40 and Duff. "Criminal Injuries Compensa-

tion and 'Violent' Crime" [1987] *Crim LR* 219.

6. *Cp R* v *Steer* [1987] 2 All ER 833 where the House of Lords held that for a person to be guilty of the offence under the Criminal Damage Act 1971, s 1(2) of destroying or damaging property with intent to endanger the life of another by the destruction or damage or being reckless whether the life of another would be thereby endangered P had to prove that the danger to life resulted from the destruction of or damage to the property; it was not sufficient for P to prove that the danger to life resulted from the act which caused the destruction or damage. D had fired a shot at V through a window; the danger to V's life did not stem from the broken window, but from D's bullet. *Cf R* v *Dudley* [1989] *Crim LR* 57.

7. Sections 143(2) and 155.

8. Compensation was awarded by the British Board in such a case where the employee had acted recklessly: CICB, *9th Annual Report* (1972–73), para 16 and *18th Annual Report* (1981–82), para 28. But see Duff, *op cit* n 5, pp 222–3.

may be guilty of the manslaughter of A,[9] but A's relatives are not entitled under (a) to claim compensation.

It may be argued that the same result can be reached by giving (a) a more common-sense interpretation – that it connotes those offences which require proof of intent to cause death, personal injury or damage to property.[10] Such an interpretation still excludes "accidental" death, etc. But it would require the courts to interpret "intended" as having the same meaning as in criminal law, *viz*

> "(1) A result is intended when it is the actor's purpose.
>
> (2) A court or jury may also infer that a result is intended, though it is not desired, where –
> (a) the result is a virtually certain consequence of the act, and
>
> (b) the actor knows that it is a virtually certain consequence."[11]

There is a lot to be said for consistency in the interpretation of "intention", but it may be that the wording used in heading (a) could lead the courts to conclude that Parliament had some wider meaning of "intention" in mind. Indeed, it is arguable that the definition given above is too narrow even in respect of the criminal law.[12] It may even be open to the courts to hold on the facts of a particular case that an actor "intended" the natural and probable consequences of the offence.[13]

Such a definition may blur the distinction between intention and recklessness; but both are included in a "violent offence" and many claims which do not fall within heading (a) will in any case succeed under heading (b) of the definition. But again the rather curious drafting of this heading could give rise to difficulty. Thus, "an offence *committed* by causing the death, etc" might mean–

(i)   an offence in which the causing of death, etc is an *essential ingredient* of the offence; or

(ii) an offence which *on the particular occasion in question* caused death, personal injury or damage to property.

---

9. *R v Conner* (1835) 7 C & P 438. See also *McNeill v Sec of State* [1989] 10 *BNIL* 27 (D guilty of offence of intimidation, but not a violent offence because no intention to cause personal injury to A).

10. This is the formula under the 1988 Act, s 109(1)(a)(ii): " . . . an offence . . . which requires proof of intent to cause death or personal injury . . . ", in effect following *R v CICB, ex parte Warner* [1986] 2 All ER 478. See further Duff, "Criminal Injuries Compensation: The Scope of the new Scheme" (1989) 52 *MLR* 518.

11. Smith and Hogan, *Criminal Law* (6th ed, 1988), p 56. *Cf* Archbold, *Pleading, Evidence and Practice in Criminal Cases* (43rd ed,

1988), pp 1336 *et seq*. See also Smith, "A Note on 'Intention'" [1990] *Crim LR* 85.

12. Thus, *R v Hancock* [1986] 1 All ER 641 suggests that intention may be inferred from knowledge of a probability, and the Criminal Justice Act (NI) 1966, s 4 also suggests that intention may be inferred from the fact that the result was a natural and probable consequence of D's act. See also *R v Nedrick* [1986] 3 All ER 1 and *R v Walker* [1990] *Crim LR* 44.

13. Albeit with reference to Lord Scarman's observation in *R v Hancock* (*supra*): "The more probable a consequence, the more likely it is that it was foreseen, and if it was foreseen, the more likely it is that it was intended."

Bingham v *Secretary of State*[14] tends to support interpretation (ii). The applicant had been attacked and injured by D's dog, and D had been convicted of an offence under Article 29 of the Dogs (NI) Order 1983. That offence can be committed even if the person attacked is not physically injured,[15] but it does not appear to have been contended in *Bingham* that the applicant had not satisfied the first part of heading (*b*). On the other hand it can be argued that had meaning (ii) been intended, Parliament would have used some formula such as "any offence committed in the course of causing the death, etc". In addition, interpretation (i) seems preferable when one refers to heading (*h*) of the meaning of "violent offence".[16]

A second question is whether the term "reckless" is to be defined as it is in criminal law (so that heading (*b*) comprises in effect only those offences which may be committed by recklessness as to whether death, etc is caused), or is not necessarily so limited. The point now has added significance in the light of criticism that the House of Lords has blurred the distinction between recklessness and negligence.[17] On a literal reading of heading (*b*) one must first consider if an offence has been committed; if so, one then considers whether the person committing that offence did so "recklessly". Since some offences can be committed without recklessness on the part of the actor (e.g. strict liability offences, negligence offences), it may be contended that "reckless" in heading (*b*) does not – or does not necessarily – connote criminal law recklessness. The advantage of this approach is two-fold; it would enable a single meaning to be given to "reckless" irrespective of the offence involved, and would also avoid the payment of criminal injuries compensation for something which may come very close to mere negligence on the part of the actor[18] (which Parliament apparently sought to have excluded from the scheme). But it could also require a decision in a particular case that a person guilty (for example) of reckless criminal damage did not have a "reckless" state of mind for the purpose of heading (*b*). For this reason, the Secretary of State and the courts may prefer the simpler approach of adopting the criminal law definition.

That definition is now based on the judgment of Lord Diplock in *R* v *Caldwell* that a person is reckless if –

---

14. Unreported, High Ct (Kelly LJ), 30 June 1987.

15. By Article 2(2) "attacking a person" includes "behaving in such a manner so as to cause a person apprehension of being attacked ...".

16. The 1986 *1WP Report*, para 4.7 refers to the 1977 Order as applying to "any offence committed by causing (i.e. any offence the essential element of which is that it caused) the death . . . ". *Cf* 1988 Act, 109(1)(*a*)(ii) applies to any offence "which requires proof of . . . recklessness as to whether death or personal injury is caused . . . "; *semble*, actual death or personal injury need not be an essential element of the offence.

17. *R* v *Caldwell* [1981] 1 All ER 961; *R* v *Lawrence* [1981] 1 All ER 974. These cases are explained with admirable clarity in Stannard, *Recent Developments in Criminal Law* (1988), pp 5–7. See also Archbold, *Pleading, Evidence and Practice in Criminal Cases* (43rd ed, 1988), pp 1346–52; Smith and Hogan, *Criminal Law* (6th ed, 1988), pp 61 *et seq*; Birch, "The Foresight Saga: The Biggest Mistake of All?" [1988] *Crim LR* 4.

18. See e.g. *Elliott* v *C* [1983] 2 All ER 1005, where (following *Caldwell*) D was held guilty of reckless damage to property in circumstances which Robert Goff LJ admitted (at p 1015) he would not have regarded as "reckless" in the ordinary sense of the word.

(1) he does an act which in fact creates an obvious (or possibly "an obvious and serious"[19]) risk[20] that a person will be killed or injured[21] or that property will be destroyed or damaged; and

(2) when he does the act he either has not given any thought to the possibility of there being any such risk or has recognised that there was some risk involved and has nonetheless gone on to do it.[22]

Applying this test in *Caldwell* itself, Lord Diplock continued:

> "If there were nothing in the circumstances that ought to have drawn the attention of an ordinary prudent individual to the possibility of that kind of harmful consequence, the accused would not be . . . 'reckless' . . . for failing to address his mind to the possibility; nor, if the risk of harmful consequences was so slight that the ordinary prudent individual on due consideration of the risk would not be deterred from treating it as negligible, could the accused be described as 'reckless' if, having considered the risk, he decided to ignore it."[23]

It has also been suggested that *Caldwell* does not apply where D honestly believes that his conduct involves no risk at all.[24]

It largely remains to be seen what the Northern Ireland courts will make of all this in criminal injury compensation claims made under heading (*b*) of the definition of "violent offence". There appear to have been only three recent cases in point, and none is fully reported. *Cummings* v *Secretary of State*,[25] a pre-*Caldwell* case, involved two soldiers who had earlier been "sky-larking" with loaded guns. D, with a pistol in his hand, later approached the applicant. D, who had over a year's military service, knew that the pistol was loaded, but had not checked to see if it was cocked. He pointed the pistol at the applicant, made some jocular remark, and pulled the trigger. The applicant was seriously wounded in the stomach. The learned county court judge followed *R* v *Parker*[26] and held that D had been reckless – D had carried out a deliberate act knowing, or closing his mind to the obvious fact, that there was some risk of injury resulting from that act, but he nevertheless continued in the performance of the act. It is submitted that a similar result is required by *Caldwell*; D had in fact created an obvious risk of injury and

---

19. The wording apparently preferred by Lord Diplock in *Lawrence*.

20. *Semble*, a risk obvious to the reasonable prudent man and not to the particular defendant: *Elliott* v *C*, *supra* n 18.

21. *Caldwell* deals only with criminal damage to property, but Lord Diplock's definition has since been applied to manslaughter (*R* v *Seymour* [1983] 2 All ER 1058), reckless driving (*R* v *Lawrence* [1981] 1 All ER 974) and rape (*R* v *Pigg* [1982] 2 All ER 591, though see also *R* v *Satnam* (1983) 78 Cr App R 149). In *Seymour*, Lord Roskill stated that the *Caldwell* definition should be used in *all* cases involving recklessness in the criminal law.

22. [1981] 1 All ER 961, 967.

23. *Ibid*, p 966.

24. *Chief Constable of Avon and Somerset* v *Shimmen* (1987) 84 Cr App R 7. This also appears to have been accepted in relation to rape – see e.g. *R* v *Satnam* (1983) 78 Cr App R 149. The offence of rape is now specifically included in the definition of "violent offence"; if *Caldwell* is followed, it is possible that sexual intercourse which does not constitute rape may nevertheless fall within heading (*b*).

25. Unreported, Cty Ct (Judge Brown), 8 Sept 1980.

26. [1977] 2 All ER 37.

either had not given any thought to the possibility or, having recognised that there was some risk, had nonetheless gone on to pull the trigger.[27]

In *Bingham* v *Secretary of State*[28] the applicant had been attacked and injured by D's dog. D had "dashed" out of her house to the shops and had no idea that the dog was following her; the dog had no previous propensity to violence and D said in evidence that she had not foreseen either that the dog would follow her or that it would attack someone. Kelly J held that D had not been reckless;[29] presumably, in the language of *Caldwell*, D had not created an obvious risk or the risk was so slight that D was entitled to treat it as negligible or even to ignore it.[30]

In *Hamilton* v *Secretary of State*[31] the applicant, an attendant at a leisure centre, pursued two youths to ensure they left the centre. They passed through a heavy door, which swung back and injured the applicant. Carswell J refused compensation; there was no evidence that the youths had foreseen the risk of injury to the applicant. This language may suggest that the learned judge had in mind the pre-*Caldwell* definition of recklessness as laid down in *R* v *Cunningham*[32] – but the decision may also be explained on the basis that although there might have been an obvious risk in fact, the youths had simply not given any thought to the possibility.

The list of specific offences contained in headings (c)–(g) of the definition of "violent offence" appears to have given rise to no difficulty in practice and their scope will be determined by the current criminal law. The broad scope of heading (h) should, however, be noted.[33] This came to the aid of the applicant in *Bellew* v *Secretary of State*[34] where a schoolboy suffered nervous shock as a result of seeing at the side of a road a dummy which he took to be the body of a police officer who had been abducted by the IRA. The dummy was in fact designed to lure members of the security forces to the area, and a bomb had been hidden nearby. The bomb exploded, but no one was injured; the body of the murdered police officer was found a few days later. The

---

27. For a case where D in fact honestly thought there was no risk – see *R* v *Larkin* [1943] 1 All ER 217.

28. Unreported, High Ct (Kelly LJ), 30 June 1987.

29. The learned judge seems also to have considered that to come within heading (b) the injury had to be caused by *the person* committing the offence, e.g. by setting his dog on the victim; here the injury had been caused by the dog.

30. Where there is evidence that a person has incited a dog to attack the applicant, the British Board will award compensation – see CICB, *25th Annual Report* (1988–89), para 16.

31. Unreported, High Ct (Carswell J), 18 Dec 1986. In *Mills* v. *Sec of State* (1989) 8 *BNIL* 20, a suspect fleeing from the police collided into A's car, smashing the windscreen; A sustained a whiplash injury and was awarded compensation on the basis that the suspect had recklessly damaged A's car. Cf *Patterson* v *Sec of State* Unreported, Cty Ct (Judge Russell), 11 Jan 1990; [1990] 2 *BNIL* 28 (D "jumped or staggered" in front of A's car; A braked but hit D; A refused compensation for injury to himself because no evidence that D had recklessly damaged A's car).

32. [1957] 2 All ER 412. Smith and Hogan, *Criminal Law* (6th ed, 1988), pp 62 *et seq* consider that "*Cunningham*" recklessness is still relevant in relation to certain statutory offences.

33. Cf 1988 Act, s 109(3)(n) refers only to "any attempt" to commit one of the specified offences.

34. [1985] 6 NIJB 86, discussed further above, p 71.

principal cause of the applicant's injury was his sight of the dummy, but Hutton J held that he was entitled to compensation on the basis that the use of the dummy to lure the security forces into the vicinity of the bomb constituted the counselling of an offence under the Explosive Substances Act 1883:

> " . . . a counsellor is one who before the commission of the offence . . . conspires to commit it . . . or knowingly gives assistance to one or more of the principals."[35]

As regards the reference to conspiracy it is important to note that counselling requires that the substantive offence must actually have been committed, as it had been in *Bellew*. In *Whiteside* v *Secretary of State*,[36] on the other hand, there may have been a conspiracy to murder the applicant; but the substantive offence had not been committed and the applicant's claim under heading (*g*) was therefore rejected.

2. Particular Provisions

(a) *Effect of age or incapacity of person causing injury*

Article 2(3) of the 1988 Order provides:

> " . . . an act shall be deemed to be a violent offence notwithstanding that the person performing it cannot be convicted of an offence arising out of the act because of his age or capacity."[37]

The intention of this provision seems clear – that compensation should not be refused merely because the "offender" is[38] exempted from criminal responsibility on grounds of youth[39] or old age,[40] by reason of insanity[41] or

---

35. *R* v *Maxwell* [1978] NI 42, 53, *per* Lowry LCJ. See further Smith and Hogan, *Criminal Law* (6th ed, 1988), pp 133 *et seq*.

36. Unreported, High Ct (MacDermott J), 27 Jan 1984.

37. The 1968 Act, s 11(1) contained a similar provision, but the wording differed in a material respect, as discussed below. The present wording replicates that of the 1977 Order, Article 2(3). *Cf* Irish Scheme, para 1: " . . . the Tribunal will not take account of any legal immunity which the person who inflicted the injury may have by reason of his mental health, his youth or otherwise."

38. It will be noted that Art 2(3) uses the word "cannot", which might be taken to mean "can never be convicted . . . ". It seems preferable, however, to regard it as here connoting

"cannot in the particular case be convicted . . . ".

39. By the Children and Young Persons Act (NI) 1968, s 69 it is "conclusively presumed" that no child under the age of 10 can be guilty of an offence. At common law a child aged between 10 and 14 is not criminally responsible unless the prosecution proves that he knew what he was doing was seriously wrong: see *e.g. JM (A minor)* v *Runeckles* (1984) 79 Cr App R 255, *R* v *Coulburn* (1988) 87 Cr App R 309 and *RUC* v *Lyttle* [1982] 8 *BNIL* 16.

40. See especially *R* v *CICB, ex parte Warner* [1986] 2 All ER 478, 482, *per* Lawton LJ.

41. Criminal Justice Act (NI) 1966, s 3(1), and see Stannard, *Northern Ireland Supplement to Smith and Hogan*, Criminal Law (1984), pp 26–40.

(possibly) because of the influence of alcohol or drugs.[42] What is not so clear is whether the applicant must prove something more than the mere perform- ance of the act which caused injury or death; must he also show that that act was intended to cause death, personal injury or damage to property or was performed recklessly? This issue arose in *Knox* v *Secretary of State*,[43] where the court had to consider the (different) wording of the 1968 Act, *viz* whether the act was one "for which a person (if he were of full age and capacity) might be fined or sentenced to imprisonment". D, a boy aged 11, threw a stone in A's direction to attract his attention. The stone hit the ground, bounced up and struck A's left eye, injuring it so badly that it had to be removed. O'Donnell LJ held that A was entitled to compensation. The learned Lord Justice accepted that "since it must be assumed that Parlia- ment was aware that an act by itself (save in exceptional cases) could not be a crime" the court had to consider the mental element necessary to make the act criminal – in this case, recklessness. The question then arose as to whether recklessness should be determined with regard to D's state of mind or to that of a person of full age and capacity. O'Donnell LJ concluded in favour of the latter:

> "If the act is to be considered as committed by a person of full age and capacity, I can see no reason for saying that the foresight and knowledge should not [also] be that of the same person of full age and capacity."[44]

Such a person would have appreciated the risk of injury in the circumstances and thus A was entitled to compensation.

The learned Lord Justice however drew attention to the new wording of the 1977 Order (which is identical to that in the 1988 Order) and implied that it would lead to a different approach. Whereas the 1968 Act referred to any act for which "*a* person" might be fined, etc, the new provision refers to "*the* person" performing the act which caused the injury. It would appear, therefore, that *Knox* would not now be followed and that regard should be had to the state of mind of the person concerned, and not to that of some hypothetical person of full age and capacity. An applicant must therefore satisfy the Secretary of State or the court that the person who performed the act and who may be exempt from criminal responsibility nonetheless intended to cause injury or was reckless whether or not he did so. This appears to have been the approach taken in *Bates* v *Secretary of State*[45] where

---

42. See generally, Smith and Hogan, *Criminal Law* (6th ed, 1988), pp 210 *et seq*, though it may be argued that a person who is so drunk as to be unable to form the necessary *mens rea* commits no crime, rather than that he can- not be convicted of a crime because of his (in)capacity. Drunkenness did not prevent compensation being awarded in two criminal damage compensation cases – *Kenneally* v *Clonmel Corp* (1955) 89 ILTR 164 and *Law- lor* v *Tralee UDC* (1954) 89 ILTR 38.

43. [1980] NI 87.

44. *Ibid*, p 89. The learned Lord Justice noted that in any case there was a rebuttable pre- sumption that D was *doli incapax* and that even D himself might have been held to have been reckless.

45. [1981] 3 *BNIL* 19. See also *L* v *Sec of State* [1989] 10 *BNIL* 28 (13 year old boy pushed 14 year old girl with "hostile intent"; compensa- tion awarded); *C* v *Sec of State* [1990] 1 *BNIL* 19 (13 year old boy acted recklessly in drag- ging 10 year old boy over broken glass).

A, a schoolboy aged nine, was playing in the school sandpit when fighting broke out between himself and two other nine-year-old boys. The court expressed itself as satisfied that A's assailants intended to injure him, and awarded compensation. On the other hand, in *K* v *Secretary of State*[46] a boy aged 11 was hit on the head by an iron bar thrown into the air by D, another boy. MacDermott J held that the applicant had failed to prove that D had acted intentionally or recklessly and dismissed the claim.

The wording of the provision in the 1977 and 1988 Orders differs from that in the British Scheme,[47] but the approach taken in *Bates* and *K* appears similar to that taken in Britain over a number of years[48] and, it is submitted, it is for that reason also preferable to that taken in *Knox*.

It seems reasonable that injuries caused by acts performed by a person with a mental incapacity should be dealt with in the same way.[49]

(b) *Act of another person*

Article 5(1) of the 1988 Order continues a requirement first introduced in 1968, *viz*

> "No compensation shall be paid unless, on a balance of probabilities, the victim sustained a criminal injury as a result of an act of another person."[50]

This provision – which is not to be found in the British or Irish Schemes[51] – appears to have been inserted *ex abundante cautela*. It covers two situations where, even if this provision were omitted, compensation would rarely, if ever, be awarded. The first is where the injury is inflicted on himself by the victim's own violent offence; a claim in such a case is in any event likely to be

---

46. [1985] 6 *BNIL* 21.

47. "In considering . . . whether any act is a criminal act, any immunity at law of an offender, attributable to his youth or insanity or other condition, will be left out of account." British Scheme (1979), para 4. The 1990 Scheme was amended to reflect the different wording of the 1988 Act, s 109(4) (which adds an express reference to "diplomatic immunity"). See further Greer, *op cit* n 5, paras 2.47–2.50.

48. See e.g. CICB, *21st Annual Report* (1984–85), para 20 (school-teacher hit on head by discus thrown by pupil on sports day; no evidence of malicious intent; compensation refused); *12th Annual Report* (1975–76), para 5 (boy hit on head when D, an 11-year-old neighbour, swung golf club; no evidence that D acted intentionally or recklessly; compensation refused); *11th Annual Report* (1974–75), para 7 (girl aged 15 struck in eye by pellet fired from blow-pipe by D, a young boy; Board satisfied that D had deliberately aimed at a group containing the applicant; compen-

sation awarded). The Board's approach has, however, been criticised by Atiyah, *Accidents, Compensation and the Law* (4th ed, 1987), pp 299–300.

49. See e.g. CICB, *20th Annual Report* (1983–84), para 21 (nurse injured when mental patient suddenly turned and punched her in the stomach; compensation awarded); *ibid*, para 22 (nurse butted in face by handicapped and mentally subnormal child aged 13; Board not satisfied that injury not accidental; compensation refused).

50. 1968 Act, s 1(3)(*a*); 1977 Order, Art 3(2)(*a*). The 1968 Act referred to "the act *or omission*" of some other person; the reference to an omission was deleted in 1977 – but see Interpretation Act (NI) 1954, s 46(2): "'Act' where used in reference to an offence or civil wrong shall include a series of acts, and words so used which refer to acts done shall extend to omissions."

51. The 1968 Act provision was apparently inspired by the New Zealand Criminal Injuries Compensation Act 1963, s 17(2).

rejected under Article 6(1).[52] But Article 5(1) may have a useful purpose in emphasising that the burden of proving that his injury has been caused by another person's violent offence lies with the applicant. Thus, in *Black* v *Secretary of State*,[53] a young boy was injured in the eye by broken glass chipped by a group of boys from a telephone kiosk. There was conflicting evidence as to whether A himself had been chipping at the glass and the court therefore decided the case on the ground that it was not satisfied on a balance of probabilities that his injury had been caused by the act of another person.

The second situation apparently envisaged by Article 5(1) arises in connection with the law enforcement limb of the definition of criminal injury and is well illustrated by *Martin* v *Ministry of Home Affairs*.[54] It will be recalled that Sergeant Martin fell through an asbestos roof after arresting three suspected burglars. His claim for compensation was rejected on the ground that his injuries were not "directly attributable" to the arrest; but, in addition, Lord MacDermott LCJ observed:

> "It seems to me that the weakness of the asbestos roof cannot be ascribed to the act or omission of anyone . . . "[55]

This application of Article 5(1) was possibly not intended, but it is submitted that it adds little if anything to the requirement that the injury be "directly attributable" to an act of law enforcement. Indeed, the questions appear to be treated as part and parcel of the one issue. If the injury is sufficiently proximate to be directly attributable to an arrest, etc the court will normally be able to find that the injury was due to the act of another; it is only when the causal connection is slender that Article 5(1) provides an additional reason for refusing compensation. In *Martin*, Jones J came close to acknowledging this connection:

> "But if the injury sustained by an applicant falls within the definition of a criminal injury it might, in many cases, be a short step to say that, on a balance of probabilities, the applicant sustained his criminal injury as a result of the act or omission of some other person or persons – as for example, as a result of the act of malefactors whose conduct necessitated an applicant having to encounter some dangerous situation in order to arrest them."[56]

Niland v *Secretary of State*[57] tends to confirm this approach. There, the applicant was a soldier injured by a flying tow-hook when an army bomb disposal team attempted to move a car suspected to contain explosives. Hutton J held that the applicant's injury was directly attributable to his giving help to the bomb disposal team who were attempting to prevent an offence, and that it was the result of the act of another person. Quoting Jones J in *Martin*, he concluded that the applicant had been injured as a result of the act of the person who drove the stolen car onto the mound of

---

52. See below, p 107 *et seq*.
53. Unreported, High Ct (MacDermott J), 22 April 1976.
54. (1970) [1979] NI 172.

55. *Ibid*, p 177.
56. *Ibid*, p 174.
57. [1982] NI 181.

earth. Alternatively the injury was the result of the act of the leader of the
bomb disposal team in trying to pull the car off the mound, since Article 5(1)
does not mean that the criminal injury must be caused by the act of a
criminal.[58]

Given this broad interpretation, it seems highly unlikely that an injury
which is considered to be "directly attributable" to an act of law enforcement
will be rejected only on the basis that it was not the result of an act of another
person.[59]

(c) *Traffic offences*

By Article 2(2) of the 1988 Order, and in line with earlier legislation,[60]
certain "traffic offences" are expressly excluded from the meaning of
"violent offence". For this purpose a "traffic offence" is–

> "an offence arising from the driving or use of a motor- vehicle[61] . . . unless the
> vehicle was, at the time of the commission of the offence, being primarily used
> for the purpose of –
>
> (*a*) causing injury; or
>
> (*b*) committing, or facilitating the commission of, a violent offence; or
>
> (*c*) avoiding arrest, or escaping detection, in connection with a violent
> offence."

The exclusion of most traffic offences from the scheme is usually justified on
the basis that compulsory third-party liability insurance, coupled with the
Motor Insurers' Bureau agreements, provide an adequate alternative source
of compensation, even if the offender is uninsured or cannot be traced.[62]
Indeed the British criminal injuries compensation scheme is interpreted so
as to complement such arrangements.[63] The 1988 Order does, however,
appear to permit some overlapping, at least where a motor-vehicle is used to

---

58. *Ibid*, p 187, referring to an example given
by Lord MacDermott LCJ in *Martin*:
"A . . . goes to the aid of a constable who is
having difficulty in making an arrest, with the
result that A is knocked down and injured
unwittingly *by the constable* in the course of
the struggle. A's injury would seem to be
within . . . section   1(3)(*a*)"   (emphasis
added). See also *Whiteside* v *Sec of State*
Unreported, High Ct (MacDermott J), 27 Jan
1984.

59. See also *Stitt* v *Sec of State* Unreported,
Cty Ct (Deputy Judge Higgins), 4 Nov 1987
(police officer chasing suspected burglar slipped and fell; injury held directly attributable
to attempted arrest of suspect and the result
of an act of the suspect).

60. 1968 Act, s 11(1); 1977 Order, Art 2(2).
See also Irish Scheme, para 12, and the
British Scheme, para 11.

61. As defined in the Road Traffic (NI) Order
1981, Art 2(2): "a mechanically-propelled
vehicle (not being a tramcar or other vehicle
running on permanent rails, or a trolley
vehicle) which is intended or adapted for use
on roads." See further Lavery, *Road Traffic
Law in Northern Ireland* (1989), pp 508–9.
Thus an injury caused by an offence involving
the use of a bicycle or a horse-drawn vehicle
may be compensated but only in the unlikely
event that the offence is also a "violent"
offence.

62. See e.g. Atiyah, *Accidents, Compensation
and the Law* (4th ed, 1987), p 302.

63. See 1986 *IWP Report*, ch 11, *R* v *CICB, ex
parte Letts* Unreported, Div'l Ct, 8 Feb 1989
and 1988 Act, s 110(7). See further Greer,
Criminal Injuries Compensation (1990), paras
2.41–2.45.

cause injury. This is one of the instances where compensation is payable under the 1988 Order – but if the offender is known,[64] the injured person may also recover from his insurance company or from the MIB. Thus, in *Gardner* v *Moore*[65] the defendant had deliberately driven his motor-vehicle at the plaintiff, and injured him. At the time of the offence D was not insured against third-party risks and P therefore sought a declaration that the MIB were liable to indemnify him against any unsatisfied judgment he might obtain against D. The House of Lords, granting the declaration, refused to take into account, in the interpretation of the MIB agreement and of the Road Traffic Acts, the fact that P was entitled to criminal injuries compensation:

> "The two remedies are not necessarily mutually exclusive alternatives and were not designed to be so. The Criminal Injuries Compensation Scheme is itself markedly less advantageous to the claimant than the MIB agreement, and since the MIB agreement and road traffic legislation came into being long before the . . . Scheme was introduced, I cannot see that the Scheme can be used as an aid to their construction."[66]

Such reasoning would appear to be equally applicable in Northern Ireland.

The exclusion of "traffic offences" does not apply to the "law enforcement" limb of the definition of criminal injury. That limb refers to the arrest, etc of "an offender" and that term is apt to cover any offence, whether or not included within the definition of a "violent" offence.[67] Thus in *R* v *CICB, ex parte Carr*[68] the applicant witnessed a road accident involving two motor-cyclists. He was injured when he tried to stop one of them from leaving the scene. Compensation was awarded on the ground that the applicant had been injured while attempting to prevent the commission of an offence under the Road Traffic Act 1972.

It will be noted that what is excluded by "traffic offence" is an *offence*, not an injury, arising from the driving and use of a motor-vehicle. Thus, if A crashes his car into an obstruction deliberately placed on the road with intent to cause an accident, there is no "traffic offence" and (assuming there is a violent offence) A is entitled to compensation.[69]

Compensation is payable where the motor-vehicle was being used "for the purpose of" causing injury. It would appear that this is a narrower test than

---

64. In other words, where a claim is made under the MIB Agreement relating to Compensation of Victims of Uninsured Drivers. If the driver cannot be traced, the claim must be made under the Agreement for the Compensation of Victims of Untraced Drivers, which specifically excludes compensation from the MIB where the untraced driver deliberately used a vehicle to kill or injure. See generally Lavery, *op cit* n 61, Part III.

65. [1984] 1 All ER 1100.

66. *Ibid*, p 1107, *per* Lord Hailsham LC. *Cf* Atiyah, *op cit* n 62, p 301: "The House seems to have ignored the fact that the Board does

not make awards in such cases where compensation is available from the MIB . . . ".

67. *Cf* the British Board's *Statement*, para 11: "Injuries caused by a motor vehicle may be within the scope of the Scheme if the incident was 'directly attributable' to persons attempting to prevent an offence or apprehend a suspected offender."

68. [1981] RTR 122.

69. Compensation was awarded by the British Board in such a case – see CICB, *15th Annual Report* (1978–79), para 22. For a similar case, see CICB, *22nd Annual Report* (1985–86), para 26.

that the driver of the motor-vehicle "intended" to cause injury. This at least appears to be the logical consequence of the use of different language from that in heading (a) of the definition of "violent offence", and tends to be confirmed by the definition of "intended" already quoted above. On the other hand a court may well take the view that such a distinction would be unduly pedantic and consider exception (a) to apply in any case where injury was intended.

The 1968 Act version of exception (b) came under scrutiny in *Cregan* v *Secretary of State*.[70] Two youths hijacked a car, drove it dangerously and caused it to collide with another car, causing serious injuries to A. The court was satisfied that at the time of the accident the youths were driving the car to some place for the purpose either of committing a terrorist offence themselves or of facilitating the commission of some offence either immediately or at some future date. The place to which the car was being driven, the precise offence in contemplation, the persons who were to commit it and the time when it was to be committed were all unknown to the court. Nevertheless the Court of Appeal held that A was entitled to compensation. The 1968 Act did not require that the vehicle was being used for the commission of a specific and identifiable offence; nor was the injury required to be immediately and contemporaneously connected with the commission of the offence.[71] Although the wording of the 1988 Order differs slightly from that construed in *Cregan*,[72] it is submitted that the reasoning and decision in that case are equally applicable thereto where the offence involved is a "violent offence" (as it presumably was in *Cregan* in any event).

LAW ENFORCEMENT

Finally, compensation is payable for injuries directly attributable to certain acts of law enforcement.

1. The Lawful Arrest or Attempted Arrest of an Offender or Suspected Offender

Unlike the British Scheme,[73] the Northern Ireland legislation has consistently referred to "the *lawful arrest* or attempted *arrest*" of an offender.[74] This would suggest that if, for any reason, the arrest is held to be unlawful, compensation cannot be awarded for any injury received in making the arrest. This interpretation is in fact supported by the English case of *R* v

---

70. [1978] NI 159.

71. These conditions were satisfied, and exception (b) applied, in *Rooney* v *Sec of State* Unreported, High Ct (McCollum J), 8 Dec 1989 (car used in deliberate attempt to damage property). *Cf R* v *CICB, ex parte Letts* Unreported, Div'l Ct, 8 Feb 1989 (no intent or recklessness by driver).

72. Under the 1968 Act, s 11(1) the car had to be used for the purpose of committing "some other offence"; the 1988 Order refers to committing "a violent offence".

73. Paragraph 4, and see 1988 Act, s 109(1)(b)(i). Both refer to "an apprehension or attempted apprehension . . . ".

74. 1968 Act, s 11(1); 1977 Order, Art 2(2); 1988 Order, Art 2(2). The Irish Scheme has no such provision – but see para 4(c).

CICB, ex parte Carr,[75] where the applicant had witnessed a road accident involving two motor-cyclists. One of the motor-cyclists attempted to leave the scene and the applicant ran after him to stop him. In so doing he burst an achilles tendon. The British Board refused compensation on the ground (*inter alia*) that " . . . none of the offences committed by the motor-cyclist were arrestable offences . . . ".[76] It is possible that an unlawful arrest constitutes an "attempted arrest", but it seems more likely that this phrase means an incomplete arrest in circumstances where a successful arrest would have been lawful. Equally, it seems clear that the "lawfulness" of the arrest is to be judged by the normal objective criteria, but this does not mean that an offence must in fact have been committed.[77]

When does an arrest or attempted arrest begin and end? In *Ince* the Board contended that "an attempt to arrest does not start until the suspected offender is located and the chase has begun", but it did not support this interpretation in the Divisional Court.[78] The Court clearly felt that the scheme should not be interpreted in so narrow a fashion, and the Board's "Statement" advises that:

> "A police officer is making 'an apprehension or attempted apprehension' from the time when he is first told of an offence or suspected offence . . . "[79]

This seems to be going too far – and, indeed, in 1982 the Board refused compensation to a police officer who had been called out from his home to investigate an offence and who was injured when he fell on the driveway:

> "No doubt it would be hoped that his investigations would ultimately lead to an arrest, but . . . the link between a potential arrest and the accident to the applicant is too remote to enable one to hold that the accident was 'directly attributable' to an arrest or attempted arrest."[80]

It may further be noted that the various instances suggested in *Martin* and the facts in subsequent Northern Ireland cases all involve situations where the suspect is in sight of, or is actually being pursued by, the hopeful arrestor.

---

75. [1981] RTR 122.

76. *Carr* was decided under the 1969 Scheme, in which the operative phrase was "arrest or attempted arrest". The Board noted that had the 1979 Scheme been in operation, "it is unlikely that his application would have been rejected." Compensation was, in fact, awarded by the Divisional Court – see above, p 93 and Greer, *op cit* n 63, para 2.57.

77. In *Niland* v *Sec of State* [1982] NI 181, 186 Hutton J considered that the reference to the attempted arrest of a suspected offender (who may not, in reality, have committed any offence at all) is "a clear indication that the legislature contemplated that compensation might be paid to a police officer who . . . was attempting to make an arrest where in fact . . . no offence had been committed."

78. [1973] 3 All ER 808, 811–2, *per* Lord Denning MR.

79. *Statement*, para 4F(4).

80. CICB, *18th Annual Report* (1981–82), para 31. It may be that the Board's *Statement* was prompted by dicta in *Ince* by Megaw LJ relating to an attempt to prevent an offence (see below p 99) and that an attempted arrest should be given a somewhat narrower interpretation.

(a) *Offender*

The word "offender" is not defined in the 1988 Order, and two interpretations are possible. The first is that "an offender" is a person who has committed a "violent offence" as defined in the Order.[81] It seems more likely, however, that the term connotes *any* criminal offence. This latter interpretation is more consistent with the policy of this part of the scheme, which has always been that those injured " 'having a go' at helping the police should receive compensation from the state".[82] And indeed in many cases compensation has been awarded in respect of injuries arising out of the arrest or attempted arrest of non-violent offenders.[83]

"Offender" means an offender against the criminal law. This point arose in *R* v *CICB, ex parte Lawton*,[84] where a person suspected of theft had been arrested and taken to a police station. He had a history of mental illness and it was decided that he should be sent to a mental hospital. While waiting to be taken there he suddenly tried to escape. The applicant police officer gave chase, and was injured. The Divisional Court *held* that the man was attempting to escape from lawful custody and that the applicant's injury arose from an attempted arrest; but had the original arrest not continued to subsist until the relevant time, compensation could not have been awarded:

> "Where a man is in lawful custody simply because . . . of the Mental Health Act . . . [and] makes his escape without committing any criminal offence . . . then although it is proper for the police to pursue and apprehend him . . . he would not be apprehended as an offender or a suspected offender."[85]

(b) *Passive bystanders*

In *R* v *CICB, ex parte Schofield*,[86] the applicant was about to enter a store when two men ran out of it. They turned out to be a store detective attempting to arrest a suspected shoplifter. One of the men knocked the applicant to the ground, and she was injured. The Board rejected her claim on the basis that the only person who could claim in respect of an arrest or attempted arrest was a person who had himself effected the arrest or attempted to do so. The Divisional Court (by a majority) disagreed; the wording of the scheme in its plain and ordinary meaning was not limited in such a way, and a literal interpretation would not render the last part of the definition ("the giving of help to any constable . . . etc") mere surplusage:

> "I think . . . that the reference to helping a constable may have been put in to cover the situation of a person who, remote from the fray and the attempted

---

81. This was apparently the view of Megaw LJ in *Ince* when (at pp 814–5) he excluded traffic offences from the scope of this paragraph. However, the justification for the exclusion of such offences (see above p 92) has no application in this context.

82. See e.g. 68 HC Debs (NI), col 625 (31 Jan 1968).
83. As e.g. in *Lawton* (below).
84. [1972] 3 All ER 582.
85. *Ibid*, p 584.
86. [1971] 2 All ER 1011.

> arrest, nevertheless decides to go in and offer his assistance. I can see that it might be found arguable, apart from the concluding words of the paragraph, . . . that his injury was not directly attributable to the arrest. [This] possibility . . . satisfies me in the end that we should give the original words their plain and ordinary meaning . . . "[87]

This approach had earlier been adopted in relation to "prevention of an offence" in *McCaughey* v *Ministry of Home Affairs*[88] and in *McCabe* v *Ministry of Home Affairs*,[89] but it was subsequently rejected in effect by MacDermott J in *Whiteside* v *Secretary of State*.[90] The applicant police officer had been told by his divisional commander that he had been "targeted" by the IRA, and he suffered nervous shock. MacDermott J considered that the divisional commander was attempting to prevent an offence, but that this was not sufficient; to qualify for compensation the applicant had to show that his injury arose from his own attempt to prevent an offence:

> "The key . . . lies in the second half of the paragraph . . . 'the giving of help to' certain people . . . To my mind the help referred to is help by the person who in the event was injured. If that be right the first half of the paragraph relates to those who themselves are injured arresting offenders or preventing offences – any other construction would appear to be absurd."

This reasoning is difficult to reconcile with the majority view in *Schofield* (which was not cited in *Whiteside*), but it has to be noted that the learned judges in *Schofield* stressed that they were not interpreting a statutory scheme. In the event MacDermott J's approach has received support from Kelly LJ who, in *Clarke* v *Secretary of State*,[91] observed that the majority view in *Schofield* was "very wide". He went on to state:

> "I have some reservations . . . whether such a wide interpretation would be or should be given . . . in this jurisdiction . . . Bridge J dissented [in *Schofield*]. I think, with respect, his reasoning and conclusion is to be preferred."[92]

McCollum J, dissenting, preferred the majority view in *Schofield* and considered that Parliament also must have done so, since the relevant wording as so interpreted had been retained unchanged in the 1977 Order.

---

87. *Ibid*, p 1014, *per* Widgery LJ. Bridge J dissented on the basis that such a situation was "rather remotely possible" and he found it "difficult to suppose that it is to cover only that remote contingency that this category . . . was included". He added that "I cannot resist the conclusion that [the majority interpretation] widens the scheme beyond the scope that it was intended to have."

88. Unreported, Cty Ct (Judge Johnson), 27 Nov 1969 (police baton-charged crowd of rioters; applicants not part of riot but injured by blows from batons; compensation awarded

on basis that injuries directly attributable to prevention or attempted prevention of riot).

89. Unreported, Cty Ct (Judge Patton), 19 March 1970 (police shot at sniper and accidentally killed soldier; held that death of soldier was directly attributable to attempt to prevent offence).

90. Unreported, High Ct (MacDermott J), 27 Jan 1984.

91. [1988] 5 NIJB 24.

92. MacDermott LJ concurred with Kelly LJ. Bridge J's dissent is summarised in n 87.

Be that as it may it would appear that Article 5(15) has now put the matter beyond doubt. This seems to require the applicant to have been taking a risk when the injury was sustained, and thus suggests that the law enforcement provision *is* restricted to those injured while arresting or attempting to arrest an offender, etc.[93]

(c) *The arrested person*

In *Clarke* v *Secretary of State*[94] the applicant had been shot by police officers who thought he was a gunman who had fired shots at them. In fact no shots had been fired by anyone and the applicant was unarmed. It was, however, accepted that the police had honestly and reasonably believed that shots had been fired and therefore they had not acted unlawfully in shooting at the applicant. The applicant contended that he was entitled to compensation on the ground (*inter alia*) that his injuries were directly attributable to his own arrest or attempted arrest. Hutton J in the High Court held that the "offender" being arrested must be someone different from the applicant, and refused compensation. This decision was upheld (by a majority) in the Court of Appeal, essentially for three reasons. First, the majority were reluctant to follow *Schofield* and preferred the general interpretation that the law enforcement provisions applied only to those injured while arresting or attempting to arrest, etc. Secondly, the interpretation contended for by the applicant was inconsistent with other provisions of the Order, which drew a clear distinction between a "victim" (or applicant) and an "offender". Thirdly, to compensate the applicant would be contrary to the intention of Parliament:

> "While it is unwise to speculate at the intention of Parliament, it must be safe at least to assume that Parliament did not intend compensation to be paid to a person who had committed a criminal offence and the criminal injury alleged is directly attributable to his resistance to his lawful arrest for that offence."

It is submitted, with respect, that only the first of these reasons is entirely convincing.[95] The second seems unduly pedantic,[96] and, in any case, like the third, fails to address the case as stated for the Court by Hutton J:

---

93. This indeed was the view of the 1986 *IWP Report*, para 6.14: "The introduction of the exceptional risk requirement . . . meant that innocent bystanders . . . no longer attracted compensation, unless their injuries were caused by the offender's reck-lessness . . . While we sympathise with those who suffer such accidental injury, we cannot find sufficient justification for recommending a change in the present position."
94. [1986] 13 NIJB 93 (High Ct); [1988] 5 NIJB 24 (CA).
95. See above.

96. Particular reference was made to Arts 3(1), (2)(*b*), 5(2) and 16 of the 1977 Order. Art 3(1) refers to a "victim", but by Art 2(2) "victim" simply means "a person . . . who has sustained a criminal injury"; Art 3(2)(*b*) prohibits compensation when "the victim was . . . living with the offender . . . ", but the applicant in *Clarke* was not an offender; Art 5(2) permits refusal of compensation for provocative or negligent behaviour – but an arrestee may be guilty of neither, and Art 16 again refers to "an offender" and thus is inapplicable to an innocent arrestee.

"Whether a suspected offender who sustains an injury directly attributable to his lawful arrest is not a victim . . . *where the injured party is innocent of the crime of which the arresting police officer or officers suspect him?*"[97]

It is the case that in certain exceptional circumstances an innocent person may lawfully be shot by the police and there is much to be said for the dissenting opinion of McCollum J:

"If by a reasonable mistake unnecessary or inappropriate force is used, I cannot see in all justice why its victim, who may be completely innocent, should not receive compensation if he is deserving of it."[98]

However, it has been suggested above that *Schofield* has now been "reversed" by the 1988 Order and, if this is correct, compensation thereunder is not payable either to a passive bystander or to the arrested person, since neither was taking an "exceptional risk" when the injury was sustained.

2. The Prevention or Attempted Prevention of an Offence

The leading case on this aspect of law enforcement is still *R v CICB, ex parte Ince*.[99] Some men were seen acting suspiciously near an army depot and PC Ince was informed by radio that suspects were actually breaking into the premises. He was rushing to the scene in a police car when he drove through a red traffic light and crashed into another police car responding to the same call. PC Ince was killed and his widow claimed compensation.

The Court of Appeal had first to decide if PC Ince was "attempting" to prevent an offence. The Board had contended that this provision applies only if the applicant was present at the scene of the crime and taking active steps to prevent its commission. The Court considered this approach to be too narrow:

" . . . if a police officer . . . has received information . . . which indicates that someone is in process of committing, or is thought to be about to commit, an offence . . . and the police officer goes towards the place . . . of the supposed offence . . . he is . . . at least unless there are some special features, attempting to prevent an offence."[1]

A similar approach was adopted in *Whiteside v Secretary of State*.[2] The police

---

97. Emphasis added.
98. As McCollum J pointed out, this may preclude the payment of compensation e.g. to persons caught in a gun-fight between police and terrorists, and accidentally shot by one side or another. It may, however, be possible to establish that the injury is directly attributable to a violent crime, *viz* the intentional or reckless shooting by the terrorists: see further above, pp 66–68.

99. [1973] 3 All ER 808. See also *R v CICB, ex parte Penny* [1982] *Crim LR* 298 (removal of violent prisoner from one cell to another *not* an attempt to prevent the commission of an offence).

1. [1973] 3 All ER 808, 814–5, *per* Megaw LJ.

2. Unreported, High Ct (MacDermott J), 27 Jan 1984.

received information that the applicant had been "targeted" by the IRA. The applicant was told of this and immediately transferred to another division. MacDermott J accepted that in passing on the information and ordering the applicant's transfer the police officers concerned could properly be said to have been attempting to prevent an offence.

A second question arose in *Ince* when it subsequently emerged that no one was, in fact, attempting to break into the depot. The Court of Appeal held that this was immaterial:

> "It cannot be necessary that an offence should *actually* have been committed. If it has been prevented, it never has been committed, and never will be committed. The words must cover an offence which it is anticipated *may* be committed unless prevented. This anticipation must be because of something the police officer has seen himself, or of some information that he has received. The information may be accurate or inaccurate; it may be mistaken; it may even be false; but, if the police officer honestly believes that an offence is about to take place, and he himself takes action to prevent it, then his action comes within the words . . . 'the prevention or attempted prevention of an offence'."[3]

PC Ince's action was prompted by the reasonable belief that the message was correct, and his widow's claim to compensation had to be tested in the light of the situation as it appeared to him at the time. This reasoning was followed in *Niland* v *Secretary of State*.[4] The applicant was one of the infantry escort of a bomb disposal team. He was seriously injured in an incident arising out of an attempt to move a car thought to contain explosives; in fact, there were no explosives in or near the car. Hutton J held that the bomb disposal team were nevertheless attempting to prevent an offence:

> "I consider it to be unlikely that it was the policy of the legislature . . . to draw a distinction between a suspect car or device which, in reality, contained a bomb and a suspect car or device which, in reality, contained no bomb although the security forces were fully justified in suspecting that it did."[5]

It would appear, however, that a particular offence must be involved or suspected. In *McBirney* v *Secretary of State*[6] the Army used explosives to crater a border road to restrict its use by terrorists. The explosion caused the applicant to suffer nervous shock, but her application for compensation was refused on the grounds that what must be prevented is "an offence" and not offences in general.

---

3. [1973] 3 All ER 808, 812, *per* Lord Denning MR.

4. [1982] NI 181. See also *Whiteside, supra*, (sufficient if offence reasonably anticipated or contemplated at the time). *Cf Patterson* v *Sec of State* [1990] 2 *BNIL* 28 (A injured when he braked sharply to avoid pedestrian; injury not attributable to attempt to prevent criminal damage to car).

5. [1982] NI 181, 186.

6. Unreported, Cty Ct (Judge Higgins), 11 Sept 1975.

3. The giving of help to any Constable,[7] Member of Her Majesty's Forces or Prison Officer[8] who is engaged in arresting or attempting to arrest an Offender or suspected Offender or in preventing or attempting to prevent an Offence

It will be recalled that it was the scope of this provision which came into question in *Schofield*,[9] where the majority of the Court of Appeal held that the wording was apt to cover some cases where the injury might not be directly attributable to an arrest or prevention of an offence, such as an injury to "a person who, remote from the fray and the attempted arrest, nevertheless decides to go in and offer his assistance". Such an injury would be directly attributable to the giving of help. What has been said above concerning the passive bystander is equally applicable here and requires no further discussion. To satisfy this aspect of law enforcement, an applicant must show –

(a) that a constable, etc was at the time engaged in arresting or attempting to arrest an offender, etc. It is submitted that this requirement is to be interpreted on the same basis as the earlier provisions of the paragraph discussed above;

(b) that the applicant "gave help to" that constable, etc. This phrase does not appear to have been subjected to scrutiny by the courts,[10] but it was considered in *Niland* to be clearly satisfied on the facts of that case. It will be recalled that the applicant was one of the infantry escort who accompanied a bomb disposal team in order to protect them against sniper attack. The bomb disposal team tried to pull a suspect car off a mound of earth, and a hook which they were using flew off and seriously injured the applicant. At the time the applicant was out in the open "in order properly to perform his duties as an escort". Hutton J was satisfied that he was at that time giving help to the leader of the bomb disposal team.[11] Another generous interpretation of this phrase was accepted in *Graham v Secretary of State*.[12] A UDR sergeant driving home was stopped by the security forces and told there was a suspicious car in front of his house. The area was sealed off and the applicant was moving his own car out of the way when he had a heart attack and died. It was held that the applicant had died while he was giving help to the security forces who were engaged in attempting to prevent an offence.

---

7. For the meaning of "constable" see Interpretation Act (NI) 1954, s 43(2), as amended by the Police Act (NI) 1970, Sch 3. See also *Sheikh* v *Chief Constable of Greater Manchester Police* [1989] 2 All ER 684.

8. These latter two categories were added in 1977. The British Scheme (para 4) applies to "constables" only; see also 1988 Act, s 109(1)(*b*).

9. See above, p 96.

10. The 1988 Act, s 109(1)(*b*)(iii) substitutes "assisting" for "the giving of help to". The Irish Scheme, para 4(*a*) uses the phrase "coming to the assistance of" a Garde, but only in five specified circumstances.

11. [1982] NI 181, 185.

12. Unreported, Cty Ct (Judge Babington), 10 Nov 1981.

If the applicant was giving help to a constable, etc, it would appear to be immaterial whether he was injured by the suspected criminal or by the constable himself:

> "A, for example, goes to the aid of a constable who is having difficulty in making an arrest, with the result that A is knocked down and injured unwittingly by the constable in the course of the struggle. A's injury would seem to be within [the] paragraph . . . "[13]

There is no *Schofield* problem here, because the giving of help to the constable was clearly the *causa causans* of A's injury.

---

13. *Per* Lord MacDermott LCJ in *Martin* v
Ministry of Home Affairs (1970) [1979] NI
172, 177.

3

Reduction or Refusal of Compensation

INTRODUCTION

As Miers observed some time ago:

> "A criminal injuries compensation scheme differs from tort law in one critical aspect: it is the taxpayer who foots the bill. This alone demands that compensation is not given to those with unclean hands . . . "[1]

In fact, a noticeable feature of the development of the Northern Ireland scheme over the past 20 years has been the refinement and extension of those provisions requiring the refusal of compensation to persons *prima facie* entitled thereto, or at least the reduction of the compensation otherwise payable. The first such provisions tended to reflect familiar common law principles relating to "contributory" conduct on the part of the victim – negligent or provocative behaviour which contributed to the criminal injury.[2] As was acknowledged in relation to the 1968 Act:

> "It would obviously be wrong for us to subsidize, as it were, fights between hooligans."[3]

But from the outset there was also a clear feeling that compensation should not be paid to "undeserving" victims whose misconduct or bad character, even though not connected with the particular injury, made it undesirable that they should receive payment from public funds. This approach was made explicit in the British Scheme which, from 1969, provided:

> "The Board will reduce the amount of compensation or reject the application altogether if, having regard to the conduct of the victim, including his conduct before and after the events giving rise to the claim, and to his character and way of life, it is inappropriate that he should be granted a full award or any award at all."[4]

---

1. *Responses to Victimisation* (1978), p 192. See also Atiyah, *Accidents, Compensation and the Law* (4th ed, 1987), p 304.

2. 1968 Act, ss 1(2) and 4(6)(*a*). See now 1988 Order, Art 6(1)(*a*), discussed below, p. 118.

3. 68 HC Debs (NI), col 626 (31 Jan 1968).

4. British Scheme, para 6(*a*), which replaced a more limited provision in para 12 of the origi-

nal (1964) Scheme and was "intended to exclude the person whose conduct is undeserving of public sympathy" (1978 *1WP Report*, para 17.3). But the Criminal Justice Act 1988 (hereafter "the 1988 Act"), s 112(2) reverts to a more limited formula – see below p 126. The Irish Scheme (para 14) adopted – and still includes – a provision based on para 6(*a*) of the 1979 British Scheme.

The 1968 Act contained no such explicit provision; but it did in section 1(2) provide:

> "In determining whether to make an order under this section, the court shall . . . have regard to all such circumstances as it considers relevant . . . "

The intention and scope of this provision, apparently derived from the New Zealand Act,[5] was not immediately obvious. But in the past 10 years or so it has been interpreted by the Northern Ireland courts to justify or require the refusal or the reduction of compensation in a wide variety of situations. In particular, "circumstances" may apparently be "relevant" even if they have not contributed to the injury sustained by the victim; it will suffice if they are "relevant" to the decision to award compensation.[6] Such an interpretation underlines the "public" nature of criminal injuries compensation and emphasises the departure from tort principles. But the uncertain generality of "relevant circumstances" has necessitated the addition of other specific provisions to ensure that compensation is not paid to certain categories of particularly undeserving applicants.[7] The overall result of these legislative stipulations and of their interpretation by the courts is that the 1988 Order now contains extensive provision for reduction or refusal of compensation to victims or applicants whose conduct or character makes them "undeserving" of compensation or full compensation from public funds.

A second set of disentitling provisions arises from the "one-sided" nature of criminal injury compensation proceedings. This was succinctly described by Hutton J in *McNamee* v *Secretary of State*:

> " . . . unlike a claim against a defendant for damages in tort or contract, where the defendant will be aware of the surrounding facts out of which the claim arises and will be able adequately to defend the claim, the respondent in a criminal injury claim will usually have no knowledge of the surrounding facts other than from the information which the applicant chooses to give . . . "[8]

For this reason a criminal injuries compensation scheme normally imposes strict procedural requirements on an applicant to ensure that "the respondent" obtains the relevant information; the sanction for failing to follow these procedural requirements is refusal or reduction of the compensation otherwise payable. The 1988 Order contains three such requirements[9]

---

5. Criminal Injuries Compensation Act 1963, s 17(3). *Cp* Compensation for Victims of Crime Act (Ontario) 1971, s 5; this and other similar Canadian legislation is discussed in Burns, *Criminal Injuries Compensation* (1980), pp 352–369.

6. See especially *Cahill* v *Sec of State* [1977] NI 53, discussed below.

7. See 1988 Order, Arts 5(9) (members of unlawful association or persons engaged in terrorism) and 6(1)(*b*) (persons with criminal convictions indicative of their character and

way of life), discussed below at pp 128 and 125 respectively. In 1984 exclusionary provisions in the British and NI schemes were thought to require a Reservation to the European Convention on Compensation of Victims of Violent Crime: Home Affairs Committee: *Compensation and Support for Victims of Crime* (1984–85 HC 43), p 6. But, following the recent changes in both Schemes, the United Kingdom ratified the Convention in February 1990.

8. [1982] NI 279, 284.

9. Art 5(3), (4) and (5).

and these are discussed briefly in this chapter and more extensively in Chapter 6.

The disentitling provisions so far discussed relate in some way to the conduct of the victim in relation to his injury, or of the applicant in relation to his application. Consideration of such "circumstances" does, in fact, occupy the main part of this chapter. But an applicant *prima facie* entitled to compensation may find that he is refused such compensation – or is awarded reduced compensation – for other reasons. Thus, a victim may be refused compensation for what is otherwise a criminal injury because of his relationship with the offender,[10] or because the injury has been "accidentally" sustained.[11] In other cases compensation is refused or reduced because of the nature of the victim's injury[12] or of the applicant's loss.[13] These latter restrictions are more appropriately considered as matters relating to the assessment of compensation, and are accordingly dealt with in the next chapter. We therefore conclude this chapter by considering two other factors which also lead to refusal or reduction of compensation, *viz* the exclusion of small claims and the deduction from compensation of unpaid public debts.

Along with the extension and refinement of these disentitling provisions has come a degree of "executive" discretion. In some instances, compensation simply "may" be refused or reduced;[14] in others, a discretion is given to pay an applicant not otherwise entitled to compensation.[15] Such powers provide a desirable element of flexibility in the disbursement of public funds. But they derogate from the legal character of a statutory scheme which generally provides that compensation "shall" or "shall not" be awarded. In addition, the bases on which these discretions are to be exercised are not clearly specified, and this can lead to uncertainty in the operation of the scheme. It appears to remain the case, however, that there is no "inherent discretion" to refuse or reduce compensation on grounds which are not set out in the Order; according to Gibson LJ in *Cahill* v *Secretary of State*:

> "Even under the Grand Jury Act 1836, where the words of enablement in section 106 were more general, it was held by a full Court of Appeal in *In re*

---

10. By Art 5(2) compensation may be refused where the victim was, at the time of the injury, living in the same household as the offender. See below, p 142.

11. By Art 5(15) compensation may not be payable where a victim, claiming in respect of an injury arising out of an act of law enforcement, was "accidentally" injured. See above p 79.

12. See e.g. Arts 5(12) (restrictions on award of compensation for nervous shock, discussed above pp 58 and 76) and 5(13) (special provision in relation to rape, discussed below p 165).

13. As e.g. in Art 5(10) and (11) (restriction

on compensation for loss of profits, discussed below p 196).

14. See e.g. Arts 12(5) (power to cancel determination), 13(4) (power to deduct certain unpaid public debts) and 9(6) (power to reduce compensation for certain consequences of rape or for bereavement).

15. As e.g. in Art 10(2) (power to make payment to a member of an unlawful association or a person who has engaged in acts of terrorism).

16. The detrimental effect of these discretionary provisions on the scope of entitlement to compensation has already been noted in Chapter 2.

Nolan's Presentment[17] . . . that the court is obliged to award compensation if the case is within the section."[18]

In the Court of Appeal Lord Lowry LCJ agreed with this interpretation of the 1968 Act,[19] and in *Annesley* v *Secretary of State*[20] MacDermott J confirmed that this reasoning applied equally to the 1977 Order. It is thus also applicable to the 1988 Order.

Finally, by way of introduction, it should be noted that, in *Cahill*, Lord Lowry further stated:

> "I also accept the proposition that, once the victim has established a *prima facie* entitlement to compensation, the respondent must accept the burden . . . of showing that the victim is not entitled to recover . . . "[21]

This matter was further considered in *Quinn* v *Secretary of State*.[22] The applicant in that case was injured when a bomb exploded in a foul water sewer inspection trap. The case for the Secretary of State was that the applicant had caused the bomb to explode while consciously trying to recover it or while handling or attempting to handle it. It was agreed that if this indeed was the case, the court should apply section 1(2) of the 1968 Act and refuse compensation. The evidence, however, was circumstantial and mostly consisted of an attempt to provide a scientific explanation of the applicant's injuries. Gibson LJ began by saying that because of the applicant's demeanour, the time and place of the explosion, etc a "guilty" explanation was "inherently unlikely", and if the scientific evidence left open any credible explanation consistent with the applicant's innocence he would accept it even though that explanation was, on the scientific evidence alone, less probable than a more sinister interpretation. If, however, there was no basis on which the known facts and the scientific evidence could be made compatible with the applicant's case and the scientific evidence weighed heavily against an innocent explanation, the applicant's claim would be rejected. Gibson LJ then examined the evidence in great detail, and concluded:

> " . . . the whole body of evidence and the picture which it gradually painted have driven me ineluctably to the conclusion that there is no explanation of the facts other than that the applicant must have been interfering with the bomb or have been taking steps preparatory to handling it when the explosion occurred."

In other words, the Secretary of State had satisfied the burden of showing that the applicant was not entitled to compensation. This approach was held

---

17. (1890) 24 *ILTSJ* 623, discussed above, p 17.
18. [1976] 9 NIJB.
19. [1977] NI 53, 55.
20. Unreported, High Ct (MacDermott J), 25 Oct 1984. See also *McLaverty* v *Sec of State* Unreported, Cty Ct (Judge Pringle), 9 Oct 1986.

21. [1977] NI 53, 55. The British Scheme (para 25) puts this burden on the applicant; *cf* 1988 Act, s 112(1) and (2) may relieve the applicant in certain cases. The Irish Scheme (para 26) provides that "It will be for the claimant to establish his case."

22. [1977] 2 NIJB.

equally applicable to the 1977 Order[23] and would appear also to apply to the 1988 Order.

RELEVANT CIRCUMSTANCES

Article 6(1) of the 1988 Order substantially[24] re-enacts earlier legislation by providing:

> "In determining whether any compensation should be paid and, if so, its amount, the Secretary of State shall have regard to all such circumstances as are relevant . . . "

The scope of the 1968 version of this provision first arose for consideration in the controversial case of *Cahill* v *Secretary of State*.[25] A, a milkroundsman, was shot during the course of his milkround; after the shooting, six rounds of ammunition (and three incriminating documents) were found in the cab of the milk van. A was subsequently convicted of possessing the ammunition in suspicious circumstances and of possessing it without holding a firearms certificate. He was sentenced to a term of imprisonment. On his release he was detained without trial as a suspected terrorist and subsequently convicted of other criminal offences and sentenced to a further term of imprisonment. In prison he was treated as a "special category" prisoner, having claimed that the offences were political in character, though he denied that he was a member of an illegal organisation. His claim for compensation was allowed in full by the county court judge, but that decision was reversed on appeal to the High Court and that reversal was upheld by the Court of Appeal.

The learned county court judge held that to be "relevant" the circumstances had in some way to be linked with the incident in which the applicant was injured; the wording of the 1968 Act did not permit an applicant to be penalised for general bad character or other conduct which, as here, had not been shown to be connected with the criminal injury.[26] Gibson LJ in the High Court disagreed:

> "The proper reading of the subsection is that the court should have regard to all relevant circumstances without limitation."

---

23. See e.g. *Annesley, supra* n 20, and *Mackie* v *Sec of State* [1986] 15 NIJB 1. See further below, p 283.

24. The 1968 Act provision was divided into two parts (s 1(2) dealt with *refusal* of compensation, s 4(6)(*a*) with *reduction* of compensation) and the wording was somewhat different; but there was no significant difference in substance. Article 5(2) of the 1977 Order introduced the present formula.

25. [1976] 9 NIJB (High Ct); [1977] NI 53 (CA).

26. The learned judge stated: "It may be that

his possession of the ammunition or . . . the fact that he sympathised with the Provisional IRA was connected with the shooting of the applicant; but that has not been established. No evidence was given in this Court to connect them. I do not think that the onus was on the applicant to disprove that there was any connection. With the evidence in that state and since I am not satisfied that the applicant was guilty of any negligent or provocative conduct which contributed to the criminal injury, I consider that I am not entitled to deprive the applicant of compensation under section 1(2)": Unreported, Cty Ct (Judge Higgins), 21 April 1976.

He then held that the issue to which the circumstances must be relevant is not the commission of the criminal injury but whether or not compensation should be awarded to the applicant in respect of that injury:

> "What the statute is requiring the court to do is to decide whether or not to award compensation in the light of all relevant circumstances. The decision for the court is a present decision as to what ought now to be done and it would be unnatural to circumscribe the decision by reference only to circumstances which existed when the right to claim originated."

The learned Lord Justice then continued with a passage which has since been quoted with approval on numerous occasions:

> "Any circumstance which logically or reasonably bears on the question whether the applicant ought to receive or be denied compensation is relevant and ought to be taken into account and given such weight as it merits."[27]

In so deciding Gibson LJ quoted with approval the following passage from the judgment of McGonigal LJ in *Moore* v *Secretary of State*:

> "There is nothing in the Act itself to limit the nature of [the circumstances to be considered] except that they must be circumstances which the court considers relevant. That, in my opinion, means circumstances related to the conduct of the applicant, circumstances in the events leading up to and subsequent to the injury, his conduct in relation to the injury after it had been received, his conduct in relation to those who inflicted the injury and who are guilty of the criminal offence, and his conduct in pursuing the claim. All these matters may be relevant to a greater or less degree depending on the facts of the particular case."[28]

In the particular case of *Cahill*, there was before the High Court fresh evidence which tended to show what had *not* been established in the county court, *viz* that the applicant had been shot because of his connection with the Provisional IRA.[29] Both Gibson LJ in the High Court and (on appeal) Lowry LCJ for the Court of Appeal held that this was a relevant circumstance to be considered in deciding whether Cahill was entitled to compensation.[30] In the words of the Lord Chief Justice:

> " . . . (without prejudice to giving to the word 'relevant' an even wider meaning), other circumstances discreditable to the victim which, like provocative or negligent behaviour, render him more likely to suffer injury or death from attack are certainly capable of being considered relevant by the court."[31]

In other words, Cahill was not entitled to compensation because his "discreditable" connections with the Provisional IRA were considered to have constituted a "circumstance" which was "relevant" because it contri-

---

27. [1976] 9 NIJB. *Cf* "When I say 'relevant' I mean this, so nearly touching the matter in issue as to be such that a judicial mind ought to regard it as a proper thing to be taken into consideration." *Tomkins* v *Tomkins* [1948] P 170, 175, *per* Lord Greene MR.

28. [1977] NI 14, 18.

29. "In this regard there is a clear distinction between the case as presented before me and that before Judge Higgins":[1976] 9 NIJB, *per* Gibson LJ.

30. See also *Ferguson* v *Sec of State* Unreported, Cty Ct (Judge Johnson), 15 Nov 1978 (compensation refused to relatives of member of IRSP shot dead by Official IRA during a feud between the two organisations).

31. [1977] NI 53, 57–8. Jones LJ and O'Donnell J concurred with the Lord Chief Justice.

buted, directly or indirectly, to his injury. The actual decision in the case is, therefore, rather narrower than some of the dicta might suggest. It is for this reason that the most important aspect of *Cahill* may be the Court of Appeal's express approval of the decision in *Moore* v *Secretary of State*.[32] In that case the court held that the applicant had not made a full disclosure of the material facts surrounding his application, and had indeed been deliberately untruthful in his report to the police. McGonigal LJ held the applicant to have been in breach of the specific requirements regarding reports to the police[33] – but he held further that the failure to give information was "relevant" to the application and a "circumstance" which he was required to consider in determining whether or not to make an award. In the event the learned judge refused to make an award. Moore's claim therefore failed because the court regarded as relevant a circumstance which neither contributed, directly or indirectly, to his injury nor was relevant to the infliction of that injury. Gibson LJ and Lowry LCJ in *Cahill* accepted that this reasoning was correct.

Moore and *Cahill* thus confirmed that the phrase "all such circumstances as are relevant" has a wide ambit – but they failed to give a clear indication of its scope. In particular the learned judges in *Cahill* considered it unnecessary to decide whether the mere fact that the applicant was a member of, or an adherent to, an illegal organisation at the time of his injury is a "relevant circumstance" if that membership or association did not in any way contribute to the injury.[34] As we shall see below this particular matter was put beyond doubt by the 1977 Order[35] and further provision has now been specifically included in the 1988 Order in relation to other "discreditable" conduct of the victim or applicant.[36] In both cases, however, these more particular provisions are expressly stated to be "without prejudice" to the general requirement to have regard to "relevant circumstances".[37] Thus it would appear that the general approach adopted in *Moore* and *Cahill* in relation to the 1968 provision is equally applicable to the interpretation of Article 6(1) of the 1988 Order.[38]

---

32. [1977] NI 14.

33. 1968 Act, s 1(3)(*e*), now 1988 Order, Art 5(4)(*a*), discussed below p 262.

34. Gibson LJ was not unsympathetic to the argument: "Such persons (i.e. members of proscribed organisations) are not outlaws, but it may be that, having joined an organisation pledged to murder and in some cases to destroy the very fabric of our society, they ought for that reason to be denied compensation . . . However . . . I prefer to leave [this matter] to an occasion when the implications are more fully argued":[1976] 9 NIJB at p 12.

35. Article 6(3), now Art 5(9) of the 1988 Order, and discussed below.

36. Article 6(1)(*b*), discussed below, p 125.

37. " . . . the words 'without limiting the generality of the foregoing' evince an intention that the general power should be given a

construction that accords with the width of the language in which it is expressed and . . . is not to be restricted by reference to the more specific character of that which follows . . . ": *Leon Fink Holdings Pty Ltd* v *Australian Film Comm'n* (1980) 53 ALJR 522, 524, *per* Mason J.

38. "I do not think that the changes made in the 1977 Order affect the validity of the proposition of law stated by Lord Lowry [in *Cahill*] . . . ": *McLaughlin* v *Sec of State* Unreported, Cty Ct (Deputy Judge Nicholson), 18 Jan 1984. Note however that the 1968 Act referred to all such circumstances "as it [i.e. the court] *considers* relevant . . . "; in *Cahill* Lord Lowry LCJ stated that these words "tend to confer a clear discretion on the court to decide what is relevant". The 1988 Order now, however, refers to "all such circumstances *as are relevant* . . . " .

What "circumstances" then are "relevant" as logically or reasonably bearing on the question whether the applicant ought to receive or be denied compensation? Some particular answers to this question are discussed below, but first it is suggested that there are three possible general approaches which the courts might adopt. First, compensation under the 1988 Order is provided by the taxpayer and it may therefore be that compensation should not be paid (or in some instances only reduced compensation should be paid) to those applicants to whom it is inappropriate or undesirable that payment should be made from public funds. There are hints of this approach in *Cahill*, where Gibson LJ observed:

> " . . . I cannot think that Parliament ever contemplated or that I should countenance the idea that such enemies of society should be awarded compensation out of public funds for injuries received because of their criminal associations directed towards the destruction of the State itself."[39]

It is, however, submitted with respect that such an approach would not be correct. The Northern Ireland scheme was traditionally, and still to a substantial extent remains, one in which an applicant has a right to compensation justiciable by the courts. To hold that compensation could be refused "in the public interest" would effectively undermine that right and, if it did not give the judges a most difficult task to determine what the public interest required, it would come perilously close to conferring on them the inherent discretion which they have always denied. The 1988 Order itself lends support to this reasoning, since it does expressly provide for some "discretionary payments" where the Secretary of State "considers it to be in the public interest" to pay compensation; but such discretionary payments are deliberately excluded from consideration by a court.[40] Moreover, it is arguable that to interpret Article 6(1) as, in effect, equivalent to the general provision in the British Scheme prior to 1990 would be contrary to the intention of Parliament. Both in 1977 and in 1988 Parliament, had it so wished, could have adopted the British formula; by failing to do so it would appear that Parliament did not intend such an extensive provision to apply in Northern Ireland.

A second general approach to the ambit of "relevant circumstances" could be to refuse or reduce compensation in Northern Ireland in any circumstance in which compensation would be refused or reduced under the British Scheme. This approach also derives support from *Cahill*:

> " . . . if in England it is recognised that it may be inappropriate to award compensation because of the applicant's character and way of life, I find some difficulty in saying that in Northern Ireland the same considerations cannot be regarded as relevant, which is here the test. To hold otherwise would be to accept the view that the British Board is entitled to refuse compensation for reasons which are irrelevant to the decision."[41]

---

39. [1976] 9 NIJB.   **41**. [1976] 9 NIJB, *per* Gibson LJ.
40. 1988 Order, Arts 10(2), 16(1).

It may indeed be incongruous to hold a person entitled to compensation from public funds in Northern Ireland in circumstances in which such compensation would not be paid in Great Britain, or vice versa. But is this not really a matter for the legislature? There have always, since the 1960s, been some differences between the two schemes; in some cases Parliament has acted to remove the differences, in other cases it has not so acted. It is submitted with respect that there is no real difficulty in saying that Parliament has stipulated and is entitled to provide that some considerations are relevant in one scheme but not in the other.

We are left then with a third possibility which, it is suggested, is the most appropriate and valid general approach to the interpretation of Article 6(1) – "circumstances" are "relevant" if Parliament has expressly or by implication indicated through the particular provisions of the 1988 Order its general intention that regard should be had to them in deciding whether or not compensation should be awarded. Thus, "circumstances" which pertain to, but are not covered by, the particular provisions of the Order may be considered "relevant" and taken into account for the purposes of the general part of Article 6(1). The validity of this approach tends if anything to be confirmed by the fact that the particular provisions in Article 6(1) are expressly stated to be "without prejudice to the generality of the foregoing . . . ". Parliament thus appears implicitly to have acknowledged a connection between the particular and the general. While it may not be possible to reconcile all the decisions with this approach, it is submitted that most of the cases since 1977 can be explained on this basis. It is to these particular decisions that we now turn.

1. Conduct of Victim

In *Cahill*, as we have seen, the court drew on the particular provisions relating to provocative or negligent behaviour to hold relevant "discreditable" conduct by Cahill which had contributed to his injury. But not all "contributory" conduct is relevant. In *Smyth* v *Secretary of State*[42] the fact that an applicant was a member of or adherent to an organisation (in this case, the UDA) which is not illegal but some of whose members have committed serious crimes was held not to be a relevant circumstance:

> "If Mr Smyth had been shot . . . simply because he was a member of or had affiliations with the UDA, it might be suggested that following *Cahill's* case the court should disallow compensation since some members of the UDA have engaged in criminal acts of violence purporting to have been committed as members of that body. In my opinion such an argument would not succeed. The UDA is not an illegal organisation and cannot be equated with the IRA."

On the other hand, in *McLaughlin* v *Secretary of State*,[43] the applicant was the victim of a "punishment" shooting. He admitted convictions for burglary, assault, criminal damage, disorderly behaviour and other offences.

---

42. Unreported, Cty Ct (Judge Johnson), 28 Aug 1979. See further below, p 130.

43. Unreported, Cty Ct (Deputy Judge Nicholson), 18 Jan 1984.

It appeared that he had been shot "by men, whether belonging to an illegal organisation or not . . . " for his "anti-social" activities. Thus the applicant's criminal injury was connected with his own criminal conduct, and the learned acting judge held that this conduct did, on the facts of the case, constitute a relevant circumstance.[44] As in *Cahill* the *contributory* nature of the applicant's conduct seems to have been the crucial factor, but the learned judge went on to observe:

> "I am not prepared to hold that there are no circumstances in which the general bad character or criminal or other anti-social activities of an applicant debar an applicant, though they did not lead directly or indirectly to the criminal injury. The point does not arise for decision in this case . . . "

Article 6(1)(*b*) now specifically provides that regard shall be had to "any criminal convictions which are indicative of the character and way of life" of the victim or of the applicant, even though these do not in any way contribute to the injury. It may, therefore, be that the courts will draw on this new provision and hold that criminal convictions not covered by Article 6(1)(*b*) may nevertheless constitute a "relevant circumstance" even though they have not caused or otherwise brought about the injury for which compensation is being sought. If that is so, then there may now be a basis for suggesting that the applicant's conduct prior to the injury may, if not covered by a particular provision of the Order, be taken into account as a "relevant circumstance" where

  (a) it was "discreditable" and contributed in some way to the injury,[45] or (more questionably)

  (b) it resulted in criminal convictions *not* indicative of his character and way of life which in no way caused or contributed to his injury.

But it would also appear that there is no basis in the 1988 Order for suggesting that the Secretary of State or the courts may now have regard to non-"contributory", non-criminal conduct on the part of the victim prior to the injury as a relevant circumstance leading to the reduction or refusal of compensation.[46]

Whatever the true scope of Article 6(1) in relation to past conduct, similar principles appear to be applicable to the victim's conduct at the time of the injury. Some support for this proposition may be found in *Corr* v *Secretary of State*[47] where Gibson LJ suggested that the court might on account of his

---

44. See also *McCabe* v *Sec of State* Unreported, High Ct (MacDermott J), 1 March 1985.

45. Following the reasoning in *Cahill, supra*. The British Scheme, para 6(*c*) now simply refers to "the conduct of the applicant . . ." but some connection with the injury is generally required – see Greer, *Criminal Injuries Compensation* (1990), paras 3.05 *et seq*. See also s 112(2)(*b*).

46. *Cf* " . . . the Board should continue to be able [to refuse or reduce compensation] . . . in exceptional cases where an applicant is considered undeserving of public sympathy for reasons other than criminal convictions": 1986 *1WP Report*, para 6.7. The 1990 Scheme, para 6(*c*) (and 1988 Act, s 112(2)(*a*)) refers to (non-contributory) criminal convictions and *unlawful conduct*.

47. Unreported, High Ct (Gibson LJ), 13 May 1977. Note that it had not been suggested that the Army had acted criminally in shooting – A's death was said to have been "directly attributable" to the offence of riot, which had provoked the Army to shoot.

conduct at the time of the incident refuse compensation to the relatives of a rioter shot dead by the Army:

> "All persons engaged in a riot are guilty of a criminal offence and if one rioter is injured or killed by another or by the Army or police in suppressing the riot, the claim is excluded because . . . the victim was engaged jointly in the activity."

A similar approach is adopted under the British Scheme.[48] "Good" conduct by an applicant at the time of his injury is equally relevant and may be taken into account as a countervailing circumstance.[49]

Insofar as "non-contributory" conduct *prior* to the injury may be relevant so also may such conduct *after* the injury.[50] Although no case has been found in which this has been expressly decided in relation to "relevant circumstances", Articles 5(9) and 6(1)(*b*) are clearly so applicable, and indeed may now even in certain instances be invoked after a determination has been made that an applicant is entitled to compensation.[51] Furthermore, in *H* v *Secretary of State*[52] the applicant was a police officer who fell and injured his back when chasing a suspected thief. Following the injury the applicant failed to try exercise or physiotherapy treatment as he did not want to take time off work, and he also failed to take distalgesic tablets which had been prescribed. Although not expressly stated it appears that the applicant's failure to mitigate his loss was considered to be a relevant circumstance requiring an (unspecified) reduction in his compensation.

2. Failure to Co-operate with Police

Several particular provisions of the 1988 Order (especially Article 5(8)) make it clear that a victim or applicant must co-operate fully with the police in their investigation of the incident which gave rise to the injury, and in the detection and prosecution of the offender. A failure so to assist the authorities has been held to constitute a relevant circumstance where there has – or may have – been no breach of the specific legislative requirements.[53] This was, of course, what *Moore*[54] decided and that decision has since been

---

48. Under the British Scheme the general rule is that a victim who is injured in the course of committing a serious crime will not receive an award: *Statement*, para 6H, and see e.g. CICB, *6th Annual Report* (1969–70), p 6 (professional housebreaker shot by occupant of house refused compensation).

49. See e.g. *McDaid* v *Sec of State* NIJB, May 1973, discussed below p 116. See also CICB, *Statement,* para 6K(4).

50. Compensation under the British Scheme has been refused e.g. to the victim of an assault who shortly afterwards himself assaulted four men – see CICB, *8th Annual Report* (1971–72), p 11.

51. 1988 Order, Art 12(5), discussed below, p 307.

52. Unreported, Cty Ct (Judge Rowland), 26 Feb 1987; [1987] 3 *BNIL* 21. See also *R* v *Sec of State* [1981] 6 *BNIL* 22. But a reasonable refusal to undergo treatment will not be held against an applicant – see e.g. *Meikle* v *Sec of State* Unreported, Cty Ct (Judge McKee), 4 Dec 1984.

53. *Cf* British Scheme, para 6(*a*), substantially enacted in the 1988 Act, s 112(1)(*a*). Article 5(8) is discussed below, p 138.

54. [1977] NI 14. See also *Dawson* v *Sec of State* Unreported, High Ct (McGonigal LJ), 15 Oct 1976.

followed in a number of cases. Thus in *Megran v Secretary of State*[55] the applicant was visiting a friend's home when a brick was thrown through the window. The applicant confronted the brick-thrower, and was stabbed by him. When the police arrived, however, the applicant failed to report the stabbing and told the police that he had been injured in a fall. His compensation was reduced from £5,000 to £3,500 because of his conduct and especially because of his failure to report the incident to the police at the scene. By reducing the compensation (instead of refusing it outright) the learned judge appears to have treated the failure to report (and the other aspects of the applicant's conduct) as a "relevant circumstance".

Similarly in *Wynne v Secretary of State*[56] the applicant had been assaulted and made a statement to the police naming her assailant. She then withdrew her complaint and requested no further police action. His Honour Judge Hart held that the withdrawal of the complaint was a "relevant circumstance" and reduced her compensation by one-third.[57] This reasoning was also applied in *McLaverty v Secretary of State*,[58] where an applicant under duress failed to give evidence at the trial of the assailant who had stabbed him; the man was acquitted. Although the applicant was held not to have breached any specific provision of the 1977 Order, the learned judge held that the refusal to give evidence at the offender's trial was a relevant circumstance.

3. Conduct in Relation to Application

Although the 1988 Order contains a number of specific provisions requiring an applicant to disclose information to, or otherwise co-operate with, the Secretary of State in connection with an application for compensation, there is no general requirement that he provide the Secretary of State with all reasonable assistance.[59] However, the courts may well regard a failure to give such assistance as a relevant circumstance, even if the applicant is not specifically required by the Order to give it. Perhaps the best example is *McNamee v Secretary of State*[60] where the applicant had been shot in the leg, but failed initially to disclose why he was in the area where the shooting took place. When his application for compensation was rejected by the Secretary

---

55. Unreported, Cty Ct (Judge Curran), 19 Nov 1986; [1987] 3 *BNIL* 26.

56. Unreported, Cty Ct (Judge Hart), 27 Feb 1986.

57. In Britain "the Board is careful to distinguish between two situations: (i) An applicant refuses to co-operate with the police; for example, he refuses to make a statement, attend an identification parade, name the assailant, attend court or suchlike conduct. The Board makes no award. (ii) An applicant expresses a wish that, for example, there should be no prosecution or makes no formal complaint. The police do not seek to persuade

him to the contrary. In no way does the applicant refuse to assist the police . . . [and] the Board makes a full award": CICB, *22nd Annual Report* (1985–86), para 20. See also *Re Killingback's Application* [1976] *CLY* 426.

58. Unreported, Cty Ct (Judge Pringle), 9 Oct 1986. See also *Dunlop v Sec of State* Unreported, Cty Ct (Judge Pringle), 18 Sept 1987, [1987] 8 *BNIL* 25 (A failed to give evidence at trial of alleged offender; compensation reduced from £2,500 to £1,250).

59. *Cf* British Scheme, para 6(*b*), enacted in the 1988 Act, s 112(1)(*b*). See also Irish Scheme, para 11.

60. [1982] NI 279.

of State, he appealed first to the county court and then to the High Court. When he gave evidence in the High Court Hutton J was satisfied that the applicant had lied when stating why he was in the area. Following *Moore* and *Cahill* the learned judge held that this was a relevant circumstance:

> " . . . in a case such as the present one . . . it is important for the court to know why the applicant was in the locality where he was shot. Moreover, the fact that the applicant has lied to the court on an important and material point is a consideration which should weigh particularly heavily against him in a criminal injury claim because . . . the respondent in [such] a . . . claim will usually have no knowledge of the surrounding facts other than from the information which the applicant chooses to give."[61]

A similar approach was adopted in *McCafferty* v *Secretary of State*[62] where each of four applicants was found to have lied on oath by testifying that he had no idea why he was shot. His Honour Judge Hart stated:

> "I consider that it is important that the court be able to decide why the appellant was shot in order to consider whether compensation should be refused or reduced . . . In order to make such a decision the court must be satisfied that so far as is possible all of the material matters have been put before it . . . "

Another possible "circumstance" is suggested by a Canadian case, *In re Sheehan and the Criminal Injuries Compensation Board*.[63] It was held that the fact that there was no evidence to indicate that the applicant had attempted to recover damages in civil proceedings against the offender (or someone liable for the offender's acts) could amount to a relevant circumstance. As we shall see, damages actually paid by the offender or any person on his behalf are deducted from the criminal injuries compensation payable to a victim, but the Order does not impose any duty on the victim to bring such proceedings.[64] *Sheehan* suggests, however, that such an obligation may be implicit in the general requirement of Article 6(1).

4. Effect of Relevant Circumstances on Award of Compensation

Where the Secretary of State (or the court) is satisfied that there is in relation to an application a relevant circumstance, he is only required by Article 6(1) to "have regard to" it. What this means in practice is that the applicant may nonetheless still be entitled to full compensation, that compensation may be reduced or no compensation at all may be awarded. In any particular case, the relevant circumstance is, as Gibson LJ observed in *Cahill*, to be "given such weight as it merits".[65] Obviously the effect of a relevant circumstance

---

61. *Ibid*, p 284.

62. Unreported, Cty Ct (Judge Hart), 26 Feb 1987.

63. (1974) 52 DLR (3d) 728 (the Ontario Compensation for Victims of Crime Act 1971, s 5 provides for "relevant circumstances" to be taken into account).

64. Article 6(2)(*a*), discussed below, p 206. See also *K* v *Sec of State* [1989] 8 *BNIL* 19.

65. [1977] NI 53, 57, as quoted by Lord Lowry LCJ. "The requirement that the board shall have regard to certain matters tends in itself to show that the board's duty in respect of these matters is limited to having regard to them. They must take them into account and give due weight to them, but they have an ultimate discretion . . . ":*Ishak* v *Thowfeek* [1968] 1 WLR 1718, 1725, *per* Lord Pearson.

depends on its seriousness in relation to all the other particular circumstances of the application. In this assessment account should be taken of all relevant circumstances – and this includes circumstances which operate to the benefit of the applicant as well as to his detriment. Thus, in *McDaid* v *Ministry of Home Affairs*[66] the applicant was shot and seriously injured during riots in Londonderry following the Apprentice Boys' march in August 1969. He went to Great James Street because of rumours he heard that St Eugene's Cathedral was being attacked by a hostile crowd who were trying to burn it down. In Great James Street he found a sectarian riot in progress with the two hostile crowds separated by a small force of police. McDaid stayed in case he was needed to protect the cathedral but did not take any part in the riot. Later, when the police force went to the aid of other policemen whose ferret car had been attacked, one crowd surged towards the cathedral and the cathedral crowd counter-attacked. McDaid went with the cathedral crowd and threw stones and "handled" a petrol bomb. The police fired tear gas into the cathedral crowd, which broke; as McDaid was running back, shots were fired from the direction of the other crowd and McDaid was hit in the back and seriously wounded. In deciding whether McDaid's application was barred by section 1(2) of the 1968 Act, McGonigal J said:

> "If this was a case simply of a person who was an active rioter and with no reason or excuse for being where he was when injured I would not consider that he would recover. His injury would have been sustained when he was engaged in a criminal act. To take any other view would be to hold, for example, that a member of a gang engaged in a gang fight with another gang could recover compensation under this Act for injuries so sustained. In my opinion the principle *ex turpi causa* would apply and such a claim could not be sustained.
>
> I am not however satisfied that that is this case. If I accept the appellant's evidence that he went initially to Great James Street because of a rumour that he had heard and remained there, not as a rioter but in view of the danger that the cathedral would be attacked . . . he had a reason for being in the area other than to take part in a riot in progress. His actual involvement followed . . . the attack and counter-attack and was part of the counter-attack movement. His actions in throwing stones and his handling of the petrol bomb were riotous but his presence there was not for the purpose of rioting and this distinction appears to me to be one which allows him to rely on the provisions of the Act.
>
> It allows him to rely on section 1(1) and say that the injury he received was a criminal injury, as undoubtedly it was. It also allows him to rely on section 1(2) and say that the Court should have regard to all the circumstances including those I have already adverted to as showing his reason for being where he was and for his involvement in the counter-attack and have regard to his involvement only as being provocative or negligent behaviour which will be taken into account . . . to reduce but not to defeat his claim."

66. NIJB, May 1973 (High Ct). See also *McCaughey* v *Ministry of Home Affairs* Unreported, Cty Ct (Judge Johnson), 27 Nov 1969 (A injured while attempting to persuade rioters to withdraw given full award) and *R* v *CICB, ex parte Chalders*, Unreported, Div'l Ct, 3 Feb 1981 (Board to take into account that A with "appalling criminal record" injured when he went to assist person being attacked).

Obviously, much will depend on all the particular circumstances of the case, but the following cases give some further indication of the courts' approach.

(a) *No reduction in compensation despite relevant circumstance*

In *McLaverty* v *Secretary of State*[67] an applicant refused, because of duress, to give evidence at the offender's trial. The refusal was held a relevant circumstance, but the applicant was nevertheless awarded full compensation. The learned judge observed:

> "As I am satisfied as to not only the making of threats to the life of the appellant and the lives of his brothers, but also that these were real threats that probably would have been carried out and but for these threats the appellant would have given evidence, I consider that it would be wrong to make any reduction in the compensation to be awarded. If all compensation were to be denied to the appellant the implication would be that he should have placed his life in the greatest jeopardy for the sake of £1,500, which would not be reasonable; the point is even stronger if the compensation were to be reduced rather than denied."[68]

However, the learned judge went on to point out that this would not always be the case:

> " . . . other applicants who refuse to give evidence against the offender because of alleged threats may find it difficult to satisfy the court as to all three elements [present in this case] i.e. the making of the threats, the reality of the threats and the threats being the only factor leading to the refusal to give evidence."

Thus in *Dunlop* v *Secretary of State*[69] an applicant who, in rather different circumstances, failed to give evidence at the trial of his assailant suffered a 50% reduction in his compensation.

(b) *Reduction in compensation because of relevant circumstance*

Two "punishment shooting" cases illustrate some of the factors which lead to reduction of compensation in the light of "relevant circumstances". In *McLaughlin* v *Secretary of State*[70] the applicant had been "knee-capped" for minor criminal activities which the court considered constituted a relevant circumstance requiring reduction of the applicant's compensation by 25%. The learned judge drew attention to the following factors:

> "There may be cases in which the criminal activities of an applicant are so grave as to debar him altogether of compensation even though he has not been negligent or provocative. But this case falls a long way short of that. In the first

---

67. Unreported, Cty Ct (Judge Pringle), 9 Oct 1986.

68. See also *Brown* v *Sec of State* Unreported, High Ct (O'Donnell LJ), 18 Oct 1985 (A who refused to give evidence because of "genuine and reasonable" fear of reprisal given full award).

69. Unreported, Cty Ct (Judge Pringle) 18 Sept 1987; [1987] 8 *BNIL* 25. See also *Wynne* v *Sec of State* Unreported, Cty Ct (Judge Hart), 27 Feb 1986 (A withdrew complaint against assailant; compensation reduced by one-third).

70. Unreported, Cty Ct (Deputy Judge Nicholson), 18 Jan 1984.

place the behaviour of the victim in this case was that of a petty criminal. Secondly, the behaviour of his assailants was outrageous, merits the strongest condemnation and involved the use of a gun . . . Thirdly, the police and the courts have been trying to deal with the applicant's anti-social behaviour . . . If the Court refuses compensation to a victim of knee-capping in circumstances such as these, will any such crime be reported to the police? Are those who claim to assert an authority alternative to the police to be allowed also to . . . inflict gun-shot wounds on a petty thief . . . and then have the courts condone such activity by debarring the victim of compensation. The plain answer is: No, to each of these questions."[71]

The learned judge concluded therefore that it would not be in the public interest to make any substantial reduction from the applicant's compensation. Similar considerations led the court in *McCabe* v *Secretary of State*[72] only to reduce by one-third the compensation payable to an applicant who had been knee-capped "because I stole cars in the area and messed about . . . ".

(c) *Refusal of compensation because of relevant circumstance*

Compensation will be refused outright in a case where the court considers that the relevant circumstance is a particularly serious one. This was, for example, the outcome in *Cahill, Moore, McNamee* and *McCafferty*.

PROVOCATIVE OR NEGLIGENT BEHAVIOUR

Article 6(1)(*a*) of the 1988 Order re-enacts Article 5(2) of the 1977 Order by providing:

"In determining whether any compensation should be paid and, if so, its amount, the Secretary of State . . . shall have regard to . . . any provocative or negligent behaviour of the victim which contributed, directly or indirectly, to the criminal injury . . . "[73]

In these cases the applicant's conduct is only taken into account if it has contributed to his injury. The use of the phrase "directly or indirectly" is calculated to provide a broad test of causation[74] and so entitle the court to

---

71. The learned judge added that "it is undesirable to set out all the factors which the court should take into account, lest one overlooks a relevant factor or appears to indicate that one is more important than another. In another case the importance of the various factors may differ from the present case."

72. Unreported, High Ct (MacDermott J), 1 March 1985.

73. There is no equivalent provision in the British Scheme, but para 6(*c*), which refers generally to "the conduct of the applicant before, during or after the events giving rise to the claim . . .", includes provocative or negligent conduct; see Greer, *Criminal Injuries Compensation* (1990), paras 3.12 *et seq*. The Irish Scheme, para 13 requires the Tribunal to consider whether "the victim was responsible, either because of provocation or otherwise, for the offence giving rise to his injuries . . .".

74. "A more remote link in the chain of causation is contemplated than the proximate and immediate cause": *Coxe* v *Employers' Liability Corp Ltd* [1916] 2 KB 629, 634, *per* Scrutton LJ.

cast its net comparatively widely in the search for behaviour to be taken into account. It may be noted further that the behaviour must contribute to the injury and not to the act or omission which caused the injury. This has two consequences. First, it means that a person's compensation may be refused – or more likely reduced – in circumstances where he has not contributed to the commission of an offence, but has through his behaviour suffered more serious injuries than he would otherwise have done – e. g. a policeman who fails to wear a "flak jacket" and is shot while on foot patrol.[75] A second consequence may be explained by reference to *McDaid* v *Ministry of Home Affairs*,[76] where the applicant, involved in a riot between rival crowds, was hit in the back and seriously wounded by shots fired from the direction of the opposing crowd. Counsel for McDaid argued that his behaviour had not contributed to his injury because —

> "the firing of the shots was a criminal act quite separate from anything that had taken place up until then and that it should be so regarded as a separate incident and unrelated to the more usual forms of rioting that had been going on . . . "

This approach, which is obviously (and, it is submitted, correctly) based on that approved, e.g. in *Jones* v *Livox Quarries Ltd*,[77] for determining whether a plaintiff's negligence has contributed to his injury, was accepted in principle by McGonigal J. But he was satisfied, on the facts, that McDaid's behaviour was so much "mixed up" with his injury that it could not be dismissed as mere history:

> " . . . [McDaid's] own behaviour . . . brought him from the back of the crowd . . . made him a part of the counter-attack and brought him in such capacity to the place where he was injured. That in my opinion was a substantial involvement."

But the same conclusion is not required had the shots been fired, for example, during a bank-robbery in an adjoining street, and McDaid been accidentally hit by a stray bullet. In such a case his behaviour cannot be said to have contributed, even indirectly, to his injury.[78]

It is for the Secretary of State to prove that the applicant's provocative or negligent behaviour did in fact contribute to his injury. In *Smyth* v *Secretary of State*[79] the deceased had made provocative statements shortly before he was murdered. There were other possible reasons for the attack on the deceased and, although the possibility could not be ruled out that his statements might have contributed to his murder, "the onus is on [the Secretary of State] to satisfy the court not merely of the possibility . . . but that on the balance of probabilities they in fact did so".

---

75. A common law analogy is the application of the Law Reform (Contributory Negligence) Act 1945 to plaintiffs who fail to wear crash-helmets or seat-belts – see e.g. *Froom* v *Butcher* [1975] 3 All ER 520.

76. NIJB, May 1973.

77. [1952] 2 QB 608.

78. See e.g. the example given by Denning LJ in *Jones, ibid*, p 616.

79. Unreported, Cty Ct (Judge Johnson), 28 Aug 1979.

It should also be noted that Article 6(1)(*a*) only provides that the Secretary of State *"shall have regard to"* provocative or negligent behaviour which contributes to the injury. Having had regard to such behaviour, it remains open to him (or the court) to make a full award, if it is not an appropriate case for refusal or reduction of compensation. It has been suggested that :

> " . . . one determines the degree by which the victim contributed to his sustaining a criminal injury by reference *either* to his responsibility for placing himself in a position which entailed the risk of injury, *or* to the relationship between his behaviour and the nature of the act which caused the injury."[80]

In *McDaid* McGonigal J appears to have preferred the first approach:

> " . . . [McDaid's] behaviour is to be assessed in relation to the extent to which it contributed to his injury, not by way of comparison with the act that injured."[81]

It is submitted with respect, however, that once the Secretary of State or the court is satisfied that the applicant's negligent or provocative behaviour did contribute to his injury then, as in tort cases involving contributory negligence,[82] regard should be had both to the causative potency of the applicant's behaviour and to the applicant's blameworthiness or culpability.

The issue of provocative or negligent conduct frequently arises in relation to street-fights, pub-brawls and other common assaults. Each case of course depends on its own particular facts, but the recent Northern Ireland decisions may be conveniently summarised by reference to the written guidelines adopted by the British Board.[83] Thus compensation may be refused – or more probably reduced:

> "a. if the victim, without reasonable cause, struck the first blow, regardless of the degree of retaliation;[84]

---

80. Miers, "Compensation and the Victim's Contribution to his Injury" (1973) 24 *NILQ* 533, 536.

81. NIJB, May 1973. The learned judge reduced the compensation payable to McDaid by one third.

82. See e.g. Salmond and Heuston, *The Law of Torts* (19th ed, 1987), pp 579–582.

83. CICB, *Statement*, para 6D. *Cf* "Our experience leads us to believe that there is seldom such a thing as a fair fight, particularly where the participants are inflamed by drink, passion, greed or aggression, and unless we adopt a realistic approach we could well end up making a full or reduced award to the one who comes out of the incident with injuries. Accordingly . . . we propose to adopt a more stringent attitude [as quoted in the text above] and will not usually award

compensation where the conduct of the victim was calculated, likely or intended to provoke violence, particularly where the injury or death occurred in a fight in which the victim had voluntarily agreed to take part." CICB, *16th Annual Report* (1979–80), para 26.

84. See e.g. *Monaghan* v *Sec of State* [1988] 4 *BNIL* 16 (A started fight; compensation refused); *Dallat* v *Sec of State* [1988] 8 *BNIL* 12 (attack on A directly linked to previous confrontation initiated by A; compensation reduced by 25%); *Mairs* v *Sec of State* [1987] 4 *BNIL* 16 (A provoked attack in context of continuing row between A and his assailants; compensation reduced by 25%); *McIntyre* v *Sec of State* [1985] 8 *BNIL* 9 (A provoked assault in context of continuing row between neighbours; compensation reduced by 66⅔%).

b. where the conduct of the victim was calculated or intended to provoke violence;[85]

c. if the injury or death occurred in a fight in which the victim had voluntarily agreed to take part;[86]

d. if the crime of violence formed part of a pattern of violence in which the victim or the applicant had been a voluntary participant;[87]

e. where the victim or the applicant had attempted to revenge himself or herself against the assailant."[88]

These guidelines have recently been amplified in the following terms:

> "The Board continues to receive a large number of applications in which drink, drugs or solvent abuse, or a combination thereof, have been a substantial cause of the victim's misfortune. Many of the incidents occur at weekends and often in places and situations which the victim might have avoided had he been sober or not willing to run some kind of risk. Occasionally it is plain that the incident occurred solely as a result of the victim's own aggressive behaviour. In these cases the Board will make no award. In other cases the most that can be levelled against the victim is his or her own lack of judgment or stupidity. In this situation the Board may make an award but only after looking very carefully at all the surrounding circumstances . . . In particular the Board will look critically at any provocative, annoying or loutish behaviour which can clearly be seen to be attributable to the applicant's own over-indulgence in alcohol or the misuse of drugs."[89]

Whether or not the applicant's conduct is sufficiently provocative or negligent to lead to *refusal* of compensation is obviously a matter of degree, but the recent Northern Ireland cases suggest that reduction of compensation is the more likely result. A good example of the court's approach is provided

---

85. See e.g. *Fletcher* v *Sec of State* [1989] 7 *BNIL* 21 (DJ at disco assaulted A after A had remonstrated with him and tried to climb into DJ's booth; A's compensation reduced by 50%); *Higginson* v *Sec of State* [1989] 4 *BNIL* 14 (A, involved in fight after party, had shouted abuse at his assailants and their girlfriends; compensation reduced by 50%); *McCreery* v *Sec of State* [1988] 8 *BNIL* 13 (A initiated confrontation with her assailant, whom A knew to be hostile; compensation reduced by 33⅓%); *Shearer* v *Sec of State* [1988] 1 *BNIL* 27 (A intervened in argument between her sister and her sister's boyfriend; compensation reduced by 25%); *Blackadder* v *Sec of State* [1987] 3 *BNIL* 23 (assault on A provoked by A's remarks; compensation reduced by 50%); *Leebody* v *Sec of State* [1986] 2 *BNIL* 12 (A tampering with car when discovered and assaulted by owner of car; compensation reduced by 33⅓%); *McA* v *Sec of State* [1984] 4 *BNIL* 29 (A, a schoolboy, insulted and acted aggressively towards his attacker; compensation reduced by 50%).

86. E.g. *McCarron* v *Sec of State* [1989] 1 *BNIL* 18 (A joined on-going fight; compensation reduced by 60%); *C* v *Sec of State* [1988] 4 *BNIL* 15 (A, aged 16, assaulted in fish and chip shop; compensation reduced by 25% because of A's own involvement in fight).

87. See e.g. *Lagan* v *Sec of State* [1986] 7 *BNIL* 10 (A had been fighting with his assailant earlier the same evening; compensation reduced by 75%); *McCullough* v *Sec of State* [1986] 7 *BNIL* 75 (A attacked partly because A had earlier assaulted his assailant's brother; compensation reduced by 50%).

88. E.g. *McCann* v *Sec of State* [1983] NI 125 discussed below.

89. CICB, *22nd Annual Report* (1985–86), para 23.

by *McCann* v *Secretary of State*.[90] The applicant was walking home after midnight when he saw two rival groups of youths. Missiles started to fly and a bottle struck the applicant on the shoulder. He was not hurt, but, having identified three or four youths as those responsible, he followed them into a house. There he was hit and injured by one of the youths. MacDermott J observed:

> "In acting as he did the appellant was not only acting foolishly but acting aggressively. He was, I am satisfied, seeking not an explanation but retribution. At the same time that does not justify his unknown assailant's assault on him. No doubt if he had not entered the house the appellant would not have been injured; but his negligent and provocative behaviour would not . . . debar him from all compensation. If this were the only point in the case I would reduce his compensation to 50% . . . "

1. Provocative Behaviour

The phrase "provocative or negligent behaviour" is not defined in the 1988 Order, but a reasonable starting point in relation to the meaning of "provocative behaviour" would appear to be the Criminal Justice Act (NI) 1966, section 7(1) of which refers to provocation "by things done or by things said or both together".[91] It would also appear that the test, as in criminal law, includes an objective element[92] – but this can give rise to some particular difficulties in the circumstances of Northern Ireland, where all too often people are "provoked" into crimes of violence by conduct which would not normally cause such a reaction. The correct approach would seem to be that adopted in *McLaughlin* v *Secretary of State*,[93] where the applicant had been "knee-capped" as a punishment for minor criminal activities. It was held that he was entitled to full compensation:

> "Whether or not [the applicant's criminal activities] could be held to be provocative must be judged by objective standards. A person providing truthful information to the security forces for the purposes of defeating terrorism might provoke a criminal injury but would not be debarred from obtaining full compensation.
>
> In my opinion a reasonable person would not be provoked to inflict a knee-capping on this applicant for the anti-social behaviour of which he was guilty."

But the learned judge added that there was in any case no evidence to suggest that those who inflicted the injury had actually been provoked.

This appears a preferable approach to that adopted in *Doherty* v *Secretary*

---

90. [1983] NI 125.
91. This provision corresponds with the Homicide Act 1957, s 3, on which see Smith and Hogan, *Criminal Law* (6th ed, 1988), pp 331 *et seq.*
92. Provocation has been defined by Lord Lowry LCJ as "something *unwarranted* which

is likely to make a reasonable person angry or indignant": *R* v *Browne* [1973] NI 96, 108 (emphasis in original). See generally Smith and Hogan, *op cit*, pp 336–340.

93. Unreported, Cty Ct (Deputy Judge Nicholson), 18 Jan 1984.

of State,[94] where an applicant, who had been "punished" at his home by masked men wielding iron bars, had his compensation reduced by one-quarter on account of his "provocative" behaviour. But conduct which "provokes" criminal retaliation may properly be regarded as provocative if it was such as would provoke a reasonable man. This would appear to have been so decided in *Smyth* v *Secretary of State*[95] where the applicant's husband had made outspoken "sectarian" statements in two published interviews. His Honour Judge Johnson held that he had thereby behaved in a provocative manner, since some of the statements were such as would arouse fear, anger or resentment in a (reasonable) section of the population.

In deciding whether an applicant provoked an attack upon himself it would appear that regard should not be had to the severity of the applicant's injuries as such; the proper approach is to look at the *conduct* of the parties and not at its consequences. This approach was endorsed by the Divisional Court in *R* v *CICB, ex parte Comerford*, in the following terms:

> "[The Board] pose the question, put in colloquial terms, 'Did the applicant ask for it?' in the sense that he asked to get hit, though of course he did not ask to get his skull fractured or his brain damaged. But the latter were the unforeseen and unforeseeable results of the blow which was 'asked for'. In those circumstances . . . one has to ask why it was that the applicant got hit. If he has got hit because 'he asked for it', then that is a situation which the Board is entitled to take into account in either rejecting or reducing his claim, regardless of the unforeseen and unforeseeable and appalling circumstances which have . . . arisen."[96]

2. Negligent Behaviour

"Negligent behaviour" would appear to cover those situations in which the victim has acted without reasonable regard for his own safety and so brought injury upon himself. But the English Court of Appeal has rejected the analogy with common law contributory negligence:

> "To my mind it would not be right to expect a policeman, in the course of his duty, to take reasonable care for his own safety. Take a case where a policeman is faced by a bank robber armed with a gun. If he thought of his own safety he would run away. If, instead, he tackles the robber and is shot dead, he may be said to be foolhardy; but his widow should not be deprived of compensation. It should not be reduced by a single penny. I would suggest, therefore, that the conduct, to be such as to reduce or reject compensation, should be something which is reprehensible or provocative, something which could fairly be described as bad conduct or misconduct, rather than failure to take reasonable care for his own safety."[97]

---

94. Unreported, Cty Ct (Judge Porter), 16 June 1987; [1987] 6 *BNIL* 14. See also *McNally* v *Sec of State* [1989] 4 *BNIL* 15 (A injured in punishment beating; compensation reduced by 50%).

95. Unreported, Cty Ct (Judge Johnson), 28 Aug 1979.

96. Unreported, Div'l Ct (Lord Parker LCJ), 19 June 1980 (and see CICB, *17th Annual Report* (1979–80), para 20(*a*)).

97. *R* v *CICB, ex parte Ince* [1973] 3 All ER 808, 813–4, *per* Lord Denning MR. It is still the case that "the Board . . . will not think in terms of 'contributory negligence' when examining the conduct of applicants" – see *Statement*, para 6C. See generally, Atiyah, *Accidents, Compensation and the Law* (4th ed, 1987), pp 303 *et seq*.

This statement must be regarded as limited to cases where the victim is a policeman (as was the case in *Ince* itself), a soldier, a fireman or some such person injured or killed in the line of duty, or indeed *any* person acting under a public duty. But where the applicant is not such a person or not so acting, the concept of reasonable care for his own safety would appear to be appropriate. This was, indeed, expressly acknowledged in *McLaughlin* v *Secretary of State*[98] and appears to have been acted on in a number of other cases. Thus, in *Banks* v *Secretary of State*[99] Mrs Banks was evacuated to a nearby garage when a car-bomb was discovered close to her home. The garage was a safe distance from the car-bomb. However the police later offered to transport the evacuees from the garage to a nearby hotel. Mrs Banks refused this offer, since it would have meant her walking through wet grass and climbing a fence to get to the police transport. The bomb was detonated with a "fairly loud bang" some hours later, and the sound of this explosion exacerbated Mrs Banks' nervous shock. His Honour Judge Higgins held that had Mrs Banks left the garage and gone to the hotel, she would not have heard the explosion and her nervous shock brought on by the whole incident would probably have been less severe. He accordingly reduced her award by one-third.

Similarly, in *Houston* v *Secretary of State*[1] the applicant deliberately went to the scene of a riot as a spectator. During the course of the riot he stood within a few feet of the rioters and in the direct line of fire of plastic bullets which the police were, with the applicant's knowledge, discharging from time to time. The applicant was struck in the face by a plastic bullet and claimed compensation. Gibson LJ reduced the amount payable to him from £27,000 to £9,000, for the reason that "There is no denying that his behaviour was at the very least negligent in the highest degree . . . ".

On the other hand an applicant may be considered to have behaved imprudently, but not negligently:

> "In our view the girl hitch-hiker who accepts a lift in a lorry should not receive less compensation on that account if she is raped by the lorry driver.[2] The man who is robbed while drunk or has been imprudent enough to show, while in a public house, that he has a large sum of money with him, presents a slightly greater difficulty. But on balance we feel that although he may have contributed by his imprudence to the loss of his money, the injuries which he sustains in the robbery are a different matter and there is no reason why he should be deprived of compensation for them."[3]

---

98. Unreported, Cty Ct (Deputy Judge Nicholson), 18 Jan 1984.

99. Unreported, Cty Ct (Judge Higgins), 7 Sept 1976. See also *Cassidy* v *Sec of State* [1988] 10 *BNIL* 9 (despite bomb alert in vicinity, A went to retrieve car; injured when bomb exploded; compensation reduced by 25%).

1. Unreported, High Ct (Gibson LJ), 25 Oct 1985. See also the common law case of

Wasson v *Chief Constable of the RUC* [1987] 8 NIJB 34 (rioter injured by baton-round: damages for trespass to the person reduced by one-half for plaintiff's contributory negligence).

2. On this issue, see Edwards, "Contributory Negligence in Compensation Claims by Victims of Sexual Assault" (1982) 132 *NLJ* 1140.

3. 1978 *IWP Report*, para 17.6.

CRIMINAL CONVICTIONS INDICATIVE OF CHARACTER AND WAY OF LIFE

In a completely new provision Article 6(1)(*b*) of the 1988 Order provides:

> "In determining whether any compensation should be paid and, if so, its amount, the Secretary of State . . . shall have regard to . . . any criminal convictions which are indicative of the character and way of life of the victim and, where the applicant is a person other than the victim, of the character and way of life of the applicant."

The general background to this provision is obvious enough, but the particular wording may give rise to considerable difficulty. The provision is clearly derived from the British Scheme, which from 1969 to 1990 provided that:

> "The Board may withhold or reduce compensation if they consider that . . . having regard to the conduct of the applicant before, during or after the events giving rise to the claim or to his character and way of life . . . it is inappropriate that a full award, or any award at all, be granted."[4]

It would appear that the Northern Ireland Working Party concluded in 1984 that, despite the wide (albeit uncertain) ambit of "relevant circumstances" and the more specific provisions relating to provocative and negligent behaviour and to members of unlawful associations or persons engaged in acts of terrorism (none of which is to be found in the British Scheme), the 1977 Order did not go far enough to prevent the payment of compensation to "undeserving" applicants. It apparently considered, for example, that that Order did not clearly allow the refusal of compensation to a person with a "non-terrorist" criminal record whose criminal activity had not been connected with his criminal injury. Nor apparently did the Order adequately cover "pub-fights" and "ordinary" criminal incidents giving rise to applications for compensation. There appears to have been little consideration given to the question why such persons should be excluded from the Scheme, other than that it is difficult to accept that such persons are deserving of public sympathy represented by payments from public funds. This issue had given rise to considerable criticism of the British Scheme;[5] but in 1984 the Chairman of the British Board expressed the view that it would be "a disastrously retrograde step" to abrogate the "character and way of life" provision,[6] and the Home Affairs Select Committee agreed that the

---

4. British Scheme, para 6(*c*). The provision was apparently introduced in 1969 (to replace a more limited provision in the original 1964 scheme) following a case in which the Board would have been obliged, but for other grounds, to award compensation to "a member of one of the most notorious London gangs" – see CICB, *21st Annual Report* (1984–85), para 19. See also Irish Scheme, para 14.

5. See especially Miers, *Responses to Victimisation* (1978), chs 1 and 5; Atiyah, *Accidents, Compensation and the Law* (4th ed, 1987), p 306. See also Burns, *Criminal Injuries Compensation* (1980), pp 362–4.

6. The text of a letter to the Chairman of the Home Affairs Select Committee is reproduced in CICB, *21st Annual Report* (1984–85), para 19.

Board should retain this power *in exceptional cases*.[7] It was thus not altogether surprising that such a provision should be included both in the Criminal Justice Bill 1987 and in the proposed Draft Order for Northern Ireland.[8] However, both proposals provoked strong criticism[9] and were in due course amended, with differing results. The provision in the 1988 Order (as quoted above) has been restricted to "any criminal convictions which are indicative of the character and way of life . . .". In Great Britain, section 112(2) of the Criminal Justice Act 1988 ultimately provided:

> "The Board may also, if they think fit, refuse an award or award less than they would otherwise have awarded because of any of the following –
>
> (a) criminal convictions or unlawful conduct of the claimant.
>
> (b) conduct on his part connected with the injury."

Somewhat ironically, the reference to "character and way of life" was thus being rejected in Great Britain at precisely the time when it was being introduced in Northern Ireland. However, the amended non-statutory Scheme still refers to "character as shown by . . . criminal convictions or unlawful conduct . . .".[10] The power of the British Board to refuse or reduce compensation will (subject to further interpretation of "relevant circumstances", etc in the 1988 Order) therefore remain more extensive than that of the Secretary of State (or the courts) in Northern Ireland.

It is difficult to predict how this new provision in the 1988 Order will be applied. Some points are, however, reasonably clear from the wording which has been used. Article 6(1)(*b*) extends only to criminal *convictions*; suspected criminal conduct for which a person has not been convicted cannot be taken into account. The convictions need not be convictions for crimes of violence – "any" criminal convictions are included. Nor need the convictions be in respect of conduct which has contributed, directly or indirectly, to the criminal injury[11] – but they may have to be "relevant", in which case as demonstrated in *Cahill*,[12] the issue to which they have to relate is the determination whether any compensation should be paid and, if so, its amount. On this basis, the Secretary of State (or the court) may have regard to any convictions entered at any time prior to the determination – i.e. including convictions made after the date of the injury.[13] But he is only required to "have regard to" them, so that Article 6(1)(*b*) may therefore lead to the refusal or reduction of compensation or to no reduction at all.

---

7. Home Affairs Committee, *Compensation and Support for Victims of Crime* (HC 43, 1984–85), para 34. See also p 104, n 7 above.

8. Clause 76(2)(*b*) and Art 6(1)(*b*) respectively.

9. In Great Britain, see especially HC Debs (Standing Committee F), cols 803 *et seq* (26 Feb 1987) and HC Debs (Standing Committee H), cols 386 *et seq* (1 March 1988); in Northern Ireland, see Standing Advisory Commission on Human Rights, *13th Annual Report* (HC 298, 1988), p 78.

10. Paragraph 6(*c*), discussed Greer, *Criminal Injuries Compensation* (1990), paras 3.26 *et seq*.

11. This requirement, expressly included in Art 6(1)(*a*), is omitted from Art 6(1)(*b*).

12. [1977] NI 53, discussed above, p 107.

13. The 1988 Act, s 112(3) specifically provides that "criminal convictions" refers to "convictions . . . at any time, including a time after the injury".

Finally, this provision applies both to victims and applicants, and may operate for example to prevent compensation from being paid either to the "innocent" wife of a deceased victim with a criminal record, or to the "guilty" father in respect of the death of his "innocent" son.

So much appears to be fairly straightforward. The difficulty lies in determining when "any criminal convictions" are "indicative" of the character and way of life of a person and, if they are, whether compensation should therefore be refused or reduced. An obvious point of departure is the practice developed over time by the British Board:

> "1. . . . Any attempts the applicant has made to reform himself will . . . be taken into consideration.
>
> 2. The Board may completely reject an application because of character and way of life if the applicant has:
>   a. a conviction for a serious crime of violence;
>   b. a conviction for some other very serious crime;
>   c. more than one recent conviction for less serious crimes or crimes of violence;
>   d. numerous convictions for dishonesty of a serious nature.
>
> 3. A person with numerous convictions for petty offences which have not caused serious trouble to anyone else, e.g. offences of drunkenness or minor breaches of the peace, will not have his application rejected completely, but may have the award reduced.
>
> 4. A past conviction, even for a serious crime, will not permanently bar an applicant from an award. The Board would be unlikely to reject the application of someone with a record of convictions who was injured during a genuine attempt to uphold the law or when giving assistance to someone who was being attacked."[14]

But can a single conviction be "indicative of" a character and way of life? In a recent case in England,[15] the applicant was an off duty bus driver who went to the assistance of a bus conductor who was being attacked. The applicant was cut in the face with a razor. Five days prior to the assault he had taken part in a robbery, and he was subsequently convicted of conspiracy to rob and of possession of a firearm. This was his only conviction – and, indeed, the sentence had reflected that he was not a full member of the conspiracy. It is submitted that in such a case the conviction was not "indicative" of his character and way of life. On the other hand, the case where an applicant has numerous convictions for serious offences would appear to be the most obvious application of Article 6(1)(b). Thus, in a case where an applicant has been injured by a person to whom he sold drugs, a number of convictions for drugs offences would obviously be indicative of the applicant's character and way of life, and would have to be taken into account.[16] Clearly the question is one of degree, depending both on the number and nature (and dates) of the applicant's convictions.

---

14. *Statement*, para 6K. See e.g. CICB, *25th Annual Report* (1988–89), para 20; *R v CICB, ex parte Thompstone and Crowe* [1984] 3 All ER 572.

15. CICB, *23rd Annual Report* (1986–87),

para 39 (the applicant received an award reduced by 50%).

16. See e.g. CICB, *20th Annual Report* (1983–84), para 28 (compensation was refused).

But even if he has a number of "indicative" convictions the issue is not altogether clear. Thus, in a Scottish case, the applicant had a string of convictions "which showed that he had lived a life of persistent dishonesty for seven years before the incident". Such convictions are clearly indicative of his character and way of life – but to what effect?[17] The British Scheme provided an explicit, albeit vague, test; was it "appropriate" that such a person should receive compensation from public funds? No such test is prescribed in the 1988 Order – the only stated requirement is that the Secretary of State "shall have regard" to such matters in determining whether compensation should be awarded. It would appear that this must be taken as a declaration by Parliament that some applicants with criminal convictions are to have their compensation refused or reduced on that account, but they are leaving it to the Secretary of State and the courts to decide particular cases. However, it is not immediately obvious how and when such convictions will be "relevant" in the *Cahill* sense. The best that can be suggested at this stage is that the Secretary of State will be most likely to refuse compensation in a case where the criminal convictions of the applicant indicate that he was, at the time of his injury, a person given to a life of violent crime whereas he may well regard as of no consequence the fact that an applicant had convictions which tended to show that many years ago he was a petty (but non-violent) criminal.

MEMBER OF UNLAWFUL ASSOCIATION OR PERSON ENGAGED IN ACTS OF TERRORISM

As we have seen above the Court of Appeal in *Cahill*[18] left open the question whether membership of an illegal organisation such as the IRA was *per se* a "relevant circumstance" requiring refusal of compensation. The public controversy surrounding the case led to considerable discussion and it was made clear that a claim by a terrorist would be rejected under the British Scheme.[19] The Government therefore resolved to put the position in Northern Ireland beyond doubt:

> " . . . we must all hesitate to pay compensation intended essentially for the innocent victims of crime to those who have put themselves far beyond public sympathy by their participation in and encouragement of the most heinous crimes of terror. I think that there will be widespread support for the view that there are notorious persons whose sole interest appears to be to destroy society and on whom it would be wrong to confer the same statutory right to compensation as the Order gives to the ordinary law-abiding citizen."[20]

As a result Article 6(3) of the 1977 Order (now re-enacted as Article 5(9) of the 1988 Order) provided:

---

17. Compensation was refused by the British Board – see CICB, *12th Annual Report* (1975–76), para 11.

18. [1977] NI 53, discussed above, p 107.

19. See CICB, *21st Annual Report* (1984–85), para 19.

20. 934 HC Debs, col 753 (1 July 1977).

"Without prejudice to Article 6(1) or 9(6), no compensation shall be paid to, or in respect of a criminal injury to, any person –

(*a*) who has been a member of an unlawful association at any time whatsoever, or is such a member; or

(*b*) who has been engaged in the commission, preparation or instigation of acts of terrorism at any time whatsoever, or is so engaged."

Three preliminary points may first be noted. The particular provisions in Article 5(9) are stated to be "without prejudice to Article 6(1) . . . ". This leaves the way open to the courts to hold that a person who does not come within Article 5(9) because e.g. like Cahill, he is not a member of, but only "adherent to", an unlawful association is not entitled to compensation by reason of a relevant "circumstance" or because of his criminal convictions. Secondly, it will be noted that Article 5(9) extends not only to victims, but also to applicants. Thus a "guilty" son cannot be awarded compensation if his "innocent" father has been killed by a crime of violence. Thirdly, this exclusion applies if the victim or the applicant was guilty of the stipulated conduct "at any time whatsoever", so that compensation must be refused e.g. to a victim who had belonged to an unlawful association only for a short time many years before the criminal injury.

However, the 1988 Order does envisage that the rigour of Article 5(9) may be mitigated in some instances; by Article 10(2):

"Where, but for Article 5(9), compensation would be payable to any person, the Secretary of State may, if he considers it to be in the public interest to do so, pay to him such sum as does not exceed the amount of that compensation."

This discretion is exercisable only by the Secretary of State – by Article 16(1) there is no appeal against a determination under Article 10(2).

1. Member of Unlawful Association

By Article 2(2) "unlawful association" means –

"any organisation which is engaged in terrorism and includes an organisation which at any relevant time is a proscribed organisation within the meaning of the Northern Ireland (Emergency Provisions) Act 1978."

(a) *Proscribed organisations*

The power to proscribe terrorist organisations is conferred by section 21 of the 1978 Act, and the organisations so proscribed are listed in Schedule 2 to the Act, which may be amended from time to time. The list at present[21] proscribes the Irish Republican Army, the Irish National Liberation Army, the Irish People's Liberation Organisation, Cumann na mBan, Fianna na hEireann, Saor Eire, the Ulster Volunteer Force, the Ulster Freedom Fighters and the Red Hand Commando.

---

21. Northern Ireland (Emergency Provisions) Act 1978, Sch 2, as amended by Northern Ireland (Emergency Provisions) Act 1978 (Amendment) Orders 1979 and 1990.

(b) *Organisations engaged in terrorism*

The definition of "unlawful association" serves two distinct purposes in the 1988 Order; as here discussed it operates to deprive a victim or applicant of compensation. But in Article 8(2) it operates to remove a limit on the compensation payable to a victim or applicant in respect of pecuniary loss.[22] That limit originally applied unless the injury or death had been caused by a member of a proscribed organisation. But during the 1970s it was found that splinter groups from such organisations, or other newly formed organisations, committed acts of terrorism before the nature of the group or organisation became sufficiently clearly established to warrant proscription. The restricted definition was, therefore, thought to be unfair and it was given its present extension in 1977.[23] The application of that extended definition in the present context is obviously required in the interests of consistency.

"Terrorism" is defined in Article 2(2) as meaning –

> "the use of violence for political ends and includes any use of violence for the purpose of putting the public or any section of the public in fear."

We discuss this definition at greater length in the next section. It does not appear to have given rise to any difficulty in the present context where, it will be noted, it applies not to the actual offender, but to the organisation of which he is a member. Thus, in a case such as *Smyth* v *Secretary of State*[24] attention would now focus not only on the deceased's own conduct, but on the nature of the offences committed by other members of the association to which he belonged.[25]

It will be noted that Article 5(9)(*a*) extends to any person who is, or "has been . . . at any time whatsoever" a member of an unlawful association. It would appear that this includes a person who was in the past a member of an organisation which at that time was proscribed, even if it is not so proscribed at the time of the injury or of the application.[26] Conversely, it will not apply to a person who was a member of an organisation only during a period when it was not proscribed.

The principal difficulty in relation to Article 5(9)(*a*) appears to be proof that the person concerned is or has been a member of an unlawful association. The burden lies with the Secretary of State and he cannot obtain in this

---

22. See below, p 173.

23. Originally in the Criminal Damage (Compensation)(NI) Order 1977, Art 2(2), discussed Greer and Mitchell, *Compensation for Criminal Damage to Property* (1982), pp 70–72. Compensation for damage to property caused by members of the UVF before that organisation was proscribed had been paid on an extra-statutory and *ex gratia* basis – see 903 HC Debs, col 97 (13 Jan 1976).

24. Unreported, Cty Ct (Judge Johnson), 28 Aug 1979, discussed above, p 111.

25. *Cf McKee* v *Chief Constable of the RUC* [1984] NI 169, 177, where Kelly J drew a distinction between a "terrorist" and "the person for example who is merely a member of a proscribed . . . organisation".

26. The definition in Art 2(2) refers to "an organisation which *at any relevant time* is a proscribed organisation . . . " (emphasis added). The special defence provided by the Northern Ireland (Emergency Provisions) Act 1978, s 21(7) would appear not to be available to an applicant for criminal injuries compensation.

context a senior police officer's certificate which can in other cases prove so helpful for an applicant. Direct evidence of membership is often not available and attempts by the Secretary of State to satisfy the burden of proof by indirect evidence have usually been rejected by the courts. Thus, in *Ferguson* v *Secretary of State*[27] "death" notices apparently inserted in a local newspaper by or on behalf of an unlawful association were held not sufficient in themselves[28] to prove that the deceased had been a member of that association. In *Corbett* v *Secretary of State*[29] the applicant had earlier been convicted of an offence which caused damage to B's property. B claimed compensation for the damage and a Chief Constable's certificate was issued to the effect that the damage had been caused by a person acting on behalf of an unlawful association. It was held that this certificate was not admissible in relation to an application for criminal injuries compensation as evidence that the applicant had engaged in an act of terrorism.

But it may be that the Secretary of State can make use of section 21(6) of the Northern Ireland (Emergency Provisions) Act 1978:

"The possession by a person of a document –

(*a*) addressed to him as a member of a proscribed organisation; or

(*b*) relating or purporting to relate to the affairs of a proscribed organisation; or

(*c*) emanating or purporting to emanate from a proscribed organisation or officer of a proscribed organisation,

shall be evidence of that person belonging to the organisation at the time when he had the document in his possession."

2. Person Engaged in Acts of Terrorism

In *Houston* v *Secretary of State*[30] Gibson LJ commented as follows on the general scope of Article 5(9)(*b*):

"The nature of the applicant's involvement with terrorism is cast in the widest terms . . . and the time during which that involvement has occurred is 'at any time whatsoever', namely, during, before or after the date of the criminal injury. There need be no connection whatsoever between the incident giving rise to the claim and the act of terrorism which may be totally unrelated in time, place, character and degree."

(a) *"Commission, preparation or instigation . . . "*

This wording has apparently been taken from the emergency legislation in respect of terrorism[31] and such consistency is, indeed, desirable. The one

---

27. Unreported, Cty Ct (Judge Johnson), 15 Nov 1978.

28. The learned judge considered, however, that they tended to corroborate other evidence.

29. Unreported, Cty Ct (Judge Higgins), 28 May 1980; High Ct (O'Donnell LJ), 22 May 1981.

30. Unreported, High Ct (Gibson LJ), 25 Oct 1985.

31. Prevention of Terrorism (Temporary Provisions) Act 1976, ss 10(1), 11(1) – see now 1989 Act, ss 14(1)(*b*), 17(1)(*a*).

aspect of the phrase to give rise to any difficulty in the criminal injuries compensation context appears to be the scope of "preparation". In *Watterson* v *Secretary of State*[32] the applicant had been convicted under section 20(1) of the Northern Ireland (Emergency Provisions) Act 1973[33] for recording information likely to be useful to terrorists, *viz* the registration numbers of vehicles used by the security forces. Kelly J held that the applicant had been "engaged in the . . . preparation of acts of terrorism . . . "; the applicant's conduct could, in broad terms, be said to be preparatory and it was not necessary that a particular act of terrorism had to be contemplated by the applicant. Nor is it necessary that the applicant be preparing to commit an act of terrorism himself. In *McCann* v *Secretary of State*[34] the applicant had been convicted of carrying a loaded sten gun to the Ardoyne area of Belfast. MacDermott J held that he was not entitled to compensation:

> "There is nothing in article 6 or in the definition article, 2, which suggests that the preparatory act has to be performed by the person who has committed or is to commit the act of violence. In my judgment carrying a loaded sten gun across a part of Belfast in times of lawless activity involving the use of such a weapon is an act of preparation for an act of terrorism to be committed by someone."

(b) *"Acts of terrorism"*

The definition of " terrorism" in Article 2(2) of the 1988 Order is also taken from the emergency legislation in respect of terrorism,[35] and it has rightly been pointed out in relation thereto that –

> "The definition . . . is a broad one and would extend to such conduct as breaking up a political meeting by force; or by force compelling people to take part in a politically motivated strike – conduct which is in both cases illegal but which would not ordinarily be thought of as terrorism."[36]

In other words, not all politically-motivated violence amounts to terrorism. But it has further been suggested that "terrorism" as defined in Article 2(2) also encompasses non-political violence. In *McCann* v *Secretary of State*[37] it was held by MacDermott J that the use of the words "and includes" which introduce the second part of the definition enlarges its scope beyond the

---

32. Unreported, High Ct (Kelly J), 16 Jan 1981. See also *R* v *Bingham* [1973] 2 All ER 89 where a similar interpretation was adopted for the purposes of the Official Secrets Act 1920, s 7.

33. See now Northern Ireland (Emergency Provisions) Acts 1978, s 22(1) and 1987, s 10.

34. [1983] NI 125, followed in *Sec of State* v *Crawford* [1985] 4 *BNIL* 15.

35. Prevention of Terrorism (Temporary Provisions) Act 1976, s 14 (see now 1989 Act, s 20(1)); Northern Ireland (Emergency Provisions) Act 1978, s 31(1). *Cf* Elected Authorities (NI) Act 1989, s 6(1)(a) (ii), where "acts of terrorism" are equated with "violence for political ends".

36. Smith and Hogan, *Criminal Law* (6th ed, 1988), pp 847–8. *Cf* the (somewhat inconclusive) critique in the [Baker] *Review of the Operation of the Northern Ireland (Emergency Provisions) Act 1978* (Cmnd 9222, 1984), ch 11. See also Bonner, *Emergency Powers in Peacetime* (1985), pp 102–3.

37. [1983] NI 125. See also *Houston* v *Sec of State* Unreported, High Ct (Gibson LJ), 25 Oct 1985.

limits imposed by the words initially used. On this basis "terrorism" consists of (a) the use of violence for political ends, and (b) any use of violence for the purpose of putting the public or any section of the public in fear, whether or not that violence has a political purpose. On the other hand it has been suggested that such a purpose *is* required to bring violence within the ambit of Article 5(9)(*b*). Thus, in *McCabe* v *Secretary of State*[38] MacDermott J himself referred to an armed robbery as lacking "the flavour of terrorism which I believe to be implicit in [this] article . . . ". In similar vein O'Donnell LJ in *Kinnear* v *Secretary of State*[39] observed:

> "The definition section appears to concentrate not so much on the act, as the underlying reasons for the act. In other words a court must look at the mind of the actor, as well as the act itself."

These differing approaches can lead – and indeed, as we shall see, have led to decisions which may be difficult to reconcile. It was apparently to avoid such uncertainty that Hutton J in *Doran* v *Secretary of State*[40] reviewed the cases to date and came out in favour of the former (and broader) approach. This may be technically correct – in *McCann*, MacDermott J drew attention to the following explanation:

> "Sometimes . . . the word 'includes' is used 'in order to enlarge the meaning of words or phrases occurring in the body of the statute; and when it is so used these words or phrases must be construed as comprehending, not only such things as they signify according to their natural import, but also those things which the interpretation clause declares that they shall include.' In other words, the word in respect of which 'includes' is used bears both its extended statutory meaning and 'its ordinary, popular, and natural sense whenever that would be properly applicable'."[41]

However, this explanation appears to apply when the definition uses the word "includes" alone; in the definition of "terrorism" the draftsman has used both "means" and "includes" – a practice which has provoked this observation:

> " . . . in certain circumstances, the first clause of a compound definition may be introduced by 'means' and a further clause may begin with 'includes'. This is only proper when the second clause is intended to remove a doubt arising from the meaning stipulated in the first clause. The 'includes' clause should not introduce matter beyond the reasonable scope of the 'means' clause or contradict the substance of the 'means' clause."[42]

This passage seems more apposite in the present context than that relied upon by MacDermott J – though, of course, the definition in Article 2(2)

---

38. Unreported, High Ct (MacDermott J), 1 March 1985.

39. [1985] 6 NIJB 93.

40. [1986] 12 NIJB 47.

41. Maxwell, *The Interpretation of Statutes* (12th ed, 1969), p 270, referring to *Dilworth* v *Commissioner of Stamps* [1899] AC 99, 105–6, *per* Lord Watson, and *Robinson* v *Burton-Eccles Local Board* (1883) 8 App Cas 798, 801, *per* Earl of Selborne LC.

42. Thornton, *Legislative Drafting* (3rd ed, 1987), p 176.

may simply provide an *improper* example of the draftsman's art. But it is submitted with respect that it is the purposive approach to the scope of "terrorism" which should in any case be preferred. As O'Donnell LJ went on to observe in *Kinnear*, such an interpretation would appear to be more consistent with the intention of Parliament in enacting Article 5(9), *viz* to prevent the payment of compensation to those involved in terrorism and not simply to those with a previous record of violent offences. This distinction is perhaps made more obvious in the 1988 Order which now makes special provision for "any criminal convictions which are indicative of the character and way of life" of the victim or applicant. It is suggested that the purposive approach to the interpretation of Article 5(9)(*b*) is, therefore, to be preferred to a literal construction of the definition of "terrorism" which does not take that context into account.

(i) *Use of firearms.* Two sets of contrasting cases illustrate the difficulty in determining whether the use of firearms constitutes an act of terrorism. In *McCann* v *Secretary of State*[43] the applicant had been convicted of offences under sections 3(4), 17 and 19A of the Firearms Act (NI) 1969 for transporting a loaded sten gun from one part of Belfast to another. MacDermott J held that he had been engaged in the preparation of an act of terrorism. However, in *McCabe* v *Secretary of State*[44] the same learned judge held that an applicant who had twice been convicted of armed robbery of shopkeepers with an imitation firearm and with three others had also hijacked a car did not come within Article 5(9)(*b*). *McCann* was distinguishable because –

> "This appellant's [i.e. McCabe's] offences, though serious, appear to have been for personal gain but more importantly lack the flavour of terrorism which I believe to be implicit in [this] article . . . "[45]

So far so good. But MacDermott J continued:

> "On some occasion it may be necessary to decide whether or not the use of a real gun or, perhaps more relevantly, a loaded firearm falls within the wide definition of terrorism . . . As at present advised, without the benefit of argument and accepting that such an observation is entirely obiter, I would . . . indicate that an offence involving the use of a real weapon (whether loaded or not) is in my view a use of violence and so within the wide definition of terrorism."

It is, with respect, difficult to understand why e.g. a robbery for personal gain using an unloaded gun should come within the definition, whereas such a robbery using an imitation firearm does not. As suggested above, the

43. [1983] NI 125.
44. Unreported, High Ct (MacDermott J), 1 March 1985. *Cf McGeough* v *Sec of State* Unreported, Cty Ct (Judge Russell), 12 June 1990 (robbery using imitation gun held act of terrorism).
45. *Semble*, the two shopkeepers involved

also did not constitute a section of the public. *Cf McCrossan* v *Sec of State* [1988] 4 *BNIL* 14 (applicant had hijacked a van with three occupants at a time of political tension; compensation refused – a section of the public had been put in fear *and* A had used violence for political ends.

better approach would appear to consider the purpose of the robbery. If for private gain, then Article 5(9)(*b*) should not apply, even if a loaded gun has been used; such a case may now come within Article 6(1)(*b*). But a robbery committed for political purposes does seem to be an act of terrorism, even if only committed with an imitation gun.

It would appear that such a distinction was recognised in *Dickson* v *Secretary of State*,[46] where the applicant had pleaded guilty to possession of a revolver and ammunition in suspicious circumstances. He said that a person unknown to him had called at his home and handed him the gun for safe-keeping in spite of his protests and reluctance to take it. Hutton J held that Article 5(9)(*b*) did not apply – it had not been proved by the Secretary of State that the applicant's intention was to assist others in acts of terrorism. The learned judge drew a distinction between possession of a firearm with intent to endanger life (an offence under section 14 of the Firearms Act (NI) 1969) as in *McCann* and possession of a firearm in suspicious circumstances (section 19A of the 1969 Act) and observed that "possession under suspicious circumstances does not in itself prove that the applicant was engaged in the preparation of acts of terrorism". The distinction drawn by the learned judge (and the importance which he attached to the burden of proof) helps to reconcile this decision with that in *Loughlin* v *Secretary of State*,[47] where the applicant had been convicted (under section 19A of the 1969 Act) as one of a group of four men armed with two guns and an air pistol who were patrolling a street on "vigilante" duty. The learned judge held that to carry a gun in the street, even an unloaded gun or a gun that will not work, for such duties was to prepare for the use of violence for political ends.

(ii) *Petrol bombing*. In four cases the courts have had to consider whether conviction of an offence in connection with petrol-bombs debars an applicant from compensation. The point was first considered in *Kinnear* v *Secretary of State*[48] where the applicant had been convicted (at the age of 17) of two offences of arson under the Criminal Damage (NI) Order 1977 and of throwing petrol bombs contrary to the Protection of the Person and Property Act (NI) 1969. It was proved or admitted that the applicant had not been motivated to commit these offences by any serious political conviction, and that there had been no member of the public in the vicinity at the time; on the other hand, the incident took place on the anniversary of the introduction of internment and the applicant had been one of a crowd of approximately 60 persons. O'Donnell LJ held that the applicant had not been engaged in an act of terrorism:

> "It is a reprehensible, but undeniable, fact that many young people now involve themselves in rioting, and in the throwing of petrol bombs, particularly at times of so called political anniversaries. It is a regrettable phenom-

46. Unreported, High Ct (Hutton J), 9 May 1986.

47. Unreported, High Ct (Murray J), 12 March 1987.

48. [1985] 6 NIJB 93. The applicant had also on another occasion thrown stones at police landrovers. O'Donnell LJ did not regard this incident as serious enough to constitute an act of terrorism, "since the police were in their landrovers at the time of the incident, and therefore unlikely to be injured or put in fear".

enon unfortunately not restricted to Northern Ireland. It would more properly be described as 'violent hooliganism' than terrorism since it lacks the ideological commitment implicit in article 6(3)(*b*) [now article 5(9)(*b*)]."

However, the learned Lord Justice commented that other cases of petrol-bombing could fall on the other side of the line:

> "There may well be cases where the throwing of petrol bombs would be masterminded, or used for political purposes, and where [this] article . ·. . would debar the instigator, or mastermind from compensation . . . "

But not, apparently, the thrower himself – a view not accepted in the more recent cases. In *Houston* v *Secretary of State*[49] the applicant had taken part in two incidents. In the first, he joined a group of 30 youths who had hijacked a bus and set it on fire. He made himself a mask and threw petrol bombs at police jeeps; later he and others hijacked a van and set it on fire. On the second occasion the applicant and others hijacked a tractor and when the police arrived he again threw petrol bombs, setting one of the police jeeps on fire. Gibson LJ held that he was not entitled to compensation:

> "There is no doubt that to engage in rioting . . . is an act calculated to arouse fear in those who either must use the streets or who live or work or have their place of business in the vicinity, and they are either the public or a section of the public, and one must conclude that this was one of the purposes of the rioters, including the applicant."

Similarly, in *Doran* v *Secretary of State*[50] the applicant had been convicted of making a number of petrol bombs contrary to section 2(*a*) of the Protection of the Person and Property Act (NI) 1969. The evidence suggested that these had been made in preparation for rioting in support of an "H-block" protest which involved the throwing of petrol bombs at the police and at property. Hutton J held that the applicant had engaged in an act of terrorism in that the petrol bombs were clearly going to be put to a violent use in serious rioting for the purpose of putting the public or a section of the public in fear. In so doing the learned judge stated that the court has to consider the question of "putting the public or a section of the public in fear" in "a common sense and realistic way" and for this purpose may adopt the approach set out by Lord MacDermott LCJ in *Devlin* v *Armstrong*,[51] *viz*:

> "This element has to be proved by [the Secretary of State] . . . , but this will be done if the evidence as a whole satisfies the court that, as a matter of fact, this requirement has been met, and irrespective of whether a witness has been called to prove a state of alarm on his own part or on that of another or others. In short, alarm may be inferred from sufficient material."

The approach adopted in *Doran* has led to the refusal of compensation to a number of applicants in similar circumstances.[52] All of these cases were

49. Unreported, High Ct (Gibson LJ), 25 Oct 1985.

50. [1986] 12 NIJB 47.

51. [1971] NI 13, 37.

52. See e.g. *Hughes* v *Sec of State* Unreported, Cty Ct (Judge Russell), 11 Feb 1986 (A convicted of making 20 petrol bombs to throw at police). Two recent decisions have gone even further – *Booth* v *Sec of State* Unreported, High Ct (Nicholson J), 3 May 1990 (placing of hoax bomb held an act of terrorism) and *McCrudden* v *Sec of State* [1990] 3 *BNIL* 15 (participation in riot at football ground held act of terrorism).

decided on the basis of a literal interpretation of the definition of "terrorism" – Article 5(9)(*b*) was held to apply if it was established simply that the applicant had used violence "for the purpose of putting the public or any section of the public fear", whether or not he had acted "for political ends". It is suggested above that this is not the correct approach to the interpretation of Article 5(9)(*b*) – but it may be thought that in each case (other than *McCrudden*) a "political flavour" had in any event been sufficiently established.

3. Discretion to make Payment "in the Public Interest"

When the provision which is now Article 5(9) of the 1988 Order was originally introduced, it was acknowledged that:

> "There may be exceptional cases in which the application of such a rigid principle would be unacceptably harsh."[53]

The Secretary of State was, therefore, given a discretion to pay compensation notwithstanding Article 5(9) if "he considers it to be in the public interest" to make such a payment.[54] This might apply, for example, where the applicant had been a member of a proscribed organisation for only a short time many years before he applied for compensation, or where the applicant had been injured as a punishment for giving information to the security forces. There are no written guidelines – each request for the exercise of the discretion is considered on its own facts and merits; by July 1989, the Secretary of State had considered a payment to be in the public interest in only three instances.[55]

The power is a purely discretionary one. By Article 16(1) there is no appeal to the county court against a refusal to make such a payment; an application for judicial review is in theory possible, but is likely to succeed only in the most exceptional circumstances.[56]

---

53. 934 HC Debs, col 754 (1 July 1977).

54. 1977 Order, Art 8(4) – see now 1988 Order, Art 10(2).

55. 157 HC Debs, cols *1, 1084* (17 and 28 July 1989).

56. *Cp R v Sec of State for the Home Dept, ex parte Harrison* [1988] 3 All ER 86, where an unsuccessful applicant for *ex gratia* compensation for wrongful imprisonment sought to challenge the Secretary of State's exercise of discretion under the royal prerogative. The court held (i) the Secretary of State was not bound to give reasons for his decision; (ii) the applicant was not entitled to be informed of the criteria applied by the Secretary of State (A had in fact obtained discovery of a document setting out these criteria), and (iii) the Secretary of State had not acted unfairly by not allowing A to see and comment on the information on which he had based the exercise of his discretion. Although the court emphasised that the case before it concerned an *ex gratia* payment under the royal prerogative, it seems likely that a similar approach would be taken to the exercise of the statutory discretion conferred by Article 5(9).

FAILURE BY VICTIM OR APPLICANT TO ASSIST POLICE

Article 5(8) of the 1988 Order now provides:

> "No compensation shall be paid unless the victim or, in the event of his death, one of his relatives or, in either event, a representative of the victim or such a relative complies with all reasonable requests for information and assistance which might lead to the identification, apprehension, prosecution and conviction of the offender."[57]

This wording modifies in three respects a provision first introduced in 1977.[58]

(a) The 1977 Order referred only to the applicant; Article 5(8) now refers to the victim or his representative or, if the victim is dead, one of his relatives or a representative of such relative. The application of this formula may give rise to difficulty in some situations.[59]

(b) The 1977 Order only gave the Secretary of State power *to withhold* the payment of all or part of the compensation until the applicant had complied with the requests for information and assistance. The scope of this wording was examined in *Scott* v *Secretary of State*[60] where the Secretary of State had, in a Notice of Decision, given the applicant's failure so to comply as one of the grounds for *refusing* to award compensation. Lord Lowry LCJ for the Court of Appeal held that Article 6(10) did not permit the Secretary of State to refuse payment altogether in an otherwise proper case:

> " . . . the presumed object of the provision . . . is not to punish the victim for failure to disclose information which may assist in combatting terrorism but to encourage and promote the disclosure of such information, even after an initial failure to disclose . . .
>
> In a new provision restricting the rights of the victim, it would not be justifiable to construe the Secretary of State's power more penally than the words of the paragraph require and allow."[61]

In *Barry* v *Secretary of State*[62] the learned Lord Chief Justice further examined the power to withhold compensation, and concluded that "the question of withholding compensation cannot arise until a decision has been reached that compensation is payable".[63] Thus where, as in *Barry*, the

---

57. *Cf* British Scheme, para 6(*a*). See to the same effect 1988 Act, s112(1)(*a*), as recommended by 1986 *1WP Report*, para 6.1. For some typical cases, see e.g. CICB, *23rd Annual Report* (1986–87), paras 25 *et seq*, and see also the Board's *Statement*, para 6B.

58. Article 6(10). There was no express equivalent in the 1968 Act, but it was stated in 1977 that "the courts, in interpreting the 1968 Act, have recently made clear that failure to provide information which could lead to the arrest of the offender may justify a complete refusal to pay compensation": HC Debs (NI Cttee), col 7 (16 Feb 1977). See e.g. *McCleery* v *Sec of State*, Unreported, Cty Ct (Judge Rowland), 11 July 1977 (failure to provide

such information a "relevant" circumstance for purposes of 1968 Act, s 1(2)).

59. This formula is identical to that used in Art 5(4), discussed below, p 263.

60. [1981] NI 185.

61. *Ibid*, p 190.

62. [1984] NI 39.

63. *Ibid*, p 43. The learned Lord Chief Justice held further that the power to withhold could not be exercised by the County Court or the High Court, although either court *could* by way of appeal affirm, reverse or vary a decision to withhold made by the Secretary of State: *ibid*, p 44.

applicant's entitlement to some compensation had been determined on appeal to the High Court, it was still open to the Secretary of State to withhold payment of the compensation so awarded to the applicant until the requirements of Article 6(10) had been satisfied.[64] If the applicant continued to refuse to comply, payment of the compensation could be withheld indefinitely. This could leave the payment of compensation in limbo and it was presumably to avoid this unsatisfactory state of affairs that Article 5(8) now uses the formula "No compensation shall be paid . . . ". But it remains the case that no time-limit is imposed upon the applicant within which he must comply with requests made under this provision. Presumably once a reasonable time has elapsed the Secretary of State may serve a Notice of Determination refusing to pay any compensation and the applicant may then decide to provide the requested information and assistance. If he does so, however, it would appear that he must enter an appeal in order to obtain payment; it would have been much more convenient surely if the Secretary of State's new power under Article 12(5) to vary a Notice of Determination in certain circumstances had been extended to cases coming under Article 5(8).

(c) The 1977 Order referred only to information and assistance which might lead to the "identification and apprehension" of the offender; Article 5(8) now refers to his "identification, apprehension, prosecution and[65] conviction . . . ". The significance of this amendment can best be understood by reference to *McLaverty* v *Secretary of State*.[66] The applicant claimed compensation for injuries received when he was stabbed by D. Shortly after the incident the applicant made "full and true disclosure"[67] to the police, but as a result of serious threats to himself and his two brothers he failed to appear as a witness to give evidence at the trial of D. The compensation payable in respect of the applicant's injuries was assessed at £1,500, but payment was refused by the Secretary of State on account of the applicant's refusal to give evidence at D's trial. On appeal the learned county court judge held that the applicant had not thereby been in breach of Article 6(10); that provision was restricted to information which might lead to identification and apprehension of the offender, but did not include the

---

64. Lord Lowry LCJ rejected the applicant's contention that the Crown Proceedings Act 1947, s 25(3) required payment in such a case: "There are two answers. The first is that section 25 is a general provision, whereas Article 6(10) is a later and particular provision which overrides section 25 in so far as it conflicts with that section. The second answer is found in the proviso to section 25(3) which allows the court . . . to direct that 'pending an appeal *or otherwise*' . . . payment shall be suspended. That means that, where Article 6(10) has been invoked, the Court could apply the proviso to section 25."

65. Although not entirely clear it would seem that "and" is used here in a disjunctive sense;

Art 5(8) will be satisfied if the information or assistance requested might lead to the identification of the offender, *or* his apprehension *or* his prosecution, etc. See e.g. *John G. Stein & Co Ltd* v *O'Hanlon* [1965] AC 890, 904, *per* Lord Reid, and generally Thornton, *Legislative Drafting* (3rd ed, 1987), pp 89–92.

66. Unreported, Cty Ct (Judge Pringle), 9 Oct 1986.

67. The relationship between Arts 3(2)(*d*) and 6(10) of the 1977 Order (now Art 5(4) and (8) of the1988 Order) was examined by Lord Lowry LCJ in *Scott* v *Sec of State* [1981] NI 185, 190–1.

giving of evidence, if so required, at the offender's trial. But His Honour Judge Pringle went on to hold that the failure to give evidence was a "relevant circumstance" for the purposes of Article 5(2) of the 1977 Order. Thus, the new wording of the 1988 Order may in practice have effected little or no change of substance in relation to an applicant's obligation to co-operate with the police. What has changed, however, is the consequence of failure to comply with those obligations. As the learned judge pointed out in *McLaverty*, Article 5(2) is discretionary, and thus "the last question is, whether weighing up all the circumstances, compensation should be denied or reduced". Convinced that the threats to the applicant and his brothers were real and that they were the only factor leading to the applicant's refusal to give evidence, His Honour Judge Pringle considered that it would be wrong to make any reduction in the compensation to be awarded to the applicant.[68] It is precisely this discretion to take factors such as intimidation into account which has been removed by the change in the wording of Article 5(8).[69]

In *Barry* Lord Lowry LCJ noted that the "reasonable requests" for information and assistance must come from the Secretary of State.[70] This suggests that the primary purpose of the provision is not the bringing of the offender to justice as such, but rather the securing of a conviction so that the Secretary of State may (at least in theory) invoke the power conferred by Article 17 to recover from the offender all or part of the compensation paid by the Secretary of State to the victim.[71]

As yet there is little authority on the ambit of "reasonable" requests. In *Scott* it appears to have been accepted as "reasonable" that the applicant should describe his attackers to the police and be prepared in due course to identify them in court. In *Barry,* the Secretary of State requested the full names and addresses of six particular persons and "any other witnesses to the incident"; the applicant was also asked to confirm that he was prepared to assist the police "in the apprehension and identification (*sic*) of his assailant". It does not appear to have been suggested that this was an unreasonable request. Similarly, it would normally be reasonable to expect a victim to attend an identification parade[72] or to identify property which may have been stolen during the attack upon him. But it must be shown that the applicant's assistance was in fact being sought. Thus, the British Board has drawn attention to the situation where "an applicant expresses a wish that . . . there should be no prosecution . . . [and] the police do not seek to

---

68. *Cp Wynne* v *Sec of State*, Unreported, Cty Ct (Judge Hart), 7 Feb 1986 (applicant made statement to police naming her assailant, but subsequently withdrew her complaint; compensation reduced by one-third by reference to 1977 Order, Art 5(2)).

69. It may be contended that a real and immediate threat to the applicant may make a request for information and assistance not a "reasonable" request; but this "reasonable"

requirement appears to qualify the request and not the applicant's failure to comply with it. *Cf* under the British Scheme, "fear of reprisals is not *as a general rule* a valid excuse for failure to co-operate with the police": CICB, *Statement*, para 6B(2).

70. [1984] NI 39, 44.

71. *Ibid*, pp 46–7, *per* Gibson LJ. Art 17 is discussed below, pp 323–326.

72. *Cp* CICB, *Statement,* para 6B(4).

persuade him to the contrary ...". In such a case there may well be no *refusal* by the applicant to assist the police because the police also consider that there should be no prosecution.[73]

It will be for the Secretary of State in the first place to decide whether the applicant has "complied" with his request. But if he refuses to award compensation and the applicant considers either that he has complied with the request or that the request is unreasonable, the applicant may appeal to the county court. Indeed, "there can be an appeal every time the Secretary of State makes a decision under Article 6(10) [of the 1977 Order]"[74] – and presumably now also under Article 5(8) of the 1988 Order.

FAILURE TO FOLLOW PROCEDURAL REQUIREMENTS

Article 5(3)–(5) of the 1988 Order provides that "no compensation shall be paid" if the victim – or, where appropriate, the applicant – fails to comply with certain procedural requirements, *viz*:

(i) If the victim fails, without reasonable cause, to undergo any medical examination requested by the Secretary of State or to produce medical records or documents relating to his injury or medical history which the Secretary of State requires to be produced.

(ii) If the victim or his representative – or, if the victim has died, a relative of the victim or his representative – fails –

  (a) to make a full report of the injury (or death) to a police constable "forthwith . . . or within 48 hours from the commission of the criminal injury . . . or . . . such period as the Secretary of State considers reasonable having regard to all the circumstances"; or

  (b) to serve a Notice of Intention to apply for compensation on the Secretary of State "within 28 days from the commission of the criminal injury . . . or . . . such period as the Secretary of State considers reasonable having regard to all the circumstances."

(iii) If an Application for Compensation is not made –

  (a) within three months from the date on which the Notice of Intention to apply for compensation was served on the Secretary of State, "unless there was reasonable cause for not making the application within that period" and

  (b) within three years from the date on which the criminal injury was sustained.

73. CICB, *22nd Annual Report* (1985–86), para 20. See also *R v CICB, ex parte Townend* Unreported, Div'l Ct, 9 June 1970.   **74**. *Barry v Sec of State* [1984] NI 39, 44, *per* Lord Lowry LCJ.

These requirements, which follow – but go further in some respects than – the 1977 Order, are examined in detail in Chapter 6.[75]

VICTIM LIVING IN SAME HOUSEHOLD AS OFFENDER

Prior to 1988 compensation could not be awarded for most injuries arising from family violence, apparently because of the difficulty of establishing precisely what had happened, the danger of collusion and the risk that any award of compensation would benefit the offender rather than the victim.[76] Such reasoning had led to a similar exception from the original British Scheme; but in 1978 the case for a blanket exception was found less convincing and the scheme was amended to allow compensation to be awarded in certain circumstances.[77] Article 5(2) of the 1988 Order now brings the Northern Ireland scheme broadly[78] into line with that amendment:

> "No compensation shall be paid in respect of an injury which is a criminal injury by virtue of [being a violent offence[79]] . . . where the victim was, at the time when the injury was sustained, living in the same household as the person or, if more than one, any of the persons responsible for causing it[80] unless the Secretary of State is satisfied –
>
> (a) in relation to the person responsible for causing the injury . . . [81]
>
>> (i) that he has been prosecuted in connection with the injury or that there is a sufficient reason why he has not been so prosecuted; and
>>
>> (ii) that he and the victim have ceased to live in the same household and are unlikely to live in the same household again or that there are exceptional circumstances which prevent them from ceasing to live in the same household; and
>
> (b) that no person who is responsible for causing the injury will benefit from the compensation if it is paid."

One noticeable difference between this provision and that in the British Scheme is that Article 5(2) makes no separate provision for minor victims.

---

75. See below pp 296, 262 and 276 respectively.

76. See 1968 Act, s 1(3)(b); 1977 Order, Art 3(2)(b).

77. British Scheme, para 8, following the recommendation made in 1978 *IWP Report*, paras 7.1 *et seq* and discussed in Wasik, "Criminal Injuries Compensation and Family Violence" [1983] *J Soc Welf L* 100. See also 1988 Act, ss 110(5) and 112(5).

78. As discussed later in the text, the British Scheme makes separate provision for adult and minor victims. Other differences are noted below.

79. As defined in Art 2(2) – see above, pp 82–88.

80. This wording is preferred to the more straightforward term "offender" apparently because it includes a person who may not actually have inflicted the injuries – see British Scheme, para 8. But such a person will invariably also be guilty of an offence.

81. Where more than one person was responsible for causing the injury, the Secretary of State must be so satisfied in relation to *each* of those persons who, when the injury was sustained, was living in the same household as the victim.

The proposed draft of the 1988 Order did (in Article 5(2)(*c*)) contain the additional requirement that if the victim was a minor when the injury was sustained, the Secretary of State had to be satisfied "that it would not be against the victim's interests that compensation be paid". Such a provision is expressly included in the British Scheme[82] to enable the payment of compensation to be withheld e.g. "in the case of a young child where the money . . . would serve no useful purpose at the time, and if held on trust could give rise to distress and antagonism when the child [later] received the money . . . and realised, perhaps for the first time, the cause of his injury."[83] No explanation was given for the omission from the 1988 Order of an express provision to this effect; but it may be that it was thought that a minor's interests would in Northern Ireland be adequately protected by Article 14, which requires any award to a minor victim to be approved by the county court. Alternatively, it may be that the victim's interests would constitute a "relevant circumstance" which the Secretary of State must take into account by reason of Article 6(1).

We have referred so far to "family" violence, but it should be noted that Article 5(2) is not intended to be limited to cases where victim and offender are related by family ties. Rather, the test is whether they are living in the same household – a test which may be satisfied in non-family cases:

> "We regard it as just as important to guard against the offender benefiting and against collusion in the case of homosexual cohabitees and in any other situation where people are living together as members of the same household, e.g. flat-sharers."[84]

Whether this intention has been realised by the wording of Article 5(2) depends on what is meant by "living in the same household". The word "household" is not defined in the Order, but did arise for consideration in *R v CICB, ex parte Staten*.[85] Relations between a husband and wife (H and W) were bad, and H had been sent to prison for persistent cruelty to W. On his release H returned to the flat where W and their children lived. For the next 11 days H and W had no sexual relations and they slept apart; W did not clean or cook for H. But in other respects "this was a family living as a family". Then they had a quarrel and H attacked W. W's claim for compensation was refused on the ground that she was living with H as a member of the family and in the same household. Counsel for W had argued that in divorce law H and W might well have been held to have been "living apart"; but Lord Widgery CJ would have none of this:

> "I deprecate the complication which would result if the whole of the mass of learning in the divorce laws were introduced into this phrase so as to make it conform with the matrimonial law itself. I think the court should look at these words and give them their ordinary sensible meaning, and very often the

---

82. Para 8(*c*). See also 1988 Act, s 112(5) which, indeed, makes it the *only* restriction on the award of compensation to a person who was under the age of 18 when he was injured by a person living in the same household.

83. 1986 *IWP Report*, para 8.4. For criticism, see Wasik, *op cit* n 77, p 104.

84. *Ibid*, para 8.5.

85. [1972] 1 All ER 1034.

question of whether the parties are living together . . . will [as here] be a pure question of fact."[86]

The Oxford Dictionary defines "household" as "the inmates of a house collectively, an organised family, including servants and attendants, dwelling in a house; a domestic establishment."[87] Unfortunately this definition did not find favour with Lord Hailsham:

> "The trouble is that the first part of the definition would cover the inmates of any house and deprive the section [sc Housing Act 1961, s 58] of any meaning at all."

His Lordship examined various other definitions, and concluded:

> " . . . both the expression 'household' and membership of it is a question of fact and degree, there being no certain indicia the presence or absence of any of which is by itself conclusive."[88]

In most cases the position will be clear on the facts;[89] where it is not the courts may have to turn to the interpretation of "household" in matrimonial,[90] social security[91] or other[92] legislation or in other contexts.[93] But such jurisprudence must be used with great care when it comes to interpreting Article 5(2). It is, however, suggested that some observations of Sachs LJ in *Santos v Santos* may provide a useful starting point:

> " . . . the word 'house' . . . relates to something physical, but 'household', which has an abstract meaning . . . essentially refers to people held together by a particular kind of tie, even if temporarily separated . . ."[94]

---

86. *Ibid*, p 1036.

87. *Cp* Longman's *Dictionary of the English Language* (1984): "all the people who live together in a dwelling and benefit from the common housekeeping".

88. *Simmons v Pizzey* [1977] 2 All ER 432, 441–2.

89. As it was in *W v Sec of State* [1987] 10 *BNIL* 21 (applicant struck in eye during party in her home).

90. See especially Matrimonial Causes (NI) Order 1978, Art 4(6): "A husband and wife shall be treated as living apart unless they are living with each other in the same household ...". See generally Bromley and Lowe, *Family Law* (7th ed, 1987), pp 190–201 and Cretney, *Principles of Family Law* (4th ed, 1984), pp 152 *et seq*.

91. See e.g. Ogus and Barendt, *The Law of Social Security* (3rd ed, 1988), pp 355–6.

92. E.g. the Housing Act under consideration in *Simmons v Pizzey*, above.

93. E.g. insurance contracts sometimes except liability in respect of members of the insured's household. In *G v Travellers Ins Co* 112 Wis 2d 18, 331 NW 2d 643 (1983) Brown J stated that " 'Residents of a household' is a phrase designative of a relationship where persons live together as a family and deal with each other in a close, intimate and informal relationship, and not at arm's length . . . Although the intended duration of the relationship is a necessary element in deciding whether a person is a resident of a household, a showing of permanency is not required. Still, something more is required than a mere temporary sojourn . . . The subjective or declared intent of the individual, while a fact to be considered, is not controlling . . . Rather, a thorough examination of all the relevant facts and circumstances surrounding the relationship is necessary . . . ". A similar definition was adopted in the Canadian case of *Wawanesa Mutual Ins Co v Bell* (1957) 8 DLR (2d) 577, 579, *per* Rand J.

94. [1972] 2 All ER 246, 255. In *R v Birmingham Juvenile Court, ex parte N (A Minor)* [1984] 2 All ER 688, "household" (as used in the Children and Young Persons Act 1969) was said to refer to "personal content" rather than to the "topographical framework".

That tie may be "living as a family" or it may be provided by the parties sharing some kind of communal life, for example through using the same living accommodation and doing household chores for each other.[95] If the latter is indeed sufficient, then Article 5(2) is not restricted to "family" violence and may, as intended, embrace other persons living together.[96] Further, if there is a sufficiently close and permanent relationship between victim and offender, the courts may even consider, as suggested by Sachs LJ in *Santos*,[97] that the parties are living in the same household despite being temporarily separated.

If the victim and offender were living in the same household when the injury was sustained, the victim will *normally* qualify for compensation only if he ceased to do so after he sustained the injury, *and* is unlikely to live again in the same household as the offender. Thus a temporary separation after the offence will not normally suffice. It may be difficult to establish what is likely to happen in the future; much will depend, no doubt, on the stated intention of the victim. But the use of the word "unlikely" suggests that what is required is an objective assessment taking into account all the relevant circumstances.[98]

Article 5(2)(*a*)(ii) recognises, however, that it may be impracticable for victim and offender to live apart and this requirement may, therefore, be waived "in exceptional circumstances".[99] It may be noted that under the British Scheme[1] the separation requirement does not apply to minors, and it may well be that the youth of the victim is one particular circumstance to be taken into account in this context.

The bringing of a prosecution is regarded as an important safeguard in this context:

> "The identity of the assailant will be known and, where serious injury has been inflicted, the principal barrier to a successful prosecution will be the unwillingness or inability of the victim to give evidence . . . The Board should be

---

95. Both Bromley and Lowe (*op cit*, p 190) and Cretney (*op cit*, p 153) suggest the "communal life" test, by reference e.g. to *Hopes* v *Hopes* [1949] P 227. See also the case discussed in CICB, *18th Annual Report* (1981–82), para 44 (H and W in same house, but W in process of divorcing H, and both led "separate and distinct lives"; W awarded compensation for injuries inflicted by H).

96. In *R* v *CICB, ex parte Fox* Unreported, Div'l Ct, 8 Feb 1972 A, her common-law husband B, and B's brother all lived in the same house; A was assaulted by B's brother; although A had no blood or legal relationship to her assailant, compensation was refused. It has also been held that a "household", for insurance purposes, is not limited to persons related by blood or marriage – see e.g. *State Farm Mutual Auto Ins Co* v *James* 80 F 2d 802 (W Va 1936). *Cf Umbarger* v *State Farm Mutual Auto Ins Co* 218 Iowa 203, 254 NW 87 (1934) (landlady who let room to boarder not a member of same household as boarder).

97. *Supra.* See also *R* v *Birmingham Juvenile Court, ex parte N, supra.* But *cf McGregor* v *H* 1983 SLT 626.

98. See e.g. CICB, *20th Annual Report* (1983–84), para 31 (compensation refused despite wife's statement that she "fully intended" not to live with husband again).

99. *Cf* 1988 Act, s 110(5)(*b*)(ii) only requires that "circumstances" prevent the victim from ceasing to live in the same household as the offender.

1. Paragraph 8, and 1988 Act, s 112(5). The British Board has published a special leaflet on compensation in child abuse cases – see *25th Annual Report* (1988–89), Appendix E.

concerned with cases in which the victim has demonstrated that he or she regards the crime as a matter of public concern."[2]

But a prosecution is not required in all cases:

> "There would inevitably be a small number of applications where the offender could not be prosecuted although his identity was known, for example because he had absconded, committed suicide, or was of unsound mind . . . The Board should be empowered to waive this requirement, but should do so only in cases where there are practical or technical reasons why the offender could not be prosecuted or other good reasons why a prosecution was not instituted."[3]

The final requirement of Article 5(2) is that the person responsible for causing the injury will not benefit from the compensation if it is paid to the victim.[4] Once again this may be difficult to establish, but the applicant may benefit from the extensive power given to the Secretary of State by Article 13(3) of the 1988 Order to pay compensation on such terms and conditions as he thinks fit. It should be possible in many cases to pay the compensation in such a way as to prevent the offender from getting his hands on it.

SMALL CLAIMS

1. General Threshold

Article 5(13) follows a policy which has been consistently adopted since the 1968 Act[5] and provides:

> "No compensation shall be paid to any person if the amount of compensation which, but for this paragraph, would be payable is less than £400."[6]

The corresponding figure under the 1977 Order was £250.[7]

---

2. 1978 *1WP Report*, para 7.6. See also 1988 Order, Art 5(8) which requires a victim to comply with all reasonable requests for information and assistance which might lead to the identification, apprehension, prosecution and conviction of the offender. The lack of a prosecution or the failure of the applicant to assist in a prosecution is a frequent reason for the refusal of compensation in "family violence" cases in Britain – see e.g. CICB, *21st Annual Report* (1984–85), para 6.

3. *Ibid*. Note that the prosecution requirement will not apply to minor victims in Great Britain: 1988 Act, s 112(5). *Cf* Scheme, para 8(*a*).

4. This is a *general* requirement of the British Scheme – see para 7, and 1988 Act, s 112(1)(*c*).

5. The 1968 Act, s 1(3)(c) used a more complicated formula which almost immediately gave rise to difficulties in *Hanlon* v *Ministry of Home Affairs* [1970] NI 167, discussed in Miers, *Note* (1971) 22 *NILQ* 188, 190–1. As a result the present approach was adopted in the 1977 Order, Art 6(5).

6. The 1988 Order, Art 23(1) provides that the Secretary of State may by order substitute a different amount. The minimum in Great Britain is £750, but this does not apply to compensation for funeral expenses: Scheme, para 5; 1988 Act, s 114(1). In the Republic the limit is £50 – Irish Scheme, para 9.

7. 1977 Order, Art 6(5), as amended from 2 April 1982 by Criminal Injuries (Compensation) (NI) Order 1977 (Amendment) Order 1982.

The Order thus follows a general pattern in compensation schemes; small claims are invariably excluded for a variety of reasons – the loss is one an applicant can reasonably be expected to bear himself, large numbers of small cases would tend to clog the administration of the scheme and they are in any event disproportionately expensive to determine, etc.[8] The only real issue in this context is the level at which the minimum threshold is set. There is sometimes a tendency to overlook the fact that what appears to administrators to be a comparatively small sum may be very important to a person of small or modest means;[9] in theory, of course, such a person may recover compensation directly from the offender by means of a compensation order.[10] It is also suggested from time to time that the threshold is simply an encouragement to exaggerate minor claims or to raise the level of compensation, so that the overall cost of compensation is increased rather than reduced by raising the minimum requirement. Determining a fair and effective minimum limit for claims can, therefore, give rise to difficulty; the justification offered for that set in 1988 was simply that it represented roughly the current value of the original minimum established in 1968.[11]

It will be noted that Article 5(13) adopts a "threshold" and not an "excess" type of approach.[12] An applicant entitled (say) to compensation of £450 is paid £450. It would seem fairer (at least to the applicant whose compensation comes to £350 and who, therefore, is now paid nothing) for a minimum sum to be deducted from all awards, particularly if, as a consequence, the relevant sum could be reduced.

The application of the provision is not clear where an application is made on behalf of more than one person. Does the limit apply to the aggregate compensation which is payable, or must Article 5(13) be read as if "to that person" were inserted after "payable"? On the former approach, compensation is payable where £600 is to be divided equally between two applicants. On the second approach no compensation can be paid. The 1977 Order clearly adopted the second approach;[13] it would seem that the change of wording can only have been intended to indicate a preference for the first approach.

---

8. See e.g. Atiyah, *Accidents, Compensation and the Law* (4th ed, 1987), p 307; Burns, *Criminal Injuries Compensation* (1980), pp 302–5.

9. See especially HC Debs (Standing Committee F), cols 735 *et seq* (24 Feb 1987). See also Editorial, [1983] *Crim LR* 210 (increase in Great Britain minimum to £400 described as "niggardly"). A particular concern is the effect of the minimum on claims by old age pensioners – see e.g. 37 HC Debs, col 394 (22 February 1983). Ashworth, "Punishment and Compensation: Victims, Offenders and the State" (1986) 6 *Oxford J Legal Stud* 86, 122n suggested that the raising of the minimum level to £400 "arguably . . . runs counter to Article 5 of the European Convention on the Compensation of Victims of Violent Crimes . . . ".

10. See below, pp 240 *et seq*.

11. 1968 Act, s 1(3)(*c*) laid down alternative criteria – £50 or three weeks' loss of earnings. According to the consumer price index £50 in 1968 is roughly equivalent to £300 in 1988, whereas three weeks' average industrial earnings (to use the test laid down in the 1988 Order, Art 8(1)) in 1987 amounted to £600.

12. *Cf* the Proposal for the Draft 1977 Order provided for up to £350 (£100 in respect of pecuniary loss and £250 in respect of non-pecuniary loss) to be deducted from *every* award. This was changed to a "threshold" of £150 following the debate on the proposal – see 934 HC Debs, col 756 (1 July 1977).

13. By Art 6(5), "Compensation shall not be payable to . . . any person if the amount of compensation which . . . would be *so payable* . . . is less than £150."

2. Special Threshold

In addition to a general minimum requirement, a special threshold may be used to exclude small claims of a particular kind. Thus, in the British Scheme there was for a time a special (higher) threshold for "family violence" cases.[14] In Northern Ireland such a threshold has applied since 1977 in relation to compensation for pain and suffering and loss of amenities arising out of "nervous shock"; this provision has been continued by Article 5(12)(c) of the 1988 Order.[15]

UNPAID PUBLIC DEBTS

Article 13(4) of the 1988 Order continues a provision first enacted in Article 12 of the 1977 Order, which brought criminal injuries compensation within the operation of the Payments for Debt (Emergency Provisions) Act (NI) 1971.[16] This empowers the Secretary of State to divert all or part of the compensation payable to a victim or to any other person under the Order to pay off or reduce unpaid "public" debts. As applied to criminal injuries compensation payments, section 1 of the 1971 Act (as amended[17]) provides in effect:

> "Where any compensation is at any time due to any person or . . . to his spouse, by the Secretary of State, the Secretary of State may put that money or any part thereof in or towards the settlement of any sum appearing to be due by that person or his spouse –
>
> (a) to the Secretary of State or any other government department or local or public authority acting as such, or to the Exchequer or Consolidated Fund; or
>
> (b) to any government department, public or local authority or other person whatsoever in respect of –
>
> (i) any tax, duty or levy, or of any local or public rates (including water rates); or
>
> (ii) any public service; or
>
> (iii) any rent due in respect of housing accommodation; or
>
> (iv) any instalment . . . due in respect of the purchase, conversion or improvement of housing accommodation."

---

14. British Scheme (1979), para 8(b). The 1988 Act, s 114(2) provides that the Home Secretary may by order specifying "the minimum amount" of compensation "make different provision for different cases or classes of case".

15. Discussed above, pp 57–61.

16. This Act was passed as an "emergency" measure in response to a rent and rates strike organised as part of a campaign of civil disobedience: see e.g. 82 HC Debs (NI), cols 1121–73 (7 Oct 1971). Although the strike soon came to an end the Act has remained in force and can no longer be regarded as a temporary measure. Cf s 18(2) of the Act provides that it shall continue in force "until six months after the end of the period of the present emergency" as defined in the Act. See generally Debt – An Emergency Situation? (CAJ Pamphlet No 13, 1989).

17. By the Payments for Debt (Amendment) (NI) Order 1978.

The granting of this power in 1977 was justified as follows:

> "It is only fair to say that money being paid out by one government department should, in a case like this, be made to be recoverable from people who owe money to public authorities or public offices."[18]

However, it was stressed that the provision is only an enabling one, and will not be applied automatically: "One would have to look at the reasons, the size of the claim and the problems within the family." There is, however, no appeal against a decision by the Secretary of State to exercise his discretion under the Act.

A question may arise as to the priority of creditors where the applicant has unpaid public debts and has also assigned his right to apply for or receive criminal injuries compensation to another.[19] The latter would appear to have first claim to the compensation; by Article 4(3) the assignee "may be treated as an applicant for the purposes of any provision of this Order". This suggests that if an effective assignment has been made the compensation (or such part of it as may have been assigned) is no longer "due" to the assignor, and the 1971 Act is, therefore, not applicable.

In June 1990, the Secretary of State announced that "the continuation of the Act is not required by present circumstances" and that it would shortly cease to be in force.[20] However:

> "The efficient collection of public debt nevertheless remains a priority and we intend to review procedures for recovering debt owed to public bodies to establish whether further legislative provision has a role to play."

---

18. HC Debs (NI Cttee), cols 8–9 (16 Feb 1977). From 1981–2 to 1987–8 deductions under the Act from criminal injury compensation awards represented less than 4% of total deductions: 127 HC Debs, cols 394–5 (12 Feb 1988) and 128 HC Debs, cols 85–6 (22 Feb 1988).

19. See below. p 278.

20. 174 HC Debs, col 522 (20 June 1990).

4

Assessment of Compensation

INTRODUCTION

Criminal injuries compensation has traditionally been assessed on principles similar to those governing the award of damages in tort actions for personal injuries or death. But the analogy is not complete. As we saw in Chapter 1, it was widely accepted that the Grand Jury (Ireland) Act 1836 did *not* put the local authority in the position of a tortfeasor; as a result, the level of *public* compensation for criminal injuries was lower than the *private* damages then recoverable at common law or under the Fatal Accidents Acts.[1] In an attempt to remedy this situation, section 1(3) of the Criminal Injuries (Ireland) Act 1919 expressly provided that the judge's power to make a decree for such compensation as he thought just and reasonable "shall include power to make a decree for *full* compensation". This wording led the Irish Court of Appeal in *O'Connell* v *Tipperary CC*[2] to make an award of compensation on a basis more favourable to the claimants than would have been warranted under the Fatal Accidents Acts.[3] O'Connor LJ dissented from this decision, however, and it appears to have been his approach, much more closely aligned to tort principles, which was preferred by the courts in Northern Ireland.[4] By 1969, at any rate, it had come to be accepted by those courts that "the measure of compensation is now analogous to that at common law for personal injuries".[5]

Criminal injuries compensation in the Republic had until recently reached much the same point by a different route. As we have seen, the 1919 Act was regarded by the Irish Parliament as imposing too great a burden on local authorities and was therefore repealed in 1923.[6] The resulting reduction in the general level of compensation continued until 1941 when another attempt was made in relation to compensation for injured police officers to

---

1. Above, pp 17 and 21.

2. [1921] 2 IR 103.

3. The majority decided, in particular, that compensation could be awarded under the 1919 Act for grief and suffering, by way of *solatium*, directly contrary to a settled line of authority on the Fatal Accidents Acts. See Veitch, "Interests in Personality" (1972) 23 *NILQ* 423.

4. See e.g. *McCann* v *Antrim CC* (1930) 64 ILTR 31.

5. *Leppington* v *Lord Mayor etc of Belfast* Unreported, CA, 18 March 1969, *per* McVeigh LJ.

6. Above, p 28.

restate the general basis of assessment.[7] But again a new statutory formula, intended to be more favourable to claimants, led to judicial uncertainty. It was not until 1974 that the obvious solution was adopted, with the new extra-statutory scheme expressly providing that compensation was in general to be assessed "on the basis of damages awarded under the Civil Liability Acts . . . ".[8]

In so providing the Irish Scheme followed the approach adopted by the British Scheme since 1964.[9] But no such general stipulation appears in the Northern Ireland legislation; the 1988 Order, like its predecessors, is silent on this point.[10] This cannot be because the basic analogy is rejected; on the contrary it must be accepted that Parliament concurs with the approach consistently taken by the courts in Northern Ireland over the past 20 years or so. The most likely explanation appears to be that the framers of the Northern Ireland scheme have taken into consideration the effect on the level of *net* compensation which results from the fact that the *object* of criminal injuries compensation differs from that of tort damages. Thus, when introducing the 1968 Bill in the Northern Ireland House of Commons, the Minister of Home Affairs emphasised that –

> "Generally the intention is *not* that the State should be given the same liability for compensation as the offender, but that the State should so far as is reasonable ensure that the victim does not suffer undue hardship."[11]

This intention was spelled out at greater length in 1978:

> "The common law basis of assessment is . . . designed to calculate the extent of the wrongdoer's liability to his victim. This can result in damages which are more than can be reasonably justified as a payment under a Government compensation scheme, especially since other Government payments to the handicapped or incapacitated . . . are based in the main on weekly allowances which do little more than provide a modest level of income. Against this background, it might seem inequitable to provide a much higher level of compensation to victims of violent crime . . . The needs of the Scheme fit neatly neither the subsistence type of payment . . . nor damages for tort . . . [T]he common law basis of assessment comes closest to providing the

---

7. Garda Siochana (Compensation) Acts 1941 and 1945, discussed above, p 40.

8. Irish Scheme, para 6.

9. 1964 Scheme, para 10; 1990 Scheme, para 12; 1988 Act, Sch 7, para 8. See further Greer, *Criminal Injuries Compensation* (1990), ch 4. The 1978 *IWP Report* concluded (at p 44) that "The common law basis of assessment . . . has served the Scheme reasonably well over the past 13 years. It is a flexible system which permits the payment of compensation for pain and suffering to those who have not suffered such severe injuries that they are required to leave their employment; it is relatively cheap to adminis-

ter largely because lump sum payments do not give rise to any continuing administrative commitment . . ." Alternatives which have been considered include industrial injury-type benefits (rejected in 1964) and a special "criminal scale" (rejected by 1986 *IWP Report*, ch 12).

10. The 1988 Order does incorporate many of the changes in the assessment of damages introduced by the Administration of Justice Act 1982.

11. 68 HC Debs (NI), col 626 (31 Jan 1968); this statement was repeated several times during the debate. A similar statement was made in relation to the 1977 Order – see HC Debs (NI Cttee), col 97 (2 March 1977).

type of compensation which is required [but it must be subject to] . . . the limitations and modifications which . . . are reasonable in this context."[12]

Whether articulated in this or some other way,[13] the extent of the public "liability" for compensation accepted by the state in Northern Ireland – as also in Britain and the Republic – does in fact fall some way short of common law levels in a number of particular respects, which are listed below. The combined effect of these derogations is now substantial, but is not yet such as to undermine the basic analogy with tort – at least where there is an explicit statutory duty generally to apply tort principles. The *absence* of such a direction in the Northern Ireland Order may mean – and may indeed have been intended to connote – that in a situation not specifically provided for in the Order the Northern Ireland courts should not automatically apply common law principles, but attempt instead to give effect to the overall intention of the Order as a whole.[14] If this is indeed the case, then the 1988 Order has continued the uncertainty as to the general level of compensation which typified the earlier legislation on this subject.

Be that as it may, the 1988 Order follows the form of previous legislation[15] by listing the specific heads under which compensation may be awarded and then stipulating certain matters for which compensation shall *not* be awarded and yet other factors to be taken into account when making an assessment. In this latter respect the Order has much in common with the criminal injuries compensation schemes in Britain and the Republic, though important differences between these schemes have now emerged. But in general the net effect of the provisions in any of these schemes is that criminal injuries compensation differs from tort damages[16] in a number of particular respects, the more important of which may be summarised as follows:

1. There is no equivalent in criminal injuries compensation of punitive or aggravated damages. In this respect the 1988 Order appears to be identical to the British and Irish Schemes.[17]

---

12. 1978 *IWP Report*, para 10.3. The Working Party had earlier observed: " . . . in deciding how much compensation should be paid and for what purpose . . . the Government must have regard both to the total demand on the national purse and to the equitable distribution of available Government funds . . . Although it is administratively convenient to use a basis of assessment that is well tried and tested . . . the level of compensation [is] very much a matter for decision from time to time in the light of the country's resources . . . ".

13. See generally, Atiyah, *Accidents, Compensation and the Law* (4th ed, 1987), pp 293 et seq.

14. As indicated by Lord Parker CJ in *R v CICB, ex parte Lain* [1967] 2 All ER 770, 776: "... paragraphs 9–13 *inclusive* must be read together as forming *the code* by which compensation is to be assessed . . . " (emphasis added).

15. Originally adopted in the New Zealand Criminal Injuries Compensation Act 1963, s 18(1). The 1968 Act followed this Act in a number of respects. The heads of compensation are not listed in either the British or the Irish Scheme.

16. See generally Kemp and Kemp, *The Quantum of Damages* (rev ed 1975), vol 1 (hereafter referred to as *"Kemp and Kemp"*); McGregor, *The Law of Damages* (15th ed, 1988)(*"McGregor"*); Munkman, *Damages for Personal Injuries and Death* (8th ed, 1989) (*"Munkman"*) and White, *The Irish Law of Damages for Personal Injury and Death* (1989) (*"White"*).

17. See further below, p 159.

2. In many cases criminal injuries compensation may be refused or reduced on account of the conduct of the victim before, at the time of or even after the injury. These provisions extend far beyond the scope of the common law defences of contributory negligence, *volenti non fit injuria* and *ex turpi causa* – and the 1988 Order goes further in this respect than either the British or Irish Scheme.[18]

3. Criminal injuries compensation for pecuniary loss is limited in certain cases. The 1988 Order imposes a ceiling on awards for loss of earnings unless the criminal injury was caused "by a person acting on behalf of or in connection with an unlawful association". No such limit is imposed in common law claims or under the Fatal Accidents legislation. On this point criminal injuries compensation in Northern Ireland comes somewhere between the British Scheme (where such a limit applies in all cases) and the Irish Scheme (where there is no such limit at all).[19]

4. Most "collateral benefits" are fully deducted from criminal injuries compensation; as a result of recent developments (in particular, Article 24 of the Social Security (NI) Order 1989) tort damages are moving in this direction, but the principle of non-deductibility still has greater application than in relation to criminal injuries compensation. Although all three compensation schemes adopt a common policy in this respect, the 1988 Order now specifies in greater detail than the other schemes what is to be deducted – but unlike those schemes provides for the effects of deduction to be offset in some cases by means of a "discretionary" payment.[20]

5. Proceedings for criminal injuries compensation cannot be continued on behalf of the estate in the event of the victim's death; but limited provision is made for the payment of compensation where certain expenses have been incurred or pecuniary loss sustained between the time of injury and the death of the victim.[21]

6. There are now a number of particular provisions affecting the assessment of criminal injuries compensation which have no equivalent at common law or under the Fatal Accidents legislation. For example:

(a) Fixed compensation can now be awarded for certain consequences of rape, as opposed to the more flexible (and probably more generous) common law rule.[22]

(b) A restriction is placed on the payment of compensation for loss of profits in certain death cases where damages therefor would be recoverable under the Fatal Accidents legislation.[23]

(c) Compensation for nervous shock is more restricted than under the common law as laid down by the House of Lords in *McLoughlin* v *O'Brian*.[24]

---

18. See generally, Chapter 3 above.

19. See further below, p 173.

20. Discussed below, pp 203 *et seq.*

21. See below, pp 201–3.

22. See below, pp 164–5.

23. See below, p 196.

24. Discussed above, pp 58–61, 76–7.

(d) A minimum threshold for compensation is imposed which has no equivalent at common law.[25]

(e) Unlike common law, future expenses are recoverable only if they result "directly" from the victim's injury or death *and* it is "reasonable and proper" to pay them out of public funds.[26]

(f) The award of compensation may be made on such terms and conditions as the Secretary of State thinks fit.[27]

GENERAL PRINCIPLES OF ASSESSMENT

1. Finality

Criminal injuries compensation is payable in a lump sum and follows the traditional common law rule of assessment on a "once and for all" basis.[28] Thus, in *MacDonald v Secretary of State*[29] an applicant was awarded compensation in 1972 for eye injuries sustained as the result of an assault. Some three years later, his eyesight unexpectedly deteriorated as a result of the injury and he applied to the county court for a review of his award. The county court judge held that he had no power to conduct such a review. A limited power to re-open an award was introduced into the British Scheme in 1979,[30] but a parliamentary request to have a similar provision inserted into the Northern Ireland legislation was rejected.[31] Hence the 1988 Order now provides in Article 16(1) that, apart from the applicant's right of appeal, a determination of compensation is "in all respects final and binding".

However, several qualifications of this principle – and some practical considerations – should be taken into account.

(i) In a new provision, Article 12(5) provides that the once and for all principle does not apply to a notice of determination issued by the Secretary of State where, shortly after service of the notice, it appears to him that the determination should be cancelled or varied under Articles 5(9), 6(1) or

---

25. Discussed above, p 146.

26. See below, p 161.

27. See below, pp 158 and 308.

28. See also Irish Scheme, para 2: "There will be no appeal against or review of a final decision of the Tribunal." *Cf* British Scheme, para 13: "Although the Board's decision in a case will normally be final, they will have a discretion to reconsider a case after a final award of compensation . . . where there has been a serious change in the applicant's medical condition . . . ".

29. Unreported, Cty Ct (Judge Watt), 25 Jan 1977.

30. British Scheme, para 13 (quoted above n 28), following a recommendation in the 1978

1WP Report, para 4.6. Interestingly, the Working Party was prepared to depart from the common law principle because "the case for finality is not so strong when compensation is being paid from Government funds." See also 1988 Act, s 111(10). For an example of the use of this power in circumstances similar to *MacDonald*, see CICB, *19th Annual Report* (1982–83), para 36. See further Greer, *op cit* n 9, paras 4.07–4.15.

31. See 3 HC Debs, cols 626–632 (27 April 1981). The Minister of State observed that the Northern Ireland scheme "is very much court-based" and should therefore adhere to a fundamental principle of assessment developed by the courts. He further pointed to the serious practical difficulties which a system of review would entail.

9(6). In such circumstances he may cancel or vary his original determination by serving the appropriate notice on the applicant, but must do so within 10 weeks from the service of the original determination and before the applicant signs a discharge or lodges a notice of appeal.[32]

(ii) By Article 13(1), the Secretary of State "may . . . make one or more payments on account of the compensation payable . . . ".[33] This power to make interim payments enables an applicant to obtain part-compensation at an early date and indeed can, in some cases, enable an applicant to put off a "final" assessment for some time:

> "Where a claimant indicates that he or she does not wish to prejudice the claim by reaching an agreed settlement before a medical condition stabilises, the claim can, within a reasonable length of time, be held in abeyance and, pending settlement, interim payments will be made so far as possible."[34]

This power can in theory be used quite extensively in cases where, at the time when the application is being considered, entitlement is clear, but there is uncertainty as to the applicant's medical condition, present or future. Indeed, in Britain before 1979, the Criminal Injuries Compensation Board made "permanent" interim awards in cases where it accepted that what was then a relatively minor injury could have serious effects in the future – e.g. where injury to an eye could result in sympathetic ophthalmia.[35] But this practice cannot be used where the applicant's condition deteriorates in a way which was not foreseen while his application was being considered.[36] Interim awards may also be used where there is some *legal* uncertainty as to the scope or assessment of the compensation to be awarded.[37] Experience suggests however that the Secretary of State is in practice rather cautious and makes interim payments in fewer cases than might have been expected.[38]

(iii) Changes which occur in the claimant's condition during the period allowed for lodging and hearing an appeal may be taken into account by the

---

32. See further below, pp 307–8. There is no equivalent provision in the Irish Scheme.

33. See also to the same effect the British Scheme, para 12 (and the 1988 Act, s 111(7)). The Irish Scheme, para 8 similarly provides that "Compensation will be by way of a lump sum payment . . . but it will be open to the Tribunal to make an interim award and to postpone making a final award in a case in which a final medical assessment of the injury is delayed."

34. 3 HC Debs, col 630 (27 April 1981).

35. 1978 *IWP Report*, para 4.6 – the interim award was treated "for all purposes as a final award unless the particular risk develops." Used in this way, interim awards can achieve much the same function as "provisional damages", one of the innovations introduced into the common law by the Administration of

Justice Act 1982 (Sch 6, para 10) which has not been extended to criminal injuries compensation in Northern Ireland, or (as yet) in Great Britain – but see 1988 Act, Sch 7, para 3.

36. Thus making an express power of review necessary, according to the 1978 *IWP Report*, para 4.6.

37. E.g. the British Board made interim awards in a number of cases from Scotland pending guidance from the Scottish courts on the method of assessing damages for "loss of society" introduced by the Damages (Scotland) Act 1976 – see e.g. CICB, *16th Annual Report* (1979–80), para 23. Final awards were made when the matter was resolved by the decision in *Dingwall v Walter Alexander & Sons (Midland) Ltd* 1982 SC 179.

38. See further p 302.

court[39] – and indeed, the court itself may adjourn the hearing of the appeal if final medical reports are not available.[40] Alternatively, as a result of section 22 of the Interpretation Act (NI) 1954,[41] the court appears to have the same power as the Secretary of State to make an interim award pending clarification of the applicant's medical condition, or for any other reason.

(iv) If all else fails, the applicant can try to persuade the Northern Ireland Office to make an *ex gratia* award.[42]

2. Lump Sum Payment

The fact that common law damages have traditionally been paid in a single lump sum was another reason for adopting the tort model for criminal injuries compensation:

> "It is relatively cheap to administer largely because lump sum payments do not give rise to any continuing administrative commitment . . . "[43]

In addition there is a feeling that a system of periodic payments, even of the limited type recommended by the Pearson Commission,[44] might "tend to destroy initiative and produce a lack of incentive towards rehabilitation".[45] Article 13(1) of the 1988 Order, therefore, re-enacts earlier provisions that, subject to the power to make interim awards, "compensation shall be a lump sum". However, the award is not a global one; Article 12(4) requires the Secretary of State to specify the amount of compensation being paid under four separate heads:

(a) pecuniary loss

(b) expenses

(c) bereavement, and

(d) other matters.[46]

---

39. In the county court the appeal takes the form of a full rehearing of the application (see e.g. *Fair Employment Agency* v *Craigavon BC* [1980] 7 NIJB), but a change in the applicant's condition may now amount to a "new matter" requiring compliance with Art 16(4) of the 1988 Order (see below, p 318). For appeals to the Court of Appeal see RSC (NI) 1981, 059, r 10(2) and see generally *McGregor*, paras 1437–1444. *Cf Dalton* v *Minister for Finance* [1989] ILRM 519.

40. "A judge may adjourn any proceedings for such period as will in his opinion best meet the ends of justice . . . ": County Courts (NI) Order 1980, Art 8(4).

41. "Where an enactment provides that an appeal against any decision or determination of a court, tribunal, authority or person (in this section called "the original tribunal") may be brought to any court, that court . . . may, for all purposes of and incidental to hearing or determining the appeal,

exercise all the powers, authority and jurisdiction of the original tribunal . . . ".

42. As e.g. (for a different reason) was ultimately granted in the *O'Hare* case – see below, p 189.

43. 1978 *1WP Report*, para 10.1.

44. *Pearson Report*, paras 555-611. See also Atiyah, *Accidents, Compensation and the Law* (4th ed, 1987), pp 150–162.

45. CICB, *14th Annual Report* (1977–78), para 54. *Cp* 1988 Act, Sch 7, para 14(1)(d) empowers the Secretary of State to "specify cases in which compensation is not to be paid as a lump sum and how it is to be paid in any such case."

46. *Cf* practice in common law cases in England and Wales – see e.g. *Kemp and Kemp*, para 1–006. *Cf* Irish practice as laid down in *Sexton* v *O'Keeffe* [1966] IR 204 and *McArdle* v *McCaughey Bros Ltd* [1968] IR 47, discussed in *White*, pp 107–8.

This itemisation is important for purposes of other provisions of the 1988 Order[47] and, as in common law damages cases, also assists an applicant in reaching a decision as to whether or not to lodge an appeal.

At common law the general rule is that provided the damages are assessed on a correct basis "it can be of no concern to the court to consider any question as to the use that will thereafter be made of the money awarded".[48] However special rules have long existed in relation to damages awarded to minors or patients.[49] Special provision for such persons is also contained in the 1988 Order,[50] but Article 13(3) further provides:

> "Compensation may be paid on such terms and conditions as the Secretary of State thinks fit as to the payment, disposal, allotment or apportionment of the compensation to the victim or his relatives, or any of them, or to any other person."

This provision appears to reflect a decision that what a successful applicant may do with compensation from public funds *is* of concern to the Secretary of State.[51] Thus, it is apt to empower the Secretary of State e.g. to require that compensation paid for private medical treatment is indeed applied to that purpose, to pay compensation to trustees where an applicant does not seem capable of handling a large sum of money, or to make appropriate arrangements where there appears to be a possibility that an offender might benefit from the payment of compensation to his victim.

3. Time of Assessment

Criminal injuries compensation is assessed on the basis of the applicant's position at the date of the determination or court hearing. As with common law damages, the Court (or the Secretary of State) will not "speculate where it knows".[52] Thus, the starting point for calculating an applicant's loss of future earnings is what the applicant would have been earning, but for his injury, at the date of the assessment.[53] This principle also applies to matters of law; should e.g. the common law "change" between the notice of determination and the hearing of the appeal, it is the law as laid down at the latter date which is applied by the court.[54]

---

47. See especially p 187 below.

48. *Per* Lord Morris in *H West & Son v Shephard* [1963] 2 All ER 625, 633.

49. See e.g. *Kemp and Kemp*, ch 18.

50. Article 14, discussed below, p 311.

51. See e.g. 1978 *1WP Report*, paras 10.4 and 18.2. Under the Irish Scheme (para 31) the Tribunal is empowered to make "any arrangements which it considers desir-able" for the administration of its awards.

52. *Per* Harman LJ in *Curwen v James* [1963] 2 All ER 619, 623. See also *McCann v Sheppard* [1973] 2 All ER 881 (P died before hearing of appeal).

53. *Graham v Dodds* [1983] NI 22, discussed below, p 172.

54. See e.g. *McGregor*, paras 1835–6.

4. Exemplary and Aggravated Damages

Section 4(2)(*a*) of the 1968 Act specifically provided that "No compensation shall be awarded by way of exemplary or vindictive damages, or by way of aggravated damages". The 1988 Order, like that of 1977, contains no such provision; but the same result appears to be achieved by the wording of Article 3(2) which omits these matters from the particular heads under which "compensation shall only be payable . . . ".

As regards exemplary (or punitive or vindictive) "damages", the 1988 Order in this respect follows a decision taken as far back as 1920[55] and consistently followed thereafter, not only in Northern Ireland, but also in Britain[56] and the Republic.[57] Since *Rookes* v *Barnard*,[58] of course, such damages can in any case be awarded at common law only in exceptional cases. However, one of these permits exemplary damages to be awarded in tort where government servants have been guilty of "oppressive, arbitrary or unconstitutional action". This exception can apply to torts committed by police officers or other members of the security forces, which are also crimes of violence.[59] The victim of improper police or army conduct may, therefore, have the option of suing in tort or claiming criminal injuries compensation. The availability of exemplary damages (and the less attention paid to his own conduct) suggest that in some cases at least he would be better advised to sue in tort.

The distinction between exemplary damages (which are punitive) and aggravated damages (which are compensatory) was explained by the House of Lords in *Rookes* v *Barnard*.[60] Aggravated damages may be awarded in tort in order to –

> "take into account the motives and conduct of the defendant where they aggravate the injury done to the plaintiff. There may be malevolence or spite or the manner of committing the wrong may be such as to injure the plaintiff's proper feelings of dignity and pride."[61]

A particularly relevant case is *W* v *Meah*[62] where two women claimed damages for personal injury in consequence of vicious sexual attacks on them by the defendant. In W's case, Woolf J awarded damages of £6,750,

---

55. *Worthington* v *Tipperary CC* [1920] 2 IR 233; *O'Connell* v *Tipperary CC* [1921] 2 IR 103.

56. British Scheme, para 14(*b*), for the reason (according to 1978 *1WP Report*, para 11.5) that: "No useful purpose would be served by requiring the State to make payments analogous to [exemplary damages] . . . ". This decision had originally been made *before* *Rookes* v *Barnard* was decided – see *Compensation for Victims of Crimes of Violence* (Cmnd 1406, 1961), paras 49, 129. See also 1988 Act, Sch 7, para 8.

57. Irish Scheme, para 6(*a*).

58. [1964] 1 All ER 367, discussed e.g.

McGregor, paras 406 *et seq*. For the "broader doctrine" in Irish law, see *White*, pp 8–16.

59. See e.g. *Lavery* v *Ministry of Defence* [1984] NI 99; *Walsh* v *Ministry of Defence* [1985] NI 62; *George* v *Metropolitan Police Comm'r The Times*, 21 March 1984; *Connor* v *Chief Constable of Cambridgeshire The Times*, 11 April 1984. See generally Clayton and Tomlinson, *Civil Actions against the Police* (1987), pp 343–7.

60. [1964] 1 All ER 367, especially pp 407–414, *per* Lord Devlin.

61. *Ibid*, p 407, *per* Lord Devlin.

62. [1986] 1 All ER 935, discussed below p 223.

including an (unspecified) award of aggravated damages in respect of five particularly "aggravating" features. An award of £10,250 to the second plaintiff likewise took certain aggravating factors into account.

The *express* exclusion of such damages by the 1968 Act may have represented a change from the pre-existing criminal injuries code[63] and at the time marked a point of departure from the British Scheme.[64] However, the change to an *implied* exclusion in the 1977 Order and again in the 1988 Order may mean that there is room for uncertainty. Thus, it is possible that some at least of the "aggravating" factors in *Meah* could have been taken into account in a claim for criminal injuries compensation under what is now Article 3(2)(*a*)(iv), i.e. "pain and suffering and loss of amenities". This indeed was the opinion expressed in Britain by the Interdepartmental Working Party:

> "We do not feel that the concept of aggravated damages is in general applicable to crimes of violence, which are always outrageous, where a degree of ill-will is always involved, and where mental distress is bound to be caused to some extent. We consider that elements of pain and suffering should and do take into account implicitly the injury to the victim's feelings and that it is therefore unnecessary for awards of compensation by the Board to allow for such injury explicitly."[65]

However, the Working Party did wish to make an exception "for offences where injury to feelings caused by an abhorrent act might be of much greater importance than any actual physical or mental injuries" and made specific reference to rape cases in this context. The level of criminal injuries compensation for rape has been criticised as being on the low side[66] and it may be that the solution suggested by the Working Party is one that might be adopted. Another possibility is suggested by Article 6(1) which provides that in determining the amount of compensation payable to an applicant, "the Secretary of State shall have regard to all such circumstances as are relevant . . . ". It has already been held that relevant circumstances of an exculpatory nature may be taken into account under this provision[67] and it seems a comparatively short step to add that "aggravating factors" such as a particularly vicious attack can also be considered in determining the appropriate compensation to be paid.

The Order establishes three classes of case for compensation:

(a) where the victim survives;

(b) where the victim dies as a result of his injuries, and

(c) where the victim dies otherwise than as a result of his injuries.

---

63. Cf *O'Connell* v *Tipperary CC* [1921] 2 1R 103, discussed Miers, "Compensating Policemen for Criminal Injuries" (1972) 7 *IJ* 241, 249–50. The Irish Scheme, para 6(*a*) now expressly excludes aggravated damages.

64. British Scheme (1964), para 11(*b*).

65. 1986 *IWP Report*, para 14.8.

66. See e.g. Temkin, *Rape and the Legal Process* (1987), p 203.

67. *McDaid* v *Ministry of Home Affairs* NIJB, May 1973, discussed above, p 116.

Compensation for Personal Injury

Where a victim survives a criminal injury, compensation is payable under Article 3(2) of the 1988 Order in respect of –

1. Expenses

    (a) Incurred by the victim.

    (b) Incurred by any person responsible for the maintenance of the victim.

2. Pecuniary loss

    (a) Incurred by the victim.

    (b) Incurred by any person responsible for the maintenance of the victim.

3. Pain and suffering and loss of amenities suffered by the victim.

Expenses

1. Incurred by the Victim

Article 3(2)(*a*)(i) allows the award of compensation to the victim in respect of –

    (a) Expenses actually and reasonably incurred as a result of his injury, and

    (b) Any other expenses resulting directly from his injury which it is reasonable and proper to make good to him out of public funds.[68]

Such expenses include the cost of medical treatment, nursing, special appliances to assist the victim, replacing ruined clothing,[69] domestic help,[70] altering a house or modifying a car to suit a now handicapped victim,[71] the cost of a holiday for convalescence,[72] etc. In deciding which expenses are

---

68. This replicates 1977 Order, Art 5(1)(*a*) and (*d*). The Irish Scheme contains no specific provisions relating to expenses, but the application form refers only to "out-of-pocket expenses resulting directly from the injuries", such as the cost of medical treatment and medicines. This suggests that common law principles are not applied: *cf White*, ch 5.

69. See e.g. *Blair* v *Sec of State* [1989] 2 *BNIL* 18 (£140 awarded for loss through damage to clothing). Under the former British Scheme, para 17 compensation was payable for loss of or damage to clothing and other personal adjuncts arising from the injury. The 1986 *IWP Report*, paras 17.1–17.3 recommended that compensation should remain payable for "personal

adjuncts" (e.g. spectacles, dentures and hearing aids), but not for lost or damaged clothing – a recommendation bitterly opposed in Parliament but ultimately implemented in the 1990 Scheme, para 17. See also 1988 Act, s 111(3). Compensation for damage to clothing or to personal effects is not payable under the Irish Scheme.

70. As e.g. in *Wootten* v *Sec of State* Unreported, Cty Ct (Judge Higgins), 7 June 1974.

71. See e.g. *McCavera* v *Sec of State* Unreported, Cty Ct (Judge Brown), 11 Jan 1980; *Roberts* v *Johnstone* [1988] 3 WLR 1247.

72. See e.g. *Munkman*, pp 80–84.

reasonable, guidance can be obtained from decisions on damages at common law where expenses reasonably incurred can likewise be recovered.[73] There are, however, some particular points to notice.

1. The expenses must be incurred "as a result of" the criminal injury. Although this requirement will be clear enough in most cases, it is not free from doubt, particularly since Article 3(2)(a)(i) appears to require a distinction to be drawn between certain expenses which "result" from the injury and others which "result directly" from it. The question appears to be one of causation, not foreseeability – but issues of remoteness cannot be ignored. A good example is provided by *Meah* v *McCreamer*[74] where P suffered brain damage in a road accident caused by D's negligence. The brain damage changed P's personality and some three years after the accident he sexually assaulted and maliciously wounded three women, and was sentenced to life imprisonment. It was held that P could recover damages in respect of the imprisonment from D, but that D was not liable to P's victims. As regards causation, Woolf J stated:

> "If it can be shown on the balance of probabilities that but for the accident and the injuries the plaintiff suffered as a result, he would not have committed the crimes referred to . . . and, therefore, would not be now serving a sentence of life imprisonment . . . the plaintiff is . . . entitled to be compensated for that . . ."[75]

Woolf J went on to state that he had to consider the case not on the basis of any issue of public policy or remoteness of damage, but as a question of fact on the basis of the medical evidence. Given the difference in wording between the two limbs of Article 3(2)(a)(i), this would appear logically to be the correct approach to the first limb – but it is always difficult to exclude policy considerations from decisions on causation. In *Steinberg* v *Secretary of State*[76] S was shot and injured in an attack on him at his home in February 1977. When he was released from hospital he was "very nervous" about a further attack. In April 1977 he decided to leave Northern Ireland and go to live in England. His claim for various expenses arising from this move was rejected; these expenses did not result from the original injury. Had S sustained "nervous shock" as a result of the incident, the expenses could have arisen "as a result of" that injury; but although S was very nervous and upset, he had not suffered nervous shock. His Honour Judge Johnson QC also justified his decision by observing:

> "If Mr Steinberg is entitled . . . to recover the expenses arising from his move to England any person who has been the subject of a terrorist attack and is

---

73. See generally *Kemp and Kemp*, para 5-008, *McGregor*, paras 1497 *et seq* and *White*, ch 5. See also Noble, Fanshawe and Hellyer, *Special Damages for Disability* (2nd ed, 1988) which provides a practical "check-list" to assist the formulation of claims.

74. *(No 1)* [1985] 1 All ER 367 (P entitled to damages for imprisonment from D) and *(No*

2) [1986] 1 All ER 943 (D not liable to victims raped by P).

75. [1985] 1 All ER 367, 371.

76. Unreported, Cty Ct (Judge Johnson), 16 March 1979. See also *Walker* v *Mullen, The Times*, 19 Jan 1984 (loss of earnings by father who stayed in England when his son was injured not recoverable as too remote).

nervous of continuing to live in Northern Ireland could allege he was suffering from nervous shock and move elsewhere, claiming compensation for the resulting expense . . . "

Much the same reasoning would apply in a case where e.g. a person is injured in a terrorist incident and is advised by the police to change his home or his job. Although it may be difficult to allocate his expenses to one or the other, it seems that he is entitled to compensation only in respect of those expenses which result from the injury itself.[77]

2. The first limb of Article 3(2)(a)(i) is limited to expenses "actually . . . incurred . . . ". This suggests expenses which can be shown to have already been incurred, and not "future" expenses.[78] Such expenses are apparently recoverable under the second limb of this sub-paragraph;[79] but that provision is narrower than the first limb and the common law in that the expenses must result "directly" from the injury and it must be "reasonable and proper" to pay them out of public funds. No explanation appears to have been given of the scope of either restriction.

3. Common law damages are governed by section 3(4) of the Law Reform (Miscellaneous Provisions) Act (NI) 1948 which provides that "there shall be disregarded, in determining the reasonableness of any expenses, the possibility of avoiding those expenses or part of them by taking advantage of facilities available under the Health Services Act (NI) 1948 or of any corresponding facilities in Great Britain". This subsection formerly applied both to claims for damages and to claims for criminal injuries compensation,[80] but its application to the latter was repealed by the 1968 Act.[81]

---

77. But cf 1978 1WP Report, para 10.10: "We considered the circumstances where a victim feels the need to move house because of the association between the house or the area and the crime, or incurs expenses in rehabilitating himself, for example in learning a new occupation. We concluded that such matters should be taken into account in assessing compensation for pain and suffering and loss of earnings, and that no special provision was necessary."

78. See e.g. Mayor etc of West Ham v Grant (1888) 40 Ch D 331, 336, where Kay J held that by the phrase "where any local authority have incurred expenses . . ." in the Public Health Act 1875, "the legislature deliberately intended not to make the estimated, but only the actual, expenses [payable] . . . ". See also O'Hare v Sec of State [1974] NI 214, discussed below, p 189.

79. Logically expenses not "actually and reasonably incurred" could be recovered as "other expenses" under the second limb of Art 3(2)(a)(i), but it is difficult to conceive of any actual but not reasonable expenses, or reasonable but not actual expenses, which it would still be reasonable and proper to make good out of public funds. The second limb of

this paragraph must therefore be intended to apply to future expenses which are clearly recoverable, in appropriate cases, at common law and have indeed been awarded in criminal injuries compensation cases – see e.g. Wootten v Sec of State Unreported, Cty Ct (Judge Higgins), 7 June 1974; McCavera v Sec of State, Unreported, Cty Ct (Judge Brown), 11 Jan 1980.

80. By s 3(6)(a) of the 1948 Act.

81. 1968 Act, s 13 and Sch 2. See also 1986 1WP Report, para 18.1: "The means by which the State provides for medical treatment is the National Health Service." Repeal in relation to the common law was proposed in the Pearson Report, paras 341–2: "If a plaintiff decides to seek private treatment for his injuries when the same treatment would have been equally available under the National Health Service, we do not think that the defendant can reasonably be expected to meet the cost." But the recommendation that damages for private medical expenses should only be recoverable if reasonably incurred on medical grounds has not been implemented – see especially 9 HC Debs, col 461 (30 July 1981) (Solicitor-General stated that 1948 Act will not be repealed).

The subsequent repeal of the 1968 Act does not revive that provision[82] and therefore if a victim now chooses private medical treatment where similar treatment is available under the National Health Service, such expenses may be disallowed as not "reasonable".[83] It is also not clear whether the issue is determined solely by medical considerations; it may be reasonable e.g. for a police officer to opt for private medical treatment on security grounds.

If the victim does make use of either private or National Health Service facilities, any savings attributable to his maintenance there may be deducted from his compensation for loss of earnings.[84]

4. Article 5(14) follows earlier legislation by providing that –

> "where the criminal injury is directly attributable to a sexual offence and, as a result of the offence, the victim gives birth to a child, no compensation shall be paid in respect of the maintenance of that child."[85]

This provision, which is also to be found in the British[86] and Irish[87] Schemes, was originally justified on three grounds: first, the welfare state makes provision by way of various grants for the mother and child; secondly, the mother can have the child fostered or adopted, and thirdly, it avoids the possibility of fraudulent claims.[88] More recently the rationale of this exclusion has been explained as follows:

> "Certainly the birth of the child may be a consequence of a crime of violence, but for the Scheme to accept full responsibility for the upkeep of the child until it reaches economic independence would be tantamount to accepting that the whole life of the child was attributable to the original crime. There is a logic to that, but it raises the same difficulty of general public policy as has prevented the courts from accepting unequivocally that the birth of a child is a disaster for which the mother must be compensated."[89]

This reasoning is not satisfactory,[90] except in so far as it asserts that the rule against compensation results from public policy, presumably to limit the liability of the taxpayer. The weakness of their argument led the Inter-

---

82. Interpretation Act (NI) 1954, s 38(2).

83. *Cp* British Scheme, para 18, and 1988 Act, Sch 7, para 9: "In assessing compensation no account shall be taken of any expenses incurred in respect of private medical treatment unless the Board are satisfied that such treatment is or was essential . . . ". In the absence of any statutory provision in Ireland along the lines of the 1948 Act or otherwise, *White* (p 231) suggests that the approach there would be similar to that suggested in the text as appropriate in Northern Ireland. But note that compensation has been held payable in Northern Ireland for the cost of private school education – *Nicholson* v *Sec of State*, Unreported, Cty Ct (Judge Russell), 20 Dec 1982.

84. See below, p 171.

85. 1968 Act, s 4(2)(*b*); 1977 Order, Art 6(6).

86. British Scheme, para 10. No equivalent provision is included in the 1988 Act, but it is implicit in s 111(6).

87. Irish Scheme, para 6(*b*).

88. 68 HC Debs (NI), cols 1237–9 (14 Feb 1968). This reasoning was criticised as putting pressure on the mother to have an abortion or to have the baby adopted, but an amendment to delete the provision was defeated.

89. 1986 *IWP Report*, para 10.3, apparently referring to *Udale* v *Bloomsbury AHA* [1983] 2 All ER 522, which has, however, since been overruled by the Court of Appeal – see e.g. *Thake* v *Maurice* [1986] 1 All ER 497.

90. Damages for (*inter alia*) the cost of upkeep of the child to the age of 17 were awarded in *Thake* v *Maurice, supra*. See also *Meah* v *McCreamer* (*No 2*) [1986] 1 All ER 943, 950, *per* Woolf J.

departmental Working Party in Britain to recommend a limited provision for compensation in such cases,[91] and that recommendation, as originally introduced in the Criminal Justice Bill 1987 (and now to be found in paragraph 10 of the British Scheme and in section 111(6) of the 1988 Act), is contained in Article 3(2)(*a*)(v), which provides for the payment of compensation for "certain consequences" of rape. These are specified in Article 9, as follows:

> "(1) Compensation shall be payable by virtue of Article 3(2)(*a*)(v) only where –
>
> > (*a*) the victim has sustained a criminal injury directly attributable to rape;[92]
> >
> > (*b*) the victim has given birth to a child conceived as a result of the rape, and
> >
> > (*c*) the victim intends to keep the child."

Where these three conditions are satisfied, a fixed sum of £5,000[93] is payable under Article 9(2), though this sum may be reduced on account of provocative or negligent behaviour of the victim, or by reason of her criminal record.[94]

2. Expenses incurred by any Person responsible for the Maintenance of the Victim

By Article 3(2)(*b*)(i), where the victim of a criminal injury survives, compensation is payable to "any person responsible for the maintenance of the victim" in respect of "expenses actually and reasonably incurred as a result of the victim's injury".

The main issue here is as to the meaning of "responsible for the maintenance of the victim". This phrase, also used in the 1968 Act and in the 1977

---

91. " . . . it would be appropriate for the Scheme to recognise, in a more limited way, the difficulties faced by a woman who bears a child conceived as a result of rape . . . In such cases the award should be increased by a fixed sum . . . " (para 10.5).

92. Presumably as defined in the Sexual Offences (NI) Order 1978, Art 3. It may be noted that Art 3(2)(*a*) of the 1988 Order is drafted inconsistently with Art 2(2), which defines a criminal injury as an injury directly attributable to a criminal offence, which is expressly stated to include rape. Presumably para (*a*) must be read to mean that the victim has sustained an injury directly attributable to rape. Violence as such does not seem to be required (by Art 2(2) rape is *per se* a violent offence) and the pregnancy itself constitutes an injury; there is therefore no need for the

victim to prove any other "impairment of her physical or mental condition" – although, of course, if she does, additional compensation is payable for such injuries.

93. A figure which "takes into account the sums awarded in damages in what appeared to be the most comparable cases in the civil courts – for example, when a woman had sued for an unexpected pregnancy following a sterilisation operation which had not worked." HC Debs (Standing Cttee H), col 362 (1 March 1988). *Cf* damages of £6,677 were awarded in *Thake* v *Maurice, supra* n 89. By Art 23(1) a different amount may by order be substituted by the Secretary of State.

94. See above, pp 118 *et seq.* This also appears to be the case under the British Scheme, para 6(*c*) – and see also the 1988 Act, s 112(2).

Order,[95] is not defined in the Order, but it would appear that the person must be under an obligation, by law or contract, to maintain the victim, or at least have accepted a continuing responsibility for the victim's maintenance (e.g. a son who looks after an elderly father). But "responsible" does not seem appropriate to include the position of a person, even if a relative, who chooses voluntarily to look after the victim. In such a case compensation for the value of the relative's services is payable directly to the victim; as Megaw LJ stated in *Donnelly* v *Joyce*:

> "The loss *is* the plaintiff's loss. The question from what source the plaintiff's needs have been met, the question who has paid the money or given the services, the question whether or not the plaintiff is or is not under a legal or moral liability to repay, are, so far as the defendant and his liability are concerned, all irrelevant. The plaintiff's loss . . . is not the expenditure of money . . . to pay for the nursing attention. His loss is the existence of the need for . . . those nursing services, the value of which for purposes of damages – for the purpose of the ascertainment of the amount of his loss – is the proper and reasonable cost of supplying [that need]."[96]

In *Donnelly* v *Joyce* the loss was in fact suffered by the infant plaintiff's mother – obviously a person responsible for her son's maintenance. But the principle is also applicable in other, less clear cases.[97] However, where such compensation is recovered by the victim of a criminal injury himself, it may, unlike common law damages,[98] be subject to "such terms and conditions as the Secretary of State thinks fit as to the payment . . . or apportionment of the compensation to the victim or his relatives . . . or to any other person".[99] In this way compensation for certain expenses or pecuniary loss actually incurred by a person not technically responsible for the victim's maintenance may nonetheless be payable to such person.

If the victim was a resident in an institution, the authority running the institution and so responsible for his maintenance may come within the meaning of "person", for section 37(1) of the Interpretation Act (NI) 1954 provides:

> "Words in an enactment importing . . . persons . . . shall include male or female persons, corporations (whether aggregate or sole) and unincorporated bodies of persons."[1]

---

95. 1968 Act, s 1(1)(*b*); 1977 Order, Art 3(1)(*b*). See also Irish Scheme, para 3(*b*). It does not appear in the British Scheme.

96. [1973] 3 All ER 475, 480. See also *Cunningham* v *Harrison* [1973] 3 All ER 463.

97. See e.g. *Housecroft* v *Burnett* [1986] 1 All ER 332, 342, *per* O'Connor LJ (principle applicable where needs of plaintiff supplied by relative or friend out of love or affection). *Cf* in *McCavera* v *Sec of State* Unreported, Cty Ct (Judge Brown) 11 Jan 1980 no compensation seems to have been awarded for help provided to a victim by her sisters.

98. *Ibid*, p 343. Earlier cases had suggested otherwise – see e.g. *Schneider* v *Eisovitch*

[1960] 1 All ER 169 (P to give undertaking to pay over damages); *Cunningham* v *Harrison* [1973] 3 All ER 463 (where Lord Denning MR suggested that P held the damages in trust for the relative). *Cf Pearson Report*, paras 348–9 thought such an approach impracticable and unnecessary.

99. Article 13(3). See e.g. *R* v *CICB, ex parte McGuffie and Smith* [1978] *Crim LR* 160 (below, p 195) and see further, below p 308.

1. In *Arouni* v *Sec of State* Unreported, High Ct (Gibson LJ), 8 Dec 1977 Gibson LJ apparently considered that a local authority which had paid boarding-out allowances was a "person" who had incurred "expenses" for which compensation may have been payable had there been no dependants of the deceased.

Although it is perhaps unlikely that a public body such as a local authority would apply for compensation, a voluntary organisation might be so reimbursed for additional expenses incurred as a result of the victim's injury, for example, the cost of nursing attention, of special equipment or of modifying a building.

PECUNIARY LOSS INCURRED BY THE VICTIM

1. Loss of Earnings Generally

By Article $3(2)(a)$(ii) an injured person is entitled to compensation in respect of "pecuniary loss to him as a result of total or partial incapacity for work".[2] This formula has remained unchanged since 1968, and clearly connotes compensation for loss of earnings and other pecuniary loss, past or future, to be assessed generally on the same basis as common law damages.[3]

But first it may be noted that Article $3(2)(a)$(ii) includes no test of causation or remoteness linking the incapacity for work to the criminal injury, and there may therefore be some uncertainty as to when, or to what extent, a victim is entitled to receive compensation.[4] In practice, however, it seems reasonable to suppose that the sub-paragraph will be interpreted as connoting incapacity for work "resulting from his injury" and that here, as elsewhere, common law precedents will be followed.[5]

The "work" referred to presumably means the victim's work at the time he received the injury. If the victim was at that time working at a job below his full potential, he cannot claim compensation for loss of earnings due to inability to work at that full potential[6] – unless, presumably, he can establish on a balance of probabilities that, had he not been injured, he would have transferred to more highly paid employment during the relevant period. Common law cases also recognise (and compensation will therefore be awarded in) the converse situation; if an injured person, despite partial incapacity, returns full-time to his pre-injury work, he is nevertheless entitled to "substantial compensation" for the real risk (if so proved) that at

---

2. Replicating 1968 Act, s 4(1)(b) and 1977 Order, Art 5(1)(b). There is no express provision in the Irish Scheme or in the Civil Liability Act 1961, but common law principles are applied, subject to any differences in practice (e.g. as to the use of actuarial evidence) which have evolved – see generally *White*, ch 4. This is also the case in England and Wales – see Scheme, para 12 and 1988 Act, Sch 7, para 8.

3. See generally *Kemp and Kemp*, chs 5-8; *McGregor*, paras 1450–1480; *White*, ch 4.

4. E.g. must the incapacity be "as a result of" or "result directly from" the criminal injury? What compensation is payable to an applicant in the position of the plaintiff in *McKew* v

Holland and Hannen & Cubitts (Scotland) Ltd [1969] 3 All ER 1621 (P's leg injured in accident; further injury to ankle when P fell while trying to descend staircase; damages not awarded for consequences of second injury because P had acted unreasonably and thus broken chain of causation)? The British Board has expressly followed *McKew* – see CICB, *7th Annual Report* (1970–71), p 13. *Cp Wieland* v *Cyril Lord Carpets Ltd* [1969] 3 All ER 1006.

5. See e.g. *McGregor*, ch 6.

6. The distinction between loss of earnings and loss of (unused) earning capacity is discussed e.g. in *Munkman*, pp 78–80 and Harris, *Remedies in Contract and Tort* (1988), pp 268–9.

some time in the future he might have to compete – at a disadvantage because of his injury – in the open labour market.[7]

It may also be noted that "incapacity" may result not only from physical injury but, as the result of the definition in Article 2(2), from sickness or any impairment of mental condition or pregnancy – provided of course that any such condition is directly attributable to the criminal injury. In particular, the restriction of "nervous shock" to certain "serious and disabling mental disorders" in Article 5(12) does not apply to reduce the much broader scope of the definition of "injury" for pecuniary loss purposes.[8]

Finally, by way of preliminary consideration, it must of course be established that the plaintiff has suffered a "loss". Thus, a victim suffers no pecuniary loss if, during any period of incapacity for work, his employer nonetheless pays him his normal earnings.[9] In some cases, however, such a payment is made on the basis that if the victim obtains criminal injuries compensation, he will reimburse his employer. In such cases the victim *has* suffered a loss. This was so held in *McCartney* v *Secretary of State*:

> "This money was paid to the applicant on the understanding that he would refund it when the claim was settled. It is an obligation which he is under a duty to honour and if he does not receive compensation equivalent to his obligation he will have sustained a pecuniary loss in that he will have to discharge his debt out of moneys which have been paid to him for other unrelated matters."[10]

However, it is arguable that such a sum may now be deducted as a "gratuity" under Article 6(2)(*b*).[11]

The normal[12] basis of assessing compensation for pecuniary loss under the 1988 Order is the traditional method of assessing damages for loss of earnings at common law, *viz* by calculating the applicant's actual loss of earnings to the date of determination and, if the loss will continue thereafter, by estimating his loss of future earnings by the application of a multiplier (representing the appropriate number of years' purchase) to a multiplicand (representing the applicant's net annual loss).[13]

---

7. See e.g. *Moeliker* v *A Reyrolle & Co Ltd* [1977] 1 All ER 9 (damages awarded for the present value of the risk of future financial loss); *Foster* v *Tyne and Wear CC* [1986] 1 All ER 567 (£35,000 awarded on this basis).

8. See above, pp 55–61.

9. See e.g. *McGregor*, paras 1483 *et seq.*

10. Unreported, Cty Ct (Judge Russell), 21 December 1979, following *Dennis* v *London Passenger Transport Board* [1948] 1 All ER 779. See also *Gaw* v *Sec of State* Unreported, High Ct (MacDermott J), 27 Feb 1987 (discussed below, p 208, *Berriello* v *Felixstowe Dock & Rly Co* [1989] 1 WLR 695 and *McElroy* v *Aldritt*, Unreported, Sup Ct, 11 June 1953, discussed *White*, pp 212–3. To avoid uncertainty in this matter, the *Pearson Report*, para 507 recommended that repayment "by custom and practice" should be replaced by a clear legal obligation.

11. See below, p 208.

12. In some cases, particularly those involving members of the security forces, a "discount method" is often used in practice. This attempts to assess an applicant's net loss on a year-by-year basis, taking into account in particular the applicant's expected earnings in terms of promotion etc, and then applying to each year's loss an appropriate discount factor. This method of assessment does not appear to have been adopted by the courts.

13. See generally *Kemp and Kemp*, chs 5-8; *McGregor*, paras 1450–1480; *Munkman*, ch 2; *White*, ch 4.

2. Past Loss of Earnings

Article 7(1) provides that the compensation payable to an injured person in respect of pecuniary loss as a result of incapacity for work –

> "shall be determined on the basis of a weekly rate which shall have regard to all relevant circumstances, and, in particular, to his actual earnings, if any, during the 6 months immediately preceding the date on which the criminal injury was sustained."

This calculation is normally fairly straightforward, but complications may arise in certain cases.

(a) It may be necessary to look at a period in excess of six months in order to establish the applicant's overall work-pattern before his injury. Thus, in *Annesley* v *Secretary of State*[14] the evidence was that the applicant had not worked for some six years, during which time he had been in and out of prison "with monotonous regularity"; no compensation was awarded for past or future pecuniary loss. Conversely, in *Deehan* v *Bell*,[15] the plaintiff had worked for 14½ years – but in the year prior to his accident, he had been unemployed for seven months. In such circumstances it would hardly have been fair or reasonable to use his earnings during that year as the basis for calculating his loss. All depends on the evidence in the particular case. In *McGeown and McAnoy* v *Ministry of Home Affairs*[16] McAnoy had been out of work at the time of his injury, but he claimed compensation for loss of earnings on the basis that had it not been for his injury he would have found employment. Had he indeed been able to prove this, he would have been entitled to compensation: but the learned judge rejected the contention on the evidence as "the merest speculation". Conversely, McGeown was in work as a labourer at the time of his injury but was unable to secure employment on his recovery. It was held that compensation was not payable during unemployment, but that a time-lag between jobs is not unusual and must be taken into account. Accordingly, McGeown was awarded compensation for loss of earnings for seven weeks, that being the period which the learned judge considered on the evidence would be the average time-lag between labouring jobs in normal economic conditions.

(b) The "relevant circumstances" include any increase in the level of remuneration which would have been payable to the applicant between the date of injury and the date of determination.[17] Thus, regard may be had both to actual pay rises which the applicant would have received and to his promotion prospects prior to the date of determination.

(c) Although Article 7(1) refers to the applicant's "actual earnings" rather than his "income", it is submitted that Article 7(4) is equally applicable, so that in calculating the applicant's loss there will be deducted from gross earnings the appropriate sum for –

---

14. Unreported, High Ct (MacDermott J), 25 Oct 1984.

15. [1983] 12 NIJB.

16. Unreported, Cty Ct (Judge Patton), 10 April 1972.

17. See e.g. *McGregor*, para 1430. Loss of family credit (formerly family income supplement) would also appear to be relevant: *Webb* v *Macauley* 1988 SLT 138.

"(a) income tax;

(b) social security contributions payable under the laws of any part of the United Kingdom or similar contributions payable under the laws of any other country, state or territory; [and]

(c) in the case of an employed person, any amount deducted from his remuneration by his employer by way of superannuation contributions."

This provision, which replicates Article 7(4) of the 1977 Order, is in line with the common law precedents,[18] and presumably includes payments which the applicant *ought* to have made.[19] But the benefits paid for by social security and superannuation contributions are generally deducted from criminal injuries compensation. The applicant is, therefore, given no credit for having paid for or contributed towards e.g. the social security benefits payable to him after his injury. In the case of pensions injustice can arise where the applicant's contributions result in a higher pension than if no such contributions had been paid. He may find that his contributions both reduce his net annual loss and increase the amount to be deducted from his compensation. This would be particularly unfair if there was no evidence to show that, had the pension been a non-contributory one, his earnings would have been correspondingly lower.[20] It will be noted however that Article 7(4)(c) refers only to *superannuation* contributions; it may be that where an applicant has contributed to an occupational pension that part of his contribution which "pays" for a disability pension to be paid during normal working years will fall to be ignored.[21]

In some recent cases[22] it has been suggested that there should also be deducted from gross earnings any expenses necessarily incurred in earning that income – e.g. travel expenses to and from work. In *Dews* v *National Coal Board,* Lord Griffiths agreed with this in principle but urged a pragmatic approach:

" . . . wherever a man lives he is likely to incur *some* travelling expenses to work which will be saved during his period of incapacity, and they are strictly expenses necessarily incurred for the purpose of earning his living. It would, however, be intolerable in every personal injury action to have an inquiry into travelling expenses to determine that part necessarily attributable to earning the wage and that part attributable to a chosen lifestyle [which would not be deductible]. I know of no case in which travelling expenses to work have been deducted from a weekly wage and, although the point does not fall for decision, I do not encourage any insurer or employer to seek to do so."[23]

---

18. *British Transport Commission* v *Gourley* [1955] 3 All ER 796 (income tax); *Cooper* v *Firth Brown* [1963] 2 All ER 31 (social security contributions) and *Dews* v *National Coal Board* [1987] 2 All ER 545 (superannuation contributions).

19. See *Donnelly* v *Hackett* [1988] 6 NIJB 6, 7–8, *per* Lord Lowry LCJ.

20. *Cp Hussain* v *New Taplow Paper Mills Ltd* [1988] 1 All ER 541.

21. The distinction between occupational *disability* pensions and occupational *retirement* pensions is noted e.g. in the *Pearson Report*, paras 517–523.

22. *Lim Poh Choo* v *Camden and Islington AHA* [1979] 2 All ER 910 and *Dews* v *National Coal Board* [1987] 2 All ER 545.

23. [1987] 2 All ER 545, 548.

But he added that he could "envisage a case where travelling expenses loomed so large . . . that further consideration of the question would be justified . . . ".[24]

(d) Article 6(7) of the 1988 Order provides:

> "Any saving to a victim which is attributable to his maintenance wholly or partly at public expense in a hospital, nursing home or other institution for a period of time shall, subject to paragraph (8), be deducted from the amount which, but for this paragraph, would be payable in respect of [pecuniary loss to the victim as a result of incapacity for work] . . . "

Paragraph (8) provides that no such deduction is to be made in respect of –

> "(a) a period of less than eight weeks; or
>
> (b) the first eight weeks of a period longer than eight weeks."

The first part of this provision replicates section 5 of the Administration of Justice Act 1982, enacted on the recommendation of the Pearson Commission[25] to "reverse" the decision in *Daish* v *Wauton*.[26] But paragraph (8) adds a concession which is unique to criminal injuries compensation.

The effect of Article 6(7) is not entirely clear. It is expressly restricted to maintenance "at public expense"; but if a victim opts for private medical treatment, he may still find that his compensation for pecuniary loss will be reduced, to avoid "overlap". Thus, in *Fletcher* v *Autocar & Transporters Ltd*[27] a plaintiff was so badly injured that he would have to spend most of the rest of his life as a paying patient in a private mental hospital. Cantley J assessed the cost of keeping the plaintiff in hospital at £1,419 per annum, but deducted from this amount £300 per annum for "saving on food and laundry at home". This approach was in general endorsed by the Court of Appeal – and indeed Diplock LJ indicated that he would have doubled the deduction, on the ground that –

> " . . . all economies, consequent on the action taken which involves the additional expenses claim, must be brought into the estimate made under the latter head . . . "[28]

Although *Fletcher* represents what McGregor[29] has called the "high point" of the overlap concept, the need to ensure that any saving in living expenses is taken into account in the computation of an award of damages for medical expenses was confirmed by the House of Lords in *Lim Poh Choo* v *Camden and Islington Area Health Authority*.[30]

---

24. *Ibid. Cf* " . . . a donation to charity which an employee agrees with his employer should be deducted at source and therefore never enters the employee's pay packet would not fall to be deducted in computing the plaintiff's loss of wages in consequence of an injury": *per* Lord Mackay at p 551.

25. *Report*, para 510 – although this recommendation was one of a number of interconnected recommendations, the remainder of which have not been implemented.

26. [1972] 1 All ER 25. *Cp* an earlier decision of the Court of Appeal to the contrary in *Oliver* v *Ashman* [1961] 3 All ER 323.

27. [1968] 1 All ER 726.

28. *Ibid*, p 742. See also *Mitchell* v *Mulholland (No 2)* [1971] 2 All ER 1205, 1225, *per* Sir Gordon Willmer. Similar views were expressed in *Reddy* v *Bates* [1983] IR 141, discussed *White*, pp 112–6.

29. *McGregor*, para 1448.

30. [1979] 2 All ER 910.

What is to be deducted under Article 6(7) as "attributable to" the victim's "maintenance" in a hospital, etc may depend on the duration of that maintenance, and the circumstances of the victim. The normal saving will be in respect of food, but there may also be savings in respect of heating, lighting, etc.[31] The "worst possible" case is exemplified by *Oliver* v *Ashman*[32] where the plaintiff was so badly injured that Willmer LJ observed:

> "He will never have the expense of maintaining a home, whether for himself alone, or for himself and dependants; and he will never have to bear the cost of food and clothing, light, heat and so forth . . . "

Article 6(7) applies to maintenance in a "hospital, nursing home *or other institution* . . . ". This would seem a clear case for the application of *ejusdem generis* – it is surely reasonable to restrict the provision to cases where the injured victim's maintenance in an institution is as a result of his injuries and not for some incidental reason. Thus, it should not apply where e.g. an injured person has been maintained at public expense in lawful custody.

(e) Finally, Article 8(1) imposes in certain cases an overall limitation on the amount of compensation which may be awarded for pecuniary loss.[33]

3. Loss of Future Earnings

(a) *Multiplicand*

The House of Lords in *Graham* v *Dodds*[34] confirmed that damages for loss of future earnings are calculated on the estimated rate of earnings at the date of assessment, not on that prevailing at the date of injury. The multiplicand therefore takes into account past inflation – i.e. increases in the level of earnings between the date of injury and the date of assessment – subject, of course, to the deductions required (as stated above) to determine the applicant's *net* annual loss.

Where the evidence establishes that the applicant had good promotion prospects or prospects of higher earnings had he not been injured, allowance for these may be made in the calculation of the multiplicand.[35] Thus in *Walker* v *Secretary of State*[36] the applicant was the owner of a small roofing business. The learned judge took as his starting point the applicant's average profits for the three years before his injury. But the evidence also established that the applicant had a good business reputation and would also have brought his sons into the business. There had, therefore, to be an increase in the multiplicand to allow for the higher future earnings arising from this expected expansion of the business. In *Payne* v *Secretary of State*,[37] Judge Rowland summarised the position in the following way:

---

31. But only insofar as these are "attributable" to maintenance in the hospital; it would not, therefore, be appropriate to think in terms of *general* savings in living expenses as e.g. envisaged in Art 7(3).

32. [1961] 3 All ER 323.

33. See below, pp 173–8.

34. [1983] NI 22.

35. See e.g. *McGregor*, para 1466.

36. Unreported, Cty Ct (Judge Higgins), 11 Feb 1982.

37. Unreported, Cty Ct (Judge Rowland), 13 May 1983.

> "In assessing the applicant's loss all various future contingencies must be taken into account providing they are not too speculative. Every claim for future loss . . . involves evaluating chances. All chances are not necessarily adverse. A particular applicant might . . . have good prospects or chances of promotion and advancement and consequently higher earnings. Some attempt must therefore be made to evaluate those chances and prospects . . . This involves an objective judgment . . . based on the evidence adduced in the case."

The learned judge considered that the existing annual loss did not provide a firm basis for calculating the future loss, since it was quite clear on the evidence that the applicant would probably have been promoted. As against this, however, was the fact that his injuries were such that he would probably not remain unemployable for the rest of his life.

In some cases the multiplicand has been adjusted upwards to take account of the fact that income tax may be payable on the investment income produced by the compensation award. Thus in *Scott* v *Pollock*[38] O'Donnell J in the High Court increased the multiplicand (in a Fatal Accidents Act case) from £2,000 to £2,500 to make allowance for increased liability to tax. Jones LJ for the Court of Appeal considered this a "correct approach in principle", though it may have been rather generous in practice. It would appear, however, that this approach is now inconsistent with the decision of the House of Lords in *Hodgson* v *Trapp*[39] that the impact of higher taxation should not normally be treated as a separate and individual consideration in the calculation of damages for loss of future earnings.

Article 8 imposes a ceiling on compensation for pecuniary loss in certain circumstances:

> "(1) Subject to paragraph (2), compensation in respect of any pecuniary loss shall not (after applying Article 6(2)(*b*)[40]) exceed 104 times the amount of average weekly industrial earnings multiplied by such factor as is appropriate having regard to the age of the victim and such other matters as are relevant.
>
> (2) Paragraph (1) does not apply where the criminal injury was caused by a person acting on behalf of or in connection with an unlawful association."

This limit on compensation for pecuniary loss thus applies, in effect, to non-terrorist cases; in the British Scheme a ceiling is imposed on such compensation in *all* cases,[41] whereas no such limitation is imposed in any case coming under the Irish Scheme.[42] The availability of "full" compensa-

---

38. [1976] NI 1.

39. [1988] 3 All ER 870. Although the decision precludes adjustment of the *multiplier*, the reasoning appears equally applicable to the multiplicand: see further below, p 179.

40. Deductions for certain pensions, gratuities and social security benefits consequent on the criminal injury – see generally below, pp 207–15.

41. Paragraph 14(*a*), discussed below n 50.

42. By implication arising from the absence of any special provision.

tion for loss of earnings by victims of terrorist offences in Northern Ireland has continued since 1968,[43] when it was defended on three grounds:

> "First, that persons are [already] entitled to unrestricted compensation under this head and it would be wrong in principle to take away a right which people have had for so many years, just because a lesser entitlement is being extended to others.

> Secondly, it can be reasonably argued that the state has a greater responsibility towards persons injured by unlawful assemblies. The Government cannot be expected to prevent all crime but they have an absolute duty to protect their citizens against civil commotion and the usurpation of lawful authority.

> Thirdly, the very nature of unlawful associations is such that their victims have no alternative remedy afforded by law in proceeding against such people."[44]

Equally, the application of a ceiling in non-terrorist cases was in line with the declared policy of the 1968 Act that "the person who inflicts the injury is really the person who is liable for full compensation. The state's contribution is to mitigate hardship."[45]

This dichotomy between terrorist and non-terrorist cases is not altogether convincing, and the 1968 Act was criticised at the time as making the amount of compensation depend not so much on the injury to the victim, nor the seriousness of the offence, but rather on the identity of the offender, with the result that some cases which are no less deserving than others are subject to a lower level of compensation.[46] In 1976[47] it was proposed to limit the amount of pecuniary loss payable in all cases, but this too was criticised[48] and then dropped, although, as something of a compromise, the 1977 provision for the first time brought injuries caused by a member of an unlawful *assembly* within the ceiling.[49] The 1988 Order retains exactly the same formula as used in the 1977 Order. In practice, the ceiling has been found to apply in very few cases.[50]

---

43. 1968 Act, s 4(4). See also 1977 Order, Art 6(1).

44. 68 HC Debs (NI), col 1243 (14 Feb 1968).

45. *Ibid,* col 1244. *Cf* 1978 *1WP Report*: "[T]he liability of the public purse can legitimately be limited . . . Those with higher incomes are more likely and better able to make some provision of their own against loss of income . . . The Scheme should not be seen to provide disproportionately large sums as compensation for loss of earnings . . . " (para 11.2). See to the same effect 1986 *1WP Report*, para 14.1.

46. 68 HC Debs (NI), cols 1239–1243, 1795–1797 (14 Feb 1968).

47. Proposal for a Draft Criminal Injuries (Compensation) (NI) Order 1976, Art 6(1).

48. See e.g. 934 HC Debs, col 766 (1 July 1977) (Mr Craig).

49. *Cp* 1977 Order, Art 6(2). The Minister of State merely observed that he was taking account of "strong representations that had been made" (*ibid,* col 753).

50. In 1968, it was estimated that only 4% of the population would be adversely affected – see 68 HC Debs (NI), col 1243 (14 Feb 1968). In 1984, however, the Chairman of the British CICB thought that the ceiling was "too low": Evidence to Home Affairs Comittee, *Report on Compensation and Support for Victims of Crime* (HC 43, 1984–1985), p 42. Conversely, the 1986 *1WP Report*, para 14.2 thought the upper limit too high and recommended reduction of the "multiplier" from 104 to 78, to yield a limit which "would not affect 70% of full-time workers". This recommendation has been implemented in the 1990 Scheme, para 14(*a*). See also 1988 Act, Sch 7, para 10(1).

(i) *Cases where the criminal injury was caused by a person acting on behalf of or in connection with an unlawful association.* By Article 2(2) –

> "'unlawful association' means any organisation which is engaged in terrorism and includes an organisation which at any relevant time is a proscribed organisation within the meaning of the Northern Ireland (Emergency Provisions) Act."

"Terrorism" is also defined in Article 2(2) as meaning –

> "the use of violence for political ends and includes any use of violence for the purpose of putting the public or any section of the public in fear."[51]

The general scope of this definition has already been examined.[52] It will be noted that it is not necessary for the victim to have been the specific "target" of an act of terrorism. This was, perhaps, clearer under the 1968 Act, section 4(4) of which required the act to have been done "maliciously". It had long been established under the criminal injuries code that this did not connote "personal malice or ill-will" against the victim, but rather "an unlawful act, done intentionally".[53] Indeed no terrorist act need be involved at all; what is required is a criminal injury – any criminal injury – caused by *a person acting on behalf of or in connection with* a terrorist organisation. This link with the unlawful association is a broad one, and it is not necessary to establish that the person concerned is a member of such an association.[54] But he must in fact have been acting on behalf of or in connection with that association when he committed the act which caused the injury – Article 8(2) will not apply e.g. where a member of an unlawful association was acting on a free-lance basis or on a frolic of his own.[55]

In practice, this link will normally be established by a senior police officer[56] acting under Article 8(3):

> "Where a senior police officer is of the opinion that any criminal injury was caused by a person acting on behalf of or in connection with an unlawful association he shall, if an applicant makes an application to him, issue to the applicant a certificate in the form . . . prescribed . . . "

By Article 8(4), this certificate –

> "shall, until the contrary is proved, be evidence that the criminal injury referred to in the certificate was caused by a person acting on behalf of or in connection with an unlawful association."

---

51. These definitions are identical to those in the 1977 Order, Art 2(2).

52. See above, pp 129–137.

53. See e.g. *McDowell* v *Dublin Corp* [1903] 2 IR 541, 544, *per* Lord Ashbourne C, discussed Greer and Mitchell, *Compensation for Criminal Damage to Property* (1982), pp 47–52.

54. " . . . the words 'in connection with' extend the persons whose acts are [included] beyond those who are members of the organisation . . . " *per* Mustill J in *Spinney's (1948)*

Ltd v *Royal Ins Co Ltd* [1980] 1 Lloyd's Rep 406, 439.

55. See criminal damage compensation cases such as *McKeever* v *Sec of State*, Unreported, High Ct (MacDermott J), 24 Oct 1979, discussed Greer and Mitchell, *op cit*, p 71.

56. By Art 8(6)(*b*) "senior police officer" means "a member of the Royal Ulster Constabulary of the rank of assistant chief constable or above". This is to the same effect as the definition of "chief constable" in the 1977 Order, Art 2(2).

It will be noted that Article 8(3) applies to all unlawful associations, and that the certificate covers not only the question of causation but also apparently the question whether what the applicant sustained was a "criminal injury".[57] It is open to the Northern Ireland Office to rebut either of these presumptions.

(ii) *Cases where the criminal injury was not caused by a person acting on behalf of or in connection with an unlawful association.* In such cases compensation "in respect of any pecuniary loss" *after* the deduction of any pension, gratuity or social security benefit as required by Article 6(2)(*b*) is limited to the maximum laid down in Article 8(1), *viz* "104[58] times the amount of average weekly industrial earnings multiplied by such factor as is appropriate . . ."[59]. By Article 8(6)(*a*) "average weekly industrial earnings" means "the average gross weekly earnings for all full-time men aged 21 and over in all industries and services (excluding those whose pay was affected by absence) as set out in the Northern Ireland Abstract of Statistics . . .". This reference is apparently[60] to Table 11.1 of the Abstract,[61] and the relevant figure there set out for April 1989 was £231.00. The Abstract is published every year.

It is unfortunate that Article 8 does not stipulate the date at which this ceiling is to be applied. Under the 1968 Act[62] that date was stated to be when the criminal injury was sustained; under Article 8 (as under the 1977 Order) the relevant date would, however, appear to be the date on which the compensation is awarded. This seems the proper implication from the wording of the Article (" . . . compensation . . . shall not . . . exceed . . .

---

57. Prior to 1977 the Chief Constable certified only that *an act* had been committed by a person acting on behalf of etc: 1968 Act, s 10(7). The wording of the 1988 Order follows the new wording introduced in 1977, and is curiously similar to that originally introduced in the Criminal Injuries Act (NI) 1957, s 3(2) and Sch 1, later amended in order "to legalise that form of certificate which the [chief constable] considers he can conscientiously give": 42 HC Debs (NI), col 1132 (29 May 1958) (Minister of Home Affairs). It had apparently been discovered in practice that the Chief Constable could not certify the extent of injury resulting from the illegal act. Under the 1977/1988 formula, the Chief Constable is expected to decide the question of causation and that the injury qualifies as a criminal injury, but he is not expected to give any detailed particulars of the injury.

58. Note that by Art 23(2) "the Secretary of State may by order substitute a different number for that for the time being specified in Art 8(1) . . . ". The equivalent number in the British Scheme is now 78 – see above n 50.

59. It is thought that the latter formula is intended to state the common law approach to the calculation of the multiplier, and, being a common factor to both the compensation and the ceiling, can be left out of account on both sides in deciding whether or not the ceiling is to be applied.

60. Strangely, there is no *exact* Table as described in Art 8(6)(*a*) to be found in the current Abstract. Table 11.1 explains that "adult employees" for purposes of that Table are those employees of *any age* on adult rates. An "adult" for this purpose is not defined. By Art 23(3) the Secretary of State may by order amend the definition of "average weekly industrial earnings" "to such extent as appears to him to be necessary or expedient in view of any change in the headings or subdivisions used in the Abstract of Statistics . . . ".

61. *Northern Ireland Abstract of Statistics* (1989), p 121.

62. Section 4(4), following the 1964 British Scheme, para 11(*a*).

average weekly industrial earnings . . . ") and from the definition of average weekly industrial earnings in Article 8(6)(*a*).[63]

It will be noted that that definition specifically refers to gross earnings, whereas compensation is calculated on the loss of net earnings – i.e. gross earnings less tax, national insurance contribution and the employee's pension contribution. In *R* v *Criminal Injuries Compensation Board, ex parte Richardson*,[64] Lord Widgery CJ observed:

> "Clearly the policy of the scheme was that there should be a ceiling above which no increase in the amount of compensation was to be paid . . . The cut-off point was in a measure arbitrary. Parliament had chosen to state that the cut-off point should be fixed by twice the average industrial earnings, and that figure was inevitably expressed as gross earnings. Naturally, gross earnings of the victim should be compared with the gross average industrial earnings. Although there was no doubt that before the end income tax [etc] was to be taken into account before the calculation was complete, one still had to begin with gross earnings."

This decision was effectively reversed when the British Scheme was revised in 1979,[65] paragraph 14(*a*) providing that "the rate of *net* loss of earnings . . . shall not exceed twice the *gross* average industrial earnings . . . " and it is submitted that it is that interpretation which is also intended to be applied to Article 8 of the 1988 Order.[66] Thus, by that Article it is the "compensation" rather than the "pecuniary loss" which is not to exceed the ceiling – and it should also be noted that the "pecuniary loss" to which the ceiling applies is not necessarily confined to the applicant's loss of earnings.[67]

It thus appears that the proper method of applying Article 8(1) and (6) is to ask:

1. What were the victim's average gross earnings per week during the six months preceding his injury (or otherwise) (A).

2. What were the victim's net weekly earnings during this period, i.e. after deduction from (A) of tax, National Insurance and superannuation contributions? (B).

---

63. The British Scheme, as amended in 1979 following a recommendation in the 1978 *IWP Report*, para 11.4, stipulates in para 14(*a*) that the ceiling is to be applied "at the date of assessment". See to the same effect 1988 Act, Sch 7, para 10(1). See also Greer, *Criminal Injuries Compensation* (1990), paras 4.33–4.36.

64. [1974] *Crim LR* 99; (1973) 118 *Sol J* 184. See also CICB, *10th Annual Report* (1973–74), para 4.

65. On the basis of a recommendation in the 1978 *IWP Report*, para 11.3.

66. This interpretation, it is submitted, is preferable to one based on the reasoning in *Richardson* which arguably could be supported by the maxim *expressio unius exclusio alterius* (the express reference to Art 6(2)(*b*) could be taken to imply that the deductions required by Art 7(4) are *not* to be taken into

account).In relation to the identical provision in the 1977 Order, the Minister of State indicated that the ceiling was intended to apply to *net* loss – see HC Debs (NI Cttee), col 4 (16 Feb 1977) and 934 HC Debs, col 752 (1 July 1977). *Cf* of the 1988 Act, Sch 7, para 10(1) suggests that the limit applies to the victim's *gross* earnings.

67. Article 8(1) applies to "*any*" pecuniary loss, which might strictly be interpreted as covering both loss to the victim himself (under Art 3(2)(*a*)(ii) *and* (iii)) and to any person responsible for his maintenance (under Art 3(2)(*b*)(ii)). No provision is made, however, for any apportionment should the combined loss exceed the ceiling and it seems likely that Art 8(1) will be held to apply in injury cases to the loss sustained by any one applicant.

3. To what collateral benefits covered by Article 6(2)(*b*) is the victim entitled during the relevant period? (C).

4. Deduct (C) from (B) and multiply the remainder by 52 to yield the net annual loss of earnings (D).

5. Does (D) exceed (E) 104 times the amount of average gross weekly industrial earnings as specified by Article 8(6)(*a*)? If no, then (D) is the multiplicand. If yes, then (E) is the multiplicand.

E.g. V's average weekly gross earnings are £430; from this he pays £80 income tax and £60 in National Insurance and superannuation contributions. After the injury he receives a statutory pension of £50 per week. At the time his compensation is assessed, the amount of average weekly industrial earnings is £231. The multiplicand in V's case is £12,480 (£430 less £(80 + 60 + 50) = £240 × 52). Since this is less than £24,024 (i.e. £231 × 104), the ceiling does not apply and V is entitled to "full" compensation for loss of earnings, notwithstanding the fact that his gross weekly earnings are almost twice the average gross weekly industrial earnings.

(b) *Multiplier*

Article 8(1) of the 1988 Order follows Article 6(1) of the 1977 Order in stipulating that the multiplier to be used in injury cases is "such factor as is appropriate having regard to the age of the victim and such other matters as are relevant". This formula incorporates into the criminal injuries compensation scheme the method by which multipliers are calculated at common law. Thus, the victim's age for this purpose is that at the date of determination,[68] and the "other matters" include the expected duration of the incapacity, the appropriate rate of discount, the contingencies of life and the other factors which the courts have recognised as relevant in capitalising the present value of a future loss.[69] The "rough and ready" nature of this approach has frequently been acknowledged:

> "Such an assessment cannot . . . by its nature be a precise science. The presence of so many imponderable factors necessarily renders the process a complex and imprecise one and one which is incapable of producing anything better than an approximate result. Essentially what the court has to do is to calculate as best it can the sum of money which will on the one hand be adequate, by its capital and income, to provide annually for the injured person a sum equal to his estimated annual loss over the whole of the period during which that loss is likely to continue, but which, on the other hand, will not, at the end of that period, leave him in a better financial position than he would have been in apart from the accident."[70]

---

68. See e.g. *Pritchard* v *JH Cobden Ltd* [1987] 1 All ER 300. The Court of Appeal refused to adopt the practice in Fatal Accidents cases where the multiplier is calculated from the date of death – see below, p 197.

69. See *Kemp and Kemp*, chs 6–9; *McGregor*, paras 1467–1480; *Munkman*, pp 56–72; *White*, ch 4.

70. *Hodgson* v *Trapp* [1988] 3 All ER 870, 879, *per* Lord Oliver.

It will be seen from this quotation that the overall objective is now stated to be to provide the injured person with an "adequate" sum to compensate him for his loss. This may result in the award of something less than "full" compensation[71] – but the courts have in recent years refused to modify the conventional approach. Thus, the appropriate discount rate is still taken to be that applicable to a stable currency (i.e. 4–5%),[72] and that rate is taken to make adequate allowance for the possibility of future inflation.[73] Similarly, although the fact that the applicant may be taxed on the capital sum is a relevant matter, it has recently been held, contrary to earlier decisions,[74] that it is not normally to be treated as "a separate, individual and independent consideration which justifies the making of additional provision" in the calculation of the multiplier.[75]

The ways in which the various factors are to be taken into account are laid down in the leading common law cases and analysed in the leading textbooks on damages. In principle, those cases will be followed in applications under the 1988 Order; in practice, however, they do not appear to have been discussed at any length in the context of criminal injury compensation in Northern Ireland. It is, therefore, somewhat difficult to give a clear indication of the courts' approach in particular cases, but some illustrative cases are given in Table 4.1. The multiplier used in each of these cases is there compared with that used in England and Wales, as reported in *Kemp and Kemp*.[76] The final column of the Table then refers to the *Actuarial Tables for Use in Personal Injury and Fatal Accident Cases* published in England in 1984.[77] Although the courts in both jurisdictions have discouraged the use of

---

71. The right to which, according to *McGregor*, para 1450, "is today a clear principle of law". *Cf* Atiyah, *Accidents, Compensation and the Law* (4th ed, 1987), pp 175–180 doubts if the judges were ever committed to the principle of "full" compensation in practice.

72. See e.g. *Cookson v Knowles* [1978] 2 All ER 604, 610-11, *per* Lord Diplock; *Hodgson v Trapp* [1988] 3 All ER 870, 885, *per* Lord Oliver. The *Pearson Report*, para 648 considered that the discount rate should be much lower – but "I think that economic and financial conditions today probably make that conclusion less valid than when it was published": *Graham v Dodds* [1983] NI 22, 29, *per* Gibson LJ. However, many recent commentators agree with Pearson – see e.g. Kemp, "Discounting compensation for future loss" (1985) 101 *LQR* 556. *Cf Munkman*, p 65: " . . . if properly applied, 4½% seems to produce an adequate award."

73. See e.g. *Cookson v Knowles* [1978] 2 All ER 604, 611, *per* Lord Diplock; *Lim Poh Choo v Camden and Islington AHA* [1979] 2 All ER 910. In both cases, however, it was acknowledged that there might be "very

exceptional" cases in which special allowance might have to be made. A more generous approach is taken in the Republic – see e.g. *Cooke v Walsh* [1984] IR 710, discussed *White*, pp 189–191.

74. E.g. *Scott v Pollock* [1976] NI 1; *Thomas v Wignall* [1987] 1 All ER 1185, and the Irish cases discussed by *White*, pp 182–7.

75. *Hodgson v Trapp* [1988] 3 All ER 870 where the House of Lords reversed the trial judge's decision to increase a multiplier from 11 to 12 to allow for higher taxation. Note, however, that Lord Oliver (at p 886) accepted that "There may . . . be cases . . . where the considerations pointing to the selection of one of two possible multipliers are so finely balanced that the future incidence of taxation may be taken into account as one, but only one, of the factors which might properly tip the balance in favour of selecting the higher rate rather than the lower . . . ".

76. Vol 1, para 6-013/1.

77. *Report of the Inter-Professional Working Party of Actuaries and Lawyers* (1984), discussed *Munkman*, p 61.

Table 4.1

Multipliers for loss of earnings from date of trial to retirement age (male applicants)

Case	Date of trial	A's age at date of trial	Multiplier	Kemp and Kemp	Actuarial Table (4½%)
Payne	1983	38	15	12	14.9
McCann	1981	40	12	8–12	14.2
Walker	1982	45	10	7–10	12.4
Starrett[78]	1984	51	8	8	9.6

such Tables,[79] it would appear that they are increasingly being referred to in practice, if only as a "check" on the figure produced by the conventional method.[80]

4. Loss of Pension

In recent years another aspect of pecuniary loss resulting from incapacity for work is the adverse effect which this may have on the pension payable to the applicant.[81] In *McCartney* v *Secretary of State*[82] the applicant's injuries caused him to retire at the age of 61. As a result his pension at age 65 would be less than it would otherwise have been, since (like many pensions) it was based on the number of pensionable years' service and on the average of the three "best" years' earnings. Had the applicant not been injured, his pension would have been £5,500 per annum; as a result of early retirement it was only £3,000 per annum. Compensation was therefore awarded on the basis of the annual loss of £2,500.[83] This reasoning follows well-established common law precedents.

---

78. *Payne* v *Sec of State* Unreported, Cty Ct (Judge Rowland), 13 May 1983; *McCann* v *Sec of State* Unreported, Cty Ct (Judge Higgins), 21 Jan 1981; *Walker* v *Sec of State* Unreported, Cty Ct (Judge Higgins), 11 Feb 1982; *Starrett* v *Sec of State* Unreported, Cty Ct (Judge Russell), 3 May 1984.

79. See e.g. *Spiers* v *Halliday, The Times,* 30 June 1984 and generally, *McGregor*, paras 1454–6. *Munkman,* p 61 asserts that the 1984 Tables are used in practice by the British Board, but see *In re Haldane* [1985] *CLY* 962 where the Board is reported to have said that "the proper course [is] . . . to apply the appropriate conventional multiplier currently applied by the courts". *Cf* "The Irish courts . . . are fully convinced . . . of the necessity of actuarial evidence . . . ": *White*, p 147 – see especially *State (Hill)* v *CICT* [1990] ILRM 36.

80. See e.g. *Mitchell* v *Mulholland (No 2)* [1971] 2 All ER 1205, 1213, *per* Edmund Davies LJ. Most commentators are in favour of greater use – see *McGregor*, para 1475, *Munkman*, pp 62, 71.

81. The leading case is now *Auty* v *National Coal Board* [1985] 1 All ER 930 (award of £1,000), which provides a detailed explanation of the assessment of damages under this head. See also *Robertson* v *Lestrange* [1985] 1 All ER 950 (award of £5,000) and *Lim Poh Choo* v *Camden and Islington AHA* [1979] 2 All ER 910 (award of £8,000).

82. Unreported, Cty Ct (Judge Russell), 21 Dec 1979.

83. It was estimated that the pension would probably be payable for eight years; making allowance for accelerated receipt, a (rather generous) multiplier of six was applied.

5. Other Pecuniary Loss

Article 3(2)(*a*)(iii) provides that compensation is payable to the victim in respect of "other pecuniary loss resulting from his injury", i.e. pecuniary loss other than that which results from incapacity for work. This category is found both in the 1977 Order and in the 1968 Act,[84] but its import has never been very clear. In the majority of cases additional cost to the victim is recoverable under Article 3(2)(*a*)(i) as expenses. As McGregor observes:

> "The plaintiff is also entitled to any other loss by way of gains prevented which he can show resulted from the injury, but losses other than of earnings will only arise in rather special cases for there are few possibilities even in theory."[85]

One possible example is a claim for loss of a deposit paid towards a holiday which the victim is now unable to take because of his injuries. Another example is provided by *Payne* v *Secretary of State*[86] where, in addition to loss of earnings, compensation was awarded for loss of army benefit entitlements in respect of a car, married quarters, assisted house purchase, medical expenses and loss of a terminal gratuity. Similarly in *McCartney* v *Secretary of State*,[87] compensation was awarded for loss of (private) use of a company car and for the loss of life insurance and private medical care premiums previously paid by the applicant's employer. Yet another example is provided by *Walsh* v *Secretary of State*[88] where, as a direct result of his injuries, the applicant was no longer able to make an active contribution to the business in which he was a partner with his brother. Contrary to their previous plans, the partners introduced their sons into the business. This caused stress resulting in the dissolution of the partnership; the applicant purchased his brother's share in the business. It was held that since the partnership would have continued but for the applicant's injury, he was entitled to be compensated in respect of the purchase price of his brother's share. In the case of an injured woman (or even a man) injuries may result in the loss of opportunity of marriage and the consequential loss of (financial) support by a husband (or wife). But as McGregor explains, although recovery for such a loss is possible, "it has become the practice . . . to allow for this loss simply by . . . declining to use a lower multiplier for loss of earning capacity than would be appropriate for a man."[89]

For a while it seemed that *Jones* v *Jones*[90] provided a further example of "other pecuniary loss" where a plaintiff's injuries led to his divorce and

---

84. 1968 Act, s 4(1)(*d*); 1977 Order, Art 5(1)(*c*).

85. *McGregor*, para 1452.

86. Unreported, Cty Ct (Judge Rowland), 13 May 1983. See further *Kemp and Kemp*, vol 1, para 5-009/6.

87. Unreported, Cty Ct (Judge Russell), 21 Dec 1979.

88. Unreported, Cty Ct (Judge Russell), 9 Jan 1981.

89. *McGregor*, para 1452, referring e.g. to *Housecroft* v *Burnett* [1986] 1 All ER 332. See also *Thomas* v *Wignall* [1987] 1 All ER 1185.

90. [1984] 3 All ER 1003.

damages were awarded for the financial loss involved in making additional financial provision for his wife and children. However in *Pritchard v J H Cobden Ltd*[91] the Court of Appeal changed its mind and held that financial orders made in matrimonial proceedings did not constitute a "loss", but represented instead a redistribution of assets. The Court also considered that any such "loss" was in any event too remote and in any case should not be recoverable on grounds of policy. Such reasoning underlines a difference in wording between sub-paragraphs (i) and (iii) of Article 3(2)(*a*) of the 1988 Order; whereas expenses other than those actually incurred are recoverable only if they result "directly" from the injury *and* it is reasonable and proper to make them good out of public funds, "other pecuniary loss" is recoverable if it simply results from the injury. It may therefore enure to the benefit of the claimant to have future financial commitments brought about by his injuries classified as the latter and not as the former.

PECUNIARY LOSS INCURRED BY A PERSON RESPONSIBLE FOR A VICTIM'S MAINTENANCE

By Article 3(2)(*b*), compensation is payable –

> "to any person responsible for the maintenance of the victim in respect of –
> . . .
> (ii) pecuniary loss resulting from the victim's injury."

This provision has already been discussed in relation to expenses and it only needs to be noted that the claim for pecuniary loss is limited to persons "responsible for the victim's maintenance". Thus, pecuniary loss resulting e.g. to a business partner of the victim is *not* recoverable under this provision.[92]

PAIN AND SUFFERING AND LOSS OF AMENITIES

Article 3(2)(*a*)(iv) provides that compensation is payable to a surviving victim of a criminal injury only in respect of "his pain and suffering and loss of amenities". This provision has remained unchanged since 1968,[93] and a similar provision is implicit in the British Scheme.[94] The Irish Scheme adopted a similar approach until 1986 when it was amended to exclude the payment of compensation for "pain and suffering".[95]

---

91. [1987] 1 All ER 300 – a "surprising" decision according to Burrows, *Remedies for Torts and Breach of Contract* (1987), pp 172–3 and regarded as incorrect by *McGregor*, para 1498.

92. See above, pp 165–6.

93. 1968 Act, s 4(1)(*f*); 1977 Order, Art 5(1)(*e*).

94. Because of the express provision in para 12 that "compensation will be assessed on the basis of common law damages . . .".

See further Greer, *op cit* n 63, paras 4.38 *et seq*.

95. Irish Scheme, para 6(*e*). It is understood that this term is intended to include compensation for other non-pecuniary loss such as loss of amenities. However, although there is no directly applicable provision in the Civil Liability Act 1961, s 7(2) does refer to "damages for any pain or suffering or personal injury . . . ". Irish common law appears to follow the familiar English analysis – see *White*, ch 6.

"Pain and suffering" is to be interpreted in the same *subjective*[96] sense as at common law.[97] Thus, compensation will be awarded (*inter alia*) for the "shock of the injury, sometimes followed by neurosis . . . physical pain at the time of the injury, during surgical operations, and perhaps during the rest of life . . . mental distress . . . inability to look after the bodily needs of life . . . disfigurement, by scars or mutilation . . . ".[98] The wording of Article 3(2)(*a*)(iv) makes it clear that compensation cannot be awarded for any loss of expectation of life as such;[99] but allowance may be made in the assessment of compensation for pain and suffering for any suffering caused by the victim's awareness that his expectation of life has been curtailed.[1]

"Loss of amenities" means the objective[2] loss or impairment of a limb or any part of the body and any consequential reduction in the victim's capacity to enjoy life.[3] The scope of this heading was considered in *Siggins* v *Ministry of Home Affairs*[4] where the applicant had suffered nervous shock and depressive illness directly attributable to his experiences when a customs post was bombed. As a result, his personality changed, he became impossible to live with and his marriage broke down. The applicant claimed compensation *inter alia* for loss of the society of his wife and children. The Ministry argued that the applicant was in effect claiming compensation for loss of consortium which was a well-established head of damage separate and distinct from loss of amenities and therefore not covered by section 4(1)(*f*) of the 1968 Act (the predecessor of Article 3(2)(*a*)(iv)). The Court of Appeal disagreed. A claim for loss of consortium, as indicated in *Best* v *Samuel Fox Ltd*,[5] was an action by a husband for an injury to his wife which deprived him of her services and company; here the injury was to the husband, whose wife had left him as a result of that injury.[6] In addition, loss

---

96. Damages for pain and suffering "depend on the plaintiff's awareness of pain, her capacity for suffering": *Lim Poh Choo* v *Camden and Islington AHA* [1979] 2 All ER 910, 919, *per* Lord Scarman. In *Wootten* v *Sec of State* Unreported, Cty Ct (Judge Higgins), 7 June 1974 an award under this head was reduced by reason of the fact that the victim was not suffering to the same extent as other applicants.

97. See further *Kemp and Kemp*, ch 2; *McGregor*, paras 1516–1521; *Munkman*, ch 4; *White*, ch 6.

98. *Munkman*, p 118.

99. Damages can no longer be awarded under this head in Northern Ireland – see Administration of Justice Act 1982, s 1(1)(*a*). Damages, but *not* criminal injuries compensation, may be awarded for loss of expectation of life in Ireland – *cp O'Sullivan* v *Dwyer* [1971] IR 275 with Irish Scheme, para 6(*c*).

1. Administration of Justice Act 1982, s 1(1)(*b*), restating the common law position – see e.g. *Hall* v *Hartill* (1968), unreported but

see *Kemp and Kemp*, vol 2, para 7-901 and *O'Sullivan* v *Dwyer*, *supra*.

2. Damages for loss of amenities "are awarded for the fact of deprivation, a substantial loss, whether the plaintiff is aware of it or not": *per* Lord Scarman in *Lim Poh Choo*, *supra*, n 96.

3. See further *Kemp and Kemp*, ch 3; *McGregor*, paras 1522–1529; *Munkman*, ch 4; *White*, ch 6.

4. NIJB, June 1973.

5. [1952] 2 All ER 394. Such damages can no longer be awarded at common law in England and Wales and Northern Ireland: Administration of Justice Act 1982, s 2. The action still exists in the Republic – see McMahon and Binchy, *The Irish Law of Torts* (2nd ed, 1990), p 597.

6. *Cf* according to McMahon and Binchy, *ibid*: "The better view [in Ireland] would appear to be that a wife does have a right of action." See also *PH and Others (Infants)* v *John Murphy & Sons Ltd* [1987] IR 621 (damages not recoverable at common law or under Constitution for loss of non-pecuniary benefits deriving from parent-child relationship).

of consortium had no relevance to the deprivation of the children's company.

Compensation for pain and suffering and loss of amenities is normally awarded as an aggregate sum and its amount depends to a large extent on the particular circumstances of each individual case. Needless to say, attaching a monetary value to such "losses" is artificial, and "all that judges and courts [and the Secretary of State] can do is to award sums which must be regarded as giving reasonable compensation".[7] An illustration of how this is done in practice is provided by *Nolan* v *Secretary of State*[8] where the applicant had been shot through the head and was totally incapacitated as a result. His Honour Judge Brown QC stated:

> "Gradually the courts build up a conventional figure for the loss of an eye, or a hand, for paraplegia, for tetraplegia and so on. These figures vary with the years and at any given moment of time, between people of different ages, and in different circumstances . . . I have been told of various recent awards in similar cases, but none of these is strictly comparable. Cases never are. Doing the best I can, I fix the figure under this head at £30,000. This is fifty per cent more than the figure approved by the Court of Appeal in England three years ago in *Mitchell* v *Mulholland (No 2)*[9] – a not dissimilar case."

It appears, however, that this sum was increased on appeal to the High Court.[10]

Some idea of the conventional figures applied by the courts in cases brought under the 1977 Order since 1980 is now available from the numerous entries in the *Bulletin of Northern Ireland Law*.[11] Now that juries have been abolished in common law personal injury actions, these will in future be supplemented by High Court damages awards and it remains to be seen how these will affect the existing "tariff". Since awards of general damages in Northern Ireland are generally accepted to be higher than those in England and Wales, it might have been thought that the abolition of the jury would lead to lower awards. But a submission to this effect was rejected by the Court of Appeal in *Simpson* v *Harland and Wolff plc*.[12] The plaintiff at the age of 59 learned that he had contracted mesothelioma through exposure to asbestos in the course of his employment. As a result, "his days are literally numbered [and] he is condemned to a future of reduced vitality and increased pain and breathlessness". The trial judge awarded damages of £75,000 for pain and suffering and loss of amenities and Lord Lowry LCJ for the Court of Appeal refused to reduce this award on the ground that it came outside the permissible range laid down in recent English cases:

---

7. *Per* Lord Morris in *H West & Son Ltd* v *Shephard* [1963] 2 All ER 625, 631.

8. Unreported, Cty Ct (Judge Brown), 14 May 1974.

9. [1971] 2 All ER 1205.

10. The overall award was increased to £52,000: judgment of Lowry LCJ delivered 6 Dec 1974.

11. Entries under the heading "Criminal Injuries" are compiled from information provided by the Northern Ireland Office.

12. [1988] 13 NIJB 10. *Cf* the suggested ceiling of £150,000 adumbrated in *Sinnott* v *Quinnsworth Ltd* [1984] ILRM 523.

" . . . the standard in this jurisdiction is that of the reasonable ordinary person, as it was in England and Wales [before juries were phased out] in 1934. One can and should logically and fairly retain that standard while *at the same time* cultivating that predictability and consistency which a group of judges can achieve . . . It would, however, be wrong for the standard of general damages to become frozen while other standards, including the standard of special and fatal accident damages, are continuously being adjusted . . . Accordingly, I would reject the suggestion that our calculations of general damages are 'wrong' if they do not conform to standards observed in other jurisdictions since Northern Ireland, like Scotland and the Republic of Ireland, constitutes a separate legal jurisdiction with its own judicial and social outlook."[13]

However, even by Northern Ireland standards, the award was "very high indeed" and the learned Lord Chief Justice substituted an award of £50,000.

Another factor to consider is the effect of inflation on such "conventional" awards. In *McKee* v *Alexander Greer Ltd*[14] Lord Lowry LCJ had stated:

"The appropriate sum for pain and suffering and loss of amenity must be considerably more now than some years ago since, whatever the difficulty of putting a figure on those aspects of damages, their value must be continuously dependent on the value of money itself."

There was, however, judicial disagreement as to how inflation should be taken into account in relation to non-pecuniary loss. On one view, inflation should automatically be taken into account;[15] on another, "an award for pain, suffering and loss of amenities is . . . dependent only in the most general way upon the movement in monetary values . . . ".[16] The former view appears to have prevailed; in *Wright* v *British Railways Board*[17] Lord Diplock referred to the judge's "duty of assessing damages for non-economic loss in the money of the day at the date of trial" and added that "this is a rule of practice that judges are required to follow . . . ". Later in his judgment Lord Diplock further observed:

"'Brackets' [of awards for non-economic loss] may call for alteration not only to take account of inflation, for which they ought automatically to be raised, but also, it may be, to take account of advances in medical science which may make particular kinds of injuries less disabling or advances in medical knowledge which may disclose hitherto unsuspected long-term effects of some kinds of injuries . . . "[18]

---

13. [1988] 13 NIJB 10, 23. The English cases are not identified in the judgment, but see e.g. *Ambrose* v *Ilford* (Unreported, 1988: award of £28,000) and other cases summarised in *Kemp and Kemp*, vol 2, part 7A.

14. [1974] NI 60, 62.

15. See especially *Walker* v *John McLean & Sons Ltd* [1979] 2 All ER 965, 970, *per* Cumming–Bruce LJ.

16. *Lim Poh Choo* v *Camden and Islington AHA* [1979] 2 All ER 910, 920, *per* Lord

Scarman, followed in *Nichol* v *Harland & Wolff Ltd* [1982] NI 1 – though see also *Hollyoak* v *Harland & Wolff Ltd* [1982] NI 371.

17. [1983] 2 All ER 698, 703.

18. *Ibid*, p 706. His Lordship did, however, warn against "too frequent alteration" of the tariff, since this would "deprive [the guidelines] of their usefulness in providing a reasonable degree of predictability . . . and so facilitating settlement of claims . . . ".

Compensation Where Victim Dies as a Result of His Injuries

The 1988 Order, like the 1977 Order,[19] distinguishes those cases where a victim dies "as a result of the injury" from those where a victim dies "otherwise than as a result of the injury". But when does an injury "result" in death? The following observations seem relevant:

> "[The question is] whether death in fact resulted from the injury. If it did in fact, it makes no matter how improbable or how unnatural the result may have been. The question whether one event 'results' from another involves an examination of the chain of causation. There must be no break in the chain. If there is a break, then the final result is not the result of the initial event. But the break must be an actual effective break, a *novus actus interveniens*, from which a new chain of causation commences. To constitute an actual effective break in the chain, the predominant and really efficient cause of the final event must be the new act intervening. Otherwise, there is no such break in the chain as to prevent the final event from being the 'result' (though an improbable result) of the initial event."[20]

It would appear that death need not be "the" result of the injury – Articles 3(3), 4(2)(*a*) and 11(2), for example, all use the phrase "where the victim . . . dies as *a* result of the injury . . . ".

As in similar provisions in the Fatal Accidents (NI) Order 1977,[21] no time limit for death is specified; it is a matter of proof of the necessary facts in each case.

In ordinary civil actions the death of a person as a result of negligence gives rise to a claim by his relatives under the Fatal Accidents Acts and by his personal representatives under the Law Reform (Miscellaneous Provisions) Act.[22] The criminal injury code has long permitted the former claim but, following a period of some uncertainty,[23] the 1988 Order has come down clearly against the latter (though some direct recovery is permitted). Where the criminal injury results in immediate death, there is only a single basis for compensation. Where a victim lives for a period before death results from the injury, however, two questions can arise.

1. If compensation has already been paid to the victim, does this bar any claim by his relatives under Article 3(3)? The 1988 Order is silent on this

---

19. Article 3(1).
20. *Dunham* v *Clare* [1902] 2 KB 292, 296, *per* Collins MR (in relation to the phrase "death results from the injury" in the Workmen's Compensation Act 1897). Thus, if a person is injured, unreasonably refuses appropriate medical treatment and then dies, his death may not "result" from the injury – see e.g. *Steele* v *Robert George Ltd* [1942] AC 497, discussed Hart and Honoré, *Causation in the Law* (2nd ed. 1985), pp 359–360, and *McGregor,* paras 158–9. See also *Gilmore* v *Belfast Corp* (1942) 76 ILTR 182.
21. Article 3(1).
22. See *Kemp and Kemp,* chs 20–26; *McGregor,* ch 34; *White,* chs 7–14. Note,

however, that *White* devotes a whole chapter (7) to the contention that there may – and should – be in the Republic a separate *common law* action for wrongful death.

23. See e.g. *McManus* v *Armagh CC* [1952] NI 38 and *Gould* v *Belfast Corp*, Unreported, High Ct (Gibson J), 11 March 1969. The matter was finally resolved in *Benson* v *Sec of State* [1976] NI 36, where the Court of Appeal, following *Peebles* v *Oswaldtwistle UDC* [1896] 2 QB 159, held that a claim for criminal injuries compensation did not come within the common law rule *actio personalis moritur cum persona* and therefore survived for the benefit of the deceased's estate.

point and various provisions of the Order by implication point in opposing directions. Thus, it would seem that in such a case compensation would still be payable under Article 3(3)(*b*) for bereavement and under Article 3(3)(*a*)(i) for expenses resulting to relatives from the victim's death. On the other hand there obviously could be no "double" recovery for pecuniary loss and Article 11(2) clearly is intended to prevent relatives recovering compensation for any pain and suffering or loss of amenities occasioned to the victim before his death.[24] The courts appear to have assumed that a successful action in tort by a living victim *does* bar any claim by his dependants under the Fatal Accidents Acts,[25] but the point does not appear to have been specifically addressed and in particular is unsupported by any decision of the House of Lords.[26] The position needs to be considered carefully in the light of recent decisions and the provision of damages (and compensation) for bereavement. There is much to be said for the view that to prevent any claim by the relatives –

> "could place [them] . . . at a disadvantage compared with those of a victim who died from his injuries but had made no application . . . before his death."[27]

2. If the victim has not applied, for compensation – or has applied, but compensation was not paid before his death – the position under the 1988 Order appears to be as follows:

(a) By Article 11(2) any compensation or balance of compensation for pain and suffering and loss of amenities to which the victim was entitled immediately prior to his death "shall cease to be payable".[28]

(b) The limited scope of Article 11(2) implies that other compensation to which the applicant was entitled remains payable after his death. This is supported by Article 11(1)(*a*) which provides that where a victim dies otherwise than as a result of the injury "*any* compen-

---

24. Damages in respect of such loss are recoverable – see e.g. *Robertson* v *Lestrange* [1985] 1 All ER 950. *Cf* " . . . we could see no justification for applying this provision to the [criminal injuries compensation] scheme in England and Wales . . . ": 1978 *IWP Report*, para 12.3.

25. See e.g. *Murray* v *Shuter* [1975] 3 All ER 375; *McCann* v *Sheppard* [1973] 2 All ER 881.

26. As noted in *Pickett* v *British Rail Eng'g Ltd* [1979] 1 All ER 774. However, according to *McGregor,* para 1538 "The point has indeed become incontrovertible now that it has been decided in *Pickett* . . . [to overrule] *Oliver* v *Ashman* . . . and thereby [give the living plaintiff] the opportunity to make provision for his dependants after his premature death." *White*, pp 315–8, citing US case-law, suggests that Irish law should not adopt this approach.

27. 1978 *IWP Report*, para 12.4, which recommended that relatives should be able to make an application, but that any compensation payable to them should be reduced by the amount already awarded to the victim. The Working Party considered that the number of cases affected by the proposal would be "very small". The British Scheme, para 15 gives effect to this recommendation, which will be continued in the 1988 Act, s 111(9).

28. Such compensation was payable to the victim's estate under the law prior to 1977 – see e.g. *Benson (supra)*, applied in *Halliday* v *Sec of State* Unreported, Cty Ct (Judge Babington), 19 Oct 1976. The position under the 1977 Order was unclear; where the victim died as a result of the injury, compensation of any kind was payable only to his "dependants", presumably as such. This would seem to preclude any payment to relatives as beneficiaries under the victim's estate.

sation . . . to which he was entitled . . . shall cease to be payable . . . ". It would therefore appear that compensation is recoverable for allowable expenses and pecuniary loss suffered by the victim
before his death. But this claim does not apparently devolve to the
victim's estate, since by Article 3(3), where the victim of a criminal
injury dies as a result of the injury, compensation is payable *only* to
his relatives.[29] It appears to follow, therefore, that where the victim
lives for a time and then dies compensation is payable to his relatives
in respect of –

   (i) allowable expenses incurred by the victim as a result of his
      injury;

  (ii) pecuniary loss to the victim resulting from his injury;

 (iii) allowable expenses incurred by the victim's relatives as a result
      of his death;

 (iv) pecuniary loss to the relatives as a result of the victim's death.[30]

Presumably the rule against double compensation will apply, and, in
relation to (i) and (ii), the Secretary of State has available to him the powers
conferred by Article 13(3) to pay the compensation to such relatives as the
Secretary of State thinks fit – normally, it is thought, to those entitled to
benefit from the victim's estate.

COMPENSATION PAYABLE TO RELATIVES

Article 3(3) provides that:

"Where the victim of a criminal injury dies as a result of the injury, compensation shall only be payable -

(*a*) to the victim's relatives in respect of –

   (i) expenses actually and reasonably incurred as a result of the victim's
      injury or death and any other expenses resulting directly from the
      victim's injury or death which it is reasonable and proper to make
      good to his relatives out of public funds;

  (ii) pecuniary loss resulting from the victim's injury or death."[31]

Where the relative concerned is the spouse or parent of the victim, compensation may also be payable for bereavement.[32]

---

29. Thus, by implication, overruling *Benson*, *supra*.

30. This interpretation is supported by the "neutral" wording of Art 3(3)(*a*) which, unlike Art 3(3)(*c*) and 3(4)(*a*), does not indi-cate by whom the expense or pecuniary loss has to be incurred.

31. This simplifies and clarifies the similar provision in the 1977 Order, Arts 3(1) and

5(1); the most important change (as noted in the text) is the substitution of "relatives" for "dependants". *Cp* British Scheme, para 15 confers the same entitlement as under the Fatal Accidents legislation: see also 1988 Act, s 111(4), (11). The Irish Scheme, para 6 like-wise incorporates the relevant provisions of the Civil Liability Act 1961.

32. Articles 3(3)(*b*) and 9(3), discussed below p 199.

1. Meaning of "Relative"

The first point to be noted is that the 1988 Order has, with one exception,[33] done away with the need to establish that a relative must have been "wholly or partially"[34] or "wholly or substantially"[35] dependent upon the deceased's income in order to qualify for compensation. As a result, it avoids a problem which plagued the earlier legislation on this subject. Under the 1968 Act, compensation was payable to non-dependent relatives only in respect of "expenses incurred".[36] In *O'Hare* v *Secretary of State*,[37] this phrase was held to extend to funeral expenses, but not to the future cost of domestic assistance required by a husband when his wife was killed.[38] In an attempt to close this gap, Article 3(1)(*c*)(iii) of the 1977 Order extended the right of recovery to "expenses necessarily incurred or to be so incurred . . . ". This amendment probably[39] covered the cost of domestic assistance, past and future – but it was not appropriate to cover earnings lost e.g. by a husband who took time off work to look after his children. Accordingly, a further amendment was made in 1982,[40] so that compensation became payable for "pecuniary loss which has been or may be suffered by him [i.e. the non-dependent relative] as a result of the victim's death" in addition to any "reasonable expenses necessarily incurred or to be so incurred by him as a result of the victim's death". Under the 1988 Order, however, any relative as defined therein is entitled to compensation, provided only that he can establish that he has or will incur expenses or pecuniary loss as provided for in the Order.

"Relative" for the purposes of Article 3(3) is defined in the 1988 Order in precisely the same terms as under the Fatal Accidents (NI) Order 1977, as amended by the Administration of Justice Act 1982,[41] *viz:*

> "'Relative', in respect of a victim, means –
>
> (*a*) the spouse or former spouse of the victim;

---

33. *Cp* Art 5(10) and (11), discussed below p 196.

34. As under the 1968 Act, s 11(1).

35. As under the 1977 Order, Art 2(2). This phrase does not appear to have been judicially explained in any case under the 1977 Order.

36. By s 1(1)(*c*)(iii).

37. [1974] NI 214, discussed Greer and Mitchell, *Compensation for Criminal Injuries to Persons in Northern Ireland* (1976), p 94. Such compensation would have been payable under the then British Scheme, para 15, and the Secretary of State subsequently agreed to make a payment to Mr O'Hare (and any other similar cases) on an extra-statutory and *ex gratia* basis, pending amendment of the 1968 Act.

38. In *O'Hare* the award of compensation for the cost of domestic assistance actually incur-

red before the hearing was not disputed; but Jones LJ observed: "But . . . it must not be taken that this Court is adjudicating on, or necessarily accepting the validity of, that part of the award . . . ".

39. In *O'Hare*, Jones LJ (at p 219) stated: "I cannot regard the cost of domestic assistance which may be . . . incurred as expenses . . . ". But it is difficult to accept this reasoning, particularly in light of the avowed legislative intention to which the new provision was designed to give effect: see Greer and Mitchell, *op cit* – 37, pp 94–5, and *Supplement*, p 47.

40. Criminal Injuries (Compensation) Amendment (NI) Order 1982, Art 5.

41. Schedule 6, para 2, following recommendations made in the *Law Commission Report*, paras 257–8 and in the *Pearson Report*, paras 400–405.

(*b*) any person who –

    (i) was living with the victim in the same household immediately before the date on which the criminal injury was sustained; and

    (ii) had been living with the victim in the same household for at least two years before that date; and

    (iii) was living during the whole of that period as the spouse of the victim:

(*c*) any parent or other ascendant[42] of the victim;

(*d*) any person who was treated by the victim as his parent;

(*e*) a child or other descendant[43] of the victim;

(*f*) any person (not being a child of the victim) who, in the case of any marriage to which the victim was at any time a party, was treated by the victim as a child of the family in relation to that marriage;

(*g*) any person who is, or is the issue of, a brother, sister, uncle or aunt of the victim."[44]

Article 2(4) further provides:

"In deducing any relationship for the purposes of this Order –

(*a*) an adopted[45] person shall be treated as the child of the person or persons by whom he was adopted and not as the child of any other person; and subject thereto,

(*b*) any relationship by affinity shall be treated as a relationship by consanguinity, any relationship of the half blood as a relationship of the whole blood, and the stepchild of any person as his child; and

(*c*) an illegitimate person shall be treated as the legitimate child of his mother and reputed father."[46]

It may be appropriate at this stage to note the changes thus introduced into the criminal injuries code by the 1988 Order.

---

42. The 1977 Order referred to grandparents and great-grandparents, so the new formula represents no change of substance.

43. The 1977 Order included grandchild and great-grandchild, and so again the new formula represents no change of substance.

44. This provision is in line with the British Scheme, para 15 (the Administration of Justice Act 1982 applied equally to the English Fatal Accidents legislation) – see also 1988 Act, s 111(11)(*a*). *Cp* the Irish Scheme is more limited, since, by the Civil Liability Act, s 47(1), a claim may only be made by a "member of the family" defined as meaning "wife, husband, father, mother, grandfather, grandmother, stepfather, stepmother, son, daughter, grandson, granddaughter, stepson, stepdaughter, brother, sister, half-brother, half-sister"; see further *White*, ch 8.

45. By Art 2(5) "adopted" means "adopted in pursuance of a court order made in any part of the United Kingdom, the Isle of Man or any of the Channel Islands or by a foreign adoption within the meaning of the Adoption (Hague Convention) Act (NI) 1969." The same definition is given in the Fatal Accidents (NI) Order 1977, Art 2(4).

46. This provision replicates the Fatal Accidents (NI) Order 1977, Art 2(3).

(a) Former spouses

Both the 1968 Act and the 1977 Order included "any wife by any former marriage",[47] but not apparently divorced husbands or other previous spouses.[48] Article 2(2) now refers to former "spouses"[49] and by Article 2(6) "former spouses" now "includes a reference to a person whose marriage to the victim has been annulled or declared void as well as a person whose marriage to the victim has been dissolved".[50] A distinction still remains, however, between a spouse and a former spouse in the assessment of compensation. By Article 6(5) of the 1988 Order, "in determining the amount of compensation payable to the widower or widow of a victim, his or her prospects of remarriage shall be disregarded". The Law Commission recognised that a question of policy arose as to whether this provision should be extended to former spouses – and the 1988 Order (as well as the Fatal Accidents legislation) appears to have followed their conclusion that to do so would be "absurd".[51]

(b) "De facto" spouses

Prior to 1983 "common law" spouses could not recover damages under the Fatal Accidents legislation, and were equally ineligible for criminal injuries compensation, although in both cases the children of such a relationship were entitled to recover.[52] Both the Law Commission and the Pearson Commission, in their examination of the Fatal Accidents legislation, rejected suggestions to extend the category of claimants to include "common law" spouses, partly because of the difficulty of definition and partly for reasons of policy.[53] However, this approach was rejected as unjust and anomalous by the House of Lords in its debate on the Administration of Justice Bill[54] and the Fatal Accidents (NI) Order 1977 was accordingly amended in 1982.[55] The provision then adopted has now been extended to the criminal injuries code.[56]

It will be noted that the definition has "some effective limits".[57] The new

---

47. 1968 Act, s 11(1); 1977 Order, Art 2(2).

48. See *Payne-Collins v Taylor Woodrow Construction Ltd* [1975] 1 All ER 898.

49. As the Law Commission pointed out (*Report*, para 259) a divorced husband may have been receiving maintenance from his former wife.

50. Replicating the new Art 2(2A) inserted into the Fatal Accidents (NI) Order 1977 by the Administration of Justice Act 1982, Sch 6, para 2, following the recommendation in the *Law Commission Report*, para 259.

51. *Law Commission Report*, para 260: " . . . a divorcee knows that the maintenance ordered to be paid to her will in any event be terminated by her remarriage . . . ".

52. See e.g. *Nicholson v Sec of State*, Unreported, Cty Ct (Judge Russell) 20 Dec 1982.

53. *Law Commission Report*, para 258; *Pearson Report*, para 405.

54. See 428 HL Debs, cols 1281–6 (30 March 1982) and 429 HL Debs, cols 1105–12 (4 May 1982).

55. Administration of Justice Act 1982, Sch 6, para 2.

56. The British Scheme did not at first follow the Fatal Accidents Act on this point, but a recommendation that it should do so was made in the 1986 *IWP Report*, para 15.6 – a recommendation implemented in the 1990 Scheme, para 15 – and see also the 1988 Act, s 111(11).

57. Considered essential by the Criminal Injuries Compensation Board and by Lord Hailsham LC – see 429 HL Debs, col 1105 (4 May 1982).

provision will not benefit "the mere kept woman" who was not living with the deceased as his wife, and the two-year requirement is intended to ensure that there is some degree of permanence about the relationship.[58] The fact that the parties are not married, however, is not to be ignored; Article 6(6) (following Article 5(3A) of the Fatal Accidents (NI) Order 1977[59]) provides that:

> "In determining the amount of compensation payable to a person who is a relative of the victim by virtue of sub-paragraph (*b*) of the definition of 'relative' . . . there shall be taken into account the fact that that person has no enforceable right to financial support by the victim as a result of their living together."

Thus, even if a person brings himself or herself within the fairly narrow scope of this definition, the element of uncertainty involved in a *de facto* relationship may be reflected in a lower award of compensation.

The wording of this definition appears to be drawn from social security and family law precedents.[60] Thus, a woman loses entitlement to various welfare benefits for any period during which she and a man to whom she is not married are "living together as husband and wife".[61] The fact that a man and woman have been living in the same household will not necessarily establish that they have been living as husband and wife; in *Crake* v *Supplementary Benefits Commission,*[62] e.g. the man had moved into a house solely to look after an injured woman and it was held that the couple were not living together as man and wife. Similarly, it has been held that neither financial support nor the existence or absence of a sexual relationship is conclusive on this issue;[63] but if a man and woman are looking after their own children, this creates "a strong presumption", as does the assumption by a woman of the man's surname.[64] Although there is much to be said for consistency in the interpretation of such phrases, the courts have frequently warned against the assumption that similar words in other statutes are to be interpreted similarly – particularly when those statutes are not *in pari materia*. We must, therefore, await a decision on the particular meaning of this definition for the purposes of the 1988 Order.

(c) *Person treated by the victim as parent or child*

The Law Commission considered that children who had been *de facto* adopted and maintained by a deceased should be entitled to claim damages

---

58. Where the new definition does not apply, the children of the relationship may still qualify for compensation. See e.g. *Nicholson* (*supra* n 52), *K* v *JMP Ltd* [1975] 1 All ER 1030 and *Dodds* v *Dodds* [1978] 2 All ER 539 (which Judge Russell in *Nicholson* considered inapplicable where "the figures upon which any assessment of the children's loss falls to be calculated are quite uncertain").

59. Inserted by Administration of Justice Act 1982, Sch 6, para 6(4).

60. See generally Ogus and Barendt, *The Law of Social Security* (3rd ed, 1988), pp 354–7, Bromley and Lowe, *Family Law* (7th ed, 1987), pp 190–200 and Cretney, *Principles of Family Law* (4th ed, 1984), pp 152 *et seq*, discussed above pp 143–5.

61. See e.g. Social Security Act 1975, ss 24(2), 25(3) and 26(3).

62. [1982] 1 All ER 498.

63. Ogus and Barendt, *op cit*, p 356.

64. *Ibid*, p 357.

in respect of his death,[65] and the Administration of Justice Act 1982 so provided.[66] Headings (c) and (f) of the definition of "relative" in the 1988 Order follow this precedent exactly. The wording of the new provision was drawn from matrimonial legislation[67] but, as the Law Commission pointed out, the child in this context need have been recognised as a child of the family only by the deceased, as under the Inheritance (Provision for Family and Dependants) (NI) Order 1979. Judicial dicta warn against attempts to define precisely the scope of these provisions and insist that each case depends on its own facts.[68] In general, however, a child will have been "treated . . . as his child" where the "parent" fed, clothed and behaved towards him as if he were his own child.[69] However, the character of the relationship between the victim and the child may carry an element of uncertainty, and, if this is so, lower compensation may be awarded.[70]

The 1977 Order specifically included a spouse's parent within the definition of "relative".[71] There is no such express reference in the 1988 Order, but such a relative is presumably covered either by heading (d) or more clearly by Article 2(4)(b) – "any relationship by affinity shall be treated as a relationship by consanguinity . . . ".

(d) Uncle or aunt of the victim

This new category is necessary to bring the 1988 Order into line with a provision which has existed in the Fatal Accidents legislation since 1959.[72]

Any relative as so defined may claim compensation, but it is not clear from the Order whether each relative is entitled to compensation for his individual loss or whether the compensation is awarded to the relatives collectively. The wording of the Order appears equivocal; thus by Article 3(3)(a) compensation is payable "to the victim's relatives . . . ".[73] But it is

---

65. *Report*, para 257.

66. Schedule 6, para 2, substituting new Art 2(2) into the Fatal Accidents (NI) Order 1977.

67. Matrimonial Proceedings and Property Act 1970, s 27(1). In Northern Ireland, see Matrimonial Causes (NI) Order 1978, Art 2(2); Domestic Proceedings (NI) Order 1980, Art 2(2).

68. See e.g. *Re Leach* [1985] 2 All ER 754, 760, *per* Slade LJ. In that case, an *adult* stepdaughter was held to have been treated by the deceased as a child of the family for purposes of the Inheritance (Provision for Family and Dependants) Act 1975, ss 1 and 2.

69. See e.g. *W (RJ) v W (SJ)* [1971] 3 All ER 303. "The obvious example is a stepchild . . . but privately fostered children or orphans being cared for by relatives are also covered": Hoggett, *Parents and Children: The Law of Parental Responsibility* (3rd ed, 1987), p 35. *Cf* "Commonsense excludes . . . young lodgers, au pair girls and

relations who are being looked after during their parents' temporary absence": Bromley and Lowe, *Family Law* (7th ed, 1987), p 292. See also Rayden and Jackson, *Law and Practice in Divorce and Family Matters* (15th ed, 1988), vol 1, p 249 and Priest, "Child of the Family" (1984) 14 *Fam L* 134.

70. See e.g. *Phipps v Cunard White Star Line Ltd* [1951] 1 Lloyd's Rep 54.

71. Article 2(2).

72. Fatal Accidents Act (NI) 1959, s 1(1).

73. *Cf* Fatal Accidents (NI) Order 1977, Art 5(1): " . . . damages . . . may be awarded as are proportioned to the injury resulting from the death to the dependants respectively". In *Pym v GNR* (1863) 4 B & S 397, 407, Erle CJ stated: "The remedy . . . given . . . is not given to a class, but to individuals . . . ". In *Mulholland v McCrea* [1961] NI 135, the Court of Appeal accepted "the personal and individual nature" of such claims. A recent example is provided by *Black v Yates, The Times,* 11 May 1989.

suggested that many of the provisions of the Order do require each relative's entitlement to compensation to be separately considered. Thus, if both the widow and father of the deceased incurred pecuniary loss as a result of his death, it can hardly be the case that the father's membership of an unlawful association would debar the widow from receiving compensation in respect of her loss. Further, in the absence of any express requirement to the contrary,[74] it seems preferable that the principles applicable to claims under the Fatal Accidents legislation should be followed.

2. Expenses

The criminal injuries legislation, unlike Fatal Accidents legislation,[75] has long provided for the payment of compensation for expenses other than funeral expenses.[76] Indeed the formula in the 1988 Order is identical to that for personal injuries cases in Article 3(2)(a)(i), which has already been discussed. In "death" cases it will in particular include:

(a) Medical and other expenses resulting from the victim's injury prior to his death. This provision allows relatives to claim compensation for what would, in a personal injuries action, be recoverable by the estate under the Law Reform (Miscellaneous Provisions) Act (NI) 1937.[77]

(b) Funeral expenses incurred by relatives. These *are* specifically provided for in the Fatal Accidents legislation[78] and it would seem reasonable for the compensation payable under the 1988 Order to follow Fatal Accidents cases on this point. Thus, the cost of embalming may be allowed,[79] together with the cost of a reasonable gravestone[80] – but not the cost of a monument.[81] The broader scope of Article 3(3)(a)(i) may, however, mean the the 1988 Order covers other "reasonable" expenses associated with a funeral.[82]

Compensation for allowable funeral and other expenses is not immune from deduction in respect of collateral benefits.[83]

---

74. Article 4(2)(a) states that an application "may be made by the victim's spouse on behalf of both the applicant and of such children . . . as are relatives of the victim . . . ". But this provision is permissive only, and in any event refers to the making of the application and not to entitlement to compensation.

75. *Cp* Fatal Accidents (NI) Order 1977, Art 5(4).

76. 1968 Act, ss 1(1)(c)(i) and 4(1)(a); 1977 Order, Arts 3(1)(c)(i) and 5(1)(a).

77. See e.g. *McGregor*, para 1608.

78. Fatal Accidents (NI) Order 1977, Art 5(4).

79. *Hart* v *Griffiths-Jones* [1948] 2 All ER 729.

80. *Gammell* v *Wilson* [1981] 1 All ER 578.

81. *Hart* v *Griffiths-Jones, supra; Stanton* v *Ewart F Youlden Ltd* [1960] 1 All ER 429, where a number of funeral expenses are considered in some detail. See also *Goldstein* v

Salvation Army Assurance Soc [1917] 2 KB 291 – and generally *Gammell* v *Wilson* in the High Court (Unreported, but judgment set out in *Kemp and Kemp*, vol 1, para 24–002).

82. Under the British Scheme (para 15, and related *Statement*) no award is made in England and Wales in respect of newspaper notices, wreaths or funeral breakfasts (such awards *are* made in Scotland). An award may be made in either jurisdiction for the reasonable cost of conveying family mourners to the funeral. *White*, ch 12 suggests that the Irish courts might take a more generous view as to recoverable expenses generally.

83. 1988 Order, Art 6(3). *Cf* 1986 *IWP Report*, para 19.2: "We take the view that the only element of an award which should be disregarded when social security benefits are taken into account is funeral expenses and we understand that this is in line with the present practice." See also 1988 Act, Sch 7, para 11(1).

3. Pecuniary Loss

In general, the compensation payable to relatives for pecuniary loss resulting from the victim's death is assessed on the same lines as damages under the Fatal Accidents (NI) Order 1977.[84] But although this is confirmed by some express provisions of the 1988 Order, other provisions require some departures from this approach.

The first point to note however is that the relative must have incurred a *loss* "resulting from the victim's injury or death". This point is neatly illustrated by *R* v *CICB, ex parte McGuffie and Smith*.[85] The applicants were the aunts of three children whose mother had been murdered by her divorced husband. After the murder the children were formally taken into care by the local authority, but were fostered by the applicants. Both aunts had to give up work to look after the children. It was held that they were not entitled to receive any award; any pecuniary loss resulting from the murder had been suffered not by them but by the children, who had indeed lost the value of their mother's services. However, the amount of this loss was in this case obviously to be measured by the loss of earnings suffered by the aunts.[86]

(a) Multiplicand

By Article 7(2) compensation for such pecuniary loss "shall be determined (a) having regard to the total annual income of the victim, both earned and unearned . . . ".[87] By Article 7(4) "income" means:

> "the amount of a person's income after taking account of –
>
> (a) income tax;
>
> (b) social security contributions payable under the laws of any part of the United Kingdom or similar contributions payable under the laws of any other country, state or territory;
>
> (c) in the case of an employed person, any amount deducted from his remuneration by his employer by way of superannuation contributions."[88]

The deceased's total annual income is only a starting point for calculating the multiplicand and may have to be varied to take into account prospects of

---

84. See generally *McGregor*, paras 1543–1593; *Kemp and Kemp*, Part III. Although Art 7(2)(*b*) of the 1988 Order (following the 1968 Act and the 1977 Order) stipulates that the compensation "shall be determined . . . without regard to the Fatal Accidents (NI) Order 1977", it is thought that this must be intended to connote the specific provisions of that Order relating e.g. to the non-deduction of collateral benefits and not the general method of assessing damages as developed by the courts.

85. [1978] *Crim LR* 160. See also CICB, *14th Annual Report* (1977–78), paras 10-13.

86. The court further indicated that under the British Scheme (para 9), the Board could direct that the money awarded to the children should be paid to the aunts; a similar solution could be adopted under the 1988 Order, Art 13(3).

87. In *Arouni* v *Sec of State*, Unreported, High Ct (Gibson LJ), 8 Dec 1977, it was held that supplementary benefits paid to a mother constituted "income" for purposes of a claim by her children under the 1968 Act.

88. Discussed above, p 170.

promotion, etc.[89] Regard may also have to be had to the value of benefits e.g. derived by the victim from his employment[90] – and to the value of services performed for his family by the victim.[91] The ceiling provided for in Article 8(1)[92] will have to be applied in appropriate cases; it will be noted that it applies not to the deceased's income, but to the applicant's pecuniary loss, *after* the deductions specified in Articles 7(4) and 6(2)(*b*) have been made. The wording suggests that the ceiling applies only after taking into account the deductions which must also be made for what the victim "required or expended for his own personal and living expenses". In Fatal Accidents cases this is a matter for decision on the evidence in each case.[93] By Article 7(3) of the 1988 Order, however:

> "In calculating the compensation payable to the relatives of a victim who dies, he shall, until the contrary is proved, be taken to have spent one-fifth of his income on himself."[94]

It is thus open either to the applicant or to the Secretary of State to show on the evidence in any particular case that the victim normally spent less or more[95] than one-fifth of his income on himself.[96]

In a new provision Article 5(10) provides:

> "Subject to paragraph 11, no compensation shall be paid to any relative of the victim . . . in respect of any pecuniary loss resulting from the victim's injury or death which consists of a loss of profits or other loss connected with any business in which the victim was engaged at the time when the criminal injury was sustained."

Paragraph (11) provides that this exclusion does not apply "if the relative was, at the time when the criminal injury was sustained, wholly or substantially dependent upon the victim's income." ·

---

89. See e.g. *McMahon* v *Sec of State* Unreported, Cty Ct (Judge Higgins), 20 Jan 1975 (deceased a "dynamic businessman" who would have earned more as business developed); *Robertson* v *Lestrange* [1985] 1 All ER 950 provides a good example of the current approach.

90. See e.g. allowance for "fringe benefits" in *Graham* v *Dodds* [1983] NI 22, 36.

91. See e.g. *Duffy* v *Sec of State* Unreported, Cty Ct (Judge Babington), 2 Feb 1978 (loss of husband's services about the home); *Donnelly* v *Hackett* [1988] 6 NIJB 6 (loss of husband's services re building of home); *Spittle* v *Bunney* [1988] 3 All ER 1031 (loss of mother's services to young child).

92. Discussed above, p 176.

93. See e.g. *Marks* v *Sec of State* Unreported, Cty Ct (Judge Brown), 16 July 1976 and generally *McGregor*, para 1559; *Kemp and Kemp*, ch 21; *White*, ch 9.

94. This provision was first introduced in the 1977 Order, Art 7(3) in order to make the assessment "rather easier and quicker" – see HC Debs (NI Cttee), col 7 (16 Feb 1977) (Mr Concannon).

95. As e.g. in *Mallett* v *McMonagle* [1969] 2 All ER 178 and *Scott* v *Pollock* [1976] NI 1 (deceased in Fatal Accidents Act case held to have spent one-third of net income on himself). Different figures may be applicable in respect of past and future loss respectively – see e.g. *Graham* v *Dodds* [1983] NI 22. *Cf McGregor*, para 1559, quoting *Robertson* v *Lestrange* [1985] 1 All ER 950, refers to the "convention" in England and Wales whereby one-third is deducted if there are no dependent children, and one-quarter where there are.

96. The suggestion in the High Court in *Graham* v *Dodds* [1983] NI 22 that 20% enshrines the *maximum* deduction is obviously incorrect.

This provision is unique to the Northern Ireland scheme and appears to have been inserted to avoid the full consequences of the omission of a general requirement that a relative had to be wholly or substantially dependent in order to recover compensation. Article 5(10) would appear to preclude compensation being paid in any case where the deceased was engaged in business and made over some of the profits from that business – in money or in kind – to some of his relatives – unless such donation represented the whole or a substantial[97] part of that relative's income. Thus, many "sleeping partners" in family firms may not qualify for compensation if the business goes downhill after the death of the person running the firm. It will be noted that this exception relates to the victim's *income*; where the business he is engaged in is a company, it would appear that no compensation is payable to any person wholly or substantially dependent on payments from the company's profits.[98]

(b) Multiplier

The method of calculating the multiplier in Fatal Accidents Act cases was authoritatively reviewed by the House of Lords in *Graham* v *Dodds*,[99] and it is submitted that the decision in that case extends to the assessment of compensation under the 1988 Order. This means in particular that the multiplier must be calculated from the date of death of the victim – not from the date of the assessment; the number of pre-assessment years for which pecuniary loss is awarded is then deducted from the multiplier. The House of Lords also considered inappropriate a multiplier of 18 for a deceased aged 41 and more generally chose to reiterate Lord Diplock's observation in an earlier Northern Ireland case – *Mallett* v *McMonagle*[1] – that a maximum multiplier of 16 should seldom be exceeded, for what Lord Bridge called "the convincing reasons which [Lord Diplock] demonstrated by reference to annuity values at different rates of interest."[2]

Under the 1988 Order the calculation of the multiplier must, in appropriate cases, take into account two special factors:

(1) Where a claim is made by a *de facto* or "common law" spouse, "there shall be taken into account the fact that that person had no enforceable right to financial support by the victim as a result of their living together."[3]

---

97. The meaning of "substantial" does not appear to have arisen for decision in any reported case under the 1977 Order.

98. *Cp Malyon* v *Plummer* [1963] 2 All ER 344.

99. [1983] NI 22.

1. [1969] 2 All ER 178.

2. [1983] 2 All ER 953, "proving" that the discount rate should be 4–4½%. But this discount rate has been widely criticised as too high – see above, p 179.

3. Article 6(6). Note that it has been argued in relation to *married* spouses that the court should take into account the prospects of divorce – see especially *Sharp-Barker* v *Fehr* (1982) 39 BCLR 19. The divorce rate was referred to in *Jones* v *Jones* [1984] 3 All ER 1003,1007, but Dunn LJ regarded that as "not in itself a sufficient foundation to justify a discount . . . "; if the marriage was not happy or stable, however, "the position might well have been different." *Cf Pearson Report*, para 417, agreed: "Such a change [by divorce] could theoretically have affected the dependency, but the chances of its taking place cannot be ascertained with any degree of certainty; and the attempt to make a forecast could lead to undesirable inquiries into the nature of the relationship."

(2) By Article 6(5):

> "In determining the amount of compensation payable to the widower or widow of a victim, his or her prospects of remarriage shall be disregarded."

This provision extends the 1977 Order (Article 5(6)) in that it applies both to widows and widowers. In this respect the paragraph must be distinguished from a similar provision contained in the Fatal Accidents (NI) Order 1977.[4] A more important distinction is that Article 6(5) does not apply to *actual* remarriage before the date of assessment, which will therefore be taken into account in criminal injuries cases.[5] This does not mean necessarily that nothing is payable in respect of the period after remarriage, but merely that the effect of the remarriage on the spouse's loss has to be considered. Thus it may be that the second husband is earning less than the deceased, and the widow will therefore have sustained a continuing loss in spite of her remarriage.

The wording of the above provision, like that in the Fatal Accidents Order, means that the prospects of remarriage *will* be taken into account in assessing the compensation payable to children on the death of their mother or father.[6] It is however suggested below[7] that the reference to "the amount of compensation" means that the prospects of remarriage are to be ignored when determining the value of any collateral benefits (and especially certain social security benefits) which must, by Article 6(2)(b), be deducted from the compensation payable to a widow or widower.

(c) Apportionment of compensation

Article 13(3) provides that "compensation may be paid . . . as the Secretary of State thinks fit as to the . . . apportionment of the compensation to [the victim's] relatives, or to any of them . . .". Any such apportionment normally reflects the pecuniary loss suffered by each relative. But, in practice, where the application is made by the victim's widow and children, the bulk of the compensation is apportioned to the widow, at least in cases where the family was stable and there is no risk that it will fail so to

---

4. Article 5(3), which applies only to widows – an anomaly which the Law Commission (*Report*, para 251) thought should be corrected. *Cf McGregor*, paras 1568 and 1598 suggests that the widower's prospects may now have to be ignored even without the benefit of specific statutory provision. For the Irish law, see *White*, pp 380–1.

5. Article 5(3) of the Fatal Accidents Order excludes "the remarriage of the widow" as well as her prospects of remarriage. The 1988 Order thus avoids the "striking example" of over-compensation noted by *Kemp and Kemp*, p 415 (young widow remarried before trial awarded £65,000, although second husband earning over £10,000 per annum). The *Pearson Report*, para 411 regarded it as a

"manifest absurdity" to award damages for a loss which is known to have ceased; but the existing law was supported in the 1986 *IWP Report*, para 15.9 and the British Scheme still follows the Fatal Accidents legislation.

6. See e.g. *Howitt v Heads* [1972] 1 All ER 491; *Thompson v Price* [1973] 2 All ER 846 – another "anomaly" criticised by the Law Commission (*Report*, para 252). *Cf Munkman*, p 151: "In fact, the sums required for the child's maintenance are normally part of the mother's damages which cannot be reduced and the balance apportioned to the child direct represents benefits other than maintenance which he might have got from his father." *Sed quaere*.

7. At|pp 214–5.

remain.[8] So long as nothing turns on such an apportionment, the practice is obviously a convenient one. But it may lead, in cases where the amount of compensation *is* affected by the apportionment, to failure to apply the proper principles. Thus, the method of apportionment became a live issue for a short time after the decision in *Gammell* v *Wilson*[9] meant that the total amount of damages payable by a defendant might well be affected by the way in which Fatal Accidents Acts awards were apportioned. As a result, the courts began to insist on a "genuine" estimate of the children's dependency.[10] It may be that the application of Article 6(2)(*b*) of the 1988 Order requires a similar approach.[11]

4. Compensation for Bereavement

Shortly after the first Fatal Accidents Act it was decided that damages were not payable thereunder for any loss of society, mental suffering, or grief caused to relatives by the death.[12] In general the criminal injuries code followed this precedent until 1920 when the power to award "full compensation" was interpreted by the majority of the Irish Court of Appeal as entitling the court to award compensation, in the case of a widow at least, for "the loss of consortium, or nervous or physical breakdown, through grief or shock . . . ".[13] The Northern Ireland courts, however, followed the Fatal Accidents Act practice; the repeal of the relevant legislation meant that the question did not at first arise in the Republic.[14] However, the British Scheme from the outset, in its application to Scotland, permitted the award of compensation for *solatium* or, from 1976, for loss of society.[15] In addition, the express reference to the Civil Liability Act 1961 in the Irish Scheme introduced in 1974 meant that compensation became payable thereunder for "mental distress" resulting to a dependant from the death of a victim.[16] The issue as to Fatal Accident cases in England and Wales was examined by the

---

8. See e.g. *Kemp and Kemp*, ch 23. It was this practice which required amendment of the provision relating to discretionary payments – see below p 215.

9. [1981] 1 All ER 578.

10. See especially *Robertson* v *Lestrange* [1985] 1 All ER 950.

11. See further below, pp 218–9.

12. *Blake* v *Midland Rly* (1852) 18 QB 93.

13. *O'Connell* v *Tipperary CC* [1921] 2 IR 103, 118, *per* Sir James Campbell C, discussed above, p 21.

14. See above, p 28.

15. According to the 1978 *IWP Report*, para 12.1 awards for *solatium* of up to £2,500 were made in cases commenced before May 1976. Thereafter compensation for "loss of society"

was awarded under the Damages (Scotland) Act 1976, as interpreted in *Dingwall* v *W Alexander & Sons (Midlands) Ltd* 1982 SC 179. According to the 1986 *IWP Report*, para 15.2: "The amount of the award is within the discretion of the court, which has to assess the value of the relationship which has been lost but without regard to the bereaved person's grief." See e.g. CICB, *20th Annual Report* (1983–84) para 41, where compensation of £7,000 and £4,000 was awarded to a widow and child respectively. The separate Scottish provision is preserved by the 1988 Act, s 111(4)(*c*).

16. Under s 49(1)(*a*)(ii), as interpreted e.g. in *McCarthy* v *Walsh* [1965] IR 246. Damages under this head were originally restricted to a total of £1,000, but that maximum was increased to £7,500 by the Courts Act 1981. See generally *White*, ch 10.

Law Commission[17] and the Pearson Commission,[18] with conflicting results. Ultimately the Administration of Justice Act 1982[19] effectively implemented the more limited recommendations of the Law Commission. This in turn was adopted for criminal injuries purposes in England and Wales[20] and an identical provision is now contained in Article 9(3) of the 1988 Order:

> "Where the victim of a criminal injury dies as a result of the injury, compensation for bereavement shall only be payable . . . to –
> (a) the spouse of the victim; or
> (b) where the victim was a minor who was never married -
>   (i) his parents, if he was legitimate; and
>   (ii) his mother, if he was illegitimate."

By Article 9(5) the amount payable as compensation for bereavement is the fixed sum of £3,500;[21] by Article 9(4), where such compensation is payable to both the parents of the victim, they each receive £1,750. In either case the amount may be reduced "by such amount as appears to the Secretary of State to be appropriate" having regard to certain provocative or negligent behaviour of the victim or in certain circumstances to the criminal record of the victim or of the applicant.[22]

In relation to these provisions it may be noted that –

(1) Compensation for bereavement is payable whether or not the spouse or parent has incurred any expenses or sustained pecuniary loss.

(2) There is to be no enquiry at all into the consequences of the bereavement in individual cases – the same amount is to be awarded to e.g. the parents of a newly born child who has been killed as to the parents of a child who has left home; a devoted wife will receive the same amount as the wife who has deserted her husband, etc. The Law Commission accepted that the effects of bereavement would be greater in some cases than in others, but they were prepared to accept this disparity "to avoid any judicial enquiry into degrees of grief".[23]

(3) The compensation can only be awarded to a spouse – i.e. the *lawful* wife or husband of the deceased. Such compensation is not payable to "former" spouses; nor is it payable to "common law" spouses, even if they satisfy the requirements laid down in Article 2(2).[24]

---

17. *Report*, paras 164–180.

18. *Report*, para 424.

19. Schedule 6, para 4.

20. 1986 *IWP Report*, para 15.1 – see now 1988 Act, s 111(4)(b).

21. By Art 23(1) the Secretary of State may by order substitute a different amount. The Government appears to accept that £3,500 is too low – see 148 HC Debs, cols 511 *et seq* (3 March 1989) and Consultative Paper issued by the Lord Chancellor in March 1990, and it now appears that an increase will be forthcoming.

22. Reduction here seems to be a matter of discretion; in other cases, the Secretary of State "shall have regard to" such matters – but it is still possible for there to be no reduction. See further above, pp 115–8.

23. *Report*, para 175. See e.g. CICB, *25th Annual Report* (1988–89), para 24.

24. This appears obvious from the wording of the definition of "relative" in Art 2(2), which draws a clear distinction between "spouses" and "former spouses" and does not treat common law spouses as "spouses" of any kind. *Cf* criminal injuries compensation for loss of society is payable to co-habitees in Scotland – see British Scheme, para 15.

(4) A "minor" is a person under the age of 18 years[25] at the date of his death, rather than at the date of injury.[26] It appears that an adopted child[27] and a stepchild also come within this provision.[28]

(5) Compensation for bereavement is a separate head of compensation and is not included with other compensation which has to be apportioned among different relatives;[29] nor is it taken into account in determining whether a widow and children qualify for a discretionary payment.[30]

(6) The right to compensation for bereavement does not survive the death of the applicant.[31]

(7) The bereavement award is not payable to children who have lost a parent – on the basis apparently that they are normally eligible for (substantial) compensation for pecuniary loss.

Compensation Payable to Non-Relatives

Finally, Article 3(3)(c) provides that where the victim of a criminal injury dies as a result of the injury and has no relatives, compensation is payable –

> "to any person who has incurred expenses as a result of the victim's injury or death in respect of such expenses actually and reasonably incurred."

This clearly covers friends of the victim and, as already pointed out, institutions or bodies, since "person" includes "corporations (whether aggregate or sole) and unincorporated bodies of persons".[32]

Compensation Where Victim Dies Otherwise Than as a Result of His Injuries

Prior to the 1977 Order it had been held that the personal representatives of a victim who died otherwise than as a result of his injuries before receiving compensation therefor could continue the application on behalf of his estate.[33] This brought criminal injuries compensation substantially into line

---

25. Age of Majority Act (NI) 1969, s 1. *Semble* compensation is payable only for the death of a live child, and not in respect of an unborn child: *Bagley v North Herts Health Authority* (1986) 136 *NLJ* 1014.

26. *Doleman v Deakin, The Times*, 30 Jan 1990.

27. As a result of Art 2(4)(a) "an adopted person shall be treated as the child of the person or persons by whom he was adopted . . . ".

28. By Art 2(4)(b). As regards illegitimate children there appears to be a conflict between Art 2(4)(c) ("an illegitimate child shall be treated as the legitimate child of his mother and reputed father") and Art 9(3)(b)(ii), which treats the reputed father as a non-parent. On a strict interpretation of Art

2(4)(c), it is arguable that Art 9(3)(b)(ii) can have no application.

29. Article 12(4). Although Art 13(3) is wide enough to permit apportionment to other relatives, this would be contrary to the whole basis of this head of compensation.

30. See below, p 216.

31. Article 11(3), discussed below, p 278.

32. Interpretation Act (NI) 1954, s 37(1), discussed above p 50. *Cf* 1986 *1WP Report*, para 15.10: " . . . funeral expenses should not be payable to a public authority . . . " – now enacted in 1988 Act, s 111(4)(a).

33. *Benson v Sec of State* [1976] NI 36, on the grounds that the common law principle *actio personalis moritur cum persona* did not apply to the *statutory* right to apply for criminal injuries compensation.

with claims for common law damages, but the decision left unresolved a number of subsidiary issues. This comparability was brought to an end by the 1977 Order, which instead made specific provision for such cases,[34] and this provision has been further refined in the 1988 Order. The position may now be summarised as follows.

1. Where compensation has been claimed by, and paid to, a victim who then dies, that compensation is simply part of the general assets of the deceased.

2. Where compensation has not been claimed by the victim, or has been claimed by, but not paid to, him before he dies, Article 11(1)(*a*) of the 1988 Order now provides that "any compensation or balance[35] of compensation to which he was entitled immediately prior to his death shall cease to be payable . . . ". This wording does not extend to cases where the compensation has been ordered by a court to be paid to an applicant, who then dies before the compensation – or some of the compensation – is actually paid to him. In *McCloskey* v *Secretary of State*[36] the applicant's wife appealed to the county court against the Secretary of State's decision that she was not entitled to compensation. The court allowed the appeal and awarded her compensation of £50,000. Part only of this sum had actually been paid when she died otherwise than as a result of her injuries. The Secretary of State, relying on Article 9(*a*) of the 1977 Order, declined to pay the balance of the compensation to the applicant. The Court of Appeal, though satisfied that the sum awarded was still "compensation",[37] held that the court order put the case beyond the stage where the applicant was merely "entitled" to that compensation. Hutton J considered that "entitled" in Article 9(*a*) means to have "a rightful claim" to compensation; where a court order has been made, the applicant is no longer a claimant, but has obtained or been awarded the compensation. The learned judge considered that "clear and unambiguous words" would be required before a court would uphold the "most unusual" construction contended for by the Secretary of State.[38] The wording of Article 11(1)(*a*) is identical in this respect to that of Article 9(*a*) of the 1977 Order.

3. By Article 3(4), however, compensation is payable –

"(*a*) to the victim's relatives in respect of –
            (i) expenses actually and reasonably incurred by the victim as a result of his injury;

---

34. Articles 3(1)(*d*)(i) and 9(*a*).

35. E.g. where an interim payment has been made.

36. [1984] NI 365.

37. "'Compensation' remains compensation after it has been awarded by the court." The learned judge rejected the argument that the "compensation" had become merged in, and therefore was properly referred to as, the county court "judgment".

38. Hutton J distinguished *Barry* v *Sec of State* [1984] NI 39 where the Court of Appeal had held that the Secretary of State could *withhold* payment under Article 6(10) even after a

court had ordered the payment of compensation: "[The] wording [of Article 6(10)] is different and does not include the word 'entitled', and the withholding of payment is authorised, not because of the chance happening of the death of the applicant, but because the applicant has been at fault in not complying with reasonable requests for information and assistance . . . ". Hutton J agreed with the Court of Appeal in *Barry* that the later and particular provisions in the 1977 Order were not overridden by any general requirements laid down in the Crown Proceedings Act 1947, s 25.

   (ii) pecuniary loss suffered by the victim as a result of his injury between the date of his injury and the date of his death;

   (b) to any person who has incurred expenses as a result of the victim's injury in respect of such expenses actually and reasonably incurred."[39]

Extended notice arrangements are made to facilitate such a claim.[40] These provisions depart from the 1977 Order in three respects:

   (1) Article 3(4)(a)(i) specifically provides for the payment of compensation in respect of expenses which had been actually and reasonably incurred by the victim before his death. Such expenses were not clearly covered by Article 3(1)(d)(ii) of the 1977 Order.

   (2) Compensation is paid under the 1988 Order for expenses "actually and reasonably incurred"; the 1977 Order was limited to "reasonable expenses necessarily incurred".

   (3) Under the 1988 Order compensation for allowable expenses and pecuniary loss sustained by the victim before his death is payable to his "relatives", but no specific provision is made as to which relatives. This question was unlikely to arise under the 1977 Order, by which such compensation was payable to the victim's dependants – i.e. those relatives who had been wholly or substantially dependent on his income at the time of his death. It would appear that the recipient of this compensation under the 1988 Order will have to be determined by the Secretary of State under the general power conferred by Article 13(3) which enables the compensation to be paid "on such terms and conditions as the Secretary of State thinks fit as to the payment . . . or apportionment of the compensation to the [victim's] . . . relatives, or any of them . . .". Presumably, this will normally mean those relatives entitled to benefit from the deceased's estate.

   The 1977 Order – and now the 1988 Order – made no specific provision for the case where the victim had before his death received part of his compensation by way of an interim payment. Presumably any compensation due to his relatives is reduced accordingly; Article 3(4)(a) stipulates that the compensation is for "expenses actually . . . incurred" and "pecuniary loss suffered" by the victim and if an interim payment was made to him in respect of these items,[41] his loss has clearly *pro tanto* been reduced.

COLLATERAL BENEFITS

The general policy of criminal injuries compensation in Northern Ireland since 1968,[42] as in Britain and Ireland,[43] is that benefits accruing to the victim

---

39. *Cf* 1978 *1WP Report*, para 13.1: " . . . compensation to dependants should be limited to the actual losses arising from the injury." The British Scheme, para 16 provides for the payment of such compensation to a dependant or relative of the deceased. See also 1988 Act, s 111(5) and Irish Scheme, para 7.

40. By Art 11(1)(b), discussed below p 282.

41. An interim payment in respect of pain and suffering and loss of amenities would *not* be taken into account in this way.

42. 1968 Act, s 4(6)(b) and (c); 1977 Order, Art 5(3)(a) and (b).

43. British Scheme, para 19 (and also 1988 Act, Sch 7, paras 11–13), discussed Greer, *Criminal Injuries Compensation* (1990), paras 4.61 *et seq*. See also Irish Scheme, paras 15 and 16.

or his relatives from "collateral" sources are deducted in full from the compensation payable under the scheme, for the reason simply, "so that public money will not be spent where it is not really needed".[44] This approach has often given rise to public criticism,[45] and was at first subject to some judicial questioning.[46] But the principle of deduction has come in recent years to be more favourably regarded by judicial opinion[47] and legislative changes (and discussions in Parliament) have been restricted to its refinement. The principle must now, therefore, be regarded as a settled part of the criminal injuries compensation code. The collateral benefits coming within this principle fall into three main categories:

(a) Compensation or damages.

(b) Pensions or gratuities.

(c) Social security benefits.

But we may first consider some special cases where collateral benefits are *not* deducted. By Article 6(10) *no* deductions in respect of any such benefits are to be made in respect of –

(i) the fixed compensation of £5,000 payable under Articles 3(2)(*a*)(v) and 9(1) for certain consequences of rape, and

(ii) the fixed compensation of £3,500 payable under Articles 3(3)(*b*) and 9(3) for bereavement.

It should also be noted that Article 7(2)(*c*) continues a provision first introduced in 1968, *viz*:

> "Where the victim of a criminal injury dies, the compensation payable in respect of [pecuniary loss resulting from his injury or death] . . . shall be determined . . .

---

44. 68 HC Debs (NI), col 627 (31 Jan 1968). It is also consistent with the stated policy of the legislation to prevent undue hardship rather than to provide "full" compensation – *ibid*, col 626.

45. See e.g. 907 HC Debs, col 1528 (18 March 1976): " . . . many of my constituents feel deeply outraged that less than £6,000 should be paid in compensation to the widow and small daughter of a British corporal . . . killed in . . . Northern Ireland, whereas up to £16,000 was paid in [damages] to an IRA detainee who suffered during interrogation . . . ". Part of the explanation of the difference results from the deduction in full of the pension payable to the corporal's widow and child.

46. "Why [a police widow's pension] . . . should not be taken into account in the case of the Fatal Accidents Acts but must be taken into account in the case of a claim under the [1968] Act for criminal injury is less than

clear. Why should an innocent victim of civil unrest be dealt with less generously than the innocent victim of a street accident?" *Rolston v Sec of State* [1975] NI 195, 202, *per* Gibson LJ. See also *Parry v Cleaver* [1969] 1 All ER 555 where some, at least, of their Lordships endorsed a general policy of non-deduction in personal injury actions at common law. That policy finds its fullest expression in the Fatal Accidents (NI) Order 1977.

47. See especially *Hodgson v Trapp* [1988] 3 All ER 870, 873–4, *per* Lord Bridge: "If, in consequence of the injuries sustained, the plaintiff has enjoyed receipts to which he would not otherwise have been entitled, *prima facie* those receipts are to be set against the aggregate of the plaintiff's losses and expenses in arriving at the measure of his damages." A principle of general "offset" of social security benefits had been recommended in the *Pearson Report*, para 482, and has now been effected in injury cases by the Social Security (NI) Order 1989, Art 24.

(c) save as expressly provided by this Order, without reference to any loss or gain to his estate consequent on the injury."[48]

It would appear that this provision was intended to reverse the general principle established in relation to the Fatal Accidents Acts and recognised by the House of Lords in *Davies v Powell Duffryn Collieries Ltd*[49] that "the damages to be awarded to a dependant . . . must take into account any pecuniary benefit accruing to that dependant in consequence of the death of the deceased". If this indeed is the case, the provision is strangely drafted[50] and it is surprising that the opportunity was not taken in the 1988 Order to amend the wording to bring it more into line with the new Article 6 introduced into the Fatal Accidents (NI) Order 1977 by the Administration of Justice Act 1982.[51] The main effect of the provision in the criminal injuries context is that no allowance is to be made, in calculating the relatives' pecuniary loss, for the accelerated payment and certainty of receipt of such matters as stocks and shares owned by the victim.[52] This result avoids what both the Law Commission[53] and the Pearson Commission[54] considered to be the unfair and arbitrary effect of the old Fatal Accidents Act approach. But in an interesting discussion of the new Fatal Accidents Act provision, McGregor[55] draws attention to two points which also have relevance to the 1988 Order:

(a) "It was the practice to counterbalance any deduction for the . . . acceleration of benefit from the estate with an addition to the award for the loss of the larger estate that the dependants would have received had the deceased lived on and built up savings . . . Is then the position that today the acceleration of the benefit is to be disregarded but the lost savings may still feature in the award?" McGregor seems to suggest a positive answer to the question, but it is difficult to see why the loss of a larger estate is not a "loss . . . to [the victim's] estate consequent on the injury."

(b) It may however be that the above loss can be categorised as *direct* pecuniary loss to the relatives rather than indirect loss to the victim's estate. As McGregor goes on to point out: " . . . benefits which accrue from the estate . . . may yet have relevance to the computation of a dependant's damages. Thus, should the deceased's sole property consist of unearned income out of which he supports the

---

48. 1968 Act, s 4(5)(*c*); 1977 Order, Art 7(2)(*c*).

49. [1942] AC 601. For the application of this principle, see e.g. *Kemp and Kemp*, ch 22.

50. It does not refer to any loss or gain *to the relatives* from the victim's estate, and it refers to any loss or gain consequent on "the injury", as opposed to the death, of the victim.

51. By Sch 6, para 7, where the effect of the wording is much clearer.

52. *Cf Bishop v Cunard White Star Line Co Ltd* [1950] 2 All ER 22. The other principal "gain" deducted from a Fatal Accidents award was in respect of damages awarded to the estate of the deceased for non-pecuniary loss, now specifically excluded by Art 11(2) of the 1988 Order.

53. *Report*, para 256.

54. *Report*, para 538.

55. *McGregor*, paras 1598–9.

dependant, and the whole estate from which he derived this income passes to the dependant, the dependant's claim fails as there is no pecuniary loss."

It would be useful to have these uncertainties clarified by judicial decision. In practice, however, the 1988 Order does in any event expressly provide for many benefits payable to the victim's relatives consequent on his death to be taken into account in the assessment of their compensation.

1. Compensation or Damages

Article 6(2)(a) provides that:

> "The Secretary of State, in determining the amount of compensation, shall deduct from the amount which, but for this paragraph, would be payable –
>
> (a) any sums paid to the victim or any of his relatives, by way of compensation or damages from the offender or any person on the offender's behalf, consequent on the criminal injury or on death resulting therefrom . . . "[56]

Article 18(1) further provides for reimbursement to the Secretary of State where criminal injuries compensation has been paid to the victim or another person and the victim or that person is subsequently paid compensation or damages by the offender or any person on the offender's behalf which has not been deducted under Article 6(2)(a).[57]

These provisions' have remained substantially unchanged since their original introduction in 1968.[58] The phrase "compensation or damages" is wide, but its most obvious components are damages recovered by an action against the offender at common law or under the Fatal Accidents (NI) Order 1977, and compensation paid by the offender to the victim or his relatives by way of a compensation order imposed by the court on his conviction for a criminal offence.[59] Neither is likely to occur very frequently.

It should be noted that the damages to be deducted must have been paid "from the offender or any person on the offender's behalf".[60] This would not cover any liability of a third party such as the police, the victim's employer or a government department.[61] Thus in *R v CICB, ex parte W*[62] a schoolboy was

56. *Cp* British Scheme, para 21 (and 1988 Act, Sch 7, para 13); Irish Scheme, para 16.

57. Discussed below, p 326.

58. 1968 Act, ss 4(6)(b) and 8; 1977 Order, Arts 5(3)(a) and 17.

59. Under Criminal Justice (NI) Orders 1983 and 1986, discussed below, p 240 *et seq*. Note that the reference here is to compensation "paid", not to compensation which perhaps ought to have been claimed but was not – nor even to compensation claimed *and* ordered to be paid, but not in fact paid. *Cp* 1986 *IWP Report*, para 21.3: "In the case of a compensation order by a criminal court, we recommend that . . . the Board should be able to deduct the total amount of the order, and not merely

the amount of compensation already paid." But the 1988 Act, Sch 7, para 13 refers to payments which the applicant has "received".

60. *Cf* the British Scheme, para 21 is not limited in this way, nor is the 1988 Act, which refers to damages which compensate the applicant "for any loss in respect of which compensation is payable to him under this Act . . . ". The Irish Scheme, para 16 on the other hand is identical to the Northern Ireland provision.

61. See e.g. the cases discussed below, pp 227–239.

62. Unreported, Div'l Ct, 18 Dec 1980 – see CICB, *17th Annual Report* (1980–81), para 20(d).

seriously injured by a fellow pupil whilst at school. He brought an action against the education authority alleging negligence by them in the supervision of the school. The action was settled for £20,000. Such damages were not paid by the offender or on the offender's behalf and are not therefore deductible.

The term "compensation" would seem also to cover any voluntary payments to the victim or his dependants by the offender or someone on his behalf. Such payments again are likely to be rare, but it is conceivable that a parent might make such a payment in respect of an offence committed by his child, or a trade union might make a voluntary payment in respect of a criminal injury caused e.g. by pickets during an industrial dispute "Compensation or damages" would also cover e.g. a payment from an insurance company or the Motor Insurers' Bureau to a person injured in a road accident where this injury was also a criminal injury e.g., where a car was used by burglars to commit a crime – provided it can be shown that such payment is by a person on the offender's behalf. However, payments to the victim or his dependants from a charitable fund, or under an accident insurance policy, or the value of gratuitous assistance from family or friends will not be deducted under Article 6(2)(a) because such payments are not "from the offender or any person on the offender's behalf".

The compensation or damages must be "consequent on" the criminal injury or on death therefrom. The phrase as used in this context is not defined in the Order, but its meaning in relation to other benefits is defined in Article 6(4)(c)[63] and it seems reasonable to suggest that, in any case of doubt, that definition will also be applied to Article 6(2)(a).

The compensation or damages must have actually been paid to the victim or any of his relatives; there is apparently no obligation to make a claim therefor, and no penalty imposed in cases where the Secretary of State might consider that such a claim should reasonably be made.[64] In such cases it may be open to the Secretary of State himself to claim against the offender under Article 17.[65]

2. Pensions or Gratuities

Article 6(2)(b) requires the deduction from compensation of –

> "any pension [or] gratuity . . . which has been or will be paid to or for the benefit of the victim or any of his relatives consequent on the criminal injury or on death resulting therefrom."[66]

---

63. Discussed below, p 214.

64. See to the same effect 1988 Act, Sch 7, para 13(a). Cp British Scheme, para 19 (in relation only to other benefits): "If, in the opinion of the Board, an applicant may be eligible for any such benefits, the Board may refuse to make an award until the applicant has taken such steps as the Board consider reasonable to claim them." Query whether a failure to claim damages may constitute a "relevant circumstance" for the purpose of Art 6(1) of the 1988 Order – see above, p 115.

65. Discussed below, pp 323–6.

66. The British Scheme (para 20 and the 1988 Act, Sch 7, para 12) also requires the deduction of many pensions and gratuities; the Irish Scheme makes no reference either to pensions or gratuities; but see the Garda Siochana (Compensation) Act 1941, s 10(3), discussed above pp 41 and 43.

A similar provision was included in both the 1968 Act and the 1977 Order,[67] but a number of uncertainties in the precise scope of the provision were revealed by experience and the 1988 Order has, therefore, attempted to deal much more specifically with this category.

By Article 6(9) "'pension' includes any payment of a lump sum in respect of a person's employment"; this general definition remains unchanged from 1968.[68] By Article 6(9) also "'gratuity' includes any payment of money whether made in consequence of a legally enforceable right or not". This new provision appears to have been inserted to avoid uncertainty as to whether a payment to which a victim was legally entitled could constitute a "gratuity".[69] This seems fair enough – the important thing is whether the applicant has in fact received the money. But it is to be hoped that "gratuity" will *not* be interpreted to cover the case where the applicant has received a payment, whether or not[70] in consequence of a legally enforceable right, which he is expected (even if not legally obliged) to repay to his employer from the compensation which he is awarded for pecuniary loss.[71] In such a case the payment is more in the nature of a loan or an advance, not a "gratuity" which a recipient is entitled to keep in any event.[72] The apparent wide meaning of the definition is restricted by Article 6(4)(*a*), which provides that only gratuities from the four sources there listed are deducted. This means e.g. that payments from insurance policies voluntarily taken out by the victim personally,[73] payments by trades unions and friendly societies, and gifts from appeal funds remain non-deductible.

We may now turn to some particular considerations affecting the deduction of "pensions" and "gratuities" as so defined.

To begin with, the 1988 Order has substituted the formula "has been or will be paid" for the word "payable" which was used in Article 5(5)(*c*) of the 1977 Order. The new formula appears to be intended to avoid the connotation that the applicant must be legally entitled to the pension or gratuity;[74] it

---

67. 1968 Act, s 4(6)(*c*); 1977 Order, Art 5(3)(*b*).

68. 1968 Act, s 4(7); 1977 Order, Art 5(7).

69. In *Holloway* v *Poplar BC* [1939] 4 All ER 165, "gratuity" was defined as "a payment made without legal obligation". *Cf Murphy* v *Cronin* [1966] IR 699, 712, *per* Kingsmill Moore J.

70. The case where an employee is *not* legally obliged to reimburse his employer is admittedly more difficult, but, as noted below we are no longer dealing in this context with legal obligation, but with what happens as a matter of fact.

71. See e.g. *McCartney* v *Sec of State*, Unreported, Cty Ct (Judge Russell), 21 Dec 1979; *Gaw* v *Sec of State*, Unreported, High Ct (MacDermott J), 27 Feb 1987.

72. This point was left open in *Gaw, supra*. MacDermott J said in passing – "even if it [the payment to the employee] could properly be

called a 'gratuity' . . . " and suggested that to be within that term, "gratuity" would have to be given "an extremely wide meaning".

73. See e.g. *Nicholson* v *Sec of State*, Unreported, Cty Ct (Judge Russell), 20 Dec 1982 (no deduction from compensation for school fees where fees already paid from proceeds of insurance policy taken out by deceased). *Cp* definition of "private pension rights" in 1988 Act, Sch 7, para 12(3).

74. Note that the position was even clearer under the 1968 Act, which referred to "any right to pension, gratuity, etc" – see *Duffy* v *Sec of State*, Unreported, Cty Ct (Judge Babington), 2 Feb 1978 (trustees of pension scheme with absolute discretion as to payee made payment to victim's widow; pension not deducted because widow had no "right" to payment). The 1988 Act uses the term "pension *rights*" (emphasis added).

will now suffice if the pension has been or will as a matter of fact be paid to him for any reason. However, the new wording will not cover e.g. a discretionary pension or gratuity which *may* at some future date be paid to the applicant.[75] But as we have seen above (p 168), a victim who is unable to work because of his injury may nonetheless continue to receive payment from his employers at their discretion and on the basis that the appropriate sum will be repaid to the employer from the compensation obtained by the victim. In *Gaw* v *Secretary of State*[76] it was held that such payment did not amount to a "gratuity" under the 1977 Order, which required any such "gratuity" to be "payable" – i.e. one which the employer was legally obliged to pay. In *Gaw's* case there was no such obligation and the payments were therefore not deducted. Now, however, "gratuities" are deducted if they are in fact paid, and it would appear that payments such as that in *Gaw* are now deductible. As MacDermott J acknowledged, this would be "a mean approach" and will hopefully be avoided by more careful interpretation of the meaning of "gratuity".[77]

Next, it would appear that when a pension or gratuity is deductible, regard should be had only to the *net* amount payable to the applicant after deduction of income tax.[78] No deduction from the amount of the pension is made for the value of any pension contributions made by the victim, which may seem unfair, since, by Article 7(4)(*c*), the amount of those contributions will have been deducted in the calculation of the applicant's net pecuniary loss. This could cause injustice.[79]

The pension or gratuity must also be paid "to or for the benefit of the victim or any of his relatives . . . ". A question may arise where a pension or gratuity is payable on death irrespective of whether the deceased has any relatives. Under the 1977 Order it could have been argued that where such a pension had, in fact, been paid to relatives, it was not "payable" to or for their benefit. Now, however, it is sufficient if the pension is in fact "paid" to the relatives and it would appear that the question has been resolved by this new and more extensive wording.

A question may also arise as to whether a pension or gratuity paid to the deceased's estate (and therefrom payable to some of his relatives) is paid "to or for the benefit of . . . any of [the victim's] relatives . . . ". It is suggested that the use of the phrase "for the benefit of" is intended specifically to cover this kind of case.

The pension or gratuity will be deducted only if it is "consequent on the criminal injury . . . ". In *Rolston* v *Secretary of State*[80] a police constable had been killed in a booby-trap explosion, and his widow therefore qualified for an "augmented" pension (i.e., a pension at a higher level than would have been payable in other circumstances). In the High Court, McGonigal LJ

---

75. *Cf* Fatal Accidents (NI) Order 1977, Art 6 (1) refers to benefits "which have accrued or will *or may* accrue" to the plaintiff.

76. Unreported, High Ct (MacDermott J), 27 Feb 1987.

77. See above, n 72.

78. See 1978 *IWP Report*, para 16.5, a con-

sideration reflected in the British Scheme, para 20 and 1988 Act, Sch 7, para 12(2).

79. Pensions paid for solely by the victim or his dependants are not deductible under Art 6(4)(*a*) – see next page. See also British Scheme, para 20.

80. [1975] 3 NIJB (HC); [1975] NI 195 (CA).

accepted the contention that only the amount by which Mrs Rolston's "ordinary" widow's pension had been increased due to husband's murder should be deducted from her compensation under the 1968 Act as "consequent on the criminal injury". Had her husband died e.g. from natural causes she would still have been entitled to an ordinary pension and its value should not, therefore, be deducted. The Court of Appeal disagreed, mainly for the reason that the 1968 Act required the deduction of many benefits which were paid in full regardless of the circumstances of the death:

> "If, therefore, one were to put the applicant's interpretation on the phrase 'consequent on', it would mean that the entire provision that 'statutory benefits' should be taken into account would probably . . . be largely incapable of application . . . "

Gibson LJ therefore concluded that –

> "the words 'consequent on' must bear the normal meaning of 'as a result or consequence of', and . . . once death has resulted from a criminal injury all pensions which are payable to dependants as a consequence of that death . . . must be taken into account."[81]

This reasoning is, in principle, equally applicable to the 1988 Order; but some doubt may arise from the fact that the Order, like the 1977 Order, has an express provision confirming the *Rolston* decision – but only in relation to social security benefits.[82] It is, therefore, arguable that this stipulative definition is not intended to be applied to other benefits – *expressio unius exclusio alterius*. But it seems highly unlikely that the courts would now wish to resuscitate McGonigal LJ's original decision and thereby apply different tests to collateral benefits which are clearly intended to be treated in generally the same way.

By Article 6(4)(*a*) a pension or gratuity is not to be deducted from compensation unless it has been or will be paid –

(i) *By or on behalf of the Crown*[83] *or the government of any country, state or territory outside the United Kingdom.* The 1988 Order extends the scope of a provision first introduced in the 1977 Order with reference only to pensions or gratuities payable by or on behalf of the Crown. The new wording adds e.g. pensions or gratuities paid to civil servants and consular officials employed by other governments.

(ii) *By or on behalf of the employer*[84] *of the victim or by any person with whom the employer has made any contract or arrangement.* This will cover e.g. contributory and non-contributory pensions, pensions paid by insurance policies taken out by the employer, etc. But the large variety of arrangements now being made between employers and employees may cause some difficulties of interpretation. A recent case in point is *Hussain* v

---

81. *Ibid*, pp 200–1.

82. Article 6(4)(*c*), discussed below p 214.

83. By Art 6(9) "the Crown" means "the Crown in right of Her Majesty's government

in the United Kingdom or in Northern Ireland".

84. By Art 6(9) "'employer' includes a former employer".

New Taplow Paper Mills Ltd.[85] The plaintiff there was employed under a contract of employment which provided that if he was injured at work he would receive his full pay for 13 weeks and then half his pre-accident pay as long-term sickness benefit under a health insurance policy taken out and paid for by his employers. The plaintiff was injured in the course of employment and he claimed that the payments he received under the policy amounted to a disability pension and should not therefore be deducted from his damages. The House of Lords, having examined the arrangement in some detail, disagreed and held that the payments made to the plaintiff were designed to compensate him for the loss or diminution of his wages resulting from the injury and so constituted sick-pay. As such they would not fall to be deducted from criminal injuries compensation under Article 6(4)(*a*)(ii). But it is submitted that to the extent that he received such payments an applicant would have suffered no pecuniary loss for the purposes of Article 3(2)(*a*)(ii)[86] and therefore this particular instance would not create any practical problem under the 1988 Order. In the *Hussain* case, however, there was no evidence that the plaintiff's wages would have been any higher if the employers had not operated the scheme; the reasoning in the case – and the argument concerning the employee's pecuniary loss – might not apply in other situations. As Kerr LJ said in the Court of Appeal:

> "[If] the plaintiff could have shown . . . that the benefits formed part of his 'wage structure', in the sense that he would have got more pay if his contract had not provided for these benefits . . . I can see no difference in principle between private sickness and accident insurance paid for out of the plaintiff's pocket on the one hand and benefits paid for by the plaintiff in some indirect manner on the other hand . . . "[87]

The former is not deductible from compensation under the 1988 Order.

(iii) *Out of the resources of an occupational pension scheme, within the meaning of the Social Security Pensions (NI) Order 1975 or of an appropriate personal pension scheme within the meaning of Article 3 of the Social Security (NI) Order 1986.*[88] Article 2(2) of the 1975 Order is one of those nightmare statutory provisions; an "occupational pension scheme" is there defined as meaning:

> "Any scheme or arrangement which is comprised in one or more instruments or agreements and which has, or is capable of having, effect in relation to one or more descriptions or categories of employment so as to provide benefits, in the form of pensions or otherwise, payable on termination of service or on death or retirement, to or in respect of earners with qualifying service in an employment of any such description or category."

---

85. [1988] 1 All ER 541.

86. See above, p 168.

87. [1987] 1 All ER 417, 429. See also *Smoker* v *London Fire and Civil Defence Authority*

The Times, 19 Jan 1990.

88. See generally Ellison, *Pensions: Law and Practice* (1990); Reardon, *Pensions Guide* (2nd ed, 1988); Ogus and Barendt, *The Law of Social Security* (3rd ed, 1988), ch 5.

"Personal pension schemes" are defined in similar terms in Article 2(2) of the 1986 Order,[89] but fortunately Article 3(8) provides a practical approach:

> "A personal pension scheme is an appropriate scheme if there is in force a certificate . . . issued by the Occupational Pensions Board in accordance with Article 4[90] that it is such a scheme."

These two categories do *not* exhaust the list of state pensions and it would appear e.g. that a Category D retirement pension payable to a person over 80 not entitled to any other category of state pension,[91] is not to be deducted from compensation.

(iv) *Under the Parliamentary and other Pensions Acts 1972 and 1987, the European Assembly (Pay and Pensions) Act 1979 or the Assembly Pensions (NI) Order 1976 or in respect of the service of the victim as a member of any parliamentary or legislative assembly in any country, state or territory outside the United Kingdom.* This new provision has been inserted into the 1988 Order apparently because doubts had arisen over the position of pensions payable to members, or to the widows of members, of the United Kingdom Parliament. Such a pension is hardly payable "by or on behalf of the Crown or the government" and, since a Member of Parliament is the holder of an office, not an employee, neither can the pension be said to be payable "by or on behalf of an employer".[92] It has been decided that such pensions should be deductible, and the provision extends not only to MPs, but also to MEPs and to members of the (former) Assembly. It also extends e.g. to members of the Irish Senate and to visiting congressmen and senators from the United States.

3. Social Security Benefits

Article 6(2)(*b*) continues the policy introduced in the 1968 Act,[93] following a fundamental principle of the British Scheme:[94]

---

89. "Any scheme or arrangement which is comprised in one or more instruments or agreements and which has, or is capable of having, effect so as to provide benefits, in the form of pensions or otherwise, payable on death or retirement to or in respect of employed earners who have made arrangements with the trustees or managers of the scheme for them to become members of the scheme."

90. By Art 4(2) a scheme can be an "appropriate" scheme only if the requirements imposed by or by virtue of Sch 1 are satisfied in its case.

91. See National Insurance Act 1971, s 5; Ogus and Barendt, *op cit*, pp 225–6.

92. *Cf* 1986 *IWP Report*, para 20.4: "For the

avoidance of doubt, . . . it [should] be made clear . . . that office-holders should be treated in the same way as employees for the purpose of the taking account of remuneration and benefits in assessing the compensation payable." The 1988 Act, Sch 7, para 12 applies to pensions payable "by virtue of any office or employment" of the victim.

93. 1968 Act, s 4(6)(*c*).

94. See e.g. 1978 *IWP Report*, para 14.1: "There should be no double payment from government funds and . . . compensation in respect of any injury or disability should be reduced on account of any other benefit payable from any other public funds for the same contingencies." See British Scheme, para 19 and 1988 Act, Sch 7, para 11. The Irish Scheme (para 15) adopts a similar approach.

"The Secretary of State, in determining the amount of compensation, shall deduct from the amount which, but for this paragraph, would be payable –

. . .

(b) any . . . social security benefit which has been or will be paid to or for the benefit of the victim or any of his relatives consequent on the criminal injury or on death resulting therefrom."

By Article 6(9), "social security benefit" means –

"(a) social security benefit payable under the laws of any part of the United Kingdom;

(b) any similar benefit under the laws of any other country, state or territory."[95]

Further, by Article 6(4)(b) –

"social security benefit shall be deemed to be payable if it would be payable but for the wilful failure at any time of the victim to pay contributions which he was liable to pay."

Somewhat strangely the 1988 Order does not specifically empower the Secretary of State to require an applicant to claim benefits for which he may be eligible, nor does it enable the Secretary of State to "claw back" any such benefits obtained by the applicant *after* compensation has been paid to him.[96] However, it may be that the applicant's eligibility – or even *apparent* eligibility – for social security benefits may be a "relevant circumstance" to which the Secretary of State must have regard under Article 6(1). Alternatively, it may be argued that the general principle of mitigation of loss is applicable. This appears to have been the basis for the decision in *Deeney* v *Secretary of State*[97] where the court deducted from the compensation payable to an applicant the value of benefits which he should have claimed.

"Social security benefit" is not defined in the 1988 Order[98] and could give rise to difficulty. Thus, in *Arouni* v *Secretary of State*[99] four infant children

---

95. See 1978 *1WP Report*, para 16.4: "The arguments about double payments from British Government funds do not apply to 'foreign' benefits, but it is relevant to take account of any other income arising from the circumstances of the criminal injury", presumably because the victim's loss is thereby diminished. This new express provision avoids the artificiality inherent in cases such as *Potter* v *Sec of State*, Unreported, Cty Ct (Judge Higgins), 28 Jan 1980 where a widow's pension paid by the Irish Department of Social Welfare, though not a social security benefit as then defined, was held to be a pension for the purposes of the 1968 Act and was deducted in full. *Cf* in *McCavera* v *Sec of State* Unreported, Cty Ct (Judge Brown), 11 Jan 1980, welfare benefits paid to the victim in the Republic were held not deductible.

96. Article 18 extends only to "compensation or damages" – see below pp 326–7. *Cf* British

Scheme, para 19 (Board may refuse to make an award until the applicant has taken such steps as the Board consider reasonable to claim benefits). The 1986 *1WP Report*, para 21.2 wished to go further: ". . . the Board should . . . be able to recover any . . . payments subsequently received [by the victim] which the Board would have been obliged to take into account if they had already been made." This recommendation is implemented in the 1988 Act, s 115(4), but not in the 1990 Scheme.

97. [1981] 4 *BNIL* 23.

98. The 1968 Act (and the 1977 Order) referred to specific statutes. Neither the British Scheme (or the 1988 Act) nor the Irish Scheme provides any definition. *Cf* Social Security (NI) Order, art 24(3).

99. Unreported, High Ct (Gibson LJ), 8 Dec 1977. See also *R* v *CICB, ex parte McGuffie and Smith* [1978] *Crim LR* 160.

were taken into care and boarded out with foster parents when their mother was murdered. Having found that the children had been financially dependent on their mother, Gibson LJ had to decide whether boarding-out allowances paid by the local authority under the Children and Young Persons Act (NI) 1968 had to be taken into account in assessing the compensation payable to them under the 1968 Act. The learned Lord Justice held that the allowances were not "statutory benefits"[1] for the purposes of the Act and therefore did not have to be deducted. Yet the principle underlying that Act – and now the 1988 Order – is to prevent "double" compensation from public funds. However, that objective can still be maintained; as Gibson LJ further held, the boarding-out allowances had to be taken into account in determining the "loss" suffered by the children.[2]

By Article 6(4)(c) social security benefit is "consequent on a criminal injury" or on a death resulting from such an injury –

> "if, but for the criminal injury or that death, the benefit would not otherwise have been paid or be payable at the same time or to the same extent as it was or will be paid following the death or injury."

This provision was first included in Article 5(5)(b) of the 1977 Order to confirm the reasoning (though not apparently the decision) of the Court of Appeal in *Rolston* v *Secretary of State*.[3] Thus, the fact that a widow would have qualified for a social security benefit had her husband died accidentally rather than as the result of a criminal injury is irrelevant; the benefit will be deducted in full since "but for the criminal injury . . . the benefit would not otherwise have been paid . . . at the same time . . . as it was . . . following the death."

The deduction may be made either by deducting the annual value of the benefits from the multiplicand or by deducting the total value of the benefits from the gross total of compensation. The latter method is frequently adopted in death cases, and may be preferable for two reasons. First, if the deceased leaves dependent children, the benefits payable to or in respect of them may cease to be payable during the dependency of the deceased's wife.[4] Secondly, it has already been seen that a widower or widow's prospects of remarriage are to be ignored "in determining the compensation payable" to him or her; it seems from this wording that such prospects are

---

1. As defined in 1968 Act, s 4(7).

2. Following *Hay* v *Hughes* [1975] 1 All ER 257. Similar reasoning was applied in *McGuffie and Smith, supra*. Care must, however, be taken in making the necessary calculations. In *McGuffie and Smith*, the court noted that a boarding-out allowance may involve two elements – a financial element which paid for food, clothing and other outgoings, and a service element for maternal care. The first was to be set against the children's dependency on their mother; only the service element was deductible from the compensation payable for loss of the mother's services (represented here by the aunts' loss of earnings). It was later established that no part of the allowance was in fact attributable to the provision of services, the whole sum was intended for the maintenance of the children – see CICB, *14th Annual Report* (1977–78), para 10.

3. [1975] NI 195.

4. See e.g. *McGregor*, para 1581.

also to be ignored in respect of the valuation of the benefits payable to him or her,[5] but not in respect of those payable to the children.

In calculating the value of the benefits to be deducted, it should be borne in mind that many of these benefits are taxable and therefore only the estimated *net* value after tax should be deducted.[6]

4. Discretionary Payments to Spouses and Children

In the mid-1970s there was considerable public concern over a number of apparently inadequate awards of compensation to the widows and families of persons, especially members of the security forces, killed as the result of criminal injuries.[7] The principal reason for such "low" awards was the operation of the "full deduction" principle established by the 1968 Act, and in particular the deduction of pensions payable to the widows or children of soldiers and police officers. A remedy was, therefore, provided by the 1977 Order in the form of "discretionary payments" which could be paid, in appropriate cases, to "top-up" the award otherwise payable under the provisions of the Order.[8] The original wording of this provision caused difficulty in practice,[9] however, and it was accordingly amended in 1982,[10] when the amounts involved were also substantially increased. Article 10(1) of the 1988 Order generally continues that amended provision:

"(1) Where the aggregate of the compensation (if any) payable [for pecuniary loss resulting from the victim's injury or death] by virtue of Article 3(3)(*a*)(ii) to the spouse[11] and child (if any) of a victim who has died as a result of a criminal injury is –

(*a*) less than the discretionary payments limit because of a deduction made by virtue of Article 6(2)(*b*); or

---

5. *Cf* 1978 *IWP Report*, para 14.2 commented: "[A] widow's prospects of remarriage should be ignored in assessing both the gross amount of her compensation and the amount of any deductions to be made from it." This recommendation was implemented in the British Scheme (para 19) – and see 1988 Act, Sch 7, para 11(4).

6. See British Scheme, para 19; 1988 Act, Sch 7, para 11(3)(*a*).

7. See e.g. "Legislation planned to resolve anomalies in Ulster compensation" *The Times*, 21 Oct 1976; "Better compensation planned for widows of Ulster Servicemen" *The Times*, 12 Jan 1977.

8. Article 8(1).

9. By Art 8(5) separate limits were set for "the widow's amount" and "the child's amount". Where a claim was made by a widow alone, no problem arose. But where a claim was made by a widow with children, a strict application of Art 8(5) required an apportionment of the gross compensation between the widow and children *before* the required deduction of the benefits, followed by a proper apportionment between them of the benefits to be deducted. In practice the gross dependency and the benefits also tend to be assessed for the family unit as a whole and any apportionment between the dependants is made only at the end of the assessment exercise. But the whole question of apportionment between relatives is one which requires further consideration – see above pp 198–9.

10. Criminal Injuries (Compensation) (Amendment) (NI) Order 1982, Art 3 – which also doubled the amount of the "discretionary payments limit". Prior to 1982, "extra-statutory arrangements [had] been made to ensure that no one . . . suffered because of this [difficulty]": 437 HC Debs, col 897 (20 Dec 1982).

11. Thus, discretionary payments may now be made to widows or widowers. The 1977 and 1982 Orders were restricted to widows.

(b) less than the discretionary payments limit and a deduction is made by virtue of Article 6(2)(b),

the Secretary of State may pay to the spouse or, if the spouse is dead,[12] to the child such sum as when added to the compensation payable to the spouse and child equals –

(i) where sub-paragraph (a) applies, the discretionary payments limit; or

(ii) where sub-paragraph (b) applies, the amount of the compensation before any deduction by virtue of Article 6(2)(b)."

By Article 10(3) "the discretionary payments limit" means "the aggregate of £10,000[13] (in respect of the spouse) and £1,300[14] (in respect of each child)".

It will be noted that Article 10(1) applies only to compensation for pecuniary loss; any compensation for expenses or for bereavement must therefore be left out of account. Equally, it applies only to deductions under Article 6(2)(b), viz in respect of a pension, gratuity or social security benefit; any other "collateral benefit" deducted under other provisions of the Order is to be left out of account.

Two examples may be given to illustrate the operation of the Article:

I. X dies as a result of a criminal injury, leaving a widow and two children. The gross compensation payable to them (apart from the bereavement award to X's widow, which, by Article 6(10), is not subject to deduction) is assessed as follows.

	£	£
Pecuniary loss	18,000	
Expenses	1,000	
Total (A)		19,000

From this is deducted:

	£	
Compensation order paid by offender	500	
Pension paid to widow and children by X's employer	8,000	
Social security benefit	5,000	
Total (B)		13,500

---

12. Presumably, where the spouse has died after the victim's death. From the wording of the first part of Art 10(1) (" . . . spouse and child (if any) . . . ") it would appear that a discretionary payment cannot be made where a person dies leaving no surviving spouse.

13. This limit remains unchanged from the 1982 Order, but it was pointed out that "by the introduction of a bereavement award of £3,500 . . . the total sum paid to a widow or

widower as an expression of public sympathy has been restored, in real terms, to the value of the adult discretionary limit when it was last raised in 1982": 493 HL Debs, col 543 (25 Feb 1988). By Art 23(1) the Secretary of State may by order substitute a different amount.

14. Raised from £1,000 in the 1982 Order – "to keep it broadly in line with inflation": 493 HL Debs, col 543 (25 Feb 1988). This amount may also be changed by order under Art 23(1).

Deducting total B from total A, X's widow and children are entitled to compensation of £5,500. In order to apply Article 10(1), however, reference is made only to the pecuniary loss figure (£18,000), from which must be deducted the pension and the social security benefit (£13,000). As a result the compensation payable for pecuniary loss is reduced to £5,000; the "discretionary payments limit" in this case is £12,600 and therefore X's widow and children are eligible for a discretionary payment of £7,600, to "top-up" the compensation of £5,500 to which they are in any case entitled.

II. Y dies as a result of a criminal injury, leaving a widower but no children. Gross compensation of £9,000 is payable for pecuniary loss, from which £3,000 must be deducted in respect of social security benefits. The net award to Y is £6,000. Since compensation payable before the necessary deduction did not exceed £10,000, Y is eligible for a discretionary payment of £3,000, to restore the compensation to the amount payable before any deduction was made.

It must be emphasised that "topping-up" under Article 10 is *discretionary*; there is no entitlement to such a payment. The basis on which the discretion is exercised has never been made clear, but two points have emerged:

(a) Payment under the pre-1988 legislation was not confined to the widows of soldiers and police officers; the widows of "civilians" benefited equally from its provisions.[15]

(b) Payment has been refused "because it was believed or known that the person who had been killed was linked to a para-military or proscribed organisation. It was felt quite improper that the deceased's relatives should benefit from his former crimes."[16]

This latter explanation points up the unsatisfactory nature of a discretionary power where no known guidelines exist for its exercise. There is no appeal from a refusal to make such an award,[17] but the decision to do so may be challenged by judicial review.[18]

5. Method of Deduction from Compensation

By Article 6(3):

"Any sum required to be deducted . . . shall be deducted from the amount of any compensation in respect of pecuniary loss and the balance (if any) of that sum shall be deducted first from the amount of any compensation in respect of expenses and then from the amount of any other compensation."[19]

---

15. Of the 240 discretionary payments made between 1977 and 1983, 123 (or 51%) were to "civilian" widows; however the average payment to such widows (at £3,709) was lower than that paid to the widows of members of the security forces (at £4,800).

16. 4th Standing Cttee on Statutory Instruments 1982–83, vol *ix*, cols 6–7 (15 Dec 1982). At that date the discretion to make no pay-

ment had been exercised in only seven cases.

17. Article 16(1).

18. See especially *R v CICB, ex parte Lain* [1967] 2 All ER 770 and *R v Sec of State for the Home Department, ex parte Harrison* [1988] 3 All ER 86, discussed above, p 137.

19. Re-enacting 1977 Order, Art 5(4). There was no equivalent provision in the 1968 Act.

But *no* such deduction is to be made from the compensation payable for bereavement or for certain consequences of rape.[20]

The principal significance of this provision lies in its effect on the operation of the system of discretionary payments provided for by Article 10. This system is "triggered" by the effect of the deductions on the compensation for pecuniary loss payable to a spouse and children.[21]

Where the compensation payable to an applicant is to be reduced e.g. because of his provocative or negligent behaviour, etc, it would appear that the benefits to be taken into account should be deducted from the full compensation *before* the necessary reduction is made.[22] A simple example shows how this approach operates to the applicant's advantage:

Total gross compensation payable	£10,000
Value of benefits etc to be deducted	£4,000
Appropriate reduction	50%
Award to applicant	
(£10,000−£4,000 = £6,000, less 50%)	£3,000

Were the 50% reduction to be made *before* the benefits were deducted, the applicant would receive only £1,000 (i.e. £10,000 less 50% = £5,000−£4,000 = £1,000).[23]

Article 6(3) fails to clarify the method of deduction where more than one person is entitled to compensation. This issue arose in *Brown* v *Secretary of State*[24] where, on the death of a soldier, an application for compensation was made by his widow and their three young children. Service pensions were payable in respect of both the widow and the children, and the court had to decide whether to deduct the aggregate value of these pensions from the total compensation payable or to assess the net compensation payable to each individual. The problem – and its significance – may be further explained by a simple example:

> On H's death, a pension worth £20,000 is payable in respect of W and £6,000 in respect of each of their two children. The gross compensation payable is £45,000 apportioned as to W (say) £35,000 and as to each child, £5,000. On the "aggregate" method, compensation of £13,000 (i.e. £45,000−£20,000 + £12,000) is payable to W and the children; on the "individual" method, £15,000 (i.e. £35,000−£20,000) is payable to W, and nothing is payable to children.

---

20. 1988 Order, Art 6(10). Compensation for funeral expenses is not protected from deduction – Art 6(3) applies generally to "expenses". *Cf* 1988 Act, Sch 7, para 11(1).

21. Article 6(3) also has relevance to the operation of the limit on compensation for pecuniary loss imposed by Art 8(1) – see above, p 176.

22. See Law Reform (Miscellaneous Provisions) Act (NI) 1948, s 3(3). A similar rule is followed in the Republic – see *White*, pp 222–3.

23. *Pearson Report*, para 497 supports the first approach as producing the fairer result; the applicant's conduct is relevant only to his criminal injuries compensation and should not reduce e.g. the value of the social security benefits payable to him.

24. Unreported, Cty Ct (Judge Rowland), 14 Feb 1984.

In *Brown* the learned judge held that the phrase "any pension . . . payable to or for the benefit of . . . any of his dependants" in Article 5(3)(*b*) of the 1977 Order (now replicated in Article 6(2)(*b*) of the 1988 Order) required him to adopt the "aggregate" method. He rejected the contention that the phrase describes only the nature of the benefits to be deducted and does not lay down the actual person from whose compensation the deduction is to be made. Such an interpretation would, according to the learned judge, mean that (as in the example given above) part of the pension would be "written out" of the case and that "is to go against the express wording of the Order as well as its policy which has been established for years".

It is suggested, with respect, that the policy of deduction is not the sole issue. What is also important is the nature of the entitlement where several relatives have suffered pecuniary loss. It has been suggested above[25] that each has an individual right to compensation; if that indeed is the case, then it does not seem correct to reduce that compensation on account of a pension payable to or for the benefit of some other relative.[26] The method of deduction is also linked to the question of apportionment of the compensation; as we have seen[27] the conventional practice, in the case of an application by a widow and children, is to award the bulk of the compensation to the widow. This practice is obviously convenient where nothing turns on the apportionment; but where the apportionment may have an effect on the amount of compensation payable, it seems that there must in principle be a genuine estimate of each relative's dependency on the deceased.[28]

---

25. Above, pp 193–4.

26. *Cp Davies* v *Powell Duffryn Associated Collieries Ltd (No 2)* [1942] AC 601, 612, *per* Lord Wright: "The actual pecuniary loss of each individual entitled to sue can only be ascertained by balancing, on the one hand, the loss to him of the future pecuniary benefit and, on the other, any pecuniary advantage which from whatever source comes to him by reason of the death." See also *McGregor*, para 1582: " . . . where collateral benefits fall to be deducted . . . it is . . . essential that these . . . deductions be made not until *after* the apportionment between the individual dependants has been arrived at . . . ". *White*, pp 354–7 agrees.

27. Above, pp 198–9.

28. See especially *Robertson* v *Lestrange* [1985] 1 All ER 950.

5

Alternative Sources of Compensation

INTRODUCTION

As already indicated,[1] the general policy of the 1988 Order, as of its predecessors, is that "collateral" payments received by the victim of a violent crime or his relatives as a result of his injury or death are normally deducted in full from the criminal injuries compensation. Such payments may come from a wide variety of sources, and a comprehensive analysis of the scope of "compensation" would require full consideration of these schemes also. It is, however, impractical in a work of this kind to examine the complex provisions relating e.g. to social security benefits or occupational pensions; these are, in any event, fully discussed elsewhere.[2] But other "alternative" sources are, perhaps, worthy of some consideration in the present context and are therefore dealt with herein.

CIVIL ACTION FOR DAMAGES

A person injured by a crime of violence will invariably have a good cause of action in trespass or negligence against the offender. The problem, of course, is that in practice the offender is all too often a man of straw and not worth suing. Indeed, it is this general inability by victims to obtain private damages that is one of the principal reasons for the development of schemes of public compensation. But funds for public compensation are not limitless, and the availability of public compensation should not necessarily operate to relieve private liability or individual responsibility. Civil liability should not, therefore, be too readily ignored in practice as a source of compensation for victims of crimes of violence. As it happens, there are already three good reasons at least why an action in tort should normally be considered. First, even if the offender himself may not be worth suing, some other person who has adequate means may be liable to the victim for injuries caused by the offender. Secondly, there may be full entitlement to private damages in a case where, because of its public nature, criminal injuries compensation would be refused or at least reduced. Finally, and again as a result of

---

1. Above, pp 203 *et seq.*
2. See e.g. Ogus and Barendt, *The Law of Social Security* (3rd ed, 1988); Calvert *et al,* *Encyclopaedia of Social Security Law* (1983); Ellison, *Pensions: Law and Practice* (1990); Reardon, *Pensions Guide* (2nd ed, 1988).

differing policy considerations, the damages recoverable at common law or under the Fatal Accidents legislation may be higher – even substantially higher – than the level of compensation payable under the 1988 Order.

It will be more convenient if we consider these three points in reverse order. But first it should perhaps be emphasised that the 1988 Order does not impose on the victim any express obligation to claim damages. Article 6(2)(*a*) provides that any sums paid to the victim "by way of . . . damages from the offender or any person on the offender's behalf, consequent on the criminal injury" must be deducted from the compensation otherwise payable under the Order. In addition, where compensation under the Order has been paid to a victim who subsequently obtains damages from the offender or any person on the offender's behalf, the victim must, under Article 18(1), *pro tanto* reimburse the Secretary of State.[3] But it will be noted that both these provisions refer solely to damages which have been or are subsequently "paid"; no reference is made to damages which are or may be "payable" nor to any "right to damages" which the victim may have.[4] It is also noticeable that both provisions refer only to damages paid by "the offender or any person on the offender's behalf . . . ";[5] this wording would not appear to extend e.g. to damages for failure to provide a safe system of work paid by an employer to an employee assaulted in the course of his employment by a non-employee.[6]

It may, however, be that the fact that the victim appears to have a good chance of recovering damages from the offender or anyone else but has taken no steps to assert that claim represents a "relevant circumstance" for the purposes of Article 6(1) and must, therefore, by implication, be taken into account. Thus in *Re Sheehan and Criminal Injuries Compensation Board*[7] a prisoner in Kingston Penitentiary was seriously injured when he was assaulted by fellow prisoners. The Ontario Board refused to award compensation on the ground (*inter alia*) that it considered as a relevant circumstance the absence of any evidence that the applicant had taken proceedings for damages against the prison authorities. This case, however, does not give clear guidance on the point[8] and the reasoning of the Ontario

---

3. These provisions are discussed further at pp 206 and 327 respectively.

4. *Cf* Irish Scheme, para 16 is couched in similar terms, but in practice "we encourage applicants to pursue their civil rights to compensation (from the wrongdoer or otherwise) . . ." – see *Workings of the Scheme*, p 1. Consideration of an application will normally be adjourned pending the outcome of such proceedings.

5. The Irish Scheme, para 16 uses the same formula.

6. As in *Chomentowski* v *Red Garter Restaurant Pty Ltd* (1970) 92 WN(NSW) 1070, discussed below, p 235. It may however be that the fact that damages have been paid by another party is a "relevant circumstance" for the purposes of Art 6(1) – it

is difficult to imagine that the court would allow a victim to recover "double" compensation. *Cf* British Scheme, para 21 requires simply that "damages . . . in respect of [his] personal injuries" obtained by the victim must be taken into account. See to the same effect 1988 Act, Sch 7, para 13(*a*) (" . . . any action for damages . . . ").

7. (1974) 52 DLR (3d) 728, discussed Miers, *Responses to Victimisation* (1978), pp 189–191.

8. The Divisional Court considered that the Board was in error on this point; the Court of Appeal expressed no opinion on the grounds that under the Ontario statute the Board was entitled to have regard to such circumstances "as it considers relevant" and its decision was therefore not subject to judicial review.

Board would, in any case, appear to be inconsistent with the express provisions of the 1988 Order. In particular it is difficult to reconcile with Article 17, which specifically empowers the Secretary of State himself to bring proceedings against an offender (but not other tortfeasors) to recover the whole or any specified part of the compensation paid to the victim. Had Parliament wished to oblige the victim to take such proceedings it would have been easy so to provide directly and such an obligation should surely not be implied in the absence of an express provision to this effect.[9]

1. Quantum of Damages

The differences between the assessment of damages (both at common law and under the Fatal Accidents legislation) and the assessment of compensation under the 1988 Order have already been summarised in Chapter 4. These differences will often mean that the sum payable as damages in civil proceedings will be greater than that payable in a similar case as criminal injuries compensation. Perhaps the most pervasive instance is provided by the rules relating to "collateral" benefits, where the plaintiff in civil proceedings will benefit e.g. from the more generous approach laid down in relation to pensions by the House of Lords in *Parry* v *Cleaver*.[10] In other specific instances, a victim may also benefit from the absence of particular restrictions imposed by the 1988 Order. A good recent example is provided by *W* v *Meah*,[11] where two women were viciously raped and assaulted by the defendant. The damages awarded by the High Court took into account the "aggravated" nature of the plaintiffs' injuries – factors which could not be (and were not) taken into account in the assessment of their criminal injuries compensation.[12]

It has, however, occasionally been suggested that the availability of criminal injuries compensation might be taken into account in the assessment of common law damages. In *Baker* v *Willoughby*[13] P received injuries to his left leg in an accident caused by D's negligence. Before the trial of his action for damages P was shot in the same leg by robbers and the injury was so severe that the leg had to be amputated. The House of Lords held that the criminal injury did not diminish the loss caused to P by D's negligence. This

---

9. In *K* v *Sec of State* [1989] 8 *BNIL* 19 a 13 year old boy was knocked off his bicycle by an assailant. The Secretary of State applied for an adjournment of his claim under the 1977 Order on the basis that he should first bring an action in tort against the assailant. His Honour Judge Gibson QC ruled that it was not for the Secretary of State to dictate which remedy the claimant should pursue and refused the application. It is not clear, however, if the "relevant circumstances" point was fully considered.

10. [1969] 1 All ER 555, and see generally McGregor, *Damages* (15th ed, 1988), paras 1481–1496, 1594–1600. But *cf* Social Security (NI) Order 1989, Art 24 (social security benefits now deducted from certain tort damages).

11. [1986] 1 All ER 935.

12. In one of the cases considered in *W* v *Meah* general damages of £10,250 were awarded in the High Court, as compared to the £3,600 compensation awarded by the Criminal Injuries Compensation Board – see *ibid*, p 942. See also *M* v *Cain, The Times*, 26 Nov 1988 where damages of £25,000 were awarded to a rape victim who had received compensation of £6,512 from the Board; a retrial was, however, ordered on the question of liability: *The Times*, 15 Dec 1989.

13. [1969] 3 All ER 1528.

decision was questioned in *Jobling* v *Associated Dairies Ltd*[14] on the ground (*inter alia*) that "no account was taken . . . of the very real possibility that the plaintiff might obtain compensation [for the second injury] from the Criminal Injuries Compensation Board". The implication was that if P did obtain an award from the Board, the decision in *Baker* would result in over-compensation. But this is surely incorrect – the provisions of the British Scheme (like those of the 1988 Order discussed above) mean that the Board will ensure that no over-compensation takes place.[15] *W* v *Meah*[16] may again provide a second example; faced with an injury for which there was no common law precedent it seems that Woolf J had some regard to the level of compensation awarded by the Criminal Injuries Compensation Board.

2. Reduction or Refusal of Damages

We have seen in Chapter 3 that criminal injuries compensation schemes (and in particular the 1988 Order) typically make extensive provision for the refusal or reduction of compensation to "undeserving" victims. In particular compensation may be refused or reduced by reason of conduct of the victim or applicant which in no way caused or contributed to the injury.[17] In tort law, on the other hand, a plaintiff's conduct is taken into account on the issue of liability[18] only if it establishes that he was *volens* or contributorily negligent.[19] Such "non-contributory" factors as a previous criminal record, membership of an unlawful association or failure to co-operate with the police do not, as such, debar a plaintiff from obtaining damages. In a limited number of cases, however, the plaintiff's criminal conduct at the time of injury has been taken into account as a matter of public policy negativing the existence of a duty of care or as a defence based on the maxim *ex turpi causa non oritur actio*.[20] The leading case is *Ashton* v *Turner*[21] where P, a passenger

---

14. [1981] 2 All ER 752, 755, *per* Lord Wilberforce. Lord Edmund-Davies (at p 758) noted Atiyah's comment ((1969) 85 *LQR* 475) that "the existence of the Criminal Injuries Compensation Board . . . plainly cast a long shadow over the entire proceedings", but observed that the Scheme "was never adverted to at any stage by anyone".

15. British Scheme, para 21 (see 1988 Act, Sch 7, para 13(*a*)); 1988 Order, Arts 6(2)(*a*) and 18(1). But Hepple and Matthews, *Tort Cases and Materials* (3rd ed, 1985), pp 255–6 point out that the damages *plus* criminal injuries compensation would not have overcompensated P in any event.

16. [1986] 1 All ER 935, 942. For comments on the interaction between common law damages and criminal injuries compensation in Northern Ireland, see *Simpson* v *Harland & Wolff plc* [1988] 13 NIJB 10, discussed above pp 184–5.

17. See especially pp 125–137.

18. Unless it amounts to contributory negli-

gence, provocative behaviour by a plaintiff is taken into account, if at all, only in relation to aggravated or exemplary damages – see *Lane* v *Holloway* [1967] 3 All ER 129. A plaintiff's criminal way of life may be taken into account in assessing compensatory damages – see e.g. *Burns* v *Edman* [1970] 1 All ER 886 (widow only able to show loss of support from deceased husband's criminal activities and therefore not entitled to any damages).

19. See in particular *Wasson* v *Chief Constable of the RUC* [1987] 8 NIJB 34 (contributory negligence may be a defence to intentional trespass to the person) and *Barnes* v *Nayer*, *The Times*, 19 Dec 1986. *Cf* Hudson, "Contributory Negligence as a defence to battery" (1984) 4 *Legal Stud* 332.

20. See generally Weinrib, "Illegality as a Tort Defence" (1976) 26 *U Toronto LJ* 28; Symmons, "*Ex Turpi Causa* in English Tort Law" (1981) 44 *MLR* 585.

21. [1980] 3 All ER 870. See also *Pitts* v *Hunt* [1989] 3 WLR 795; *Lindsay* v *Poole* 1984 SLT 269.

in a car, was seriously injured by the negligence of D, the driver of the car. Shortly before the accident P and D had participated jointly in a burglary and the accident occurred as they tried to get away from the scene of the crime. Ewbank J held that P was not entitled to damages:

> "[T]he law of England may in certain circumstances not recognise the existence of a duty of care by one participant in a crime to another participant in the same crime, in relation to an act done in connection with the commission of that crime. That law is based on public policy, and the application of the law depends on a consideration of all the facts."[22]

In *Ashton* the defendant had acted negligently; what if he had *intentionally* injured the plaintiff – i.e. had committed a crime of violence? The orthodox statement of principle was made by Lord Asquith in *National Coal Board* v *England*:

> "[T]he plaintiff cannot be precluded from suing simply because the wrongful act is committed after the illegal agreement is made and during the period involved in its execution. The act must . . . at least be a step in the execution of the common illegal purpose . . . [Thus] if A and B are proceeding to the premises which they intend burglariously to enter, and before they enter them, B picks A's pocket and steals his watch, I cannot prevail on myself to believe that A could not sue in tort . . . The theft is totally unconnected with the burglary."[23]

In more recent times, however, several attempts have been made to extend the scope of the *ex turpi* defence. *Farrell* v *Secretary of State for Defence*[24] is a particular case in point. P's husband was apparently attempting to commit a robbery when he was shot dead by an army patrol who reasonably believed that he was, with others, engaged in a terrorist bombing attempt. One ground of defence was that P's death arose *ex turpi causa*, since at the time he was shot he was engaged in a serious crime. This contention was firmly rejected in the Court of Appeal:

> "*Ex turpi* does not mean that a plaintiff who is guilty of a crime cannot recover from a defendant whose tort is independent of the plaintiff's crime . . . A criminal is not an outlaw and the maxim is not *turpe factum delet actionem*."[25]

---

22. *Ibid*, p 877. See to the same effect *Smith* v *Jenkins* (1970) 119 CLR 397; *Tomlinson* v *Harrison* (1971) 24 DLR (3d) 26. See also *O'Connor* v *McDonnell*, Unreported, High Ct (Murnaghan J), 30 June 1970, discussed O'Reilly, (1972) 7 *IJ* 98 (P and D (along with others) poaching deer; P negligently shot by D; shooting held to be in furtherance of a common illegal purpose and P therefore not entitled to damages).

23. [1954] AC 403, 428. His Lordship did, however, note that there was "a surprising dearth of authority" on this point.

24. [1980] NI 55.

25. *Ibid*, p 64, *per* Lord Lowry LCJ, who added that "even if . . . the *ex turpi* doctrine applied, it could only have been related to the robbery attempt and not to the alleged bombing, because the possible barring of the action has to be related to a plaintiff's . . . actual discreditable conduct and not to something of which he is wrongly suspected." The Court of Appeal's decision in favour of the plaintiff was reversed by the House of Lords, which did not consider this particular point. *Cp* [Irish] Civil Liability Act 1961, s 57(1): "It shall not be a defence in an action of tort merely to show that the plaintiff is in breach of the . . . criminal law."

This passage was relied on by Hutton J in *Lynch* v *Ministry of Defence*,[26] where P drove a stolen car through an army road-block and was shot by one of the soldiers. D contended that P was shot because he had attempted to run down and injure a soldier and relied (*inter alia*) on the defence of *ex turpi causa*. Hutton J was not satisfied on the evidence that P had deliberately attempted to injure a soldier and considered that *ex turpi* did not apply. The main question in the case was whether the force used by the soldiers was reasonable in the circumstances, as required by section 3 of the Criminal Law Act (NI) 1967. The learned judge was not satisfied that it was – and this finding meant further that *ex turpi causa* could not succeed:

> " . . . when Parliament has expressly enacted in section 3(1) [of the 1967 Act] that a person may use such force as is reasonable in the circumstances in the prevention of crime, and has gone on to state in section 3(2) that the provisions of subsection (1) shall replace the rules of the common law as to the matters dealt with by that subsection, the common law should not permit a soldier or police officer . . . to say: 'True it is that I . . . used unreasonable force against the plaintiff, but because my . . . force was occasioned by the plaintiff's criminal or improper conduct, he is not entitled to damages'."[27]

This reasoning is, with respect, not convincing. It would appear that section 3 merely replaces the rules of the common law relating to the use of force in the prevention of crime, etc. In other words it defines when the use of force will give rise to *prima facie* liability in tort (and in criminal law). But it is presumably still open to a defendant unable to rely on section 3 to lead a defence such as contributory negligence – section 3 can hardly have replaced *that* rule. It should, therefore, in theory be open to the defence to plead *ex turpi causa*. But it is further submitted, with respect, that the learned judge's *decision* to reject that defence in this case was correct. A person's criminal conduct should not, as a matter of policy, excuse unreasonable force; it should rather be taken into account in deciding whether the use of force was reasonable in the circumstances (the nature of the plaintiff's conduct being an important "circumstance" for the purposes of section 3[28]).

The *ex turpi* defence was also rejected in *Lane* v *Holloway*.[29] P, a "rather cantankerous" man aged 64, became involved in an altercation with D, another man some 40 years his junior. P threw the first punch (to D's shoulder), whereupon D punched P severely in the eye, causing serious injury. When P claimed damages for battery, D pleaded (*inter alia*) *ex turpi causa*. The Court of Appeal held this defence inapplicable:

> "To say in circumstances such as those that *ex turpi causa non oritur actio* is a defence seems to me to be quite absurd. Academically of course one can see the argument, but one must look at it . . . from a practical point of view. To say that this old gentleman was engaged jointly with the defendant in a criminal venture is a step which . . . I feel wholly unable to take."[30]

26. [1983] NI 216.

27. *Ibid*, p 235. For this reason *ex turpi causa* was not pleaded in *Wasson* v *Chief Constable of the RUC* [1987] 8 NIJB 34.

28. *Ibid*, p 232. See also *Wasson, supra*.

29. [1967] 3 All ER 129.

30. *Ibid*, p 133, *per* Salmon LJ. Nor was P *volenti*: "I agree that in an ordinary fight with fists there is no cause of action to either [partici-pant] for any injury suffered . . . *Volenti non fit injuria*. But [a participant] does not take on him-self the risk of a savage blow out of all proportion to the occasion": *per* Lord Denning MR at p 131.

This orthodox application of *ex turpi causa* has not, however, been followed consistently. In *Murphy* v *Culhane*[31] D struck P's husband on the head with a plank and killed him. The defence to an action by P (the widow of the deceased) was that the assault occurred during and as part of a criminal affray initiated by the deceased. The Court of Appeal held that P was not entitled to judgment on the pleadings; in the words of Lord Denning MR:

> "A man who takes part in a criminal affray may well be said to have been guilty of such a wicked act as to deprive himself of a cause of action or, alternatively, to have taken on himself the risk . . . [S]uppose that a burglar breaks into a house and the householder . . . picks up a gun and shoots him, using more force maybe than is reasonably necessary. The householder may be guilty of manslaughter . . . But I doubt very much whether the burglar's widow could have an action for damages. The householder might well have a defence either on the ground of *ex turpi causa* . . . or *volenti non fit injuria*. So in the present case it is open to [D] to raise both those defences."[32]

This statement, and other "straws in the wind",[33] suggest that *ex turpi causa* may be coming to be considered more frequently as a defence in actions of tort – or at least that judges as a matter of public policy are now somewhat more reluctant to allow "criminal" plaintiffs to obtain damages. One reason for such a change could be that the judges may become unwilling to continue awarding what may be substantial damages to persons considered by Parliament to be undeserving of any criminal injuries compensation. But as the law stands at present this is still possible in a considerable number of cases.

3. Liability of Person other than Offender

As the scope of public compensation becomes more restricted, either by limitations on entitlement or reductions in quantum, it seems likely that there will be a corresponding increase in efforts on behalf of victims to find a tort defendant other than the offender liable – and able – to pay "private" damages. In the United States, where criminal injury compensation schemes have generally been more limited than in the United Kingdom, some notable developments have already taken place.[34] The English courts,

---

31. [1976] 3 All ER 533. See also *Wade* v *Martin* [1955] 3 DLR 635 (P, who agreed to "have it out" with D and was injured, not entitled to damages because *ex turpi*).

32. *Ibid*, p 536. But with respect the burglar would seem to be entitled to damages – see e.g. *Bird* v *Holbrook* (1828) 4 Bing 628 and Occupiers' Liability (NI) Order 1987; see also *Bigcharles* v *Merkel* [1973] 1 WWR 324 (fleeing burglar shot and killed by occupier; *ex turpi* not applicable but burglar held 75% contributorily negligent).

33. Weir, *A Casebook on Tort* (6th ed, 1988), pp 226-7, referring in addition to *obiter dicta* e.g. in *Cummings* v *Grainger* [1977] 1 All ER 104 (defence of illegality might apply to burglar bitten by guard-dog) and *Nettleship* v *Weston* [1971] 3 All ER 581 (*ex turpi* may

apply to passenger who accepts lift from driver he knows to be drunk and is injured by driver's negligence). See also *Marshall* v *Osmond* [1983] 2 All ER 225 and *Barnes* v *Nayer, The Times*, 19 Dec 1986.

34. See e.g. Brown and Doyle, "Growing Liability for Premises Owners" (1986) 72 *ABAJ* 64; McLaughlin, "The Foreseeable Risks of Apartment Living" (1986) 31 *Vill L Rev* 627; Yelnosky, "Business Inviters' Duty to Protect Invitees from Criminal Acts" (1986) 134 *U Pa L Rev* 883; Annotation, "Liability of Land Carrier to passenger who becomes victim of third party's assault on or about Carrier's vehicle or premises" (1984) 34 ALR 4th 1054; Annotation, "Tavernkeeper's Liability to Patron for Third Person's Assault" (1986) 43 ALR 4th 277; Carrington and Rapp, *Victims' Law and Litigation* (1988).

on the other hand, have in recent years shown considerable reluctance (even deliberate refusal) as a matter both of principle and of policy to impose liability on one negligent defendant for the intentional wrongdoing of another, while at the same time acknowledging that there are "exceptional" cases where a negligent defendant may be so liable.[35] The issues may be illustrated by two contrasting cases – *Home Office* v *Dorset Yacht Ltd*[36] and *Hill* v *Chief Constable of West Yorkshire*.[37]

The facts of *Dorset Yacht* are familiar enough. Some borstal boys working on Brownsea Island escaped from the custody of their officers, boarded a boat moored nearby and caused it to collide with P's yacht. The boys then boarded P's yacht and caused further damage to it. P alleged that the escape resulted from the officers' negligent breach of their orders, for which D was vicariously liable. The House of Lords (by a majority of 4–1) held that on the facts as alleged D did owe P a duty of care capable of giving rise to liability in damages.[38]

Although the judgments differ in some respects, the basic reasoning of their Lordships appears to be agreed. As a general principle D, even though he has been at fault and some injury or damage to P is reasonably foreseeable, is not liable to P for an injury which X, an independent third party, has deliberately chosen to inflict on P. This non-liability of D may be because in the circumstances D owes no duty to safeguard P or, if he does or may owe such a duty, the injury to P is too remote because X's intentional act operates as a *novus actus interveniens* to break the chain of causation between D's negligence and P's injury. To this general principle, however, there are a number of exceptions, and in particular liability may arise where there is a "special relationship" between P and D or between D and X. In *Dorset Yacht* such a "special relationship" did exist because –

(i)   the geographical proximity of P's yacht and the foreseeable nature of the damage inflicted made that damage "very likely" and therefore gave rise to a special relationship between P and D, and

(ii) the fact that the boys had been under the supervision and control of D's servants created a special relationship between D and X.

In these circumstances, D did owe a duty to safeguard P's yacht from damage by the borstal boys.

In *Hill*, on the other hand, no duty was owed by D to safeguard P from injury by X. There, X had committed 13 murders and eight attempted murders in a period of five years; all the offences had occurred in West Yorkshire, the victims were all young women and the *modus operandi* in

---

35. See e.g. *Smith* v *Littlewoods Organisation Ltd* [1987] 1 All ER 710, 729–730, *per* Lord Goff: "That there are special circumstances in which a defender may be held responsible in law for injuries suffered by the pursuer through a third party's deliberate wrongdoing is not in doubt."

36. [1970] 2 All ER 294.

37. [1988] 2 All ER 238. Liability of the police generally is discussed at some length in Clayton and Tomlinson, *Civil Actions against the Police* (1987), pp 297 *et seq*.

38. Technically, their Lordships dismissed the appeal on a preliminary issue of law and allowed the case to go for trial on the issues of fact.

each case was the same. P, the mother of X's last victim, claimed damages from D for negligent failure by the police to detect and apprehend X before he murdered her daughter. The House of Lords held D not liable; the police, in the absence of a special relationship or ingredient over and above the reasonable foreseeability of likely harm, did not owe a general duty of care to individual members of the public to identify and apprehend an unknown criminal. *Dorset Yacht* was distinguishable on two grounds, *viz* here there was no special relationship between D and P – P's daughter was simply "one of a vast number of potential victims at risk . . . ". Nor was there any special relationship between D and X, given that X had never been in police custody *before* the murder of P's daughter.

In addition there were in *Hill* various considerations of public policy which had to be taken into account. Of particular interest in this context are some observations of Fox LJ in the Court of Appeal:

> "If the state made no provision at all for criminal injuries that might be a reason for imposing a legal duty of care on the police in the conduct of their investigations . . . In fact the state has provided a scheme of compensation for criminal injuries since 1964 . . . [which makes] . . . quite wide provision for compensation . . . as a result of a crime of violence. It is not desirable that inequalities should be produced by providing additional remedies for negligence. Either such remedies will merely duplicate the scheme, or they will give rise to inequalities which may be offensive to the families of other victims of crimes of violence in cases where no negligence . . . was involved . . . [T]he problems of compensation for injury from crimes of violence are best dealt with in the framework of the scheme . . . which has been developed for more than 20 years with a view to dealing with the particular difficulties of the subject matter and to the establishment of an acceptable system of compensation."[39]

Such reasoning is, with respect, not very convincing[40] and it is noticeable that no reference to this point was made in the House of Lords. It is true, of course, that one justification for a scheme of public compensation is that the state should accept "liability" for the breakdown of law and order which is reflected in the commission of crimes of violence and in one sense there would be duplication in holding the police liable essentially for the same reason. But the "liability" of the state can only be so justified in very general terms, and it has never been suggested that such a moral or political responsibility should supersede a well-established *legal* principle such as liability for fault. This could, of course, be done by Parliament, which could, in turn allow the Board as its agent to sue the offender or anyone else who

---

39. [1987] 1 All ER 1173, 1181-2. See also Samuel, "Legal Reasoning and Liability for People" (1982) 98 *LQR* 358, 361: "The availability of a public loss spreading scheme is a relevant factor to be taken into account in deciding whether one person should be liable for the wrongful act of another."

40. It is described as "flawed" by Bailey, "Beyond the Call of Duty" (1987) 50 *MLR* 956, 959. Clayton and Tomlinson (*op cit* n 37, p 307) consider that *Hill* was wrongly decided. It has, however, been followed in *Alexandrou* v *Oxford, The Times*, 19 Feb 1990. *Cf Donaldson* v *Chief Constable of the RUC* Unreported, High Ct (Carswell J), 14 July 1989.

might be legally liable for a victim's injury. But although Parliament in the 1988 Order and in the 1988 Act has made some provision along these lines,[41] it would still appear that the state is intended to be a secondary source of compensation for criminal injuries, to be availed of only when and because damages in tort cannot be recovered. Thus, although there may be other policy reasons for not imposing liability for negligence (whether on the police or any other person or organisation), the existence of the criminal injuries compensation scheme does *not* appear to provide a valid justification for not doing so.

It has nonetheless to be accepted that the current judicial climate in the United Kingdom is against the extension of liability for the deliberate acts of third parties.[42] But just how far does the existing law go in imposing such liability? It is suggested that four requirements must be satisfied:

  (i) There must exist between D and P, or between D and X (the third party) a special relationship such as to impose on D a duty to safeguard P from X's wrongful conduct;

 (ii) D must have been in breach of that duty;

(iii) The injury to P must have been not only a reasonably foreseeable consequence of D's negligent act or omission, but also closely related to, a highly likely consequence of, or the natural and probable result of, D's negligence, and

 (iv) At least in any novel situation (such as *Hill*) it must not be unfair to make D liable.

Such an attempt to summarise the law by reference to the familiar division of duty, breach and damage is, however, rather artificial.[43] We shall, therefore, look more closely at some of the "special relationships" which may, in an appropriate case, give rise to liability.

(a) Injury inflicted by person in D's custody

We have seen that the fact that the borstal boys had been under the supervision and control of D's servants was an important factor in making the Home Office liable in the *Dorset Yacht* case. In fact a duty to safeguard P may arise (a) where X is in D's control, (b) where X is in the act of escaping from D's control and (c) where X has been released from D's control.

In a number of cases the prison authorities have been sued by one prisoner injured by a fellow prisoner. The leading case is *Ellis* v *Home Office*,[44] where

---

41. In Art 17 and ss 115–116, respectively – but proceedings may only be taken against the offender, and after conviction.

42. At least where such acts cause damage to property – see especially *Lamb* v *Camden London BC* [1981] 2 All ER 408; *P Perl (Exporters) Ltd* v *Camden LBC* [1983] 3 All ER 161 and *Smith* v *Littlewoods Organisation Ltd* [1987] 1 All ER 710.

43. Various attempts have been made to synthesise the case law, without great success –

see especially *Smith* v *Littlewoods Organisation Ltd* [1987] 1 All ER 710, 728, *per* Lord Goff, and Prosser and Keeton, *The Law of Torts* (5th ed, 1984), pp 383 *et seq. Cf* Street, *The Law of Torts* (8th ed, 1988), p 169: "There is alas . . . no one principle applicable to all cases where a duty may arise in respect of the wrongdoing of others."

44. [1953] 2 All ER 149, approved in *Home Office* v *Dorset Yacht Ltd* [1970] 2 All ER 294, 309, *per* Lord Morris.

a prison officer had left a cell door open, allowing a prisoner thought to be mentally defective to escape and injure P, another prisoner. It was assumed that the Home Office owed a duty to P to safeguard him from such injury;[45] but on the facts the court found that there had been no breach of that duty. There was no reason for the authorities to have known that X was more dangerous or violent than any ordinary prisoner.[46] On the other hand, in *Steele* v *Northern Ireland Office*[47] the plaintiff, while on remand in prison charged with the rape and incest of his daughter, was assaulted by fellow prisoners on three occasions. The prison authorities knew that, because of the nature of the offences charged, it was highly likely that P would be attacked. Kelly LJ, stating that "with this knowledge, reasonable care would inevitably require greater care, supervision and protection than in the case of a prisoner who was not at risk", held that the prison authorities had, in relation to the first assault, failed to take all reasonable steps to protect P. However, P had on that occasion been guilty of contributory negligence and the learned Lord Justice therefore reduced the damages from £9,000 to £6,000.

The principles applied in these cases were extended by the House of Lords in *Dorset Yacht*[48] to damage done or injuries inflicted in the course of escaping from lawful custody. Their Lordships however stressed the limited scope of their decision – D was liable only because the Borstal officers had acted negligently outside any discretion delegated to them and a duty was owed to P because in the circumstances a special relationship existed between D and P which exposed him to a particular risk of damage in consequence of the escape:

> " . . . any duty of a borstal officer to use reasonable care to prevent a borstal detainee from escaping from his custody was owed only to persons whom he could reasonably foresee had property situate in the vicinity of the place of detention of the detainee which the detainee was likely to steal or to appropriate and damage in the course of eluding immediate pursuit and recapture."[49]

---

45. "The duty on those responsible for one of Her Majesty's prisons is to take reasonable care for the safety of those who are within . . . " [1953] 2 All ER 149, 154, *per* Singleton LJ.

46. See also *Muldoon* v *Ireland* [1988] ILRM 367 (prison authorities not liable where attack on prisoner unprovoked and took place without warning). Cf *D'Arcy* v *Prison Comm'rs* [1956] *Crim LR* 56 (D liable when P had his throat cut by three fellow prisoners; P found 5% contributorily negligent).

47. [1988] 12 NIJB 1. The NIO was also held liable in *Taggart* v *NIQ* [1989] 2 *BNIL* 88 (but P 50% at fault). Cf *Egerton* v *Home Office* [1978] *Crim LR* 494 (P serving sentence for sexual offences against young girls, attacked by fellow prisoners and badly injured; D not liable because supervisory staff adequate for the reasonable care of the prisoners in general and of P in particular, and attack on P spontaneous and could not reasonably have been anticipated by an experienced prison officer). The Home Office was again exonerated in *Porterfield* v *Home Office*, *The Times*, 9 March 1988.

48. [1970] 2 All ER 294.

49. *Ibid*, p 334. Lord Diplock added that: "Whether or not any person fell within this category would depend on the facts of the particular case including the previous criminal and escaping record of the individual trainee concerned and the nature of the place from which he escaped." See e.g. *Vicar of Writtle* v *Essex CC* (1979) 77 LGR 656 (D liable when 12 year old boy escaped from home and set fire to P's church; D knew boy had fire-raising propensities but failed to inform person in charge of home); *Marti* v *Smith* (1981) 131 *NLJ* 1028 (boy escaped from borstal and stole car; some miles from borstal drove over P and injured him. Held, Home Office not liable because injury to P too remote).

The application of this principle to a case of personal injury was considered briefly in *Leeds CC* v *West Yorkshire Metropolitan Police*.[50] A 12-year-old boy in the care of a local authority was allowed home for a week-end to visit his parents. During the week-end he attacked and robbed an old lady. The question in issue was whether the criminal court which convicted the boy of robbery and unlawful wounding could make a compensation order against the local authority;[51] but in the course of his judgment Lord Scarman drew attention to *Dorset Yacht* and observed that:

> "The local authority . . . is . . . liable at common law if it should fail to take such care as was reasonable in all the circumstances to prevent a child in its care from causing damage to others."[52]

It is not thought that his Lordship was suggesting that the local authority would be liable on the facts of the case; but the case may be taken to show the potential application of *Dorset Yacht* to a crime of violence.

Negligence may also occur in the release of persons from custody. In *Holgate* v *Lancashire Mental Health Board*[53] D was held liable for an assault on P by X, a "mental defective". X, who had a record of violent assault, had been sentenced to be detained during Her Majesty's pleasure. He was subsequently transferred to a mental hospital and later was released on licence. The assault on P occurred during the period of the licence, which was held to have been granted without due regard to X's character and past history. Although doubted in *Dorset Yacht*[54] this decision may still be followed in an appropriate case.

(b) Injury inflicted by servant of D in course of his employment

In what amounts to a particular aspect of (*a*) above, an employer may be liable for an intentional injury inflicted by an employee – but only if the employee is considered to have been acting in the course of his employment. The case-law on this difficult issue has been summarised as follows:

> "[The servant's act] is deemed to be so done [i.e. in the course of employment] if it is either (1) a wrongful act authorised by the master, or (2) a wrongful and unauthorised mode of doing some act authorised by the master . . . On the other hand, if the unauthorised and wrongful act of the servant is not so connected with the authorised act as to be a mode of doing it, but is an independent act, the master is not responsible, for in such a case the servant is not acting in the course of his employment, but has gone outside of it."[55]

---

50. [1982] 1 All ER 274.

51. The House of Lords held that an order could not be made – see below, p 245.

52. [1982] 1 All ER 274, 279. See further Samuel, "Legal Reasoning and Liability for People" (1982) 98 *LQR* 358.

53. [1937] 4 All ER 19.

54. Their Lordships considered that due account might not have been given to the discretion which exists in such a case. Thus Lord Reid considered that the decision in *Holgate* "could only be supported if it could be said that the release was authorised so carelessly that there had been no real exercise of discretion." But *cf* Clayton and Tomlinson, *Civil Actions against the Police* (1987), p 308.

55. Salmond and Heuston, *The Law of Torts* (19th ed, 1987), pp 521–2 – a summary which has been judicially approved on many occasions.

The problem is to decide on which side of the line a particular case falls.[56] We may consider some illustrative cases. The employer was held liable in *Dyer* v *Munday*,[57] where an employee was sent by D to recover furniture bought by P on hire purchase, for which several instalments had not been paid. When P demurred, the employee assaulted her. D was held liable because the assault was considered to have been committed in furtherance of D's business – it was a wrongful and unauthorised mode of doing an authorised act. In *Daniels* v *Whetstone Entertainments Ltd*[58] a steward in a dance hall twice assaulted a customer in the course of ejecting him from the dance hall. On the first occasion the steward acted in the course of his employment; but on the second occasion he was considered to have acted out of personal vengeance. The manager of the dance hall was therefore vicariously liable for the first assault, but not for the second. More recent cases have also gone either way. In *Keppel Bus Co Ltd* v *Sa'ad bin Ahmad*,[59] D was held not liable for an assault by a bus conductor on a passenger; a conductor's duties may include the keeping of order among passengers, but there was in the case no evidence of any disorder or other circumstances calling for forcible action by the conductor. However, in *Nahhas* v *Pier House (Cheyne Walk) Management Ltd*[60] jewellery was stolen from P's flat by a porter employed by the company responsible for managing the property. The porter had gained access to the flat by means of a key left by P at the porter's desk. D argued that the porter had merely taken advantage of the situation, and had not been acting in the course of his employment. Although the porter was neither permitted nor required by the terms of his employment to enter P's flat and was in fact expressly forbidden to do so, D was held liable. The court took the broad view that the porter was employed to preserve the security of P's flat and to steal from it was a wrongful and unauthorised exercise of that task.

Nahhas further demonstrates that an employer may even in an exceptional case be *directly* liable for the deliberate wrongdoing of an employee. The porter who stole the jewellery from P's flat was, in fact, a professional thief who had numerous convictions for burglary or theft. D was held directly liable to P for negligence in their recruitment procedure – had they made adequate inquiries into the porter's background they would have discovered his criminal record and never have given him the job.[61] Thus, an

---

56. The cases involving deliberate infliction of personal injury are examined in detail by Rose, "Liability for an Employee's Assaults" (1977) 40 *MLR* 420. See also Clerk and Lindsell, *Torts* (16th ed, 1989), para 3.26.

57. [1895] 1 QB 742. *Cf Kinsella* v *Hamilton* (1890) 26 LR Ir 671 (death of person resisting distress occasioned by bailiffs: land agent not liable); *McNamara* v *Brown* [1918] 2 IR 215 (D employed watcher to prevent poaching; when attempting to apprehend some poachers watcher shot and killed poacher's son: D not liable). See the discussion of these and other Irish cases in McMahon and Binchy, *The Irish Law of Torts* (2nd ed 1990), p 759.

58. [1962] 2 Lloyd's Rep 1.

59. [1974] 2 All ER 700. See also *Deatons Pty Ltd* v *Flew* (1949) 79 CLR 370 (employer not liable for barmaid who used excessive force to repel a drunken customer).

60. (1984) 270 *EG* 328. See also *Johnson & Johnson (Ireland) Ltd* v *CP Security Ltd* [1986] ILRM 559. For US cases see generally Annotation, "Security Guard Company's liability for negligent hiring, supervision, retention or assignment of guard" (1986) 44 ALR 4th 620.

61. (1984) 270 *EG* 328, 330. See also *Morris* v *CW Martin & Sons Ltd* [1965] 2 All ER 725, 731, *per* Salmon LJ.

employer might also be personally liable for an assault by an employee whose propensity for violence was known to or ought to have been known by the employer.

Several commentators have suggested that the availability of criminal injuries compensation has largely removed the need for any development of the law relating to vicarious liability for personal injuries inflicted by employees.[62] But it would surely be anomalous to have one law for the intentional infliction of personal injury and another for deliberate damage to or theft of property by an employee. In any case:

> " . . . if it is right and proper to hold the employer liable, . . . it is preferable for the plaintiff's claim to be satisfied out of his pocket than out of public funds . . . "[63]

(c) Injury inflicted on servant of D in course of employment

An employer's duty to provide his employees with a safe system of work may mean that he is liable if an employee is assaulted in the course of his employment:

> "[I]t is an employer's duty to take reasonable care to see that his employees are not exposed to unnecessary risks, even if it be the risk of injury by criminals."[64]

The existence of this duty is clear; but P may have difficulty in proving that D was in breach of his duty. The issues were carefully examined in *Charlton* v *Forrest Printing Ink Co Ltd*[65] where P received serious eye injuries when he was attacked by robbers after having collected money from a bank to pay the D company's wages. P alleged that he had been exposed to unnecessary risk, and in particular that D had been negligent in not employing an outside firm of security specialists to collect the wages. The Court of Appeal held D not liable – the evidence did not suggest that they ought to have employed a security firm,[66] and P had been given clear instructions to vary the method used for collecting the money.[67] The defendants had, therefore, done what

---

62. E.g. Veitch and Miers, "Assault on the Law of Tort" (1975) 38 *MLR* 139, Winfield and Jolowicz, *Tort* (13th ed. 1989), p 574n.

63. Rose, *op cit*, p 428n, who goes on to call for "a more liberal approach in applying the traditional tests of vicarious liability and a greater readiness to hold the employer liable for assaults arising out of circumstances connected with the servant's employment . . . " (*ibid*, pp 432–3).

64. *Houghton* v *Hackney BC* (1961) 3 KIR 615, 617, *per* Diplock J. See also *West Bromwich Building Soc* v *Townsend* [1983] ICR 257, 268, *per* McNeill J.

65. [1980] IRLR 331. See also *Donaldson* v *Chief Constable of the RUC* Unreported,

High Ct (Carswell J), 14 July 1989 (D under duty to exercise reasonable care to ensure that police officers not exposed to unnecessary danger in the performance of their duties).

66. The great majority of firms in the area dealing with similar amounts of money used their own staff to collect those sums from the bank.

67. "It would have been different if it had been established that [D] . . . had not taken proper steps or had not given proper directions as to the making of variations or the giving of proper assistance to the employees in collecting money from the bank": *per* Lord Denning MR at p 333.

was reasonable in the circumstances to eliminate the risk of injury from robbery.[68]

On the other hand in *Chomentowski v Red Garter Restaurant Pty Ltd*[69] D was held liable when a head-waiter was robbed on the way to deposit the evening's takings from a restaurant in the night safe of a bank. The robbery occurred in the early hours of the morning, the employee was on his own, and the court held that it was clearly open to the jury to conclude from the circumstances that there was a reasonably foreseeable risk of robbery and of injury to P.

Once again it has been suggested (in relation to *Chomentowski*) that it is preferable for the injured victim to claim criminal injuries compensation than to make the employers liable for what might be regarded as "a pardonable want of foresight".[70] But as before this reasoning seems misconceived:

> "[I]t is not at all clear why the employers' liability insurers, who have received a premium to cover the very risk that has materialised, i.e. the employers' negligence, should be permitted to transfer the burden of this risk to the taxpayer."[71]

(d) Occupier's liability

The occupier's common duty of care to his (lawful) visitors is capable of extending in appropriate cases to the prevention of injury by a third party:

> "The occupier has the power of immediate supervision and control and the power of permitting or prohibiting the entry of other persons and he is under a duty to take reasonable care to prevent damage, at least from unusual danger, arising from such acts of third parties as could reasonably be foreseen."[72]

There does not appear to be any English case in which an injured visitor has claimed for such a breach of duty, but a Scottish case comes close to this point. In *Hosie v Arbroath Football Club*[73] a crowd of would-be football spectators made a "deliberate attack" on a closed wooden gate set in the perimeter wall of D's ground; they broke it down and surged through the opening. In so doing the crowd engulfed P who was knocked down and badly injured. D were held liable under section 2(1) of the Occupiers' Liability (Scotland) Act 1960.[74] The crucial factors in the case were that the gate was

---

68. So also in *Houghton v Hackney BC* (1961) 3 KIR 615 (P employed by D as rent collector; tenants came to a particular room to pay rent; P in room when robbed by three men; P injured in attack. D not liable – D had taken precautions which complied in all the circumstances with that standard of reasonable care required of D); *Williams v Grimshaw* (1967) 3 KIR 610 (P employed as part-time stewardess in D's clubhouse; at end of evening P took home money from bar and other takings; attempted robbery as she was leaving clubhouse one night. D not liable – precautions taken by D were reasonable in the circumstances).

69. (1970) 92 WN (NSW) 1070; (1971) 45 ALJR 713n.

70. See *Lamb v Camden London BC* [1981] 2 All ER 408, 413, *per* Lord Denning MR.

71. Jones, "Paying for the Crimes of Others" (1984) 47 *MLR* 223, 228.

72. Salmond and Heuston, *The Law of Torts* (19th ed, 1987), p 307. *Cp* Restatement, *Torts* (2d), para 344.

73. 1978 SLT 122.

74. This may be taken as identical to the English and Northern Ireland Acts of 1957, and indeed the learned judge relied on the *Dorset Yacht* case.

defective in that it lacked "commonplace and effective" safety devices and that on the evidence[75] an attack by the crowd was considered reasonably foreseeable.

The potential scope of this liability is considerable:

> "Parking garages, for example, must make efforts to protect customers against robbers and rapists; even more obviously must places of entertainment protect customers from each other."[76]

There is considerable American authority on both these matters,[77] but possibly more persuasive in this jurisdiction is *Allison* v *Rank City Wall Canada Ltd*[78] where P was brutally attacked and injured by an intruder in the garage of her apartment building. The owner of the building was held liable because the security measures taken in respect of the garage were "totally inadequate" in the circumstances.[79]

(e) Liability arising out of contract between P and D

In some cases where a contractual relationship exists between P and D, there may be an express or implied undertaking by D to accept responsibility for P's protection. Thus, the employer's duty to provide a safe system of work can be viewed as an implied term of the employee's contract of employment. *Allison* suggests that in certain circumstances a landlord may accept an obligation to safeguard a tenant as an implied term of the lease. Similarly, the well-known case of *Stansbie* v *Troman*[80] can be classified in this way.[81] There, a painter and decorator entered into a contract with D to do work in D's house.[82] When P was working in the house at a time when he knew both D and his wife were out, he left the house to obtain some more wallpaper. He left the front door unlocked, and was away for two hours. When he returned he discovered that someone had entered the house in his absence and stolen jewellery belonging to D's wife. The Court of Appeal held P liable; he owed a duty of care to D and was in breach of that duty. The damage to D, albeit the deliberate act of a thief, was not too remote:

---

75. In particular, there had been an unsuccessful attack on the gate at a previous match.

76. Fleming, *The Law of Torts* (7th ed, 1987), p 435 citing (*inter alia*) *Glasgow Corp* v *Muir* [1943] AC 448 (a case of *accidental* injury for which the occupier was *not* held liable).

77. See especially *Kline* v *1500 Massachusetts Avenue Apartment Corp* 439 F 2d 477 (DC Cir 1970). The issues are interestingly analysed by Zacharias, "The Politics of Torts" (1986) 95 *Yale LJ* 698. See also Annotation, "Tavernkeeper's Liability to Patron for Third Person's Assault" (1986) 43 ALR 4th 277 and *Note*, "Tort liability of Mall Owners for criminal conduct of third parties" (1986) 36 *Drake L Rev* 755.

78. (1984) 6 DLR (4th) 144. See also *Q* v *Minto Management Ltd* (1985) 15 DLR (4th) 581. In several Canadian cases the occupier of

a restaurant or bar has been held liable for the actions of intoxicated patrons – e.g. *Brown* v *Wilson* (1975) 66 DLR (3d) 295.

79. The evidence showed that the garage was in an urban area in which there had in recent years been numerous assaults. The court also took into account the fact that P had emphasised to D the importance of a secure garage and D had given P assurances to this effect.

80. [1948] 1 All ER 599.

81. See e.g. *Morris* v *CW Martin & Sons Ltd* [1965] 2 All ER 725, 731, *per* Lord Denning MR.

82. The case originated as a claim by the painter for breach of contract – he had not been paid for the work done. The owner of the house counterclaimed for the value of the stolen jewellery.

"[T]he very act of negligence itself consisted in the failure to take reasonable care to guard against the very thing that in fact happened . . . [Therefore] if . . . the plaintiff was negligent in leaving the house in this condition, it was a direct result of his negligence that the thief got in through this door which was left unlocked and stole these valuable goods."[83]

A similar principle applies, albeit only in appropriate and, to date, rare cases, in respect of other contractual relationships. Thus, as regards carriers and their passengers, it has been stated that:

"Railway authorities are not liable, if one passenger negligently or wilfully injures another . . . If, however, the railway authorities know that a person, whether by reason of disease, drunkenness or avowed intention, is likely to be a danger to other passengers, they are under a duty to prevent him from · entering the train."[84]

A similar principle applies to road carriers.[85] In theory, this principle extends to liability for deliberate acts, but no English or Irish case has been found in which this has been done.[86] *Pounder* v *North Eastern Rly Co*[87] might well have provided such an opportunity. P, who was employed to evict pit-men from their homes, boarded D's train. He was followed on board by a number of pit-men, obviously displeased with P's activities. During the journey P was assaulted and injured by the pit-men. Although there was evidence that D's employees knew that the pit-men had threatened P, D was held not liable on the ground that it could not know that the pit-men would break the law and assault a fellow-passenger. This may now seem rather a harsh decision[88] – and indeed it is unfortunate that the relevant case-law on this point dates almost entirely from the late nineteenth century. It may well now be the case that a carrier would be held liable if, in the circumstances, it knew or ought to have known of a particular danger from a third party to a passenger which was likely (or very likely) to, and did, result in injury to that passenger.

---

83. [1948] 1 All ER 599, 600, *per* Tucker LJ. See to the same effect *Petrovitch* v *Callinghams Ltd* [1969] 2 Lloyd's Rep 386. In somewhat similar vein, a negligent security contractor may be liable to the owner of a building when defective work facilitates burglary – see *Dove* v *Banhams Patent Locks Ltd* [1983] 2 All ER 833 and *McNeil* v *Village Locksmiths Ltd* (1981)129 DLR (3d) 543. For American cases, see Annotation, "Liability of persons furnishing, installing or servicing burglary or fire alarm systems . . . " (1985) 37 ALR 4th 47.

84. Charlesworth and Percy, *Negligence* (7th ed, 1983), para 10.70 – see e.g. *Adderley* v *Great Northern Rly Co* [1905] 2 IR 378, 406, *per* FitzGibbon LJ.

85. Charlesworth and Percy, *op cit*, para 10.98.

86. *Cp Gordon* v *Chicago Transit Authority* (1984) 470 NE 2d 1163 (P assaulted and raped by another passenger on D's train; D liable for failure to exercise due care and vigilance). See generally Annotation, "Liability of Land Carrier to Passenger who becomes a victim of another passenger's assault" (1986) 43 ALR 4th 173.

87. [1892] 1 QB 385. See also *Cobb* v *GWR* [1894] AC 419 (P, a passenger in D's train robbed by group of passengers, alleged D negligent in permitting carriage to be overcrowded and thus facilitating robbery; held, D not liable, because P had not shown that overcrowding conduced to robbery) and *Kerr* v *Belfast & Co Down Rly* (1897) 31 *ILTSJ* 256 (P injured during disturbance in overcrowded carriage; D not liable because injury to P not the natural and necessary result of the overcrowding).

88. It is criticised e.g. in Rose, "Liability for an Employee's Assaults" (1977) 40 *MLR* 420, 431–2.

Much the same may be said of a hotelier's liability to his guests. Thus Halsbury states:

> "No absolute liability to insure the personal safety of his guests is, however, imposed on [an innkeeper] such as exists with respect to the safety of their goods, so that if a guest is attacked in an inn the innkeeper is not liable. There is, however, an implied warranty by the innkeeper that, for the purpose of personal use by the guest, the inn premises are as safe as reasonable care and skill on the part of anyone can make them."[89]

In other words, in an appropriate case an innkeeper *may* be liable if a guest is attacked in an inn. Thus, in *Winkworth v Raven*,[90] Swift J said:

> "The innkeeper is not an insurer of the person of the guest . . . he is only responsible in case of injury to the guest . . . if negligence on the part of the innkeeper is proved."

Again there appears to be no modern English authority on this point but it may well be that some at least of the American cases in which an innkeeper has been held liable would now be followed in this jurisdiction.[91]

(f) Where D has created a special source of danger

According to Street:

> "Where the defendant has created some special source of danger, or presented a third party with the means of committing a tort, he may be under a duty to those placed at risk by his folly."[92]

The example given is where D hands a loaded gun to a small boy in the street, who then shoots P, a passer-by; in such a case, it is suggested, D is liable. No authority is given[93] and a warning is added " . . . this is a category which must be carefully confined". *Meah v McCreamer (No 2)*[94] appears to provide support for this warning. P was badly injured in an accident caused by D's negligence. He underwent a marked personality change and, as a result, developed a propensity to attack women. He raped and sexually assaulted two women who were awarded damages against P. P's claim to recover the amount of those damages from D was rejected. Woolf J held that the damages, although a consequence of D's negligence, were too remote

---

89. *Laws of England* (4th ed, 1979), vol 24, para 1224.

90. [1931] 1 KB 652, 657.

91. See e.g. *Orlando Executive Park Inc v PDR* (1981) 433 So 2d 491 (P attacked in motel: D, operator of motel, held liable for inadequate security precautions); *cf Courtenay v Remler* (1983) 566 F Supp 1225 (P assaulted in D's hotel; D not liable because security measures reasonable). See generally Annotation, "Liability of Hotel or Motel Operator for Injury to Guest resulting from assault by a third party" (1984) 28 ALR 4th 80.

92. *The Law of Torts* (8th ed, 1988), p 170. See e.g. *Smith v Littlewoods Organisation Ltd* [1987] 1 All ER 710, applied in *Connor v NI Housing Executive* [1989] 9 BNIL 93.

93. But see *Dixon v Bell* (1816) 105 ER 1023 and *Sullivan v Creed* [1904] 2 IR 317.

94. [1986] 1 All ER 943.

therefrom to be recoverable by P from D.[95] He held further that claims by the two victims against D would also have been rejected on the basis that their injuries were too remote.[96]

4. Conclusion

In addition to the cases discussed above, there are a number of other situations in which a negligent defendant may be liable to a plaintiff injured by the deliberate wrongdoing of a third party.[97] Nor is the potential liability confined to the tort of negligence. Thus, according to Fleming:

> "Organisers of fairs, races and other public entertainment have been repeatedly held liable for 'creating' a nuisance by attracting bad elements who misbehave . . . "[98]

Similarly, liability could arise under the rule in *Rylands* v *Fletcher*. For instance, in *Perry* v *Kendricks Transport Ltd*[99] some boys threw a lighted match into the empty petrol tank of D's motor-coach; the petrol fumes exploded and injured P. D were held not liable on the grounds that P's injuries were caused by the acts of a stranger for which D could not be responsible. But Jenkins LJ observed that D would have been liable –

> " . . . if it can be shown that . . . the dangerous thing was left by the defendants in such a condition that it was a reasonable and probable consequence of their action, which they ought to have foreseen, that children might meddle with the dangerous thing and cause it to escape."[1]

It is therefore suggested that although the general principle of non-liability may remain intact, there is a fair degree of scope for clarification or development of the recognised exceptions to it to provide the victim of a crime of violence with an alternative defendant in a significant number of cases. The potential is there – but it is unlikely to be realised unless or until the courts are prepared to give further consideration to the proper relationship between private liability and public compensation.

---

95. The learned judge held that it would in any case be contrary to public policy for P to be indemnified for the consequences of his crimes.

96. P's liability to the victims was dealt with in *W* v *Meah* [1986] 1 All ER 935, discussed above p 159. See also *Marx* v *AG* [1974] 1 NZLR 164 (P's husband severely injured by D's negligence; husband suffered personality change and assaulted P; held, P not entitled to damages from D).

97. Thus, an education authority may be liable for the assault of one pupil by another – see e.g. *R* v *CICB, ex parte W* Unreported, Div'l Ct (Donaldson LJ), 18 Dec 1980 (case settled out of court). Similarly, a negligent parent may be liable for an assault committed by his child – see e.g. *Newton* v *Edgerley* [1959] 3 All ER 337 and generally Salmond and Heuston, *The Law of Torts* (19th ed, 1987), pp 488–490. See further Irish Law Reform Commission, *Report on Liability in Tort of Minors and Liability of Parents for Children's Torts* (LRC 17, 1985).

98. *The Law of Torts* (7th ed, 1987), pp 399–400 – albeit probably only for damage to property. See e.g. *Page Motors Ltd* v *Epsom & Ewell BC* (1980) 78 LGR 505; *Dunton* v *Dover DC, The Times*, 31 March 1977.

99. [1956] 1 All ER 154.

1. *Ibid*, p 160. See also the example given by Lord Goff in *Smith* v *Littlewoods Organisation Ltd* [1987] 1 All ER 710, 731 (occupier stores fireworks in unlocked garden shed; boys enter as trespassers and cause fire which destroys neighbour's home; "liability might well be imposed . . . ").

CRIMINAL COURT COMPENSATION ORDERS

Since 1980 crown courts and magistrates' courts in Northern Ireland have had a general power, on convicting a person for any offence, to order the offender to pay to his victim compensation "for any personal injury, loss or damage resulting from that offence, or any other offence which is taken into consideration by the court in determining sentence".[2] A similar power had been introduced in England and Wales in 1973,[3] and has been gradually enlarged in both jurisdictions as a result of government policy that, whenever possible and practicable, such compensation should be paid. Thus, in 1986, the court was empowered to make a compensation order *instead of* dealing with the offender in any other way, and it was further provided that –

"When the court considers –

(a) that it would be appropriate both to impose a fine and to make a compensation order; but

(b) that the offender has insufficient means to pay both an appropriate fine and appropriate compensation,

the court shall give preference to compensation (though it may impose a fine as well)."[4]

In theory these provisions create an alternative source of compensation for the victim of a crime of violence where the offender has been apprehended and convicted, of particular import in a case which falls outside the ambit of the criminal injuries compensation scheme. In practice, however, the criminal courts appear to make compensation orders only in respect of a minority of offenders convicted of offences against the person,[5] and even

---

2. Criminal Justice (NI) Order 1980, Arts 3–5 ("the 1980 Order"), as amended by the Criminal Justice (NI) Order 1986 ("the 1986 Order"), Art 6. See generally, Boyle and Allen, *Sentencing Law and Practice* (2nd ed, 1990) Part III.

3. Criminal Justice Act 1972, ss 1–5, implementing recommendations made by the Advisory Council on the Penal System in its Report, *Reparation by the Offender* (1970) (the *Widgery Report*). The 1972 provisions were re-enacted in the Powers of Criminal Courts Act 1973, ss 35–38, which was in turn amended by the Criminal Justice Act 1982, s 67. Further amendments are made by the Criminal Justice Act 1988, ss 104–5, discussed by Miers, [1989] *Crim LR* 32 and Thomas, *ibid*, pp 48–9.

4. 1986 Order, Art 6 (identical to 1982 Act, s 67). The Chairman of the Criminal Injuries Compensation Board regarded these changes as making "a radical alteration in the way in which sentencers in criminal courts should consider compensation for victims" – see

Ogden, "Compensation Orders in Cases of Violence" [1985] *Crim LR* 500.

5. Statistics relating to the making of compensation orders in Northern Ireland are not available. The position in England and Wales in 1988 in relation to indictable offences may be summarised as follows:

Nature of Indictable Offence	Offenders ordered to pay compensation as % of all offenders dealt with	
	Magistrates' Courts	Crown Courts
Offences against the Person	34	19
Burglary	36	7
Criminal Damage	67	23
All offences	22	9

Criminal Statistics (England and Wales) 1988 (C'm 847, 1989), Table 7.24.

where such orders are made, the amount ordered to be paid is usually small.[6] Many reasons have been suggested for this situation[7] and these may best be considered as part of a closer examination of the statutory provisions as they apply in particular to compensation for personal injury.

1. Nature and Scope of Compensation Orders

It has frequently been stated that compensation orders were introduced –

> "as a convenient and rapid means of avoiding the expense of resorting to civil litigation when the criminal clearly has means which would enable the compensation to be paid . . . "[8]

But the scope of the remedy so provided is necessarily limited by its hybrid nature. A compensation order must to some extent be regarded as a sentence which may be imposed upon a convicted offender – indeed, since the 1986 Order, it may be made *instead of* dealing with the offender in any other way. But it is hardly a punishment to order an offender to pay to his victim compensation for which he may in any event be civilly liable. This point was brought out in *R v Dorton*,[9] where D had been convicted of assault occasioning actual bodily harm and of criminal damage. He was sentenced to two years' immediate imprisonment and ordered to pay £2,850 in compensation. D appealed against this sentence on the ground that it was wrong to impose both a substantial sentence of imprisonment and a large compensation order. The Court of Appeal disagreed:

> "[I]t is not right, certainly not right in every case and certainly not right in this case, to regard the imposition of a compensation order as being by way of additional punishment . . . Had the victim in the instant case not been given the benefit of a compensation order she might well . . . have brought civil proceedings against [D] . . . quite independently of any sentence that the Crown Court . . . might have imposed . . . It may indeed be painful for the offender to have to pay compensation, but it would be equally painful if . . . the victim chose to bring civil proceedings."[10]

---

6. In 1988 the average compensation awarded in magistrates' courts in respect of indictable offences against the person was £87 (as compared with an overall average of £128 for indictable offences), and in crown courts it was £233 (as compared with an overall average of £1,144 for indictable offences): *ibid.*

7. See especially Home Affairs Committee, *Compensation and Support for Victims of Crime* (1984–85 HC 43) – *Report*, pp xiv–xvi, and *Minutes of Evidence*, pp 6–10. See also Hodgson Committee, *The Profits of Crime*

and their Recovery (1984), ch 5 and Newburn, *The Use and Enforcement of Compensation Orders in Magistrates' Courts* (Home Office Research Study, 1988), pp 8 *et seq.*

8. *R v Inwood* (1975) 60 Cr App R 70, 73, *per* Scarman LJ. In *R v Chappell* (1984) 80 Cr App R 31, 34, Lord Lane CJ adopted counsel's "striking turn of phrase" in describing a compensation order as "a kind of criminal Order 14 procedure".

9. (1988) 9 Cr App R (S) 514.

10. *Ibid*, p 516, *per* French J.

But a compensation order may be made even if the offender is not, or may not be, civilly liable to the victim. Thus, in *R* v *Chappell*,[11] Lord Lane CJ observed:

> "It does not . . . follow that because Parliament envisaged that in many, or indeed most, cases the criminal remedy would be exercised against the background of a potential action in the civil courts, an intention must be inferred to make that remedy conditional on the existence of a civil cause of action . . . Indeed it plainly is not so, for the [criminal] court has a discretion . . . and will take into account factors such as the offender's means and the moral desirability or otherwise of making him pay[12] . . . which have no relevance at all in the context of civil litigation . . . Thus a compensation order could properly be withheld in whole or in part where the civil court would have no alternative but to make an order in full."[13]

Thus, even if a compensation order is not (or is not always) an additional punishment, it has to be seen as part of the sentencing process. The payment of compensation may be taken into account as a factor mitigating the punishment imposed on an offender;[14] conversely, the punishment considered appropriate by the court may inhibit the making of a compensation order.[15]

The scope of compensation orders is also affected by the nature of the process by which they are made. Thus, it has been stated that compensation orders are not intended to be "straight alternatives" to the civil process;[16] it has frequently been emphasised that they may be used only in straightforward cases, and normally only when the amounts involved are not too substantial.[17] The limitations imposed by the criminal process may be illustrated by a further reference to *Dorton*. The Court of Appeal there upheld an order for substantial compensation, since D was buying a flat on a mortgage in which he had an equity of about £2,000. But the practical benefit of the award for the victim was open to doubt:

---

11. (1984) 80 Cr App R 31. D was convicted under the Customs and Excise Management Act 1979, s 167(1) for recklessly making VAT returns which understated the value of supplies made by his company.

12. See e.g. *R* v *Bradburn* (1973) 57 Cr App R 948 (compensation order may be made to remind D of the evil he has done).

13. (1984) 80 Cr App R 31, 34–5. *Cf* Atiyah, "Compensation Orders and Civil Liability" [1979] *Crim LR* 504 who argues that "the anomalies which . . . result from this view are manifest."

14. See e.g. *R* v *Roberts* (1987) 9 Cr App R (S) 275, discussed below p 250. *Cf R* v *Barney*, *The Times*, 12 Oct 1989.

15. See e.g. *R* v *Inwood* (1974) 60 Cr App R

70 (court should not refrain from imposing sentence of imprisonment in order to enable D to pay compensation). See generally Softley and Tarling, "Compensation Orders and Custodial Sentences" [1977] *Crim LR* 720 and Newburn, *op cit* n 7, p 13.

16. *R* v *Ramsey* (1987) 9 Cr App R (S) 251, 253, where Stephen Brown LJ explained that a compensation order "is not in any sense to be regarded as equivalent to the judgment of a civil court."

17. See e.g. *Hyde* v *Emery* (1984) 6 Cr App R (S) 206, 210, *per* Watkins LJ: "Courts should not be invited, and if invited should decline the invitation, to . . . make compensation orders upon evidence out of which arise questions difficult to resolve of either fact or law or both."

"It seems highly likely that the effect of the sentence of [two years'] imprisonment on [D] . . . would be that he would default on his mortgage, and the lender . . . would foreclose . . . By the time the compensation order may be payable,[18] such funds as had survived the foreclosure might well have been dissipated. If the victim had been left to her civil remedy, she might have obtained a summary judgment from the county court . . . and secured a charge on the house so that any remaining proceeds after the sale by the mortgagor would be payable to her."[19]

Of course the making of the compensation order did not prevent the victim from instituting such county court proceedings. But it is suggested that *Dorton* illustrates some of the difficulties inherent in conferring on the criminal courts a jurisdiction in respect of which a complex law and procedure has been developed in the civil courts.

If we add to those factors the suggestion that criminal courts frequently assume that the provision of compensation for a victim who has been physically injured is more properly a matter for the criminal injuries compensation scheme,[20] then we can see that the general nature and scope of criminal court compensation orders may not be particularly appropriate or conducive to their use in personal injury cases.

2. When Compensation may be Ordered

Although the power to make a compensation order is a general one, and may be exercised whether or not the offender pleads guilty and irrespective of whether the offence charged is a crime of violence, there are a number of specific restrictions or qualifications which limit its availability in personal injury cases.

1. The victim has no *right* to compensation – the legislation prescribes only that the court "may . . . make an order".[21] The Criminal Justice Act 1988 has, however, put a rather heavier burden on the criminal courts in England and Wales – by section 104(1) it is stated that "a court shall give reasons, on passing sentence, if it does not make such an order in a case where [the statute] empowers it to do so". It seems reasonable to expect that a similar provision will be enacted for Northern Ireland in due course.[22]

2. Compensation orders may not be made in respect of road traffic offences – or, more strictly, by Article 3(3) of the 1980 Order:

"No compensation order . . . shall be made in respect of injury, loss or damage due to an accident arising out of the presence of a motor vehicle on a road or other public place . . . "[23]

---

18. £2,600 of the award was to be paid within six months of D's release from prison.

19. Thomas, [1988] *Crim LR* 255. *Cf* a criminal court has power under the Criminal Justice Act (NI) 1953, s 10 to prohibit D from disposing of property.

20. *Cf* the British Board has expressed the hope that "magistrates will not feel that the existence of the Board should be a factor which causes them to limit such orders . . . " CICB, *19th Annual Report* (1982–83), p 31.

21. See especially *Brown v Normand* 1988 SCCR 229 (Court declined to make order because V would have been refused criminal injuries compensation).

22. On the basis that this was done in respect of the earlier legislation on compensation orders.

23. 1980 Order, Art 3(2), (3), which contains some exceptions in relation to certain property damage – as to which see further 1988 Act, s 104(2). Most cases of personal injury caused by road traffic offences will come within the MIB arrangements.

3. Article 3(3) of the 1980 Order also provides that compensation cannot be ordered in respect of loss suffered by his dependants when a victim has died as a result of the offence.[24] To this general rule there may soon be two exceptions – section 104(1) of the 1988 Act in England and Wales now provides that an order may require the payment of funeral expenses (to the person who incurred those expenses) or compensation for bereavement (on the same basis as is now provided in the 1988 Order).[25]

4. Compensation is payable for "personal injury, loss and damage". This phrase is not defined in the Order, but "personal injury" was given a generous interpretation by the Divisional Court in *Bond* v *Chief Constable of Kent*.[26] In the early hours of the morning the occupier of a house was awakened by noises in the front garden and discovered D behaving strangely. The police were called, but before they could arrive, D threw a stone through a window of the house. The occupier, fearing a sustained attack, was terrified for himself and his family. However, the police soon arrived and arrested D. On conviction for criminal damage D was ordered to pay the occupier compensation for the fright and distress he had suffered.[27] This award was upheld on appeal:

"I . . . have no doubt that the terror directly occasioned by this attack on the occupier's house falls either within 'personal injury' or alternatively within the word 'damage' . . . and the magistrates were fully entitled to award the modest sum of £25."[28]

It will be interesting to see if this approach will be maintained following the restrictions on the award of compensation for "nervous shock" imposed by the 1988 Order and the 1988 Act.[29]

5. The injury must "result from" the offence for which the offender has been convicted. Here again the courts have adopted a broad approach; in *R* v *Thomson Holidays Ltd*[30] Lawton LJ stated:

"Parliament . . . never intended to introduce into the criminal law the concepts of causation which apply to the assessment of damages under the law of contract and tort . . . Wherever the making of an order for compensation is appropriate the court must ask itself whether loss or damage can fairly be said to have resulted to anyone from the offence . . ."[31]

---

24. Apparently because of the difficulty of assessment – see *Widgery Report*, para 51.

25. See above, pp 194 and 199.

26. [1983] 1 All ER 456.

27. In addition to compensation for the broken window.

28. [1983] 1 All ER 456, 459, *per* Griffiths LJ, following *R* v *Thomson Holidays Ltd* [1974] 1 All ER 823 (compensation order of £50 made against a company convicted of an offence under the Trade Descriptions Act 1968, in respect of the "disappointment and inconvenience of a ruined holiday"). But *cf Smillie* v *Wilson* 1990 SCCR 133.

29. See above, pp 55–61 and 68–77.

30. [1974] 1 All ER 823.

31. *Ibid*, p 829. In *Bond, supra*, McCullough J observed: ". . . the sense of that observation is this: in assessing whether compensation should be awarded . . . the court should approach the matter in a broad commonsense way and should not allow itself to become enmeshed in . . . refined questions of causation . . .". See also *R* v *Boardman* (1987) 9 Cr App R (S) 74, 75 (phrase to be given "a wide and commonsense meaning ...").

However, some injury may still be too remote. Thus, in *Berkeley* v *Orchard*[32] D was convicted of possession of a controlled drug. He had possession of one tablet of Lysergide, part of which had been taken by V who, as a result, became ill. V was awarded compensation of £75, but on appeal this order was quashed on the grounds that V's illness did not "result from" the offence (of simple possession) for which D had been convicted.

6. Where an offence has been committed by a child or young person, the court may in certain cases order compensation to be paid by the offender's parent or guardian. Section 76(1) of the Children and Young Persons Act (NI) 1968 provides that where a child or young person has been convicted of an offence and the court considers that the case would best be met by an award of compensation (whether with or without any other punishment), the court –

"(*a*) may in any case, and

(*b*) shall if the offender is a child,

order that the . . . compensation be paid by the parent or guardian[33] of the child or young person . . . unless the court is satisfied that there is good reason[34] for not so doing."

3. Assessment of Compensation for Personal Injuries

By Article 3(1A) of the 1980 Order:

"Compensation . . . shall be of such amount as the court considers appropriate, having regard to any evidence and to any representations that are made by or on behalf of the accused or the prosecution . . . "[35]

In determining the amount of compensation to be awarded, it would appear that there are three principal factors, *viz* (a) the jurisdiction of the court, (b) the nature of the injuries to the victim, and (c) the means of the defendant.

(a) The jurisdiction of the court

A crown court can make a compensation order for any amount; but by Article 3(5) of the 1980 Order:

"The compensation to be paid under a compensation order made by a magistrates' court in respect of any offence of which the court has convicted the offender shall not exceed £2,000."[36]

It will be noted that this maximum applies in relation to any *one* offence for which the offender has been convicted; separate orders may be made where

---

32. [1975] *Crim LR* 225.

33. A local authority is not a "parent or guardian" for the purposes of this legislation: *Leeds CC* v *West Yorkshire Metropolitan Police* [1982] 1 All ER 274.

34. See e.g. *R* v *Sheffield Crown Court, ex*

parte Clarkson (1986) 8 Cr App R (S) 454.

35. As inserted by the 1986 Order, Art 6.

36. The 1980 Order fixed a maximum of £1,000, but this was increased to £2,000 by Criminal Penalties etc (Increase) (NI) Order 1984, Sch 1(3).

an offender has been convicted of more than one offence.[37] A separate rule governs the maximum award of compensation in respect of offences taken into consideration.[38]

(b) The nature of the victim's injuries

It is obvious that the court will take into account the nature of the victim's injuries when considering the amount of compensation to be awarded. This principle has given rise to two difficulties in practice. First, there may be difficulty in ensuring that the court has sufficient and up-to-date details of the victim's injuries; we deal with this problem later. Secondly, the court, being a criminal court, may not be familiar with the principles on which damages for personal injuries are assessed in the civil courts, and the "going rate" for particular injuries.[39] The obvious solution is to refer to damages awards in similar cases – a practice apparently approved in *R* v *Broughton*.[40] In that case D pleaded guilty to assault occasioning actual bodily harm and was ordered to pay £475 by way of compensation to the victim for breaking his nose. The figure of £475 had been determined by reference to a scale published by the Criminal Injuries Compensation Board.[41] D contended on appeal that the award was excessive, but the Court of Appeal held that the trial court's approach "cannot be criticised". The availability of such guidelines is likely to be particularly helpful to magistrates' courts[42] and indeed it has been the practice in England and Wales since 1978 for such guidelines to be issued at regular intervals.[43] It does not appear that any similar steps have been taken in Northern Ireland.

As the seriousness of the victim's injuries increases so the criminal court becomes more aware of its limitations. In *R* v *Cooper*[44] D pleaded guilty to assault occasioning actual bodily harm. The victim sustained a cut to his right

---

37. See e.g. *R* v *Inwood* (1974) 60 Cr App R 70; *R* v *Oddy* [1974] 2 All ER 666.

38. By 1980 Order, Art 3(5): " . . . the compensation or total compensation to be paid under a compensation order or compensation orders made by a magistrates' court in respect of any offence or offences taken into consideration in determining sentence shall not exceed the difference (if any) between the amount or total amount which . . . is the maximum for the offence or offences of which the offender has been convicted and the amount or total amounts (if any) which are in fact ordered to be paid in respect of that offence or those offences."

39. It appears to have been consistently assumed that common law principles and levels should be followed. *Cf* the proposal for a "criminal scale" of compensation discussed in 1986 *IWP Report*, para 12.2.

40. (1986) 8 Cr App R (S) 379.

41. Guidelines figures are adopted following

an "assessment exercise" involving a number of judges and members of the legal profession; the Board emphasises that the figure given is a starting-point and may be increased or decreased according to circumstances – see e.g. CICB, *23rd Annual Report* (1986–87), para 41.

42. See e.g. Vennard, "Magistrates' Assessments of Compensation for Injury" [1979] *Crim LR* 510. *Cf* Newburn, *op cit* n 7, pp 28–30.

43. At first these were prepared for and approved by the Council of the Magistrates' Association. But these guidelines were criticised as setting the level of compensation too low – see especially, Ogden, "Compensation Orders in Cases of Violence" (1985) 41 *Magistrate* 5. The most recent guidelines (published in 1988) have been prepared by the Criminal Injuries Compensation Board – see Home Office Circular No 85/1988; *Guidelines on Compensation in the Criminal Courts*.

44. [1982] *Crim LR* 308.

eye with associated bruising, and five chipped front teeth; he had to stay in hospital over-night. D was ordered to pay compensation of £750, but on appeal, the order was quashed. The Court is reported to have stated:

"Where a substantial sum of compensation was contemplated in respect of personal injury then there should be up-to-date and detailed information before the court as to the extent of the injury, such as medical reports and photographs. The proper course in such a case was [however] to leave the matter to the county court where the extent of the injuries could be fully investigated, if the victim wished to take such proceedings."[45]

A somewhat more helpful approach was taken in *R* v *Welch*.[46] There D again admitted assault occasioning actual bodily harm. The victim suffered cuts to his nose and on examination in hospital it was found that the tip of his nose was broken. He was awarded compensation of £400 and this award was upheld on appeal. Ackner LJ considered this case "significantly different" from *Cooper*:

"[F]irst, because the amount of compensation [in *Cooper*] was nearly twice the sum with which we are concerned . . . and, secondly . . . the court there had no information at all in regard to the seriousness of the chipping [of the victim's teeth] . . . But here, we do know . . . just what was the nature of the assault and what were the consequences . . . [I]f one anticipated what could have occurred in the county court . . . there would be nothing extravagant in the figure of £400."[47]

(c) The means of the offender

By Article 3(4) of the 1980 Order:

"In determining whether to make a compensation order against any person and in determining the amount to be paid by any person under such an order, the court shall have regard to his means so far as they appear or are known to the court."

In addition, by Article 3(1A), the court must take into account "any representations that are made by or on behalf of the accused . . . ".

In practice, it is the means of the offender which determine the size of a compensation order,[48] and it is the court's assessment of the offender's means and what he can properly be asked to pay which account for a large percentage of reported appeals from the making of compensation orders. As a result there is an extensive case-law on the subject and we deal here only with what appear to be the principal matters to be taken into account.[49]

45. *Ibid*, p 309.

46. (1984) 6 Cr App R (S) 13.

47. *Ibid*, p 15.

48. In an attempt to reduce this reliance – and to make compensation more readily available – the Hodgson Committee in its *Report* (pp

63–5) proposed the setting up of a "Victims' Compensation Fund".

49. See generally Thomas, *Current Sentencing Practice* (1988), Part J(2); Archbold, *Pleading, Evidence and Practice in Criminal Cases* (43rd ed, 1988), ch 5, s II (J); Morrish and McLean, *The Crown Court* (12th ed, 1987).

The criminal court does not require a precise calculation of D's assets – a broad picture is sufficient, provided it is adequately supported by reliable evidence.[50] If D has capital, the court will take this into account in determining an award, but normally only if that capital is readily disposable.[51] In the absence of clear evidence that D has such capital,[52] the award must be based on D's expected income,[53] less necessary outgoings. The fact that D has no income at present is not *per se* a ground for refusing to make an order, but it is wrong to award compensation on the basis that the order could be activated at some date in the future when D comes into funds or obtains employment.[54] D can, however, be ordered to pay compensation by instalments – and indeed this is the usual practice.[55] In such cases it appeared until recently to have been settled – at least in England and Wales – that D should not be ordered to pay a greater sum than he could afford to pay by instalments over a period of one year.[56] However, in *R* v *Olliver*[57] the Court of Appeal has now held that there is nothing wrong in principle with the period of payment being longer than one year, indeed much longer,[58] provided that it was not an undue burden on the offender and therefore too severe a punishment, having regard to the nature of the offence and of the offender.

D's means may, of course, be significantly affected by his sentence. Thus, if D is given a custodial sentence, compensation will rarely be awarded

---

50. *R* v *Howell* (1978) 66 Cr App R 179. Many compensation orders have been quashed as based on inadequate or unreliable information as to D's means – see e.g. *R* v *Huish* (1985) 7 Cr App R (S) 272; *R* v *Bond* (1986) 8 Cr App R (S) 11.

51. See e.g. *R* v *Stewart* (1983) 5 Cr App R (S) 320 (D required to sell car). Cf *R* v *Hackett* (1988) 10 Cr App R (S) 388 and *R* v *Holah* (1989) 11 Cr App R(S) 282 (unreasonable to require D to sell family home). Of course the victim may still bring civil proceedings against D and attempt to enforce a civil judgment by compelling D e.g. to sell the house.

52. Normally it will be for the prosecution to establish to the court's satisfaction that D has, at the time of sentence, the means to pay compensation. But the court may be prepared to infer this from the evidence as in *R* v *Bolden* (1987) 9 Cr App R (S) 83, where the evidence showed that D had clearly been in possession of substantial assets at an earlier time and had given no satisfactory explanation as to where those assets had gone.

53. Difficulties may arise if events turn out differently from expected – see e.g. *R* v *Math-ieson* (1989) 9 Cr App R(S) 54 (D given suspended prison sentence and ordered to pay compensation from earnings; D committed further offences and suspended sentence activated; compensation order

quashed because D no longer able to pay).

54. See e.g. *R* v *Daly* [1974] 1 All ER 290: *R* v *Diggles* (1988) 10 Cr App R (S) 279 and *R* v *Scott* (1986) 83 Cr App R 221.

55. According to a recent survey in England and Wales, over 80% of compensation orders are paid by instalments, usually of less than £10 per week – see Newburn, *The Use and Enforcement of Compensation Orders in Magistrates' Courts* (Home Office Research Study, 1988), p 15.

56. See e.g. *R* v *Diggles* (1988) 10 Cr App R (S) 279; *R* v *Broughton* (1986) 8 Cr App R (S) 379.

57. (1989) 11 Cr App R(S) 10. See also *R* v *Bagga* [1990] *Crim LR* 128.

58. "A two-year period will seldom be too long, and in an appropriate case three years will be unassailable ...": *ibid*, p 15, *per* Lord Lane LCJ. However, earlier cases have suggested that a compensation order will not normally be made if (a) there is no realistic possibility of the order being complied with (*R* v *Webb* [1979] *Crim LR* 466); (b) the difference between V's loss and the amount D can pay is so great as to make the order appear derisory (*R* v *Legros* Unreported, CA, 23 Jan 1976), or (c) the order imposes such a burden on D that he may commit other offences in order to comply with it (*R* v *Morgan* (1982) 4 Cr App R (S) 358).

unless D has substantial capital assets, has substantially benefited from the crime, or the sentence is a short one and D is expected to resume employment on his release.[59]

4. Practice and Procedure

Although the 1980 Order states that a compensation order may be made "on application or otherwise", there is no formal procedure by which a victim may make an application for compensation. It is of course open to the court to raise the matter of compensation of its own motion, but the evidence suggests that this may not always be done.[60] Since the victim does not appear to have any right to speak in court otherwise than as a witness,[61] otherwise than as a witness,[61] it became obvious that any representation on his behalf would have to be made by the prosecution. In 1988 a systematic procedure was introduced in England and Wales[62] to ensure that the police and the Crown Prosecution Service obtained all the necessary information and evidence to give to the Court in appropriate cases and similar steps have recently been taken in Northern Ireland.[63] Thus the police will normally obtain the relevant details of his personal injury, loss or damage from the applicant, and forward them to the DPP.[64] Should the police investigation file not contain sufficient details, the DPP will specify further enquiries to be made by the investigating police officer, including such consultation with the victim as may be appropriate. The DPP will normally[65] draw to the court's attention its power to award compensation, tender the relevant information and make such representations as may be necessary. In the event of dispute either as to the extent of the injury or as to its cause, evidence will be called to allow the court to adjudicate upon this; in appropriate cases an application may be made to adjourn the proceedings so that such evidence (or further evidence) can be produced.

In some cases it is the defendant himself who raises the question of compensation, usually with a view to having this taken into account (in his

---

59. *R v McKinley* [1975] *Crim LR* 924; *R v Townsend* (1980) 2 Cr App R (S) 328. See also Softley and Tarling, "Compensation Orders and Custodial Sentences" [1977] *Crim LR* 720. Under the 1988 Act, s 105 a compensation order may be discharged or reduced if there is a "substantial reduction" in the defendant's means.

60. Shapland, Willmore and Duff, *Victims in the Criminal Justice System* (1985), p 137.

61. He may, however, be allowed or even encouraged by the court to address it.

62. See Home Office Circular No 20/1988, *Victims of Crime*. An attempt in 1988 to provide a formal mechanism to enable the victim himself to apply for compensation was rejected as infringing the fundamental principle that a victim has no active role in the criminal process – see HC Debs (Standing Ctte F), cols 329–336 (25 Feb 1988).

63. Information supplied by DPP.

64. As regards personal injury there should be up-to-date and detailed evidence concerning the nature and extent of the injury; this may involve medical reports or photographs. The injuries should be described in detail and evidence as regards treatment, length of hospitalisation, time off work, the likely prognosis and the like should be provided.

65. An "application" may not be necessary if the issue of compensation is otherwise sufficiently before the court, and an "application" will not be made where the police report states that the victim has indicated an unwillingness to seek or accept compensation.

favour) in the determination of the sentence. When this is done, difficulties can arise if the court has not been given accurate information.[66] *R* v *Roberts*[67] is a case in point. D was convicted of obtaining property by deception; he was sentenced to two years' imprisonment and ordered to pay £4,370 compensation. The compensation order had been made on the basis that D could pay the greater part of such a sum from the proceeds of the sale of a house and pay the remainder from earnings from the employment he had been offered on release from prison. D's willingness to pay compensation of this amount was "very much" taken into account in determining the sentence of imprisonment. But it transpired that D in fact had neither any substantial equity in the house nor did he have a firm offer of employment. In such circumstances the Court of Appeal had no option but to quash the compensation order – and to reiterate the necessity in such cases of a proper investigation of the offender's means by his solicitor:

> "[I]t is the duty of those who put before the Court proposals for compensation that are themselves likely to affect the length of any sentence imposed to ensure that the information placed before the Court is not just as accurate as may be but that it has been investigated, so that those who are called upon to put those matters before the Court are satisfied that the information is in fact accurate."[68]

How much information is required by the court? At first the courts set a high standard of proof[69] both as to the victim's injury or loss, and as to the offender's means, but Parliament intervened with the intention of encouraging a more flexible approach.[70] In *R* v *Swann*[71] Kilner Brown J observed that the provision which is now Article 3(1A) of the 1980 Order was intended to ameliorate the strict requirement in respect of the burden of proof before a compensation order could be made. But he added:

> "There is nothing in these new statutory provisions which indicates that a trial judge, when considering compensation, should simply pluck a figure out of the air and have no regard to whether or not the offender is in a position to meet all or any of it."[72]

In the particular case, there was "simply no evidence of means" and therefore an order for compensation was quashed. It was argued in *R* v

---

66. Thomas [1983] *Crim LR* 270 argues that "It is possible that the . . . amendment [allowing a compensation order to be made 'instead of' any other sentence] will tempt sentencers to ignore the offence and simply make a compensation order, on the basis of estimates of [the offender's] ability to pay which are . . . unrealistic . . . Once the compensation order has been made, a different picture of the offender's financial state may emerge, with the result that the compensation order will be quashed, and the offender will escape any effective penalty."

67. (1987) 9 Cr App R (S) 275. See also *R* v *Bond* (1986) 8 Cr App R (S) 11 and *R* v *Phillips* (1988) 10 Cr App R (S) 419.

68. (1987) 9 Cr App R (S) 275, 278, *per* Turner J, referring in particular to *R* v *Huish* (1985) 7 Cr App R (S) 272 in which it had been stated that documents should be obtained and evidence should be given, orally or on affidavit. It was also suggested that the proceedings should be adjourned if necessary to arrive at a true statement of D's means.

69. *R* v *Vivian* [1978] 1 All ER 48; *R* v *Amey* [1983] 1 All ER 865.

70. Criminal Justice Act 1982, s 67.

71. (1984) 6 Cr App R (S) 22. See also *R* v *Chappell* (1984) 80 Cr App R 31.

72. (1984) 6 Cr App R (S) 22, 25.

Horsham Justices, ex parte Richards[73] that a compensation order could now be made even though the court had heard no evidence of the victim's loss, since under Article 3(1A) "representations" would suffice. The Divisional Court disagreed:

> "The court has no jurisdiction to make a compensation order without receiving any evidence where there are real issues raised as to whether the claimants have suffered any, and if so what, loss. The new subsection seems to contemplate that the court can make assessments and approximations where the evidence is scanty or incomplete. It can then make an order which is 'appropriate'. But here the [defendant] was challenging the basis on which *any* compensation could be paid . . . He was declining to accept that there was any loss. In these circumstances . . . justice required that the defendant should have a proper opportunity to test the grounds on which the order was to be made against him.[74]

5. Enforcement

By Article 3(6) of the 1980 Order:

> "A compensation order shall be enforceable –
>
> (*a*) if made by a magistrates' court, in the same manner as any other sum adjudged to be paid by a conviction of that court;
>
> (*b*) if made by any other court, in the same manner as any fine which has been or might have been imposed, in respect of the offence for which the person has been convicted, by the court making the order."

The manner of enforcing payment of a sum adjudged to be paid by a conviction in a magistrates' court is specified in Articles 92–94 of the Magistrates' Courts (NI) Order 1981; a fine imposed by a crown court is enforced according to section 35 of the Criminal Justice Act (NI) 1945. These provisions do not warrant discussion in the present context.[75]

6. Relationship with Criminal Injuries Compensation and Civil Liability

(*a*) *Criminal injuries compensation*

Payments received by the victim under a compensation order are deducted from the compensation otherwise payable under the 1988 Order. Article 6(2)(*a*) is clearly applicable – but only, it may be noted, in relation to any sums "paid".[76] This would appear to exclude sums due to be paid (e.g. by instalments), but it would appear that the Secretary of State follows the practice of the British Board, *viz* with the applicant's agreement any further

---

73. [1985] 2 All ER 1114.

74. *Ibid*, p 1121, *per* Neill LJ.

75. See Valentine and Hart, *Criminal Procedure in Northern Ireland* (1989), ch 19. See also Lomax and Reynolds, *Enforcement in the Magistrates' Courts* (1988), chs 1, 2 and 8. A Home Office Research Study found that some 80% of those ordered to pay compensation had completed payment within 18 months: Newburn, *op cit* n 55, p 42.

76. This provision is discussed at p 206 above.

sums paid to the criminal court by the offender under the compensation order are paid to the Board.[77]

(b) Civil liability

The relationship between compensation orders and civil damages is governed by Article 5 of the 1980 Order. Where a compensation order has been made in favour of a person who subsequently claims damages in civil proceedings:

> "(a) The damages . . . shall be assessed without regard to the order; but where the whole or part of the amount awarded by the order has been paid, the damages . . . shall not exceed the amount (if any) by which . . . they exceed the amount paid under the order.
>
> (b) Where the whole or part of the amount awarded by the [compensation] order remains unpaid and the court awards damages . . . then unless the person against whom the order was made has ceased to be liable to pay the amount unpaid . . . the court shall direct that the judgment –
>
> > (i) if it is for an amount not exceeding the amount unpaid under the order, shall not be enforced; or
> >
> > (ii) if it is for an amount exceeding the amount unpaid under the order, shall not be enforced as to a corresponding amount,
>
> without the leave of the court."

Thus, suppose the criminal court has ordered D to pay compensation of £500 and at the time when damages are being assessed by the civil court D has paid £300 compensation. The civil court then decides that P is otherwise entitled to damages of £1000. P is awarded damages of £700, but may only enforce judgment for £500; presumably the leave of the court to enforce the remaining £200 will depend on whether or not D pays up under the compensation order.

The Northern Ireland legislation does not appear to cater for the situation where the civil court decides that the damages to which the victim is entitled are lower than the sum awarded to him by way of a compensation order. In such a case the compensation order appears to stand – but, of course, the victim receives no damages. However, there is provision in England and Wales for the compensation order to be reviewed in such a case, so that (unless the compensation has already been paid) it can be reduced to the level thought appropriate by the civil court.[78]

A victim may incur costs in bringing civil proceedings, but it would appear that he cannot recover such costs by way of a compensation order. In *Hammertons Cars Ltd* v *London Borough of Redbridge*[79] car dealers were convicted of offences under the Trade Descriptions Act. The buyer of one of

---

77. See e.g. CICB, *16th Annual Report* (1979–80), p 24.

78. Powers of Criminal Courts Act 1973, s 37. It has however been pointed out that there is no provision for D to recover any excess paid under the compensation order: Atiyah, "Compensation Orders and Civil Liability" [1979] *Crim LR* 504, 506.

79. [1974] 2 All ER 216.

the cars brought civil proceedings against the dealers; the out-of-court settlement of the action did not include the buyer's costs (£195). On conviction of D the justices made a compensation order for £195, but this was quashed on appeal. According to Lord Widgery CJ:

> "It seems to me to be abundantly clear that if the victim brings civil proceedings, and those civil proceedings are brought to an end, then they should be regarded as quite independent of the criminal proceedings, and no compensation order should be made . . . in respect of liabilities which arose, or might have arisen, in the civil proceedings . . . If in the civil proceedings the judge had been asked to make an order for costs and had refused, it would be almost ludicrous to suggest that the dissatisfied party could come to the justices and get them to countermand the High Court judge's order in the civil case."[80]

7. Conclusion

It would seem that much remains to be done, both in terms of theory and practice, to implement more fully the policy of requiring offenders to compensate their victims. A major theoretical difficulty arises from the tension which may frequently exist between punishing the offender and requiring him to compensate his victim. The major practical difficulty is the limitation imposed by the offender's means: "No legislation . . . can easily increase the ability of offenders to pay."[81] But this is not to say that compensation orders cannot provide a useful and convenient method of providing some compensation for victims of crimes of violence and, at the same time, help to create a more positive attitude by victims to the criminal justice system.[82]

PRIVATE INSURANCE

A criminal injury may entitle the victim (or, if he is killed, one of his relatives) to payments under a contract of insurance entered into by the victim or by someone on his behalf (such as his employer). The most relevant types of policy in this context are life assurance, personal accident insurance and loss of income (or permanent health) insurance.[83] The incidence of life assurance is high,[84] but of course does not provide any payment for the injury of the insured person. Insurance cover for personal injury as such is much less common[85] and, even where obtained, tends to

80. *Ibid*, p 219. In so holding Lord Widgery CJ did "not think it necessary to decide" whether the phrase "loss or damage resulting from [the] offence" was inappropriate to cover such costs, or whether the loss, if loss it be, was not too remote.

81. Shapland, Willmore and Duff, *Victims in the Criminal Justice System* (1985), p 147.

82. *Ibid*, pp 139 *et seq*.

83. See especially Harris *et al*, *Compensation and Support for Illness and Injury* (1984), ch 8 (hereafter referred to as "*Harris*").

84. See *Insurance Statistics 1984–1988* (1989), pp 8–9.

85. *Ibid*, p 40. For Northern Ireland see *Family Expenditure Survey Report for 1983–1986* (1989), Table 15. *Harris* (p 224) reported that personal accident insurance was held by only 6.2% of his sample of victims of illness or injury. The Pearson Report (*Report of the Royal Commission on Civil Liability and Compensation for Personal Injury* (Cmnd 7054, 1978), vol 1, para 154) found that about 10% of those injured in 1973 had relevant private insurance cover. However, both surveys are now rather out of date.

provide a comparatively low level of benefit.[86] There is no particular reason why this should be so,[87] and, as we shall see, such insurance could represent an important source of compensation – or further compensation – to victims of violent crime.

At common law it has long been settled that payments received under private insurance policies are not deducted from damages for personal injury,[88] and by statute such payments are also ignored in the assessment of damages under the Fatal Accidents legislation.[89] The same approach appears to apply to criminal injuries compensation, albeit by implication rather than by express statutory provision. Thus, Article 6(2) of the 1988 Order, which requires various sums to be deducted from the compensation otherwise payable to a victim, makes no reference to insurance moneys. More positively, Article 7(2)(c) in effect applies the Fatal Accidents rule by providing that the compensation payable where a person has died as the result of a criminal injury is to be assessed "without reference to any . . . gain to [the victim's] estate consequent on the injury".

To this extent the 1988 Order merely replicates the 1977 Order[90] and there does not appear to have been any intention to adopt a new approach. But some doubt may arise from the new (and extended) definition of "gratuity" in Article 6(9) of the 1988 Order as including "any payment of money . . . made in consequence of a legally enforceable right . . . ". The limited scope of Article 6(4) ensures that this definition cannot possibly apply to payments under an insurance policy taken out by the victim himself. But it might now be argued that payments to a victim under a policy taken out by his employer have to be deducted under Article 6(4)(a)(ii) as constituting a "gratuity" paid "on behalf of the employer . . . or by any person with whom the employer has made any contract or arrangement". The immediate response to this argument is that, in spite of Article 6(9), it still does not seem appropriate to describe payment under a contract of insurance as a "gratuity" in the usual sense of "an acknowledgment of service".[91] In addition the new definition in Article 6(9) is intended to catch payments legally enforceable *by the victim*[92] and therefore cannot be taken to extend the ambit of "gratuity" by reference to rights legally enforceable

---

86. According to *Harris* (pp 225–6), the mean amount received by holders of private insurance was £81 (in respect of personal accident insurance only, the mean was £47); the *Pearson Report* (para 154) reported a mean payment of £70. Unfortunately more up-to-date data does not appear to be available.

87. The issues are considered in *Harris*, pp 224 *et seq*.

88. *Bradburn* v *Great Western Rly Co* (1874) LR 10 Ex 1, confirmed by the House of Lords in *Parry* v *Cleaver* [1969] 1 All ER 555.

89. Fatal Accidents (Damages) Act 1908, s 1, reversing *Hicks* v *Newport etc Rly Co* (1857) 4 B & S 403n. See now Fatal Accidents (NI) Order 1977, Art 6(1).

90. Articles 5(3) and 7(2)(c) respectively.

91. But see *Harris* (p 221): "Group loss of income and personal accident insurances are in effect a form of occupational sick pay when they are provided through an employer's scheme . . . ".

92. See above, pp 208–9. An employee may have enforceable rights under an insurance arrangement made by his employer – see e.g. *Bowskill* v *Dawson (No 2)* [1954] 2 All ER 649 (group life policy created trust under which employee was a beneficiary). *Cf* the arrangement in *Green* v *Russell* [1959] 2 All ER 525 gave the employee no legal or equitable right to payment.

by the employer. It might also be contended that payment under an insurance policy is not a payment "consequent on the criminal injury" as required by Article 6(2)(*b*).[93] None of these arguments is conclusive, however, and it would be desirable for the matter to be authoritatively resolved.

We shall now consider briefly the three types of insurance most relevant in the present context.

1. Life Assurance

A life insurance policy normally covers death resulting from a criminal injury:

> "An ordinary [life] policy covers the risk of the assured being murdered by third parties just as it covers the risk of death by accident or disease . . . "[94]

There is usually little scope for argument about the extent of cover, but two problems may briefly be mentioned. First, it may be that the assured is obliged, when obtaining the insurance, to disclose threats against his life, at least if he has reason to believe that they might be carried out.[95] Secondly, payment under the policy may not be made if the assured has been killed as a result of his own participation in criminal conduct.[96] This latter issue arose in *Hewitson* v *Prudential Assurance Co*[97] where P was the beneficiary under a policy which provided for the payment of various sums in the event of the death of her husband. P's husband was shot dead after attempting (with P herself and two others) to commit an armed robbery. Gibson LJ stated the law as follows:

> "A plaintiff guilty of an atrocious crime which shocks the public conscience will not be debarred from recovering on foot of a policy of insurance unless the event giving rise to the contractual obligation to pay the insurance moneys (namely, the death of the life assured) was so connected with the crime that it is properly regarded as a result of it. Again, even though the event giving rise to the contractual liability may have been the result of a crime or other anti-social conduct, the policy holder will be entitled to recover unless he or a person through whom he claims has been involved in the crime or other act. The anti-social act does not render the contract illegal; it merely prevents a person from claiming on foot of it as a matter of public policy in any case where he is so tainted by the act that the courts would regard it as immoral that he should benefit thereby."[98]

---

93. According to Pigott B in *Bradburn, supra* at p 3: "[The injured person] does not receive that sum of money because of the accident, but because he has made a contract providing for the contingency; an accident must occur to entitle him to it, but it is not the accident, but his contract, which is the cause of his receiving it". But this reasoning appears to have been rejected in *Rolston* v *Sec of State* [1975] NI 195, discussed above pp 209–210.

94. *Wainewright* v *Bland* (1835) 1 Moo & Rob 481, 486, *per* Lord Abinger. See generally Colinvaux, *The Law of Insurance* (5th ed, 1984), ch 16.

95. Colinvaux, *op cit*, pp 324.

96. *Ibid*. See also MacGillivray and Parkington, *Insurance Law* (8th ed, 1988), p 184.

97. [1985] 12 NIJB 65.

98. *Ibid*, p 72.

It was accepted that the attempted armed robbery was such anti-social conduct;[99] the only question for the court was whether there was the requisite causal connection between that crime and the death of P's husband. In the circumstances of the particular case Gibson LJ concluded that "in law . . . the plaintiff must be regarded as having caused the death of her husband by his participation in the crime" and therefore she was not entitled to any payment under the policy.

2. Personal Accident Insurance[1]

Personal accident insurance enables a person – or his employer – to provide for the payment of a sum of money in the event of the insured sustaining bodily injury[2] or death "by accident". Although the meaning of "accident" gives rise to some difficulties, it has long been established that the standpoint is that of the victim and therefore injury or death resulting from a crime of violence is "accidental" for this purpose, provided the victim is not a party or privy to the crime,[3] or the contract is not otherwise unenforceable as a matter of public policy.[4] The "really decisive case"[5] on this point is *Trim Joint District School Board of Management* v *Kelly*.[6] An assistant master at an industrial school was assaulted and killed by two pupils of the school acting in pursuance of a preconcerted plan of attack. The House of Lords, by a narrow majority, held that he had been killed "by accident" for the purposes of compensation under the Workmen's Compensation Act 1906. Viscount Haldane adopted an earlier definition of this term as denoting –

> "in the popular and ordinary sense of the word . . . an unlooked-for mishap or an untoward event which is not expected or designed . . . "[7]

---

99. The learned Lord Justice went on to observe: "As the plaintiff and her husband were both party to the plan to rob . . . and to carry imitation firearms to facilitate the robbery, it is a matter of indifference whether one directs one's attention to the plaintiff or her husband in judging the immorality of the deed and the propriety of denying a remedy to the plaintiff" (pp 73–4).

1. See generally MacGillivray and Parkington, *Insurance Law* (8th ed, 1988), ch 26; Colinvaux, *The Law of Insurance* (5th ed, 1984), ch 17; Halsbury's *Laws of England* (4th ed, 1978), paras 592–616.

2. "Bodily injury" is usually defined to exclude sickness or disease and gradual physical or mental decline. It does appear, however, to include nervous shock – see e.g. *Pugh* v *London, Brighton and South Coast Rly Ltd* [1896] 2 QB 248 and *Seamann* v *National Ins Co of New Zealand Ltd* (1986) 84 FLR 389 –

and may be expressly extended to include death or disablement resulting from "exposure" to the elements.

3. This proviso arises from cases such as *Midland Ins Co* v *Smith* (1881) 6 QBD 561.

4. As e.g. in *Beresford* v *Royal Ins Co Ltd* [1938] AC 586 and *Hewitson* v *Prudential Assurance Co Ltd* [1985] 12 NIJB 65, discussed above.

5. So described by Paull J in *Mills* v *Smith* [1963] 2 All ER 1078, 1086.

6. [1914] AC 667, in effect following *Nisbet* v *Rayne* [1910] 2 KB 689 and *Anderson* v *Balfour* [1910] 2 IR 497.

7. See *Fenton* v *Thorley* [1903] AC 443, 448, *per* Lord MacNaghten. See also *Nisbet* v *Rayne* [1910] 2 KB 689, 693, *per* Farwell LJ: "The intention of the murderer is immaterial; so far as any intention on the part of the victim is concerned, his death was accidental . . . ".

His Lordship then explained that "designed" here means "designed by the sufferer". Although a decision under the Workmen's Compensation Act – and one in which that particular context played an important part in their Lordships' reasoning[8] – the *Trim* case has consistently been followed in the interpretation of personal accident insurance policies.[9]

The precise scope of a personal accident policy may however be affected by the particular language used in the policy.[10] Thus, the policy may refer to injury caused by "accidental means" rather than "by accident". Taken literally the former term could be held to exclude injury caused by intentional crimes of violence, but it appears that this interpretation would not be adopted in this jurisdiction.[11] Similarly, the policy may be stated to cover only bodily injury "by violent, accidental, external and visible means". This phrase appears to have been intended to cut down the ambit of "by accident", but the courts and commentators do not appear to consider that "anything of substance has been achieved by the change of formula",[12] at least in the present context.

An injury is not accidental if invited or provoked by the insured,[13] but it may still qualify if it has been brought about by the insured's negligence.[14] Thus, in *Cornish* v *Accident Insurance Co*,[15] the insured, while attempting to cross a railway track in broad daylight, was killed by a train. Lindley LJ stated:

> "[T]he deceased met his death by what may be properly called an accident, although his own want of care unquestionably contributed to his death."[16]

But if the cause of injury or death was the insured's own *deliberate* act the injury or death will not normally[17] be regarded as "accidental".[18] The issue

---

8. See the caveat expressed e.g. in *MacGillivray and Parkington*, s 1762 and in *Halsbury*, para 594n.

9. See e.g. *MacGillivray and Parkington*, s 1785; *Halsbury*, para 600. Surprisingly there is no clear English authority on the point in relation to personal accident insurance, though see *Mills* v *Smith* [1963] 2 All ER 1078 in relation to property damage insurance. The *Trim* case was not followed in respect of the "hearth and home" indemnity policy in issue in *Gray* v *Barr* [1971] 2 All ER 949.

10. Thus, "the word 'accidental' is quite different from the words 'by accident'; so are 'from any accident which may happen', [and] 'by accident' has a different meaning from 'by an accident'": *Mills* v *Smith supra* at p 1084, *per* Paull J.

11. See *MacGillivray and Parkington*, s 1792, referring to *Hamlyn* v *Crown Accidental Ins Co* [1893] 1 QB 750.

12. See e.g. *Halsbury*, paras 601-604, *MacGillivray and Parkington*, paras 1789-1795. *Cf*

In re United London and Scottish Ins Co, Brown's Claim [1915] 2 Ch 167, 170, where Cozens-Hardy MR sardonically observed: "[I]t is open to doubt whether this [wording] does not exempt the company upon every occasion that is likely to occur."

13. *MacGillivray and Parkington*, para 1785.

14. *Ibid*, para 1787.

15. (1889) 23 QBD 453.

16. *Ibid*, p 455. However, the case was held to fall within an exception to the policy on the grounds that the insured had exposed himself to an obvious risk of injury – see below p 259.

17. It may be otherwise if the insured was mentally disordered at the time of the act – see *Halsbury*, para 600, referring to *Gray* v *Barr* [1971] 2 All ER 949.

18. See e.g. *Beresford* v *Royal Ins Co Ltd* [1938] AC 586, 595, *per* Lord Atkin. Thus, as *MacGillivray and Parkington* (para 1815) explain, suicide or attempted suicide are not "accidental" deaths – unless perhaps the insured was insane or drunk.

of causation, however, poses familiar problems, as evidenced by *Marcel Beller Ltd* v *Hayden*.[19] The plaintiffs in that case had insured an employee's life against accidental bodily injury resulting in death. The insured crashed his car and killed himself; before setting out he had consumed a considerable amount of alcohol and the plaintiffs contended that as a result his death was not "accidental". The court disagreed:

> "A clear distinction can be drawn between cases where the predisposing cause is the deliberate taking of an appreciated risk[20] and the cases such as the present where the predisposing cause, although it leads to the taking of risks, involves risk which was neither deliberately run nor actually appreciated."[21]

This distinction may be difficult to apply in practice.[22]

The general cover provided by a personal accident insurance policy is of course subject to any exceptions stated in the policy.[23] Unlike fire insurance, there is no general "overriding exclusion"[24] in relation to accidental bodily injury in Northern Ireland. However, some policies do except injury occurring or arising as a consequence of riot or civil commotion in Northern Ireland. Others except only injury *caused by taking part in* civil commotion or riot[25] of any kind – a particular example of a more common provision excepting injury due to the insured participating in a criminal act or to the insured's own criminal act. The scope of this latter exception also arose in *Marcel Beller Ltd* v *Hayden*[26] where the insured killed himself in a road accident. He had committed the offences of dangerous driving and driving while under the influence of drink, and the court held his employers could not recover under a policy which excluded death resulting from the insured's own "criminal act". The learned judge was –

> "disposed to think that it would be right to find an implied term limiting that phrase so as to exclude acts of inadvertence or negligence. But I can find no justification for confining it to cases where a subjective test of conscious wrong-doing is applied . . . In my judgment I am concerned with criminal acts other than those of inadvertence or negligence."[27]

Payment under the policy was, therefore, refused.

An accident insurance policy may also exclude liability for accidents caused by the insured exposing himself to an obvious risk of injury.

---

19. [1978] 3 All ER 111.

20. As e.g. in *Greenway* v *Saskatchewan Govt Ins Office* (1967) 59 WWR 673, where P was injured when he crashed his car while attempting to negotiate a T junction at high speed and the court held that P had deliberately taken the risk with full knowledge of the facts.

21. [1978] 3 All ER 111, 119, *per* Judge Fay QC.

22. For a critical analysis of the decision, see *MacGillivray and Parkington*, paras 1763–5A.

23. See generally *MacGillivray and Parkington*, paras 1815–1847.

24. *Cf* Greer and Mitchell, *Compensation for Criminal Damage to Property* (1982), pp 282–3.

25. For an analysis of these terms see *ibid*, pp 283–8.

26. [1978] 3 All ER 111.

27. *Ibid*, p 120. The learned judge continued: "If I were wrong and the limitation on the criminal acts was that they be crimes of moral culpability or turpitude I am satisfied that [these] offences . . . are sufficiently serious to qualify."

It appears that such an exception applies only if the insured has been negligent and where the risk of injury is obvious to the insured or would have been obvious to him had he paid reasonable attention to what he was doing.[28] Here again the degree of care required of the insured may turn on the precise wording of the exclusion. Thus, in the *Marcel Beller* case the court held that the insured, by driving his car after having consumed a considerable amount of alcohol, had not thereby "deliberately exposed himself to danger". The learned judge reasoned as follows:

> "In *Cornish* v *Accident Insurance Co*[29] the phrase was 'by exposure . . . to obvious risk of injury'. A farmer was killed by a train when crossing the line between two of his fields. The risk was obvious to anyone who paid attention and the exception applied. This was distinguished . . . in *Lehman* v *Great Eastern Casualty and Indemnity Co of New York*[30] where the words were 'voluntary exposure to unnecessary danger'. The court here applied a subjective test. See *per* Adam J: 'one cannot be said to be guilty of a voluntary exposure to danger unless he intentionally and consciously assumes the risk of an obvious danger' . . . The word 'deliberately' is stronger than the word 'voluntarily' . . . and imports the subjective test. In the absence of evidence I am not prepared to assume that the deceased thought about his condition or about the risk he was taking and deliberately chose to run the risk."[31]

However, a policy may specifically except bodily injury sustained by the insured when intoxicated or under the influence of drink or drugs.[32]

The benefits payable under an accident insurance policy usually consist of stated lump sums payable respectively on death, loss of one or more limbs, other specified injuries or permanent total inability to attend to the insured's usual occupation or a suitable alternative occupation.[33] A periodic payment of a stated sum per week or month may be payable for a maximum period (usually two years) in respect of any one injury for a temporary inability to work – but often only if that inability is total. Other payments (e.g. hospitalisation benefit) may be included in the table of benefits provided by the policy. All these sums vary according to the premium paid by or on behalf of the insured.

3. Permanent Health Insurance

Loss of income or permanent health insurance provides periodic payments in lieu of income if the insured becomes unable, because of sickness or accident, to follow his normal occupation. A policy may be issued either to an individual, or to an employer to cover his employees on a group basis. According to Harris, "it is permanent in the sense that once an insurer has accepted a proposal, the terms of the policy are that renewal cannot be refused until some prearranged expiry date, usually the retirement of the

---

28. *Halsbury*. para 609.

29. (1889) 23 QBD 453.

30. (1896) 7 App Div NY 424.

31. [1978] 3 All ER 111, 119, *per* Judge Fay QC.

32. Unless perhaps the insured can establish that the taking of alcohol was not a factor contributing to the happening of the injury.

33. See e.g. *Halsbury*, paras 606–7.

insured."[34] Payments do not usually begin until six or 12 months after the injury and are usually limited to a stated maximum benefit. Although the incidence of such insurance appears to be growing,[35] the Harris survey found that only 1% of the victims interviewed held loss of income insurance, and that the mean amount received per claim was only £30.[36]

34. Harris, *op cit* n 83, p 222.

35. See *Pearson Report*, para 153. In 1988 an estimated 5 million persons in the United Kingdom were covered by permanent health insurance – see *Insurance Statistics 1984–1988* (1989), p. 11. *Cf* Harris, *op cit* n 83, p 222: "In general, insurers appear to be very cautious and conservative in their approach to the marketing of permanent health contracts, and the choice available . . . is poor in comparison with that available in the life insurance market."

36. *Ibid*, pp 224 and 226.

6

Practice and Procedure

INTRODUCTION

Prior to 1977 the initial determination of applications for compensation was a matter for the county courts, though in many instances the court was merely giving its formal approval to a settlement agreed between the parties.[1] In the mid 1970s it came to be thought that this process caused delays in the determination of applications and possibly also added to the costs of administration.[2] The Government therefore resolved to move to the system which had been introduced in 1973 to deal with applications for criminal damage compensation.[3] This gave the power of initial determination to the Secretary of State – in practice, the Northern Ireland Office – but with a wide right of appeal on any point of fact or law to the county court and beyond. In spite of considerable opposition to this proposal,[4] the new procedure was enacted in the 1977 Order and appears to have worked sufficiently well that the administration of the scheme gave rise to little discussion during the passage of the 1988 Order.[5] Despite this apparent satisfaction, and notwithstanding that the 1988 Order provides for judicial review in most instances, it is still *in principle* a matter of concern that a government department, as opposed to an independent tribunal, should be given such wide powers to determine the legal rights of individual applicants. The exercise of those powers *in practice* also gives rise from time to time to adverse comment, the validity (or otherwise) of which is difficult to assess in the absence of regular and systematic information. There is

---

1. 1968 Act, s 1(1). "In practice . . . nearly 70% of claims are now agreed on the basis of an offer . . . and half of the remainder are settled after further negotiation . . . ": HC Debs (NI Cttee), col 2 (16 Feb 1977).

2. See especially *ibid*, cols 94–6.

3. Criminal Injuries to Property (Compensation) Act (NI) 1971, discussed Greer and Mitchell, *Compensation for Criminal Damage to Property* (1982), ch 9.

4. See e.g. HC Debs (NI Cttee), col 21 (16 Feb 1977), where Rev Paisley referred to "a quasi-court made up of civil servants ...".

5. 128 HC Debs, cols 540-544 (25 Feb 1988). The NIO comes within the jurisdiction of the Parliamentary Commissioner for Administration, and it appears that only one complaint (which was rejected as regards the NIO) has been made in relation to the administration of criminal injuries compensation – see *Annual Report for 1985* (1985–86 HC 275), pp 47–49. *Cf* both the British and Irish Schemes are administered by an independent Board or Tribunal – see British Scheme, para 1 and 1988 Act, s 108 and Sch 6, and Irish Scheme, paras 17 *et seq*.

therefore a strong case for making the operation of the scheme more amenable to public scrutiny and, to that end, publishing an annual report, on the lines of that issued by the Criminal Injuries Compensation Board in Great Britain.[6]

The scheme is administered on behalf of the Secretary of State by the Compensation Division of the Northern Ireland Office, which is comprised of administrative staff and solicitors. The administrative staff gather whatever documentation and information is necessary to decide the outcome of claims and have authority to negotiate settlements within limits which vary according to the grade of the officer. Solicitors, who act in support of the administration, provide legal advice, deal with the more complex and high value claims and also take charge of those which are the subject of appeal.

Applications (of which there are some 9,000 per annum) are dealt with by the Division up to the stage where a notice of determination is issued; if an applicant appeals against the notice, one of the Division's solicitors will normally brief counsel for the court hearing. Although the Secretary of State is ultimately responsible for the scheme, neither he nor the Minister of State for the Northern Ireland Office is often involved in the decision-making process.[7]

MAKING AN APPLICATION

The 1988 Order follows its predecessors in requiring three steps to be taken in relation to the making of an application for compensation, *viz*

1. Reporting the commission of the injury to the police.

2. Serving on the Secretary of State a Notice of Intention to Apply for Compensation, and

3. Serving on the Secretary of State an Application for Compensation.

1. Reporting to the Police

Article 5(4) slightly amends earlier provisions[8] by providing:

> "No compensation shall be paid unless the victim or, in the event of his death, one of his relatives or, in either event, a representative of the victim or such a relative –

---

6. See now the statutory requirement in the 1988 Act, Sch 6, para 10. The Government has, in fact, acknowledged in respect of the NI Scheme that "there is a requirement for improved statistical information', but this is apparently dependent on "additional computer facilities": 128 HC Debs, col 544 (25 Feb 1988).

7. Information provided by the Northern Ireland Office.

8. *Cp* 1968 Act, s 1(3)(*e*); 1977 Order, Art 3(2)(*d*). As will be seen below, the 1977 Order varied the 1968 Act by deleting a power to dispense with a report on "reasonable cause"; the 1988 Order does likewise, but also adds the details of what the report is to contain. The other schemes have similar provisions of a less detailed nature – see British Scheme, para 6(*a*) and 1988 Act, s 112(1)(*a*): Irish Scheme, para 23.

(a) makes forthwith to a constable or, within 48 hours from the commission of the criminal injury, to a constable at a police station in Northern Ireland, a report of the commission of the injury containing full and true disclosure of all facts, within his knowledge or belief, which might lead to the identification and apprehension of the offender or otherwise be material to the investigation of the matter by the police . . . "[9]

Paragraph (4) goes on to provide that the report may alternatively be made "within such period as the Secretary of State considers reasonable having regard to all the circumstances" and, by Article 16(6)(a):

"The county court may, on an application made to it on notice to the Secretary of State and in accordance with County Court Rules . . . extend the time for making . . . any report . . . referred to in Article 5(4) . . . "

As we have seen,[10] prompt reporting of incidents to the authorities has long been a feature of the Irish criminal injuries compensation code; the purposes of this and similar provisions in the modern scheme have been explained by McGonigal LJ as follows:

"They are necessary in order to enable the facts of the incident and the bona fides of the claim to be investigated at the earliest opportunity. They are also important for another reason. These claims are based on injuries received as a result of a criminal act by some person or persons. It is not only in the interests of justice that the guilty party should be made amenable for the offence . . . [but also that] the Secretary of State may recover from a person convicted of the criminal offence, the whole or part of any compensation paid to the injured party. This . . . [provision] puts a duty on the injured party who chooses to exercise his right to apply for compensation to report the criminal act and injury at a very early date and to make full and true disclosure as a condition of any award being made to him."[11]

Four particular points arise for consideration.

(a) By whom the report is to be made

Article 5(4) appears to provide for the necessary report to be made by the injured victim or his "representative" or, where the victim has died, by a relative or his "representative".[12] "Relative" is defined in Article 2(2) of the Order, but "representative" is not. It is unlikely that it connotes only a *legal* representative; but bearing in mind the purpose of the paragraph, the

---

9. See also the further requirement in Art 5(8) that an applicant comply with all reasonable requests for information and assistance which might lead to the identification, apprehension, prosecution and conviction of the offender, discussed above, pp 138–141.

10. Above pp 2 and 4. Prompt reporting to the police is also required under the British Scheme, para 6(a), discussed Greer, *Criminal Injuries Compensation* (1990), paras 3.36–

3.42. See also 1988 Act, s 112(1)(a) and Irish Scheme (para 23).

11. *Moore* v *Sec of State* [1977] NI 14, 16.

12. The drafting is not as precise as it might have been; strictly interpreted, "in either event" suggests that if the victim is injured, he, a representative or a representative of a relative can make the report! The word "of" also appears to have been omitted before the phrase "such a relative".

"representative" should presumably be someone sufficiently well informed to be able to provide all requisite information. A "second-hand" report by a person who does not know the full circumstances of the incident may not satisfy this requirement[13] – although the paragraph does not specifically require the representative to be properly informed, and it will apparently suffice if he informs the police of "all facts, within his knowledge or belief . . . ". It is difficult to believe that the courts would permit the purpose of Article 5(4)(a) to be frustrated by the use of uninformed "representatives".

It should be noted that compensation is payable in certain circumstances to non-relatives;[14] it would, perhaps, be prudent for such persons in appropriate cases to regard themselves as "representatives" and ensure that a report is made to the police to avoid any difficulty over their claim.

In *Hughes* v *Secretary of State*[15] it was emphasised that the Order "places the duty of complying . . . upon either the applicant or his representative, so that whatever one elects to undertake the responsibility of issuing the notice [of intention to apply for compensation] . . . must do it." This reasoning is equally applicable to the report to the police; in *Hughes* the applicant's claim was rejected because, by reason of oversight, his solicitor failed to serve the Notice of Intention within a reasonable time.

(b) Form and content of the report

With reference to the earlier provision in the 1968 Act it was observed:

> " . . . such a report is not a bare report of the injury, but is a report of all the relevant circumstances pointing to the commission of a criminal offence and of an injury resulting therefrom. It is such a report as a complainant would normally make to a police officer concerning the commission of a criminal offence."[16]

This observation, which was treated as equally applicable to the 1977 Order,[17] must now be read in the light of the new wording inserted into the 1988 Order, *viz* that the report is to contain "full and true disclosure" of "all facts, within his knowledge or belief, which might lead to the identification and apprehension of the offender or otherwise be material to the investigation of the matter by the police . . . ". The report is, therefore, to assist the police to investigate the incident rather than to provide details of the applicant's injuries:

> "The onus is on the applicant to prove his case and to prove that he has fully co-operated with the police in doing all within his power and knowledge to bring the criminals to justice."[18]

---

13. This is specifically noted in the *Statement* accompanying the British Scheme, para 6(a).

14. See e.g. Art 3(2)(b), 3(3)(c) and 3(4)(b), discussed above pp 182, 201 and 203 respectively.

15. Unreported, Cty Ct (Judge Rowland), 14 April 1978.

16. *Moore* v *Sec of State* [1977] NI 14, 16, *per* McGonigal LJ.

17. See *McLaverty* v *Sec of State* Unreported, Cty Ct (Judge Pringle), 9 Oct 1986.

18. *McCleery* v *Sec of State*, Unreported, Cty Ct (Judge Rowland), 11 July 1977.

The applicant will thus be expected e.g. to give the police the name of the offender (if known to him) or his description, details of any vehicle used by the offender, possible motives for the offence, background details leading up to the incident, etc. The applicant is not, however, obliged to make a full statement immediately if he might himself be suspected of a criminal offence.[19]

It has been pointed out that:

> "It is . . . difficult to see how [the Secretary of State] will find . . . out [whether the applicant has made full and true disclosure] or how the question can be tested."[20]

But a number of checks *are* available. Thus, the police in their report to the Secretary of State may indicate whether or not the applicant had provided them with appropriate information and assistance. The applicant's statement to the police can also be scrutinised with reference to subsequent evidence, including the applicant's own testimony. In *McCleery v Secretary of State*[21] the applicant had given the police a brief description of his attackers; he did not say whether they were masked, but did say that they had warned him to give "no identification". Subsequently the applicant testified that his attackers *were* masked and that they had warned "no *description*". These changes of story – and a general attitude of non-co-operation with the police – were held to give rise to "serious questions regarding the quality of the disclosure made by the applicant", and his application for compensation was rejected.

Article 5(4) must also be considered in connection with the (amended) requirement in Article 5(8) that a victim must (apparently at all times) comply with "all reasonable requests for information and assistance which might lead to the identification, apprehension, prosecution and conviction of the offender".[22] The increased sychronisation[23] of these two provisions is designed in particular to put an even greater onus on the victims of "kneecapping", paramilitary feuds, pub brawls, etc to reveal what they know about the identity of their assailants or else forego the right to compensation.[24] But whereas by Article 5(8) the applicant is bound only to

---

19. In *Gouck v Sec of State* [1988] 8 *BNIL* 11 A was attacked and injured by a group of youths. He reported the incident to the police on the day of the incident but refused to make a full statement when advised by a police officer that the statement had to be taken under caution. Subsequently he made a full statement in the presence of his solicitor. It was held that he was not in breach of the 1977 Order. The form of caution has since been altered as a result of the Criminal Evidence (NI) Order 1988, but an applicant must surely still be entitled, for the purposes of Art 5(4), to a reasonable time within which to consult his solicitor before making a statement to the police.

20. *Scott v Sec of State* [1981] NI 185, 191, *per* Lord Lowry LCJ.

21. *Supra* n 18 (a case under the 1968 Act, but equally applicable to the 1988 Order).

22. See above, Chapter 3.

23. In *McLaverty, supra* n 17, His Honour Judge Pringle QC had taken into account "the restricted ambit" of Art 6(10) of the 1977 Order (the predecessor of Art 5(8) of the 1988 Order) in the interpretation of the scope of the reporting requirement.

24. Failure to give information to the police may also constitute a criminal offence – see especially Criminal Law Act (NI) 1967, s 5.

comply "with all reasonable requests", it would appear that Article 5(4)(*a*) requires him to volunteer *all* the relevant information.

It should also be noted that any failure by the applicant to continue to co-operate fully with the police may constitute a "relevant circumstance" to which, under Article 6(1), the Secretary of State must have regard "in determining whether any compensation should be paid and, if so, its amount".[25]

It appears that it is not necessary for the report to the police to be in writing or signed by the applicant; most apparently are oral. In *Dawson* v *Secretary of State*,[26] the applicant gave the police an oral account of what had happened, but refused to make a written statement or to sign the note of his account as taken down in writing by the investigating police officer. The note of the interview was, nonetheless, put in evidence and accepted as admissible. The court appears to have accepted the note as an acceptable form of "report", but compensation was refused on the ground that there had not been "full and true disclosure" of the identity of the applicant's assailants.

(c) Time-limits

The normal time-limit for reporting to the police is "forthwith . . . or within 48 hours" of the commission of the offence. Although the wording makes it immaterial which course is pursued, there appears to be a judicial preference in favour of prompt reporting.[27] In *McLaughlin* v *Secretary of State*[28] an application was initially refused on account of the applicant's failure to make the necessary report to the police. On appeal it emerged that the applicant had been shot twice, once in each leg, and was taken to hospital at midnight. There he was visited by the police, but at first refused to make a statement. However, about 36 hours after the shooting he did give details to the police. In what should have been a straightforward case Nicholson J felt it necessary to observe:

> "He did make a report within 48 hours from the commission of the offence and his refusal to speak to [the police on the earlier occasion] . . . was explained by the Appellant on the basis that . . . he did not want to see anybody. Drugs were not relieving his pain, he felt unfit and he was about to have an operation or had just had it. In my view the claim should not fail on this ground."

Megran v *Secretary of State*[29] illustrates another aspect of this requirement. The applicant was stabbed in an incident at a friend's home. When the police

---

25. See above, Chapter 3.

26. Unreported, High Ct (McGonigal LJ), 15 Oct 1976 (the applicant had told the police that he had "a good idea" of his assailants' identity).

27. The British Board "attach great importance to the duty of every victim of violent crime to report the matter personally to the police at the earliest opportunity . . . ": CICB, *23rd Annual Report* (1986 –87), para 25.

28. Unreported, High Ct (Nicholson J), 6 Jan 1984. The form requesting evidence in support of an Application for Compensation under the 1977 Order asked whether a report had been made to the police "within the specified period of 48 hours . . . ". The new form of Application simply asks for the date when the incident was reported.

29. Unreported, Cty Ct (Judge Curran), 19 Nov 1986; [1987] 3 *BNIL* 26.

arrived, the applicant did not "forthwith" report the stabbing but said instead that he had fallen and injured himself. His compensation was reduced from £5,000 to £3,500 because of his conduct "and particularly because of his failure to report the incident at the scene . . . ". This was a decision under the 1977 Order, and (like the 1988 Order) the reporting requirement was an "all-or-nothing" one; if not satisfied "no compensation shall be paid . . . ". It would seem, therefore, that the learned judge must have been intending to refer to the falsity of the report and to have regarded the applicant's failure to give *true* information to the police as a "relevant circumstance" to which, by Article 6(1), regard must be had "in determining whether any compensation should be paid and, if so, its amount . . . ".[30] As regards the timing of the report as such, it would be undesirable if the *general* provision in Article 6(1) as to "relevant circumstances" were to be held to qualify or operate inconsistently with the *particular* rule laid down in Article 5(4)(*a*).

Where the 48-hour requirement has not been satisfied, a valid report may still be made "within such period as the Secretary of State considers reasonable having regard to all the circumstances". The requirement to make a prompt report to the police is an important one, and where no reason for delay is given by the applicant, such an extension – and therefore compensation – will usually be refused. Thus in *McNally* v *Secretary of State*[31] the applicant was assaulted on 17 May, but did not report the incident to the police until 29 May. Compensation was refused and an appeal therefrom dismissed on the ground that he had given no satisfactory reason why the incident could not have been reported on the night it happened, or at least on the following day. Obviously the causes of delay are infinite; those which have been considered in this context include the following:

(i) The applicant at first reasonably believed that his injuries were trivial and only later discovered them to be sufficiently serious to warrant an application.[32]

(ii) The applicant reasonably believed that the incident had been reported to the police by a third party, and then discovered that it had not been.[33]

---

30. As e.g. in *McNamee* v *Sec of State* [1982] NI 279, discussed below p 272.

31. Unreported, Cty Ct (Judge Rowland), 23 March 1984; [1984] 4 *BNIL* 32. See also *Reilly* v *Sec of State* [1987] 7 *BNIL* 13 (A notified police on 10 January of assault which had taken place on 3 January; appeal against refusal of award for breach of Art 3(2)(*d*)(i) of 1977 Order dismissed by Recorder).

32. Accepted by the British Board as a valid excuse in CICB, *8th Annual Report* (1971–72), para 8(1), provided a report is made

when the injury is discovered. In CICB, *23rd Annual Report* (1986–87), para 30, no report at all was made and compensation was refused.

33. The report must be made by the victim's "representative"; it would not appear that he can necessarily rely e.g. on a doctor or ambulance driver to make the report for him – see *ibid*, paras 31 and 33. If such reliance was, in the circumstances, reasonable and a report was not made, the victim should himself make a report without delay.

(iii) The applicant's physical or mental condition as a result of his injury was such that he could not reasonably have been expected to make a full report to the police within 48 hours.[34]

(iv) The applicant was at first unaware that his injuries were or may have been directly attributable to a crime of violence.[35]

(v) The applicant was genuinely unaware of the duty to report "forthwith".[36]

(vi) The applicant was a person of low intelligence without sufficient understanding to know that he should have reported the details to the police.[37]

(vii) The applicant had made a prompt report to a person in authority.[38]

Where an applicant has a valid reason for the delay, he must, however, notify the police as soon as possible after he becomes aware of "all the circumstances".

The courts have in the past held that duress or fear of reprisal, though genuine, does not constitute "reasonable cause" for failure to make a prompt report to the police. The leading case is *Moore v Secretary of State*,[39] where McGonigal LJ stated:

> "Fear of reprisal is not a reasonable excuse [for the purposes of section 1(3)(*e*) of the 1968 Act]; if it were, a claimant need only say that he was injured but refuse to give any other information on the ground that he was afraid and the Court would then have to award compensation in the dark, without the police having any opportunity to investigate the occurrence relied on or the bona fides of the complaint . . . "

However, in *Hobbs v Secretary of State*,[40] *Moore* was distinguished on two grounds:

---

34. See e.g. *Doherty v Sec of State* [1988] 1 *BNIL* 29 (applicant received head injuries in assault reported 10 days later to police. Held: given nature of injuries, applicant could not have made an earlier report and in any case there was no real probability of the police apprehending the assailants even if he had done so). See also *Hobbs v Sec of State*, Unreported, Cty Ct (Judge Curran), 30 Oct 1981 (threats made to A led to "a supervening medical condition"; this was one factor justifying grant of extension).

35. Accepted in CICB, *8th Annual Report* (1971–72), para 8.

36. In *McNally v Sec of State* Unreported, Cty Ct (Judge Rowland), 23 March 1984 the applicant's explanation that he had failed to make a report because he was unaware of the statutory time-limit was apparently rejected. Ignorance of the law is usually not a defence –

but in *Jennings v Sec of State* Unreported, High Ct (Gibson LJ), 7 Dec 1977 it was regarded as possibly providing a reasonable cause for delay where the applicant was "a genuine individual".

37. See e.g. *Lunney v Sec of State* Unreported, Cty Ct (Judge Babington), 8 Dec 1980 (such circumstances could constitute "good cause" for not reporting promptly to the police, but not on particular facts of case).

38. *Hobbs v Sec of State, supra* n 34 (assaulted employee gave details of incident to employer (and to doctor), but did not report to police because of threats; extension granted).

39. [1977] NI 14, 16. See also *Dawson v Sec of State* Unreported, High Ct (McGonigal LJ), 15 Oct 1976.

40. Unreported, Cty Ct (Judge Curran), 30 Oct 1981.

(i) The applicant in *Hobbs* had no information as to the identity of his assailants which could in any way have assisted the police. It would appear that the learned Recorder thus considered that the failure to report had not in this respect prejudiced the police in their investigation of the incident; but this is not to say that a prompt report would not in some way have assisted their enquiries.[41]

(ii) The threats to the applicant in *Hobbs* led not to "a generalised fear of reprisal" but to an actual "anxiety state . . . supported by medical evidence". But again the learned judge did not consider whether it was the applicant's medical condition as such, as opposed to the fear of reprisal, which had brought about his failure to report.

Harsh though it may appear, the principle laid down in *Moore* is still applicable:[42] the fact that the 1977 and 1988 Orders make no provision for any "reasonable excuse" tends to confirm this. The decision in *Hobbs*, however, may suggest that fear of reprisal may provide an acceptable basis for extending the time within which such a report may be made.

If an extension of the time for reporting to the police is not allowed by the Secretary of State, the applicant may, under Article 16(6)(*a*), apply to the county court for such an extension. By the County Court (Criminal Injuries to the Person) (Compensation) Rules (NI) 1988,[43] such application is made by notice in writing in the prescribed form[44] to the county court for the division in which the criminal injury was sustained.[45] A copy of this notice must be served on the solicitor for the Secretary of State, and the procedure thereafter follows that for interlocutory applications made on notice in the course of an action or matter as laid down in the County Court Rules,[46] but "with any necessary modifications". On the hearing of the application the county court "may make such order as [it] considers just".[47]

---

41. *Cf* "Often the applicant says that he could not identify his assailant and saw no point in reporting [the assault]. However, even if there is little action the police can take, they will still make a record of the incident and are usually able to supply . . . helpful information about the nature of the injuries sustained": CICB, *23rd Annual Report* (1986 –87), para 26. But the reasoning in *Hobbs* appears to have also been accepted in *Doherty* (*supra* n 34) and in *McCarron* v *Sec of State* [1989] 1 *BNIL* 18 (late report caused no prejudice and therefore accepted).

42. "Irrespective of the provisions of the Scheme, it is essential, if the rising tide of crime is to be stemmed, that all victims of crime should, without delay, report the circumstances of the incident . . . to the police and thereafter co-operate fully with the police in their enquiries . . . There is no soft option, no practical alternative if we are to walk our streets free from fear and injury . . . ": CICB, *19th Annual Report* (1982–83), para 27.

43. Rule 12.

44. Form 13. An affidavit is not necessary "unless the judge or circuit registrar . . . otherwise directs . . . ": CCR O 14, r 1(*c*).

45. By lodging it in the office of the chief clerk. The notice so lodged "shall be duly endorsed as to service and accompanied by any certificate of posting": 1988 Rules, r 12(7) and (8).

46. O 14, r 1 – see Valentine and Glass, *County Court Procedure in Northern Ireland* (1985), pp 101–2.

47. CCR O 14, r 1(*d*). Any order made on the application is endorsed on the notice; an order dismissing the application is in Form 14: 1988 Rules, r 12(4).

The judges appear to be divided as to whether the making of a report is a procedural or substantive requirement. In *Mackie* v *Secretary of State*[48] MacDermott J stated that "Article 3(2) is not a procedural requirement. It is a bar to the payment of compensation if an applicant has not complied with the statutory requirements." In *McA* v *Secretary of State*,[49] however, the applicant schoolboy had been assaulted at 10.50 am on 15 May, but the incident was only reported to the police at 8.15 pm on 17 May (i.e. some 57 hours later). The Secretary of State and the County Court rejected the application for compensation on the ground (*inter alia*) that the required report to the police had not been made in time. On appeal to the High Court, however, Carswell J considered "the substance of the appeal" more important than the applicant's failure to comply with Article 3(2)(*d*)(i), and awarded compensation.

(*d*) *Failure to make a report*

Prior to the 1977 Order a failure to make a report to the police could be excused for "reasonable cause".[50] This provision is not to be found, however, in the 1977 Order, and has likewise been omitted from the 1988 Order. The requirement to report is, therefore, an absolute one. As has been said in relation to the second limb of Article 5(4):

> " . . . Parliament was deliberately reducing the Court's power to alleviate against non-compliance with the statutory provision. Since 1977 the only discretionary power in this field is to vary the stated time-limits."[51]

This intention has, if anything, been made even clearer in the 1988 Order by the more direct wording of Article 5(8).

2. Notice of Intention to Apply for Compensation

By Article 5(4)(*b*):

> "No compensation shall be paid unless the victim or, in the event of his death, one of his relatives, or, in either event, a representative of the victim or such a relative – . . .
>
> (*b*) serves on the Secretary of State within 28 days from the commission of the criminal injury, a notice of intention to apply for compensation containing full and true disclosure of all facts, within his knowledge or belief, material to the determination of the application . . . "

This time-limit also may be extended – but a Notice of Intention *must* be served at some time; as with the report to the police, no "reasonable cause"

---

48. [1986] 15 NIJB 1, 6. The learned judge was referring to Art 3(2)(*d*)(ii) of the 1977 Order, but his reasoning is equally applicable to the first limb of that paragraph, and to the 1988 Order.

49. [1984] 4 *BNIL* 29. The applicant had also failed to comply with Art 3(2)(*d*)(ii). See also *Brown* v *Sec of State* Unreported,

High Ct (O'Donnell LJ), 18 Oct 1985.

50. 1968 Act, s 1(3)(*c*).

51. *Mackie* v *Sec of State* [1986] 15 NIJB 1, 4, *per* MacDermott J, following Lord Lowry LCJ in *Scott* v *Sec of State* [1981] NI 185, 191. *Cf* British Scheme, para 6(*a*) (and 1988 Act, s 112(1)(*a*)) requires an applicant to take "all reasonable steps" to inform the police.

can excuse the failure to do so. Thus, this second step is clearly complementary to the first and much of what has been said above – particularly in relation to "full and true disclosure" – is equally relevant here. But other considerations must also be taken into account.

(a) By whom the Notice is to be served

The wording of Article 5(4)(b) again leaves open a possible lacuna in that the notice is to be served by the victim, a relative of a deceased victim, or "a representative". In the vast majority of cases this will cover all those entitled to compensation. But in some cases it may not, since compensation is also payable in appropriate circumstances to a non-relative responsible for the maintenance of the victim or to a non-relative who has incurred expenses as a result of the victim's injury or death. If it appears unlikely that the victim or a relative will claim compensation, therefore, it would be prudent for such other applicants to regard themselves as "representatives" (even though they will be claiming on their own behalf) and serve the appropriate notice of their intention to make a claim.

(b) Form and content of the Notice

The form of the Notice of Intention has not been prescribed, but a new form (Form PI/1) for cases coming under the 1988 Order has been adopted by the Secretary of State. The opportunity has been taken to deal with some of the less specific aspects of the previous form and the applicant is now required to give personal information concerning the victim and the applicant (where the victim is deceased or under a disability), details of the location, date and time of the incident, and of the report to the police, the identity of the alleged offender, the name and address of any witness to the incident, particulars of the injuries suffered and of how the alleged injury was received.[52]

In considering the scope of the information required, regard must be had to two further provisions of the 1988 Order:

(i) By Article 20(1)(b), a person is guilty of a criminal offence if –

> "for the purposes of obtaining any compensation, [he] knowingly, in or in connection with an application to the Secretary of State or otherwise, makes a false or misleading statement or a statement which he does not believe to be true or fails to disclose a material fact."

(ii) By Article 18(4):

> "Where, on an application made to it by the Secretary of State, the county court is satisfied –

---

52. As compared with the previous form, the new form specifically requests information as to the identity of the alleged offender and whether, when the incident took place, the victim was living in the same household as the offender. The request for the name and address of any witness to the incident is also new, and instead of "precise details" of the circumstances in which the injury was sustained, the applicant must now give "a full and true account" of the incident. He no longer has to indicate whether any other person will be applying for compensation in respect of the same incident.

(*a*) that the Secretary of State has paid compensation to any person; but

(*b*) that that person failed to make full and true disclosure of all the facts material to the determination of the application,

the county court may make an order requiring that person to reimburse to the Secretary of State the compensation or such part of it as the court may specify."

What has to be disclosed to the Secretary of State is any fact "*material to the determination of the application*". This wording obliges the applicant to give to the Secretary of State a somewhat different range of information than is required in the report to the police,[53] but the principle of full disclosure is equally applicable, for the reason that –

" . . . unlike a claim against a defendant for damages in tort or contract, where the defendant will be aware of the surrounding facts out of which the claim arises and will be able adequately to defend the claim, the respondent in a criminal injury claim will usually have no knowledge of the surrounding facts other than from the information which the applicant chooses to give."[54]

It would appear further that service of a valid Application for Compensation will not cure a defect in, or failure to serve, a Notice of Intention.[55]

The starting point for deciding the precise information to be given is McGonigal LJ's injunction in *Moore* v *Secretary of State* that the applicant makes a "full and true disclosure of all the facts within his knowledge . . . ".[56] To this may now be added MacDermott J's "salutory reminder" that "It is not for the applicant to pick and choose from his recollection – what to him may be a trifling matter may well be an important clue to the authorities."[57]

The detailed scope of the requirement was considered in *McNamee* v *Secretary of State*.[58] In his notice of intention to apply for compensation the applicant stated that he "was walking on the Springfield Road at Turf Lodge when he was approached by two men who shot him in the leg". The court considered that the case "has the marks of a punishment shooting" and that one of the facts material to the determination of the claim was the reason why the applicant was in the locality where he was shot:

"Where an applicant is shot in a punishment shooting one possibility which has to be investigated . . . is the possibility that he was shot by members of a

---

53. The difference between the wording here and in the other "disclosure" provision in Art 5(8) [formerly Art 6(10) of the 1977 Order] was underlined by Lord Lowry LCJ in *Scott* v *Sec of State* [1981] NI 185.

54. *McNamee* v *Sec of State* [1982] NI 279, 284, *per* Hutton J. See also *McCafferty* v *Sec of State* [1987] 6 *BNIL* 19.

55. *Cp Cole* v *Sec of State* [1983] 9 *BNIL* 29 (a criminal damage compensation case).

56. [1977] NI 14, 16. The remainder of this frequently-quoted passage is given at pp 263–4 above. According to MacDermott J in *McCabe* v *Sec of State* (see next footnote): "The relevance of all that is there said is as true today as it was eight years ago."

57. *McCabe* v *Sec of State* Unreported, High Ct (MacDermott J), 1 March 1985.

58. [1982] NI 279.

terrorist organisation because he was a member of another terrorist organisation, or the possibility that he was shot because he had transgressed the rules of a terrorist organisation to which he belonged. And the reason why the applicant was in the place where he was shot is relevant to that investigation because a person shot by reason of his connection with a terrorist organisation is sometimes lured to the place where he was shot or is sometimes ordered to go to that place."

By failing to state the true reason why he was in the area in which he was shot the applicant had, therefore, failed to disclose a fact "material to the determination of the application".[59] Hutton J further observed:

"'The facts . . . material to the determination of the application' will, of course, vary from case to case, and I am not holding that in every case the applicant must make disclosure . . . of the reason why he was in the area where he was injured. In many cases [this fact] . . . will not be material; for example, when a woman is injured by a bomb planted in a shop, it would not be necessary for her to state in her notice of intention to apply for compensation that she was in the shop to make a purchase, or where a man is injured by a bomb planted in a train, it would not be necessary for him to state . . . that he was travelling in the train to his work."

But the reasoning in *McNamee* was stated by MacDermott J in *Mackie* v *Secretary of State* "to apply with even greater force to the question of failing to disclose the name of a known assailant."[60]

It should perhaps be noted at this stage that the disclosure requirement is a continuing one. Any relevant information not known to the applicant at the time of service of the Notice of Intention should be included in the Application itself.[61] Thereafter, it should be notified in writing to the Secretary of State.[62] Although the 1988 Order, like its predecessors, contains no general provision that compensation may be refused or reduced if the applicant fails to give "all reasonable assistance" to the Secretary of State in connection with the application,[63] such a requirement does appear to be implicit in the general provisions of Article 6(1); a failure to keep the Secretary of State informed would be a "relevant circumstance"[64] which the Secretary of State must take into account in determining whether to award compensation and, if so, its amount.

---

59. *Ibid*, pp 282–3. The applicant's claim was also rejected on the ground that the court was satisfied that the applicant had lied as to the reason why he was in the area; this was a "relevant circumstance" for the purposes of s 1(2) of the 1968 Act (now Art 6(1) of the 1988 Order).

60. [1986] 15 NIJB 1, 7. The learned judge added: "Indeed in this case the applicant not only fails to name his attacker but falsely in the initial notice states that he

was approached by unknown men."

61. As expressly indicated in the Application form.

62. *Ibid*.

63. *Cp* British Scheme, para 6(*b*) – see e.g. CICB, *18th Annual Report* (1981–82), para 33. See also 1988 Act, s 112(1)(*b*) to the same effect.

64. See above, p 114.

(c) Time-limits

By Article 5(4)(*b*) the Notice of Intention should normally be served on the Secretary of State within 28 days *from the commission of the criminal injury*. However, this limit may be extended to such period "as the Secretary of State considers reasonable having regard to all the circumstances" and, by Article 16(6)(*a*), the county court may also extend the time for serving such a notice.[65] It would appear from these provisions that there may be more flexibility in relation to this time-limit as compared with that governing the report to the police, as indeed would be understandable given that the latter will already have given the authorities full details of the incident. However –

> "In personal injury cases it is generally essential that the respondents should have the earliest opportunity of assessing the medical position, though the fact that the applicant must provide copies of his medical evidence reduces the risk of the respondent being put at a disadvantage by late notice of an intended claim. None the less, whenever an applicant fails to comply with the rules he runs the grave risk that the time will not be extended and secondly, the Court will scrutinise the evidence very carefully to ensure as far as possible that he is not allowed to take advantage of his own neglect. Furthermore, as memory of the incident fades, any inconsistencies in the applicant's testimony or that of his witnesses may affect his claim adversely."[66]

A further consideration arose in *Hughes* v *Secretary of State*,[67] where the Notice of Intention was served some two and a half years after the commission of the alleged criminal injury. Apparently the necessary instructions had been duly taken in the applicant's solicitor's office by a recently qualified assistant who drafted the necessary Notice, but failed to serve it on the Secretary of State. The assistant then resigned from the office. The principal assumed that the Notice had been served and only discovered at a much later date that it had not been. The case arose under the 1968 Act where service of the Notice could be excused altogether for "reasonable cause";[68] but, although that provision is no longer applicable, the reasoning of the court rejecting the claim is, it is submitted, still relevant:

> " . . . the giving of notice . . . is no mere formality. On the contrary, it is a matter of great importance for the reasons stated [by McGonigal LJ in *Moore* v *Secretary of State*[69]] . . . As well as the purpose of the legislation the possible prejudice to either side has to be considered."

Possible prejudice to the Secretary of State was the "deciding factor" in *Robinson* v *Secretary of State*,[70] another case under the 1968 Act. The applicant alleged that he had been assaulted in 1972, when he was four years old. The incident was not reported to the police apparently because A's father felt that it would be pointless to do so and he made no claim for

---

65. For details of this procedure, see above p 269.

66. *Hobbs* v *Sec of State*, Unreported, Cty Ct (Judge Curran), 30 Oct 1981.

67. Unreported, Cty Ct (Judge Rowland), 14 April 1978.

68. Section 1(3)(*e*).

69. [1977] NI 14, 16, quoted above, p 263.

70. Unreported, High Ct (McCollum J), 17 Nov 1989; [1990] 2 *BNIL* 25.

compensation because he did not know enough about the law to realise he could or should consult a solicitor. In 1982, however, A applied for compensation. McCollum J refused to grant an extension under section 10(2) of the 1968 Act (the predecessor of Article 16(6)(a) of the 1988 Order). The learned judge considered five factors to be relevant to the exercise of his discretion in relation to the late notice of intention to apply for compensation:

(i) *The age of the applicant.* "Unless it can clearly be shown that it would be unjust to the respondent to do so, the discretion should be exercised in favour of a minor to cover such period of time as would have given him a reasonable opportunity to bring proceedings after achieving his majority."[71] That period is now subject to the absolute bar imposed by Article 5(6) of the 1988 Order, by which an application in respect of an injury to a minor must be made at the latest "within three years from the date on which the victim attains the age of 18 years".[72]

(ii) *The reasons for failing to report the incident.* Good reasons for delay could be taken into account. But in this case, the explanation offered by A's father was "quite unconvincing" and did not in any way advance A's cause.

(iii) *The nature of the injury sustained.* "Obviously if serious permanent injuries were caused, and even more so if catastrophic injuries were caused or injuries which in any case would have affected the livelihood of the applicant, a court would lean towards exercising the discretion in his favour." In this case A's hand had been crushed down on a broken bottle; although the injury was "undoubtedly serious", it was "not such as to merit any special consideration" for A.

(iv) *The length of time since the incident.* Ten years is "an extremely prolonged period and of itself is so long as to incline the court very strongly towards refusing to exercise its discretion on the basis that it is now virtually impossible to investigate fairly the circumstances of this alleged criminal injury".

(v) *Injustice to the respondent.* The court has to consider the nature and cogency of the available evidence and determine whether the Secretary of State is in a proper position to defend the application. Had there been "objective evidence or any contemporary account . . . which would be helpful in identifying the truth", the learned judge "would have been swayed strongly towards allowing the application to proceed". But there was no such evidence and, therefore, the application had to be refused.

---

71. McCollum J noted that A's right to bring a civil action for damages would have continued until July 1989.

72. Discussed below, p 282.

The normal 28-day time-limit does not apply in two cases:

(i) Where the victim was an unborn child when the injury was sustained, the Notice of Intention is, by Article 5(7)(a), to be served on the Secretary of State "within three months from the date of birth of the child".

(ii) Where the victim of a criminal injury dies otherwise than as a result of the injury, Article 11(1)(b) provides that "so much of Article 5(4)(b) . . . as requires a notice to be served . . . within a specified time shall not apply" to an application for compensation by the victim's relatives or any person who incurred expenses as a result of the victim's injury.[73] In most of these cases a notice will in practice have been duly served by the victim himself; but the above wording suggests that if he had not done so for any reason, there is nevertheless *no* requirement for a Notice to be served by a would-be applicant, provided that a proper Application is duly made.

(d) Method of service

In all cases the Notice of Intention should be served on the Secretary of State by personal service or by registered or recorded delivery post, using the advice of delivery form.[74]

3. Application for Compensation

The third step in the procedure for making a claim is now governed by Article 4(1) of the 1988 Order, which provides simply that "An application for compensation shall be made in such manner as may be prescribed." By Article 2(2), "'prescribed' means prescribed by regulations made by the Secretary of State". No such regulations have been made, but two application forms have been issued by the Secretary of State, one (Form PI/2) for use where the victim is still alive, the other (Form PI/3) for cases where the victim has died. On receipt of a Notice of Intention, the Secretary of State sends the applicant or his solicitor two copies[75] of the appropriate form of application, and the procedure thereafter to be followed may be summarised as follows.

(a) Who may apply for compensation?

Article 4(2) of the 1988 Order provides that an application for compensation may be made by any person who may be entitled to compensation, *viz*

(i) where the victim has survived, by –
    (a) the victim himself;
    (b) any person responsible for the maintenance of the victim.

---

73. See further below, p 282.

74. Interpretation Act (NI) 1954, s 24(2).

75. One for the applicant's solicitor to retain, the other to be returned to the Northern Ireland Office.

(ii) Where the victim has died as a result of his injuries, by –

    (*a*) any of his relatives. By Article 4(2)(*a*) the application "may" be made by the victim's spouse on his or her own behalf and of such children as are "relatives" of the victim. By Article 4(2)(*b*), where there is no surviving spouse, the application may be made by such person "as may be prescribed". No person has been prescribed by regulations; in practice the application can be made by any relative entitled to compensation.

    (*b*) if he has no relatives, any person who has incurred expenses as a result of the victim's injury or death.

(iii) Where the victim has died otherwise than as a result of his injuries, by –

    (*a*) a relative. It would appear that Article 4(2)(*b*) again applies, so that if there is no surviving spouse, the application may be made by such person "as may be prescribed"; in practice, again, any relative entitled to compensation may apply.

    (*b*) any person who has incurred expenses as a result of the victim's injury

In addition to the above, the Order makes special provision for two further categories of applicant, *viz* where the victim or applicant is under a disability and where the right to apply for compensation has passed to another person.

By Article 4(2)(*b*), "where . . . the victim or other person entitled to apply for compensation is under a disability" the application may be made by such person "as may be prescribed". By Article 2(7) a person is under a disability while –

(*a*) he is a minor, or

(*b*) he is incapable, by reason of mental disorder within the meaning of Article 3 of the Mental Health (NI) Order 1986, of managing and administering his property and affairs.[76]

No persons have been formally prescribed to be applicants in such cases by regulations made by the Secretary of State; in practice the application form provides for an application by a victim under a disability to be made by the victim's parent, guardian "or other representative over 18 years of age".[77]

By Article 4(3):

"Where, by virtue of any assignment or act or event in the law, the right of any person to apply for or receive any compensation has passed to any other

---

76. Special rules also apply in England and Wales where the victim is a ward of court – see *Practice Direction (Fam D) (Wards: CICB)*, 10 December 1987 [1988] 1 All ER 182.

77. Cf *Child Abuse and the Criminal Injuries Compensation Scheme* (see 25th Annual Report (1988–89), p 39) advises: " . . . if the child has been subjected to abuse within the immediate family [application by a parent] may be impossible. If the child is in care the Board will expect the claim to be lodged by or on behalf of the authority to whom care has been granted. Usually the claim will be signed by the Director of Social Services or other responsible officer. In other cases the Board will look to the person having parental rights over the child for the time being."

person, that other person, or, if he is under a disability, the person appearing to the Secretary of State to be entitled to act on his behalf, may be treated as an applicant for the purposes of any provision of this Order."

(i) *Assignment*. Since a right of action in tort is not in general assignable,[78] it would appear that an applicant may not assign his right to apply for compensation under the 1988 Order.[79] But as with a common law action, he *may* assign the compensation to be recovered from the Secretary of State, and can do so before he makes the application or at any time before the compensation is paid to him.[80] As Salmond and Heuston observe:

> "This is not the assignment of an existing cause of action. It is merely the equitable assignment of future property defined or identified by reference to such a cause of action. It confers upon the assignee no right to institute or intervene in the action, and is therefore free from the objectionable element of maintenance."[81]

Given that what is involved here is *public* compensation paid to prevent undue hardship, it is arguable that the right to assign criminal injuries compensation should be more limited than in respect of *private* damages. But any such restriction would have to be expressly provided for by statute.[82] A form of involuntary assignment is provided for in Article 13(4).[83] *Voluntary* assignments of compensation might, for example, be made in favour of an insurance company which has paid out money in respect of the injury under a policy which does not have a provision for subrogation,[84] or in favour of a bank which has lent an applicant money on the strength of his application for compensation.

(ii) *Act or event in law*. The 1988 Order makes specific provisions for the situation where the victim dies as a result of his injury or otherwise and these have already been discussed.[85] What happens when an applicant other than the victim dies before he or she receives the compensation? With one exception the 1988 Order is silent on this point. Article 11(3) provides:

> "Where a person dies, any compensation or balance of compensation to which he was entitled immediately prior to his death in respect of [bereavement] . . . shall cease to be payable."[86]

78. See generally Crossley Vaines, *Personal Property* (5th ed, 1973), ch 11.

79. The leading tort case is *Defries* v *Milne* [1913] 1 Ch 98. *Cf Dawson* v *GNR Co* [1905] 1 KB 260 (claim for statutory compensation is assignable but only if it is not in the nature of a claim for damages against a wrongdoer). See also *Trendtex Trading Corp* v *Credit Suisse* [1981] 3 All ER 520.

80. See e.g. *Glegg* v *Bromley* [1912] 3 KB 474; *Laurent* v *Sale & Co* [1963] 2 All ER 63. A right to criminal damage compensation was apparently assigned in *Northern Bank Ltd* v *McNeill* [1987] 11 NIJB 1.

81. *The Law of Torts* (19th ed, 1987), pp 675–6.

82. *Cf* 1988 Act, s 117: "Every assignment . . . of, or charge on, an award of compensation . . . and every agreement to assign or charge such an award shall be void . . . ".

83. See above, p 148.

84. *King* v *Victoria Insurance Co* [1896] AC 250; *Compania Colombiana de Seguros* v *Pacific Steam Navigation Co* [1964] 1 All ER 216.

85. Above, pp 186 *et seq*.

86. Following Administration of Justice Act 1982, Sch 6, para 9 (amending to this effect the Law Reform (Miscellaneous Provisions) Act (NI) 1937, s 14).

This understandable provision appears, on the basis of *expressio unius exclusio alterius*, to permit or imply the survival for the benefit of the (non-victim) applicant's estate of the right to compensation in all other respects.[87] Any application commenced by the deceased should, therefore, be continued by his administrator or executor.

Bankruptcy also constitutes an "act or event in law". In the words of Winfield and Jolowicz:

> "One of the rules of bankruptcy law is that demands in the nature of unliquidated damages arising otherwise than by reason of a contract, promise or breach of trust are not provable. Hence, as actions in tort are usually for unliquidated damages . . . the right of action of the injured party ought [not] in general, to pass to the trustee in bankruptcy . . . "[88]

This is particularly the case where the tort is "a purely personal one" such as assault.[89] That being so, it would seem unlikely that an application for criminal injuries compensation, which is equally a "purely personal" matter, should pass to a trustee in bankruptcy.[90] The fact that the applicant's business has gone into liquidation may, however, have serious implications for the amount of compensation to which the applicant is entitled.

(b) *Form and content of Application*

As already indicated, separate application forms have been issued for (i) personal injury cases where the victim has survived, and (ii) where the victim has died. But each form requires the applicant to give information which is "true and complete to the best of my knowledge" on all matters relevant to his claim. He is asked specifically to confirm that the Notice of Intention gave a "full and true" account of the incident and for details of any new facts (such as the identity of the offender) which may be relevant. In personal injury cases further details are sought of the victim's injury and the medical treatment he has undergone. In all cases the applicant is requested to provide the necessary information for calculating the pecuniary loss and expenses which have resulted from the injury or death. Details must be given of any proceedings (past or intended) for damages arising out of the incident and whether the applicant has received compensation from any other source. Finally, the applicant must indicate whether the victim or the applicant (if a person other than the victim) has been convicted of a criminal

---

87. See also *Benson v Sec of State* [1976] NI 36, discussed above p 186. The Irish Scheme seems to be to the same effect, since the Civil Liability Act 1961, s 7(1) provides that "On the death of a person . . . all causes of action . . . vested in him shall [with certain exceptions] survive for the benefit of his estate." *Cf R v CICB, ex parte Tong* [1977] 1 All ER 171, 174, *per* Lord Denning MR: "[I]t is quite plain that the award of compensation under the [British] scheme is personal to the applicant. In that respect it is like damages for personal injuries at common law before the Law Reform Act 1934. *Actio personalis moritur cum persona.*"

88. *Tort* (12th ed, 1984), p 749.

89. *Ibid.* The devolution of tort claims is not affected by the Insolvency Act 1986 – see *Winfield and Jolowicz* (13th ed, 1989), p 733.

90. The 1988 Act, s 117 expressly so provides.

offence.[91] The applicant is then required to acknowledge his understanding that it is a criminal offence to give false or misleading information or to fail to disclose relevant information.

The form is therefore designed to provide the Secretary of State with all relevant information or to alert him to matters relevant to the application which require further investigation.[92] With the latter in mind, the form also obliges the applicant to authorise the Secretary of State to obtain further information from various specified sources and generally "from any other source [which may be able to provide] any information which is relevant to this application". The applicant also acknowledges that he understands that the Secretary of State may inform such sources of the application and his decision thereon.

Finally, the form requires the applicant to acknowledge his continuing responsibilities. He is required to state that he will inform the Secretary of State if there is any change in the details given, and to acknowledge his understanding that it is a criminal offence to fail to inform the Secretary of State if he receives other compensation or damages in respect of the injury or death.

(c) Time-limits

The general rule is laid down in Article 5(5):

> "No compensation shall be paid in respect of a criminal injury unless an application for compensation is made –
>
> (a) within 3 months from the date on which a notice [of intention to apply for compensation] is served on the Secretary of State . . . in relation to the application unless there was reasonable cause for not making the application within that period; and
>
> (b) within 3 years from the date on which the criminal injury was sustained."

The first part of this provision substantially replicates earlier legislation.[93] The general approach to the interpretation of "reasonable cause" was considered in *Hughes* v *Secretary of State*.[94] The "overriding consideration"

---

91. This is a new requirement prompted by the decision in *Reaney* v *Sec of State* Unreported, Cty Ct (Judge Russell), 3 Feb 1988. The Secretary of State sought reimbursement of compensation paid to an applicant for failure to make "full and true disclosure" of a material fact, *viz* that he had been convicted of a "terrorist" offence. The learned county court judge refused to make the order on the ground that neither the notice of intention nor the application form specifically required the applicant to give such information.

92. Under the 1977 Order the Application form was supplemented by a separate form of Evidence in Support of Application for Compensation, which was not required to be served by the applicant within three months. The amalgamation of the two forms under the 1988 Order means that *all* the relevant

information and evidence should be forwarded to the Secretary of State within the normal time-limit. The format of the new form means, however, that the applicant is no longer required to repeat much of the information given in the Notice of Intention.

93. 1968 Act, s 2(1); 1977 Order, Art 4(1)(*b*). *Cf* British Scheme, para 22 only requires the application to be made "as soon as possible after the event"; see also 1988 Act, Sch 7, para 4(1). The Irish Scheme, para 21 sets a three-month limit "except in circumstances determined by the Tribunal to justify exceptional treatment . . . " .

94. Unreported, Cty Ct (Judge Rowland), 14 April 1978, citing *Moore* v *Naval Colliery Co* [1912] 1 KB 28, *King* v *Port of London Authority* [1920] AC 1 and *Lackie* v *Merry* [1915] 3 KB 83.

is the reason advanced for not complying with the three-month requirement; whether this amounts to "reasonable cause" is a matter of law to be considered by the court by reference to all the circumstances, and in particular the purpose and general object of the legislation, the importance of complying with the statutory requirement and any possible prejudice which might result to *either* side. If the "cause" offered by the applicant is not considered reasonable by the Secretary of State, the applicant may apply to the county court for an extension of the time for making an application.[95]

The three-year limitation imposed by Article 5(5)(*b*) is new. Neither the 1968 Act nor the 1977 Order stipulated any period after which the right to make a claim was extinguished, although the power to extend the time for reporting to the police, serving a notice of intention and then making an application could result in the lapse of a substantial period before the substance of the application came to be considered.

The case for a limitation period similar to that applicable in claims for damages for personal injuries[96] was made in relation to the British Scheme in 1978:

> "Although in practice few applications are made as long as several years after the incident occurred, those which are received cause disproportionate work because of the difficulty of obtaining reliable statements or reports from witnesses. After several years, it is clearly more difficult to establish the facts, and the possibility that such applications will succeed is considerably diminished. We think it reasonable that there should be a limit of three years within which an application should be made."[97]

Such a limit was, therefore, introduced into the British Scheme in 1979[98] and the 1988 Order now follows suit, and not only for claims thereunder – by Schedule 2, paragraph 3(2):

> "No compensation shall be paid *under the 1977 Order* in respect of a criminal injury unless an application for compensation under that Order –
>
> (*a*) has been made before the coming into operation of this Order; or
>
> (*b*) is made within the period of 3 years beginning with the date on which the criminal injury was sustained."

In the British Scheme the Board may "in exceptional cases" waive this three-year limitation.[99] Such discretion is expressly prohibited under the 1988 Order, by Article 16(7)(*a*):

---

95. 1988 Order, Art 16(6)(*b*). The application is made on notice to the Secretary of State and in accordance with the County Court (Criminal Injuries to the Person) (Compensation) Rules (NI) 1988, r 12 – see above, p 269.

96. By Limitation (NI) Order 1989, Art 7.

97. 1978 *IWP Report*, para 5.8.

98. British Scheme, para 4. See also 1988 Act, Sch 7, para 2.

99. *Ibid*, on the recommendation of the Working Party, which considered that "This would be broadly in line with the principles of the Limitation Act 1975."

> "Nothing in this Article or in any other statutory provision shall authorise the county court to extend . . . the time referred to in Article 5(5)(b) for making an application."[1]

Such an absolute rule may give rise to injustice. Thus, an application was made in Great Britain by a widow whose husband had disappeared six years previously. His body was found in a shallow grave five and a half years later, and his widow then claimed compensation: "The Board had no difficulty in deciding that the three-year limit should be waived".[2] No such relief can be granted under the 1988 Order – unless, perhaps, on an *ex gratia* basis.

The 1988 Order also makes provision for three special time-limits:

(i) *Injury to minor*. By Article 5(6), where the victim was under the age of 18 years when the injury was sustained, the application should normally be made within the general time limit; it *must* be made within three years from the date on which the injury was sustained, "or, if there was reasonable cause for not making the application at any earlier time, within three years from the date on which the victim attains the age of 18 years."

(ii) *Injury to unborn child*. By Article 5(7)(b), where the victim was an unborn child when the injury was sustained, the application for compensation should normally be made within six months from the date of birth of the child, unless there was reasonable cause for not making the application within that period. In every case, the application must be made within three years from the date of birth of the child.[3]

(iii) *Where the victim dies otherwise than as a result of his injuries*. By Article 11(1)(b) where the victim of a criminal injury dies otherwise than as a result of the injury:

> "so much of Article 5(4)(b) and (5)(a) as requires a notice to be served or an application made within a specified time shall not apply to an application made by virtue of Article 3(4), but any such application shall be made within 3 months from the date of the victim's death unless there was good cause for not making the application within that period."

By Article 16(6)(b) this time-limit may be extended by the county court. But Article 5(5)(b) is apparently still applicable; this can make sense only if it is interpreted as barring any application not made within three years from the date on which the victim died.

---

1. Note that this provision does not prevent a county court from granting an extension of the initial three-month period within which an application should normally be made. Note further that in relation to criminal damage compensation it was accepted by the Court of Appeal in *Tansey* v *Sec of State* [1981] NI 193 that the county court has no *inherent* jurisdiction to extend the time for serving a preliminary notice: "the powers of the [county court] can only be found in the statute . . .".

2. CICB, *19th Annual Report* (1982–83), para 23.

3. Article 5(7)(c), which qualifies Art 5(5)(b) to this effect. Note that Art 5(5)(b) is also amended in relation to minor victims (see above) and that amendment might be argued to apply also to unborn children (giving a maximum limitation period of 21 years). But the drafting of the Order suggests that an unborn child is not to be considered for this purpose as "a victim . . . under the age of 18 years".

(d) Service of Application

As with the Notice of Intention, the Application for Compensation should be served on the Secretary of State by personal service or by registered or recorded delivery post, using the advice of delivery form.

EVIDENCE

1. Burden and Standard of Proof

The 1988 Order, like its predecessors, contains no *general* provision relating to the incidence of the legal burden of proof. In particular instances the onus is fairly clearly on the applicant; thus, in Article 5(2) compensation is not payable where a victim was living in the same household as the offender "unless the Secretary of State is satisfied" that certain conditions exist.[4] The Order also contains a number of presumptions: some of these are irrebuttable, as e.g. in Articles 2(3) and 13(4); others are rebuttable, as in Articles 7(3), 8(4) and 19(1)(*b*)(*i*). But the Order gives no general indication as to which party must prove what,[5] and it would appear reasonable to apply the general rule[6] that he who asserts must prove. This would mean in practice that it is for the applicant to establish that he is *prima facie* entitled to compensation and for the Secretary of State to establish any circumstance which leads to refusal or reduction of that compensation.[7] Thus, in *Cahill* v *Secretary of State*,[8] Lord Lowry LCJ observed:

> "I also accept the proposition that, once the victim has established a *prima facie* entitlement to compensation, the respondent must accept the burden [under section 1(2) of the 1968 Act] of showing that the victim is not entitled to recover . . . "

This statement has since been adopted in a number of cases,[9] and in *Smyth* v *Secretary of State*[10] was carried one stage further:

> "Where the respondent [i.e. the Secretary of State] is contending for a *reduction* of compensation . . . it seems to me that the burden is also upon him of showing that such a reduction should be made."

---

4. See also Art 5(15).

5. *Cf* British Scheme, para 25: "It will be for the applicant to make out his case at the hearing, and where appropriate this will extend to satisfying the Board that compensation should not be withheld or reduced under [various] terms [of the Scheme] . . . ". See further *Statement*, para 25. The Irish Scheme, para 26 states that "It will be for the claimant to establish his case".

6. See generally Cross, *Evidence* (6th ed, 1985), pp 110 *et seq*.

7. *Cf* "[Under the Criminal Injuries to Property (Compensation) Act (NI) 1971] the onus of proof is not placed on either party,

with the result that in practice it tends to be left to the NIO to prove unreasonableness . . . We regard this as wrong and consider that the onus . . . should rest squarely upon the applicant": *Report of a Committee to Review the Principles and Operation of the Criminal Injuries to Property (Compensation) Act (NI) 1971* (1976), para 131.

8. [1977] NI 53, 55.

9. See e.g. *Annesley* v *Sec of State* Unreported, High Ct (MacDermott J), 25 Oct 1984; *Mackie* v *Sec of State* [1986] 15 NIJB 1.

10. Unreported, Cty Ct (Judge Johnson), 28 Aug 1979.

Although made in relation to the 1968 Act, these statements appear equally applicable to the 1977 and 1988 Orders.[11] The incidence of the burden of proof may be particularly important in relation to Article 6(1) (provocative or negligent behaviour and criminal convictions indicative of the character of the victim or applicant). A similar provision in the 1969 British Scheme exercised the Divsional Court in *R* v *Criminal Injuries Compensation Board, ex parte Lloyd*,[12] where an applicant alleged that he had been injured in a fight. The Board rejected his claim, *inter alia*, because it was not satisfied that A had not started the fight. A sought judicial review of this decision on the grounds that the burden of proof on this issue did not lie on him. Lord Lane CJ agreed that he did not have the legal burden,[13] but added:

> "The legal burden must not be confused with the evidential burden. If there is *prima facie* evidence against the applicant . . . it is up to him to discharge the resulting evidential burden."

In the present case there was *prima facie* evidence that A might have started the fight and the court therefore held that the Board's decision to refuse compensation was not unfair or unreasonable.

The standard of proof would appear to be the normal civil standard of proof on the balance of probabilities.[14] This is indeed specified for one particular matter in Article 5(1) and, although this express reference might be taken to suggest a different standard in respect of other matters, this would be quite unprecedented[15] and contrary to established principles.[16]

2. Proof of Entitlement

Entitlement to compensation is normally proved in one or more of the following ways:

---

11. Both *Annesley* and *Mackie* (*supra* n 9) involved applications under the 1977 Order. See also *K* v *Sec of State* [1985] 6 *BNIL* 21 (A, injured by iron bar thrown by boy, not entitled to compensation because of failure to prove any criminal or reckless act). *Cf R* v *CICB, ex parte Sorrell*, Unreported, Div'l Ct, 2 March 1987.

12. Unreported, Div'l Ct, 4 July 1980 (but see CICB, *17th Annual Report* (1980–81), para 20(*b*)).

13. Note that in *Lloyd* the court did not go on to hold that the legal burden relating to matters of refusal or reduction lay with the Board, but rather accepted that the wording of paragraph 17 was neutral in this regard. However, the British Scheme was amended in 1979 to put the legal burden on the applicant – see now 1990 Scheme, para 25 (quoted above, n 5). But *cf* 1988 Act, s 112(2) appears to return to the 1969 position.

14. See e.g. *Black* v *Sec of State* Unreported, Cty Ct (Judge Rowland), 7 Nov 1975; *R* v *CICB, ex parte Crangle, The Times,* 14 Nov 1981. The 1988 Act, s 111(1) contains an express provision to this effect.

15. After some uncertainty this was established for criminal damage compensation claims in *Cavendish Ltd* v *Dublin Corp* [1974] IR 171, and was expressly written into the Irish Scheme, para 30.

16. See e.g. *Hornal* v *Neuberger Products Ltd* [1956] 3 All ER 970. But note *Bater* v *Bater* [1951] P 35, 37, *per* Denning LJ: "The case may be proved by a preponderance of probability . . . but [proof of a criminal charge] does require a degree of probability which is commensurate with the occasion". See also *M* v *Cain, The Times,* 15 Dec 1989 and *Dept of the Environment* v *Fair Employment Agency* [1989] 2 NIJB 13.

(a) Senior police officer's certificate

If the claim for compensation is being made in respect of a criminal injury caused by a person acting on behalf of or in connection with an unlawful association, the applicant will normally apply for a certificate as provided for in Article 8(3):

> "When a senior police officer[17] is of the opinion that any criminal injury was caused by a person acting on behalf of or in connection with an unlawful association he shall, if an applicant makes an application to him, issue to the applicant a certificate in the [prescribed] form . . . "[18]

Article 8(4) adds that such a certificate "shall, until the contrary is proved, be evidence" that the criminal injury to the person named in the certificate[19] was so caused. Although principally designed for use in establishing whether the applicant is entitled to unlimited compensation for pecuniary loss,[20] the certificate necessarily provides evidence that the applicant has suffered a criminal injury. In neither case, however, does the certificate provide conclusive evidence. Thus, in *Smith* v *Secretary of State*,[21] a certificate had been issued, but the applicant himself did not appear to give evidence. The court considered that the facts of the case were not clear and there was not sufficient evidence to establish what had happened. The onus was on the applicant to prove his case and the certificate by itself was not sufficient for this purpose. Although rebuttable, in certain cases the certificate will in practice be indefeasible, *viz* where, in accordance with Article 8(5), the senior police officer further certifies that it is in the public interest not to disclose the information on which the certificate is based. In theory it is open to the Secretary of State even in such cases to adduce rebutting evidence; in practice this opportunity is likely to be availed of only when the basis on which a certificate is issued can be disclosed for consideration by the court. In any such case it is presumably open to the Secretary of State to prove either that the applicant did not sustain a criminal injury or that, if he did,

---

17. By Art 8(6)(*b*), "'senior police officer' means a member of the Royal Ulster Constabulary of the rank of assistant chief constable or above." This effects no substantial change from the 1977 Order, which provided for a *Chief Constable's* Certificate, but in Art 2(2) defined "Chief Constable" as including an assistant chief constable and a deputy chief constable. Presumably the new formula is designed to allow for any modifications in the senior command of the RUC.

18. The "Chief Constable's certificate" was first introduced by the Criminal Injuries Act (NI) 1957, s 3. The form of the certificate (see now 1988 Order, Sch 1) has undergone some change from time to time but in this respect the 1988 Order is identical to Art 6 of the 1977 Order. *Cf* by 1968 Act, s 10(7) the certificate referred only to an "act" – as also the Criminal

Damage (Compensation) Order 1977, discussed *Greer and Mitchell*, p 302.

19. A claim for compensation by A cannot be founded on a certificate issued to B – see *Coyle* v *Sec of State* [1981] 5 *BNIL* 15. Further, a certificate issued in relation to a claim by B for compensation for criminal damage cannot be used as evidence in a later claim by A for criminal injuries compensation – see e.g. *Corbett* v *Sec of State* Unreported, High Ct (O'Donnell LJ), 22 May 1981 (court rejected use of certificate as evidence that A, who had been convicted of causing the damage for which B had claimed compensation, had thereby been involved in the commission of an act of terrorism).

20. See above p 175.

21. Unreported, Cty Ct (Judge Rowland), 1 Dec 1976.

that it was not caused by a person acting on behalf of or in connection with an unlawful association.

If a certificate is not issued, it would appear that the basis for that decision need not (and will not) be disclosed, and there is no procedure for appeal or for requiring the senior police officer to explain or justify his decision. It is, of course, open to the applicant to establish his case by other evidence.

(b) Police reports

In his Application for Compensation the applicant authorises the Secretary of State to obtain from the police all relevant information, including copies of any statements made in connection with the incident. Such an authorisation is probably strictly unnecessary. The whole basis of the scheme has long assumed the closest co-operation between the police and the Secretary of State in relation to its administration[22] and it is presumably because such co-operation has in practice been forthcoming that the 1988 Order, like its predecessors, contains no express provision *obliging* the police to give their assistance.[23] Indeed, information provided by the police plays a major role in determining whether an application for compensation is successful.

On receipt of an application the Secretary of State writes to the police requesting relevant information and, in particular, copies of any statements made to the police, the names of witnesses, comments on any relevant circumstances surrounding the incident itself and in the immediate aftermath thereof, details of the criminal record (if any) of the victim (or applicant) and whether any criminal proceedings have taken place in respect of an offence connected with the incident. The relevant information will in due course be given to the Secretary of State, and is normally regarded as confidential to him. It will normally be privileged from disclosure to the applicant[24] and may also be subject to public interest immunity.[25] However the police also complete for the Secretary of State a "Police Report of Alleged Criminal Injury to the Person", a copy of which *is* given to the applicant or his solicitor. This gives a brief summary of the facts relating to the incident as ascertained by the police, and states whether anyone has been convicted of an offence connected with the incident. If the victim has made a statement to the police, a copy will normally[26] be attached to the report. Although necessarily vague and incomplete, this report may in a

---

22. See especially Art 5(4)(a) and its predecessors.

23. *Cf* Criminal Damage (Compensation) (NI) Order 1977, Art 21(3): "Regulations . . . may require the Chief Constable to furnish to the Secretary of State such reports and information as the Secretary of State may require . . .", and see Criminal Damage (Compensation) (NI) Regulations 1978, reg 6. *Cp* 1986 *IWP Report*, para 23.9: "With regard to the police, if there had been any general problem relating to the supply of information it might have been necessary to

consider whether the police should be placed under a statutory duty to assist the Board . . . ".

24. See further below p 288.

25. See e.g. *Monaghan* v *Chief Constable of the RUC* [1988] 7 NIJB 16. See also *Neilson* v *Laugharne* [1981] 1 All ER 829 and *cf Peach* v *Comm'r of Police of the Metropolis* [1986] 2 All ER 129.

26. The police reserve the right to withhold the statement if it cannot be released at that stage e.g. because enquiries are still proceeding.

number of instances provide the applicant with some indication at least as to whether the police accept his version of the incident giving rise to his claim. We shall see below, however,[27] that the applicant may find it difficult to obtain more precise details of other evidence available to the police and thereby also to the Secretary of State.

(c) Applicant's own evidence

In most cases the applicant himself is the person best able to give evidence relating to the incident and he will usually do so in his report to the police and in the Notice of Intention and the Application to the Secretary of State. In theory the evidence of the applicant alone is sufficient to prove entitlement; in practice, such evidence will require to be supported by "independent" evidence:

> "There is no statutory requirement for corroboration in the technical sense, or even in the wider sense of supportive evidence. The tribunal of fact is nevertheless entitled to insist that it be satisfied that the event occurred as described [by the applicant] . . ."[28]

If the applicant's evidence is supported e.g. by the police report to the Secretary of State, there is likely to be little difficulty. The problem for the applicant will arise when there is no such support. Thus, in *McCourt* v *Secretary of State*,[29] an applicant claimed compensation for gunshot wounds to both legs. He alleged that he had been approached by masked men who pushed him into his own car and then shot him. The court concluded that the incident could not have occurred in the way the applicant suggested, given the nature of his injuries, the fact that no bullets were found and there were no strike marks on the car. His Honour Judge Higgins observed that it was not sufficient to rely on the evidence of the applicant alone and hope that the court would ignore any gaps in the testimony. On the other hand, in *McMaster* v *Secretary of State*,[30] the applicant had been shot outside a bar frequented by members of the UDA. The physical evidence and the applicant's own evidence indicated that there had been a two-sided shooting incident of some kind, but the applicant maintained that he had been an innocent bystander caught in the cross-fire. Although the learned judge felt that the way in which the applicant had presented his case gave rise to a strong suspicion that he was not telling the whole truth, nothing adverse to the applicant had been proved; on the state of the entire evidence the "assumptions" (sic) against the applicant were unwarranted. The applicant was, therefore, entitled to compensation in full.

It would appear that much may depend on whether the court treats the issue as one of *prima facie* entitlement (so that the burden of proof is on the applicant) or, being satisfied that the applicant has sustained a criminal injury, is dealing with the question whether compensation should be refused or reduced (so that the burden of proof is (or is at least more heavily) on the Secretary of State).

---

27. Pp 289 *et seq.*

28. *Per* MacDermott J in *Annesley* v *Sec of State*, Unreported, High Ct, 25 Oct 1984.

29. Unreported, Cty Ct (Judge Higgins), 22 Nov 1983.

30. Unreported, High Ct (Lord Lowry LCJ), 24 Sept 1981.

(d) Evidence of other witnesses

If the applicant can locate eye-witnesses to the incident and obtain statements from them, such statements can obviously provide cogent evidence in support of his own evidence. In some cases, however, the applicant may not be able to identify or locate all the relevant witnesses, but it may be that they have made statements to the police (which will, therefore, be available to the Secretary of State). This situation will cause the applicant little difficulty if the evidence of those witnesses tends to support his application. His position may be more problematical if that evidence does not support the applicant or positively conflicts with his version of the incident. The question may then arise as to whether the applicant can obtain details of the case against him in order to refute it, if possible. The 1988 Order, like its predecessors, contains no relevant provisions on this point, but it would appear than an applicant may in due course be able to invoke two general procedures.

By the County Court Rules (NI) 1981, Order 15, rule 1(1):

> "Any party to any proceedings may give notice in writing to any other party requiring him to make discovery on oath of the documents relating to any question in the proceedings which are or have been in his possession or power . . . "

Further, by Order 15, rule 2(1):

> "Any party to any proceedings may at any time give to the other party notice to produce any document in his possession or power which is relevant to the issues, for the inspection of the party giving the notice and to permit him to take copies thereof."

The term "any proceedings" appears to include criminal injury compensation appeals and "party" includes the Crown.[31] It may be noted, however, that the rules refer only to any party to "the proceedings", so that (unlike certain personal injury cases[32]) discovery is not available against non-parties (such as the RUC).[33] In addition, discovery is a matter for the discretion of the court and "shall not be ordered if and so far as the judge is of the opinion that it is not necessary either for disposing fairly of the proceedings or for saving costs".[34] In the exercise of this discretion the court may have regard (*inter alia*) to the confidentiality of the information, the sensitivity of the type of information concerned and the extent to which the interests of third parties may be affected by disclosure.[35] It may, therefore, be difficult for an applicant to show that disclosure is necessary for disposing fairly of the proceedings.

In any event, many of the relevant documents are likely to be covered by legal professional privilege, which has been held to apply to salaried legal

---

31. Crown Proceedings Act 1947, s 28.

32. *Cf* Administration of Justice Act 1970, ss 32, 34.

33. For general discussion of Order 15, see Valentine and Glass, *County Court Pro-* *cedure in Northern Ireland* (1985), ch 11.

34. *CCR*, O 15, r 1(4).

35. See especially *Science Research Council* v *Nassé* [1979] 3 All ER 673.

advisers such as the solicitors employed by the Secretary of State.[36] As a result communications between those solicitors and the RUC (and other bodies) will be privileged in so far as they were made "for the purpose of pending or contemplated litigation".[37] Since those communications will be made only after an applicant has applied for compensation, and for the purposes of determining that application, that condition will normally be satisfied. However, the privilege extends only to documents brought into existence for the "dominant" purpose of litigation.[38] This qualification might give rise to some uncertainty as regards original documents such as witness statements obtained for other purposes such as the investigation of crime. In such cases, however, what is supplied to the Northern Ireland Office will be a copy, not the original, and that copy may be privileged as having itself been made for the purpose of the proceedings.[39] This analysis appears to be supported by the decision in *Duffy* v *Secretary of State*,[40] where the applicant claimed compensation for injuries received in an assault. The police had investigated the incident, taken statements from witnesses and supplied copies of these statements to the Secretary of State in connection with the application for compensation. The county court judge refused to grant discovery of the statements to the applicant. It has to be said, however, that the matter is a technical and complex one which awaits an authoritative decision of the High Court or Court of Appeal. On the other hand, legal professional privilege may be waived by the client[41] – in this case by the Secretary of State – and in this context reference may be made to the practice of the Criminal Injuries Compensation Board in England and Wales. This arose for consideration in *R* v *Chief Constable of Cheshire, ex parte Berry*,[42] where B, an applicant for criminal injuries compensation, sought an order of mandamus requiring the Cheshire police to disclose to him in advance copies of statements made by witnesses to an incident in which B had been injured, together with details of the criminal record (if any) of those witnesses. Differences in the procedure of the Board make the analysis of B's claim inconclusive from a Northern Ireland perspective, but the case nevertheless

---

36. *Alfred Crompton Amusement Machines Ltd* v *Customs and Excise Commrs* [1972] 2 All ER 353, 376, *per* Lord Denning MR [this point was not queried in the subsequent appeal to the House of Lords]; *Geraghty* v *Minister of Local Govt* [1975] IR 300.

37. See generally Cross, *Evidence* (6th ed, 1985), ch 12, s 2; Style and Hollander, *Documentary Evidence* (1984), Part III; Phipson, *Evidence* (13th ed, 1982), ch 15, s 1.

38. *Waugh* v *British Railways Board* [1979] 2 All ER 1169, considered in *Hughes* v *Law* [1988] 12 NIJB 30 and *Downey* v *Murray* [1988] 13 NIJB 84. For the Irish law see e.g. *Silver Hill Duckling Ltd* v *Min for Agriculture* [1987] IR 289.

39. As in *O'Sullivan* v *Herdman's Ltd* [1986] 8 NIJB 51 (copy of document obtained for purposes of litigation privileged even though

original *not* privileged). But *cf Dubai Bank Ltd* v *Galadari* [1989] 3 All ER 769 (original affidavit not privileged, therefore copy of affidavit not privileged even though made for purpose of obtaining legal advice) and (to the same effect) *Tromso Sparebank* v *Beirne* [1989] ILRM 257.

40. Unreported, Cty Ct (Judge Brown), 6 Oct 1981.

41. See e.g. Cross, *op cit* m 37, p 397. *Cf Downey* v *Murray, supra.*

42. Unreported, QBD (Nolan J), 30 July 1985 (evidence of the Board's procedure was given by its Chairman). See also *R* v *CICB, ex parte Brady, The Times*, 11 March 1987 (and see CICB, *23rd Annual Report* (1986–87), para 54) and *R* v *CICB, ex parte Gould*, Unreported, Div'l Ct, 16 Feb 1989.

merits consideration. In England and Wales, an applicant whose claim has been rejected by a single member of the Board may apply for a hearing of his case by a three-member panel. On the morning of the hearing (or, in some cases, during the hearing itself), the applicant *will* be shown copies of witness statements and details of the criminal record (if any) of those witnesses. At the applicant's request the hearing may then be adjourned to give him adequate time to study this information before the case is heard. The Board, however, retains custody and control of the statements and recovers them from the applicant before he leaves. Two reasons are given in support of this practice:

(i) The need to preserve confidentiality.
(ii) The belief that if an applicant was given earlier access to the statements he might adapt his evidence to avoid any criticism of his conduct that might be contained therein.

In *Berry*, Nolan J rejected B's claim, and in doing so concluded that the lateness of the disclosure of the statements to the applicant, in the context of the Board's practice at hearings, did not conflict with the rules of natural justice. The reasons given by the Board in support of its procedure appear equally important in Northern Ireland. Nonetheless, and although it is clear that there are significant procedural differences between the two schemes, it is submitted that the Board's practice of limited disclosure suggests that there is some basis for a rather more flexible approach in this regard by the Secretary of State in Northern Ireland.

However, apart from any question of privilege, the information provided to the Secretary of State may be subject to public interest immunity, and this cannot be waived by any party.[43]

If the evidence is not obtainable from the Secretary of State, may it be obtained instead directly from the RUC? The current practice of the police in Northern Ireland appears to be that they will normally provide an applicant only with a copy of his own statement. Requests by an applicant for copies of witness statements by "civilians" will not normally be acceded to unless the maker of the statement has expressly given his consent to the statement being forwarded to other interested parties. In the case of police officers, an applicant will, on payment of the requisite fee, be supplied with copies of statements of fact relating to the occurrence which can be proved by members of the RUC. But in all such cases it must be considered that the applicant has given adequate reasons for acquiring the statements and that their provision would not be objectionable on grounds of public policy or amount to a breach of confidence.[44] The reasonableness or otherwise of this practice is susceptible to judicial review – according to Nolan J in *Berry*,[45] Chief Constables come within the class of persons described by Lord

---

43. See e.g. *Air Canada* v *Sec of State for Trade (No 2)* [1983] 1 All ER 910, 917, *per* Lord Fraser. Public interest immunity is discussed briefly below, pp 291–2.

Monaghan v *Chief Constable of the RUC* [1988] 7 NIJB 16 (statements of police and civilian witness produced to plaintiff in action against police for alleged assault).

44. Information supplied by RUC. See e.g.

45. *Supra* n 42.

Diplock in *O'Reilly* v *Mackman*[46] as "having legal authority to determine questions affecting the common law or statutory rights or obligations of other persons as individuals". A decision not to disclose a witness statement could affect an applicant's statutory right to compensation and such a decision therefore is amenable –

> " . . . to the remedy of an order to quash [the] decision either for error of law in reaching it or for failure to act fairly towards the person who will be adversely affected by the decision by failing to observe either one or other of the two fundamental rights accorded to him by the rules of natural justice or fairness, *viz* to have afforded to him a reasonable opportunity of learning what is alleged against him and of putting forward his own case in answer to it . . . "[47]

In *Berry* the Cheshire police drew a distinction between statements made by "civilian" witnesses and those made by police witnesses. Copies of the former were supplied to the applicant if the maker had given his written consent for this to be done; but the police refused outright to disclose statements made by police officers.[48] They also refused to give B details of any criminal records relating to any of the witnesses. As indicated above, however, copies of all the statements and criminal records had been supplied to the Criminal Injuries Compensation Board on the basis that the Board would disclose them to the applicant, albeit only on the morning of the hearing. Nolan J was satisfied that the police had not acted perversely – on the contrary, "the reasonableness of the general policy of preserving the confidentiality of witness statements (and lists of convictions) is . . . indisputable".[49]

But overriding all these considerations is the question of public interest immunity – that the documents are being withheld by the Secretary of State or the Chief Constable on the ground that their production would be contrary to the public interest.[50] Indeed, specific provision for the application of this principle is made in Article 8(5) of the 1988 Order in relation to the information on which a senior police officer's certificate has been issued. The precise scope of the public interest immunity is not settled,[51] nor is its particular application to documents and other material relevant to the determination of an application for criminal injuries compensation.[52] It would appear, however, that there is no general public interest which

---

46. [1982] 3 All ER 1124.

47. *Ibid*, p 1130.

48. However A was offered facilities to interview the police officers concerned, on proof that civil proceedings (or apparently criminal injury compensation proceedings) had been commenced.

49. The learned judge considered that "ample support" for this conclusion could be found in the judgment of the Court of Appeal in *Neilson* v *Laugharne* [1981] 1 All ER 829.

50. See generally Cross, *Evidence* (6th ed, 1985), pp 413–425; Phipson, *Evidence* (13th

ed, 1982), ch 14 and Archbold, *Pleading, Evidence and Practice in Criminal Cases* (43rd ed, 1988), ch 12.

51. "The categories of public interest are not closed and must alter from time to time whether by restriction or extension as social conditions and social legislation develop." *D* v *NSPCC* [1977] 1 All ER 589, 605, *per* Lord Hailsham LC. See generally Cross, *loc cit*.

52. Since copies of the statements would be disclosed to A on the morning of the hearing, the question whether they could be withheld in the public interest from disclosure to A did not arise in *Berry*.

requires blanket non-disclosure e.g. of statements made by witnesses to the police.[53] But the possibility of disclosure of some statements or other information could in a particular case either hamper the work of the police in their investigation of crime and of circumstances relevant to an application for compensation,[54] or inhibit the Secretary of State in the fulfilment of his public duty in determining applications.[55] It seems likely therefore that the Secretary of State and the RUC will continue to adopt a cautious approach in practice. This matter is one which can only be resolved satisfactorily by the courts on a case-by-case basis.

(e) Other evidence

(i) *Conviction of criminal offence.* Article 19(1)(a) of the 1988 Order replicates an earlier provision:[56]

> "The fact that a person has been convicted of an offence by or before any court[57] in the British Islands[58] shall be admissible in evidence for the purpose of proving the acts, omissions or conduct on which the conviction[59] was based, whether he was so convicted upon a plea of guilty or otherwise,[60] but no conviction other than a subsisting conviction shall be admissible in evidence . . . "

This provision is similar to the general provision for civil proceedings contained in the Civil Evidence Act (NI) 1971,[61] but is broader in one

---

53. Thus, in *Monaghan* v *Chief Constable of the RUC* [1988] 7 NIJB 16, 17 no objection was taken to the production to a plaintiff in an action for alleged assault of statements made by civilian and police witnesses of the incident. See also *Peach* v *Comm'r of Police of the Metropolis* [1986] 2 All ER 129 and *Tipene* v *Apperley* [1978] NZLR 761.

54. See e.g. *Evans* v *Chief Constable of Surrey* [1989] 2 All ER 594 (police report to DPP immune from disclosure on grounds of public interest). In *Monaghan, supra*, Hutton J held that it was not in the public interest that certain reports prepared by police officers investigating the alleged assault be produced to the plaintiff, but only because the plaintiff had failed to establish that the reports were "very likely" to contain material which would give him "substantial support" and that without them he might be deprived of "the means of . . . proper presentation" of his case. In a second application heard with *Monaghan* the learned judge did order that certain police investigation reports should be produced.

55. See e.g. *Alfred Crompton Amusement Machines Ltd* v *Comm'rs of Customs and Excise (No 2)* [1973] 2 All ER 1169; *Neilson* v *Laugharne* [1981] 1 All ER 829.

56. 1977 Order, Art 18(1), which substantially re-enacted 1968 Act, s 10(4).

57. By Art 19(2), "'court' includes a court-martial".

58. "The United Kingdom, the Channel Islands, the Isle of Man and the Republic of Ireland": Interpretation Act (NI) 1954, s 43(1). Thus convictions for offences committed in Northern Ireland but tried in courts in the Republic under the Criminal Law (Jurisdiction) Act 1976 are admissible in evidence.

59. By Art 19(2) " 'conviction' includes, notwithstanding section 8 of the Probation Act (NI) 1950, a conviction for an offence in respect of which an order is made under that Act placing the offender on probation or discharging him absolutely or conditionally."

60. By Art 19(2), "subsisting conviction" includes "where a conviction for an offence has been replaced on appeal by a conviction for another offence, the conviction for that other offence". A conviction subject to appeal is subsisting – see *Re Raphael* [1973] 3 All ER 19, but the determination of a criminal injuries application to which the criminal case was material would normally be postponed or adjourned pending the outcome of the appeal.

61. Section 7, following legislation in England and Wales implementing the recommendations of the Law Reform Committee, *Fifteenth Report on the Rule in Hollington* v *Hewthorn* (Cmnd 3391, 1967). *Cf* Police and Criminal Evidence (NI) Order 1989, Arts 71–73.

respect. The 1988 Order refers to the conviction as providing evidence of "the acts, omissions or conduct" on which the conviction was based, whereas the 1971 Act refers only to the conviction as "being admissible" in evidence for the purpose of proving . . . that [the person] committed that offence . . . ". This distinction suggests that in criminal injuries cases the conviction may be used as evidence of acts, etc necessarily accepted in relation to the conviction, in addition to the conviction itself. Thus if D's defence of provocation to a charge of the murder of V was accepted and he was convicted of manslaughter, the conviction is apparently evidence both that V died as the result of a crime of violence and that he was guilty of provocative behaviour.

The restrictions on the use of "spent" convictions imposed by Article 5(1) of the Rehabilitation of Offenders (NI) Order 1978 do not apply to proceedings in respect of an application for criminal injuries compensation.[62]

Article 19(1)(a) makes it clear (as does section 7(2) of the 1971 Act) that the conviction is not *conclusive* evidence, but is simply "admissible . . . as evidence". As Cross points out,[63] the Court of Appeal in *Stupple* v *Royal Insurance Co*[64] expressed different views on the weight to be attached to such evidence; he suggests however that the evidence arising from the conviction will only "give way to evidence establishing the contrary on the balance of probability".[65]

Details of a conviction are outlined in a Certificate of Conviction from the relevant court. This gives only the "bare bones" – the offence(s) charged, whether the defendant pleaded guilty or not guilty, and the sentence imposed by the court. Should further information be required in the case of conviction following trial on indictment, it may be possible to obtain copies of the depositions taken on the preliminary investigation. Alternatively, the investigating police officer – or the applicant himself – may be asked for further details.

As in the general law,[66] an acquittal is not normally admissible as evidence of any matter of fact material to a criminal injuries application; but the evidence tendered at proceedings which result in an acquittal is admissible and may have greater probative value because of the outcome of the proceedings. Thus, in *R* v *Criminal Injuries Compensation Board, ex parte Lloyd*,[67] the applicant was injured in a fight which he alleged had been

---

62. Rehabilitation of Offenders (Exceptions) Order (NI) 1979, Art 4 and Sch III, para 15. *Cf* "We would expect the Board to comply with the spirit of the legislation in taking these convictions into account": 1978 *IWP Report*, para 17.9.

63. *Evidence* (6th ed, 1985), pp 99–100.

64. [1970] 3 All ER 230.

65. *Per* Buckley LJ at p 239. *Cf* Lord Denning MR at p 236. The reference here is to the equivalent of Art 19(b), but it is suggested that a similar approach is applicable to Art 19(a). Cross adds: "The House of Lords has affirmed [in *Hunter* v *Chief Constable of West Midlands* [1981] 3 All ER 727, 735–6] that the burden is the ordinary civil one, but nonetheless characterised as 'uphill' the task of a defendant to persuade the court of the contrary of a verdict beyond reasonable doubt."

66. Cross, *op cit*, pp 102–3. See e.g. *Collins* v *Sec of State* [1981] 5 *BNIL* 16 (criminal damage case).

67. Unreported, Div'l Ct, 4 July 1980 (see CICB, *17th Annual Report* (1980–81), para 20(b)).

started by two other men. They had been prosecuted for assault but the prosecution accepted pleas of not guilty to that charge on the basis that it was by no means clear that they had not acted in reasonable self-defence. Evidence was given to the Criminal Injuries Compensation Board by the applicant and by the police officer who had taken statements from the two men; the applicant's claim was rejected.[68]

(ii) *"Accident" reports*. If the applicant has been injured in an incident arising out of and in the course of his employment, an "accident" report may have been completed by his employers. Subject to any claim of privilege,[69] a copy of this report may be tendered in evidence in relation to a claim for criminal injuries compensation arising out of the incident.

(iii) *Reports from private investigators*. It is open either to the applicant himself or to the Secretary of State to employ private investigators to obtain additional evidence in relation to an application. Thus, in *Keyes v Secretary of State*,[70] some of the medical evidence apparently led the Secretary of State to suspect that an applicant, now living in the Republic, was malingering. Private investigators were employed to visit the applicant and they discovered that the applicant, who claimed that she was completely deaf, could hear perfectly well!

3. Evidence of Circumstances leading to Reduction or Refusal of Compensation

The circumstances in which the compensation to which an applicant is *prima facie* entitled may be reduced or refused have been considered in Chapter 3. The burden of proving such circumstances generally lies with the Secretary of State[71] and we consider here briefly the sources of evidence which may be available for this purpose.

The routine request by the Secretary of State to the police for a report on the incident for which compensation has been claimed asks specifically whether there was any provocative act or negligent behaviour by the applicant and generally provides the police with an opportunity to make "any other observations arising from the incident". Any such information will normally have to amount to evidence admissible in court – rumour and opinion will not suffice. Thus, in *McCleery v Secretary of State*[72] – a suspected "punishment shooting" case – the police intimated that intelligence reports showed that the applicant had associations with an illegal organisation. The court observed however that the probative value of this evidence had to be

---

68. The Divisional Court, relying on *R v Deputy Industrial Injuries Commission, ex parte Moore* [1965] 1 All ER 81, held that the Board could accept hearsay evidence and that to do so in this case would not be unfair to the applicant or contrary to the rules of natural justice. Such a course would not generally be open to the courts in Northern Ireland.

69. See e.g. *Waugh v BRB* [1979] 2 All ER 1169.

70. [1979] 4 NIJB.

71. See above, p 283.

72. Unreported, Cty Ct (Judge Rowland), 11 July 1977.

regarded as "fairly small" and "not determinative" of the present case. It would appear, however, that the courts are bound by the technical rules of evidence even in circumstances where the evidence tendered does have some clear probative value.[73]

The police will also provide the Secretary of State with the criminal record (if any) of the victim or the applicant, and the use of convictions as evidence of matters of fact has already been discussed. If the formal record does not contain the necessary detail, further particulars can usually be obtained by direct evidence from the investigating officers. If necessary, the applicant himself can be asked to give further details;[74] if he does not do so to the satisfaction of the Secretary of State, this may constitute a "relevant circumstance" for the purposes of Article 6(1).[75]

The applicant's own evidence in his report to the police or in his application for compensation may also provide relevant information or at least suggest lines of enquiry to be followed up by the Secretary of State. The applicant can be requested to provide further particulars and ultimately, if the case is appealed to the courts, the applicant can be cross-examined on his testimony. Thus, in *McNamee* v *Secretary of State*,[76] Hutton J, "observing the appellant giving his evidence", was satisfied that he was lying on a particular point and added: "The fact that the appellant lied [on that point] gives rise to a strong inference that he was in the area [where the incident occurred] for some reason which he wished to conceal from the court". The fact that the appellant had lied in court on an important point was held to constitute a "relevant circumstance" justifying rejection of his application.

Out-of-court statements by the victim may also be adduced in evidence. In *Smyth* v *Secretary of State*[77] the applicant's husband had given interviews to the BBC and to a newspaper some two months before his murder. In those interviews he was described as a spokesman for the UDA and made outspoken remarks which the court held were "provocative". The court held further, however, that the Secretary of State had not established that his provocative conduct had contributed to the victim's death.

4. Evidence relating to the Assessment of Compensation

In broad terms the evidence required to establish the amount of compensation payable to an applicant falls into two categories, *viz* (a) medical evidence, and (b) evidence of financial loss.

---

73. *Cf* British Scheme, para 25: "The Board will be entitled to take into account any relevant hearsay, opinion or written evidence, whether or not the author gives oral evidence at the hearing." See e.g. *R* v *CICB, ex parte Lloyd* Unreported, Div'l Ct, 4 July 1980. "This system appears to work well and we propose no change":1986 *IWP Report*, para 23.7. See also 1988 Act, Sch 7, para 4(2)(*d*).

74. As e.g. in *McLaughlin* v *Sec of State*

Unreported, Cty Ct (Acting Judge Nicholson), 18 Jan 1984.

75. *Cf* CICB, *16th Annual Report* (1979–80), para 18 (A refused to give Board details of conviction for arson: application for compensation rejected).

76. [1982] NI 279.

77. Unreported, Cty Ct (Judge Johnson), 28 Aug 1979. But see Valentine and Glass, *County Court Procedure in Northern Ireland* (1985), para 15.29.

(a) Medical evidence

Extensive provision for obtaining medical evidence is made by Article 5(3) of the 1988 Order:

> "No compensation shall be payable if the victim fails, without reasonable cause –
>
> (a) to undergo any medical examination which he may be required by the Secretary of State to undergo;
>
> (b) to produce or cause or permit to be produced to the Secretary of State any medical records, X-rays or other documents relating to his injury or medical history which the Secretary of State may require to be produced, or
>
> (c) to produce or cause or permit to be produced to the Secretary of State any medical report relating to his injury obtained by or on behalf of the victim in contemplation of or for the purpose of an application for compensation or civil proceedings."

Paragraphs (a) and (b) re-enact earlier provisions,[78] but (c) is new, and is apparently designed to "overrule" judicial interpretation of those provisions. In *Porter* v *Scott*[79] S, the defendant in a common law action for negligence, sought discovery of a medical report from the plaintiff P. That report had been made in connection with an application by P for criminal injuries compensation and P contended that it was therefore privileged from disclosure.[80] Kelly J held that the report had initially been privileged but that that privilege had been waived by P when the report had become the agreed medical report in the criminal injury proceedings.[81] The report had been forwarded by P's solicitors to the Crown Solicitor's Office (the predecessor of the Compensation Division of the Northern Ireland Office) in an effort to get it agreed and thus avoid the necessity of calling medical witnesses. Kelly J was satisfied that the privilege originally attaching to the report was waived as between P and the Crown Solicitor[82] when the report was sent to his office and *a fortiori* when it became the agreed report in the proceedings. This finding made it strictly unnecessary for the learned judge to decide whether section 1(3)(d)(ii) of the 1968 Act had in any case removed the privilege in criminal injury compensation proceedings, but he nonetheless observed:

---

78. Paragraph (a) is identical to Art 3(2)(c)(i) of the 1977 Order, which in turn re-enacted s 1(3)(d)(i) of the 1968 Act; para (b) re-enacts Art 3(2)(c)(ii) of the 1977 Order and s 1(3)(d)(ii) of the 1968 Act. Cf British Scheme, para 6(b) and 1988 Act, s 112(1)(b) simply requires an applicant to give the Board "all reasonable assistance". See to the same effect Irish Scheme, para 11.

79. [1979] NI 6.

80. For the scope of this kind of legal profes-

sional privilege see e.g. Cross, *Evidence* (6th cd, 1985), pp 390–2, and above, pp 288–289.

81. The waiver was *not* a qualified one limited to the criminal injury compensation proceedings and the medical report was therefore not a privileged document for the purpose of the common law proceedings.

82. The learned judge found as a fact that P had not sent the report to the Crown Solicitor's office in fulfilment of an obligation under s 1(3)(d)(ii).

"My view is that this subsection was not intended to include medical reports made in contemplation of or for the purpose of litigation. Its aim was to make available to the Ministry (now the Secretary of State for Northern Ireland) those documents relating to the hospitalisation of the claimant e.g. the admission and examination notes made in hospital, records of surgical and laboratory investigations made there, X-rays taken there, records of hospital treatment as an in-patient and out-patient . . . And it would seem that the purpose of the subsection was merely to afford an alternative proof to a medical examination of the victim on behalf of the Ministry . . . that an injury had in fact been sustained by the victim . . . [I]f it had been the intention to abrogate privilege from medical reports made in contemplation of litigation arising under the statute the legislation would have done so not in an oblique nor implied way but in express terms . . . "[83]

This (*obiter*) view was accepted as correct in *Hughes* v *Secretary of State*.[84] Following an explosion A suffered a depressive illness and applied for compensation. She obtained a psychiatric report "for the purpose of advancing [her] claim . . . and in contemplation thereof". When A refused to disclose this report, the Secretary of State contended that she was obliged to do so under the 1977 Order. His Honour Judge Russell disagreed:

"I consider that the view of [Kelly J in *Porter* v *Scott*] . . . ought to be given full weight . . . and ought to be followed. I consider further that the clear opinion of Kelly J provides the appellant with "reasonable cause" in the words of Article 3(2)(c) for not producing [this] report."

The Northern Ireland Office apparently considered that as a result of this decision an applicant need only submit to it medical reports obtained for the purpose of the application which were favourable to the applicant. On the other hand the 1977 Order already gave the Secretary of State extensive (and some might have thought sufficient) powers to obtain medical evidence relating to an applicant, including the power to require the applicant to undergo a special medical examination. Be that as it may, the 1988 Order now "in express terms" enables the Secretary of State to override the normal privilege attaching to medical reports obtained by an applicant in contemplation or for the purpose not only of an application for criminal injuries compensation but also of common law proceedings. Unlike Article 5(3)(b), however, paragraph (c) applies only to "any medical report relating to [the applicant's] injury"; privilege may apparently still attach to earlier reports forming part of the applicant's medical *history*. Thus, although *Hughes* is clearly superseded, there is room for argument should the converse of *Porter* v *Scott* arise.

Such legal issues rarely arise in practice. In his Application for Compensation the applicant not only gives brief details of any medical treatment he has received for his injury, but also authorises the Secretary of State to obtain any relevant medical records and reports from any doctor, dentist, consultant or hospital attended by the victim. In the first instance such medical

---

83. [1979] NI 6, 10.

84. Unreported, Cty Ct (Judge Russell), 31 May 1985.

evidence is forwarded by the applicant;[85] it is only if further information is required that the Secretary of State will himself request it. In some cases (particularly "nervous shock" claims) the applicant will be required to attend for examination by a doctor or consultant nominated by the Secretary of State. It appears to be the general policy of the Secretary of State to agree medical reports where possible. If reports cannot be agreed the Secretary of State will issue a notice of determination and, if the applicant appeals, the relevant medical witnesses will give oral evidence in court.

In most cases the medical evidence is clear and straightforward, but difficulties can arise both in relation to diagnosis (particularly where the applicant has a prior medical history which makes it difficult to assess whether or to what extent his present condition was caused by the incident in question) and prognosis. A good example of the complexities which may arise is *Rainey* v *Secretary of State*,[86] where oral evidence was given by two physicians and two psychiatrists, and agreed written reports were obtained from three other medical practitioners. The applicant was a security man at a bank when it was robbed by armed men. The applicant claimed that in the course of the robbery he sustained a "whiplash" injury to his neck which had since kept him out of work. The Secretary of State accepted that the applicant had indeed received a whiplash injury, but did not accept that the applicant's subsequent condition was wholly attributable to this injury. Three issues arose for decision by the court; (a) whether the applicant's symptoms were referable to an organic cause, or whether there was functional overlay, either consciously or unconsciously motivated; (b) whether loss of earnings since the incident were attributable solely to the criminal injury or whether the applicant would have become unemployed in any event by reason of a heart condition totally unconnected with the robbery, and (c) whether the applicant's subsequent depression was a consequence of the criminal injury. The learned judge had, therefore, to examine the medical evidence carefully in order to distinguish those aspects of the applicant's medical condition which had been established on the balance of probabilities to be attributable to the criminal injury from those which had not been so established. Carswell J found that the applicant's heart condition would in any event have compelled him to cease employment some six months after the robbery and that the applicant's description of the symptoms of the whiplash injury was "considerably motivated by the claim for compensation . . . ". Further, an examination of the applicant's medical history before the robbery showed that the applicant had suffered to quite a material degree from psychiatric symptoms of depression long before the criminal injury, with the result that the learned judge was not satisfied that the depression from which the applicant now suffered was a reactive depression attributable to a criminal injury. However, Carswell J accepted

---

85. The applicant's solicitor is asked to arrange for the medical examination of the applicant and to forward the report to the Secretary of State. Production of the victim's up-to-date medical records, as well as the records for a period of 3–5 years prior to the injury, is also normally required. If the applicant's claim is successful, "reasonable costs and expenses" incurred in obtaining such evidence will be paid by the Secretary of State.
86. Unreported, High Ct (Carswell J), 18 Sept 1987.

that the whiplash injury brought about by the robbery had genuinely caused the applicant symptoms of a painful and incapacitating kind and awarded compensation for pain and suffering of £10,000, plus a small amount for loss of six months' earnings.

Keyes v *Secretary of State*[87] provides another example of a difficult medical issue. The applicant claimed compensation *inter alia* for deafness caused by an explosion. The applicant testified that she was completely deaf in both ears, and, with one exception, this was supported by a number of medical specialists. Compensation on this basis was awarded at the county court – but it subsequently became clear that the applicant had been able for some time to hear without any difficulty, and had in fact successfully deceived the medical specialists who had examined her for the purposes of her application. Accordingly, her compensation was substantially reduced by the High Court.

It should perhaps finally be noted that Article 5(3) of the 1988 Order does permit an applicant to withhold medical evidence where he has "reasonable cause" to do so. Apart from *Hughes*, which has already been discussed, there appear to have been no criminal injuries compensation cases on this point, although in *Farrell* v *Secretary of State*[88] Gibson LJ drew attention to the importance of this aspect of the legislation.

(b) Evidence of financial loss

In his Application for Compensation an applicant will indicate whether he is making any claim for pecuniary loss resulting from his injury (or the death of the victim) and authorises the Secretary of State to obtain from his employers information about his earnings, conditions of service, pension rights and any other information which may be relevant in assessing that loss. Thus both the applicant's solicitor and the Secretary of State will want to know the applicant's normal pay, the amount and frequency of overtime, promotion prospects, details of taxable and non-taxable allowances, arrangements for "sick-pay", pension provisions, etc. The applicant also authorises the Secretary of State to obtain from the Department of Health and Social Services details of any social security payments made or due to be made to the applicant. If there is evidence of any other "collateral" benefits to be deducted under Article 6(2) precise details of these will also be obtained. The object is to build up a detailed picture of the applicant's net pecuniary loss on a week-by-week basis prior to the date of assessment and to provide as accurately as possible the necessary data for assessing any continuing net loss. It is in the first instance for the applicant, in appropriate cases with the assistance of an accountant, to submit a detailed assessment of his pecuniary loss. If this assessment appears to be based on incorrect calculations or the claim is a complex one, the Northern Ireland Office will prepare its own assessment, if necessary with the assistance of one of its own accountants. This assessment will then provide the basis for any offer to the applicant of compensation for pecuniary loss (one of the heads of compensation which

---

87. [1979] 4 NIJB.

88. Unreported, High Ct (Gibson LJ), 23 April 1980.

must, by Article 12(4)(*a*), be separately identified in any Notice of Determination). Before deciding whether or not to accept any such offer the applicant may ask for a copy of the Northern Ireland Office's calculations and these will be furnished to him in appropriate cases. If not agreed, a process of negotiation will follow. If agreement still cannot be reached, a Notice of Determination, based on the Secretary of State's assessment, will be issued.

Since it may take several years to determine the compensation payable in a more complex case, the process of assessment of pecuniary loss may have to be revised a number of times as circumstances change or further information becomes available.

DETERMINATION OF APPLICATION AND PAYMENT OF COMPENSATION

1. Delay by the Secretary of State

In a survey made at the end of August 1988, it was found that approximately 30% of claims are settled in under a year, a further 35% within two years and most of the balance within three years.[89] This compares favourably with the time taken to dispose of common law claims for damages.[90] But during the debates on the 1977 Draft Order serious concern was expressed as to the excessive time which could elapse before an application for compensation was determined by the courts. Although the avoidance of delay was one of the reasons being advanced by the Government for transferring the power to make the initial determination from the county court to the Secretary of State, some Northern Ireland MPs felt that this would only exacerbate the situation.[91] As a result a new provision, apparently derived from Article 24 of the Planning (NI) Order 1972,[92] was inserted in the 1977 Order, and this provision has now been replicated in Article 15 of the 1988 Order.

An applicant who is aggrieved by the failure of the Secretary of State to make a prompt determination may be able to force the case out of his hands and into the county court. The procedure may be summarised as follows:

1. The applicant serves notice on the Secretary of State of his intention to apply to the county court for a "delay" declaration.[93] No form of notice has been prescribed – presumably a letter setting out the relevant facts and the applicant's intention will suffice.

---

89. Information provided by the Northern Ireland Office.

90. An action for damages for personal injuries which goes to the High Court normally takes 3–4 years from the date of the cause of action: *Judicial Statistics for Northern Ireland 1988* (1989), Table C.5. The average time taken to settle a case out of court is not known.

91. See e.g. HC Debs (NI Cttee), cols 20 (Mr Paisley), 38 (Mr Craig), 69 (Rev Bradford)

(16 Feb and 2 March 1977). A number of speakers accepted that the responsibility for delay was not that of the Northern Ireland Office alone.

92. This analogy was suggested by Mr Powell – *ibid*, col 50, only to be rejected by him on the ground that "the difference in cases is so wide that it might be to the disadvantage of the citizen to have a hard and fast time limit imposed upon the Secretary of State."

93. Article 15(2)(*b*).

2. Not less than one month later, and not less than six months from the date of the application for compensation,[94] the applicant makes a special application to the county court for the division in which the criminal injury was sustained. This application must be "in accordance with county court rules",[95] which provide that the application is to be made as if it were an interlocutory application in the course of an action or matter under the provisions of Order 14, rule 1 of the County Court Rules "with any necessary modifications".[96] The form of the notice of application is specified,[97] and this notice must be lodged in the office of the chief clerk duly endorsed as to service and accompanied by any certificate of posting.[98] A copy of the notice must be served on the solicitor for the Secretary of State.

3. The county court must afford to the Secretary of State an opportunity of being heard before it deals with the application.[99]

4. The court may then make a declaration that the Secretary of State has not determined the application within a reasonable period if, having regard to all the circumstances, it considers –

   (a) that the Secretary of State has had sufficient information to enable him to determine the application, and

   (b) that he has not determined the application within such period after he received or obtained that information as is reasonable.[1]

   If the court makes a declaration it is endorsed, in the form specified, on the notice of application. Alternatively, the court may dismiss the application and award costs in respect thereof to the Secretary of State.[2]

5. Where a county court has made such a declaration and the Secretary of State does not, within two months after the date of that declaration, determine the application, the Secretary of State is deemed to have determined that no compensation is payable and to have served on the applicant a notice to that effect,[3] thereby enabling the applicant forthwith to appeal to the county court.

6. There is no appeal by *either* side against the decision of the county court whether or not to make such a declaration.[4]

This provision therefore sets a target of approximately eight months from the date of the application for making a determination. However, this target is conditional upon the Secretary of State having received "sufficient information" to enable him to determine the application and this will require

---

94. Article 15(2). *Semble* the application must still be a live one in the sense that it has not been withdrawn or abandoned by the applicant.

95. Article 15(1) – see County Court (Criminal Injuries to the Person) (Compensation) Rules (NI) 1988, Part IV (hereafter referred to as "1988 Rules").

96. 1988 Rules, r 12(1).

97. *Ibid*, Form 15.

98. *Ibid*, r 12(7), (8).

99. Article 15(3).

1. Article 15(2).

2. 1988 Rules, Forms 15 and 16 respectively.

3. Article 15(4).

4. Article 21(4).

equivalent expedition and efficiency on the part of the applicant's advisers, both legal and medical, as well as others from whom relevant information must be obtained.[5] It would appear that some use has been made of Article 15 and that it is a useful "long-stop" in case of delay in the making of a determination.[6]

2. Interim Payments

Article 13(1) of the 1988 Order replicates the 1977 Order[7] by providing:

> "The Secretary of State may, if he thinks fit, make one or more payments on account of the compensation payable . . . "

This power is a useful one both to offset the principle of finality of compensation and to mitigate any delay which that principle or other factors may cause in the making of a final determination. To facilitate the making of payments, the Secretary of State requires an applicant to sign and have witnessed the following form of discharge:

> "I accept the offer of an interim payment of £   on the understanding that the terms and conditions relating to the payment of compensation specified in the Criminal Injuries (Compensation) (NI) Order 1988 have been or will be fulfilled and I undertake to refund any overpayment should the final settlement be less than the amount now advanced."

On this basis it should be possible in many cases for a payment to be made on account once entitlement is satisfactorily established. But the Secretary of State tends to adopt a cautious approach, having apparently found it impossible or difficult in some cases to recover overpaid sums. The risk of overpayment is increased by two particular rules relating to criminal injuries compensation which do not apply to claims for common law damages, *viz* (a) the extensive range of circumstances which may lead to the reduction or refusal of compensation to an applicant *prima facie* entitled thereto, and (b) the fact that entitlement to compensation ceases if the applicant dies otherwise than as a result of his injuries. In addition, there is always the possibility of deception. As a result, interim payments are made in a comparatively small number of cases – an approach which compares unfavourably with practice under the British Scheme.[8] The usual practice is for

---

5. Applications under Art 15 are usually contested by the Secretary of State on the basis that any failure to determine the claim arises from insufficiency of information.

6. Obviously the factors governing the time for determination are many and inter-related and their combined effect will vary from case to case. *Cf* "It is certainly not our intention to handle any claim in such a way that a declaration of delay can be obtained against us, but I believe that the very existence of this provision will be a reassurance to applicants and to those who may feel that the withdrawal of initial jurisdiction from the courts could lead to undue delays": 934 HC Debs, col 757 (1 July 1977).

7. Article 11(1). *Cf* 1968 Act, s 4(3) only empowered the court to make "an interim award" where, at the time of the hearing, it was only possible to make a provisional medical assessment of the applicant's injuries. The Irish Scheme, para 8 still contains such a provision.

8. The British Board have found that prompt payment of an interim award has a beneficial effect on many victims (*7th Annual Report* (1970–71), pp 7–8); interim awards are now made in 16% of successful applications: *25th Annual Report* (1989), para 5.1. Note, however, that the Board never requests repayment of an interim award.

the applicant's solicitor to request that an interim payment be made. The Secretary of State will consider whether entitlement has been or is likely to be clearly established; if so, a payment will usually be made where the applicant has sustained a net financial loss and/or reasonable expenses directly attributable to his injuries – particularly if there is some evidence which suggests that the applicant is in financial difficulties. It is not the practice to make interim payments in respect of anticipated compensation for pain and suffering and loss of amenities; these are considered too vulnerable to the factors mentioned above.

Although the wording of the form of discharge is not entirely clear on this point, it would appear to be open to the Secretary of State, notwithstanding that an interim payment has been made, to determine that the applicant is not entitled to *any* compensation. This issue arose in another context in *R v CICB, ex parte Brindle*.[9] The Board, having heard evidence of an applicant's previous convictions, informed him that an award would be made, reduced by two-thirds in view of his criminal record. The matter was then adjourned (no interim award was paid) so that further information could be obtained for assessment purposes. The applicant was subsequently arrested on very serious criminal charges and the Board further adjourned consideration of the application pending the outcome of those charges. Woolf J held that they were entitled to do so in the circumstances:

> "Having announced the determination which they did . . . it would clearly be unfair for the Board to go back on that determination in relation to the matters which were then before it . . . But if thereafter something happens which substantially alters the position as it then was before the Board, they can go into that new matter because there would be no unfairness in doing so . . . But unless there is something which can be regarded as creating a new situation, it would be wrong for them to do so."[10]

3. Determination of Application

(a) The determination

The process of collecting and evaluating evidence relating to entitlement and to the assessment of the amount of compensation payable to the applicant continues until the Secretary of State considers that he has sufficient information on which to determine the application. Where any compensation is payable to any person who at the date of that determination is under a disability, the determination must, by Article 14 of the 1988 Order, be approved by the county court. In all other cases, one of three possibilities may arise.

---

9. Unreported, Div'l Ct (Woolf J), 4 Feb 1982 (see CICB, *18th Annual Report* (1981–82), para 26B). See also *Williams* v *Boag* [1940] 4 All ER 246 (D, who had paid money into court with admission of liability, subsequently given leave to withdraw notice of admission).

10. The British Scheme subsequently provided (para 12): "In a case in which an interim award has been made, the Board may decide to make a reduced award, increase any reduction already made or refuse to make any further payment at any stage before receiving notification of acceptance of a final award." The 1988 Act, s 111(7) confirms that the Board may make an interim order "without prejudice to their powers on a final determination".

(i) *The Secretary of State determines that no compensation is payable to the applicant.* Where the Secretary of State considers that the applicant is not entitled to any compensation for any reason, he must serve a Notice of Determination[11] to that effect under Article 12(1). By Article 12(3) any such Notice must inform the applicant of his right to appeal to the county court under Article 16(1). Like its predecessors, the 1988 Order does not require the Secretary of State to give reasons for a refusal to pay compensation, but the form of Notice used by the Secretary of State does in fact provide for reasons to be given.[12] It is, in any case, likely that prior correspondence between the parties will have given the applicant a good indication of the Secretary of State's concerns.

It is open to the Secretary of State under the procedure described below[13] to vary a Notice of Determination that no compensation is payable to an applicant, but it would appear that this power is limited to the addition of a further ground for such refusal. If the determination arose from a failure by the applicant to comply with some requirement of the Order – e.g. failure to undergo a medical examination (Article 5(3)(*a*)) or failure to comply with a reasonable request for information which might lead to the identification of the offender (Article 5(8)) – and the applicant, on receipt of the Notice, is then able to redeem that failure, the Secretary of State is *not* able to cancel or vary the notice under Article 12(5);[14] the only remedy for the applicant is to appeal to the county court.

(ii) *The Secretary of State determines that compensation is payable in an amount acceptable to the applicant.* Where the Secretary of State considers that an applicant is entitled to compensation, the usual practice is to make him an offer "without prejudice" in "final and binding settlement" of the application. This written offer specifies the *gross* amount considered payable in respect of (a) pecuniary loss, (b) expenses, (c) bereavement (if applicable) and (d) other matters (principally compensation for pain and suffering and for loss of amenities), and the extent (if any) by which that amount has been reduced for any reason – e.g. because of provocative or negligent conduct by the applicant. The applicant then has to decide whether the *net* amount offered by the Secretary of State is acceptable. If it is, then Article 13(5) of the 1988 Order applies:

"Where –

(*a*) the Secretary of State determines the amount of compensation payable on an application . . .

---

11. The 1988 Order appears to have eschewed any reference to a "Notice of Decision", the term apparently used in the 1977 Order (Art 14(1)) to connote a decision that *no compensation* was payable (as opposed to a determination of *the amount* where compensation was payable).

12. See e.g. *Scott* v *Sec of State* [1981] NI 185. The case for giving reasons was made forcibly during the debates on the draft 1977 Order – see e.g. HC Debs (NI Cttee), col 50 (16 Feb 1977) (Mr Powell); in reply for the Government it was said "We do not want the individual to be at a disadvantage or more disadvantaged than he is at this moment" (*ibid*, col 92).

13. Page 307.

14. Article 12(5) applies only in relation to Arts 5(9), 6(1) and 9(6).

(*b*) none of that compensation is payable to any person who at the date of the determination is a person under a disability, and

(*c*) the applicant notifies the Secretary of State that he and all other persons to whom that compensation or any part of it is payable wish to accept the amount of compensation so determined in full satisfaction of the claim for compensation,

the applicant shall, as a condition of the payment of such compensation by the Secretary of State, sign a discharge in the prescribed form[15] and, on such signing, the determination of the Secretary of State shall become in all respects final and binding."

This new provision does little more than give statutory recognition to what had become established practice under the 1977 Order. But it is apparently intended to clarify a point which that Order had left uncertain – that no formal Notice of Determination is required when the parties can reach an agreed settlement. Given, however, that the relationship between this provision and Article 12(2) is not entirely clear, it is perhaps unfortunate that this intention was not more definitely expressed.

By Article 13(5), the Secretary of State's determination only becomes "final and binding" when the applicant signs the prescribed discharge form. This will normally be done shortly after the determination is made – but, until the discharge form has been signed, it appears that the Secretary of State may (without resort to Article 12(5)) vary the determination if fresh evidence becomes available. This issue arose in effect in *R* v *CICB, ex parte Brindle*,[16] where the British Board determined that an applicant was entitled to compensation (albeit reduced by two-thirds in view of his criminal record), the amount of compensation to be assessed when further information was received. The applicant was then arrested on "very serious" criminal charges. The Divisional Court held that the Board were entitled to adjourn further consideration of the application pending the outcome of these new criminal proceedings and then reconsider their determination.

The outcome of the fresh criminal proceedings could operate adversely to the applicant; but, as Woolf J pointed out, there could be many circumstances where taking account of a new development could operate in favour of the applicant – e.g. if he unexpectedly lost his job or failed to gain an expected promotion.

When the applicant has signed the discharge form, the determination becomes "in all respects final and binding". This wording appears to conflict with Article 12(2) which provides for the issue, on certain conditions, of a formal Notice of Determination "in relation to *any* application for compensation". Is it therefore open to an applicant who has accepted a determination under Article 13(5) to request the Secretary of State to issue a Notice of Determination under Article 12(2)(*b*), thereby entitling the applicant to

---

15. By the Criminal Injuries (Compensation) (NI) Regulations 1989. This form, which must be signed by the applicant and a witness, includes a declaration that the applicant is "aware that upon acceptance of the amount specified . . . the determination becomes in all respects final and binding".
16. *Supra* n 9.

change his mind and challenge the determination on appeal? The scope of Article 12(2) is not qualified by any express reference to Article 13(5), but this limitation must surely have been intended. Such an interpretation receives support from Article 12(6)(*b*), which provides that once an applicant has signed an Article 13(5) discharge, the Secretary of State cannot vary his determination; *a fortiori* he cannot issue a Notice of Determination under Article 12(2)(*c*) for that purpose.[17]

On the other hand, Article 13(5) appears to be limited by Article 12(2)(*a*), which provides that a Notice of Determination must be issued in every case where "the applicant, or any person to whom the compensation or any part of it is payable, is at the time of the determination under a disability . . . ".

When an application has not been "settled" under Article 13(5) and the Secretary of State has issued a Notice of Determination under Article 12(2), the applicant may, of course, accept the compensation so determined. In such a case it appears from Article 12(6)(*b*) that he must still sign a discharge in the form prescribed under Article 13(5).

(iii) *The Secretary of State determines that compensation is payable in an amount not acceptable to the applicant.* If the applicant does not consider the offer made by the Secretary of State to be acceptable, he may suggest why the amount is insufficient and make representations to the Secretary of State to reconsider the case. If those representations are accepted, a second offer may be made. This process may continue until either agreement is reached or the Secretary of State refuses to go any further. If no agreement can be reached, a Notice of Determination will be issued under Article 12(2):

> "Where, in relation to any application for compensation, the Secretary of State determines the amount of compensation payable to the applicant, he shall serve notice of that determination on the applicant in any case where . . .
>
> (*b*) the applicant requests the Secretary of State in writing to do so, or
>
> (*c*) it appears to the Secretary of State to be appropriate to do so."

Thus, either side can bring the negotiations to a conclusion, and the Secretary of State's "final offer" will be entered in a formal Notice and served on the applicant. The Notice will, as required by Article 12(4), itemise the compensation determined to be payable and inform the applicant of the terms of Article 16(1) governing his right of appeal to the county court. It is then up to the applicant to decide whether to accept the amount so offered, or enter an appeal.

In what appears to be an oversight the 1988 Order neither lays down any time-limit within which a Notice of Determination must be requested by an applicant or served by the Secretary of State,[18] nor does it make any provision for such time-limits to be prescribed. Perhaps it was thought

---

17. Further support may arise from the fact that Art 13(5), unlike Art 16(1), has no express provision qualifying the phrase "in all respects final and binding" in relation to appeals.

18. There is, of course, the procedure laid down in Art 15 and discussed above, p 300, but it is submitted that this is not designed for the situation now envisaged by Art 12(2).

sufficient to give either party the power to force the issue. But it will undermine the fairly strict limitations laid down in Articles 12(6)(*a*) and 16(1) if Article 12(2)(*b*) and (*c*) are not interpreted and applied as requiring prompt action.

(*b*) Service of Notice of Determination

By Article 12(1) and (2) a Notice of Determination is to be served "on the applicant". In *In re Tully*[19] a Notice of Determination by the Secretary of State under the 1977 Order was served on the applicant's solicitors, but not on the applicant personally. The applicant sought to appeal against the determination and the question arose whether the Notice of Determination had been validly served. MacDermott J noted that the applicant had stated in two forms that solicitors were acting for her and concluded that those solicitors had in fact a general authority to act for the applicant throughout her application for compensation. In such circumstances service of the Notice of Determination on the applicant's solicitors did constitute good service.[20] The retention of the wording of the 1977 Order in Article 12 of the 1988 Order suggests that the decision in *Tully* is equally applicable thereto. In any event, it was – and appears to remain – the practice of the Secretary of State to serve a "courtesy" copy of the Notice of Determination on the applicant himself, as well as on his solicitor.

(*c*) Cancellation or variation of Notice of Determination

By Article 16(1) a Notice of Determination which has been duly served on the applicant is "in all respects final and binding" – with two exceptions, *viz*:

(a) Any person aggrieved by the determination may appeal therefrom to the county court. This right of appeal is discussed below.

(b) In a new provision, Article 12(5) of the 1988 Order provides that in certain circumstances the Secretary of State may cancel or vary a Notice of Determination. This power can, however, only be exercised if two conditions are satisfied:

  (i) *After* service of the Notice it appears to the Secretary of State that his determination should be cancelled or varied by reason of the application of Articles 5(9) (membership of unlawful association or involvement in acts of terrorism), 6(1) (relevant circumstances, provocative or negligent behaviour or criminal convictions indicative of character and way of life) or 9(6) (provocative or negligent behaviour or criminal convictions indicative of character and way of life in relation to compensation for rape or for bereavement); and

---

19. Unreported, High Ct (MacDermott J), 21 March 1985.

20. The decision in *Tully* is supported by *Anderton* v *Kinnaird* [1986] RTR 11 where the Divisional Court held good, for the purposes of the Road Traffic Act 1972, s 10, the service to D's solicitors (who had authority to receive and deal with documents) of a certificate relating to an offence of drunken driving required to be served "on the accused". See also *R* v *Bott* [1968] 1 All ER 1119 (similar decision re service of copy of written statement to be tendered in evidence under Criminal Justice Act 1967, s 2(2)(*c*)).

(ii) He serves on the applicant notice of the cancellation or variation within 10 weeks from the service of the Notice of Determination *and* before the applicant signs a formal discharge or lodges notice of appeal.[21]

This provision is clearly designed to enable the Secretary of State to cancel or vary a determination where further evidence becomes available shortly after a Notice has been issued. Under the 1977 Order, such evidence had to be disregarded unless the applicant for some reason decided to appeal to the county court. The Secretary of State is now given the same maximum period as that within which an appeal must be lodged to discover fresh evidence relating to the specified matters which may justify refusal or reduction of the compensation awarded to the applicant. A Notice will now, therefore, in such cases operate as an award *nisi* – it only becomes absolute after the expiration of 10 weeks (or sooner, if the applicant signs a discharge or lodges notice of appeal). It remains to be seen whether the Secretary of State will in practice defer the actual payment of the compensation until this period has elapsed.

(*d*) *Terms and conditions attaching to compensation*

Article 13(3) replicates the 1968 Act[22] and the 1977 Order[23] by providing:

> "Compensation may be paid on such terms and conditions as the Secretary of State thinks fit as to the payment, disposal, allotment or apportionment of the compensation to the victim or his relatives, or any of them, or to any other person."

As already indicated this provision gives the Secretary of State an extensive control over the persons to whom and the purposes for which compensation is paid. It is particularly applicable where the compensation is to be divided between several applicants and to ensure proper expenditure in cases where compensation has been awarded for particular expenses to be incurred by an applicant. Successful operation of the power may, however, require administrative supervision by the Northern Ireland Office and it may be for this reason that the power has not been extensively exercised.

Under Article 6(10) of the 1977 Order, the Secretary of State could –

> "withhold payment of all or part of compensation until the applicant [had] complied with all reasonable requests for information and assistance which might lead to the identification and apprehension of the offender."

In *Scott* v *Secretary of State*[24] the Secretary of State had refused to pay

---

21. Article 12(6)(*b*) also provides that the Secretary of State loses the right to cancel or vary if the requisite notice is not served "before the applicant signs the discharge mentioned in Article 13(5) . . .". It would appear that the whole point of that provision is to formalise the settlement procedure and obviate the need for a Notice of Determination in many cases. But the cancellation or variation procedure only applies where a Notice of Determination has been served.

22. Section 5(1), apparently based on s 20(1) of the New Zealand Act of 1963.

23. Article 11(3).

24. [1981] NI 185.

compensation to an applicant on the ground (*inter alia*) that he had failed to comply with a reasonable request for information and was therefore in breach of Article 6(10). Lord Lowry LCJ held that this was not a valid ground for *refusing* compensation:

> "In a new provision restricting the rights of the victim, it would not be justifiable to construe the Secretary of State's power more penally than the words of the paragraph require and allow . . . Article 6(10) does not permit the Secretary of State to refuse payment altogether in an otherwise proper case . . ."[25]

By this provision the Secretary of State could, therefore, only *withhold* compensation, albeit possibly indefinitely. Not surprisingly this interpretation was apparently felt to leave the matter in an inconclusive state and as a result the 1988 Order has in Article 5(8) converted this provision into one where compensation may be refused outright and as such the provision (the scope of which has also been amended) has been discussed in Chapter 3.

4. Payment of Compensation

Payment of compensation is made by a payable order issued by the Secretary of State some two weeks or so from the date of receipt of the form of discharge or other notice that the applicant has accepted the determination of the Secretary of State.[26] Where the applicant has been in receipt of legal aid (e.g. for an appeal to the county court) the order will in accordance with that scheme[27] be made payable to the applicant's solicitor. Before any actual payment is made the Secretary of State will make a final check to discover whether the applicant has any unpaid "public debts" to which Article 13(4) may apply.[28] Subject to this possibility the applicant will normally in due course receive payment of the agreed or determined amount.

However, some recent cases in England and in Northern Ireland have required the courts to decide when precisely the right to payment of criminal injuries compensation vests in a successful applicant so that if, for example, he dies before payment has actually been received, the compensation must nonetheless be paid to his estate. In *McCloskey v Secretary of State*[29] the question arose as to the application of Article 9(*a*) of the 1977 Order (now Article 11(1)(*a*) of the 1988 Order):

---

25. *Ibid*, p 190. See also *Barry v Sec of State* [1984] NI 39, where the Court of Appeal held that the power to withhold only arose after a determination had been made that compensation was payable and that the power may be exercised by the Secretary of State *after* the court has determined that an applicant is entitled to compensation. Lord Lowry LCJ further held (p 44): "The court can by way of appeal affirm, reverse or vary the Secretary of State's decision to withhold, but cannot . . . itself decide to withhold."

26. Where the application has been settled at or determined by a court, a payable order is issued thereafter, a Certificate of Order is not required and the applicant is told that the Secretary of State will not reimburse any expenses incurred in respect of the extraction of any such Certificate.

27. Legal Aid (General) Regulations (NI) 1965, reg 17.

28. See above, p 148.

29. [1984] NI 365.

"Where the victim of a criminal injury dies otherwise than as a result of the
,injury –

(a) any compensation or balance of compensation to which he was entitled
immediately prior to his death shall cease to be payable . . . "

The applicant had been held by the county court in June 1980 to be entitled
to compensation of £50,000. Payment of the compensation was made in
stages at her request and by November 1980 she had received £22,500.
Before any further payment was made, however, the applicant died otherwise than as a result of her injury. The Secretary of State declined to pay the
balance of the compensation to the applicant's personal representative. The
Court of Appeal held that the balance was so payable; Article 9(a) did not
apply to justify non-payment where a court had made an order for the
payment of compensation. The case turned on the meaning of the word
"entitled" and it is necessary to quote in full Hutton J's interpretation of this
term:

"If counsel were acting for a pedestrian injured by the negligent driving of a
motorist and the pedestrian had been awarded damages by the court, counsel,
on the day after the award and before the damages had actually been
paid . . . would not say: 'my client is entitled to damages', he would say: 'my
client has been awarded damages' or 'my client has obtained damages'.
Similarly, the day after the victim of a criminal injury had been awarded
compensation by the county court, his counsel would not say: 'my client is
entitled to compensation', he would say: 'my client has been awarded
compensation' . . . A layman would use the word 'entitled' in the same
way . . . I consider that this is the meaning of the word 'entitled' in Article
9(a) and that it means a person who has a right to compensation before the
compensation has been awarded by a court, and that accordingly the Article
does not apply where a county court has made an order for the payment of
compensation."[30]

Such reasoning is equally applicable to the 1988 Order. But what if the
applicant dies at an earlier stage? This point may be regarded as having been
settled by implication in *McCloskey* – but it is arguable that the Court of
Appeal in that case was concerned only with the situation where a court
order had in fact been made.[31] Where no such order has been made, the
issue may still be an open one. In *R v CICB, ex parte Tong*[32] an applicant
under the British Scheme died otherwise than as a result of his injury after a
single member of the Board had decided he was entitled to compensation
but before he had been so notified (and *a fortiori* before he received

---

30. *Ibid*, p 369. The learned judge rejected a
submission that Mrs McCloskey's right to
"compensation" had, by reason of the court
order, merged into and become a "judgment
debt". He held further, following *Barry* v *Sec
of State* [1984] NI 39, that s 25(3) of the Crown
Proceedings Act 1947, being a general provision, did not override the later and particular
provision contained in the 1977 Order.

31. It seems contrary to the whole scheme of
the 1977 and 1988 Orders that a court award
should be treated in some way as more "final"
or "binding" than a determination of the
Secretary of State. It is true that such a determination is subject to appeal – but so also is a
county court order.

32. [1977] 1 All ER 171.

payment). The English Court of Appeal held that the compensation vested in him as soon as the single member of the Board made his decision. Lord Denning MR adopted this approach by analogy with the common law "which held that a man's damages for personal injuries became vested in him as soon as the verdict was given, even though he died before judgment was entered." In addition, an applicant or his estate should not suffer through the Board's delay in paying compensation. Waller J added a third consideration – that if the applicant was satisfied with the single member's decision, that decision was final. All three reasons appear equally applicable to a determination by the Secretary of State which has been notified to the applicant.[33] To adapt Hutton J's approach in *McCloskey*, would not an applicant's solicitor, on being notified that the Secretary of State had determined that compensation was payable to the applicant, not say: "my client has obtained compensation", instead of: "my client is entitled to compensation"? In this regard it is noticeable that the Order never refers to a determination by the Secretary of State that an applicant is "*entitled* to" compensation; rather, the Order says " . . . where the Secretary of State determines that compensation is [or is not] payable . . . " or "compensation [or no compensation] *shall be paid* . . . ".

On the other hand the British Scheme being interpreted in *Tong* had no provision equivalent to Article 11(1)(*a*). More conclusive perhaps is a side-effect of Article 12(5) of the 1988 Order which empowers the Secretary of State in certain instances to cancel or vary a Notice of Determination. One such instance is the application of Article 6(1), and it may well be that the death of the applicant after a Notice has been served but before payment has been made is a "relevant circumstance" requiring the Notice to be cancelled. No such power exists where the determination has been accepted by the applicant in accordance with Article 13(5).[34]

5. Approval of Awards to Persons under a Disability

As in common law cases[35] the 1988 Order makes special provision for court approval of criminal injury compensation awards to applicants under a disability, i.e. minors and mental patients.[36] By Article 14(1):

"Where –

(*a*) the Secretary of State determines the amount of compensation payable on an application . . . and

---

33. Note the particular wording of Art 16(1): " . . . unless [the applicant] . . . appeals . . . the determination shall become *in all respects* final and binding . . . ". *Cp R v CICB, ex parte Earls* Unreported, CA, 21 Dec 1982 (see CICB, *19th Annual Report* (1982–83), para 18) (A died after lodging "appeal" against decision of a single member; held, award of single member not vested in A).

34. See above, p 308. Note that the current British Scheme provides in para 22 that an applicant has no title to an award until the

Board has received notification in writing that he accepts it. See to the same effect 1988 Act, Sch 7, para 6(3).

35. See e.g. Kemp and Kemp, *The Quantum of Damages* (Rev ed, 1975), vol 1, ch 18.

36. Defined in Art 2(7) (as in common law cases) as a person "incapable, by reason of mental disorder within the meaning of the Mental Health (NI) Order 1986, of managing and administering his property and affairs." The 1977 Order made no provision for such persons.

(*b*) all or part of that compensation is payable to any person who at the date of
the determination is a person under a disability,

none of that compensation shall be paid by the Secretary of State unless the
determination is approved by the county court on an application made in
accordance with county court rules by or on behalf of the person under
disability or any other person to whom any of the compensation is payable."

It will be noted that the application for approval is now made by an applicant
(or, more strictly, by any person to whom any compensation is payable in
respect of the application), not (as under the 1977 Order[37]) by the Secretary
of State. It was apparently considered more satisfactory to follow the normal
practice in common law actions and in any case the relevant details were in
practice under the 1977 Order normally given to the court by the applicant's
solicitor or counsel since he was better informed than the Secretary of State
about the applicant's injuries and circumstances.

An application is required when "all or part" of the compensation is
payable to a person under a disability. This wording is designed to make
clear that county court approval is required not only in appropriate injury
cases, but also in applications for compensation for the death of a victim
where one or more of the persons to whom compensation is payable is a
relative who is a minor or otherwise under a disability. The Article comes
into operation in respect of *all* the persons to whom compensation is payable
even if only one such person is under a disability and entitled perhaps only to
a small part of the compensation.

An application for approval is made to the county court for the division in
which the criminal injury was sustained.[38] The notice of application[39] must
be served on the Secretary of State and a copy lodged in the office of the chief
clerk duly endorsed as to service, together with any certificate of posting.[40]
The procedure thereafter follows Order 44 of the County Court Rules (NI)
1981 "as if the amount determined as payable . . . by the Secretary of
State had been damages agreed to be paid in proceedings in the county
court".[41]

If the county court is satisfied that the determination is in the interests of a
person under a disability, it will approve the determination and is further
empowered by Article 14(2) to "make such an order as to the apportionment, investment or payment of the compensation as appears to it to be
just." Such part of the compensation as is payable to persons *not* under a
disability will be ordered to be paid to them directly. As regards the
compensation payable to a person who is under a disability the court will
order the Secretary of State "forthwith upon the privity of the Chief Clerk"
to lodge the appropriate sum in court to the separate credit of that person.[42]

---

37. Article 13(1).

38. County Court (Criminal Injuries to the
Person) (Compensation) Rules (NI) 1988
("the 1988 Rules"), rr 3(1), 11(2).

39. *Ibid*, Form 10.

40. *Ibid*, r 11(3). A court fee of £11 is payable

– see County Court Fees (Amendment)
Order (NI) 1990, Section VI.

41. 1988 Rules, r 11(1). See generally Valentine and Glass, *County Court Procedure in
Northern Ireland* (1985), paras 16.51–16.53.

42. *Ibid*, Form 11.

The court will further order how that sum is to be invested, that it is to be invested in accordance with the directions of the Accountant General or that it is otherwise to be dealt with, and if necessary will appoint a guardian "of his fortune" for the person under disability. The sum is then paid by the Secretary of State to the credit of the Accountant General (County Court Account) and is thereafter dealt with, subject to any order of the court, in accordance with Court Funds Rules.

If the county court is *not* satisfied that the determination is in the interests of a person under a disability, Article 14(2)(*b*) provides that it shall make "such an order as it could have made under Article 16 if there had been an appeal to it against that determination".[43] In effect the court may itself decide what compensation is payable and substitute that sum for the amount determined by the Secretary of State. Thereafter the procedure follows that described in the preceding paragraph.

6. Payment into Court where Assignment or Act or Event in Law affects Compensation

By Article 21(1)(*a*):

> "Where . . . the Secretary of State receives notice of any assignment, or any act or event in the law, affecting any compensation . . . the Secretary of State may, in accordance with county court rules, pay the compensation . . . into such county court as appears to him to be appropriate."

By Article 21(2)(*a*), such a payment "shall to that extent be a sufficient discharge to the Secretary of State . . . ".

A payment into court under this provision is made in accordance with Order 28 of the County Court Rules relating to payment into court by trustees, subject to certain modifications.[44] The Secretary of State files in the County Court office an affidavit[45] giving details (*inter alia*) of the persons concerned and pays the money into court in accordance with Court Funds Rules. The affidavit is filed by the chief clerk who sends to each person concerned notice[46] of the payment; provision is also made for the issuing by the chief clerk of a certificate of payment into court.[47] The persons named in the affidavit may then apply to the judge *ex parte*[48] respecting the investment, payment out or mode of dealing with the compensation. By Article 21(2)(*b*), any such application –

---

43. 1988 Rules, Form 12.

44. *Ibid,* r 16. For discussion of *CCR* O 28 see Valentine and Glass, *County Court Procedure in Northern Ireland* (1985), p 147, who note that by the Court Funds Rules (NI) 1979, r 6, the Accountant-General maintains *inter alia* a Criminal Injuries Account in the Bank of Ireland in each county court division.

45. In Form 132 of the County Court Rules

"modified as may be necessary": 1988 Rules, r 16(*a*).

46. 1988 Rules, Form 22.

47. *Ibid,* Form 23.

48. *CCR* O 28, r 2. Note that "The judge on the hearing of the *ex parte* application may require notice of the application to be served on such persons as he thinks fit, and fix a day for a further hearing": *CCR* O 28, r 2(*b*).

"shall, subject to any county court rules regarding money paid into court under section 63 of the Trustee Act (NI) 1958,[49] be dealt with in accordance with the orders of the court."

7. Costs and Expenses

Article 13(2) follows the principle established by earlier legislation[50] by providing:

"Where on an application . . . the Secretary of State pays compensation to any person, the Secretary of State shall also pay to that person, in respect of the costs and expenses incurred by him in making out and verifying his claim to compensation, such sum as is reasonable having regard to the circumstances . . . "

In short, the applicant's costs and expenses follow the event; if the Secretary of State determines that *no* compensation is payable, then (subject to an appeal therefrom), the applicant must bear his own costs and expenses.

In practice costs and expenses usually fall into three categories:

(a) Medical reports

As already indicated,[51] the applicant's solicitor will normally obtain medical reports in respect of the applicant's injuries. Details of the costs incurred in obtaining such reports will be furnished to the Secretary of State and will be paid on a scale agreed between the Secretary of State and the British Medical Association.

(b) Other expenses

The Secretary of State will also pay other reasonable expenses incurred by the applicant in support of his application. Thus, as we have seen, an applicant may employ an accountant to advise and assist with the assessment of compensation payable for pecuniary loss; the fee payable for such assistance will, provided it is reasonable, be paid by the Secretary of State. It would be prudent for the applicant's solicitor to check in advance with the Secretary of State whether payment will be made for any unusual expenses.

(c) Legal costs

Solicitors' and counsel's costs are paid by the Secretary of State on scales agreed with the Law Society and the Executive Council of the Bar respectively.[52]

---

49. See generally Carswell, *Trustee Act (NI) 1958* (1964), pp 131–5. Underhill and Hayton, *The Law Relating to Trusts and Trustees* (14th ed, 1987), pp 714–5 advise trustees that this procedure "can only be used with safety in somewhat rare cases . . . ". But this is because most questions of doubt or difficulty can more easily be resolved by originating summons; no such alternative procedure is available to the Secretary of State.

50. 1968 Act, s 6; 1977 Order, Art 11(2). *Cf*

British Scheme, para 25: " . . . the Board will not pay the cost of legal representation. They will, however, have discretion to pay the expenses of the applicant and witnesses at a hearing." The Irish Scheme, paras 27 and 28, follows the British Scheme in this regard. The costs of witnesses appearing at a hearing under the 1988 Order are dealt with below, p 321.

51. Above, pp 297–298.

52. Information supplied by the Northern Ireland Office.

APPEALS

1. To County Court

(a) General nature of appeal

The 1988 Order follows the 1977 Order[53] in providing a disappointed applicant with an unrestricted right of appeal to the county court from a determination by the Secretary of State. To this extent it continues the distinctive Irish judicial tradition in determining the payment of compensation for criminal injuries.[54] Although not specifically so provided in Article 16(1), this appeal takes the form of a full rehearing of the application.[55] This is confirmed by the relevant County Court rule which provides for the lodging of a notice of appeal by the applicant:

> "Nothing in this rule shall prevent the court from considering other items specified in the determination or from considering grounds of appeal not referred to in the notice."[56]

The evidence is therefore heard *de novo*, and the burden of proof is on the applicant to prove either that he is entitled to compensation or (if that is accepted by the Secretary of State) that he is entitled to compensation over and above that determined by the Secretary of State. In practice, many appeals are entered and many of these are successful. Thus, in the four years to 1988–89, a Notice of Determination was issued in 10,225 cases; an appeal was entered in 6,829 (67%) of these; of the appeals disposed of by June 1989 (3,104), some 2,420 (78%) were upheld.[57]

(b) Legal aid

An applicant who appeals to the county court may apply for legal aid under the Legal Aid, Advice and Assistance (NI) Order 1981.[58] If he satisfies the financial requirements as specified in Article 9 of that Order, he is eligible for legal aid under Article 10 if he can show that –

(i) he has reasonable grounds for taking an appeal, and

(ii) it does not, in the particular circumstances of the case, appear unreasonable that he should receive legal aid.

---

53. Article 14(1). *Cf* 1988 Act, s 113 (appeal only on point of law – a new provision) and Irish Scheme, para 2 (no appeal against or review of final decision of Tribunal).

54. See generally Chapter 1 above.

55. See *CCR* O 32, r 1(2). In *Kennedy* v *Limerick CC* (1903) 3 NIJ 87, Lord O'Brien LCJ observed: "... the judges . . . should give their judgments wholly independently of the decision arrived at below. An appeal is a rehearing, and a judge on appeal should form his own opinion of the effect of the evidence as given before him." See also *Belfast Corporation* v *Goldring* [1954] NI 107 and *Fair*

Employment Agency v *Craigavon BC* [1980] 7 NIJB.

56. County Court (Criminal Injuries to the Person) (Compensation) Rules (NI) 1988, r 3(5) (the "1988 Rules").

57. Information supplied by the Northern Ireland Office.

58. See generally, Greer, *The Legal Aid, Advice and Assistance (NI) Order 1981* (1981), pp 19–42; Moeran, *Practical Legal Aid* (3rd ed, 1982), Part II; Hansen and Levenson, *Legal Aid – How to use it* (1985), Part I.

It is inappropriate here to discuss the detailed provisions governing the award of legal aid, but attention may be drawn to four particular points, *viz:*

    (a) Where a person receives legal aid for any proceedings, the legal aid fund will, by Article 11(1)(*a*) of the 1981 Order, pay "the expenses incurred in connection with those proceedings . . . ". But it will *not* pay expenses incurred *before* the legal aid certificate was obtained nor those incurred thereafter in relation to proceedings not covered by the certificate.

    (b) The legal aid fund may, under Article 12(5), have a first charge on any compensation "recovered or preserved" for the applicant as a result of the appeal or of any compromise arrived at to settle the appeal out of court.

    (c) If the appeal is successful, the compensation due to the applicant is payable not to him but to his solicitor, who must comply with the requirements of the 1981 Order relating to the legal aid fund before making any payment to the applicant.

    (d) If the appeal is unsuccessful, the costs payable to the applicant's solicitor and counsel will be paid out of the legal aid fund according to the scale laid down in Schedule 2 to the 1981 Order.

(*c*) *Entering an appeal*

An appeal from a determination of the Secretary of State lies to the County Court for the division in which the criminal injury was sustained.[59] The procedure for entering the appeal is governed by Article 16 of the 1988 Order and by the County Court (Criminal Injuries to the Person) (Compensation) Rules (NI) 1988, and may be summarised as follows.

(i) *Notice of appeal.* By rule 3 of the 1988 Rules, an appeal is by notice in the prescribed form.[60] It must state whether the appeal is against the entire determination or against only part thereof, and in every case must state the grounds of appeal.[61] In practice these "grounds" are normally stated in quite general terms and this does not appear to cause any difficulty. A copy of the completed notice must be served on the Secretary of State – failure to observe this requirement nullifies the appeal.[62]

    The notice of appeal is lodged with the court by delivering it to the chief clerk at his office[63] duly endorsed as to service and with the following documents attached:

---

59. 1988 Rules, r 3(1).

60. *Ibid*, Form 1.

61. *Ibid*, r 3(4).

62. As was accepted in *Gray* v *Sec of State* [1987] 2 *BNIL* 24 (notice of appeal received by county court office, but not by Secretary of State, within six weeks; *held* that county court had no jurisdiction to hear appeal). But *cf Kinsella* v *Sec of State* Unreported, Cty Ct (Judge Hart), 1 June 1989 (county court *has*

discretion under *CCR* O 43, r 10 to extend time for service of notice of appeal on Secretary of State).

63. In *In re Tully* Unreported, High Ct (MacDermott J), 21 March 1985 the applicant's solicitors failed to give notice to the court and it was accepted that the attempted appeal was a nullity. See also *Goodall* v *Sec of State* Unreported, Cty Ct (Judge Pringle), 20 Jan 1988 to the same effect.

(a) any certificate of posting;
(b) a copy of the Notice of Determination endorsed with a certificate as to the date of service of the Notice on the appellant;
(c) a copy of the notice of intention to apply for compensation,[64] and
(d) a copy of the original form of application for compensation.

It has occasionally been suggested that (b) results in the county court judge knowing, before or at the time of hearing, the amount of compensation determined by the Secretary of State and using it as a "base" from which to increase the compensation. There is no evidence that this, in fact, occurs and, in any case, it is the normal practice for an appellate tribunal to be aware of the decision appealed against. It would appear that this view has again been accepted in the drafting of the 1988 Rules.

Since 1986, a court fee has been payable on lodgment of the notice of appeal; in April 1990, this fee was increased from £50 to £55.[65]

When the applicant is ready for the appeal to be heard, he delivers to the chief clerk a certificate of readiness in the prescribed form, and serves a copy thereof on the Secretary of State.[66] The chief clerk will then enter the appeal for hearing at the first sitting he deems practicable, and gives notice of such hearing to both parties. Alternatively, the chief clerk may enter an appeal for hearing "notwithstanding that a certificate of readiness has not been delivered by the appellant".

(ii) *Time-limit.* Article 16(1) extends from six to 10 weeks the time-limit for bringing an appeal. This limit is an absolute one, since Article 16(7) goes on to provide:

> "Nothing in this Article or in any other statutory provision shall authorise the county court to extend – . . . (b) the time for bringing an appeal under this Article."

The 10 week period runs from the date of service of the Notice of Determination by the Secretary of State.[67] Such service will normally be effected by post and, by section 24(1) of the Interpretation Act (NI) 1954, –

> "unless the contrary is proved, the [notice] shall be deemed to have been served at the time at which such [notice] would have been delivered in the ordinary course of post."[68]

---

64. This is a new requirement not to be found in the previous (1983) Rules.

65. County Court Fees (Amendment) Order (NI) 1986, Part 2; see now County Court Fees (Amendment) Order (NI) 1990, Section VI. The introduction of this fee attracted considerable criticism, but it was justified as having been calculated in accordance with Government policy that fees levied in the civil courts should cover the full cost of civil proceedings, less judicial costs, and it was comparable with other fees charged for the initiation of proceedings in the county court and the High Court – see 107 HC Debs, col *1* (8 Dec 1986) (Attorney-General).

66. 1988 Rules, r 3(6)–(8).

67. By Art 16(2), where the Secretary of State has exercised the power conferred by Art 12(5) to vary a notice of determination, the time-limit for appeal runs from the date of service of the later notice of determination.

68. See *Doogan v Colquhoun* (1886) 20 LR Ir 361; *R(Petty)* v *County Court Judge of Down* [1946] NI 12; *In re Bird Mayer* (1964) 88 ILTR 202.

In practical terms[69] time begins to run from the date on which the Notice of Determination was delivered to the applicant or his solicitor.

(iii) *Special notice of new matters.* In a new provision Article 16(4) of the 1988 Order provides:

> "At the hearing of any appeal . . . the appellant shall not adduce evidence of any new matter unless –
>
> (*a*) the Secretary of State consents to that evidence being adduced, or
>
> (*b*) the applicant has, not less than 7 days before the day on which the appeal is heard, served on the Secretary of State a notice[70] specifying that matter."

By Article 16(5), "new matter" means –

> "any fact, information, report or other matter which would have been material to the determination of the appellant's application for compensation by the Secretary of State but which, for whatever reason, was not available to the Secretary of State on the date on which he made the determination against which the appeal is brought."

It would appear that the purpose of this provision is to prevent the Secretary of State from being put at a disadvantage by the appellant adducing new evidence – e.g. medical reports or details of pecuniary loss – only at the hearing in the county court. A strict seven day requirement might have operated harshly on an appellant who obtains evidence of "new matters" after that dead-line has been passed, and Article 16(4) therefore tempers its application in two respects. Provided notice is given promptly to the Secretary of State, it seems reasonable to suppose that he will normally give his consent to that evidence being adduced. Alternatively, the appellant may request an adjournment to allow the requisite time to elapse.

The 1988 Order places no reciprocal duty on the Secretary of State but, curiously,[71] the 1988 Rules *do* impose on him a limited "notice" requirement – by rule 4(2):

> "Where the Secretary of State intends at the hearing of the appeal to adduce evidence of any matter relevant to Article 5(9) [involvement in terrorism or membership of an unlawful association] or 6(1)(*b*) [criminal convictions indicative of applicant's character and way of life] . . . such evidence shall not be admitted at the hearing of the appeal unless –
>
> (*a*) the Secretary of State, not less than 7 days before the day on which the appeal is to be heard, serves on the appellant written notice specifying particulars of that evidence, including a list of any convictions which he intends to adduce in evidence; or

---

69. See wording of Notice of Appeal in 1988 Rules, Form 1.
70. In Form 25 – see 1988 Rules, r 4(1).
71. There does not appear to be any specific power in the 1988 Order to make such a rule, but it is presumably a valid exercise of the general power conferred by the County Courts (NI) Order 1980, Art 48(*a*).

(b) the appellant consents to that evidence being adduced, or

(c) the court gives leave for that evidence to be adduced."

As an alternative to (c) the court may adjourn the appeal to allow the required notice to be served on the appellant.[72]

Though not required to do so the Secretary of State will normally inform an appellant if he intends to rely at the hearing on some ground for rejecting the application additional to those originally stated in the Notice of Determination.

(d) Payment into court by Secretary of State

Article 16(3) replicates Article 14(4) of the 1977 Order by providing:

> "Where an appeal . . . relates to the amount of compensation or costs to be paid by the Secretary of State . . . [he] shall have the like right to make a payment into the county court as a defendant has in an action in that court and –
>
> (a) where such a payment is made by the Secretary of State it shall . . . have the like consequences as regards liability to pay the costs of the appeal as a payment made into court by a defendant has as regards liability to pay the costs of such an action . . . "[73]

According to Valentine and Glass:

> "Where the plaintiff does not obtain, against the defendant who lodged, a decree for an amount exclusive of costs and expenses greater than the sum lodged he has 'failed to beat the lodgment' and O21/4(1) applies."[74]

Order 21, rule 4(1) of the County Court Rules (NI) 1981 in turn provides:

> "Where the money has been paid into court by any defendant and the plaintiff does not serve notice of acceptance . . . and does not obtain a decree against that defendant for an amount, exclusive of costs and expenses, greater than that paid into court, then –
>
> (a) where the plaintiff is not under legal disability, he shall not be entitled to any costs against the defendant and shall be liable for the costs of that defendant based on the amount lodged; or
>
> (b) where the plaintiff is under legal disability, costs shall be in the discretion of the judge."

---

72. 1988 Rules, r 4(2), which also provides that "any costs occasioned by any such adjournment shall be in the discretion of the judge."

73. This provision is stated to be "notwithstanding any provision to the contrary contained in section 22(c) of the Interpretation Act (NI) 1954 or in any other statutory provi-

sion . . . ". Section 22(c) provides that the court "may . . . make such order as to costs and expenses as [it] . . . may think proper . . . ".

74. County Court Procedure in Northern Ireland (1985), p 144. The authors add that "whether the defendant disputed liability, or only quantum, is irrelevant . . .".

In fact the County Court (Criminal Injuries to the Person) (Compensation) Rules (NI) 1988 themselves provide:

(i) Where the appellant accepts the amount paid into court by the Secretary of State in satisfaction of his claim, the appellant is entitled to any costs or expenses reasonably incurred by him between the date of service of the Notice of Determination and the date of the payment into court.[75]

(ii) Where the appellant does not accept the amount paid into court and on appeal does not obtain, in relation to such items in the determination of the Secretary of State as are the subject of the appeal, an order for the recovery of an amount greater than the amount paid into court, the appellant is not entitled to any costs against the Secretary of State; on the contrary, he is liable for the costs of the Secretary of State in such amount as the court may determine.[76]

The procedure relating to payments into court is also governed by the 1988 Rules. By rule 4, such payment may be made at any time within 21 days from service on the Secretary of State of the copy of the notice of appeal. The sum considered appropriate by the Secretary of State to satisfy so much of the appellant's claim for compensation and/or costs as is the subject of the appeal is lodged in the County Court Bank to the credit of the Criminal Injuries Account. The Secretary of State must also lodge with the court a written undertaking to pay to the appellant any costs or expenses reasonably incurred by him between the date of service of the Notice of Determination and the date of the payment in. Notice of the lodgment and of the undertaking is at the same time given in the prescribed form[77] to the appellant, and a copy of this notice must be lodged with the chief clerk and the county court bank.

The appellant may accept the payment into court by serving a notice in the prescribed form[78] on the Secretary of State and lodging a copy thereof with the chief clerk. Such notice must be served –

(i) within 21 days of the date of service on him of the notice of payment in, or

(ii) before the commencement of the sittings at which the appeal is to be heard,

whichever first occurs. Later service may be made with the consent of the Secretary of State.

If the appellant does not accept the payment in by serving the appropriate notice, the appeal proceeds to hearing. In such a case it is important to note that by rule 6 of the 1988 Rules:

---

75. Rule 5(6). By r 5(7) if these costs and expenses cannot be agreed between the parties, they will be settled by the circuit registrar subject to an appeal to the judge. By r 5(9) special rules apply where a payment into court is accepted by an appellant who is a person under a disability.

76. Rule 5.

77. Form 4.

78. Form 5.

> "Where money has been paid into court . . . that fact shall not be communi-
> cated to the judge before the determination of the appeal."

(e) Powers of the county court on hearing the appeal

It has already been indicated that the appeal to the county court is by way of a full rehearing of the application for compensation. In practice, however, some aspects of the application will not be in dispute, having been agreed or at least accepted by the parties.[79] The main significance of the hearing is that evidence relating to the matters in dispute will for the first time be given orally by the appropriate witnesses – and be subject to cross-examination. This may be particularly important in relation to medical evidence, especi-ally in "nervous shock" cases, and to the evidence of the applicant himself. By way of corollary the procedure at the hearing follows the normal "adversary" process. As a result the substance of the application as it appears at the hearing may vary substantially from that determined by the Secretary of State and it is not altogether surprising that the rate of "success" for appellants is quite high. But the process is not one way; many an appellant has found that his case cannot withstand examination in court.

Having heard all the evidence the county court judge has a wide range of powers. Although these are not specified in the 1988 Order, section 22 of the Interpretation Act (NI) 1954 applies:

> "Where an enactment provides that an appeal against any . . . determination
> of a . . . person (in this section called 'the original tribunal') may be brought
> to any court, that court (in this section called 'the appellate court') may, for all
> purposes of and incidental to hearing or determining such appeal, exercise all
> the powers, authority and jurisdiction of the original tribunal and, in addition,
> may –
>
> (a) confirm, reverse or vary the decision or determination of the original
>   tribunal;
>
> (b) remit the appeal or any matter arising thereon to the original tribunal with
>   such declarations or directions as the appellate court may think proper; or
>
> (c) make such order as to costs and expenses as the appellate court may think
>   proper . . . "

This provision would appear to give the county court all the powers it may wish to exercise on appeal and two comments only are appropriate. First, as has already been indicated, this section would appear to give the court power to make interim awards, and thus mitigate the principle of finality of compensation; and secondly, it would appear that the power of remittal to the Secretary of State is seldom, if ever, exercised in practice.

(f) Costs of appeal

By Article 21(3):

> "Subject to Article 16(3) [payment into court by Secretary of State] and to
> section 21A of the Crown Proceedings Act 1947 [provision for costs in civil

---

79. See eg *Scott* v *Sec of State* [1981] NI 185 (court dealt only with grounds 1, 4 and 5 of the Secretary of State's notice of determin-ation).

proceedings to which the Crown is a party[80]] the county court may award costs to or against any party to or person appearing on any proceedings before it under this Order."

Schedule 2 to the County Court (Criminal Injuries to the Person) (Compensation) Rules (NI) 1988 sets out the relevant scale of party and party costs payable to solicitors and counsel.[81] It should be noted that for these costs to apply, an award must be obtained in excess of the Secretary of State's determination. If the appeal is dismissed, the court may order the appellant to pay to the Secretary of State an amount for his costs.

(g) *Interest on award*

Interest at the current rate is payable on an award of compensation by the county court from the date of the award to the date of payment of the compensation.[82]

2. Further Appeals

Article 21(4) of the 1988 Order replicates Article 20(5) of the 1977 Order:

> "Without prejudice to section 22 of the Crown Proceedings Act 1947,[83] an appeal from any order made by a county court on or in connection with any proceedings under this Order (except an application under Article 15[84]) shall lie at the instance of –
>
> (*a*) the Secretary of State; or
>
> (*b*) any person who appeared or might have appeared on the hearing of those proceedings,
>
> as if the order had been made in exercise of the jurisdiction conferred by Part III of the County Courts (NI) Order 1980 and the appeal were brought under Part VI of that Order."

The formula in the latter part of this provision brings this matter within the normal practice and procedure governing appeals from the county court, which is fully discussed by *Valentine and Glass*.[85]

---

80. See Crown Proceedings (NI) Order 1981, Art 16.

81. Where the case is one of exceptional complexity or difficulty the judge may certify an amount exceeding the scale figure: 1988 Rules, Sch 2, n 4.

82. Judgments Enforcement (NI) Order 1981, Art 127(1): *CCR* O 33, r 2.

83. " . . . all enactments [and] rules of

court . . . relating to appeals . . . shall, with any necessary modifications, apply to civil proceedings by or against the Crown as they apply to proceedings between subjects."

84. Declaration by County Court as to delay by Secretary of State in determining application – see above, p 300.

85. *County Court Procedure in Northern Ireland* (1985), ch 19.

OTHER PROCEEDINGS

1. Recovery of Compensation from Offender

Article 17 of the 1988 Order provides:

"(1) Where –

(*a*) any person is convicted of a violent offence; and

(*b*) compensation[86] has been paid or is payable in respect of a criminal injury directly attributable to that offence,

a county court may, on an application made to it by the Secretary of State, make an order directing the offender to reimburse to the Secretary of State the whole or any specified part of the amount of the compensation paid or payable."

The benefit of such a provision in a criminal injuries compensation scheme has long been a matter for debate, given that one of the reasons for such schemes in the first instance is the impecuniosity of most offenders.[87] Although the sums recovered from offenders in Northern Ireland appear never to have risen above 1% of the total compensation paid,[88] provision for reimbursement has been consistent policy since the 1968 Act:[89]

"This is the way to punish the criminal without doing him any injustice and at the same time to ensure that the state is not put under obligation to pay for a criminal act by a person who is able to make some contribution."[90]

It will be noted however that Article 17 extends only to offenders; there is no provision e.g. for reimbursement by persons who may be vicariously or otherwise liable in tort for the injuries inflicted by the offender.[91]

Application is made by notice in the prescribed form at any time after the conviction of the offender.[92] This application may be dealt with *either* –

---

86. By Art 17(7). "'compensation' includes –

(*a*) any costs awarded, on an appeal under Article 16, to any person other than the Secretary of State;

(*b*) any expenses incurred by the Secretary of State in recovering, or attempting to recover, any compensation from the offender in pursuance of this Article."

By Art 13(2), "compensation" here also includes any sum paid to an applicant in respect of the costs and expenses incurred by him in making out and verifying his claim.

87. Thus, the British Board does not consider it worthwhile to have such a power. The 1986 *IWP Report* disagreed, however (para 21.7), and recommended a provision similar to that in Northern Ireland. This has been enacted in the 1988 Act, s 115.

88. Information supplied by Northern Ireland Office.

89. 1968 Act, s 7 (apparently based on s 23 of the New Zealand Criminal Injuries Compensation Act 1963); 1977 Order, Art 16. No changes of substance have been made in the 1988 Order.

90. 68 HC Debs (NI), col 634 (31 Jan 1968).

91. *Cf* by Art 6(2), damages which have been paid to the victim by any person "on the offender's behalf" are deducted from the compensation payable by the Secretary of State – see above, p 206. Difficulties may also arise as to the apportionment of liability between joint offenders – see e.g. *Kingston-Lee* v *Hunt* (1986) 42 SASR 136.

92. County Court (Criminal Injuries to the Person) (Compensation) Rules (NI) 1988 (the " 1988 Rules"), r 13(1) and Form 18.

(i) At any ordinary sitting of the county court for the division in which the criminal injury was sustained – in which case a copy of the notice of application must be served on the offender *and* on the chief clerk not less than 15 days before the day appointed for the commencement of the sitting at which the application is to be heard, *or*

(ii) Where on appeal to a county court an offender's summary conviction of an offence causing a criminal injury is affirmed, the application may be made at the time of that affirmation by furnishing the offender forthwith with a copy of the application made to the court.[93]

An application can be made in any case; there is e.g. no requirement that the Secretary of State should have reason to believe that the offender has sufficient financial resources.[94] In practice, however, the Secretary of State asks the police to indicate the financial status of any person convicted for the offence, whether he is employed or unemployed and whether, in their opinion, the offender would be in a position to reimburse any compensation paid to the victim. In the event of a negative report from the police or any other indication that proceedings would be fruitless, an application is unlikely.[95]

Article 17(3) then provides:

"Before making an order under this Article, the court shall –

(*a*) give the offender an opportunity to be heard;[96] and

(*b*) have regard to the financial position of the offender, his employment, the possibilities of his future employment, his liabilities to his family and otherwise and such other circumstances as the court considers relevant . . . "[97]

The scope of this provision, as contained in the 1968 Act, came under scrutiny in *Secretary of State* v *McKinney*.[98] In that case one Martin had been injured by McKinney in a brawl in a public house. McKinney pleaded guilty to a charge of unlawfully and maliciously inflicting grievous bodily harm to Martin, who was subsequently awarded compensation of £15,000. The Secretary of State then applied to the county court for an order requiring McKinney to make a contribution towards that award.

The first issue raised in the county court was whether McKinney could re-open in the civil court the issue to which he had pleaded guilty in the criminal proceeding and seek to prove either that there had been no assault or at least that it had been provoked by Martin. The learned county court judge held that he had no power to treat the plea as if it had never been made and McKinney was, therefore, estopped from seeking to go behind it.[99] However, since provocation would not have been a defence to the crime

---

93. *Ibid*, r 13(2), (4).
94. *Cf* 1988 Act, s 115(2).
95. Reimbursement may also be sought if the offender is himself awarded compensation on a subsequent occasion.
96. See *Williams* v *Crimes Compensation Tribunal* [1968] NZLR 711.

97. The court may, for these purposes, obtain and consider a report from a probation officer.

98. Unreported, Cty Ct (Judge Rowland), 13 Sept 1976; High Ct (Kelly J), 22 April 1977.

charged (though relevant to the sentence therefor), there seems no reason why McKinney should have been barred by his plea of guilty from raising the issue of "provocative behaviour" at the subsequent civil proceedings. Any such evidence is surely relevant to the county court's decision whether or not to exercise its discretion to order reimbursement and, if so, the amount to be reimbursed. This question was not pursued on appeal.

The learned county court judge next held that the reference in sub-paragraph (*b*) to "such other circumstances as the court considers relevant" is to be read *ejusdem generis* with the preceding particular circumstances – i.e. "the financial position of the offender, his employment, etc", and so must be confined to financial and family matters. If this is correct, then the county court has no discretion to have regard to the offender's conduct in relation to the injury. On appeal Kelly J unfortunately did not advert to this point. However, in *Secretary of State* v *B*[1] Higgins J appears to have adopted this approach by holding that the court was not permitted to take into account, as a relevant circumstance, the offender's moral culpability. The offender in that case assaulted a woman after he had received injuries in a road accident which changed his personality and made him aggressive and assertive. He was ordered to repay in full the amount of compensation paid by the Secretary of State to his victim.

The final question is whether the offender is in a financial position to make a contribution. In *McKinney*, His Honour Judge Rowland in the county court thought not; McKinney's "family liabilities" exceeded his personal income, and his wife's income could not be taken into account. On appeal, Kelly J disagreed with this approach:

> " . . . The details of [McKinney's] monthly budget indicate that with care he is able to enjoy much more than the bare necessities of life. A conclusion on the evidence before me at least that the respondent is not in a position to make a partial reimbursement, even small, would be an unrealistic one."

In adopting this approach the learned judge acknowledged that he was following views expressed by the Court of Appeal in England in relation to the making of compensation orders by criminal courts.[2] In broad terms, this may be correct; but the court may have to take into account that different considerations may apply where compensation is being sought by the victim, as opposed to the state.

In the event, McKinney was ordered[3] to pay £1,500 in two equal instalments.[4] The power to make such an order is now conferred by Article 17(2):

---

99. But *cf* Art 19(1) – a conviction "whether . . . upon a plea of guilty or otherwise . . . " is admissible in evidence to show that the convicted person was guilty of the acts etc on which the conviction was based, "except in so far as the contrary is proved . . . ". *Cf* 1988 Act, s 115(3): " . . . the court shall have regard . . . to such other matters (not including the question whether he was properly convicted) as the court thinks relevent . . .". See also *Hunter* v *Chief Constable of the West Midlands* [1981] 3 All ER 727.

1. [1988] 4 *BNIL* 17.

2. Particularly *R* v *Bradburn* (1973) 57 Cr App R 948. See further above, pp 247–248.

3. The form of an order for reimbursement is specified in the 1988 Rules, Form 21.

4. In doing so the learned judge stressed that the amount "does not at all reflect . . . [McKinney's] responsibility for the criminal injury he inflicted . . . ".

"Any such order may be for the payment by the offender of a lump sum or of periodical payments during a specified period, or both . . . "

Payment by way of a single lump sum is more likely where the offender is known to have substantial capital assets.[5]

Article 17(4) further provides that the court may, at any time, on the application of the Secretary of State *or* of the offender,[6] vary any order "in such manner as it thinks fit". But before doing so, the court must have regard to –

"(*a*) any fresh evidence which has become available;

(*b*) any change of circumstances which has occurred since the making of the order or, as the case may be, any previous variation of the order, or which is likely to occur; and

(*c*) any other matter which the court considers relevant."

Reimbursement orders are enforceable "in the same manner as a county court decree for a debt is enforceable . . . ".[7]

Finally Article 17(6) provides that, in the somewhat unlikely event that the total amount reimbursed by the offender (and the victim[8]) to the Secretary of State exceeds the amount of compensation paid in respect of the criminal injury, "the Secretary of State shall repay the excess to the offender".

2. Recovery of Compensation from Applicant

(*a*) *Where compensation or damages subsequently paid to applicant by or on behalf of offender*

We have already seen[9] that in determining the amount of compensation payable to an applicant, the Secretary of State must deduct –

"any sums paid to the victim or any of his relatives, by way of compensation or damages from the offender or any person on the offender's behalf, consequent on the criminal injury or on death resulting therefrom . . . "

This provision thus deals with the situation where such compensation or damages were paid to the applicant *before* the Secretary of State makes his determination. Where such compensation or damages are paid *after* that determination, two procedures for the reimbursement of the Secretary of State are laid down in Article 18,[10] *viz*:

---

5. As in *Sec of State* v *B*, *supra* n 93, where the offender was ordered to reimburse the sum of £12,500 from the damages award which at the relevant time amounted to almost £175,000. *Cp* compensation order cases cited above p 248, n 51.

6. The form of application is prescribed in the 1988 Rules (Form 20) and must be served on the respondent and the chief clerk not less than 15 days before the day appointed for the commencement of the sitting at which the application is to be heard.

7. Article 17(2). See generally Judgments (Enforcement) (NI) Order 1981.

8. Under Art 18, discussed below.

9. Above, p 206.

10. Re-enacting 1977 Order, Art 17.

(i) *Direct payment to Secretary of State.* By Article 18(1):

> "Where –
>
> (*a*) compensation is paid to any victim or other person consequent on any criminal injury; and
>
> (*b*) there has been or is subsequently paid to the victim or that person, by way of compensation or damages from the offender or any person on the offender's behalf, any sum which has not been deducted under Article 6(2)(*a*),
>
> the person receiving any such sum shall forthwith notify the Secretary of State and shall [subject to paragraph 2 – see below] . . . forthwith reimburse to the Secretary of State –
>
> (i) the amount of the compensation paid to the victim or that person, if that amount is equal to or less than that sum; or
>
> (ii) that sum, if the amount of the compensation paid is greater."

Failure to comply with this provision without reasonable cause is specifically made a criminal offence by Article 18(6).

(ii) *Payment into court.* By Article 18(2):

> "Where compensation is paid to any victim or other person consequent on a criminal injury and civil proceedings have been or are subsequently instituted in any court against the offender as a result of the injury and –
>
> (*a*) that court awards damages against the offender in favour of the victim or that other person . . . or
>
> (*b*) the parties agree to settle the proceedings in consideration of the payment by the offender to the victim or that other person of an agreed amount of damages,
>
> the court may order the offender to pay the damages so awarded or agreed, or any part thereof, into court."

In such a case the amount due to the Secretary of State will be paid to him and the balance of the money paid into court will be "paid to the victim or the other person . . . or otherwise dealt with for the benefit of the victim or person as the court may, in the circumstances of the case, consider proper".[11]

(*b*) *Where applicant failed to disclose material facts*

By Article 18(4):

> "Where, on an application made to it by the Secretary of State, the county court is satisfied –
>
> (*a*) that the Secretary of State has paid compensation to any person; but
>
> (*b*) that that person failed to make full and true disclosure of all the facts material to the determination of the application,

---

11. Article 18(3).

the county court may make an order requiring that person to reimburse to the Secretary of State the compensation or such part of it as the court may specify."[12]

The scope of the requirement to make full and true disclosure has already been considered.[13] The procedure for making such an application is for the first time specified in the 1988 Rules. The application is by notice in the prescribed form[14] stating the facts material to the determination of the application of which the applicant did not make full and true disclosure. This notice must be served on –

(i) the person to whom the compensation was paid, and
(ii) the chief clerk of the county court for the division in which the criminal injury was sustained,

not less than 15 days before the commencement of the sittings at which the application is to be heard.[15] On receipt of the application, the chief clerk enters it for hearing at any ordinary sitting of the court. If the court, having heard the evidence, is satisfied that the applicant had failed to make full and true disclosure of some material facts, it will make an order stating the sum to be reimbursed[16] (by instalments, if necessary) to the Secretary of State.

If a person fails to reimburse the Secretary of State in any of the circumstances described in this section, the appropriate sum is recoverable as a debt due to the Secretary of State and, without prejudice to any other available remedy, is recoverable in the county court by civil bill or summarily in the magistrates' court as a civil debt.

---

12. Re-enacting 1977 Order, Art 17(4). Cf the earlier provision in the 1968 Act, s 8(3) expressly required the court to give the applicant an opportunity to be heard.

13. Above, pp 272–273.

14. 1988 Rules, Form 26.

15. Ibid, r 15.

16. Ibid, Form 27. This sum may include the costs and witnesses' fees and expenses incurred on the hearing of the application, as well as all or part of the compensation originally paid to the applicant.

INDEX